ISBN 978-0-282-19332-4
PIBN 10844137

1 MONTH OF
FREE
READING

at
www.ForgottenBooks.com

By purchasing this book you are eligible for one month membership to ForgottenBooks.com, giving you unlimited access to our entire collection of over 700,000 titles via our web site and mobile apps.

To claim your free month visit:
www.forgottenbooks.com/free844137

AUTHOR'S PREFACE.

This popular account of the voyage of the *Vega* round Asia and Europe is herewith presented to the friends of geographical research in an English translation. Along with the sketch of the voyage itself, of the natural conditions on the north coast of Siberia, of the animal and vegetable life prevailing there, and of the races with whom we came in contact in the course of the voyage, the work contains a review, as complete as space permitted, of preceding exploratory voyages to the Polar Sea of Europe and Asia, from King Alfred's account of the first North-East voyage under the Northman, Othere, down to the expeditions for sport and hunting of the past decade. For it would have been too ungrateful, in an account of the voyage of the *Vega*, not to have referred at some length to our predecessors, who, with indescribable struggles and difficulties, and generally with the sacrifice of health and life, paved the way along which we advanced, made possible the victory we achieved. In this way, besides, the work itself has gained a much-needed variety, for nearly all the narratives of the older North-East voyages contain in abundance what a sketch of our own adventures has not to offer, but what many readers, perhaps, will expect to find in a book such as this—accounts of dangers and misfortunes of a thousand sorts by land and sea.

May the prominent part which England and America have played in the history of Polar Exploration, and the lively interest that everywhere in these countries has been taken in the voyage of the *Vega*, secure for this work a friendly reception ; and, above all, may the voyage of the *Vega* conduce to maintain the desire for Arctic Research till the veil which still conceals the lands round the North and South Poles be completely removed. Many a problem of great importance to mankind still waits for a solution from the ice-deserts of the Polar Seas and the Polar Lands ; many a splendid victory in the service of science is still to be won in those distant regions.

A. E. NORDENSKIÖLD.

London, *November*, 1881.

TRANSLATOR'S PREFACE.

HAVING been honoured by a request from Baron Nordenskiöld that I would undertake the translation of the work in which he gives an account of the voyage by which the North-East Passage was at last achieved, and Asia and Europe circumnavigated for the first time, I have done my best to reproduce in English the sense of the Swedish original as faithfully as possible, and at the same time to preserve the style of the author as far as the varying idioms of the two languages permit.

I have to thank two ladies for the help they kindly gave me in reading proofs, and my friend Herr GUSTAF LINDSTRÖM, for valuable assistance rendered in various ways.

Where not otherwise indicated, temperature is stated in degrees of the Centigrade or Celsius thermometer. Longitude is invariably reckoned from the meridian of Greenwich.

Where distance is stated in miles without qualification, the miles are Swedish (one of which is equal to 6·64 English miles), except at page 282, where the geographical square miles are German, each equal to sixteen English geographical square miles.

ALEX. LESLIE.

CHERRYVALE, ABERDEEN,
24th November, 1881.

CONTENTS.

CONTENTS.   xv

PORTRAITS.

Engraved on Steel by G. J. Stodart of London.

LITHOGRAPHED MAPS.

LIST OF WOOD-CUTS.

The Wood-cuts, when not otherwise stated below, were engraved at Herr Wilhelm Meyer's Xylographic Institute in Stockholm.

h

INTRODUCTION.

THE voyage, which it is my purpose to sketch in this book, owed its origin to two preceding expeditions from Sweden to the western part of the Siberian Polar Sea, in the course of which I reached the mouth of the Yenisej, the first time in 1875 in a walrus-hunting sloop, the *Proeven*, and the second time in 1876 in a steamer, the *Ymer*.

After my return from the latter voyage, I came to the conclusion, that on the ground of the experience thereby gained, and of the knowledge which, under the light of that experience, it was possible to obtain from old, especially from Russian, explorations of the north coast of Asia, I was warranted in asserting that the open navigable water, which two years in succession had carried me across the Kara Sea, formerly of so bad repute, to the mouth of the Yenisej, extended in all probability as far as Behring's Straits, and that a circumnavigation of the old world was thus within the bounds of possibility.

It was natural, that I should endeavour to take advantage of the opportunity for making new and important discoveries which thus presented itself. An opportunity had arisen for solving a geographical problem—the forcing a north-east passage to China and Japan—which for more than three hundred years had been a subject of competition between the world's foremost commercial states and most daring navigators, and which,

B

if we view it in the light of a circumnavigation of the old world, had, for thousands of years back, been an object of desire for geographers. I determined, therefore, at first to make use, for this purpose, of the funds which Mr. A. SIBIRIAKOFF, after my return from the expedition of 1876, placed at my disposal for the continuation of researches in the Siberian Polar Sea. For a voyage of the extent now contemplated, this sum, however, was quite insufficient. On this account I turned to His Majesty the King of Sweden and Norway, with the inquiry whether any assistance in making preparations for the projected expedition might be reckoned upon from the public funds. King OSCAR who, already as Crown Prince, had given a large contribution to the Torell Expedition of 1861, immediately received my proposal with special warmth, and promised within a short time to invite the Swedish members of the Yenisej expeditions and others interested in our voyages of exploration in the north, to meet him for the purpose of consultation, asking me at the same time to be prepared against the meeting with a complete exposition of the reasons on which I grounded my views— differing so widely from the ideas commonly entertained—of the state of the ice in the sea off the north coast of Siberia.

This assembly took place at the palace in Stockholm, on the 26th January, 1877, which may be considered the birth-day of the *Vega* Expedition, and was ushered in by a dinner, to which a large number of persons were invited, among whom were the members of the Swedish royal house that happened to be then in Stockholm ; Prince JOHN OF GLÜCKSBURG ; Dr. OSCAR DICKSON, the Gothenburg merchant ; Baron F. W. VON OTTER, Councillor of State and Minister of Marine, well known for his voyages in the Arctic waters in 1868 and 1871 ; Docent F. R. KJELLMAN, Dr. A. STUXBERG, the former a member of the expedition which wintered at Mussel Bay in 1872-73, and of that which reached the Yenisej in 1875, the latter, of the Yenisej Expeditions of 1875 and 1876 ; and Docents HJALMAR THEEL and Å. N, LUNDSTRÖM, both members of the Yenisej Expedition of 1875.

After dinner the programme of the contemplated voyage was laid before the meeting, almost in the form in which it after-wards appeared in print in several languages. There then arose a lively discussion, in the course of which reasons were advanced for and against the practicability of the plan. In particular the question concerning the state of the ice and the marine currents at Cape Chelyuskin gave occasion to an exhaustive discussion. It ended by His Majesty first of all declaring himself convinced of the practicability of the plan of the voyage, and prepared not only as king, but also as a private individual, to give substantial support to the enterprise. Dr. Oscar Dickson shared His Majesty's views, and promised to contribute to the not

inconsiderable expenditure, which the new voyage of exploration would render necessary. This is the sixth expedition to the high north, the expenses of which have been defrayed to a greater or less extent by Dr. O. Dickson.[1] He became the banker of the *Vega* Expedition, inasmuch as to a considerable extent he advanced the necessary funds, but after our return the expenses were equally divided between His Majesty the King of Sweden and Norway, Dr. Dickson, and Mr. Sibiriakoff.

I very soon had the satisfaction of appointing, as superintendents of the botanical and zoological work of the expedition in this new Polar voyage, my old and tried friends from previous expeditions, Docents Dr. Kjellman and Dr. Stuxberg, observers so well known in Arctic literature. At a later period, another member of the expedition that wintered on Spitzbergen in 1872-3, Lieutenant (now Captain in the Swedish Navy) L. PALANDER, offered to accompany the new expedition as commander of the vessel—an offer which I gladly accepted, well knowing, as I did from previous voyages, Captain Palander's distinguished ability both as a seaman and an Arctic explorer. Further there joined the expedition Lieutenant GIACOMO BOVE, of the Italian Navy; Lieutenant A. HOVGAARD, of the Danish Navy; Medical candidate E. ALMQUIST, as medical officer; Lieutenant O. NORDQUIST, of the Russian Guards; Lieutenant E. BRUSEWITZ, of the Swedish Navy; together with twenty-one men—petty officers and crew, according to a list which will be found further on.

An expedition of such extent as that now projected, intended possibly to last two years, with a vessel of its own, a numerous well-paid *personnel*, and a considerable scientific staff, must of course be very costly. In order somewhat to diminish the expenses, I gave in, on the 25th August, 1877, a memorial to the Swedish Government with the prayer that the steamer *Vega*, which in the meantime had been purchased for the expedition, should be thoroughly overhauled and made completely seaworthy at the naval dockyard at Karlskrona: and that, as had been done in the case of the Arctic Expeditions of 1868 and 1872-3, certain grants of public money should be given to the officers and men of the Royal Swedish Navy, who might take part as volunteers in the projected expedition. With reference to this petition the Swedish Government was pleased, in terms of a letter of the Minister of Marine, dated the 31st December, 1877, both to grant sea-pay, &c., to the officer and eighteen men of the Royal Navy, who might take part in the expedition in

---

[1] The expeditions to Spitzbergen in 1868, to Greenland in 1870, to Spitzbergen in 1872-73, and to the Yenisej in 1875 and 1876.

THE VEGA.

Longitudinal section.

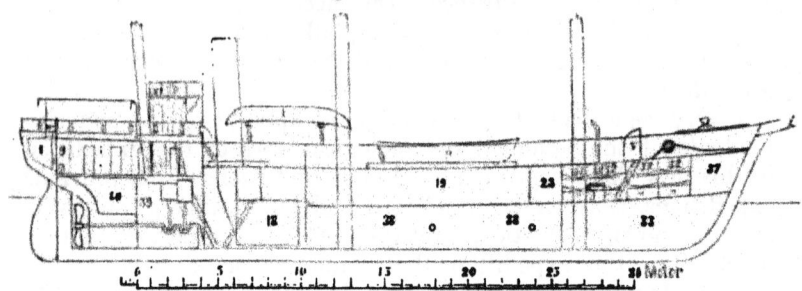

Plan of arrangement under deck.

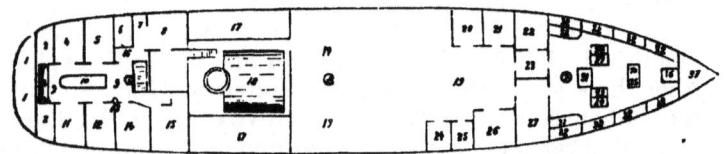

1. Powder magazine.
2. Instrument room.
3. Sofa in gunroom.
4. Cabin for Lieut. Brusewitz
5. Cabin for Lieuts. Bove and Hovgaard
6. Pantry during winter.
7. Corridor.
8. Cabin for Dr. Stuxberg and Lieut. Nordquist.
9. Gunroom.
10. Table in gunroom.
11. Cabin for Dr. Almquist.
12. Cabin for Dr. Kjellman.
13. Stove
14. Cabin for Capt. Palander.
15. Cabin for Prof. Nordenskiold.
16. Corridor(descent to gunroom)
17. Coal bunkers.
18. Boiler.
19. Storeroom 'tween decks.
20. Pilot's cabin } built in
21. Cabin for Lieut. Bove } Japan.
22. Cabin for two petty officers.
23. Petty officers' mess
24. Cabin for Carpenter's } built
    effects. } in
25. Cabin for collections. } Japan.
26. Cabin for library.
27. Gunroom pantry.
28. Hatch to provision room.
29. Hatch to the cable-tier.
30. Hatch to room set apart for scientific purposes.
31. Galley.
32. Bunks for the crew — double rows.
33. Cable-tier and provision store.
34. Hatch to store-room.
35. Hatch to room for daily giving out of provisions.
36. Hatch to rope-room.
37. Sail-room.
38. Storeroom for water and coal.
39. Engine-room.
40. Cellar.

Plan of upper deck.

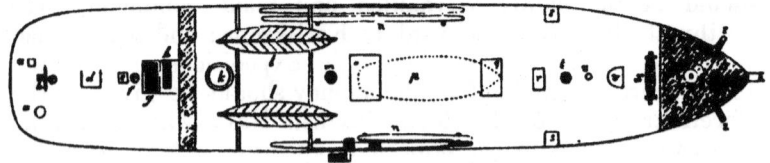

a. Thermometer case.
b. The rudder.
c. Binnacle with compass.
d. } Skylights to the gunroom.
e. }
f. Mizenmast
g. Descent to the gunroom } companion common
h. Descent to the engine } to both.
i. Bridge.
k. Funnel.
l. Boats lying on gallows.
m. Mainmast.
n. Rooms (for reserve masts, yards, &c.).
o. Main hatch.
p. Steam launch.
q. Fore hatch.
r. Hencoops.
s. Water closet.
t. Foremast.
u. Smoke-cowl.
v. Descent to lower deck (companion)
x. Windlass.
y. Capstan on the forecastle.
z. Catheads.

THE LENA.

Longitudinal section.

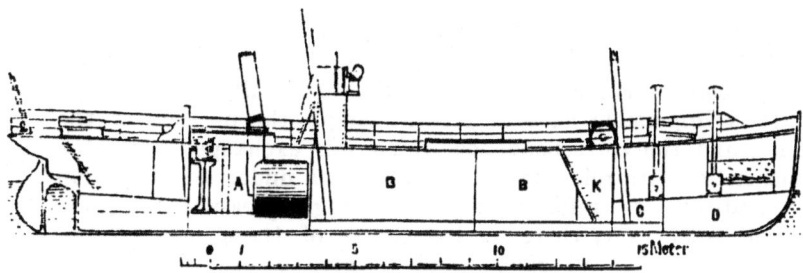

Plan of arrangement under deck.

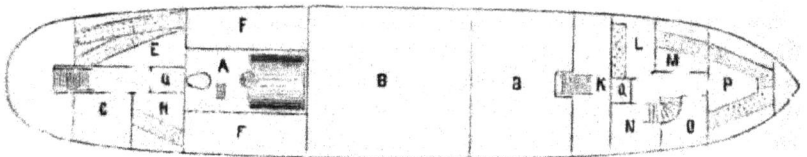

Plan of upper deck.

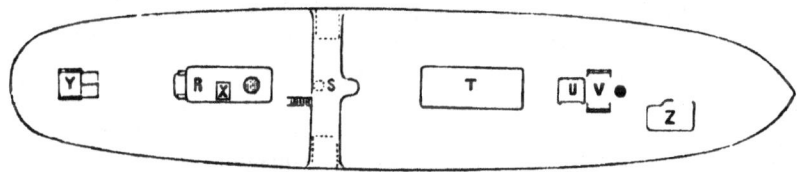

A.   Engine-room.
B. B. Hold.
C   Cable.
D.   Water ballast tank.
E.   Forecastle.
F. F.   Coal bunkers.
G.   Fireman's cabin.
H.   Engineer's cabin.
K.   Provision-room.
L.   Captain's cabin.
M.   Mate's cabin.
N.   Kitchen.
O.   Pantry.
P.   Saloon.
Q. Q. Presses.
R.   Engine-room companion.
S.   Bridge.
T.   Hatch to hold.
U.   Descent to provision-room.
V.   Winch.
X.   Descent to engine-room.
Y.   Descent to forecastle and engineer's cabin.
Z.   Descent to captain's cabin, saloon, &c.

question, and at the same time to resolve on making a proposal to the Diet in which additional grants were to be asked for it.

The proposal to the Diet of 1878 was agreed to with that liberality which has always distinguished the representatives of the Swedish people when grants for scientific purposes have been asked for; which was also the case with a private motion made in the same Diet by the President, C. F. WÆRN, member of the Academy of Sciences, whereby it was proposed to confer some further privileges on the undertaking.

It is impossible here to give at length the decision of the Diet, and the correspondence which was exchanged with the authorities with reference to it. But I am under an obligation of gratitude to refer to the exceedingly pleasant reception I met with everywhere in the course of these negotiations, from officials of all ranks, and to give a brief account of the privileges which the expedition finally came to enjoy, mainly owing to the letter of the Government to the Marine Department, dated the 14th June, 1878.

Two officers and seventeen men of the Royal Swedish Navy having obtained permission to take part in the expedition as volunteers, I was authorised to receive on account of the expedition from the treasury of the Navy, at Karlskrona—with the obligation of returning that portion of the funds which might not be required, and on giving approved security—full sea pay for two years for the officers, petty officers, and men taking part in the expedition; pay for the medical officer, at the rate of 3,500 Swedish crowns a year, for the same time; and subsistence money for the men belonging to the Navy, at the rate of one and a half Swedish crowns per man per day. The sum, by which the cost of provisions exceeded the amount calculated at this rate, was defrayed by the expedition, which likewise gave a considerable addition to the pay of the sailors belonging to the Navy. I further obtained permission to receive, on account of the expedition, from the Navy stores at Karlskrona, provisions, medicines, coal, oil, and other necessary equipment, under obligation to pay for any excess of value over 10,000 Swedish crowns (about 550l.); and finally the vessel of the expedition was permitted to be equipped and made completely seaworthy at the naval dockyard at Karlskrona, on condition, however, that the excess of expenditure on repairs over 25,000 crowns (about 1,375l.) should be defrayed by the expedition.

On the other hand my request that the *Vega*, the steamer purchased for the voyage, might be permitted to carry the man-of-war flag, was refused by the Minister of Marine in a letter of the 2nd February 1878. The *Vega* was therefore inscribed in the following month of March in the Swedish

Yacht Club. It was thus under its flag, *the Swedish man-of-war flag with a crowned O in the middle,* that the first circumnavigation of Asia and Europe was carried into effect.

The *Vega,* as will be seen from the description quoted further on, is a pretty large vessel, which during the first part of the voyage was to be heavily laden with provisions and coal. It would therefore be a work of some difficulty to get it afloat, if, in sailing forward along the coast in new, unsurveyed waters, it should run upon a bank of clay or sand. I therefore gladly availed myself of Mr. Sibiriakoff's offer to provide for the greater safety of the expedition, by placing at my disposal funds for building another steamer of a smaller size, the *Lena,* which should have the river Lena as its main destination, but, during the first part of the expedition, should act as tender to the *Vega,* being sent before to examine the state of the ice and the navigable waters, when such service might be useful. I had the *Lena* built at Motala, of Swedish Bessemer steel, mainly after a drawing of Engineer R. Runeberg of Finland. The steamer answered the purpose for which it was intended particularly well.

An unexpected opportunity of providing the steamers with coal during the course of the voyage besides arose by my receiving a commission while preparations were making for the expedition of the *Vega,* to fit out, also on Mr. Sibiriakoff's account, two other vessels, the steamer *Fraser,* and the sailing vessel *Express,* in order to bring to Europe from the mouth of the Yenisej a cargo of grain, and to carry thither a quantity of European goods. This was so much the more advantageous, as, according to the plan of the expedition, the *Vega* and the *Lena* were first to separate from the *Fraser* and the *Express* at the mouth of the Yenisej. The first-named vessels had thus an opportunity of taking on board at that place as much coal as there was room for.

I intend further on to give an account of the voyages of the other three vessels, each of which deserves a place in the history of navigation. To avoid details I shall only mention here that, at the beginning of the voyage which is to be described here, the following four vessels were at my disposal :—

1. The *Vega,* commanded by Lieutenant L. Palander, of the Swedish Navy; circumnavigated Asia and Europe.

2. The *Lena,* commanded by the walrus-hunting captain, Christian Johannesen; the first vessel that reached the river Lena from the Atlantic.

3. The *Fraser,* commanded by the merchant captain, Emil Nilsson.

4. The *Express,* commanded by the merchant captain,

Gundersen, the first which brought cargoes of grain from the Yenisej to Europe.[1]

When the *Vega* was bought for the expedition it was described by the sellers as follows :—

"The steamer *Vega* was built at Bremerhaven in 1872-73, of the best oak, for the share-company 'Ishafvet,' and under special inspection. It has twelve years' first class ³/₃ I.I. Veritas, measures 357 register tons gross, or 299 net. It was built and used for whale fishing in the North Polar Sea, and strengthened in every way necessary and commonly used for that purpose. Besides the usual timbering of oak, the vessel has an ice-skin of greenheart, wherever the ice may be expected to come at the vessel. The ice-skin extends from the neighbourhood of the under chain bolts to within from 1·2 to 1·5 metres of the keel. The dimensions are :—

Length of keel	37·6 metres
Do. over deck	43·4 „
Beam extreme	8·4 „
Depth of hold	4·6 „

"The engine, of sixty-horse power, is on Wolff's plan, with excellent surface condensers. It requires about ten cubic feet of coal per hour. The vessel is fully rigged as a barque, and has pitch pine masts, iron wire rigging, and patent reefing topsails. It sails and manœuvres uncommonly well, and under sail alone attains a speed of nine to ten knots. During the trial trip the steamer made seven and a half knots, but six to seven knots per hour may be considered the speed under steam. Further, there are on the vessel a powerful steam-winch, a reserve rudder, and a reserve propeller. The vessel is besides provided in the whole of the under hold with iron tanks, so built that they lie close to the vessel's bottom and sides, the tanks thus being capable of offering a powerful resistance in case of ice pressure. They are also serviceable for holding provisions, water, and coal." [2]

We had no reason to take exception to this description,[3] but, in any case, it was necessary for an Arctic campaign, such as that now in question, to make a further inspection of the

---

[1] The first cargo of goods from Europe to the Yenisej was taken thither by me in the *Ymer* in 1876. The first vessel that sailed from the Yenisej to the Atlantic was a sloop, *The Dawn*, built at Yeniseisk, commanded by the Russian merchant captain, Schwanenberg, in 1877.

[2] In order to obtain sufficient room for coal and provisions most of these tanks were taken out at Karlskrona.

[3] The consumption of coal, however, was reckoned by Captain Palander at twelve cubic feet or 0·3 cubic metre an hour, with a speed of seven knots.

vessel, to assure ourselves that all its parts were in complete order, to make the alterations in rig, &c., which the altered requirements would render necessary, and finally to arrange the vessel, so that it might house a scientific staff, which, together with the officers, numbered nine persons. This work was done at the Karlskrona naval dockyard, under the direction of Captain Palander. At the same time attention was given to the scientific equipment, principally in Stockholm, where a large number of instruments for physical, astronomical, and geological researches was obtained from the Royal Academy of Sciences.

The dietary during the expedition was fixed upon, partly on the ground of our experience from the wintering of 1872-73, partly under the guidance of a special opinion given with reference to the subject by the distinguished physician who took part in that expedition, Dr. A. Envall. Preserved provisions,[1] butter, flour, &c., were purchased, part at Karlskrona, part in Stockholm and Copenhagen; a portion of pemmican was prepared in Stockholm by Z. Wikström; another portion was purchased in England; fresh ripe potatoes [2] were procured from the Mediterranean, a large quantity of cranberry juice from Finland; preserved cloudberries and clothes of reindeer skins, &c., from Norway, through our agent Ebeltoft, and so on —in a word, nothing was neglected to make the vessel as well equipped as possible for the attainment of the great object in view.

What this was may be seen from the following

PLAN OF THE EXPEDITION,

PRESENTED TO HIS MAJESTY THE KING OF SWEDEN AND NORWAY, *July* 1877.

THE exploring expeditions, which, during the recent decades, have gone out from Sweden towards the north, have long ago acquired a truly national importance, through the lively interest that has been taken in them everywhere, beyond, as well as within, the fatherland; through the considerable sums of money that have been spent on them by the State, and above all by private persons; through the practical school they have formed for more than thirty Swedish naturalists; through the important

---

[1] The preserved provisions were purchased part from Z. Wikström of Stockholm, part from J. D. Beauvois of Copenhagen.

[2] The potatoes were to be delivered at Gothenburg on the 1st July. In order to keep, they had to be newly taken up and yet *ripe*. They were therefore procured from the south through Mr. Carl W. Boman of Stockholm. Of these, certainly one of the best of all anti-scorbutics, we had still some remaining on our arrival at Japan.

scientific and geographical results they have yielded; and
through the material for scientific research, which by them has
been collected for the Swedish Riks-Museum, and which has
made it, in respect of Arctic natural objects, the richest in the
world. To this there come to be added discoveries and investigations which already are, or promise in the future to become, of
practical importance; for example, the meteorological and hydrographical work of the expeditions: their comprehensive inquiries
regarding the Seal and Whale Fisheries in the Polar Seas; the
pointing out of the previously unsuspected richness in fish, of
the coasts of Spitzbergen; the discoveries, on Bear Island and
Spitzbergen, of considerable strata of coal and phosphatic
minerals which are likely to be of great economic importance
to neighbouring countries; and, above all, the success of the two
last expeditions in reaching the mouths of the large Siberian
rivers, navigable to the confines of China—the Obi and Yenisej
—whereby a problem in navigation, many centuries old, has at
last been solved.

But the very results that have been obtained incite to a continuation, especially as the two last expeditions have opened
a new field of inquiry, exceedingly promising in a scientific, and
I venture also to say in a practical, point of view, namely, the
part of the Polar Sea lying east of the mouth of the Yenisej.
Still, even in our days, in the era of steam and the telegraph, there
meets us here a territory to be explored, which is new to science,
and hitherto untouched. Indeed, the whole of the immense
expanse of ocean which stretches over 90 degrees of longitude
from the mouth of the Yenisej past Cape Chelyuskin—the
Promontorium Tabin of the old geographers—has, if we except
voyages in large or small boats along the coast, never yet been
ploughed by the keel of any vessel, and never seen the funnel
of a steamer.

It was this state of things which led me to attempt to procure
funds for an expedition, equipped as completely as possible,
both in a scientific and a nautical respect, with a view to
investigate the geography, hydrography, and natural history
of the North Polar Sea beyond the mouth of the Yenisej, if
possible as far as Behring's Straits. It may be affirmed without
any danger of exaggeration, that since Cook's famous voyages
in the Pacific Ocean, no more promising field of research has
lain before any exploring expedition, if only the state of the
ice permit a suitable steamer to force a passage in that sea. In
order to form a judgment on this point, it may perhaps be
necessary to cast a brief glance backwards over the attempts
which have been made to penetrate in the direction which the
projected expedition is intended to take.

The Swedish port from which the expedition is to start will

probably be Gothenburg. The time of departure is fixed for the beginning of July, 1878. The course will be shaped at first along the west Coast of Norway, past North Cape and the entrance to the White Sea, to Matotschkin Sound in Novaya Zemlya.

The opening of a communication by sea between the rest of Europe and these regions, by Sir Hugh Willoughby and Richard Chancellor in 1553, was the fruit of the first exploring expedition sent out from England by sea. Their voyage also forms the first attempt to discover a north-east passage to China. The object aimed at was not indeed accomplished; but on the other hand, there was opened by the voyage in question the sea communication between England and the White Sea; the voyage thus forming a turning-point not only in the navigation of England and Russia, but also in the commerce of the world. It also demanded its sacrifice, Sir Hugh Willoughby himself, with all the men in the vessels under his command, having perished while wintering on the Kola peninsula. In our days thousands of vessels sail safely along this route.

With the knowledge we now possess of the state of the ice in the Murman Sea—so the sea between Kola and Novaya Zemlya is called on the old maps—it is possible to sail during the latter part of summer from the White Sea to Matotschkin without needing to fear the least hindrance from ice. For several decades back, however, in consequence of want of knowledge of the proper season and the proper course, the case has been quite different—as is sufficiently evident from the account of the difficulties and dangers which the renowned Russian navigator, Count Lütke, met with during his repeated voyages four summers in succession (1821-1824) along the west coast of Novaya Zemlya. A skilful walrus-hunter can now, with a common walrus-hunting vessel, in a single summer, sail further in this sea than formerly could an expedition, fitted out with all the resources of a naval yard, in four times as long time.

There are four ways of passing from the Murman Sea to the Kara Sea, viz:—

a. Yugor Sound—the Fretum Nassovicum of the old Dutchmen—between Vaygats Island and the mainland.

b. The Kara Port, between Vaygats Island and Novaya Zemlya.

c. Matotschkin Sound, which between 73° and 74° N. Lat. divides Novaya Zemlya into two parts, and finally,

d. The course north of the double island. The course past the northernmost point of Novaya Zemlya is not commonly clear of ice till the beginning of the month of September, and perhaps ought, therefore, not to be chosen for an expedition having for its object to penetrate far to the eastward in this sea. Yugor Sound and the Kara Port are early free of fast ice, but instead, are long rendered difficult to navigate by considerable masses of drift ice, which are carried backwards and forwards in the bays on both sides of the sound by the currents which here alternate with the ebb and flow of the tide. Besides, at least in Yugor Sound, there are no good harbours, in consequence of which the drifting masses of ice may greatly inconvenience the vessels, which by these routes attempt to enter the Kara Sea. Matotschkin Sound, again, forms a channel nearly 100 kilometres long, deep and clear, with the exception of a couple of shoals, the position of which is known, which indeed is not usually free from fast ice until the latter half of July, but, on the other hand, in consequence of the configuration of the coast, is less subject to be obstructed by drift ice than the southern straits. There are good harbours at the eastern mouth of the sound. In 1875 and 1876 both the sound and the sea lying off it were completely open in the end of August, but the ice was much earlier broken up also on the eastern side, so that a vessel could without danger make its way among the scattered pieces of drift ice. The part of Novaya Zemlya which is first visited by the walrus-hunters in spring is usually just the west coast off Matotschkin.

In case unusual weather does not prevail in the regions in question during the course of early and mid-summer, 1878—for instance, very steady southerly winds, which would early drive the drift ice away from the coast of the mainland—I consider, on the grounds which I have stated above, that it will be safest for the expedition to choose the course by Matotschkin Sound.

We cannot, however, reckon on having, so early as the beginning of August, open water *direct* to Port Dickson at the mouth of the Yenisej, but must be prepared to make a considerable detour towards the south in order to avoid the masses of drift ice, which are to be met with in the Kara Sea up to the beginning of September. The few days' delay which may be caused by the state of the ice here, will afford, besides, to the expedition an opportunity for valuable work in examining the natural history and hydrography of the channel, about 200 fathoms deep, which runs along the east coast of Novaya Zemyla. The Kara Sea is, in the other parts of it, not deep, but evenly shallow (ten to thirty fathoms), yet without being fouled by shoals or rocks. The most abundant animal life is found in the before-mentioned deep channel along the east coast, and it was from it that our two foregoing expeditions brought home several animal types, very peculiar and interesting in a systematic point of view. Near the coast the algæ, too, are rich and luxuriant. The coming expedition ought, therefore, to endeavour to reach Matotschkin Sound so early that at least seven days' scientific work may be done in those regions.

The voyage from the Kara Sea to Port Dickson is not attended, according to recent experience, with any difficulty. Yet we cannot reckon on arriving at Port Dickson sooner than from the 10th to the 15th August. In 1875 I reached this harbour with a sailing-vessel on the 15th August, after having been much delayed by calms in the Kara Sea. With a steamer it would have been possible to have reached the harbour, that year, in the beginning of the month. In 1876 the state of the ice was less favourable, in consequence of a cold summer and a prevalence of north-east winds, but even then I arrived at the mouth of the Yenisej on the 15th August.

It is my intention to lie to at Port Dickson, at least for some hours, in order to deposit letters on one of the neighbouring islands, in case, as is probable, I have no opportunity of meeting there some vessel sent out from Yeniseisk, by which accounts of the expedition may be sent home.

Actual observations regarding the hydrography of the coast between the mouth of the Yenisej and Cape Chelyuskin are for the present nearly wholly wanting, seeing that, as I have already stated, no large vessel has ever sailed from this neighbourhood. Even about the boat voyages of the Russians along the coast we know exceedingly little, and from their unsuccessful attempts to force a passage here we may by no means draw any unfavourable conclusion as to the navigability of the sea during certain seasons of the year. If, with a knowledge of the resources for the equipment of naval expeditions which Siberia now possesses, we seek to form an idea of the equipment of the Russian expeditions [1] sent out with extraordinary perseverance during the years 1734-1743 by different routes to the north coast of Siberia, the correctness of this assertion ought to be easily perceived. There is good reason to expect that a well-equipped steamer will be able to penetrate far beyond the point where they were compelled to return with their small but numerously manned craft, too fragile to encounter ice, and unsuitable for the open sea, being generally held together with willows.

[1] A carefully written account of these voyages will be found in *Reise des Kaiserlich-russischen Flotten-Lieutenants Ferdinand von Wrangel längs der Nordküste von Siberien und auf dem Eismeere*, 1820-1824, bearbeitet von G. Engelhardt, Berlin, 1839 ; and G. P. Müller, *Voyages et Découvertes faites par les Russes le long des Côtes de la Mer Glaciale*, &c. Amsterdam : 1766.

There are, besides these, only three sea voyages, or perhaps more correctly coast journeys, known in this part of the Kara Sea, all under the leadership of the mates Minin and Sterlegoff. The first attempt was made in 1738 in a "double sloop," 70 feet long, 17 broad, and 7½ deep, built at Tobolsk and transported thence to the Yenisej by Lieutenant Owzyn. With this vessel Minin penetrated off the Yenisej to 72° 53′ N.L. Hence a jolly boat was sent further towards the north, but it too was compelled, by want of provisions, to return before the point named by me, Port Dickson, was reached. The following year a new attempt was made, without a greater distance being traversed than the summer before. Finally in the year 1740 the Russians succeeded in reaching, with the double sloop already mentioned, 75° 15′ N.L., after having survived great dangers from a heavy sea at the river mouth. On the 2nd September, just as the most advantageous season for navigation in these waters had begun, they returned, principally on account of the lateness of the season.

There are, besides, two statements founded on actual observations regarding the state of the ice on this coast. For Middendorff, the Academician, during his famous journey of exploration in North Siberia, reached from land the sea coast at Tajmur Bay (75° 40′ N.L.), *and found the sea on the 25th August,* 1843, *free of ice as far as the eye could reach from the chain of heights along the coast.*[1] Middendorff, besides, states that the Yakoot Fomin, the only person who had passed a winter at Tajmur Bay, declared that the ice loosens in the sea lying off it in the first half of August, and that it is driven away from the beach by southerly winds, yet not further than that the edge of the ice can be seen from the heights along the coast.

The land between the Tajmur and Cape Chelyuskin was mapped by means of *sledge* journeys along the coast by mate Chelyuskin in the year 1742. It is now completely established that the northernmost promontory of Asia was discovered by him in the month of May in the year already mentioned, and at that time the sea in its neighbourhood was of course covered with ice. We have no observation as to the state of the ice during summer or autumn in the sea lying immediately to the west of Cape Chelyuskin; but, as the question relates to the possibility of navigating this sea, this is the place to draw attention to the fact that Prontschischev, on the 1st September, 1736, in an open sea, with coasting craft *from the east,* very nearly reached the north point of Asia, which is supposed to be situated in 77° 34′ N. Lat. and

---

[1] Th. von Middendorff, *Reise in dem äussersten Norden und Osten Sibeieriens,* vol. iv. I., pages 21 and 508 (1867).

105° E. Long., and that the Norwegian walrus-hunters during late autumn have repeatedly sailed far to the eastward from the north point of Novaya Zemlya (77° N. Lat., and 68° E. Long.), *without meeting with any ice.*

From what has been already stated, it is evident that for the present we do not possess any complete knowledge, founded on actual observations, of the hydrography of the stretch of coast between the Yenisej and Cape Chelyuskin. I, however, consider that during September, and possibly the latter half of August, we ought to be able to reckon with complete certainty on having here ice-free water, or at least a broad, open channel along the coast, from the enormous masses of warm water, which the rivers Obi, Irtisch, and Yenisej, running up through the steppes of High Asia, here pour into the ocean, after having received water from a river territory, everywhere strongly heated during the month of August, and more extensive than that of all the rivers put together, which fall into the Mediterranean and the Black Seas.

Between Port Dickson and White Island, there runs therefore a strong fresh-water current, at first in a northerly direction. The influence which the rotation of the earth exercises, in these high latitudes, on streams which run approximately in the direction of the meridian, is however, very considerable, and gives to those coming from the south an easterly bend. In consequence of this, the river water of the Obi and Yenisej must be confined as in a proper river channel, at first along the coast of the Tajmur country, until the current is allowed beyond Cape Chelyuskin to flow unhindered towards the north-east or east. Near the mouths of the large rivers I have, during calm weather in this current, in about 74° N. L., observed the temperature rising off the Yenisej to + 9·4° C. (17th August, 1875), and off the Obi to + 8° C. (10th August of the same year). As is usually the case, this current coming from the south produces both a cold under-current, which in stormy weather readily mixes with the surface water and cools it, and on the surface a northerly cold ice-bestrewn counter-current, which, in consequence of the earth's rotation, takes a bend to the west, and which evidently runs from the opening between Cape Chelyuskin and the northern extremity of Novaya Zemlya, towards the east side of this island, and perhaps may be the cause why the large masses of drift ice are pressed during summer against the east coast of Novaya Zemlya. According to my own experience and the uniform testimony of the walrus-hunters, *this ice melts away almost completely during autumn.*

In order to judge of the distance at which the current coming from the Obi and the Yenisej can drive away the drift ice, we ought to remember that even a very weak current exerts an influence on the position of the ice, and that, for instance, the current from the Plata River, whose volume of water, however, is not perhaps so great as that of the Obi and Yenisej, is still clearly perceptible at a distance of 1,500 kilometres from the river mouth, that is to say, about three times as far as from Port Dickson to Cape Chelyuskin. The only bay which can be compared to the Kara Sea in respect of the area, which is intersected by the rivers running into it, is the Gulf of Mexico,[1] The river currents from this bay appear to contribute greatly to the Gulf Stream.

The winds which, during the autumn months, often blow in these regions from the north-east, perhaps also, in some degree, contribute to keep a broad channel, along the coast in question, nearly ice-free.

The knowledge we possess regarding the navigable water to the east of Cape Chelyuskin towards the Lena, is mainly founded on the observations of the expeditions which were sent out by the Russian Government, before the middle of last century, to survey the northern part of Asia. In order to form a correct judgment of the results obtained, we must, while fully recognising the great courage, the extraordinary perseverance, and the power of bearing sufferings and overcoming difficulties of all kinds, which have always distinguished the Russian Polar explorers, always keep in mind that the voyages were carried out with small sailing-vessels of a build, which, according to modern requirements, is quite unsuitable for vessels intended for the open sea, and altogether too weak to stand collision with ice. They wanted, besides, not only the powerful auxiliary of our time, steam, but also a proper sail rig, fitted for actual manœuvring, and were for the most part manned with crews from the banks of the Siberian rivers, who never before had seen the water of the ocean, experienced a high sea, or tried sailing among sea ice. When the requisite attention is given to these circumstances, it appears to me that the voyages referred to below show positively that even here we ought to be able during autumn to reckon upon a navigable sea.

The expeditions along the coast, east of Cape Chelyuskin, started from the town Yakoutsk, on the bank of the Lena, in 62° N. L., upwards of 900 miles from the mouth of the river. Here also were built the vessels which were used for these voyages.

---

[1] Compare von Middendorff, *Reise im Norden u. Osten Siberiens* (1848), part i., page 59, and a paper by von Baer, *Ueber das Klima des Tajmur-landes.*

The first started in 1735, under the command of Marine-Lieutenant Prontschischev. After having sailed down the river, and passed, on the 14th August, the eastern mouth-arm of the Lena, he sailed round the large delta of the river. On the 7th September he had not got farther than to the mouth of the Olonek. Three weeks had thus been spent in sailing a distance which an ordinary steamer ought now to be able to traverse in one day. Ice was seen, but not encountered. On the other hand, the voyage was delayed by contrary winds, probably blowing on land, whereby Prontschischev's vessel, if it had incautiously ventured out, would probably have been cast on the beach. The late season of the year induced Prontschischev to lay up his vessel for the winter here, at some summer yourts built by fur-hunters in 72° 54′ N. L. The winter passed happily, and the following year (1736) Prontschischev again broke up, as soon as the state of the ice in Olonek Bay permitted, which, however, was not until the 15th August. The course was shaped along the coast toward the north-west. Here drift ice was met with, but he nevertheless made rapid progress, so that on the 1st September he reached 77° 29′ N. L., as we now know, in the neighbourhood of Cape Chelyuskin. Compact masses of ice compelled him to turn here, and the Russians sailed back to the mouth of the Olonek, which was reached on the 15th September. The distinguished commander of the vessel had died shortly before of scurvy, and, some days after, his young wife, who had accompanied him on his difficult voyage, also died. As these attacks of scurvy did not happen during winter, but immediately after the close of summer, they form very remarkable contributions to a judgment of the way in which the Arctic expeditions of that period were fitted out.

A new expedition, under Marine-Lieutenant Chariton Laptev, sailed along the same coast in 1739. The Lena was left on the 1st August, and Cape Thaddeus (76° 47′ N. L.) reached on the 2nd September, the navigation having been obstructed by drift ice only off Chatanga Bay. Cape Thaddeus is situated only fifty or sixty English miles from Cape Chelyuskin. They turned here, partly on account of the masses of drift ice which barred the way, partly on account of the late season of the year, and wintered at the head of Chatanga Bay, which was reached on the 8th September. Next year Laptev attempted to return along the coast to the Lena, but his vessel was nipped by drift ice off the mouth of the Olonek. After many difficulties and dangers, all the men succeeded in reaching safely the winter quarters of the former year. Both from this point and from the Yenisej, Laptev himself and his second in command, Chelyuskin, and the surveyor, Tschekin, the following year made a number of sledge journeys, in order to survey the peninsula which projects farthest to the north-west from the mainland of Asia.

With this ended the voyages west of the Lena. The northern-most point of Asia, which was reached from land in 1742 by Chelyuskin, one of the most energetic members of most of the expeditions which we have enumerated, could not be reached by sea, and still less had any one succeeded in forcing his way with a vessel from the Lena to the Yenisej. Prontschischev had, however, turned on the 1st September, 1736, only some few minutes, and Laptev on the 2nd September, 1739, only about 50' from the point named, after voyages in vessels, which clearly were altogether unsuitable for the purpose in view. Among the difficulties and obstacles which were met with during these voyages, not only ice, but also unfavourable and stormy winds played a prominent part. From fear of not being able to reach any winter station visited by natives, the explorers often turned at that season of the year when the Polar Sea is most open. With proper allowance for these circumstances, we may safely affirm that no serious obstacles to sailing round Cape Chelyuskin would probably have been met with in the years named, by any steamer properly fitted out for sailing among ice.

From the sea between the Lena and Behring's Straits there are much more numerous and complete observations than from that further west. The hope of obtaining tribute and commercial profit from the wild races living along the coast tempted the adventurous Russian hunters, even before the middle of the 17th century, to undertake a number of voyages along the coast. On a map which is annexed to the previously quoted work of Müller, founded mainly on researches in the Siberian archives, there is to be found a sea route pricked out with the inscription, " *Route anciennement fort fréquentée. Voyage fait par mer en* 1648 *par trois vaisseaux russes, dont un est parvenu jusqu'à la Kamschatka.*" [1]

Unfortunately the details of most of these voyages have been completely forgotten ; and, that we have obtained some scanty accounts of one or other of them, has nearly always depended on some remarkable catastrophe, on lawsuits or other circum-stances which led to the interference of the authorities. This is even the case with the most famous of these voyages, that of the Cossack, Deschnev, of which several accounts have been preserved, only through a dispute which arose between him and one of his companions, concerning the right of discovery to a walrus bank on the east coast of Kamschatka. This voyage, however, was a veritable exploring expedition undertaken with the approval of the Government, partly for the discovery of some large islands in the Polar Sea, about which a number of reports

---

[1] The map bears the title, " Nouvelle carte des découvertes faites par des vaisseaux Russiens, etc., dressée sur des mémoires authentiques de ceux qui ont assisté à ces découvertes, et sur d'autres connaissances dont on rend raison dans un mémoire séparé.   St Pétersbourg à l'Académie Impériale des Sciences, 1758."

were current among the hunters and natives, partly for extending the territory yielding tribute to the Russians, over the yet
unknown regions in the north-east.

Deschnev started on the 1st July, 1648, from the Kolyma in
command of one of the seven vessels (*Kotscher*),[1] manned with
thirty men, of which the expedition consisted. Concerning the
fate of four of these vessels we have no information. It is
probable that they turned back, and were not lost, as several
writers have supposed; three, under the command of the
Cossacks, Deschnev and Ankudinov, and the fur-hunter, Kolmo-
gorsov, succeeding in reaching Chutskojnos through what appears
to have been open water. Here Ankudinov's vessel was shipwrecked; the men, however, were saved and divided among
the other two, which were speedily separated. Deschnev continued his voyage along the east coast of Kamschatka to the
Anadir, which was reached in October. Ankudinov is also
supposed to have reached the mouth of the Kamschatka River,
where he settled among the natives and finally died of scurvy.

The year following (1649) Staduchin sailed again, for seven
days, eastward from the Kolyma to the neighbourhood of
Chutskojnos, in an open sea, so far as we can gather from the
defective account. Deschnev's own opinion of the possibility
of navigating this sea may be seen from the fact, that, after
his own vessel was lost, he had timber collected at the Anadir
for the purpose of building new ones. With these he intended
to send to Yakoutsk the tribute of furs which he had received
from the natives. He was, however, obliged to desist from his
project by an easily understood want of materials for the building of the new vessels; he remarks also in connection with this
that the sea round Chutskojnos is not free of ice every year.

A number of voyages from the Siberian rivers northward, were
also made after the founding of Nischni Kolymsk, by Michael
Staduschin in 1644, in consequence of the reports which were
current among the natives at the coast, of the existence of large
inhabited islands, rich in walrus tusks and mammoth bones,
in the Siberian Polar Sea. Often disputed, but persistently taken
up by the hunting races, these reports have finally been verified
by the discovery of the islands of New Siberia, of Wrangel's
Land, and of the part of North America east of Behring's Straits,
whose natural state gave occasion to the golden glamour of
tradition with which the belief of the common people incorrectly adorned the bleak, treeless islands in the Polar Sea.

All these attempts to force a passage in the open sea from the
Siberian coasts northwards, failed, for the single reason, that an

---

[1] Pretty broad, flat-bottomed, keelless vessels, 12 fathoms long, generally moved forward by rowing; sail only used with fair wind (*Wrangels
Reise*, p. 4).

open sea with a fresh breeze was as destructive to the craft which were at the disposal of the adventurous, but ill-equipped Siberian polar explorer as an ice-filled sea; indeed, more dangerous, for in the latter case the crew, if the vessel was nipped, generally saved themselves on the ice, and had only to contend with hunger, snow, cold, and other difficulties to which the most of them had been accustomed from their childhood; but in the open sea the ill-built, weak vessel, caulked with moss mixed with clay, and held together with willows, leaked already with a moderate sea, and with a heavier, was helplessly lost, if a harbour could not be reached in time of need.

The explorers soon preferred to reach the islands by sledge journeys on the ice, and thus at last discovered the whole of the large group of islands which is named New Siberia. The islands were often visited by hunters for the purpose of collecting mammoth tusks, of which great masses, together with the bones of the mammoth, rhinoceros, sheep, ox, horse, etc., are found imbedded in the beds of clay and sand here. Afterwards they were completely surveyed during Hedenström's expeditions, fitted out by Count Rumänzov, Chancellor of the Russian Empire, in the years 1809-1811, and during Lieutenant Anjou's in 1823. Hedenström's expeditions were carried out by travelling with dog-sledges on the ice, before it broke, to the islands, passing the summer there, and returning in autumn, when the sea was again covered with ice. As the question relates to the possibility of navigating this sea, these expeditions, carried out in a very praiseworthy way, might be expected to have great interest, especially through observations from land, concerning the state of the ice in autumn; but in the short account of Hedenström's expeditions which is inserted in Wrangel's *Travels*, pp. 99-119, the only source accessible to me in this respect, there is not a single word on this point.[1] Information on this subject, so important for our expedition, has, however, by Mr. Sibiriakoff's care, been received from inhabitants of North Siberia, who earn their living by collecting mammoths' tusks on the group of islands in question. By these accounts the sea between the north coast of Asia and the islands of New Siberia, is every year pretty free of ice.

A very remarkable discovery was made in 1811 by a member of Hedenström's expedition, the Yakoutsk townsman Sannikov; for he found, on the west coast of the island Katelnoj, remains of a roughly-timbered winter habitation, in the neighbourhood of the wreck of a vessel, differing completely in build from those which are common in Siberia. Partly from this, partly from a

---

[1] Wrangel's own journeys were carried out during winter, with dog-sledges on the ice, and, however interesting in many other respects, do not yield any other direct contribution to our knowledge of the state of the ice in summer and autumn.

number of tools which lay scattered on the beach, Sannikov drew the conclusion, that a hunter from Spitzbergen or Novaya Zemlya had been driven thither by the wind, and had lived there for a season with this crew. Unfortunately the inscription on a monumental cross in the neighbourhood of the hut was not translated.

During the great northern expeditions,[1] several attempts were also made to force a passage eastwards from the Lena. The first was under the command of Lieutenant Lassinius in 1735. He left the most easterly mouth-arm of the Lena on the 21st of August, and sailed 120 versts eastward, and there encountered drift ice, which compelled him to seek a harbour at the coast. Here the winter was passed, with the unfortunate result, that the chief himself, and most of the fifty-two men belonging to the expedition, perished of scurvy.

The following year, 1736, there was sent out, in the same direction, a new expedition under Lieutenant Dmitri Laptev. With the vessel of Lassinius he attempted, in the middle of August, to sail eastward, but he soon fell in with a great deal of drift ice. So soon as the end of the month—the time when navigation ought properly to begin—he turned towards the Lena on account of ice.

In 1739 Laptev undertook his third voyage. He penetrated to the mouth of the Indigirka, which was frozen over on the 21st September, and wintered there. The following year the voyage was continued somewhat beyond the mouth of the Kolyma to Cape Great Baranov, where further advance was prevented by drift ice on the 26th September. After having returned to the Kolyma, and wintered at Nischni Kolymsk, he attempted, the following year, again to make his way eastwards in some large boats built during winter, but, on account of fog, contrary winds, and ice, without success. In judging of the results these voyages yielded, we must take into consideration the utterly unsuitable vessels in which they were undertaken— at first in a double sloop built at Yakoutsk, in 1735, afterwards in two large boats built at Nischni Kolymsk. If we may judge of the nature of these craft from those now used on the Siberian rivers, we ought rather to be surprised that any of them could venture out on a real sea, than consider the unsuccessful voyages just described as proofs that there is no probability of being able to force a passage here with a vessel of modern build, and provided with steam power.

It remains, finally, for me to give an account of the attempts that have been made to penetrate westward from Behring's Straits.

[1] This is a common name for the many Russian expeditions which, during the years 1734-1743, were sent into the North Polar Sea from the Dwina, Obi, Yenisej, Lena, and Kamschatka.

Deschnev's voyage, from the Lena, through Behring's Straits to the mouth of the Anadir, in 1648, became completely forgotten in the course of about a century, until Müller, by searches in the Siberian archives, recovered the details of these and various other voyages along the north coast of Siberia. That the memory of these remarkable voyages has been preserved to after-times, however, depends, as has been already stated, upon accidental circumstances, lawsuits, and such like, which led to correspondence with the authorities. Of other similar undertakings we have certainly no knowledge, although now and then we find it noted that the Polar Sea had in former times often been traversed. In accounts of the expeditions fitted out by the authorities, it, for instance, often happens that mention is made of meeting with hunters and traders, who were sailing along the coast in the prosecution of private enterprise. Little attention was, however, given to these voyages, and, eighty-one years after Deschnev's voyage, the existence of straits between the north-eastern extremity of Asia and the north-western extremity of America was quite unknown, or at least doubted. Finally, in 1729, Behring anew sailed through the Sound, and attached his name to it. He did not sail, however, very far (to 172° W. Long.) along the north coast of Asia, although he does not appear to have met with any obstacle from ice. Nearly fifty years afterwards Cook concluded in these waters the series of splendid discoveries with which he enriched geographical science. After having, in 1778, sailed a good way eastwards along the north coast of America, he turned towards the west, and reached the 180th degree of longitude on the 29th August : the fear of meeting with ice deterred him from sailing further westward, and his vessel appears to have scarcely been equipped or fitted for sailing among ice.

After Cook's time we know of only three expeditions which have sailed westwards from Behring's Straits. The first was an American expedition, under Captain Rodgers, in 1855. He reached, through what appears to have been open water, the longitude of Cape Yakan (176° E. from Greenwich). The second was that of the English steam-whaler Long, who, in 1867, in search of a new profitable whale-fishing ground, sailed further west than any before him. By the 10th August he had reached the longitude of Tschaun Bay (170° E. from Greenwich). He was engaged in whale-fishing, not in an exploring expedition, and turned here ; but, in the short account he has given of his voyage, he expresses the decided conviction that a voyage from Behring's Straits to the Atlantic belongs to the region of possibilities, and adds that, even if this sea-route does not come to be of any commercial importance, that between the Lena and Behring's Straits ought to be useful for turning to account the products of Northern Siberia.[1] Finally, last year a Russian expedition was sent out to endeavour to reach Wrangel's Land from Behring's Straits. According to communications in the newspapers, it was prevented by ice from sailing thence, as well as from sailing far to the west.

Information has been obtained through Mr. Sibiriakoff, from North Siberia, regarding the state of the ice in the neighbouring sea. The hunting in these regions appears to have now fallen off so seriously, that only few persons were found who could give any answers to the questions put.

Thus in Yakoutsk there was only one man (a priest) who had been at the coast of the Polar Sea. He states that when the wind blows off the land the sea becomes free of ice, but that the ice comes back when the wind blows on to the land, and thereby exposes the vessels which cannot reach a safe harbour to great danger.

Another correspondent states, on the ground of observations made during Tschikanovski's expedition, that in 1875 the sea off the Olonek was *completely* free of ice, but adds at the same time that the year in this respect was an exceptional one. The Arctic Ocean, not only in summer, but also during winter, is *occasionally* free of ice, and at a distance of 200 versts from the coast, the sea is open even in winter, in what direction, however, is uncertain. The latter fact is also confirmed by Wrangel's journeys with dog-sledges on the ice in 1821-1823.

A third person says, "According to the information which I have received, the north coast, from the mouth of the Lena to that of the Indigirka, is free from ice from July to September. The north wind drives the ice towards the coast, but not in large masses. According to the observations of the men who search for mammoth tusks, the sea is open as far as the southern part of the New Siberia Islands. It is probable that these islands form a protection against the ice in the Werchnojan region. It is otherwise on the Kolyma coast; and if the Kolyma can be reached from Behring's Straits, so certainly can the Lena."

The circumstance that the ice during summer is driven from the coast by southerly winds, yet not so far but that it returns, in larger or smaller quantity, with northerly winds, is further confirmed by other correspondents, and appears to me to show that the New Siberian Islands and Wrangel's Land only form links in an extensive group of islands running parallel with the north coast of Siberia, which, on the one hand, keeps the ice from the intermediate sea from drifting away altogether, and favours the formation of ice during winter, but, on the other

---

[1] Petermann's *Mittheilungen*, 1868, p. 1, and 1869, p. 32.

hand, protects the coast from the Polar ice proper, formed to the north of the islands. The information I have received besides, refers principally to the summer months. As in the Kara Sea, which formerly had a yet worse reputation, the ice here too, perhaps, melts away for the most part during autumn, so that at this season we may reckon on a pretty open sea.

Most of the correspondents, who have given information about the state of the ice in the Siberian Polar Sea, concern themselves further with the reports current in Siberia, that American whalers have been seen from the coast far to the westward. The correctness of these reports was always denied in the most decided way; yet they rest, at least to some extent, on a basis of fact. For I have myself met with a whaler, who for three years in a steamer carried on trade with the inhabitants of the coast from Cape Yakan to Behring's Straits. He was quite convinced that some years at least it would be possible to sail from Behring's Straits to the Atlantic. On one occasion he had returned through Behring's Straits as late as the 17th October.

From what I have thus stated, it follows,—

That the ocean lying north of the north coast of Siberia, between the mouth of the Yenisej and Tschaun Bay, has never been ploughed by the keel of any proper sea-going vessel, still less been traversed by any steamer specially fitted out for navigation among ice :

That the small vessels with which it has been attempted to traverse this part of the ocean never ventured very far from the coast :

That an open sea, with a fresh breeze, was as destructive for them, indeed more destructive, than a sea covered with drift ice :

That they almost always sought some convenient winter harbour, just at that season of the year when the sea is freest of ice, namely, late summer or autumn :

That, notwithstanding the sea from 'Cape Chelyuskin to Behring's Straits has been repeatedly traversed, no one has yet succeeded in sailing over the whole extent at once :

That the covering of ice formed during winter along the coast, but probably not in the open sea, is every summer broken up, giving origin to extensive fields of drift ice, which are driven, now by a northerly wind towards the coast, now by a south wind out to sea, yet not so far but that it comes back to the coast after some days' northerly wind ; whence it appears probable that the Siberian Sea is, so to say, shut off from the Polar Sea proper, by a series of islands, of which, for the present, we know only Wrangel's Land and the islands which form New Siberia.

In this connection it seems to me probable that a well-equipped steamer would be able without meeting too many difficulties, at least obstacles from ice, to force a passage this way during autumn in a few days, and thus not only solve a geographical problem of several centuries' standing, but also, with all the means that are now at the disposal of the man of science in researches in geography, hydrography, geology, and natural history, survey a hitherto almost unknown sea of enormous extent.

The sea north of Behring's Straits is now visited by hundreds of whaling steamers, and the way thence to American and European harbours therefore forms a much-frequented route. Some few decades back, this was, however, by no means the case. The voyages of Behring, Cook, Kotzebue, Beechey, and others were then considered as adventurous, fortunate exploring expeditions of great value and importance in respect of science, but without any direct practical utility. For nearly a hundred and fifty years the same was the case with Spangberg's voyage from Kamschatka to Japan in the year 1739, by which the exploring expeditions of the Russians, in the northernmost part of the Pacific Ocean, were connected with those of the Dutch and the Portuguese to India and Japan ; and in case our expedition succeeds in reaching the Suez Canal, after having circumnavigated Asia, there will meet us there a splendid work, which, more than any other, reminds us, that what to-day is declared by experts to be impossible, is often carried into execution to-morrow.

I am also fully convinced that it is not only possible to sail along the north coast of Asia, provided circumstances are not too unfavourable, but that such an enterprise will be of incalculable practical importance, by no means directly, as opening a new commercial route, but indirectly, by the impression which would thereby be communicated of the practical utility of a communication by sea between the ports of North Scandinavia and the Obi and Yenisej, on the one hand, and between the Pacific Ocean and the Lena on the other.

Should the expedition, contrary to expectation, not succeed in carrying out the programme which has been arranged in its entirety, it ought not to be looked upon as having failed. In such a case the expedition will remain for a considerable time at places on the north coast of Siberia, suitable for scientific research. Every mile beyond the mouth of the Yenisej is a step forward to a complete knowledge of our globe—an object which sometime or other must be attained, and towards which it is a point of honour for every civilised nation to contribute in its proportion.

Men of science will have an opportunity, in these hitherto unvisited waters, of answering a number of questions regarding the former and present state of the Polar countries, of which

more than one is of sufficient weight and importance to lead to
such an expedition as the present. I may be permitted here
to refer to only a few of these.

If we except that part of the Kara Sea which has been
surveyed by the two last Swedish expeditions, we have for the
present no knowledge of the vegetable and animal life in the
sea which washes the north coast of Siberia. Quite certainly we
shall here, in opposition to what has been hitherto supposed,
meet with the same abundance of animals and plants as in the
sea round Spitzbergen. In the Siberian Polar sea, the animal
and vegetable types, so far as we can judge beforehand, exclusively
consist of survivals from the glacial period, which next preceded
the present, which is not the case in the Polar Sea, where the
Gulf Stream distributes its waters, and whither it thus carries
types from more southerly regions. But a complete and exact
knowledge of which animal types are of glacial, and which of
Atlantic origin, is of the greatest importance, not only for zoology
and the geography of animals, but also for the geology of Scandinavia, and especially for the knowledge of our loose earthy layers.

Few scientific discoveries have so powerfully captivated the
interest, both of the learned and unlearned, as that of the colossal
remains of elephants, sometimes well preserved, with flesh and
hair, in the frozen soil of Siberia. Such discoveries have more
than once formed the object of scientifice expeditions, and careful researches of eminent men ; but there is still much that is
enigmatical with respect to a number of circumstances connected
with the mammoth period of Siberia, which *perhaps* was contemporaneous with our glacial period. Specially is our knowledge of the animal and vegetable types, which lived contemporaneously with the mammoth, exceedingly incomplete, although
we know that in the northernmost parts of Sibeira, which are
also most inaccessible. from land, there are small hills covered
with the bones of the mammoth and other contemporaneous
animals, and that there is found everywhere in that region so-
called Noah's wood, that is to say, half-petrified or carbonised
vegetable remains from several different geological periods.

Taking a general view of the subject, we see that an
investigation, as complete as possible, of the geology of the
Polar countries, so difficult of access, is a condition indispensable to a knowledge of the former history of our globe. In
order to prove this I need only point to the epoch-making
influence which has been exerted on geological theories by the
discovery, in the rocks and earthy layers of the Polar countries,
of beautiful fossil plants from widely separated geological
periods. In this field too our expedition to the north coast of
Siberia ought to expect to reap abundant harvests. There are
besides to be found in Siberia, strata which have been deposited

almost contemporaneously with the coal-bearing formations of South Sweden, and which therefore contain animal and vegetable petrifications which just now are of very special interest for geological science in our own country, with reference to the discoveries of splendid fossil plants which of late years have been made at several places among us, and give us so lively an idea of the sub-tropical vegetation which in former times covered the Scandinavian peninsula.

Few sciences perhaps will yield so important practical results as meteorology is likely to do at some future date—a fact, or rather an already partly realised expectation, which has won general recognition, as is shown by the large sums which in all civilised countries have been set apart for establishing meteorological offices and for encouraging meteorological research. But the state of the weather in a country is so dependent on the temperature, wind, pressure of the air, etc., in very remote regions, that the laws of the meteorology of a country can only be ascertained by comparing observations from the most distant regions. Several international meteorological enterprises have already been started, and we may almost consider the meteorological institutions of the different countries as separate departments of one and the same office, distributed over the whole world, through whose harmonious co-operation the object in view shall one day be reached. But, beyond the places for which daily series of observations may be obtained, there are regions hundreds of square miles in extent from which no observations, or only scattered ones, are yet to be had, and here notwithstanding we have just the key to many meteorological phenomena, otherwise difficult of explanation, within the civilised countries of Europe. Such a meteorological territory, unknown, but of the greatest importance, is formed by the Polar Sea lying to the north of Siberia, and the land and islands there situated. It is of great importance for the meteorology of Europe and of Sweden to obtain trustworthy accounts of the distribution of the land, of the state of the ice, the pressure of the air, and the temperature in that in these respects little-known part of the globe, and the Swedish expedition will here have a subject for investigation of direct importance for our own country.

To a certain extent the same may be said of the contributions which may be obtained from those regions to our knowledge of terrestrial magnetism, of the aurora, etc. There are, besides, the examination of the flora and fauna in those countries, hitherto unknown in this respect, ethnographical researches, hydrographical work, etc.

I have of course only been able to notice shortly the scientific questions which will meet the expedition during a stay of some length on the north coast of Siberia, but what has been said

may perhaps be sufficient to show that the expedition, even
if its geographical objects were not attained, ought to be a
worthy continuation of similar enterprises which have been set
on foot in this country, and which have brought gain to science
and honour to Sweden.

Should the expedition again, as I hope, be able to reach
Behring's Straits with little hindrance, and thus in a comparatively short time—in that case indeed the time, which on
the way can be devoted to researches in natural history, will be
quite too short for solving many of the scientific questions I
have mentioned. But without reckoning the world-historical
navigation problem which will then be solved, extensive contributions of immense importance ought also to be obtainable,
regarding the geography, hydrography, zoology, and botany
of the Siberian Polar Sea, and, beyond Behring's Straits, the
expedition will meet with other countries having a more
luxuriant and varied nature, where other questions which
perhaps concern us less, but are not on that account of less
importance for science as a whole, will claim the attention
of the observer and yield him a rich reward for his labour
and pains.   These are the considerations which formed the
grounds for the arrangement of the plan of the expedition which
is now in question.

It is my intention to leave Sweden in the beginning of
July, 1878, in a steamer, specially built for navigation among
ice, which will be provisioned for two years at most, and
which, besides a scientific staff of four or five persons, will
have on board a naval officer, a physician, and at most eighteen
men—petty officers and crew, preferably volunteers, from your
Royal Majesty's navy. Four walrus-hunters will also be hired
in Norway. The course will be shaped at first to Matotschkin
Sound, in Novaya Zemlya, where a favourable opportunity
will be awaited for the passage of the Kara Sea. Afterwards
the voyage will be continued to Port Dickson at the mouth
of the Yenisej, which I hope to be able to reach in the first
half of August. As soon as circumstances permit, the
expedition will continue its voyage from this point in the open
channel which the river-water of the Obi and the Yenisej must
indisputably form along the coast to Cape Chelyuskin, possibly
with some short excursions towards the north-west in order
to see whether any large island is to be found between the
northern part of Novaya Zemlya and New Siberia.

At Cape Chelyuskin the expedition will reach the only
part of the proposed route which has not been traversed by
some small vessel, and this place is perhaps rightly considered
as that which it will be most difficult for a vessel to double
during the whole north-east passage. As Prontschischev, in

1736, in small river craft built with insufficient means reached within a few minutes of this north-westernmost promontory of Asia, our vessel, equipped with all modern appliances, ought not to find insuperable difficulties in doubling this point, and if that be accomplished, we will probably have pretty open water towards Behring's Straits, which ought to be reached before the end of September.

If time, and the state of the ice permit, it would be desirable that the expedition during this voyage should make some excursions towards the north, in order to ascertain whether land is not to be found between Cape Chelyuskin and the New Siberian group of islands, and between it and Wrangel's Land. From Behring's Straits the course will be shaped, with such stoppages as circumstances give rise to, for some Asiatic port, from which accounts may be sent home, and then onwards round Asia to Suez. Should the expedition be prevented from forcing a passage east of Cape Chelyuskin, it will depend on circumstances which it is difficult to foresee, whether it will immediately return to Europe, in which case the vessel with its equipment and crew may be immediately available for some other purpose, or whether it ought not to winter in some suitable harbour in the bays at the mouths of the Tajmur, Pjäsina, or Yenisej. Again, in case obstacles from ice occur east of Cape Chelyuskin, a harbour ought to be sought for at some convenient place on the north coast of Siberia, from which, during the following summer, opportunities would ¦be found for important surveys in the Polar Sea, and during the course of the summer some favourable opening will also certainly occur, when southerly winds have driven the ice from the coast, for reaching Behring's Straits. Probably also, if it be necessary to winter, there will be opportunities of sending home letters from the winter station.

CHAPTER I.

Departure—Tromsoe—Members of the Expedition—Stay at Maosoe—Limit of Trees—Climate—Scurvy and Antiscorbutics—The first doubling of North Cape—Othere's account of his Travels—Ideas concerning the Geography of Scandinavia current during the first half of the sixteenth century—The oldest Maps of the North—Herbertstein's account of Istoma's voyage — Gustaf Vasa and the North-east Passage — Willoughby and Chancelor's voyages.

THE *Vega* left the. harbour of Karlskrona on the 22nd June, 1878. Including Lieutenants Palander and Brusewitz, there were then on board nineteen men belonging to the Swedish navy, and two foreign naval officers, who were to take part in the expedition — Lieutenants Hovgaard and Bove. The two latter had lived some time at Karlskrona in order to be present at the fitting out and repairing of the vessel.

On the 24th June the *Vega* called at Copenhagen in order to take on board the large quantity of provisions which had been purchased there. On the 26th June the voyage was resumed to Gothenburg, where the *Vega* anchored on the 27th. During the passage there was on board the famous Italian geographer, Commendatore CHRISTOFORO NEGRI, who, for several years back, had followed with special interest all Arctic voyages, and now had received a commission from the Government of his native country to be present at the departure of the *Vega* from Sweden, and to make himself acquainted with its equipment, &c. At Gothenburg there embarked Docent Kjellman, Dr. Almquist, Dr. Stuxberg, Lieutenant Nordquist, and an assistant to the naturalists, who had been hired in Stockholm; and here were taken on board the greater part of the scientific equipment of the expedition, and various stocks of provisions, clothes, &c., that had been purchased in Sweden.

On the 4th July the *Vega* left the harbour of Gothenburg. While sailing along the west coast of Norway there blew a fresh head wind, by which the arrival of the vessel at Tromsoe was delayed till the 17th July. Here I went on board. Coal, water, reindeer furs[1] for all our men, and a large quantity of

---

[1] In many Polar expeditions, sealskin has been used as clothing instead of reindeer skin. The reindeer skin, however, is lighter and warmer, and ought therefore to have an unconditional preference as a means of protection against severe cold. In mild weather, clothing made of reindeer skin in the common way has indeed the defect that it is drenched through with water, and thereby becomes useless, but in such weather it

TROMSÖ.

After a photograph by Claus Knudsen, Christiania.

other stores, bought in Finmark for the expedition, were taken in here; and three walrus-hunters, hired for the voyage, embarked.

On the 21st July the whole equipment of the *Vega* was on board, the number of its crew complete, all clear for departure, and the same day at 2.15 P.M. we weighed anchor, with lively hurrahs from a numerous crowd assembled at the beach, to enter in earnest on our Arctic voyage.

The members of the expedition on board the *Vega* were—

A. E. Nordenskiöld, Professor, in command of the expedition	born 18th Nov. 1832
A. A. L. Palander, Lieutenant, now Captain in the Royal Swedish Navy, chief of the steamer *Vega*	„ 2nd Oct. 1840
F. R. Kjellman, Ph.D., Docent in Botany in the University of Upsala, superintendent of the botanical work of the expedition	„ 4th Nov. 1846
A. J. Stuxberg, Ph.D., superintendent of the zoological work	„ 18th April 1849
E. Almquist, Candidate of Medicine, medical officer of the expedition, lichenologist	„ 8th Aug. 1852
E. C. Brusewitz, Lieutenant in the Royal Swedish Navy, second in command of the vessel	„ 1st Dec. 1844
G. Bove, Lieutenant in the Royal Italian Navy, superintendent of the hydrographical work of the expedition . . .	„ 23rd Oct. 1853
A. Hovgaard, Lieutenant in the Royal Danish Navy, superintendent of the magnetical and meteorological work of the expedition	„ 1st Nov. 1853
O. Nordquist, Lieutenant in the Imperial Russian Regiment of Guards, interpreter, assistant zoologist . . .	„ 20th May 1858
R. Nilsson, sailing-master	„ 5th Jan. 1837

is in general unnecessary to use furs. The coast Chukchis, who catch great numbers of seals, but can only obtain reindeer skins by purchase, yet consider clothing made of the latter material indispensable in winter. During this season they wear an overcoat of the same form as the Lapps' *pesk*, the suitableness of whose cut thus appears to be well proved. On this account I prefer the old-world Polar dress to that of the new, which consists of more closely fitting clothes. The Lapp shoes of reindeer skin (*renskallar, komager*) are, on the other hand, if one has not opportunity to change them frequently, nor time to take sufficient care of them, quite unserviceable for Arctic journeys.

F. A. Pettersson, first engineer	. . .	born	3rd July 1835
O. Nordström, second engineer	. . .	„	24th Feb. 1855
C. Carlström, fireman	. . . .	„	14th Dec. 1845
O. Ingelsson, fireman	. . . .	„	2nd Feb. 1849
O. Oeman, seaman	. . . .	„	23rd April 1843
G. Carlsson, seaman	. . . .	„	22nd Sep. 1843
C. Lundgren, seaman	. . . .	„	5th July 1851
O. Hansson, seaman	. . . .	„	6th April 1856
D. Asplund, boatswain, cook	. . . .	„	28th Jan. 1827
C. J. Smaolaenning, boatswain	. . .	„	27th Sep. 1839
C. Levin, boatswain, steward	. . . .	„	24th Jan. 1844
P. M. Lustig, boatswain	. . . . . .	„	22nd April 1845
C. Ljungström, boatswain	. . . . .	„	12th Oct. 1845
P. Lind, boatswain	. . . .	„	15th Sep. 1856
P. O. Faeste, boatswain	. . . . . .	„	23rd Sep. 1856
S. Andersson, carpenter	. . . . . .	„	3rd Sep. 1847
J. Haugan, walrus-hunter [1]	. . . . .	„	23rd Jan. 1825
P. Johnsen, walrus-hunter	. . . . .	„	15th May 1845
P. Sivertsen, walrus-hunter	. . . . .	„	2nd Jan. 1853
Th. A. Boström, assistant to the scientific men	. . . .	„	21st Sep. 1857

There was also on board the *Vega* during the voyage from Tromsoe to Port Dickson, as commissioner for Mr. Sibiriakoff, Mr. S. J. Serebrenikoff, who had it in charge to oversee the taking on board and the landing of the goods that were to be carried to and from Siberia in the *Fraser* and *Express*. These vessels had sailed several days before from Vardoe to Chaborova in Yugor Schar, where they had orders to wait for the *Vega*. The *Lena*, again, the fourth vessel that was placed at my disposal, had, in obedience to orders, awaited the *Vega* in the harbour of Tromsoe, from which port these two steamers were now to proceed eastwards in company.

After leaving Tromsoe, the course was shaped at first within the archipelago to Maosoe, in whose harbour the *Vega* was to make some hours' stay, for the purpose of posting letters in the post-office there, probably the most northerly in the world. But during this time so violent a north-west wind began to blow, that we were detained there three days.

Maosoe is a little rocky island situated in 71° N. L., thirty-two kilometres south-west from North Cape, in a region abounding in fish, about halfway between Bred Sound and Mageroe Sound. The eastern coast of the island is indented by a bay, which

---

[1] Haugan had formerly for a long series of years carried his own vessel to Spitzbergen and Novaya Zemlya, and was known as one of the most fortunate walrus-hunters of the Norwegian Polar Sea fleet.

forms a well protected harbour. Here, only a few kilometres
south of the northernmost promontory of Europe, are to be
found, besides a large number of fishermen's huts, a church,
shop, post-office, hospital, &c.; and I need scarcely add, at
least for the benefit of those who have travelled in the north
of Norway, several friendly, hospitable families in whose society
we talked away many hours of our involuntary stay in the
neighbourhood. The inhabitants of course live on fish. All

OLD-WORLD POLAR DRESS.
Lapp, after original in the Northern Museum, Stockholm.

agriculture is impossible here. Potatoes have indeed sometimes yielded an abundant crop on the neighbouring Ingoe
(71° 5′ N. L.), but their cultivation commonly fails, in consequence of the shortness of the summer; on the other hand,
radishes and a number of other vegetables are grown with
success in the garden-beds. Of wild berries there is found here
the red whortleberry, yet in so small quantity that one can
seldom collect a quart or two; the bilberry is somewhat more
plentiful; but the grapes of the north, the cloudberry (*multer*),

grow in profuse abundance. From an area of several square fathoms one can often gather a couple of quarts. There is no wood here—only bushes.

In the neighbourhood of North Cape, the wood, for the present, does not go quite to the coast of the Polar Sea, but at sheltered places, situated at a little distance from the beach, birches,[1] three to four metres high, are already to be met with.

NEW-WORLD POLAR DRESS.

Greenlanders, after an old painting in the Ethnographical Museum, Copenhagen [2]

[1] The birch which grows here is the sweet-scented birch (*Betula odorata*, Bechst.), not the dwarf birch (*Betula nana*, L.), which is found as far north as Ice Fjord in Spitzbergen (78° 7′ N. L.), though there it only rises a few inches above ground.

[2] The original of this drawing, for which I am indebted to Councillor of Justice H. Rink, of Copenhagen, was painted by a German painter at Bergen, in 1654. The painting has the following inscription:—

Mit Lebern Schifflein auff bem Meer
De grönleinber fein bein unbt her
Von Thieren unbt Bögelen haben see Ire Tracht
Das kalte Lanbs von Winter nacht.

In former times, however, the outer archipelago itself was covered with trees, which is proved by the tree-stems, found imbedded in the mosses on the outer islands on the coast of Finmark, for instance, upon Renoe.   In Siberia the limit of trees runs to the beginning of the estuary delta, *i.e.* to about 72° N. L.[1]   As the latitude of North Cape is 71° 10', the wood in Siberia at several places, viz., along the great rivers, goes considerably farther north than in Europe.   This depends partly on the large quantity of warm water which these rivers, in summer, carry down from the south, partly on the transport of

LIMIT OF TREES IN NORWAY.
At Præstevandet, on Tromsoen, after a photograph.

seeds with the river water, and on the more favourable soil, which consists of a rich mould, yearly renewed by inundations, but in Norway again for the most part of rocks of granite and gneiss or of barren beds of sand.   Besides, the limit of trees has a quite dissimilar appearance in Siberia and Scandinavia:

[1] According to Latkin, *Die Lena und ihr Flussgebiet* (*Petermann's Mittheilungen*, 1879, p. 91).   On the map which accompanies Engelhardt's reproduction of Wrangel's *Journey* (Berlin, 1839), the limit of trees at the Lena is placed at 71° N. L.

in the latter country, the farthest outposts of the forests towards the north consist of scraggy birches, which, notwithstanding their stunted stems, clothe the mountain sides with a very lively and close green; while in Siberia the outermost trees are gnarled and half-withered larches (*Larix dahurica*, Turcz.), which stick up over the tops of the hills like a thin grey brush.[1]   North of this limit there are to be seen on the Yenisej luxuriant bushes of willow and alder.   That in Siberia, too, the large wood, some hundreds or thousands of years ago, went farther north than now, is shown by colossal tree-stumps found still standing in the *tundra*, nor is it necessary now to go far

LIMIT OF TREES IN SIBERIA.
At Boganida, after Middendorf.

south of the extreme limit, before the river banks are to be seen crowned with high, flourishing, luxuriant trees.

The climate at Maosoe is not distinguished by any severe winter cold,[2] but the air is moist and raw nearly all the year

[1] On the Kola Peninsula, and in the neighbourhood of the White Sea, as far as to Ural, the limit of trees consists of a species of pine (*Picea obovata*, Ledeb.), but farther east in Kamschatka again of birch.—Th. von Middendorff, *Reise in dem äussersten Norden und Osten Sibiriens*, vol. iv. p. 582.

[2] An idea of the influence exerted by the immediate neighbourhood of a warm ocean-current in making the climate milder may be obtained from the following table of the mean temperatures of the different months at 1. Tromsoe (69° 30′ N. L.); 2. Fruholm, near North Cape (71° 6′ N. L.);

round. The region would however be very healthy, did not
scurvy, especially in humid winters, attack the population,

THE CLOUDBERRY (RUBUS CHAMÆMORUS, L.).
Fruit of the natural size.   Flowering stalks diminished.

3. Vardoe (70° 22′ N. L.); 4. Enontekis and Karesuando, on the river
Muonio, in the interior of Lapland (68° 26′ N. L.).

	Tromsoe.	Fruholm.	Vardoe.	Enontekis.
January	− 4·2°	− 2·7°	· 6·0°	- 13·7°
Februar	− 4·0	− 4·7	·· 6·4	−17·1
March	− 3·8	−· 3·2	·· 5·1	−11·4
April	− 0·1	− 0·9	− 1·7	− 6·0
May	+ 3·2	+2·7	+1·8	+ 0·9
June	+ 8·7	+7·5	+5·9	+ 8·0
July	+11·5	+9·3	+8·8	+11·6
August	+10·4	+9·9	+9·8	+12·0
September	+ 7·0	+5·8	+6·4	+ 4·5
October	+ 2·0	+2·5	+1·3	− 4·0
November	- 1·7	− 1·1	− 2·1	− 9·9
December	−· 3·2	− 1·9	− 4·0	−11·3

The figures are taken from H. Mohn's *Norges Klima* (reprinted from C. F.
Schübeler's *Væxtlivet i Norge*, Christiania, 1879), and A. J. Ångström, *Om
lufttemperaturen i Enontekis* (Öfvers. af Vet. Akad. Förhandl., 1860).

educated and uneducated, rich and poor, old and young. According to a statement made by a lady resident on the spot, very severe attacks of scurvy are cured without fail by preserved cloudberries and rum. Several spoonfuls are given to the patient daily, and a couple of quarts of the medicine is said to be sufficient for the complete cure of children severely attacked by the disease. I mention this new method of using the cloudberry, the old well-known antidote to scurvy, because I am convinced that future Polar expeditions, if they will avail themselves of the knowledge of this cure, will find that it conduces to the health and comfort of all on board, and that the medicine is seldom refused, unless it be by too obstinate abstainers from spirituous liquors.

It enters into the plan of this work, as the *Vega* sails along, to give a brief account of the voyages of the men who first opened the route along which she advances, and who thus, each in his measure, contributed to prepare the way for the voyage whereby the passage round Asia and Europe has now at last been accomplished. On this account it is incumbent on me to begin by giving a narrative of the voyage of discovery during which the northernmost point of Europe was first doubled, the rather because this narrative has besides great interest for us, as containing much remarkable information regarding the condition of the former population in the north of Scandinavia. This voyage was accomplished about a thousand years ago by a Norwegian, OTHERE, from Halogaland or Helgeland, that part of the Norwegian coast which lies between 65° and 66° N. L. Othere, who appears to have travelled far and wide, came in one of his excursions to the court of the famous English king, Alfred the Great. In presence of this king he gave, in a simple, graphic style, a sketch of a voyage which he had undertaken from his home in Norway towards the north and east. The narrative has been preserved by its having been incorporated, along with an account of the travels of another Norseman, Wulfstan, to the southern part of the Baltic, in the first chapter of Alfred's Anglo Saxon reproduction of the history of PAULUS OROSIUS : *De Miseria Mundi.*[1] This work has since been

---

[1] Orosius was born in Spain in the fourth century after Christ, and died in the beginning of the fifth. He was a Christian, and wrote his work to show that the world, in opposition to the statements of several heathen writers, had been visited during the heathen period by quite as great calamities as during the Christian. This is probably the reason why his monotonous sketch of all the misfortunes and calamities which befell the heathen world was long so highly valued, was spread in many copies and printed in innumerable editions, the oldest at Vienna in 1471. In the Anglo-Saxon translation now in question, Othere's account of his journey is inserted in the first chapter, which properly forms a geogra-

the subject of translation and exposition by a great number
of learned men, among whom may be named here the
Scandinavians, H. G. PORTHAN of Åbo, RASMUS RASK and C.
CHR. RAFN of Copenhagen.

Regarding Othere's relations to King Alfred, statements
differ. Some inquirers suppose that he was only on a visit at
the court of the king, others that he had been sent out by King
Alfred on voyages of discovery, and finally, others say that he
was a prisoner of war, who incidentally narrated his experience
of foreign lands. Othere's account of his travels runs as
follows:—

" Othere told his lord, King Alfred, that he dwelt northmost
of all the Northmen. He said that he dwelt in the land to
the northward, along the West-Sea; he said, however, that that
land is very long north from thence, but it is all waste, except
in a few places where the Fins at times dwell, hunting in the
winter, and in the summer fishing in that sea. He said that he
was desirous to try, once on a time, how far that country extended
due north, or whether any one lived to the north of the waste.
He then went due north along the country, leaving all the way
the waste land on the right, and the wide sea on the left. After
three days he was as far north as the whale-hunters go at the
farthest. Then he proceeded in his course due north, as far as
he could sail within another three days; then the land there
inclined due east, or the sea into the land, he knew not which;
but he knew that he waited there for a west wind or a little
north, and sailed thence eastward along that land as far as he
could sail in four days. Then he had to wait for a due north wind
because the land inclined there due south, or the sea in on that
land, he knew not which. He then sailed along the coast due
south, as far as he could sail in five days. There lay a great river
up in that land; they then turned in that river, because they
durst not sail on up the river on account of hostility; because
all that country was inhabited on the other side of the river.
He had not before met with any land that was inhabited since
he left his own home; but all the way he had waste land on his
right, except some fishermen, fowlers, and hunters, all of whom
were Fins; and he had constantly a wide sea to the left. The

phical introduction to the work written by King Alfred. This old
Anglo-Saxon work is preserved in England in two beautiful manuscripts
from the ninth and tenth centuries. Orosius' history itself is now for-
gotten, but King Alfred's introduction, and especially his account of
Othere's and Wulfstan's travels, have attracted much attention from in-
quirers, as appears from the list of translations of this part of King
Alfred's Orosius, given by Joseph Bosworth in his *King Alfred's Anglo-
Saxon version of the Compendious History of the World by Orosius.*
London, 1859.

Beormas had well cultivated their country, but they (Othere and his companions) did not dare to enter it. And the Terfinna[1] land was all waste, except where hunters, fishers, or fowlers had taken up their quarters.

"The Beormas told him many particulars both of their own land and of other lands lying around them; but he knew not what was true because he did not see it himself. It seemed to him that the Fins and the Beormas spoke nearly the same language. He went thither chiefly, in addition to seeing the country, on account of the walruses,[2] because they have very noble bones in their teeth, of which the travellers brought some to the king; and their hides are very good for ship-ropes. These whales are much less than other whales, not being longer than seven ells. But in his own country is the best whale-hunting. There they are eight-and-forty ells long, and the largest are fifty ells long. Of these he said he and five others had killed sixty in two days.[3] He was a very wealthy man in those possessions in which their wealth consists, that is, in wild deer. He had at the time he came to the king, six hundred unsold tame deer. These deer they call rein-deer, of which there were six

[1] By Fins are here meant Lapps; by Terfins the inhabitants of the Tersk coast of Russian Lapland.

[2] Walruses are still captured yearly on the ice at the mouth of the White Sea, not very far from the shore (cf. A. E. Nordenskiöld, *Redogörelse för en expedition till mynningen af Jenisej och Sibirien år 1875*, p. 23; *Bihang till Vetenskaps-Akad. Handl.* B. iv. No. 1). Now they occur there indeed only in small numbers, and, it appears, not in the immediate neighbourhood of land; but there is scarcely any doubt that in former days they were common on the most northerly coasts of Norway. They have evidently been driven away thence in the same way as they are now being driven away from Spitzbergen. With what rapidity their numbers at the latter place are yearly diminished, may be seen from the fact that during my many Arctic journeys, beginning in 1858, I never saw walruses on Bear Island or the west coast of Spitzbergen, but have conversed with hunters who ten years before had seen them in herds of hundreds and thousands. I have myself seen such herds in Hinloopen Strait in July 1861, but when during my journeys in 1868 and 1872-3 I again visited the same regions, I saw there not a single walrus.

As it appears to be impossible for six men to kill sixty great whales in two days, this passage has caused the editors of Othere's narrative much perplexity, which is not wonderful if great whales, as the *Balæna mysticetus*, are here meant. But if the narrative relates to the smaller species of the whale, a similar catch may still, at the present day, be made on the coasts of the Polar countries. For various small species go together in great shoals; and, as they occasionally come into water so shallow that they are left aground at ebb, they can be killed with ease. Sometimes, too, a successful attempt is made to drive them into shallow water. That whales visit the coast of Norway in spring in large shoals dangerous to the navigator is also stated by Jacob Ziegler, in his work, *Quæ intus continentur Syria, Palestina, Arabia, Ægyptus, Schondia, &c.* Argentorati, 1532, p. 97.

decoy rein-deer, which are very valuable among the Fins, because they catch the wild rein-deer with them.

" He was one of the first men in that country, yet he had not more than twenty horned cattle, twenty sheep and twenty swine, and the little that he ploughed he ploughed with horses. But their wealth consists mostly in the rent paid them by the Fins. That rent is in skins of animals and birds' feathers, and whalebone, and in ship-ropes made of whales'[1] hides, and of seals'. Every one pays according to his birth ; the best-born, it is said, pay the skins of fifteen martens, and five rein-deers, and one bear's skin, ten ambers of feathers, a bear's or otter's skin kyrtle, and two ship-ropes, each sixty ells long, made either of whale or of seal hide."

NORSE SHIP OF THE TENTH CENTURY.
Drawn with reference to the vessel found at Sandefjord in 1880. under the superintendence of Ingvald Undset. Assistant at the Christiania University's collection of Northern antiquities.

The continuation of Othere's narrative consists of a sketch of the Scandinavian peninsula, and of a journey which he undertook from his home towards the south. King Alfred then gives an account of the Dane, Wulfstan's voyage in the Baltic. This part of the introduction to Orosius, however, has too remote a connection with my subject to be quoted in this historical sketch.

It appears from Othere's simple and very clear narrative that

---

[1] In this case is meant by "whale" evidently the walrus, whose skin is still used for lines by the Norwegian walrus-hunters, by the Eskimo, and the Chukchis. The skin of the true whale might probably be used for the same purpose, although, on account of its thickness, perhaps scarcely with advantage without the use of special tools for cutting it up.

undertook a veritable voyage of discovery in order to explore
unknown lands and sea lying to the north-east. This
yage was also very rich in results, as in the course of it
e northernmost part of Europe was circumnavigated. Nor
rhaps is there any doubt that during this voyage Othere
netrated as far as to the mouth of the Dwina or at least
the Mesen in the land of the Beormas.[1] We learn from
e narrative besides, that the northernmost part of Scandinavia
as already, though sparsely, peopled by Lapps, whose mode of
fe did not differ much from that followed by their descendants,
ho live on the coast at the present day.

The Scandinavian race first migrated to Finmark and settled
here in the 13th century, and from that period there was
aturally spread abroad in the northern countries a greater
nowledge of those regions, which, however, was for a long time
exceedingly incomplete, and even in certain respects less correct
han Othere's. The idea of the northernmost parts of Europe,
which was current during the first half of the 16th century, is
shown by lithographed copies of two maps of the north, one
dated 1482, the other 1532,[2] which are appended to this work.
On the latter of these Greenland is still delineated as connected
with Norway in the neighbourhood of Vardoehus. This map,
however, is grounded, according to the statement of the author
in the introduction, among other sources, on the statements of
two archbishops of the diocese of Nidaro,[3] to which Greenland
and Finmark belonged, and from whose inhabited parts
expeditions were often undertaken both for trade and plunder,
by land and sea, as far away as to the land of the Beormas. It
is difficult to understand how with such maps of the distribution
of land in the north the thought of the north-east passage could
arise, if voices were not even then raised for an altogether
opposite view, grounded partly on a survival of the old idea,

---

[1] It ought to be remarked here that the distances which Othere in that
case traversed every day, give a speed of sailing approximating to that
which a common sailing vessel of the present day attains *on an average*.
This circumstance, which on a cursory examination may appear somewhat
strange, finds its explanation when we consider that Othere sailed only
with a favourable wind, and, when the wind was unfavourable, lay still.
It appears that he usually sailed 70′ to 80′ in twenty-four hours, or perhaps
rather *per diem*.

[2] The maps are taken from *Ptolemæi Cosmographia latine reddita a Jac.
Angelo, curam mapparum gerente Nicolao Donis Germano, Ulmæ* 1482, and
from the above-quoted work of Jacobus Ziegler, printed in 1532. That
portion of the latter which concerns the geography of Scandinavia is
reprinted in *Geografiska Sektionens Tidskrift*, B. I. Stockholm, 1878.

[3] These were the Dane, Erik Valkendorff, and the Norwegian, Olof Engel-
brektsson. The Swedes, Johannes Magnus, Archbishop of Upsala, and Peder
Maonsson, Bishop of Vesteraos, also gave Ziegler important information
regarding the northern countries.

we may say the old popular belief, that Asia, Europe and
Africa were surrounded by water, partly on stories of Indians
having been driven by wind to Europe, along the north coast of
Asia.[1] To these was added in 1539 the map of the north by the
Swedish bishop OLAUS MAGNUS,[2] which for the first time gave
to Scandinavia an approximately correct boundary towards the
north. Six hundred years,[3] in any case, had run their course

[1] Of these much-discussed narratives concerning *Indians*—probably
men from North Scandinavia, Russia, or North America, certainly not
Japanese, Chinese, or Indians—who were driven by storms to the coasts
of Germany, the first comes down to us from the time before the birth of
Christ. For B.C. 62 Quintus Metellus Celer, "when as proconsul he
governed Gaul, received as a present from the King of the Bæti [Pliny says
of the Suevi] some Indians, and when he inquired how they came to those
countries, he was informed that they had been driven by storm by the
Indian Ocean to the coasts of Germany" (Pomponius Mela, lib. iii. cap. 5,
after a lost work of Cornelius Nepos. Plinius, *Hist. Nat.*, lib. ii. cap. 67).
Of a similar occurrence in the middle ages, the learned Æneas Sylvius,
afterwards Pope under the name of Pius II., gives the following account
of his cosmography:—"I have myself read in Otto [Bishop Otto, of
Freising], that in the time of the German Emperor an Indian vessel and
Indian merchants were driven by storm to the German coast. Certain it
was that, driven about by contrary winds, they came from the east, which
had been by no means possible, if, as many suppose, the North Sea were
unnavigable and frozen" (Pius II., *Cosmographiu in Asiæ et Europæ eleganti
descriptione, etc.*, Parisiis, 1509, leaf 2). Probably it is the same occurrence
which is mentioned by the Spanish historian Gomara (*Historia general de
las Indias*, Saragoça, 1552-53), with the addition, that the Indians stranded
at Lübeck in the time of the Emperor Frederick Barbarossa (1152-1190).
Gomara also states that he met with the exiled Swedish Bishop Olaus
Magnus, who positively assured him that it was possible to sail from
Norway by the north along the coasts to China (French translation of the
above-quoted work, Paris, 1587, leaf 12). An exceedingly instructive
treatise on this subject is to be found in *Aarböger for nordisk Oldkyn-
dighed og Historie*, Kjöbenhavn, 1880. It is written by F. Schiern, and
entitled *Om en etnologisk Gaade fra Oldtiden.*
[2] Olaus Magnus, *Auslegung und Verklerung der neuen Mappen von den
alten Gœttenreich*, Venedig, 1539. Now perhaps (according to a communication from the Librarian-in-chief, G. E. Klemming) there is scarcely any
copy of this edition of the map still in existence, but it is given unaltered
in the 1567 Basel edition of Olaus Magnus, "*De gentium septentrionalium
variis conditionibus*," &c. The edition of the same work printed at Rome
in 1555, on the other hand, has a map, which differs a little from the
original map of 1539.
[3] To interpret Nicolò and Antonio Zeno's travels towards the end of the
fourteenth century, which have given rise to so much discussion, as Mr. Fr.
Krarup has done, in such a way as if they had visited the shores of the
Arctic Ocean and the White Sea, appears to me to be a very unfortunate
guess, opposed to innumerable particulars in the narrative of the Zenos,
and to the accompanying map, remarkable in more respects than one,
which was first published at Venice in 1558, unfortunately in a somewhat
"improved" form by one of Zeno's descendants. On the map there is
the date MCCCLXXX. (Cf. *Zeniernes Reise til Norden, et Tolknings Forsög*,
af Fr. Krarup, Kjöbenhavn, 1878 ; R. H. Major, *The Voyages of the Venetian
Brothers Nicolò and Antonio Zeno*, London, 1873, and other works concerning
these much-bewritten travels).

Map labels:

UPSALIA
FIERINGIA
PIRCMO
RASBVR GHVM
INGIA
VIDVRGI
STOKHOLM
OONEAE
HANGOO
OX ILIA
TVVM
ALBVS
LAGVS
OVIS DI GOTH IA
ARE DAL
NEOGRODA
BORISTHENES
RESAN
VOLODE
SAR
MOSKAVA
REVALIA
SMOLE ZKI
CHOLOBA
ORZRA
LNA

before Othere found a successor in Sir Hugh Willoughby; and it is usual to pass by the former, and to ascribe to the latter the honour of being the first in that long succession of men who endeavoured to force a passage by the north-east from the Atlantic Ocean to China. Here however it ought to be remarked that while such maps as those of Ziegler were published in western Europe, other and better knowledge of the regions in question prevailed in the north. For it may be considered certain that Norwegians, Russians and Karelians often travelled in boats on peaceful or warlike errands, during the fifteenth and beginning of the sixteenth century, from the west coast of Norway to the White Sea, and in the opposite direction, although we find nothing on record regarding such journeys except the account that SIGISMUND VON HERBERTSTEIN [1] gives, in his famous book on Russia, of the voyage of GREGORY ISTOMA and the envoy DAVID from the White Sea to Trondhjem in the year 1496.

The voyage is inserted under the distinctive title *Navigatio per Mare Glaciale*,[2] and the narrative begins with an explanation that Herbertstein got it from Istoma himself, who, when a youth, had learned Latin in Denmark. As the reasons for choosing the unusual, long, " but safe " circuitous route over the North Sea, in preference to the shorter way that was usually taken, Istoma gives the disputes between Sweden and Russia, and the revolt of Sweden against Denmark, at the time when the voyage was undertaken (1496). After giving an account of his journey from Moscow to the mouth of the Dwina, he continues thus :—

" After having gone on board of four boats, they kept first along the right bank of the ocean, where they saw very high

[1] The first edition, entitled *Rerum Moscoviticarum Commentarii, &c.*, Vienna, 1549, has three plates, and a map of great value for the former geography of Russia. It is, however, to judge by the copy in the Royal Library at Stockholm, partly drawn by hand, and much inferior to the map in the Italian edition of the following year (*Comentari della Moscovia et parimente della Russia, &c., per il Signor Sigismondo libero Barone in Herbetstain. Neiperg et Guetnbag, tradotti nuaomente di Latino in lingua nostra volgare Italiana*, Venetia, 1550, with two plates and a map, with the inscription " per Giacomo Gastaldo cosmographo in Venetia, MDL "). Von Herbertstein visited Russia as ambassador from the Roman Emperor on two occasions, the first time in 1517, the second in 1525, and on the ground of these two journeys published a sketch of the country, by which it first became known to West-Europeans, and even for Russians themselves it forms an important original source of information regarding the state of civilisation of the empire of the Czar in former times. Von Adelung enumerates in *Kritisch-literärische Übersicht der Reisenden in Russland bis 1700*, St. Petersburg and Leipzig, 1846, eleven Latin, two Italian, nine German, and one Bohemian translation of this work. An English translation has since been published by the Hakluyt Society.

[2] *Von Herbertstein*, first edition, leaf xxviii., in the second of the three separately-paged portions of the work.

mountain peaks; [1] and after having in this way travelled sixteen miles, and crossed an arm of the sea, they followed the
western strand, leaving on their right the open sea, which like
the neighbouring mountains has its name from the river Petzora.
They came here to a people called Finn-Lapps, who, though they
dwell in low wretched huts by the sea, and live almost like wild
beasts, in any case are said to be much more peaceable than the
people who are called wild Lapps.   Then, after they had passed
the land of the Lapps and sailed forward eighty miles, they came
to the land Nortpoden, which is part of the dominions of the
King of Sweden.   This region the Rutheni call Kayenska
Selma, and the people they call Kayeni.   After sailing thence
along a very indented coast which jutted out to the right, they
came to a peninsula, called the Holy Nose,[2] consisting of a
great rock, which like a nose projects into the sea.   But in this
there is a grotto or hollow which for six hours at a time
swallows up water, and then with great noise and din casts out
again in whirls the water which it had swallowed.   Some call
it the navel of the sea, others Charybdis.   It is said that this
whirlpool has such power that it draws to itself ships and other
things in its neighbourhood and swallows them.   Istoma said
that he had never been in such danger as at that place, because
the whirlpool drew the ship in which he travelled with such
force, that it was only by extreme exertion at the oars that
they could escape.   After passing this *Holy Nose* they came to
a rocky promontory, which they had to sail round.   After having
waited here some days on account of head winds, the skipper
said : 'This rock, which ye see, is called Semes, and we shall
not get so easily past it if it be not propitiated by some offering.'   Istoma said that he reproved the skipper for his foolish
superstition, on which the reprimanded skipper said nothing
more.   They waited thus the fourth day at the place on account of the stormy state of the sea, but after that the storm
ceased, and the anchor was weighed.   When the voyage was
now continued with a favourable wind, the skipper said : 'You
laughed at my advice to propitiate the Semes rock, and considered it a foolish superstition, but it certainly would have
been impossible for us to get past it, if I had not secretly by
night ascended the rock and sacrificed.'   To the inquiry what
he had offered, the skipper replied : 'I scattered oatmeal
mixed with butter on the projecting rock which we saw.'
As they sailed further they came to another great promontory,
called Motka, resembling a peninsula.   At the end of this

----

[1] An erroneous transposition of mountains seen in Norway, the north-
eastern shore of the White Sea being low land.

[2] An unfortunate translation, which often occurs in old works, of
Swjatoinos, "the holy headland."

there was a castle, Barthus, which means *vakthus*, watch-house, for there the King of Norway keeps a guard to protect his frontiers. The interpreter said that this promontory was so long that it could scarcely be sailed round in eight days, on which account, in order not to be delayed in this way, they carried their boats and baggage with great labour on their shoulders over land for the distance of about half a mile. They then sailed on along the land of the Dikilopps or wild Lapps to a place which is called Dront (Trondhjem) and lies 200 miles north of [1] the Dwina. And they said that the prince of Moscow used to receive tribute as far as to this place."

The narrative is of interest, because it gives us an idea of the way in which men travelled along the north coast of Norway, four hundred years ago. It may possibly have had an indirect influence on the sending of Sir Hugh Willoughby's expedition, as the edition of Herbertstein's work printed at Venice in 1550 probably soon became known to the Venetian, Cabot, who, at that time, as Grand Pilot of England, superintended with great care the fitting out of the first English expedition to the north-east.

There is still greater probability that the map of Scandinavia by Olaus Magnus, already mentioned, was known in England before 1553. This map is an expression of a view which before that time had taken root in the north, which, in opposition to the maps of the South-European cosmographers, assumed the existence of an open sea-communication in the north, between the Chinese Sea and the Atlantic, and which even induced GUSTAF VASA to attempt to bring about a north-east expedition. This unfortunately did not come to completion, and all that we know of it is contained in a letter to the Elector August of Saxony, from the Frenchman HUBERT LANGUET, who visited Sweden in 1554. In this letter, dated 1st April 1576, Languet says :—" When I was in Sweden twenty-two years ago, King Gustaf often talked with me about this sea route. At last he urged me to undertake a voyage in this direction, and promised to fit out two vessels with all that was necessary for a protracted voyage, and to man them with the most skilful seamen, who should do what I ordered. But I replied that I preferred journeys in inhabited regions to the search for new unsettled lands." [2] If Gustaf Vasa had found a man fit to carry out his great plans, it might readily have happened that Sweden

---

[1] Instead of " north of," the true reading probably is " beyond " the Dwina.

[2] Huberti Langueti *Epistolæ Secretæ*, Halæ, 1699, i. 171. Compare also a paper by A. G. Ahlquist, in *Ny Illustrerad Tidning* for 1875, p. 270.

would have contended with England for the honour of opening the long series of expeditions to the north-east.[1]

England's navigation is at present greater beyond comparison than that of any other country, but it is not of old date. In the middle of the sixteenth century it was still very inconsiderable, and mainly confined to coast voyages in Europe, and a few fishing expeditions to Iceland and Newfoundland.[2] The great power of Spain and Portugal by sea, and their jealousy of other countries rendered it impossible at that period for foreign seafarers to carry on traffic in the East-Asiatic countries, which had been sketched by Marco Polo with so attractive accounts of unheard-of richness in gold and jewels, in costly stuffs, in spices and perfumes. In order that the merchants of northern Europe might obtain a share of the profit, it appeared to be necessary to discover new routes, inaccessible to the armadas of the Pyrenean peninsula. Here lies the explanation of the zeal with which the English and the Dutch, time after time, sent out vessels, equipped at great expense, in search of a new way to India and China, either by the Pole, by the north-west, along the north coast of the new world, or by the north-east, along the north coast of the old. The voyages first ceased when the maritime supremacy of Spain and Portugal was broken. By none of them was the intended object gained, but it is remarkable that in any case they gave the first start to the development of England's ocean navigation.

Sir HUGH WILLOUGHBY's in 1553 was thus the first maritime expedition undertaken on a large scale, which was sent from

---

[1] The first to incite to voyages of discovery in the polar regions was an Englishman, Robert Thorne, who long lived at Seville. Seeing all other countries were already discovered by Spaniards and Portuguese, he urged Henry VIII. in 1527 to undertake discoveries in the north. After reaching the Pole (going sufficiently far north) one could turn to the east, and, first passing the land of the Tartars, get to China and so to Malacca, the East Indies, and the Cape of Good Hope, and thus circumnavigate the " whole world." One could also turn to the west, sail along the back of Newfoundland, and return by the Straits of Magellan (Richard Hakluyt, *The Principael Navigations, Voiages, and Discoveries of the English Nation, &c.*, London, 1589, p. 250). Two years before, Paulus Jovius, on the ground of communications from an ambassador from the Russian Czar to Pope Clement VII., states that Russia is surrounded on the north by an immense ocean, by which it is possible, if one keeps to the right shore, and if no land comes between, to sail to China. (Pauli Jovii *Opera Omnia*, Basel, 1578, third part, p. 88; the description of Russia, inserted there under the title " Libellus de legatione Basilii ad Clementem VII.," was printed for the first time at Rome in 1525.)

[2] In the year 1540, London, exclusive of the Royal Navy, had no more than four vessels whose draught exceeded 120 tons (Anderson, *Origin of Commerce*, London, 1787, vol. ii. p. 67). Most of the coast towns of Scandinavia have thus in our days a greater sea-going fleet than London had at that time.

SIR HUGH WILLOUGHBY.
After a portrait in the Great Picture Hall, Greenwich.

(*To face page* 49.)

England to far distant seas. The equipment of the vessels
was carried out with great care under the superintendence of
the famous navigator, Sebastian Cabot, then an old man, who
also gave the commander precise instructions how he should
behave in the different incidents of the voyage. Some of these
instructions now indeed appear rather childish,[1] but others
might still be used as rules for every well-ordered exploratory
expedition. Sir Hugh besides obtained from Edward VI. an
open letter written in Latin, Greek, and several other languages,
in which it was stated that discoveries and the making of com-

SEBASTIAN CABOT.
After a portrait in E. Vale Blake's Arctic Experiences, London, 1874.[2]

mercial treaties were the sole objects of the expedition; and the
people with whom the expedition might come in contact, were
requested to treat Sir Hugh Willoughby as they themselves
would wish to be treated in case they should come to England.
So sanguine were the promoters of the voyage of its success in

---

[1] For instance Article 30 : "Item, if you shall see them [the foreigners
met with during the voyage] weare Lyons or Bears skinnes, hauing long
bowes, and arrowes, be not afraid of that sight : for such be worne often-
times more to feare strangers, then for any other cause." (*Hakluyt*, 1st
edition, p. 262.)

[2] The endeavour to procure for this work a copy of an original portrait
of Cabot, stated to be in existence in England, has unfortunately not been
crowned with success.

reaching the Indian seas by this route, that they caused the ships that were placed at Sir Hugh Willoughby's disposal to be sheathed with lead in order to protect them from the attacks of the teredo and other worms.[1] These vessels were:—

1. The *Bona Esperanza*, admiral of the fleet, of 120 tons burden, on board of which was Sir Hugh Willoughby himself, as captain general of the fleet. The number of persons in this ship, including Willoughby, the master of the vessel, William Gefferson, and six merchants, was thirty-five.

2. The *Edward Bonaventure*, of 160 tons burden, the command of which was given to Richard Chancelor, captain and pilot major of the fleet. There were on board this vessel fifty men, including two merchants. Among the crew whose names are given in Hakluyt we find the name of Stephen Burrough, afterwards renowned in the history of the north-east passage, and that of Arthur Pet.

3. The *Bona Confidentia*, of ninety tons, under command of Cornelius Durfoorth, with twenty-eight men, including three merchants.

The expense of fitting out the vessels amounted to a sum of £6,000, divided into shares of £25. Sir Hugh Willoughby was chosen commander "both by reason of his goodly personage (for he was of tall stature) as also for his singular skill in the services of warre."[2] In order to ascertain the nature of the lands of the east, two "Tartars" who were employed at the royal stables were consulted, but without any information being obtained from them. The ships left Ratcliffe the 20th May 1553.[3] They were towed down by the boats, "the mariners being apparelled in watchet or skie coloured cloth," with a favourable wind to Greenwich, where the court then was. The King being unwell could not be present, but "the courtiers came running out, and the common people flockt together, standing very thicke upon the shoare; the Privie Consel, they lookt out at the windowes of the court, and the rest ran up to the toppes of the towers; the shippes hereupon discharge their ordinance, and shoot off their pieces after the maner of warre, and of the sea, insomuch that the tops of the hilles sounded therewith, the valleys and the waters gave an echo, and the mariners

---

[1] According to Clement Adams' account of the voyage. (*Hakluyt*, 1st edition, p. 271.)

[2] "Cum ob corporis formam (erat enim procerae staturae) tum ob singularem in re bellica industriam." Clement Adams' account.—*Hakluyt* p. 271.

[3] Ten days earlier or later are of very great importance with respect to the state of the ice in summer in the Polar seas. I have, therefore, in quoting from the travels of my predecessors, reduced the old style to the new.

they shouted in such sort, that the skie rang again with the noise thereof." [1] All was joy and triumph; it seemed as if men foresaw that the greatest maritime power, the history of the world can show, was that day born.

The voyage itself was, however, very disastrous for Sir Hugh and many of his companions. After sailing along the east coast of England and Scotland the three vessels crossed in company to Norway, the coast of which came in sight the $\frac{24}{14}$th July in 66° N. L. A landing was effected and thirty small houses were found, whose inhabitants had fled, probably from fear of the foreigners. The region was called, as was afterwards ascertained, "Halgeland," and was just that part of Norway from which Othere began his voyage to the White Sea. Hence they sailed on along the coast. On the $\frac{6\text{th Aug.}}{27\text{th July}}$ they anchored in a harbour, "Stanfew" (perhaps Steenfjord on the west coast of Lofoten), where they found a numerous and friendly population, with no articles of commerce, however, but dried fish and train oil. In the middle of September the *Edward Bonaventure*, at Senjen during a storm, parted company with the two other vessels. These now endeavoured to reach Vardoehus, and therefore sailed backwards and forwards in different directions, during which they came among others to an uninhabited, ice-encompassed land, along whose coast the sea was so shallow that it was impossible for a boat to land. It was said to be situated 480' east by north from Senjen, in 72° N. L.[2] Hence they sailed first to the north, then to the south-east. Thus they reached the coast of Russian Lapland, where, on the $\frac{21}{18}$th September they found a good harbour, in which Sir Hugh determined to pass the winter. The harbour was situated at the mouth of the river Arzina "near Kegor." Of the further fate of Sir Hugh Willoughby and

---

[1] "Vibrantur bombardarum fulmina, Tartariæ volvuntur nubes, Martem sonant crepitacula, reboant summa montium juga, reboant valles, reboant undæ, claraque Nautarum percellit sydera clamor." Clement Adams' account.—*Hakluyt*, p. 272.

[2] At the time when the whale-fishing at Spitzbergen commenced Thomas Edge, a captain of one of the Muscovy Company's vessels, endeavoured to show that the land which Willoughby discovered while sailing about after parting company with Chancelor was Spitzbergen (*Purchas*, iii. p. 462). The statement, which was evidently called forth by the wish to monopolise the Spitzbergen whale-fishing for England, can be shown to be incorrect. It has also for a long time back been looked upon as groundless. Later inquiries have instead supposed that the land which Willoughby saw was Gooseland, on Novaya Zemlya. For reasons which want of space prevents me from stating here, this also does not appear to me to be possible. On the other hand, I consider it highly probable that "Willoughby's Land" was Kolgujev Island, which is surrounded by shallow sand-banks. Its latitude has indeed in that case been stated 2° too high, but such errors are not impossible in the determinations of the oldest explorers.

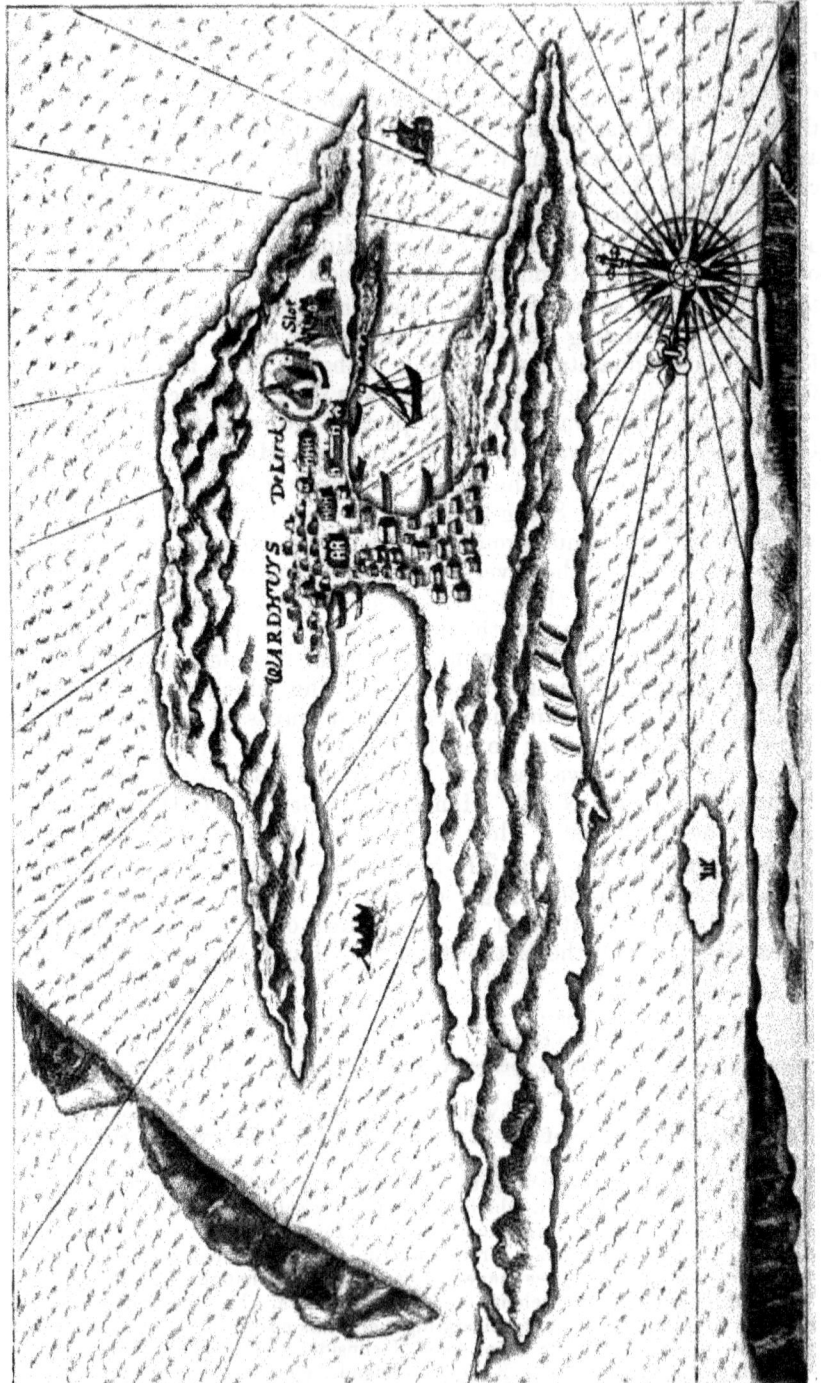

VARDOE IN 1594.
After Lindschoten.

VARDOZ IN OUR DAYS.
After a photograph.

his sixty-two companions, we know only that during the course of the winter they all perished, doubtless of scurvy. The journal of the commander ends with the statement that immediately after the arrival of the vessels three men were sent south-south-west, three west, and three south-east, to search if they could find people, but that they all returned "without finding of people or any similitude of habitation." The following year Russian fishermen found at the wintering station the ships and dead bodies of those who had thus perished, together with the journal from which the extract given above is taken, and a will witnessed by Willoughby,[1] from which it appeared that he himself and most of the company of the two ships were alive in January, 1554.[2] The two vessels, together with Willoughby's corpse, were sent to England in 1555 by the merchant George Killingworth.[3]

With regard to the position of Arzina it appears from a statement in Anthony Jenkinson's first voyage (*Hakluyt*, p 335) that it took seven days to go from Vardoehus to Swjatoinos, and that on the sixth he passed the mouth of the river where Sir Hugh Willoughby wintered. At a distance from Vardoehus of about six-sevenths of the way between that town and Swjatoinos, there debouches into the Arctic Ocean, in 68° 20' N. L. and 38° 30' E. L. from Greenwich, a river, which in recent maps is called the Varzina. It was doubtless at the mouth of this river that two vessels of the first North-East Passage Expedition wintered with so unfortunate an issue for the officers and men.

The third vessel, the *Edward Bonaventure*, commanded by Chancelor, had on the contrary a successful voyage, and one of great importance for the commerce of the world. As has been already stated, Chancelor was separated from his companions during a storm in August. He now sailed alone to Vardoehus. After waiting there seven days for Sir Hugh Willoughby, he set out again, resolutely determined "either to bring that to passe which was intended, or else to die the death;" and though "certaine Scottishmen" earnestly attempted to persuade him to return, "he held on his course towards that unknown part of the world, and sailed so farre that hee came at last to the place where hee found no night at all, but a continuall light and brightnesse of the sunne shining

---

[1] The testator was Gabriel Willoughby, who, as merchant, sailed in tho commander's vessel.

[2] *Hakluyt*, p. 500; *Purchas*, iii. p. 249, and in the margin of p. 463.

[3] It is of him that it is narrated in a letter written from Moscow by Henrie Lane, that the Czar at an entertainment "called them to his table, to receave each one a cuppe from his hand to drinke, and tooke into his hand Master George Killingworths beard, which reached over the table, and pleasantly delivered it the Metropolitane, who seeming to bless it, sad in Russe, 'this is God's gift.'"—*Hakluyt*, p. 500.

clearly upon the huge and mighty sea."[1] In this way he finally reached the mouth of the river Dwina in the White Sea, where a small monastery was then standing at the place where Archangel is now situated. By friendly treatment he soon won the confidence of the inhabitants, who received him with great hospitality. They, however, immediately sent off a courier to inform Czar Ivan Vasilievitsch of the remarkable occurrence. The result was that Chancelor was invited to the court at Moscow, where he and his companions passed a part of the winter, well entertained by the Czar. The following summer he returned with his vessel to England. Thus a commercial connection was brought about, which soon became of immense importance to both nations, and within a few years gave rise to a number of voyages, of which I cannot here give any account, as they have no connection with the history of the North-east Passage.[2]

Great geographer or seaman Sir Hugh Willoughby clearly was not, but his and his followers' voluntary self-sacrifice and undaunted courage have a strong claim on our admiration. Incalculable also was the influence which the voyages of Willoughby and Chancelor had upon English commerce, and on the development of the whole of Russia, and of the north of Norway. From the monastery at the mouth of the Dwina a flourishing commercial town has arisen, and a numerous population has settled on the coast of the Polar Sea, formerly so desolate. Already there is regular steam and telegraphic communication to the confines of Russia. The people of Vardoe can thus in a few hours get accounts of what has happened not only in Paris or London, but also in New York, the Indies, the Cape, Australia, Brazil, &c., while a hundred years ago the post came thither only once a year. It was then that a journal-loving commandant took the step, giving evidence of strong self-command, of not " devouring" the post at once, but reading the newspapers day by day a year after they were published. All this is now different, and

---

[1] As the Dwina lies to the south of Vardoehus, these remarks probably relate to an earlier part of the voyage than that which is referred to in the narrative.

[2] Writings on these voyages are exceedingly numerous. An account of them was published for the first time in Hakluyt, *The principael Navigations, Voiages, and Discoveries of the English Nation*, &c., London, 1589; *Ordinances, King Edward's Pass*, &c., p. 259; *Copy of Sir Hugh Willoughby's Journal, with a List of all the Members of the Expedition*, p. 265; *Clement Adams' Account of Chancelor's Voyage*, p. 270, &c. The same documents were afterwards printed in Purchas' *Pilgrimage*, iii. p. 211. For those who wish to study the literature of this subject further, I may refer to Fr. von Adelung *Kritisch-literärische Übersicht der Reisenden in Russland*, St. Petersburg and Leipzig, 1846, p. 200; and I. Hamel, *Tradescant der Aeltere 1618 in Russland*, St. Petersburg and Leipzig, 1847.

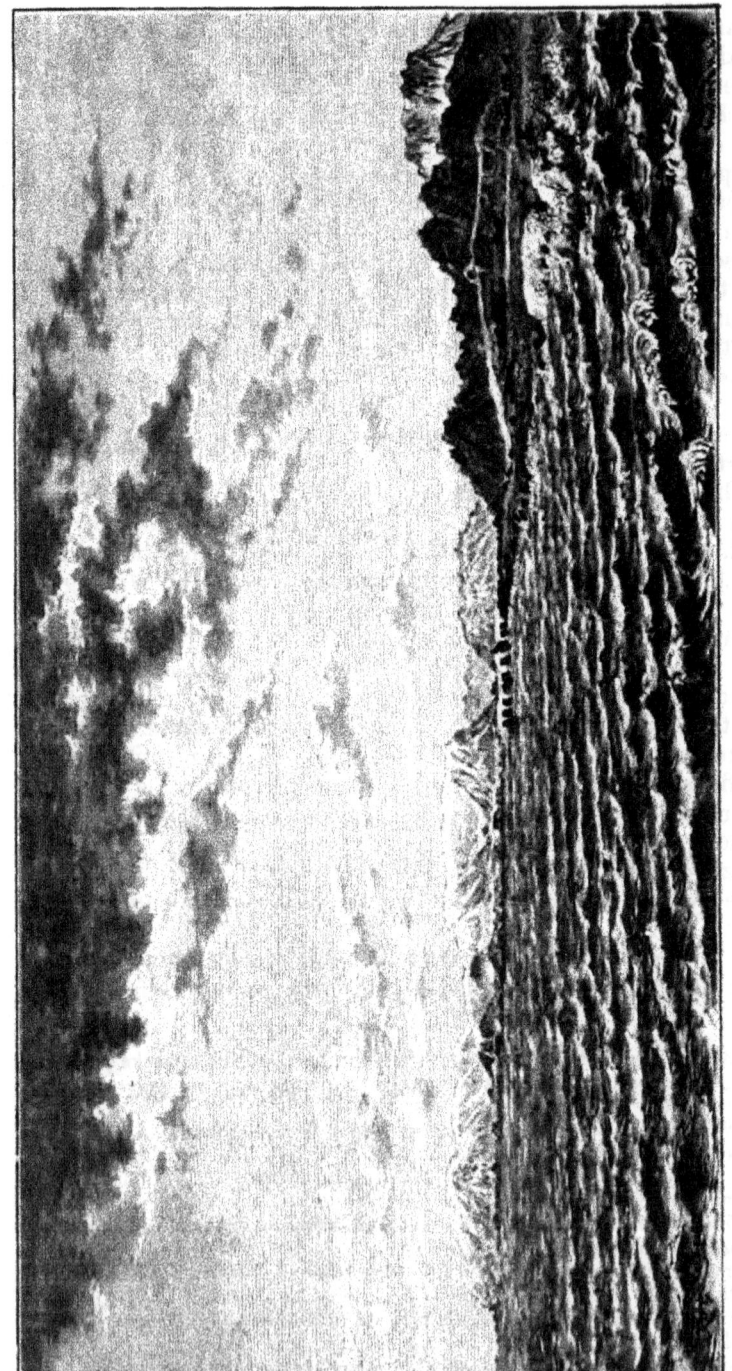

COAST LANDSCAPE FROM MATOTSCHKIN M'HAR.

After Svenske.

yet men are not satisfied. The interests of commerce and the fisheries require railway communication with the rest of Europe. That will certainly come in a few years, nor will it be long before the telegraph has spun its net, and regular steam communication has commenced along the coast of the Arctic Ocean far beyond the sea which was opened by Chancelor to the commerce of the world.

CHAPTER II.

Departure from Maosoe—Gooseland—State of the Ice—The Vessels of the Expedition assemble at Chabarova—The Samoyed town there—The Church—Russians and Samoyeds—Visit to Chabarova in 1875—Purchase of Samoyed Idols—Dress and Dwellings of the Samoyeds—Comparison of the Polar Races—Sacrificial Places and Samoyed Grave on Vaygats Island visited—Former accounts of the Samoyeds—Their place in Ethnography.

THE *Vega* was detained at Maosoe by a steady head wind, rain, fog, and a very heavy sea till the evening of the 25th July. Though the weather was still very unfavourable, we then weighed anchor, impatient to proceed on our voyage, and steamed out to sea through Mageroe Sound. The *Lena* also started at the same time, having received orders to accompany the *Vega* as far as possible, and, in case separation could not be avoided, to steer her course to the point, Chabarova in Yugor Schar, which I had fixed on as the rendezvous of the four vessels of the expedition. The first night, during the fog that then prevailed, we lost sight of the *Lena*, and did not see her again until we had reached the meeting place.

The course of the *Vega* was shaped for South Goose Cape. Although, while at Tromsoe, I had resolved to enter the Kara Sea through Yugor Schar, the most southerly of the sounds which lead to it—so northerly a course was taken, because experience has shown that in the beginning of summer so much ice often drives backwards and forwards in the bay between the west coast of Vaygats Island and the mainland, that navigation in these waters is rendered rather difficult. This is avoided by touching Novaya Zemlya first at Gooseland, and thence following the western shore of this island and Vaygats to Yugor Schar. Now this precaution was unnecessary; for the state of the ice was singularly favourable, and Yugor Schar was reached without seeing a trace of it.

During our passage from Norway to Gooseland we were favoured at first with a fresh breeze, which, however, fell as we

approached Novaya Zemlya; this notwithstanding, we made
rapid progress under steam, and without incident, except that
the excessive rolling of the vessel caused the overturn of some
boxes containing instruments and books, fortunately without
any serious damage ensuing.

Land was sighted on the 28th July at 10.30 P.M. It was
the headland which juts out from the south of Gooseland in
70° 33′ N. L. and 51° 54′ E. L. (Greenwich). Gooseland is a low
stretch of coast, occupied by grassy flats and innumerable
small lakes, which projects from the mainland of Novaya
Zemlya between 72° 10′ and 71° 30′ N. L. The name is a translation of the Russian Gusinnaja Semlja, and arises from the
large number of geese and swans (*Cygnus Bewickii,* YARR.) which
breed in that region. The geese commonly place their exceedingly inconsiderable nests on little hillocks near the small
lakes which are scattered over the whole of Gooseland; the
powerful swans, which are very difficult of approach by the
hunter, on the other hand breed on the open plain. The swans'
nests are so large that they may be seen at a great distance.
The building material is moss, which is plucked from the
ground within a distance of two metres from the nest, which
by the excavation which is thus produced, is surrounded by a
sort of moat. The nest itself forms a truncated cone, 0·6 metre
high and 2·4 metres in diameter at the bottom. In its upper
part there is a cavity, 0·2 metre deep and 0·6 metre broad, in
which the four large grayish-white eggs of the bird are laid.
The female hatches the eggs, but the male also remains in the
neighbourhood of the nest. Along with the swans and geese, a
large number of waders, a couple of species of Lestris, an owl
and other birds breed on the plains of Gooseland, and a few
guillemots or gulls upon the summits of the strand cliffs. The
avifauna along the coast here is besides rather poor. At least
there are none of the rich fowl-fells, which, with their millions
of inhabitants and the conflicts and quarrels which rage amongst
them, commonly give so peculiar a character to the coast
cliffs of the high north. I first met with true loom and
kittiwake fells farther north on the southern shore of Besim-
manaja Bay.

Although Gooseland, seen from a distance, appears quite level
and low, it yet rises gradually, with an undulating surface, from
the coast towards the interior, to a grassy plain about sixty metres
above the sea-level, with innumerable small lakes scattered over
it. The plain sinks towards the sea nearly everywhere with a
steep escarpment, three to fifteen metres high, below which
there is formed during the course of the winter an immense
snowdrift or so-called "snow-foot," which does not melt until
late in the season. *There are no true glaciers here, nor any*

erratic blocks, to show that circumstances were different in former times. Nor are any snow-covered mountain-tops visible from the sea. It is therefore possible at a certain season of the year (during the whole of the month of August) to sail from Norway to Novaya Zemlya, make sporting excursions there, and return without having seen a trace of ice or snow. This holds good indeed only of the low-lying part of the south island, but in any case it shows how erroneous the prevailing idea of the natural state of Novaya Zemlya is. By the end of June or beginning of July the greater part of Gooseland is nearly free of snow, and soon after the Arctic flower world develops during a few weeks all its splendour of colour. Dry, favourably situated spots are now covered by a low, but exceedingly rich flower bed, concealed by no high grass or bushes. On moister places true grassy turf is to be met with, which, at least when seen from a distance, resembles smiling meadows.

In consequence of the loss of time which had been caused by the delay in sailing along the coast of Norway, and our stay at Maosoe, we were unable to land on this occasion, but immediately continued our course along the west coast of Novaya Zemlya towards Yugor Schar, the weather being for the most part glorious and calm. The sea was completely free of ice, and the land bare, with the exception of some small snow-fields concealed in the valleys. Here and there too along the steep strand escarpments were to be seen remains of the winter's snow-foot, which often, when the lower stratum of air was strongly heated by the sun, were magnified by a strong mirage, so that, when seen from a distance, they resembled immense glaciers terminating perpendicularly towards the sea. Coming farther south the clear weather gave us a good view of Vaygats Island. It appears, when seen from the ·sea off the west coast, to form a level grassy plain, but when we approached Yugor Schar, low ridges were seen to run along the east side of the island, which are probably the last ramifications of the north spur of Ural, known by the name of Paj-koi.

When we were off the entrance to Yugor Schar, a steamer was sighted. After much guessing, the *Fraser* was recognised. I was at first very uneasy, and feared that an accident had occurred, as the course of the vessel was exactly the opposite of that which had been fixed beforehand, but found, when Captain Nilsson soon after came on board, that he had only come out to look for us. The *Express* and the *Fraser* had been waiting for us at the appointed rendezvous since the 20th. They had left Vardoe on the 13th, and during the passage had met with as little ice as ourselves. The *Vega* and the *Fraser* now made for the harbour at Chabarova, where they anchored on the evening of the 30th July with a depth of fourteen metres and a clay bottom. The *Lena* was still wanting. We feared that the little steamer had had some difficulty in keeping afloat in the sea which had been encountered on the other side of North Cape. A breaker had even dashed over the side of the larger *Vega* and broken in pieces one of the boxes which were fastened to the deck. Our fears were unwarranted. The *Lena* had done honour to her builders at Motala works, and behaved well in the heavy sea. The delay had been caused by a compass deviation, which, on account of the slight horizontal intensity of the magnetism of the earth in these northern latitudes, was greater than that obtained during the examination made before the departure of the vessel from Gothenburg. On the 31st the *Lena* anchored alongside the other vessels, and thus the whole of our little Polar Sea squadron was collected at the appointed rendezvous.

Chabarova is a little village, situated on the mainland, south of Yugor Schar, west of the mouth of a small river in which at certain seasons fish are exceedingly abundant. During summer the place is inhabited by a number of Samoyeds, who pasture their herds of reindeer on Vaygats Island and the surrounding *tundra*, and by some Russians and Russianised Fins, who come hither from Pustosersk to carry on barter with the Samoyeds, and with their help to fish and hunt in the neighbouring sea. During winter the Samoyeds drive their herds to more southern regions, and the merchants carry their wares to Pustosersk, Mesen, Archangel, and other places. Thus it has probably gone on for centuries back, but it is only in comparatively recent times that fixed dwellings have been erected, for they are not mentioned in the accounts of the voyages of the Dutch in these regions.

The village, or "Samoyed town" as the walrus-hunters grandiosely call it, consists, like other great towns, of two portions, the town of the rich—some cabins built of wood, with flat turf-covered roofs—and the quarter of the common people, a collection of dirty Samoyed tents. There is, besides, a little church, where, as at several places along the shore, votive crosses have been erected. The church is a wooden building, divided by a partition wall into two parts, of which the inner, the church proper, is little more than two and a half metres in height and about five metres square. On the eastern wall during the time the region is inhabited, there is a large number of sacred pictures placed there for the occasion by the hunters. One of them, which represented St. Nicholas, was very valuable, the material being embossed silver gilt. Before the lamps hung large dinted old copper lamps or rather light-holders, resembling inverted Byzantine cupolas, suspended by three chains. They were set full of numerous small, and some few thick wax lights which were lighted on the occasion of our visit. Right above our landing-place there were lying a number of sledges laden with goods which the Russian merchants had procured by barter, and which were to be conveyed to Pustosersk the following autumn. The goods consisted mainly of train oil and the skins of the mountain fox, common fox, Polar bear, glutton, reindeer, and seal. The bears' skins had often a very close, white winter coat, but they were spoiled by the head and paws having been cut off. Some of the wolf skins which they showed us were very close and fine. The merchants had besides

CHURCH OF CHABAROVA.
After a photograph by L. Palander

collected a considerable stock of goose quills, feathers, down, and ptarmigans' wings. For what purpose these last are used I could not learn. I was merely informed that they would be sold in Archangel. Perhaps they go thence to the dealers in fashions in Western Europe, to be afterwards used as ornaments on our ladies' hats. Ptarmigans' wings were bought as long ago as 1611 at Pustosersk by Englishmen.[1]

[1] "Letter of Richard Finch to Sir Thomas Smith, Governor ; and to the rest of the Worshipful Companie of English Merchants, trading into Russia."—*Purchas*, iii. p. 534.

At the same time I saw, among the stocks of the merchants, walrus tusks and lines of walrus hide. It is noteworthy that these wares are already mentioned in Othere's narrative.

As I was not myself sufficiently master of the Russian language, I requested Mr. Serebrenikoff to make inquiries on the spot, regarding the mode of life and domestic economy of the Russians in the neighbourhood, and I have received from him the following communication on the subject :—

"The village consists of several cabins and tents. In the cabins nine Russian householders live with their servants, who are Samoyeds.[1] The Russians bring hither neither their wives nor children. In the tents the Samoyeds live with their families. The Russians are from the village Pustosersk on the Petchora river, from which they set out immediately after Easter, arriving at Chabarova about the end of May, after having traversed a distance of between 600 and 700 versts. During their stay at Chabarova they employ themselves in the management of reindeer, in catching whales, and in carrying on barter with the Samoyeds. They bring with them from home all their household articles and commercial wares on sledges drawn by reindeer, and there is a poor ruinous chapel there, they bring also pictures of St. Nicholas and other saints. The holy Nicholas also figures as a shareholder in a company for the capture of whales. Part of their reindeer is left during summer on Vaygats, and after their arrival at Chabarova they still pass over on the ice to that island. Towards the close of August, when the cold commences, the reindeer are driven across Yugor Schar from Vaygats to the mainland. About the 1st October, old style, the Russians return with their reindeer to Pustosersk. Vaygats Island is considered by them to afford exceedingly good pasturage for reindeer ; they therefore allow a number of them to winter on the island under the care of some Samoyed families, and this is considered the more advantageous, as the reindeer there are never stolen. Such thefts, on the contrary, are often committed by the Samoyeds on the

---

[1] Mr. Serebrenikoff writes *Samodin* instead of *Samoyed*, considering the latter name incorrect. For *Samoyed* means "self-eater," while *Samodin* denotes "an individual," "one who cannot be mistaken for any other," and, as the Samoyeds never were cannibals, Mr. Serebrenikoff gives a preference to the latter name, which is used by the Russians at Chabarova, and appears to be a literal translation of the name which the Samoyeds give themselves. I consider it probable, however, that the old tradition of man-eaters (*androphagi*) living in the north, which originated with Herodotus, and was afterwards universally adopted in the geographical literature of the middle ages, reappears in a Russianised form in the name "Samoyed." (Compare what is quoted further on from Giles Fletcher's narrative.)

mainland. For thirty years back the Siberian plague has raged severely among the reindeer. A Russian informed me that he now owned but two hundred, while some years ago he had a thousand; and this statement was confirmed by the other Russians. Men too are attacked by this disease. Two or three days before our arrival a Samoyed and his wife had eaten the flesh of a diseased animal, in consequence of which the woman died the following day, and the man still lay ill, and, as the people on the spot said, would not probably survive. Some of the Samoyeds are considered rich, for instance the ' eldest ' (starschina) of the tribe, who owns a thousand reindeer. The Samoyeds also employ themselves, like the Russians, in fishing. During winter some betake themselves to Western Siberia, where ' corn is cheap,' and some go to Pustosersk.

" The nine Russians form a company (artell) for whale-fishing. There are twenty-two shares, two of which fall to the holy Nicholas, and the other twenty are divided among the share-holders. The company's profit for the fishing season commonly amounts to 1,500 or 2,000 pood train oil of the white whale (*Beluga*), but this season there had been no fishing on account of disagreements among the shareholders. For in the Russian ' artell ' the rule is, ' equal liability, equal rights,' and as the rich will never comply with the first part of the rule, it was their arrogance and greed which caused contention here, as everywhere else in the world.

" Neither the Russians nor the Samoyed carry on any agriculture. The former buy meal for bread from Irbit. The price of meal varies; this season it costs one rouble ten copecks per pood in Pustosersk. Salt is now brought from Norway to Mesen, where it costs fifty to sixty copecks per pood. The Samoyeds buy nearly everything from the Russians. There were many inquiries for gunpowder, shot, cheap fowling-pieces, rum, bread, sugar, and culinary vessels (tea-cups, &c.). The Samoyed women wear clothes of different colours, chiefly red. In exchange for the goods enumerated above there may be obtained fish, train oil, reindeer skins, walrus tusks, and furs, viz., the skins of the red, white, and brown fox, wolf, Polar bear, and glutton.

" The Russians in question are ' Old Believers,' but the difference between them and the orthodox consists merely in their not smoking tobacco, and in their making the sign of the cross with the thumb, the ring finger, and the little finger, while the orthodox Russians, on the other hand, make it with the thumb, the forefinger and the middle finger. All Samoyeds are baptised into the orthodox faith, but they worship their old idols at the same time. They travel over a thousand versts as pilgrims to their sacrificial places. There are several such places on Vaygats, where their idols are to be found. The

Russians call these idols 'Bolvany.'[1] Both the Russians and
Samoyeds are very tolerant in regard to matters of faith. The
Russians, for instance, say that the Samoyeds attribute to their
'bolvans' the same importance which they themselves attach
to their sacred pictures, and find in this nothing objectionable.
The Samoyeds have songs and sagas, relating among other
things to their migrations.

"The Samoyed has one or more wives; even sisters may
marry the same man. Marriage is entered upon without any
solemnity. The wives are considered by the men as having
equal rights with themselves, and are treated accordingly, which
is very remarkable, as the Russians, like other Christian nations,
consider the woman as in certain respects inferior to the man."

I visited the place for the first time in the beginning of
August, 1875. It was a Russian holiday, and, while still a
long way off at sea, we could see a large number of Russians
and Samoyeds standing in groups on the beach. Coming
nearer we found them engaged in playing various different
games, and though it was the first time in the memory of
man that European gentlemen had visited their "town," they
scarcely allowed themselves to be more disturbed in their occupation than if some stranger Samoyeds had suddenly joined
their company. Some stood in a circle and by turns threw a
piece of iron, shaped somewhat like a marlinspike, to the
ground ; the art consisting in getting the sharp end to strike it
just in front of rings placed on the ground, in such a way that
the piece of iron remained standing. Others were engaged in
playing a game resembling our nine-pins; others, again, in
wrestling, &c. The Russians and Samoyeds played with each
other without distinction. The Samoyeds, small of stature,
dirty, with matted, unkempt hair, were clad in dirty summer
clothes of skin, sometimes with a showy-coloured cotton shirt
drawn over them; the Russians (probably originally of the
Finnish race and descendants of the old Beormas) tall, well-
grown, with long hair shining with oil, ornamentally parted,
combed and frizzled, and held together by a head band, or
covered with a cap resembling that shown in the accompanying
woodcut, were clad in long variegated blouses, or "mekkor,"
fastened at the waist with a belt. Notwithstanding the feigned
indifference shown at first, which was evidently considered good
manners, we were received in a friendly way. We were first
invited to try our luck and skill in the game in turn with the
rest, when it soon appeared, to the no small gratification of our

---

[1] This name, which properly denotes a coarse likeness, has passed into
the Swedish, the word *bulvan* being one of the few which that language
has borrowed from the Russian.

hosts, that we were quite incapable of entering into competition either with Russian or Samoyed. Thereupon one of the Russians invited us to enter his cabin, where we were.entertained with tea, Russian wheaten cakes of unfermented dough, and brandy. Some small presents were given us with a naïve notification of what would be welcome in their stead, a notification which I with pleasure complied with as far as my resources permitted. A complete unanimity at first prevailed between our Russian and Samoyed hosts, but on the following day a sharp dispute was like to arise because the former invited one of us to drive with a reindeer team standing in the neighbourhood of a Russian hut. The Samoyeds were much displeased on this account, but declared at the same time, as well as they could by signs, that they themselves were willing to drive us, if we so desired, and they showed that they were serious in their declaration by there and then breaking off the quarrel in order to take a short turn with their reindeer teams at a rapid rate among the tents.

SAMOYED WOMAN'S HOOD.
One-eighth of natural size.

The Samoyed sleigh is intended both for winter travelling on the snow, and for summer travelling on the mosses and water-drenched bogs of the *tundra.* They are, therefore, constructed quite differently from the "akja" of the Lapp. As the woodcut on p. 66 shows, it completely resembles a high sledge, the carriage consisting of a low and short box, which, in convenience, style, and warmth, cannot be compared to the well-known equipage of the Lapps. We have here two quite different types of sleighs. The Lapp "akja" appears from time immemorial to have been peculiar to the Scandinavian north ; the high sleigh, on the contrary, to northern Russia. Thus we find "akjas" of the kind still in common use, delineated in Olaus Magnus (Rome edition, 1555, page 598) ; Samoyed sleighs, again, in the first works we have on those regions, for instance, in HUYGHEN VAN LINSCHOTEN'S *Schip-vaert van by Noorden,* &c., Amsterdam,

F

1601, as a side drawing on the principal map. Such high
sleighs are also used on the Kanin peninsula, on Yalmal,
and in Western Siberia. The sleighs of the Chukchis, on
the other hand, as will be seen by a drawing given farther
on, are lower, and thus more resemble our "kaelkar," or
work-sledges.

The neighbourhood of the tents swarmed with small black
or white long-haired dogs, with pointed nose and pointed ears.
They are used exclusively for tending the herds of reindeer, and
appear to be of the same race as the "renvallhund," the reindeer
dog. At several places on the coast of the White Sea, however, dogs are also employed as beasts of draught, but according

SAMOYED SLEIGH.
After a drawing by 1 j. Theel.

to information which I procured before my departure for
Spitzbergen in 1872—it was then under discussion whether
dogs should be used during the projected ice journey—these
are of a different race, larger and stronger than the Lapp or
Samoyed dogs proper.

Immediately after the *Vega* came to anchor, I went on land
on this occasion also; in the first place with a view to take some
solar altitudes, in order to ascertain the chronometer's rate of
going; for during the voyage of 1875 I had had an opportunity
of determining the position of this place as accurately as is

possible with the common reflecting circle and chronometer, with the following result :—

The Church at Chabarova { Latitude 69° 38′ 50″.
{ Longitude 60° 19′ 49″ E. from Greenwich.

When the observations were finished I hastened to renew my acquaintance with my old friends on the spot. I also endeavoured to purchase from the Samoyeds dresses and household articles; but as I had not then with me goods for barter, and ready money appeared to be of small account with them, prices were very high; for instance, for a lady's beautiful "pesk,"

LAPP AKJA.
After original in the Northern Museum, Stockholm.

twenty roubles; for a cap with brass ornaments, ten roubles; for a pair of boots of reindeer skin, two roubles; for copper ornaments for hoods, two roubles each; and so on.

As I knew that the Samoyeds during their wanderings always carry idols with them, I asked them whether they could not sell me some. All at first answered in the negative. It was evident that they were hindered from complying with my requests partly by superstition, partly by being a little ashamed, before the West European, of the nature of their gods. The metallic lustre of some rouble pieces which I had procured in Stockholm, however, at last induced an old woman to set aside

F 2

all fears. She went to one of the loaded sledges, which appeared
to be used as magazines, and searched for a long time till she
got hold of an old useless skin boot, from which she drew a fine
skin stocking, out of which at last four idols appeared. After
further negotiations they were sold to me at a very high price.
They consisted of a miniature "pesk," with belt, without body ; a
skin doll thirteen centimetres long, with face of brass ; another
doll, with a bent piece of copper plate for a nose ; and a stone,
wrapped round with rags and hung with brass plates, a corner
of the stone forming the countenance of the human figure it
was intended to resemble.

*Samoiedarum, trahis a rangiferis protractis infidentium,
Nec non Idolorum ab ijfdem cultorum effigies.*

SAMOYED SLEIGH AND IDOLS.
After an old Dutch engraving.

More finely-formed gods, dolls pretty well made, with bows
forged of iron, I have seen, but have not had the good fortune
to get possession of. In the case now in question the traffic
was facilitated by the circumstance that the old witch, Anna
Petrovna, who sold her gods, was baptised, which was naturally
taken advantage of by me to represent to her that it was wrong
for her as a Christian to worship such trash as " bolvans," and
the necessity of immediately getting rid of them. But my argu-
ments, at once sophistic and egoistic, met with disapproval, both
from the Russians and Samoyeds standing round, inasmuch as

they declared that on the whole there was no great difference between the "bolvan" of the Samoyed and the sacred picture of the Christian. It would even appear as if the Russians themselves considered the "bolvans" as representatives of some sort of Samoyed saints in the other world.

When the traffic in gods was finished, though not to my full satisfaction, because I thought I had got too little, we were invited by one of the Russians, as in 1875, to drink tea in his cabin. This consisted of a lobby, and a room about four metres square, and scarcely two metres and a half high. One corner was occupied by a large chimney, at the side of which was the very low door, and right opposite the window opening, under which were placed some chests, serving as tea-table for the occasion. Along the two remaining sides of the room there were fastened to the wall sleeping places of boards covered with reindeer skin. The window appeared to have been formerly

SAMOYED IDOLS.
One-third of natural size

filled with panes of glass, but most of these were now broken and replaced by boards. It need scarcely surprise us if glass is a scarce article of luxury here.

We had no sooner entered the cabin than preparations for tea commenced. Sugar, biscuits, teacups and saucers, and a brandy flask were produced from a common Russian travelling trunk. Fire was lighted, water boiled, and tea made in the common way, a thick smoke and strong fumes from the burning fuel spreading in the upper part of the low room, which for the time was packed full of curious visitors. Excepting these trifling inconveniences the entertainment passed off very agreeably, with constant conversation, which was carried on with great liveliness, though the hosts and most of the guests could only with difficulty make themselves mutually intelligible.

Hence we betook ourselves to the skin tents of the Samoyeds

which stood apart from the wooden huts inhabited by the Russians. Here too we met with a friendly reception. Several of the inhabitants of the tents were now clad with somewhat greater care in a dress of reindeer skin, resembling that of the Lapps. The women's holiday dress was particularly showy. It consisted of a pretty long garment of reindeer skin, fitting closely at the waist, so thin that it hung from the middle in

SAMOYED HAIR ORNAMENTS
One-third of natural size.

beautiful regular folds. The petticoat has two or three differently coloured fringes of dogskin, between which stripes of brightly coloured cloth are sewed on. The foot-covering consists of boots of reindeer skin beautifully and tastefully embroidered. During summer the men go bare-headed. The women then have their black straight hair divided behind into two tresses, which are braided with straps, variegated ribbons

and beads, which are continued beyond the point where the
hair ends as an artificial prolongation of the braids, so that, including the straps which form this continuation, loaded as they
are with beads, buttons, and metal ornaments of all kinds, they
nearly reach the ground.   The whole is so skilfully done, that
at first one is inclined to believe that the women here were
gifted with a quite incredible growth of hair.   A mass of other

SAMOYED WOMAN'S DRESS.
After a drawing by Hj. Theel

bands of beads ornamented with buttons was besides often
intertwined with the hair in a very tasteful way, or fixed to the
perforated ears.   All this hair ornamentation is naturally very
heavy, and the head is still more weighed down in winter, as it
is protected from the cold by a thick and very warm cap of reindeer skin, bordered with dogskin, from the back part of which
hang down two straps set full of heavy plates of brass or copper.

The young woman also, even here as everywhere else, bedecks herself as best she can ; but fair she certainly is not in our eyes. She competes with the man in dirt. Like the man she is small of stature, has black coarse hair resembling that of a horse's mane or tail, face of a yellow colour, often concealed by dirt, small, oblique, often running and sore eyes, a flat nose, broad projecting cheekbones, slender legs and small feet and hands.

The dress of the man, which resembles that of the Lapps, consists of a plain, full and long " pesk," confined at the waist with a belt richly ornamented with buttons and brass mounting, from which the knife is suspended. The boots of reindeer skin commonly go above the knees, and the head covering consists of a closely fitting cap, also of reindeer skin.

SAMOYED BELT WITH KNIFE.
One-sixth of natural size.

The summer tents, the only ones we saw, are conical, with a hole in the roof for carrying off the smoke from the fireplace, which is placed in the middle of the floor. The sleeping places in many of the tents are concealed by a curtain of variegated cotton cloth. Such cloth is also used, when there is a supply of it, for the inner parts of the dress. Skin, it would appear, is not a very comfortable material for dress, for the first thing, after fire-water and iron, which the skin-clad savage purchases from the European, is cotton, linen, or woollen cloth.

Of the Polar races, whose acquaintance I have made, the reindeer Lapps undoubtedly stand highest ; next to them come the Eskimo of Danish Greenland. Both these races are Christian and able to read, and have learned to use and require a large number of the products of agriculture, commerce, and the industrial arts of the present day, as cotton and woollen cloth, tools of forged and cast iron, firearms, coffee, sugar, bread, &c. They are still nomads and hunters, but cannot be called savages; and the educated European who has lived among them for a considerable time commonly acquires a liking for many points of their natural disposition and mode of life. Next to them in civilisation come the Eskimo of North-western America, on whose originally rough life contact with the American whale-fishers appears to have had a very beneficial influence. I form my judgment from the Eskimo tribe at Port Clarence. The members of this tribe were still heathens, but a few of them were far travelled, and had brought home from the Sandwich Islands not only cocoa-nuts and palm mats, but also a trace of the South Sea islander's greater love for ornament and order. Next come the Chukchis, who have as yet come in contact with men of European race to a limited extent, but whose resources appear to have seriously diminished in recent times, in consequence of which the vigour and vitality of the tribe have decreased to a noteworthy extent. Last of all come the Samoyeds, or at least the Samoyeds who inhabit regions bordering on countries inhabited by the Caucasian races; on them the influence of the higher race, with its regulations and ordinances, its merchants, and, above all, its fire-water, has had a distinctly deteriorating effect.

When I once asked an Eskimo in North-western Greenland, known for his excessive self-esteem, whether he would not admit that the Danish Inspector (Governor) was superior to him, I got for answer: "That is not so certain: the Inspector has, it is true, more property, and appears to have more power, but there are people in Copenhagen whom he must obey. I receive orders from none." The same haughty self-esteem one meets with in his host in the "gamma" of the reindeer Lapp, and the skin tent of the Chukchi. In the Samoyed, on the other hand, it appears to have been expelled by a feeling of inferiority and timidity, which in that race has deprived the savage of his most striking characteristics.

I knew from old travels and from my own experience on Yalmal, that another sort of gods, and one perhaps inferior to those which Anna Petrovna pulled out of her old boot, was to be found set up at various places on eminences strewn with the bones of animals that had been offered in sacrifice. Our Russian host informed us the Samoyeds from far distant regions are accustomed to make pilgrimages to these places in order to offer sacrifices and make vows. They eat the flesh of the animals they sacrifice, the bones are scattered over the sacrificial height, and the idols are besmeared with the blood of the sacrificed animal. I immediately declared that I wished

to visit such a place. But for a long time none of the Russians
who were present was willing to act as guide. At last however a young man offered to conduct me to a place on Vaygats
Island, where I could see what I wished. Accordingly the
following day, accompanied by Dr. Almquist, Lieutenant
Hovgaard, Captain Nilsson, and my Russian guide, I made
an excursion in one of the steam launches to the other shore
of Yugor Straits.

The sacrificial eminence was situated on the highest point of
the south-western headland of Vaygats Island, and consisted
of a natural hillock which rose a couple of metres above the

SACRIFICIAL EMINENCE ON VAYGATS ISLAND.
After a drawing by A. Hovgaard.

surrounding plain. The plain terminated towards the sea
with a steep escarpment. The land was even, but rose gradually
to a height of eighteen metres above the sea. The country
consisted of upright strata of Silurian limestone running
from east to west, and at certain places containing fossils
resembling those of Gotland. Here and there were shallow
depressions in the plain, covered with a very rich and uniformly
green growth of grass. The high-lying dry parts again made a
gorgeous show, covered as they were with an exceedingly
luxuriant carpet of yellow and white saxifrages, blue *Eritrichia*,
Polemonia and *Parryæ*, and yellow *Chrysosplenia*, &c. The last

named, commonly quite modest flowers, are here so luxuriant that they form an important part of the flower covering. Trees are wholly wanting. Even bushes are scarcely two feet high, and that only at sheltered places, in hollows and at the foot of steep slopes looking towards the south. The sacrificial mound consisted of a cairn of stones some few metres square, situated on a special elevation of the plain. Among the stones there were found :—

1. Reindeer skulls, broken in pieces for the purpose of extracting the brains, but with the horns still fast to the coronal bone ; these were now so arranged among the stones that they formed a close thicket of reindeer horns, which gave to the sacrificial mound its peculiar character.

2. Reindeer skulls with the coronal bone bored through, set up on sticks which were stuck in the mound. Sometimes there was carved on these sticks a number of faces, the one over the other.

3. A large number of other bones of reindeer, among them marrow bones, broken for the purpose of extracting the marrow.

4. Bones of the bear, among which were observed the paws and the head, only half flayed, of a bear which had been shot so recently that the flesh had not begun to decompose ; alongside of this bear's head there were found two lead bullets placed on a stone.

5. A quantity of pieces of iron, for instance, broken axes, fragments of iron pots, metal parts of a broken harmonicon, &c.; and finally,

6. The mighty beings to which all this splendour was offered.

They consisted of hundreds of small wooden sticks, the upper portions of which were carved very clumsily in the form of the human countenance, most of them from fifteen to twenty, but some of them 370 centimetres in length. They were all stuck in the ground on the south-east part of the eminence. Near the place of sacrifice there were to be seen pieces of driftwood and remains of the fireplace at which the sacrificial meal was prepared. Our guide told us that at these meals the mouths of the idols were besmeared with blood and wetted with brandy, and the former statement was confirmed by the large spots of blood

IDOLS FROM THE SACRIFICIAL CAIRN.
One-twelfth of natural size.

which were found on most of the large idols below the holes
intended to represent the mouth.

After a drawing had been made of the mound, we robbed it
discreetly, and put some of the idols and the bones of the animals
offered in sacrifice into a bag which I ordered to be carried down
to the boat. My guide now became evidently uncomfortable
and said that I ought to propitiate the wrath of the "bolvans"
by myself offering something. I immediately said that I was
ready to do that, if he would only show me how to go to
work. A little at a loss, and doubting whether he ought to
be more afraid of the wrath of the "bolvans" or of the punishment which in another world would befal those who had
sacrificed to false gods, he replied that it was only necessary
to place some small coins among the stones. With a solemn
countenance I now laid my gift upon the cairn. It was certainly the most precious thing that had ever been offered
there, consisting as it did of two silver pieces. The Russian
was now satisfied, but declared that I was too lavish, "a
couple of copper coins had been quite enough."

The following day the Samoyeds came to know that I had
been shown their sacrificial mound. For their own part
they appeared to attach little importance to this, but they
declared that the guide would be punished by the offended
"bolvans." He would perhaps come to repent of his deed
by the following autumn, when his reindeer should return
from Vaygats Island, where they for the present were tended
by Samoyeds; indeed if punishment did not befall him now,
it would reach him in the future and visit his children and
grandchildren—certain it was that the gods would not leave him
unpunished. In respect to God's wrath their religious ideas
were thus in full accordance with the teaching of the Old
Testament.

This place of sacrifice was besides not particularly old, for
there had been an older place situated 600 metres nearer the
shore, beside a grotto which was regarded by the Samoyeds
with superstitious veneration. A larger number of wooden
idols had been set up there, but about thirty years ago a
zealous, newly-appointed, and therefore clean-sweeping archimandrite visited the place, set.fire to the sacrificial mound,
and in its place erected a cross, which is still standing. The
Samoyeds had not sought to retaliate by destroying in their
turn the symbol of Christian worship. They left revenge to
the gods themselves, certain that in a short time they would
destroy all the archimandrite's reindeer, and merely removed
their own place of sacrifice a little farther into the land.
There no injudicious religious zeal has since attacked their
worship of the "bolvans."

The old place of sacrifice was still recognisable by the number of fragments of bones and rusted pieces of iron which lay strewed about on the ground, over a very extensive area, by the side of the Russian cross. Remains of the fireplace, on which the Schaman gods had been burned, were also visible. These had been much larger and finer than the gods on the present eminence, which is also confirmed by a comparison of the

SACRIFICIAL CAVITY ON VAYGATS ISLAND.
After a drawing by A. Hovgaard.

drawings here given of the later with those from the time of the Dutch explorers. The race of the Schaman gods has evidently deteriorated in the course of the last three hundred years.

After I had completed my examination and collected some contributions from the old sacrificial mound I ordered a little boat, which the steam-launch had taken in tow, to be carried

over the sandy neck of land which separates the lake shown on
the map from the sea, and rowed with Captain Nilsson and my
Russian guide to a Samoyed burying-place farther inland by
the shore of the lake.

Only one person was found buried at the place. The grave
was beautifully situated on the sloping beach of the lake, now
gay with numberless Polar flowers. It consisted of a box
carefully constructed of broad stout planks, fixed to the ground
with earthfast stakes and cross-bars, so that neither beasts of
prey nor lemmings could get through. The planks appeared
not to have been hewn out of drift-wood, but were probably

SAMOYED GRAVE ON VAYGATS ISLAND.

brought from the south, like the birch bark with which the
bottom of the coffin was covered. As a " pesk," now fallen in
pieces, lying round the skeleton, and various rotten rags showed,
the dead body had been wrapped in the common Samoyed
dress. In the grave were found besides the remains of an iron
pot, an axe, knife, boring tool, bow, wooden arrow, some copper
ornaments, &c. Rolled-up pieces of bark also lay in the coffin,
which were doubtless intended to be used in lighting fires
in another world. Beside the grave lay a sleigh turned upside
down, evidently placed there in order that the dead man should
not, away there, want a means of transport, and it is probable

that reindeer for drawing it were slaughtered at the funeral banquet.

As it may be of interest to ascertain to what extent the Samoyeds have undergone any considerable changes in their mode of life since they first became known to West-Europeans, I shall here quote some of the sketches of them which we find in the accounts of the voyages of the English and Dutch travellers to the North-East.

That changes have taken place in their weapons, in other words, that the Samoyeds have made progress in the art of war or the chase, is shown by the old drawings, some of which are here reproduced. For in these they are nearly always

SAMOYED ARCHERS
After Linschoten.

delineated with bows and arrows. Now the bow appears to have almost completely gone out of use, for we saw not a single Samoyed archer. They had, on the other hand, the wretched old flint firelocks, in which lost pieces of the lock were often replaced in a very ingenious way with pieces of bone and thongs. They also inquired eagerly for percussion guns, but breechloaders were still unknown to them. In this respect they had not kept abreast of the times so well as the Eskimo at Port Clarence.

One of the oldest accounts of the Samoyeds which I know is that of Stephen Burrough from 1556. It is given in

Hakluyt (1st edition, page 318). In the narrative of the voyage of the *Searchthrift* we read :—

"On Saturday the 1st August 1556 I went ashore,[1] and there saw three morses that they (Russian hunters) had killed: they held one tooth of a morse, which was not great, at a roble, and one white beare skin at three robles and two robles : they further told me, that there were people called Samoeds on the great Island, and that they would not abide them nor us, who have no houses, but only coverings made of Deerskins, set ouer them with stakes : they are men expert in shooting, and have great plenty of Deere. On Monday the 3rd we weyed and went roome with another Island, which was five leagues (15′) East-north-east from us : and there I met againe with Loshak,[2] and went on shore with him, and he brought me to a heap of Samoeds idols, which were in number aboue 300, the worst and the most unartificiall worke that ever I saw : the eyes and mouthes of sundrie of them were bloodie, they had the shape of men, women, and children, very grosly wrought, and that which they had made for other parts, was also sprinkled with blood. Some of their idols were an olde sticke with two or three notches, made with a knife, in it. There was one of their sleds broken and lay by the heape of idols, and there I saw a deers skinne which the foules had spoyled : and before certaine of their idols blocks were made as high as their mouthes, being all bloody, I thought that to be the table whereon they offered their sacrifice : I saw also the instruments whereupon they had roasted flesh, and as farre as I could perceiue, they made the fire directly under the spit. Their boates are made of Deers skins, and when they come on shoare they cary their boates with them upon their backs : for their cariages they haue no other beastes to serve them but Deere only. As for bread and corne they have none, except the Russes bring it to them : their knowledge is very base for they know no letter."

Giles Fletcher, who in 1588 was Queen Elizabeth's ambassador to the Czar, writes in his account of Russia of the Samoyeds in the following way :—[3]

"The *Samoyt* hath his name (as the *Russe* saith) of eating himselfe : as if in times past they lived as the *Cannibals*, eating

[1] Probably on one of the small islands near Vaygats.

[2] A Russian hunter who had been serviceable to Stephen Burrough in many ways.

[3] *Treatise of Russia and the adjoining Regions*, written by Doctor Giles Fletcher, Lord Ambassador from the late Queen, Everglorious Elizabeth, to Theodore, then Emperor of Russia. A.D. 1588. *Purchas*, iii. p. 413.

one another. Which they make more probable, because at this time they eate all kind of raw flesh, whatsoeuer it bee, euen the very carrion that lyeth in the ditch. But as the *Samoits* themselves will say, they were called *Samoie*, that is, *of themselves*, as though they were *Indigenæ*, or people bred upon that very soyle that never changed their seate from one place to another, as most Nations have done. They are clad in Seale-skinnes, with the hayrie side outwards downe as low as the knees, with their Breeches and Netherstocks of the same, both men and women. They are all Blacke hayred, naturally beardless. And therefore the Men are hardly discerned from the Women by their lookes: saue that the Women weare a locke of hayre down along both their eares."

In nearly the same way the Samoyeds are described by G. DE VEER in his account of Barents' second voyage in 1595. Barents got good information from the Samoyeds as to the navigable water to the eastward, and always stood on a good footing with them, excepting on one occasion when the Samoyeds went down to the Dutchmen's boats and took back an idol which had been carried off from a large sacrificial mound.

The Samoyeds have since formed the subject of a very extensive literature, of which however it is impossible for me to give any account here. Among other points their relations to other races have been much discussed. On this subject I have received from my learned friend, the renowned philologist Professor AHLQUIST of Helsingfors the following communication:—

The Samoyeds are reckoned, along with the Tungoose, the Mongolian, the Turkish and the Finnish-Ugrian races, to belong to the so-called Altaic or Ural-Altaic stem. What is mainly characteristic of this stem, is that all the languages occurring within it belong to the so-called agglutinating type. For in these languages the relations of ideas are expressed exclusively by terminations or suffixes—inflections, prefixes and prepositions, as expressive of relations, being completely unknown to them. Other peculiarities characteristic of the Altaic languages are the vocal harmony occurring in many of them, the inability to have more than one consonant in the beginning of a word, and the expression of the plural by a peculiar affix, the case terminations being the same in the plural as in the singular. The affinity between the different branches of the Altaic stem is thus founded mainly on analogy or resemblance in the construction of the languages, while the different tongues in the material of language (both in the words themselves and in the expression of relations) show a very limited affinity

G

or none at all. The circumstance that the Samoyeds for the
present have as their nearest neighbours several Finnish-Ugrian
races (Lapps, Syrjaeni, Ostjaks, and Voguls), and that these

SAMOYEDS

From Schleissing's Neu-entdecktes Sieweria, worinnen die Zobeln gefangen werden.
Zittau 1693.[1]

[1] A still more extraordinary idea of the Samoyeds, than that which this
woodcut gives us, we get from the way in which they are mentioned in
the account of the journey which the Italian Minorite, Joannes de Plano
Carpini, undertook in High Asia in the years 1245-47 as ambassador from
the Pope to the mighty conqueror of the Mongolian hordes.   In this book
of travels it is said that Occodai Khan, Chingis Khan's son, after having
been defeated by the Hungarians and Poles, turned towards the north,
conquered the Bascarti, i e. the Great Hungarians, then came into collision
with the Parositi—who had wonderfully small stomachs and mouths, and
did not eat flesh, but only boiled it and nourished themselves by inhaling
the steam—and finally came to the Samogedi, who lived only by the chase
and had houses and clothes of skin, and to a land by the ocean, where
there were monsters with the bodies of men, the feet of oxen and the faces
of dogs (Relation des Mongols ou Tartares, par le frère Jean du Plan de
Carpin, publ. par M. d'Avezac, Paris 1838. p. 281. Compare Ramusio,
Delle navigationi e viaggi, ii. 1583, leaf 236). At another place in the
same work it is said that " the land Comania has on the north immediately
after Russia, the Mordvini and Bileri, i.e. the Great Bulgarians, the
Bascarti, i.e. the Great Hungarians, then the Parositi and Samogedi, who
are said to have the faces of dogs" (Relation des Mongols, p. 351.
Ramusio, ii., leaf 239).

to a great extent carry on the same modes of life as themselves
has led some authors to assume a close affinity between the
Samoyeds and the Fins and the Finnish races in general. The
speech of the two neighbouring tribes however affords no
ground for such a supposition. Even the language of the
Ostjak, which is the most closely related to that of the
Samoyeds, is separated heaven-wide from it and has nothing
in common with it, except a small number of borrowed words
(chiefly names of articles from the Polar nomad's life), which the
Ostjak has taken from the language of his northern neighbour.
With respect to their language, however, the Samoyeds are
said to stand at a like distance from the other branches of the
stem in question. To what extent craniology or the modern
anthropology can more accurately determine the affinity-relation-
ship of the Samoyed to other tribes, is still a question of
the future.

CHAPTER III.

From the Animal World of Novaya Zemlya—The Fulmar Petrel—The
Rotge or Little Auk—Brünnich's Guillemot—The Black Guillemot—
The Arctic Puffin—The Gulls—Richardson's Skua—The Tern—Ducks
and Geese—The Swan—Waders—The Snow Bunting—The Ptarmigan
—The Snowy Owl—The Reindeer—The Polar Bear—The Mountain Fox
—The Lemming—Insects—The Walrus—The Seal—Whales.

IF we do not take into account the few Samoyeds who of
recent years have settled on Novaya Zemlya or wander about
during summer on the plains of Vaygats Island, all the lands
which in the old world have formed the field of research of
the Polar explorer—Spitzbergen, Franz-Josef Land, Novaya
Zemlya, Vaygats Island, the Taimur Peninsula, the New
Siberian Islands, and perhaps Wrangel's Land also—are uninhabited. The pictures of life and variety, which the native,
with his peculiar manners and customs, commonly offers to the
foreigner in distant foreign lands, are not to be met with here.
But, instead, the animal life, which he finds there in summer—
for during winter almost all beings who live above the surface of
the sea disappear from the highest North—is more vigorous and
perhaps even more abundant, or, to speak more correctly, less
concealed by the luxuriance of vegetation than in the south.
    It is not, however, the larger mammalia—whales, walruses,
seals, bears and reindeer—that attract attention in the first place,
but the innumerable flocks of birds that swarm around the Polar
traveller during the long summer day of the North.

G 2

BREEDING-PLACE FOR LITTLE AUKS.

Long before one enters the region of the Polar Sea proper, the vessel is surrounded by flocks of large grey birds which fly, or rather hover without moving their wings, close to the surface of the sea, rising and sinking with the swelling of the billows, eagerly searching for some eatable object on the surface of the water, or swim in the wake of the vessel in order to snap up any scraps that may be thrown overboard.   It is the Arctic *stormfogel* [1] (Fulmar, " Mallemuck," " Hafhaest," *Procellaria glacialis*, L.). The fulmar is bold and voracious, and smells villanously, on which account it is only eaten in cases of necessity, although its flesh, if the bird has not recently devoured too much rotten blubber, is by no means without relish, at least for those who have become accustomed to the flavour of train oil, when not too strong.   It is more common on Bear Island and Spitzbergen than on Novaya Zemlya, and scarcely appears to breed in any considerable numbers on the last-named place. I know three places north of Scandinavia where the fulmar breeds in large numbers : the first on Bear Island, on the slopes of some not very steep cliffs near the so-called south harbour of the island,[2] the second on the southern shore of Brandywine Bay on North-East Land, the third on ledges of the perpendicular rock-walls in the interior of Ice Fjord. At the two latter places the nests are inaccessible. On Bear Island, on the other hand, one can without very great difficulty plunder the whole colony of the dirty grey, short eggs, which are equally rounded at both ends. · The eggs taste exceedingly well. The nest is very inconsiderable, smelling badly like the bird itself.

When the navigator has gone a little further north and come to an ice-bestrewed sea, the swell ceases at once, the wind is hushed and the sea becomes bright as a mirror, rising and sinking with a slow gentle heaving. Flocks of little auks (*Mergulus alle*, L.) Brünnich's guillemots (*Uria Brünnichii*, Sabine), and black guillemots (*Uria grylle*, L.) now swarm in the air and swim among the ice floes. The *alke-kung* (little auk), also called the "sea king," or rotge, occurs only sparingly off the southern part of Novaya Zemlya, and does not, so far as I know, breed there. The situation of the land is too southerly, the accumulations of stones along the sides of the mountains too

---

[1] The name *stormfogel* is also used for the Stormy Petrel (*Thalassidroma pelagica*, Vig.). This bird does not occur in the portions of the Polar Sea with which we are now concerned.

[2] At Bear Island, Tobiesen, on the 28th May, 1866, saw fulmars' eggs laid immediately on the ice which still covered the rock. At one place a bird sitting on its eggs was even frozen fast by one leg to the ice on the 11 August, 1596. Barents found on the north part of Novaya Zemlya that some fulmars had chosen as a hatching-place a piece of ice covered with a little earth. In both these cases the under part of the egg during hatching could never be warmed above the freezing-point.

inconsiderable, for the thriving of this little bird. But on Spitzbergen it occurs in incredible numbers, and breeds in the talus, 100 to 200 metres high, which frost and weathering have formed at several places on the steep slopes of the coast mountain sides; for instance, at Horn Sound, at Magdalena Bay, on the Norways (near 80° N. L.), and other places. These stone heaps form the palace of the rotge, richer in rooms and halls than any other in the wide round world. If one climbs up among the stones, he sees at intervals actual clouds of fowl suddenly emerge from the ground either to swarm round in the air or else to fly out to sea, and at the same time those that remain make their presence underground known by an unceasing cackling and din, resembling, according to Friedrich Martens, the noise of a crowd of quarrelling women. Should this sound be stilled for a few moments, one need only attempt in some opening among the stones to imitate their cry

THE LITTLE AUK, OR ROTGE.
Swedish, Alkekung. (*Mergulus Alle*, L.)

(according to Martens: *rott-tet-tet-tet-tet*) to get immediately eager and sustained replies from all sides. The fowl circling in the air soon settle again on the stones of the mountain slopes, where, squabbling and fighting, they pack themselves so close together that from fifteen to thirty of them may be killed by a single shot. A portion of the flock now flies up again, others seek their safety like rats in concealment among the blocks of stone. But they soon creep out again, in order, as if by agreement, to fly out to sea and search for their food, which consists of crustacea and vermes. The rotge dives with ease. Its single bluish-white egg is laid on the bare ground without a nest, so deep down among the stones that it is only with difficulty that it can be got at. In the talus of the mountains north of Horn Sound I found on the 18th June, 1858, two eggs of this bird lying directly on the layer of ice between the stones. Probably the hatching season had not then begun. Where the main body of these flocks of birds passes the winter, is unknown,[1] but they return to the north early—sometimes too early. Thus in 1873 at the end of April I saw a large number of rotges frozen to death on

---

[1] It deserves to be investigated whether some little auks do not, like the Spitzbergen ptarmigan, pass the winter in their stone mounds, flying out to sea only at pretty long intervals in order to collect their food.

the ice in the north part of Hinloopen Strait. When cooked
the rotge tastes exceedingly well, and in consequence of the
great development of the breast muscles it affords more food
than could be expected from its small size.

Along with the rotge we find among the ice far out at sea
flocks of *alkor* (looms, or Brünnich's guillemots), and the nearer
we come to the coast, the more do these increase in number,
especially if the cliffs along the shore offer to this species of sea-
fowl—the most common of the Polar lands—convenient hatching
places. For this purpose are chosen the faces of cliffs which rise
perpendicularly out of the sea, but yet by ledges and uneven

THE LOOM OR BRÜNNICH'S GUILLEMOT.
Swedish, Alka. (*Uria Brünnichii*, Sabine.)

places afford room for the hatching fowl. On the guillemot-
fells proper, eggs lie beside eggs in close rows from the crown of
the cliff to near the sea level, and the whole fell is also closely
covered with seafowl, which besides in flocks of thousands and
thousands fly to and from the cliffs, filling the air with their
exceedingly unpleasant scream. The eggs are laid, without trace
of a nest, on the rock, which is either bare or only covered with
old birds' dung, so closely packed together, that in 1858 from a
ledge of small extent, which I reached by means of a rope from
the top of the fell, I collected more than half a barrel-full
of eggs. Each bird has but one very large egg, grey pricked

with brown, of very variable size and form. After it has been sat upon for some time, it is covered with a thick layer of birds' dung, and in this way the hunters are accustomed to distinguish uneatable eggs from fresh.

If a shot be fired at a "loomery," the fowl fly away in thousands from their hatching places, without the number of those that are not frightened away being apparently diminished. The clumsy and short-winged birds, when they cast themselves out of their places, fall down at first a good way before they get "sufficient air" under their wings to be able to fly. Before this takes place, many plump down into the water, sometimes even into the boat which may be rowed along the foot of the fell.

An unceasing, unpleasant cackling noise indicates that a continual gossip goes on in the "loomery"; and that the unanimity there is not great, is proved by the passionate screams which are heard now and then. A bird squeezes forward in order to get a place on a ledge of rock already packed full, a couple of others quarrel about the ownership of an egg which has been laid on a corner of the rock only a few inches broad, and which now during the dispute is precipitated into the abyss. By the beginning of July most of the eggs are uneatable. I have seen the young of the size of a rotge accompany their mothers in the middle of August. The loom breeds on Walden Island and the north coast of North-East Land, accordingly far north of 80°. I found the largest "loomeries" on Spitzbergen south of Lomme Bay in Hinloopen Strait, at the southern entrance to Van Meyen Bay in Bell Sound, and at Alkornet in Ice Fjord. In respect to the large number of fowl, however, only the first of these can compete with the south shore of Besimannaja Bay (72° 54′ N. L.) and with the part of Novaya Zemlya that lies immediately to the south of this bay. The eggs of the loom are palatable, and the flesh is excellent, though not quite free from the flavour of train oil. In any case it tastes much better than that of the eider.

Along with the rotge and the loom two nearly allied species of birds, *lunnefogeln*, the Arctic puffin (*Mormon arcticus*, L.) and *tejsten* or *tobis-grisslan*, the black guillemot (*Uria grylle*, L.) are to be seen among the drift-ice. I do not know any puffin-fells on Spitzbergen. The bird appears to breed there only in small numbers, though it is still found on the most northerly part of the island. On Novaya Zemlya, too, it occurs rather sparingly. The black guillemot, on the other hand, is found everywhere, though never collected in large flocks, along the shores of Spitzbergen, and Novaya Zemlya, even as far north as Parry Island in 80° 40′ N. L., where in 1861

I saw several of their nests. These are placed near the summits of steep cliffs along the shore. The black guillemots often swim out together in pairs in the fjords. Their flesh has about the same taste as Brünnich's guillemot, but is tougher and of inferior quality; the eggs, on the other hand, are excellent.

The sea fowl mentioned above are never met with inland. They never settle on a grassy sward or on a level sandy beach. The steep fowl-fell· sides, the sea, ground-ice, pieces of drift-ice and small stones rising above the water, form· their habitat. They swim with great skill both on, and under the water. The black guillemots and rotges fly swiftly and well; Brünnich's guillemots, on the contrary, heavily and ill. The latter therefore do not perhaps remove in winter farther from their hatching

THE ARCTIC PUFFIN.
Swedish, Lunnefogel. (*Mormon Arcticus*, L.)

THE BLACK GUILLEMOT.
Swedish, Tejst. (*Uria Grylle*, L.)

places than to the nearest open water, and it is probable that colonies of Brünnich's guillemots are not located at places where the sea freezes completely even far out from the coast. On this perhaps depends the scarcity of Brünnich's guillemot in the Kara Sea.

While sailing in the Arctic Ocean, vessels are nearly always attended by two kinds of gulls, the greedy *stormaosen* or *borgmaesteren*, glaucous gull (*Larus glaucus*, Brünn.), and the gracefully formed, swiftly flying *kryckian* or *tretaoiga maosen*, kittiwake (*Larus tridactylus*, L.), and if the hunter lies to at an ice-floe to flense upon it a seal which has been shot, it is not long till a large number of snow-white birds with dark blue bills and black legs settle down in the neighbourhood in order

that they may get a portion of the spoil. They belong to the third kind of gull common in the north, *ismaosen*, the ivory gull (*Larus eburneus*, Gmel.).

In disposition and mode of life these gulls differ much from each other. The glaucous gull is sufficiently strong to be able to defend its eggs and young against the attack of the mountain fox. It therefore breeds commonly on the summits of easily accessible small cliffs, hillocks or heaps of stones, preferably in the neighbourhood of "loomeries" or on fowl-islands, where the young of the neighbouring birds offer an opportunity for prey and hunting during the season when its own young are being fed. Sometimes, as for instance, at Brandywine Bay on Spitzbergen, the glaucous gull breeds in great flocks on the ledges of steep fell-sides, right in the midst of Brünnich's guillemots. On Bear Island I have seen it hatch on the very beach, at a place, for instance, under the arch of a waterfall leaping down from a precipitous cliff. The nests, which, to judge from the quantity of birds' dung in their neighbourhood, are used for a long succession of years, are placed in a depression in the rock or the ground, and lined with a little straw or a feather or two. The number of the eggs is three or four. After boiling they show a jellylike, half transparent white, and a reddish yellow, and are exceedingly delicious. The young birds have white flesh, resembling chicken. The burgomaster is common everywhere along the coasts of Novaya Zemlya and Spitzbergen. Yet I have not seen the nest of this gull on the north coast of North-East Land or on the Seven Islands.

Still more common than the glaucous gull in the lands of the High North is *kryckian*, the kittiwake. It is met with far out at sea, where it accompanies the vessel whole days, circling round the tops of the masts, and sometimes—according to the statements of the walrus-hunters, when a storm is approaching—pecking at the points of the pendant. When the vessel is in harbour, the kittiwakes commonly gather round it to pick out anything eatable in the refuse that may be thrown away. They breed in great flocks on the steep escarpments in some separate part of the fowl-fells, in connection with which, it is evident that the kittiwakes always endeavour to choose the best places of the fell—those that are most inaccessible to the fox and are best protected against bad weather. Among the birds of the north the kittiwake is the best builder; for its nest is walled with straw and mud, and is very firm. It juts out like a great swallow's nest from the little ledge to which it is fixed. Projecting ends of straw are mostly bent in, so that the nest, with its regularly rounded form, has a very tidy appearance. The interior is further lined with a soft, carefully arranged layer of moss, grass and seaweed, on which the bird lays three to four well-flavoured eggs. The soft warm underlayer is, however, not without its inconvenience; for Dr. Stuxberg during the voyage of ·1875 found in such a nest no fewer than twelve kinds of insects, among them *Pulex vagabundus*, Bohem. in nine specimens, a beetle, a fly, &c.

The ivory gull, called by Fr. Martens "Rathsherr," the Councillor, is found, as its Swedish name indicates, principally out at sea in the *pack*, or in fjords filled with drift-ice. It is a true ice-bird, and, it may almost be said, scarcely a water-bird at all, for it is seldom seen swimming on the surface, and it can dive as little as its relatives, the glaucous gull and the kittiwake.

A. THE KITTIWAKE.
Swedish. Kryckla. (*Larus tridactylus*. L.)   B. THE IVORY GULL
Swedish, Ismaos. (*Larus eburneus*. L.)

In greed it competes with the fulmar. When any large animal has been killed among the drift-ice, the ivory gull seldom fails to put in an appearance in order to quench its hunger with flesh and blubber. It consumes at the same time the excrements of the seal and the walrus, on which account from three to five ivory gulls may often be seen sitting for a long time round a seal-hole, quiet and motionless, waiting patiently the arrival of the seal (Malmgren).

The proper breeding places of this bird scarcely appear to be yet known. So common as it is both on the coasts of Spitzbergen from the Seven Islands to South Cape and on the north coast of Novaya Zemlya and America, its nest has only been found twice, once in 1853 by McClintock at Cape Krabbe in North America in 77° 25′ N.L., the second time by Dr. Malmgren at Murchison Bay, in 82° 2′ N.L. The two nests that Malmgren found consisted of depressions, twenty-three to twenty-six centimetres in diameter, in a heap of loose gravel, on a ledge of a steeply-sloping limestone-rock wall. In each nest was found only one egg, which, on the 30th July, already contained a down-covered young bird. For all the ivory gulls which have their home on Spitzbergen there were doubtless required several hundred such breeding-places as that at Murchison Bay. When to this is added the fact that we never

RARE NORTHERN GULLS.

A Sabine's Gull. (*Larus Sabinii*, Sabine.)   B. Ross's Gull. (*Larus Rossii*, Richards.)

in autumn saw on Spitzbergen any full-grown young of this kind of gull, I assume that its proper breeding-place must be found farther north, on the shores of some still unknown Polar land, perhaps continually surrounded by ice. It deserves to be mentioned with reference to this, that Murchison Bay was covered with ice when Malmgren found the nests referred to above.

Besides these varieties of the gull, two other species have been found, though very rarely, in the Polar regions, viz., *Larus Sabinii*, Sabine, and *Larus Rossii*, Richards. Although I have myself only seen the latter, and that but once (on the Chukchi Peninsula), I here give drawings of them both for the use of future Polar explorers. They are perhaps, if they be pro erly observed, not so rare as is commonly supposed.

Often during summer in the Arctic regions one hears a penetrating shriek in the air. When one inquires into the reason of this, it is found to proceed from a kittiwake, more rarely from a glaucous gull, eagerly pursued by a bird as large as a crow, dark-brown, with white breast and long tail-feathers.

A. THE COMMON SKUA.
Swedish, Labben   (*Lestris parasitica*, L.)

B. BUFFON'S SKUA.
Swedish, Fjellabben. (*Lestris Buffonii*, Boie.)

C. THE POMARINE SKUA.
Swedish, Bredstjertade Labben. (*Lestris pomarina*, Tem.)

It is *labben*, the common skua (*Lestris parasitica*, L.), known by the Norwegian walrus-hunters under the name of *tjufjo*, derived from the bird's cry, " *I o-i-o*," and its shameless thief-nature. When the "tjufjo" sees a kittiwake or a glaucous gull fly off with a shrimp, a fish, or a piece of blubber, it instantly attacks it. It flies with great swiftness backwards and forwards around its victim, striking it with its bill, until the attacked

bird either drops what it has caught, which is then immediately
snapped up by the skua, or else settles down upon the surface
of the water, where it is protected against attack. The skua
besides eats eggs of other birds, especially of eiders and geese.
If the eggs are left but for a few moments unprotected in the
nest, it is immediately to the front and shows itself so voracious
that it is not afraid to attack nests from which the hatching
birds have been frightened away by men engaged in gathering
eggs only a few yards off. With incredible dexterity it pecks
a hole in the eggs and sucks their contents. If speed is
necessary, this takes place so quickly and out of so many eggs
in succession that it sometimes has to stand without moving,
unable to fly further until it has thrown up what it had
swallowed. The skua in this way commonly takes part in
the plundering of every eider island. The walrus-hunters are
very much embittered against the bird on account of this intrusion on their industry, and kill it whenever they can. The
whalers called it "struntjaeger"—refuse-hunter—because they
believed that it hunted gulls in order to make them void their
excrements which "struntjaegeren" was said to devour as a
luxury.

The skua breeds upon low, unsheltered, often water-drenched
headlands and islands, where it lays one or two eggs on the
bare ground, often without trace of a nest. The eggs are so
like the ground that it is only with difficulty that they can be
found. The male remains in the neighbourhood of the nest
during the hatching season. If a man, or an animal which
the bird considers dangerous, approaches the eggs, the pair
endeavour to draw attention from them by removing from the
nest, creeping on the ground and flapping their wings in the
most pitiful way. The bird thus acts with great skill a
veritable comedy, but takes good care that it is not caught.

As is well known, we know only two varieties of colour in
this bird, a self-coloured brown, and a brown on the upper part
of the body with white below. Of these I have only once in
the Arctic regions seen the self-coloured variety, viz. at Bell
Sound in 1858. All the hundreds of skuas which I have
seen, besides, have had the throat and lower part of the body
coloured white.

This bird is very common on Spitzbergen and Novaya
Zemlya. Yet perhaps it scarcely breeds on the north part of
North-East Land. Along with the bird now described there
occur, though sparingly, two others:—*bredstjertade labben*, the
Pomarine skua (*Lestris pomarina*, Tem.) and *fjellabben*, Buffon's
skua (*Lestris Buffonii*, Boie). The latter is distinguished by its
more slender build and two very long tail-feathers, and it is
much more common farther to the east than on Spitzbergen.

I have not had an opportunity of making any observations on the mode of life of these birds.

As the skua pursues the kittiwake and the glaucous gull, it is in its turn pursued with extraordinary fierceness by the little swiftly-flying and daring bird *taernan*, the Arctic tern (*Sterna macroura*, Naum.). This beautiful bird is common everywhere on the coasts of Spitzbergen, but rather rare on Novaya Zemlya. It breeds in considerable flocks on low grass-free headlands or islands covered with sand or pebbles. The eggs, which are laid on the bare ground without any trace of a nest, are so like lichen-covered pebbles in colour, that it is only with difficulty one can get eyes upon them; and this is the case in a yet higher degree with the newly-hatched young, which notwithstanding their thin dress of down have to lie without anything below them among the bare stones. From the shortness of their legs and the length of their wings it is only with difficulty that the tern can go on the ground. It is therefore impossible for it to protect its nest in the same way as the "tjufjo." Instead, this least of all the swimming birds of the Polar lands does not hesitate to attack any one, whoever he may be, that dares to approach its nest. The bird circles round the disturber of the peace with evident exasperation, and now and then goes whizzing past his head at such a furious rate that he must every moment fear that he will be wounded with its sharp beak.

Along with the swimmers enumerated above, we find everywhere along these shores two species of eider, the *vanliga eidern*, common eider (*Somateria mollissima*, L.) and *praktejdern*, king-duck (*Somateria spectabilis*, L.). The former prefers to breed on low islands, which, at the season for laying eggs, are already surrounded by open water and are thus rendered inaccessible to the mountain foxes that wander about on the mainland. The richest eider islands I have seen in Spitzbergen are the Down Islands at Horn Sound. When I visited the place in 1858 the whole islands were so thickly covered with nests that it was necessary to proceed with great caution in order not to trample on eggs. Their number in every nest was five to six, sometimes larger, the latter case, according to the walrus hunters, being accounted for by the female when she sits stealing eggs from her neighbours. I have myself seen an egg of *Anser bernicla* in an eider's nest. The eggs are hatched by the female, but the beautifully coloured male watches in her nighbourhood and gives the signal of flight when danger approaches. The nest consists of a rich, soft, down bed. The best down is got by robbing the down-covered nest, an inferior kind by plucking the dead birds. When the female is driven from the nest she seeks in haste to scrape down over the eggs in order that they may not be visible. She besides squirts over them a very stinking fluid, whose disgusting smell adheres to the collected eggs and down. The stinking substance is however so volatile or so easily decomposed in the air that the smell completely disappears in a few hours. The eider, which some years ago was very numerous on Spitzbergen,[1] has of late years considerably diminished in numbers, and perhaps will soon be completely driven thence, if some restraint be not laid on the heedless way in which not only the Eider Islands are now plundered, but the birds too killed, often for the mere pleasure of slaughter. On Novaya Zemlya, too, the eider is common. It breeds, tor instance, in not inconsiderable numbers on the high islands in Karmakul Bay. The eider's flesh has, it is true, but a slight flavour of train oil, but it is coarse and far inferior to that of Brünnich's guillemot. In particular, the flesh of the female while hatching is almost uneatable.

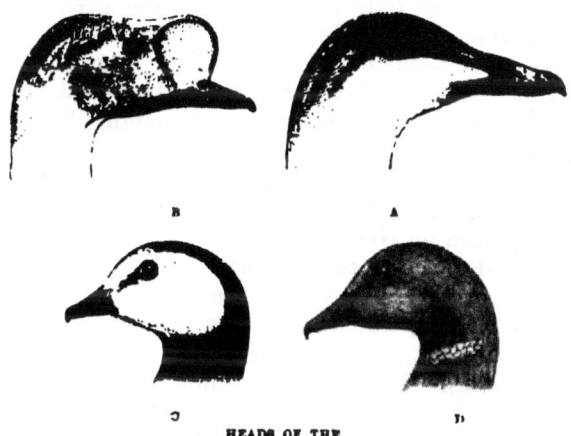

HEADS OF THE
A. EIDER ; B. KING DUCK ; C. BARNACLE GOOSE ; D. WHITE-FRONTED GOOSE.

The king-duck occurs more sparingly than the common eider. On Spitzbergen it is called the " Greenland eider," on Greenland the " Spitzbergen eider," which appears to indicate that in neither place is it quite at home. On Novaya Zemlya, on the other hand, it occurs in larger numbers. Only once have I seen the nest of this bird, namely, in 1873 on Axel's Islands in Bell Sound, where it bred in limited numbers together with the common eider. In the years 1858 and 1864, when I visited the same place, it did not breed there. Possibly its proper breeding

---

[1] The quantity of eider-down which was brought from the Polar lands to Tromsoe amounted in 1868 to 540, in 1869 to 963, in 1870 to 882, in 1871 to 630, and in 1872 to 306 kilograms. The total annual yield may be estimated at probably three times as much.

place is on Novaya Zemlya at the inland lakes a little way from the coast. The walrus-hunters say that its eggs taste better than those of the common eider. They are somewhat smaller and have a darker green colour.

On the Down Islands hatches, along with the eiders, the long-necked *prutgaessen*, barnacle goose (*Anser bernicla*, L.) marked on the upper part of the body in black and brownish grey. It lays four to five white eggs in an artless nest without down, scattered here and there among the eiders' nests rich in down. This variety of goose is found in greatest numbers during the moulting season at small inland lakes along the coast, for instance on the line of coast between Bell Sound and Ice Fjord and on Gooseland. The walrus-hunters sometimes call them "rapphoens"—partridges—a misleading name which in 1873 induced me to land on the open coast south of Ice Fjord, where "rapphoens" were to be found in great numbers. On landing I found only moulting barnacle geese. The barnacle goose finds its food more on land and inland lakes than in the sea. Its flesh accordingly is free from the flavour of train oil and tastes well, except that of the female during the hatching season, when it is poor and tough. The eggs are better than the eider's.

On Spitzbergen besides the barnacle goose we meet with the closely allied species *Anser leucopsis*, Bechst. It is rather rare, but more common on Novaya Zemlya. Further there occurs at the last-named place a third species of goose, *vildgaosen*, the "grey goose" or "great goose" of the walrus-hunters; the bean goose (*Anser segetum*, Gmel.), which is replaced on Spitzbergen by a nearly allied type, the pink-footed goose (*Anser brachy-rhynchus*, Baillon). These geese are much larger than both the eider and the barnacle goose, and appear to be sufficiently strong to defend themselves against the fox. They commonly breed high up on some mossy or grassy oasis, among the stone mounds of the coast mountains, or on the summit of a steep strand escarpment in the interior of the fjords. During the moulting season the grey geese collect in flocks at the small fresh-water lakes along the coast. The flesh of this species of goose is finer than that of the common tame goose and has no trace of any train flavour.

Among the swimming birds that give the summer life on Novaya Zemlya its peculiar character, we may further reckon the scaup-duck and the swan. *Alfogel* or *allan*, the long-tailed duck (*Fuligula glacialis*, L.) is rare on Spitzbergen, but occurs very generally on Novaya Zemlya, and especially in the Kara Sea, on whose coasts it is seen in summer collected in large flocks. *Mindre saongsvanen*, Bewick's swan (*Cygnus Bewickii*, Yarr.), is the most nobly formed and coloured bird of the north. I have already described its nest, which is found in considerable numbers in Gooseland. The bird is blinding white, resembling the common swan, but somewhat smaller, and with a considerable difference in the formation of the windpipe and the "keel" of the breastbone. The flesh is said to be coarse and of inferior flavour.

BEWICK'S SWAN.
Swedish, Mindre Saongsvanen. (*Cygnus Bewickii*, Yarr.)

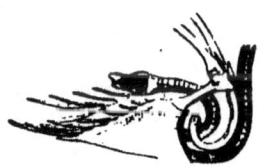

BREASTBONE
of Cygnus Bewickii, showing the peculiar position of the windpipe. After Yarrell.

The land-birds in the Arctic regions are less numerous both in species and individuals than the sea-birds. Some of them, however, also occur in large numbers. Almost wherever one lands, some small greyish brown waders are seen running quickly to and fro, sometimes in pairs, sometimes in flocks of ten to twenty. It is the most common wader of the north, the *fjaerplyt* of the walrus-hunters, the purple sandpiper (*Tringa maritima*, Brünn.). It lives on flies, gnats, and other land

insects. Its well-filled crop shows how well the bird knows
how to collect its food even in regions where the entomologist
can only with difficulty get hold of a few of the animal forms
belonging to his field of research. The purple sandpiper lays
its four or five eggs in a pretty little nest of dry straw on open
grassy or mossy plains a little distance from the sea. It also
endeavours to protect its nest by acting a comedy like that of
the *tjuffo*. Its flesh is delicious.

In the company of the purple sandpiper there is often seen a
somewhat larger wader, or, more correctly, a bird intermediate
between the waders and the swimming birds. This is the
beautiful *brednaebbade simsnaeppan*, the grey (or red) phalarope
(*Phalarcpus fulicarius*, Bonap.). It is not rare on Spitzbergen,
and it is exceedingly common, perhaps even the commonest
bird on the north coast of Asia. I imagine therefore that it is
not absent from Novaya Zemyla, though there has hitherto been
observed there only the nearly allied *smalnaebbade simsnaeppan*,
the red - necked phalarope (*Phalaropus hyperboreus*, Lath.).
This bird might be taken as the symbol of married love, so
faithful are the male and female, being continually to be seen
in each other's company. While they search for their food in
pools of water along the coast, they nearly always bear each
other company, swimming in zig-zag, so that every now and
then they brush past each other. If one of them is shot, the
other flies away only for a short time until it observes that its
mate is left behind. It then flies back, swims with evident
distress round its dead friend, and pushes it with its bill to get
it to rise. It does not, however, spend any special care on its
nest or the rearing of its young, at least to judge by the nest
which Dunér found at Bell Sound in 1864. The position of
the nest was indicated by three eggs laid without anything
below them on the bare ground, consisting of stone splinters.
The flesh of the phalarope is a great delicacy, like that of other
waders which occur in the regions in question, but which I
cannot now stay to describe.

During excursions in the interior of the land along the coast,
one often hears, near heaps of stones or shattered cliffs, a
merry twitter. It comes from an old acquaintance from the
home land, the *snoesparfven* or *snoelaerken*, the snow-bunting
(*Emberiza nivalis*, L.). The name is well chosen, for in winter
this pretty bird lives as far south as the snow goes on the
Scandinavian peninsula, and in summer betakes itself to the
snow limit in Lapland, the *tundra* of North Siberia, or the
coasts of Spitzbergen and Novaya Zemlya. It there builds
its carefully-constructed nest of grass, feathers and down, deep
in a stone heap, preferably surrounded by a grassy plain.
The air resounds with the twitter of the little gay warbler,

which makes the deeper impression because it is the only true bird's song one hears in the highest north.[1]

On Spitzbergen there is sometimes to be met with in the interior of the country, on the mountain slopes, a game bird, *spetsbergsripan,* the rock ptarmigan (*Lagopus hyperboreus,* Sund.). A nearly allied type occurs on the Taimur peninsula, and along the whole north coast of Asia. It perhaps therefore can scarcely be doubted that it is also to be found on Novaya Zemlya, though we have not hitherto seen it there. On Spitz-

PTARMIGAN FELL.
Mussel Bay on Spitzbergen, after a photograph taken by A. Envall on the 21st June, 1872

bergen this bird had only been found before 1872 in single specimens, but in that year, to our glad surprise, we discovered an actual ptarmigan-fell in the neighbourhood of our winter colony, immediately south of the 80th degree of latitude. It formed the haunt of probably a thousand birds; at least a couple of hundred were shot there in the course of the winter. They probably breed there under stones in summer, and creeping in among the stones pass the winter there, at certain seasons doubtless in a kind of torpid state.

[1] There are, however, various other song-birds found already on south Novaya Zemlya, for instance, *lappsparfven,* the Lapland bunting (*Emberiza lapponica,* L.), and *berglaerkan,* the shore-lark (*Alauda alpestris,* L.). They hatch on the ground under bushes, tufts of grass, or stones, in very carefully constructed nests lined with cotton-grass and feathers, and are not uncommon.

The mode of life of the Spitzbergen ptarmigan is thus widely different from that of the Scandinavian ptarmigan, and its flesh also tastes differently. For the bird is exceedingly fat, and its flesh, as regards flavour, is intermediate between black-cock and fat goose.[1] We may infer from this that it is a great delicacy.

When I was returning, in the autumn of 1872, from an excursion of some length along the shore of Wijde Bay, I fell in with one of our sportsmen, who had in his hand a white bird marked with black spots, which he showed me as a "very large ptarmigan." In doing so, however, he fell into a great ornithological mistake, for it was not a ptarmigan at all, but another

THE SNOWY OWL.
Swed sh, Fjelluggla. (*Strix nyctea.* L.)

kind of bird, similarly marked in winter, namely, *fjellugglan*, the walrus-hunter's *isoern*, the snowy owl (*Strix nyctea*, L.). It evidently breeds and winters at the ptarmigan-fell, which it appears to consider as its own poultry-yard. In fact, the marking of this bird of prey is so similar to that of its victim that the latter can scarcely perhaps know how to take care of itself. On Spitzbergen the snowy owl is very rare; but on Novaya Zemlya and the north coast of Asia—where the lemming, which is wanting on Spitzbergen, occurs in great crowds

[1] Hedenström also states (*Otryvki o Sibiri*, St. Petersburg, 1830, p. 130,) that the ptarmigan winters on the New Siberian Islands, and that there it is fatter and more savoury than on the mainland.

—it is common. It commonly sits immovable on an open
mountain slope, visible at a great distance, from the strong
contrast of its white colour with the greyish-green ground.
Even in the brightest sunshine, unlike other owls, it sees
exceedingly well. It is very shy, and therefore difficult to
shoot. The snow ptarmigan and the snowy owl are the only
birds of which we know with certainty that they winter on
Spitzbergen, and both are, according to Hedenström, native
to the New Siberian Islands (*Otryuki o Sibiri*, p. 112).

In the cultivated regions of Europe the larger mammalia
are so rare that most men in their whole lifetime have never
seen a wild mammal so large as a dog. This is not the case
in the high north. The number of the larger mammalia here
is indeed no longer so large as in the seventeenth century, when
their capture yielded an abundant living to from twenty to
thirty thousand men ; but sport on Novaya Zemlya and Spitzbergen still supports several hundred hunters, and during
summer scarcely a day passes without a visitor to the coasts of
these Islands seeing a seal or a walrus, a reindeer or a Polar
bear. In order to present a true picture of the Polar traveller's
surroundings and mode of life, it is absolutely necessary to
give a sketch of the occurrence and mode of life, of the wild
mammalia in the Polar lands.

I shall make a beginning with the reindeer. This graminivorous animal goes nearly as far to the north as the land in
the old world. It was not, indeed, observed by Payer on Franz
Josef Land, but traces of the reindeer were seen by us on
the clay beds at Cape Chelyuskin ; remnants of reindeer were
observed at Barents' winter harbour on the northernmost part
of Novaya Zemlya ; some very fat animals were killed by
Norwegian walrus hunters on King Karl's land, east of Spitzbergen, and for some years back the reindeer was very numerous
even on the north coast of North East Land, and on Castrén's,
Parry's, Marten's, and Phipps' Islands, lying still farther to the
north. Although these regions are situated between 80° and
81° N.L., the reindeer evidently thrives there very well, and
finds, even in winter, abundant food on the mountain slopes
swept clear of snow by storms, as is shown by the good condition in which several of the animals shot by us were, and by
the numerous reindeer traces and tracks which we saw on
Castrén's Island in the month of May 1873. Nor does a
winter temperature of −40° to −50° appear to agree particularly ill with these relatives of the deer of the south. Even
the Norwegian reindeer can bear the climate of Spitzbergen,
for some of the selected draught reindeer which I took with
me to Spitzbergen in 1872, and which made their escape soon
after they were landed, were ·shot by hunters in 1875. They

then pastured in company with wild reindeer, and were, like them, very fat. It is remarkable that the reindeer, notwithstanding the devastating pursuit to which it is exposed on Spitzbergen,[1] is found there in much larger numbers than on North Novaya Zemlya or the Taimur peninsula, where it is almost protected from the attacks of the hunter. Even on the low-lying part of South Novaya Zemlya, the reindeer, notwithstanding the abundance of the summer pasture, is so rare that, when one lands there, any reindeer-hunting is scarcely to be counted on. It first occurs in any considerable numbers farther to the north, on both sides of Matotschkin Schar.

It deserves to be mentioned here that three hundred years ago, when the north part of Novaya Zemlya was for the first time visited by man, reindeer do not appear to have been more numerous there than now. In the narrative of Barents' third voyage (De Veer, *Diarium Nauticum*, 21st June, 1596) it is expressly stated : " Here it may be remarked that, although the land, which we consider as Groenland (the present Spitzbergen), lies under and over the 80th degree of latitude, there grow there abundant leaves and grass, and there are found there such animals as eat grass, as *reindeer*, while on the other hand, on Novaya Zemlya, under the 76th degree of latitude, there are neither leaves nor grass, nor any grass-eating animal." After this, however, traces of reins were found even at the winter station ; a bear, for instance, was killed that had devoured a reindeer.

On Spitzbergen the reindeer have been considerably diminished in numbers by the hunting first of the Dutch and English, and afterwards of the Russians and Norwegians. In the north-western part of the island where the Dutch had their train-boiling establishments, the animal has been completely extirpated.[2]

---

[1] The hunters from Tromsoe brought home, in 1868, 996 ; in 1869, 975 ; and in 1870, 837 reindeer. When to this we add the great number of reindeer which are shot in spring and are not included in these calculations, and when we consider that the number of walrus-hunting vessels which are fitted out from Tromsoe is less than that of those which go out from Hammerfest, and that the shooting of reindeer on Spitzbergen is also carried on by hunters from other towns, and by tourists, we must suppose that at least 3,000 reindeer have been killed during each of those years. Formerly reindeer stalking was yet more productive, but since 1870 the number killed has considerably diminished.

[2] When Spitzbergen was first mapped a great number of places were named after reindeer, which shows that the reindeer were found there in large numbers, and now just at these places it is completely absent. On the other hand, the Dutch and English explorers during the sixteenth century saw no reindeer on Novaya Zemlya. During the Swedish expedition of 1875 no reindeer were seen on the west coast of this island south of Karmakul Bay, while a number were shot at Besimannaja Bay and Matot-schkin Schar. When some of the companions of the well-known walrus-

It still, however, occurs on Ice Fjord in very great numbers which, were the animal protected, would speedily increase.

That so devastating a pursuit as that which goes on year after year on Spitzbergen can be carried on without the animal being extirpated, has even given rise to the hypothesis of an immigration from Novaya Zemlya. But since I have become better acquainted with the occurrence of the reindeer in the latter place, this mode of explanation does not appear to me to be correct. If, therefore, as several circumstances in fact indicate, an immigration of reindeer to Spitzbergen does take place, it must be from some still unknown Polar land situated to the north-north-east. In the opinion of some of the walrus-hunters there are indications that this unknown land is inhabited, for it has repeatedly been stated that *marked* reindeer have been taken on Spitzbergen. The first statement on this point is to be found in Witsen (*Noort ooster gedeelte van Asia en Europa*, 1705, ii. page 904), where the reins are said to have been marked on the horns and the ears : and I have myself heard hunters, who in Norway were well acquainted with the care of reindeer, state positively that the ears of some of the Spitzbergen reindeer they shot were clipped—probably, however, the whole has originated from the ears having been marked by frost. That no immigration to Spitzbergen of reindeer from Novaya Zemlya takes place, is shown besides by the fact that the Spitzbergen reindeer appear to belong to a race differing from the Novaya Zemlya reindeer, and distinguished by its smaller size, shorter head and legs, and plumper and fatter body.

The life of the wild reindeer is best known from Spitzbergen. During summer it betakes itself to the grassy plains in the ice-free valleys of the island, in late autumn it withdraws—according to the walrus-hunters' statements—to the sea-coast, in order to eat the seaweed that is thrown up on the beach, and in winter it goes back to the lichen-clad mountain heights in the interior of the country, where it appears to thrive exceedingly well, though the cold during winter must be excessively severe ; for when the reindeer in spring return to the coast they are still very fat, but some weeks afterwards, when the snow has

hunting captain, Sievert Tobiesen, were compelled in 1872-73 to winter at North Goose Cape, they shot during winter and spring only eleven reindeer. Some Russians, who by an accident were obliged to pass six years in succession somewhere on the coast of Stans Foreland (Maloy Broun), and who, during this long time, were dependent for their food on what they could procure by hunting without the use of fire-arms (they had when they landed powder and ball for only twelve shots), when the three survivors were found and taken home in 1749, had killed two hundred and fifty reindeer (P. L. le Roy, *Relation des Aventures arrivées à quatre matelots Russes jettés par une tempête près de l' Isle déserte d'Ost-Spitzbergen, sur laquelle ils ont passé six ans et trois mois.* 1766).

frozen on the surface, and a crust of ice makes it difficult for
them to get at the mountain sides, they become so poor as
scarcely to be eatable. In summer, however, they speedily eat
themselves back into condition, and in autumn they are so fat
that they would certainly take prizes at an exhibition of fat
cattle. In the museum at Tromsoe there is preserved the
backbone of a reindeer, shot on King Karl's Land, which had a
layer of fat seven to eight centimetres in thickness on the loin.

The reindeer, in regions where it has been much hunted, is
very shy, but, if the ground is not quite even, one can creep

REINDEER PASTURE.
Green Harbour on Spitzbergen, after a photograph taken by A. Envall on the 20th July, 1873.

within range, if the precaution be taken not to approach it
from the windward. During the rutting season, which falls in
late autumn, it sometimes happens that the reindeer attacks
the hunter.

The Spitzbergen reindeer is not tormented, like the reindeer in Lapland and on Novaya Zemlya, by " gorm " (inch-long
larvæ of a fly, which are developed under the animal's skin).
Its flesh is also better than that of the Lapp reindeer. None
of the contagious diseases which of late years have raged so

dreadfully among the reindeer in northern Europe has ever, at least during the last fifty years, been common on Spitzbergen.

The Polar bear occurs principally on coasts and islands which are surrounded by drift-ice, often even upon ice-fields far out at sea, for his best hunting is among the ice-floes. Now he is rather rare on the south-western coasts of Spitzbergen and Novaya Zemlya which are almost free of ice during summer, but more common on the northern parts of these islands, which are almost always surrounded by ice. Thus for instance during my many landings at Horn Sound, Bell Sound, Ice Fjord, Foreland Sound, and King's Bay, on the west coast of Spitzbergen, I have never seen a single bear. On the other hand, bears were seen at nearly every resting-place during the boat-voyage I made in 1861 with Torell in Hinloopen Strait and along the shores of the most northerly islands on Spitzbergen, also during the sledge journey which Palander and I made in the spring of 1873 round North East Land. The Polar bear is besides found everywhere along the north coast of Asia and America, apparently in greater numbers the farther north we go. Sometimes too, first on ice and then swimming, he has reached the north coast of Norway, for instance, in March 1853, when according to a statement in *Tromsoe Stifstidende* (No. 4 for 1869), a Polar bear was killed in Kjoellefjord in East Finmark.

The bear is not difficult to kill. When he observes a man he commonly approaches in hope of prey, with supple movements, and in a hundred zigzag bends, in order to conceal the direction he intends to take, and thus keep his prey from being frightened. During his approach he often climbs up on blocks of ice, or raises himself on his hind legs, in order to get a more extensive view, or else stands snuffing up the air with evident care in all directions, in order, by the aid of smell, which he seems to rely upon more than sight, to ascertain the true kind and nature of the surrounding objects. If he thinks he has to do with a seal, he creeps or trails himself forward along the ice, and is said then to conceal with the fore-paws the only part of his body that contrasts with the white colour of the snow—his large black nose. If one keeps quite still, the bear comes in this way so near that one can shoot him at the distance of two gun-lengths. or, what the hunters consider safer, kill him with the lance. If an unarmed man falls in with a Polar bear, some rapid movements and loud cries are generally sufficient to put him to flight, but if the man himself flies, he is certain to have the bear after him at full speed. If the bear is wounded, he always takes to flight. He often lays snow upon the wound with his fore-paws; sometimes in his death struggles he scrapes with his fore-feet a hole in the snow, in which he buries his head.

When a vessel lies at anchor, the bear sometimes swims out to it, and if one encamps in distant regions one often finds on getting up in the morning a Polar bear in the neighbourhood, who during the night has gone and nosed round the tent, without daring to attack it. I remember only one case of a bear venturing to look into an inhabited tent; it was during Kane's journey. He was frightened on that occasion by the lighting of some lucifers. I have myself with my comrades encamped without a watch in regions where we were certain that our encampment would be visited, while we lay in deep

POLAR BEARS.
Drawn by G. Mützel of Berlin.

sleep, by some bear, that seldom, when the cook rose to make coffee, failed to come within range of shot.

The bear on the other hand has a special fancy for taking an inventory of depôts of provisions, of abandoned vessels or of boats that have been left drawn up on the beach. Most Arctic travellers have remarkable adventures to relate, which both men and bears have gone through on such occasions. During our expedition in 1864, for instance, a large bear came and closely examined the contents of a boat covered with a tent, which we had left unwatched for a few hours at the bottom of Stor Fjord. He ate up a carefully-cooked reindeer roast, tore the reserve clothes, scattered about the ship-biscuit, &c.; and after we had returned in the evening, gathered our things together in a heap, closed the tent and lain down to sleep, the same bear returned, and, while we slept, appropriated all the reindeer beef we had cooked to be used, in place of the roast we had lost, during the following day's journey. During one of the English expeditions in search of Franklin, there was killed on one occasion, a bear in whose stomach there was found, among many other articles, the stock of sticking-plaster from a neighbouring depôt. The bear can also roll away very large stones, but a layer of frozen sand is too much for him.

The Polar bear swims exceedingly well, but not so fast as that he can escape in this way, if he be pursued in a boat; if a boat and stout rowers are at hand he is accordingly done for, if, as often happens, he in attempting to escape seeks his deliverance in the sea. There, he is, as the hunters say, "as easy to kill as a sheep," but one has to make haste to get hold of the killed animal with a harpoon or in some other way, for it speedily sinks, unless it is very fat.

The walrus-hunting vessels from Tromsoe brought home in 1868 twenty, in 1869 fifty-three, in 1870 ninety-eight, in 1871 seventy-four, and in 1872 thirty-three bears. It may be inferred from this that the Norwegian walrus-hunters kill yearly on an average at least a hundred bears. It is remarkable that in this large number a pregnant female or one with newly-born young is never found.[1] The female bear appears to keep herself well concealed during the time she is pregnant; perhaps in some ice-hole in the interior of the country.

Whether the Polar bear hibernates during winter is not quite settled; various facts, however, point in this direction. For instance, he disappears almost completely from wintering stations during the dark time, and holes have sometimes been met with in which bears were concealed. Thus it once happened to Tobiesen that he went down with one foot into such a hole, to the no small dismay not only of the experienced walrus-hunter, but also of the bear.

It is also stated that the bear during the dark time goes to the edge of the ice to seek his food. I cannot say positively whether this is the case or not; but the fact points in an opposite direction, that while only a single bear was seen in the course of winter in the open water in the neighbourhood of our winter station at Mussel Bay in 1872-73, Palander and I

---

[1] During the wintering of 1869-70 on East Greenland, Dr. Pansch once saw a female bear with quite small young (*Die zweite deutsche Nordpolarfahrt*, Leipzig, 1873-74. Vol. II. p. 157).

almost daily saw bears on the hard frozen sea north of North East Land. Tracks of bears were visible there in all directions on the ice, and along with them light, sinuous traces of the fox. There were, on the other hand, no seal holes to be found, and it was accordingly difficult to understand wherefore the bears had chosen just this desolate stretch of ice as their haunt. The bears that were killed were besides uncommonly lean, the fat which they yielded being scarcely available as fuel for the sledge-party's cooking apparatus.

During their extended excursions after prey the male and the female, the latter generally attended by one or two large young ones, keep each other company. Large numbers are seldom seen together, unless at places where a good many carcases of walruses, seals, or white fish are lying.

In former times the sight of a bear created great dismay in Polar travellers, but now the walrus-hunters do not hesitate a moment to attack, lance in hand, a large number of bears. They have sometimes in this way killed as many as twelve within a short time. They depend less on the gun. During the expedition of 1861 Carl Chydenius shot three in a few minutes, close to his tent-covered boat.

I do not know a single case in which any Norwegian walrus-hunter has been seriously wounded by a bear. It appears, however, as if this animal were bolder and more dangerous in regions where he has not made acquaintance with man's dangerous hunting implements. During the first English and Dutch voyages to Novaya Zemlya, bears were met with at nearly every place where a landing was effected, in regions where the Polar bear is now wholly absent, and the travellers were compelled to undertake actual combats—combats which cost several human lives. During Barents' second voyage some men on the $\frac{26th}{16th}$ September, 1595, landed on the mainland near the eastern mouth of Yugor Schar, in order to collect "a sort of diamonds occurring there" (valueless rock crystals), when a large white bear, according to De Veer, rushed forward and caught one of the stone collectors by the neck. On the man screaming "Who seizes me by the neck?" a comrade standing beside answered, "A bear," and ran off. The bear immediately bit asunder the head of his prey, and sucked the blood. The rest of the men who were on land now came to his relief, attacking the bear with levelled guns and lances. But the bear was not frightened, but rushed forward and laid hold of a man in the rank of the attacking party, and killed him too, whereupon all the rest took to flight. Assistance now came from the vessel, and the bear was surrounded by thirty men, but against their will, because they had to do with a "grim undaunted, and greedy beast." Of these thirty men only three ventured to attack the bear, whom these "courageous" men finally killed, after a rather severe struggle.

A large number of occurrences of a similar nature, though commonly attended with fortunate results, are to be found recorded in most of the narratives of Arctic travel. Thus a sailor was once carried off from a whaler caught in the ice in Davis' Straits, and in 1820, among the drift-ice in the sea between Greenland and Spitzbergen, the same fate was like to befall one of the crew of a Hull whaler; but he succeeded in effecting his escape by taking to flight, and throwing to the bear, first his only weapon of defence, a lance, and then his articles of clothing, one after the other.[1] On the 6th of March 1870, Dr. Boegen was attacked by a bear, and dragged a considerable distance.[2] It is remarkable that the bear did not this time either kill his prey, but that he had time to cry out, "A bear is dragging me away;" and that, after the bear had dragged him several hundred yards and he had got free, he could, though very badly scalped, himself make his way back to the vessel. The scalping had been done by the bear attempting to crush the skull in its mouth, as it is accustomed to do to the seals it catches. Scoresby considers it dangerous to hunt the Polar bear in deep snow. The well-known Dane, C. Petersen, guide to McClintock, Kane and others, on the other hand, considered it as little dangerous to attack a bear as to slaughter a sheep. The Siberian traveller, Hedenström, says that a man may venture to do so with a knife tied to a walking-stick, and the Norwegian hunters, or at least the Norwegian-Finnish harpooners, express themselves in much the same way regarding "this noble and dangerous" sport.

The bear's principal food consists of the seal and walrus. It is said that with a single stroke of his powerful paw he can cast a walrus up on the ice. On the other hand he seldom succeeds in catching the reindeer, because it is fleeter than the bear. I have, however, in North East Land, on two occasions, seen blood and hair of reindeer which had been caught by bears. There is not the least doubt that, along with flesh, the bear also eats vegetable substances, as seaweed, grass, and lichens. I have several times, on examining the stomach of a bear that had been shot, found in it only remains of vegetable substances; and the walrus-hunters know this so well that they called a large old Polar bear, which Dr. Theel shot at Port Dickson in 1875, "an old Land-king" that was too fat to go a hunting, and therefore ate grass on land. He makes use besides of food of many different kinds; a bear, for instance, in the winter 1865-66

[1] W. Scoresby's des Jüngern, *Tagebuch einer Reise auf dem Wallfischfang. Aus dem engl. übers.* Hamburg, 1825, p. 127.
[2] *Die zweite deutsche Nordpolarfahrt*, Vol. I. p. 465.

consumed for Tobiesen the contents of two barrels of salt-fish, which he had left behind in a deserted hut.

The flesh of the bear, if he is not too old or has not recently eaten rotten seal-flesh, is very eatable, being intermediate in taste between pork and beef. The flesh of the young bear is white and resembles veal. The eating of the liver causes sudden illness.

Although, as already mentioned, the Polar bear sometimes drifts to land and is killed in the northernmost part of Norway, his skin is not enumerated by Othere among the products of Finmark. It thus appears to have become known in Europe first after the Norwegians' discovery of Iceland and Greenland, and was at first considered an extraordinary rarity. A Norwegian of importance, who had emigrated to Iceland, and there succeeded in getting hold of a female bear with two young, sent them in 880 to the King of Norway, and got in return a small vessel laden with wood. This animal had not then been seen in Norway before. The old sagas of the north are said to relate further that the priest Isleif, in order to be nominated bishop of Iceland, in the year 1056 presented a white bear to Kejsar Henrik. In the year 1064 the King of Denmark gave in exchange for a white bear from Greenland a well-equipped, full rigged, trading vessel, a considerable sum of money, and a valuable gold ring.[1]

Marco Polo also says in his account of the country of the peace-loving nomad Tatar tribes living in the north, that there are to be found there white bears most of them twenty hands long, large black foxes, wild asses (reindeer), and a little animal called "rondes," from which we get the sable fur.[2] As the Polar bear is only to be found on the coast of the Arctic Ocean, these statements prove that in the thirteenth century the northernmost part of Asia was inhabited or at least visited by hunters. Olaus Magnus even describes the bear's mode of life not incorrectly, with the addition that it was customary to present their skins to the altars of cathedrals and parish churches in order that the feet of the priest might not freeze during mass.[3] The Polar bear however first became more generally known in Western Europe by the Arctic voyages of the English and Dutch, and its price has now sunk so much that its skin, which was once considered an article of extraordinary value, is now, in adjusting accounts between the owners of a vessel and the walrus-hunters, reckoned at from twenty-five to fifty Scandinavian crowns (say twenty-eight to fifty-six shillings).

---

[1] *Grönlands historiske Mindesmärker.* Kjöbenhavn, 1838, III. p. 384.
[2] Ramusio, Part II., Venice, 1583, p. 60.
[3] Ol. Magnus. Rome edition, 1555, p. 621.

In 1609 Stephen Bennet, during his seventh voyage to Bear Island, captured two young Polar bears, which were brought to England and kept at Paris Garden (Purchas, iii. p. 562). Now such animals are very frequently brought to Norway in order to be sent from thence to the zoological gardens of Europe, in which the Polar bear is seldom wanting. The capture is facilitated by the circumstance that the young bears seldom leave their mother when she is killed.

Along with the reindeer and the bear there are found in the regions now in question only two other land-mammalia, the mountain-fox (*Vulpes lagopus* L.) and the lemming (*Myodes obensis*, Brants).[1] The fox is rather common both on Spitzbergen and Novaya Zemlya. Its abode sometimes consists of

POLAR BEARS.
After Olaus Magnus (1555).

a number of passages excavated in the ground and connected together, with several openings. Such a nest I saw on Wahlberg's Island in Hinloopen Strait on the summit of a fowl-fell; it was abundantly provided with a stock of half-rotten guillemots, concealed in the passages. The old foxes were not visible while we were there, but several young ones, some black, some variegated red and white, ran hither and thither from out the openings and played with supple movements in the neighbourhood of the nest. A similar nest also, with young that ran between its openings, played and hunted each other, I have seen on the north shore of Matotschkin

[1] It is stated that wolves also occur on Novaya Zemlya as far up as to Matotschkin Sound. They are exceedingly common on the north coasts of Asia and Eastern Europe.

Schar, and uninhabited fox-holes and passages at several places on the west coast of Novaya Zemlya, commonly in the tops of dry sandy knolls.

The lemming is not found on Spitzbergen, but must at certain seasons occur in incredible numbers on Novaya Zemlya. For at the commencement of summer, when the snow has recently melted away, there are to be seen, everywhere in the level fertile places in the very close grass of the meadows, foot-paths about an inch and a half deep, which have been formed during winter by the trampling of these small animals, under the snow, in the bed of grass or lichens which lies immediately above the frozen ground. They have in this way united with each other the dwellings they had excavated in the ground, and constructed for themselves convenient ways, well protected against the severe cold of winter, to their fodder-places. Thousands and thousands of animals must be required in order to carry out this work even over a small area, and wonderfully keen must their sense of locality be, if, as seems probable, they can find their way with certainty in the endless labyrinth they have thus formed. During the snow-melting season these passages form channels for running off the water, small indeed, but everywhere to be met with, and contributing in a considerable degree to the drying of the ground. The ground besides is at certain places so thickly strewed with lemming dung, that it must have a considerable influence on the condition of the soil.

In the Arctic regions proper one is not tormented by the mosquito,[1] and viewed as a whole the insect fauna of the entire Polar area is exceedingly scanty, although richer than was before supposed. Arachnids, acarids, and podurids occur most plentifully, Dr. Stuxberg having been able during the Yenisej expedition of 1875 to collect a very large number of them, which were worked out after his return—the podurids by Dr. T. TULLBERG of Upsala, the arachnids by Dr. T. KOCH of Nürnberg. These small animals are found in very numerous individual specimens, among mouldering vegetable remains, under stones and pieces of wood on the beach, creeping about on grass, straws, &c.

Of the insects proper there were brought home from Novaya

---

[1] That is to say, not on Spitzbergen and Novaya Zemlya, for it is otherwise on the coast of the mainland. In West Greenland the mosquito as far north as the southern part of Disco Island is still so terrible, especially to the new comer during the first days, that the face of any one who without a veil ventures into marshy ground overgrown with bushes, becomes in a few hours unrecognisable. The eyelids are closed with swelling and changed into water-filled bladders, suppurating tumours are formed in the head under the hair, &c. But when a man has once undergone this unpleasant and painful inoculation, the body appears, at least for one summer, to be less susceptible to the mosquito-poison.

Zemlya, during the same expedition, nine species of coleoptera, which were determined by Professor F. W. Mäklin, of Helsingfors.[1] Some few hemiptera and lepidoptera and orthoptera, and a large number of hymenoptera and diptera from the same expedition have been examined by Lector A. E. Holmgren of Stockholm. Dr. Stuxberg also collected a large number of land-worms, which have been described by our countryman Dr. G. Eisen, now settled in California. The occurrence of this animal group in a region where the ground at the depth of a few inches is continually frozen, appears to me exceedingly remarkable—and from a general point of view the occurrence of insects in a land which is exposed to a winter cold below the freezing-point of mercury, and where the animal cannot seek protection from it by creeping down to a stratum of earth which never freezes, presupposes that either the insect itself, its egg, larva, or pupa, may be frozen stiff without being killed. Only very few species of these small animals, however, appear to survive such a freezing test, and the actual land-evertebrate-fauna of the Polar countries is therefore exceedingly scanty in comparison with that of more southerly regions.

It is quite otherwise as regards the sea. Here animal life is exceedingly abundant as far as man has succeeded in making his way to the farthest north. At nearly every sweep the dredge brings up from the sea-bottom masses of decapods, crustacea, mussels, asterids, echini,[2] &c., in varying forms, and the surface of the sea on a sunny day swarms with pteropods, beroids, surface-crustacea, &c. Dr. Stuxberg will give farther on, a sketch of this department of animal life, which in the high north is so rich in variety. In the meantime I can but refer to the large number of papers on this subject which have been issued in the publications of the Swedish Academy of Sciences.

Of the higher animal types a greater number within the Polar territory occur in the sea than on the land. Thus by far the greater

---

[1] As the *only* Chrysomela, which von Baer found at Matotschkin Schar, played so great a *rôle* in Arctic-zoological literature, I shall here enumerate the species of coleoptera, now known—after Professor Mäklin's determination of the collections which we·brought home with us—to exist on Novaya Zemlya. These are :— *Feronia borealis* Ménétr., *F. gelida* Mäkl., *Amara alpina* Fabr., *Agabus subquadratus* Motsch., *Homalota sibirica* Mäkl., *Homalium angustatum* Mäkl., *Cylletron* (?) *hyperboreum* Mäkl., *Chrysomela septentrionalis* (?) Ménétr., *Prasocuris hannoverana* Fabr., v. *degenerata*. From Vaygats Island we brought home seven species more, which were not found on Novaya Zemlya. The insects occur partly under stones, especially at places where lemming dung is abundant, or in tracts where birds'-nests are numerous, partly in warm days on willow-bushes.

[2] Echini occur only very sparingly in the Kara Sea and the Siberian Polar Sea, but west of Novaya Zemlya at certain places in such numbers that they almost appear to cover the sea-bottom.

number of the birds' I have enumerated above belong to the sea, not to the land, and this is the case with nearly all the animals which for three or four hundred years back have been the objects of capture in the Arctic regions. This industry, which during the whale-fishing period yielded a return perhaps equal to that of the American oil-wells in our time, has not now in the most limited degree the importance it formerly had. For the animal whose capture yielded this rich return, the right whale (*Balæna mysticetus* L.), is now so extirpated in these navigable waters, that the whalers were long ago compelled to seek new fishing-places in other parts of the Polar seas. It is therefore no longer the whale, but other species of animals which attract the hunter to the coasts of Spitzbergen and Novaya Zemlya.

Of these animals the most important for the last fifty years has been the walrus, but it too is in course of being extirpated. It is now seldom found during summer on the west coast of Novaya Zemlya south of Matotschkin Schar. During our visits to that island in 1875, 1876, and 1878 we did not see one of these animals. But in the Kara Gate, on the east coast of Novaya Zemlya, and at certain places in the Kara Sea, abundant hunting is still to be had. Earlier in the year the walrus is also to be met with among the drift-ice on the west coast, and to the south, off the mouth of the Petchora, although the number of the animals that are captured by the Samoyeds at Chabarova appears to be exceedingly small. On the other hand the Dutch, in their first voyages hither, saw a considerable number of these gregarious animals. The walrus, however, did not then occur here in such abundance as they did at the same time on Spitzbergen and Bear Island, which evidently formed their principal haunts.

During Stephen Bennet's third voyage to Bear Island in 1606, 700 to 800 walruses were killed there in six hours, and in 1608 nearly 1,000 in seven hours. The carcases left lying on the beach attracted bears thither in such numbers that, for instance, in 1609 nearly fifty of them were killed by the crew of a single vessel. At one place eighteen bears were seen at once (Purchas, iii. p. 560). A Norwegian skipper was still able during a wintering in 1824-25 to kill 677 walruses. But when Tobiesen wintered there in 1865-66 he killed only a single walrus, and on the two occasions of my landing there I did not see one. Formerly the hunters almost every year, during late autumn when the drift-ice has disappeared, found " walrus on land," *i.e.* herds of several hundred walruses which had crept up on some low, even, sandy beach, to pass days and weeks there in an almost motionless state. During this period of rest most of them appear to be sunk in deep sleep, yet not all, for—according to the concurrent statements of all the walrus-hunters with

whom I have conversed on this subject—they keep a watch to
warn their comrades when danger is near. If necessary precautions are observed, *i.e.* if the hunters approach the beach
where the animals are assembled when the wind blows from the
land, and kill with the lance those that lie nearest the water, the
rest are slaughtered without difficulty, being prevented by the
carcases of their dead comrades from reaching the sea. Now
such an opportunity for the hunter happens exceedingly seldom;
there are famous headlands on which in former times the
walrus was·found by hundreds, in whose neighbourhood now not
a single one is to be seen.

In the sea too there are certain places which the walrus
principally haunts, and which are therefore known by the
hunters as walrus-banks. Such a bank is to be found in the
neighbourhood of Muffin Island, situated on the north coast
of Spitzbergen in 80° north latitude, and the animals that have
been killed here must be reckoned by thousands. Another bank
of the same kind is to be met in 72° 15′ north latitude, on
the coast of Yalmal. The reason why the walruses delight to
haunt these places is doubtless that they find there abundant food,
which does not consist, as has often been stated, of seaweed, but
of various living mussels from the bottom of the sea, principally
Mya truncata and *Saxicava rugosa*. Their fleshy parts are freed,
before they are swallowed, so remarkably well from the shells,
and cleaned so thoroughly, that the contents of the stomach
have the appearance of a dish of carefully-shelled oysters. In
collecting its food the walrus probably uses its long tusks to
dig up the mussels and worms which are deeply concealed in
the clay.[1] Scoresby states that in the stomach of a walrus he
found, along with small crabs, pieces of a young seal.

The largest walrus tusks I have seen were two of a male
walrus purchased·in the summer of 1879 at St. Lawrence Island,
in the north part of Behring's Sea. They measured 830 and
825 millimetres in length, their largest circumference was 227
and 230 millimetres, and they weighed together 6,680 gram.
I have seen the tusks of females of nearly the same length, but
they are distinguished from those of the male by being much
more slender. The surface of the tusks is always full of cracks,
but under it there is a layer of ivory free of cracks, which again
incloses a grained kernel of bone which at some places is semi-
transparent, as if drenched with oil.

When the walrus ox gets very old, he swims about by

---

[1] Compare Malmgren's instructive papers in the publications of the
Royal (Swedish) Academy of Sciences and Scoresby's *Arctic Regions,*
Edinburgh, 1820, i., p. 502. That the walrus eats mussels is already
indicated in the Dutch drawing from the beginning of the seventeenth
century reproduced below, page 123.

himself as a solitary individual, but otherwise animals of the
same age and sex keep together in large herds. The young
walrus long follows its mother, and is protected by her with
evident fondness and very conspicuous maternal affection. Her
first care, when she is pursued, is accordingly to save her young
even at the sacrifice of her own life. A female walrus with
young is nearly always lost, if they be discovered from a hunting
-boat. However eagerly she may try by blows and cuffs to get
her young under water or lead her pursuers astray by diving

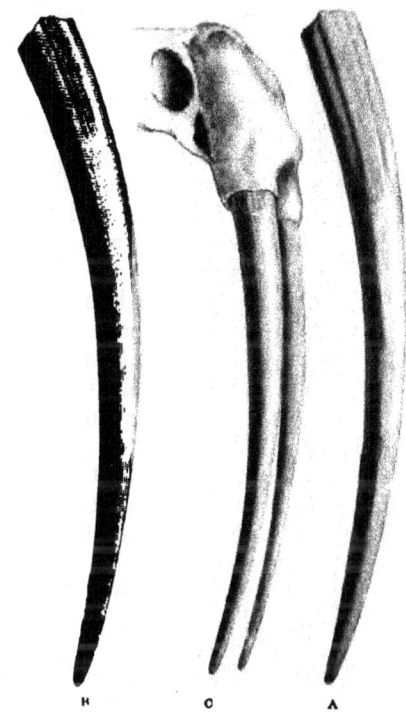

H C A

WALRUS TUSKS,

A. Tusk of male, outside. B. Tusk of male, inside. C. Tusks of female.
One-tenth of natural size.

with it under her forepaw, she is generally overtaken and killed.
Such a hunt is truly grim, but the walrus-hunter knows no
mercy in following his occupation. The walrus, especially the
old solitary male, sleeps and rests during autumn, when the
drift-ice has disappeared, also in the water, with his head now
above the surface, now under it, and with his lungs so strongly
inflated that the body is kept floating, with part of the back
projecting out of the water. The latter way of sleeping is
indeed possible only for so long at once as the animal can keep

below, but this is said to be a very long time. If a hunting boat meets a walrus sleeping in this way it is first wakened with a loud "strike up" before it is harpooned, "in order that in its fright it may not knock a hole in the boat with its tusks." The walrus sinks and is lost, if he is killed by a shot while in the water, or if he be shot while lying on a piece of ice, but without being killed so instantaneously that he cannot cast himself into the water in his death struggles. He is killed accordingly almost exclusively with the harpoon or lance.

The harpoon consists of a large and strong iron hook, very sharp on the outer edge, and provided with a barb. The hook is loosely fixed to the shaft, but securely fastened to the end of a slender line ten fathoms long, generally made of walrus hide. The line is fastened at its other end to the boat, in the forepart of which it lies in a carefully arranged coil. There are from five to ten such harpoon lines in every hunting boat. When the hunters see a herd of walrus, either on a piece of drift-ice or in the water, they endeavour silently and against the wind to approach sufficiently near to one of the animals to be able to harpoon it. If this is managed, the walrus first dives and then endeavours to swim under water all he can. But he is fixed with the line to the boat, and must draw it along with him. His comrades swim towards the boat, curious to ascertain the cause of the alarm. A new walrus is fixed with another harpoon, and so it goes on, one after another, until all the harpoons are

3   2   1
HUNTING IMPLEMENTS.
(1)Harpoon, and (2) Lance for Walrus-hunting. (3)"Skottel" for the capture of the White Whale.
One-fifteenth of natural size.

in use. The boat is now drawn forward at a whizzing speed, although the rowers hold back with the oars; but there is no actual danger as long as all the animals draw in the same direction. If one of them seeks to take a different course from that of his comrades in misfortune, his line must be cut off, otherwise the boat capsizes. When the walruses get exhausted by their exertions and by loss of blood, the hunters begin to haul in the lines. One animal after the other is drawn to the stem of the boat, and there they commonly first get a blow on the head with the flat of a lance, and when they turn to guard against it, a lance is thrust into the heart. Since breechloaders have begun to be used by the walrus-hunters, they often prefer to kill the harpooned walruses with a ball instead of "lancing" them. To shoot an unharpooned walrus, on the other hand, the walrus hunters formerly considered an unpardonable piece of thoughtlessness, because the animal was in this way generally wounded or killed without any advantage accruing. They therefore expressed themselves with great irritation against the tourists who sometimes came to Spitzbergen, and in this way destroyed the hunting. It cannot however be denied that they themselves in recent times have often followed the bad example, and many consider that this is one of the main reasons of the great diminution in the numbers of the walrus of late years. Should an international code be established for hunting in the Polar sea, all shooting of unharpooned walruses ought to be forbidden in the first place.

Gregariousness and curiosity appear to be the main characteristics of the walrus. These qualities of theirs I had an opportunity of observing when once, on a glorious northern summer day, I rowed forward over a mirror-bright, drift-ice-bestrewn sea right into the midst of a considerable herd of these animals. Part followed the boat long distances quite peaceably, now and then emitting a grunting sound ; others swam quite close, and raised themselves high out of the water in order to take a view of the foreigners ; others, again, lay so closely packed on pieces of drift-ice as to sink them down to the water's edge, while their comrades swimming about in the sea endeavoured with violence to gain a place on the already overfilled resting-places, though a number of unoccupied pieces of ice floated up and down in the neighbourhood.

When the hunters have killed a female walrus, it often happens that they take the young living. It is easily tamed, and soon regards its keeper with warm attachment. It seeks, as best it can—poorly equipped as it is for moving about on dry land—to follow the seamen on the deck, and gives itself no rest if it be left alone. Unfortunately, one does not succeed in keeping them long alive, probably because it is impossible to provide them with suitable food. There are instances, however, of the young of the walrus being brought to Europe alive. Thus it is said (Purchas, iii., p. 560), that Master Welden and Stephen Bennet, on the 24th July, 1608, caught two young walruses alive, one a male and the other a female. The female died before they reached England, but the male lived ten weeks. He was carried to court, shown to the king and many honourable gentlemen, and excited general admiration for his extraordinary form and great docility.

A young walrus that was taken to St. Petersburg in 1829-30, also died in a short time. It gave occasion to K. E. von BAER's famous treatise: "Anatomische und zoologische Untersuchungen über das Wallross," printed in *Mémoires de l'Académie Impériale des Sciences de St. Petersbourg,* ser. vi., t. iv. 2, 1838, p. 97.

The walrus is hunted for its skin, blubber, and oil. The value of a full-grown walrus was calculated at Tromsoe, in 1868, in settling accounts between the owners of hunting sloops and the hunters, at eighty Scandinavian crowns (say

WALRUS HUNTING.
After Olaus Magnus (1555).

4*l.* 10*s.*), but it sank in 1871 to only forty-eight crowns (say 2*l.* 15*s.*). The flesh of the walrus is coarse and train-flavoured, and is eaten by the hunters only in cases of necessity. From my own experience, however, I can certify that its comparatively small tongue is very delicious. By the Eskimo and the Chukchis the flesh of the walrus is considered a delicacy.

The walrus was doubtless hunted by the Polar tribes long before the historic period,[1] but it is mentioned for the first time in writing in the sketch of Othere's Arctic journey. The narrative shows that it was then captured on the north coast of Scandinavia. This appears the less improbable, as a walrus now and then even in our days drifts to land on the Norwegian coast, and walruses are still annually killed off Swjatoinos on the Kola peninsula.[2] The walrus is very correctly described in the well-known Norse confession written in the end of the eleventh

---

[1] Implements of walrus-bone occur among the Northern grave *finds.*
[2] Compare note [2] at page 41 above.

century, "Konungs skuggsjá" (the King's Mirror), as an animal resembling the seal,[1] except that, besides several smaller teeth, it has two large tusks which project beyond the upper jaw. This clear and unexaggerated sketch is however replaced in the later writings of the middle ages by the most extraordinary accounts of the animal's appearance and mode of capture. Thus Albertus Magnus,[2] who died in 1280, says that the walrus is taken by the

WALRUSES (female with young).
Old Dutch drawing.[3]

hunter, while the sleeping animal hangs by its large tusks to a cleft of the rock, cutting out a piece of its skin and fastening to

[1] I saw in 1858 a *Phoca barbata* with tusks worn away by age, which in its reddish-brown colour very much resembled a walrus, and was little inferior to it in size.

[2] Albertus Magnus, *De animalibus*, Mantua, 1479, Lib. xxiv. At the same place however is given a description of the whale-fishery grounded on actual experience, but with the shrewd addition that what the old authors had written on the subject did not correspond with experience.

[3] This drawing is made after a facsimile by Frederick Müller from Hessel Gerritz, *Descriptio et delineatio geographica detectionis freti*, &c. Amsterodami, 1613. The same drawing is reproduced coloured in Blavii *Atlas major*, Part I., 1665, p. 25, with the inscription: "Ad vivum delineatum ab Hesselo G.A."

it a strong rope whose other end is tied to trees, posts, or large rings fixed to rocks. The walrus is then wakened by throwing large stones at its head. In its attempts to escape it leaves its hide behind. It perishes soon after, or is thrown up half dead on the beach. He further states that walrus lines on account of their strength are suitable for lifting great weights, and that they are always on sale at Cologne. They were probably used at the

JAPANESE DRAWING OF THE WALRUS.[1]

building of the Cathedral there. Similar extraordinary representations of the appearance and mode of life of the walrus are

[1] The drawing is taken from a Japanese manuscript book of travels— No. 360 of the Japanese library which I brought home. According to a communication by an attaché of the Japanese embassy which visited Stockholm in the autumn of 1880, the book is entitled *Kau-kai-i-fun*, "Narrative of a remarkable voyage on distant seas." The manuscript, in four volumes, was written in 1830. In the introduction it is stated that when some Japanese, on the 21st November, 1793 (?), were proceeding with a cargo of rice to Yesso, they were thrown out of their course by a storm, and were driven far away on the sea, till in the beginning of the following June they came to some of the Aleutian islands, which had recently been taken by the Russians. They remained there ten months, and next year in the end of June they came to Ochotsk. The following year in autumn they were carried to Irkutsk, where they remained eight years, well treated by the Russians. They were then taken to St. Petersburg, where they had an audience of the Czar, and got furs and splendid food. Finally they were sent back by sea round Cape Horn to Japan in one of Captain von Krusenstern's vessels. They were handed over to the Japanese authorities in the spring of 1805, after having been absent from their native country about thirteen years. From Nagasaki they were carried to Yeddo, where they were subjected to an examination. One person put questions, another wrote the answers, and a third showed by drawings all the remarkable events they had survived. They were then sent to their native place. In the introduction it is further said that the shipwrecked were unskilful seamen, by whom little attention was often given to the most important matters. A warning accordingly is given against full reliance on their accounts and the drawings in the book. The latter occupy the fourth part of the work, consisting of more than 100 quarto pages. It is remarkable that the first Russian circumnavigation of the globe, and the first journey of the Japanese round the world, happened at the same time.

repeated in a more or less altered form even by Olaus Magnus, whose representation of the walrus is shown by the woodcut on page 123.

The $\frac{11th}{1st}$ of August 1556, the year after the publication of the work of Olaus Magnus, a West European saw for the first time some actual walruses, which had been killed by Russian hunters at Vaygats Island. No description of the animal, however, is given, but from that period all the members of the English and Dutch north-east expeditions had opportunities of seeing walruses in hundreds and thousands. It was now first that man learned actually to know this remarkable animal which had been decked out in so many fables. To this period belongs the beautiful and natural delineation of the walrus which is given above.

A peculiarity of the walrus may be mentioned here. The hide, especially in old males, is often full of wounds and scratches, which appear to be caused partly by combats and scraping against sharp pieces of ice, partly by some severe disease of the skin. Mr. H. W. Elliot has remarked this of the walrus in Behring's Sea.[1] The walrus is also troubled with lice, which is not the case, so far as I know, with any kind of seal. Masses of intestinal worms are found instead in the stomach of the seal, while on the contrary none are found in that of the walrus.

With reference to the other animals that are hunted in the Polar Sea I am compelled to be very brief, as I have scarcely any observations to make regarding them which are not already sufficiently known by numerous writings.

There are three kinds of seals on Novaya Zemlya. *Storsaelen,* the bearded seal (*Phoca barbata,* Fabr.) occurs pretty generally even on the coasts of Spitzbergen, though never in large flocks. The pursuit of this animal is the most important part of the seal-fishing in these waters, and the bearded seal is still killed yearly by thousands. Their value is reckoned in settling accounts between owners and hunters at twenty to twenty-five Scandinavian crowns (say 22s. to 27s. 6d.

Groenlands or *Jan-Mayen-saelen,* the Greenland seal (*Phoca Groenlandica,* Müller), which at Jan Mayen gives occasion to so profitable a fishing, also, is of general occurrence among the drift-ice in the Murman and Kara seas.

Snadden, the rough or bristled seal (*Phoca hispida,* Erxl.) is also common on the coast. These animals in particular are seen to lie, each at its hole, on the ice of fjords, which has not been broken up. It also many times follows with curiosity in the

---

[1] *A Report upon the Condition of Affairs in the Territory of Alaska.* Washington, 1875, p. 160.

YOUNG OF THE GREENLAND SEAL.
After a drawing by A. W. Quennerstedt (1864).

wake of a vessel for long distances, and can then be easily shot, because it is often so fat that, unlike the two other kinds of seals, it does not ·sink when it has been shot dead in the water.

Klapmytsen, the bladdernose seal (*Cystophora cristata,* Erxl.), the walrus-hunters say they have never seen on Novaya Zemlya,

THE BEARDED SEAL.
Swedish. Storsäl. (*Phoca barba a,* Fabr)

THE ROUGH SEAL.
Swedish, Snadd. (*Phoca hispida,* Erxl)

but it is stated to occur yearly in pretty large numbers among the ice W.S.W. of South Cape on Spitzbergen. Only once during our many voyages in the Polar Sea has a *Klapmyts* been seen, viz., a young one that was killed in 1858 in the neighbourhood of Bear Island.

Of the various species of whales, the narwhal, distinguished by its long and valuable horn projecting in the longitudinal direction of the body from the upper jaw, now occurs so seldom on the coast of Novaya Zemlya that it has never been seen there by the Norwegian walrus-hunters. It is more common at Hope Island, and Witsen states (P. 903) that large herds of narwhals have been seen between Spitzbergen and Novaya Zemlya.

The white whale or beluga, of equal size with the narwhal, on the other hand, occurs in large shoals on the coasts of Spitzbergen and Novaya Zemlya, especially near the mouths of fresh-water streams. These animals were formerly captured, but not with any great success, by means of a peculiar sort of harpoon, called by the hunters "skottel." Now they are caught with nets of extraordinary size and strength, which are laid out from the shore at places which the white whales are wont to frequent. In this way there were taken in the year 1871, when the fishing appears to have been most productive, by vessels belonging to Tromsoe alone, 2,167 white whales. Their value was estimated at fifty-four Scandinavian crowns each (about 3*l*.).

THE WHITE WHALE. (*Delphinapterus leucus*, Pallas.)
After a drawing by A. W. Quennerstedt (1864).

The fishing, though tempting, is yet very uncertain; it sometimes falls out extraordinarily abundant, as in the spring of 1880, when a skipper immediately on arriving at Magdalena Bay caught 300 of these animals at a cast of the net. Of the whales thus killed not only the blubber and hide are taken away, but also, when possible, the carcases, which when cheap freight can be had, are utilised at the guano manufactories in the north of Norway. After having lain a whole year on the beach at Spitzbergen they may be taken on board a vessel without any great inconvenience, a proof that putrefaction proceeds with extreme slowness in the Polar regions.

With its blinding milk-white hide, on which it is seldom possible to discover a spot, wrinkle, or scratch, the full-grown white whale is an animal of extraordinary beauty. The young whales are not white, but very light greyish brown. The white whale is taken in nets not only by the Norwegians at Spitzbergen, but also by the Russians and Samoyeds at Chabarova. In former times they appear to have been also caught at the mouth of the Yenisej, to judge by the large number of vertebræ that are found at the now deserted settlements there. The white whale there goes several hundred kilometres up the river. I have also seen large shoals of this small species of whale on the north coast of Spitzbergen and the Taimur peninsula.

Other species of the whale occur seldom on Novaya Zemlya. Thus on this occasion only two small whales were seen during our passage from Tromsoe, and I do not remember having seen more than one in the sea round Novaya Zemlya in the course of my two previous voyages to the Yenisej. At the north part of the island, too, these animals occur so seldom, that a hunter told me, as something remarkable, that towards the end of July, 1873, W.N.W. of the western entrance to Matotschkin Schar 20' to 30' from land, he had seen a large number of whales, belonging to two species, of which one was a *slaethval*, and the other had as it were a top, instead of a fin, on the back.

It is very remarkable that whales still occur in great abundance on the Norwegian coast, though they have been hunted there for a thousand years back, but, on the other hand, if we except the little white whale, only occasionally east of the White Sea. The whale fishing which was carried on on so grand a scale on the west coast of Spitzbergen, has therefore never been prosecuted to any great extent on Novaya Zemlya; and fragments of skeletons of the whale which are found thrown up in such quantities on the shores of Spitzbergen, are not to be found, so far as my experience reaches, either on the shores of Novaya Zemlya, on the coast of the Kara Sea, or at the places on the north coast of Siberia between the Yenisej and the Lena, at which we landed. The sacrifices which were so long made in vain in the endeavour to find a passage to China in this direction accordingly were not compensated, as on Spitzbergen, by the rise of a profitable whale fishery. Meeting with a whale is spoken of by the first seafarers in these regions as something very remarkable and dangerous; for instance, in the account of Stephen Burrough's voyage in 1556 : — " On St. James his day, there was a monstrous whale aboord of us, so neere to our side that we might have thrust a sworde or any other weapon in him, which we durst not doe for feare he should have over-throwen our shippe ; and then I called my company together, and all of us shouted, and with the crie that we made he departed from us ; there was as much above water of his back as the bredth of our pinnesse, and at his falling down he made such a terrible noise in the water, that a man would greatly have marvelled, except he had known the cause of it ; but, God be thanked, we were quietly delivered of him." [1] When Nearchus sailed with the fleet of Alexander the Great from the Indus to the Red Sea, a whale also caused so great a panic that it was

[1] Hakluyt, first edition, p. 317.

K

only with difficulty that the commander could restore order among the frightened seamen, and get the rowers to row to the place where the whale spouted water and caused a commotion in the sea like that of a whirlwind. All the men now shouted, struck the water with their oars, and sounded their trumpets, so that the large, and, in the judgment of the Macedonian heroes, terrible animal, was frightened. Is seems to me that from these incidents we may draw the conclusion that great whales in Alexander's time were exceedingly rare in the sea which surrounds Greece, and in Burrough's time in that which washes the shores of England. Quite otherwise was the whale regarded on Spitzbergen some few years after Burrough's voyage by the Dutch and English whalers. At the sight of a whale all men were out of themselves with joy, and rushed down into the boats in order from them to attack and kill the valuable animal. The fishery was carried on with such success, that, as has already been stated, the right whale (*Balæna mysticetus* L.), whose pursuit then gave full employment to ships by hundreds, and to men by tens of thousands, is now practically extirpated. Thus during our many voyages in these waters we have only seen one such whale, which happened on the 23rd June, 1864, among the drift-ice off the west coast of Spitzbergen in 78° N.L. As the right whale still occurs in no limited numbers in other parts of the Polar Sea, and as there has been no whale fishing on the coast of Spitzbergen for the last forty or fifty years, this state of things shows how difficult it is to get an animal type to return to a region where it has once been extirpated, or from which it has been driven away.

The whale which Captain Svend Foeyn has almost exclusively hunted on the coast of Finmark since 1864 belongs to quite another species, *blaohvalen* (*Balænoptera Sibbaldii* Gray); and there are likewise other species of the whale which still in pretty large numbers follow shoals of fish to the Norwegian coast, where they sometimes strand, and are killed in considerable numbers. A *tandhval*, killer or sword-fish (*Orca gladiator*, Desm.) was even captured some years ago in the harbour of Tromsoe. This whale was already dying of suffocation, caused by an attempt to swallow an eider which entered the gullet, not, as the proper way is, with the head, but with the tail foremost. When the mouthful should have slidden down, it was prevented by the stiff feathers sticking out, and the bird stuck in the whale's throat, which, to judge by the extraordinary struggles it immediately began to make, must have caused it great inconvenience, which was increased still more when the inhabitants did not neglect to take advantage of its helpless condition to harpoon it.

CHAPTER IV.

The Origin of the names Yugor Schar and Kara Sea—Rules for Sailing through Yugor Schar—The "Highest Mountain" on Earth—Anchorages—Entering the Kara Sea—Its Surroundings—The Inland-ice of Novaya Zemlya—True Icebergs rare in certain parts of the Polar Sea—The Natural Conditions of the Kara Sea—Animals, Plants, Bog Ore—Passage across the Kara Sea—The Influence of the Ice on the Sea-bottom—Fresh-water Diatoms on Sea-ice—Arrival at Port Dickson—Animal Life there—Settlers and Settlements at the Mouth of the Yenisej—The Flora at Port Dickson—Evertebrates—Excursion to White Island—Yalmal—Previous Visits—Nummelin's Wintering on the Briochov Islands.

In crossing to Vaygats Island I met the *Lena*, which then first steamed to the rendezvous that had been fixed upon. I gave the captain orders to anchor without delay, to coal from the *Express*, and to be prepared immediately after my return from the excursion to weigh anchor and start along with the other vessels. I came on board the *Vega* on the evening of the 31st July, much pleased and gratified with what I had seen and collected in the course of my excursion on Vaygats Island. The *Lena*, however, was not quite ready, and so the start was put off till the morning of the 1st August. All the vessels then weighed anchor, and sailed or steamed through Vaygats Sound or Yugor Schar into the Kara Sea.

We do not meet with the name Yugor Schar in the oldest narratives of travel or on the oldest maps. But it is found in an account dating from 1611, of a Russian commercial route between "Pechorskoie Zauorot and Mongozei," which is annexed to the letter of Richard Finch to Sir Thomas Smith, already quoted (Purchas, iii. p. 539). The name is clearly derived from the old name, Jugaria, for the land lying south of the sound, and it is said, for instance, in the map to Herberstein's work, to have its name from the Hungarians, who are supposed to derive their origin from these regions. The first Dutch north-east explorers called it Vaygats Sound or Fretum Nassovicum. More recent geographers call it also Pet's Strait, which is incorrect, as Pet did not sail through it.

There was at first no special name for the gulf between the Taimur peninsula and Novaya Zemlya. The name "Carska Bay" however is to be found already in the information about sailing to the north-east, communicated to the Muscovie Companie by its principal factor, Antonie Marsh (Purchas, iii. p. 805). At first this name was applied only to the estuary of the Kara river, but it was gradually transferred to the whole of the neighbouring sea, whose oldest Samoyed name, also derived from a river, was in a somewhat Russianised form, "Neremskoe" (compare Purchas, iii. p. 805, Witsen, p. 917). I shall in the following part of this work comprehend under the name "Kara Sea" the whole of that gulf which from 77° N.L. between Cape Chelyuskin and the northern extremity of Novaya Zemlya extends towards the south to the north coast of Europe and Asia.

Captain Palander gives the following directions for sailing through the sound between Vaygats Island and the mainland :—

"As Yugor Straits are difficult to discover far out at sea, good solar observations ought to be taken on approaching them, where such can be had, and after these the course is to be shaped in the middle of the strait, preferably about N.E. by the compass. On coming nearer land (three to four English miles) one distinguishes the straits with ease. Afterwards there is nothing else to observe than on entering to keep right in the middle of the fairway.

"If one wishes to anchor at the Samoyed village one ought to keep about an English mile from the land on the starboard, and steer N.E. by the compass, until the Samoyed huts are seen, when one bends off from starboard, keeping the church a little to starboard. For larger vessels it is not advisable to go in shallower water than eight to nine fathoms, because the depth then diminishes rather suddenly to from three to four fathoms.

"From the Samoyed village the course is shaped right to the south-east headland of Vaygats Island (Suchoi Nos), which ought to be passed at the distance of half an English mile. Immediately south-west of this headland lies a very long shoal, which one ought to take care of.

"From this headland the vessel is to be steered N.$\frac{1}{4}$E. out into the Kara Sea. With this course there are two shoals on starboard and two on port at the distance of half an English mile.

"The depth is in general ten fathoms; at no place in the fairway is it less than nine fathoms.

"Vessels of the greatest draught may thus sail through Yugor Schar. In passing the straits it is recommended to keep a good outlook from the top, whence in clear weather the shoals may easily be seen."

In the oldest narratives very high mountains, covered with ice and snow, are spoken of as occurring in the neighbourhood of the sound between Vaygats Island and the mainland. It is even said that here were to be found the highest mountains on earth, whose tops were said to raise themselves to a height of a hundred German miles.[1] The honour of having the highest

---

[1] *Les moeurs et usages des Ostiackes*, par Jean Bernard Muller, Capitaine de dragon au service de la Suède, pendant sa captivité en Sibérie (*Recueil de Voiages au Nord*. T. VIII., Amsterdam, 1727, p. 389).

mountains on earth has since been ascribed by the dwellers
on the plains of Northern Russia to the neighbourhood of
Matotschkin Schar, "where the mountains are even much higher
than Bolschoj Kamen," a rocky eminence some hundreds of feet
high at the mouth of the Petchora—an orographic idea which
forms a new proof of the correctness of the old saying :—" In the
kingdom of the blind the one-eyed is king." Matotschkin Schar
indeed is surrounded by a wild Alpine tract with peaks that
rise to a height of 1,000 to 1,200 metres. On the other hand
there are to be seen around Yugor Straits only low level plains,
terminating towards the sea with a steep escarpment. These
plains are early free of snow, and are covered with a rich turf,
which yields good pasture to the Samoyed reindeer herds.

Most of the vessels that wish to sail into the Kara Sea through
Yugor Schar require to anchor here some days to wait for favourable winds and state of the ice. There are no good harbours
in the neighbourhood of the sound, but available anchorages
occur, some in the bay at Chabarova, at the western entrance
of the sound ; some, according to the old Dutch maps, on the
eastern side of the sound, between Mestni Island (Staten Eiland)
and the mainland. I have, however, no experience of my own
of the latter anchorages, nor have I heard that the Norwegian
walrus-hunters have anchored there. Perhaps by this time they
are become too shallow.

When we sailed through Yugor Schar in 1878, the sound was
completely free of ice. The weather was glorious, but the wind
was so light that the sails did little service. In consequence
of this we did not go very rapidly forward, especially as I wished
to keep the three vessels together, and the sailing ship *Express*,
not to be left behind, had to be towed by the *Fraser*. Time was
lost besides in dredging and taking specimens of water. The
dredgings gave at some places, for instance off Chabarova, a rich
yield, especially of isopods and sponges. The samples of water
showed that already at a limited depth from the surface it had
a considerable salinity, and that therefore no notable portion
of the mass of fresh water, which the rivers Kara, Obi, Tas, and
Yenisej and others pour into the Kara Sea, flows through this
sound into the Atlantic Ocean.

In the afternoon of the 1st August we passed through the
sound and steamed into the sea lying to the east of it, which
had been the object of so many speculations, expectations, and
conclusions of so many cautious governments, merchants eager
for gain, and learned cosmographers, from the sixteenth and
seventeenth centuries, and which even to the geographer and
man of science of the present has been a *mare incognitum* down
to the most recent date. It is just this sea that formed the
turning-point of all the foregoing north-east voyages from

Burrough's to Wood's and Vlamingh's, and it may therefore not
be out of place here, before I proceed further with the sketch
of our journey, to give some account of its surroundings and
hydrography.

If attention be not fixed on the little new-discovered island
"Ensamheten" the Kara Sea is open to the north-east. It
is bounded on the west by Novaya Zemlya and Vaygats Island;
on the east by the Taimur peninsula, the land between the
Pjaesina and the Yenisej and Yalmal; and on the south by the
northernmost portion of European Russia, Beli Ostrov, and the
large estuaries of the Obi and the Yenisej. The coast between
Cape Chelyuskin and the Yenisej consists of low rocky heights,
formed of crystalline schists, gneiss, and eruptive rocks, from
the Yenisej to beyond the most southerly part of the Kara
Sea, of the Gyda and Yalmal *tundras* beds of sand of equal
fineness, and at Vaygats Island and the southern part of
Novaya Zemlya (to 73° N.L.) of limestone and beds of schist [1]
which slope towards the sea with a steep escarpment three
to fifteen metres high, but form, besides, the substratum of a
level plain, full of small collections of water which is quite
free of snow in summer. North of 73° again the west coast
of the Kara Sea is occupied by mountains, which near Matotschkin are very high, and distributed in a confused mass of
isolated peaks, but farther north become lower and take the form
of a plateau.

Where the mountains begin, some few or only very inconsiderable collections of ice are to be seen, and the very mountain tops are in summer free of snow. Farther north glaciers
commence, which increase towards the north in number and
size, till they finally form a continuous inland-ice which, like
those of Greenland and Spitzbergen, with its enormous ice-sheet,
levels mountains and valleys, and converts the interior of the
land into a wilderness of ice, and forms one of the fields for the
formation of icebergs or glacier-iceblocks, which play so great
a *rôle* in sketches of voyages in the Polar seas. I have not
myself visited the inland-ice on the northern part of Novaya
Zemlya, but doubtless the experience I have previously gained
during an excursion with Dr. Berggren on the inland-ice of
Greenland in the month of July 1870, *after all the snow on it
had melted*, and with Captain Palander on the inland-ice of
North-East Land in the beginning of June 1873, *before any
melting of snow had commenced*, is also applicable to the ice-
wilderness of north Novaya Zemlya.

[1] I come to this conclusion from the appearance of the strata as seen
from the sea, and from their nature on Vaygats Island and the west coast
of Novaya Zemlya. So far as I know, no geologist has landed on this part
of the east coast.

As on Spitzbergen the ice-field here is doubtless interrupted by deep bottomless clefts, over which the snowstorms of winter throw fragile snow-bridges, which conceal the openings of the abysses so completely that one may stand close to their edge without having any suspicion that a step further is certain death to the man, who, without observing the usual precaution of being bound by a rope to his companions, seeks his way over the blinding-white, almost velvet-like, surface of this snow-field, hard packed indeed, but bound together by no firm crust. If a man, after taking necessary precautions against the danger of tumbling down into these crevasses, betakes himself farther into the country in the hope that the apparently even surface of the snow will allow of long day's marches, he is soon disappointed in his expectations; for he comes to regions where the ice is everywhere crossed by narrow depressions, *canals*, bounded by dangerous clefts, with perpendicular walls up to fifteen metres in height. One can cross these depressions

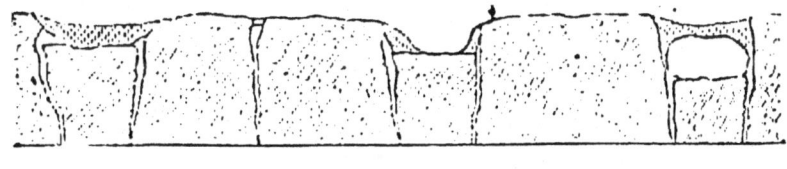

D   D   D   D   D

SECTION OF INLAND-ICE.

A. Open glacier-canal. B. Snow-filled canal. c. Canal concealed by a snow-vault.
D. Glacier-clefts.

only after endless zigzag wanderings, at places where they have become filled with snow and thereby passable. In summer again, when the snow has melted, the surface of the ice-wilderness has quite a different appearance. The snow has disappeared and the ground is now formed of a blue ice, which however is not clean, but everywhere rendered dirty by a grey argillaceous dust, carried to the surface of the glacier by wind and rain, probably from distant mountain heights. Among this clay, and even directly on the ice itself, there is a scanty covering of low vegetable organisms. The ice deserts of the Polar lands are thus the habitat of a peculiar flora, which, insignificant as it appears to be, forms however an important condition for the issue of the conflict which goes on here, year after year, century after century, between the sun and the ice. For the dark clay and the dark parts of plants absorb the warm rays of the sun better than the ice, and therefore powerfully promote its melting. They eat themselves down in perpendicular cylindrical holes thirty to sixty centimetres in depth, and from a few milimetres to a whole metre in diameter. The surface of the ice is thus destroyed and broken up.

After the melting of the snow there appears besides a number of inequalities, and the clefts previously covered with a fragile snow-bridge now gape before the wanderer where he goes forward, with their bluish-black abysses, bottomless as far as we can depend on ocular evidence. At some places there are

VIEW FROM THE INLAND ICE OF GREENLAND
After a drawing by S. Berggren, 23rd July, 1870.

also to be found in the ice extensive shallow depressions, down whose sides innumerable rapid streams flow in beds of azure-blue ice, often of such a volume of water as to form actual rivers. They generally debouch in a lake situated in the middle of the depression. The lake has generally an underground outlet through a grotto-vault of ice several thousands of feet high. At other places a river is to be seen, which has bored itself a hole through the ice-sheet, down which it suddenly disappears with a roar and din which are heard far and wide,

SLOWLY-ADVANCING GLACIER,
At Foul Bay, on the west coast of Spitzbergen. after a photograph taken by A. Enva ,
30th August, 1872.

GLACIER WITH STATIONARY FRONT,
Udde Bay, on Novaya Zemlya, after a drawing by Hj. Théel (1875).

and at a little distance from it there is projected from the ice a column of water, which, like a geyser with a large intermittent jet in which the water is mixed with air, rises to a great height.

Now and then a report is heard, resembling that of a cannon shot fired in the interior of the icy mass. It is a new crevasse that has been formed, or if one is near the border of the ice-desert, an ice-block that has fallen down into the sea. For, like ordinary collections of water, an ice-lake also has its outlet into the sea. These outlets are of three kinds, viz., *ice-rapids*, in which the thick ice-sheet, split up and broken in pieces, is

GREENLAND ICE FJORD.
After a design drawn and lithographed by a Greenland Eskimo.

pressed forward at a comparatively high speed down a narrow steeply-sloping valley, where ice-blocks tumble on each other with a crashing noise and din, and from which true icebergs of giant-like dimensions are projected in hundreds and thousands ; *broad, slowly-advancing glaciers*, which terminate towards the sea with an even perpendicular face, from which now and then considerable ice-blocks, but no true icebergs, fall down; and *smaller stationary glaciers*, which advance so slowly that the ice in the brim melts away about as fast as the whole mass of ice glides forward, and which thus terminate at the beach not with a perpendicular face but with a long ice-slope covered with clay, sand, and gravel.

The inland-ice on Novaya Zemlya is of too inconsiderable extent to allow of any large icebergs being formed. There are none such accordingly in the Kara Sea,[1] and it is seldom that even a large glacier ice-block is to be met with drifting about.

The name ice-house, conferred on the Kara Sea by a famous Russian man of science, did not originate from the large number of icebergs,[2] but from the fact that the covering of ice, which during winter, on account of the severity of the cold and the slight salinity of the surface-water, is immensely thick, cannot, though early broken up, be carried away by the marine currents and be scattered over a sea that is open even during winter.[3] Most of the ice formed during winter in the Kara Sea, and perhaps some of that which is drifted down from the Polar basin, is on the contrary heaped by the marine currents against the east coast of Novaya Zemlya, where during early summer it blocks the three sounds which unite the Kara Sea with the Atlantic. It was these ice-conditions which caused the failure of all the older north-east voyages and gave to the Kara Sea its

---

[1] Sometimes, however, icebergs are to be met with in the most northerly part of the Kara Sea and on the north coast of Novaya Zemlya, whither they may drive down from Franz Josef Land or from other yet unknown Polar lands lying farther north.

[2] In most of the literary narratives of Polar journeys colossal icebergs play a very prominent part in the author's delineations both with the pencil and the pen. The actual fact, however, is that icebergs occur in far greater numbers in the seas which are yearly accessible than in those in which the advance of the Polar travellers' vessel is hindered by impenetrable masses of ice. If we may borrow a term from the geography of plants to indicate the distribution of icebergs, they may be said to be more *boreal* than *polar* forms of ice. All the fishers on the coast of Newfoundland, and most of the captains on the steamers between New York and Liverpool, have some time or other seen true icebergs, but to most north-east voyagers this formation is unknown, though the name iceberg is often in their narratives given to glacier ice-blocks of somewhat considerable dimensions. This, however, takes place on the same ground and with the same justification as that on which the dwellers on the Petchora consider Bolschoj-Kamen a very high mountain. But although no true icebergs are ever formed at the glaciers so common on Spitzbergen and also on North Novaya Zemlya, it however often happens that large blocks of ice fall down from them and give rise to a swell, which may be very dangerous to vessels in their neighbourhood. Thus a wave caused by the falling of a piece of ice from a glacier on the 23rd (13th) of June, 1619, broke the masts of a vessel anchored at Bell Sound on Spitzbergen, threw a cannon overboard, killed three men, and wounded many more (Purchas, iii., p. 734). Several similar adventures, if on a smaller scale, I could relate from my own experience and that of the walrus-hunters. Care is taken on this account to avoid anchoring too near the perpendicular faces of glaciers.

[3] It may, however, be doubted whether the *whole* of the Kara Sea is completely frozen over in winter.

bad report and name of ice-house.   Now we know that it is not
so dangerous in this respect as it was formerly believed to be—
that the ice of the Kara Sea melts away for the most part, and
that during autumn this sea is quite available for navigation.

In general our knowledge of the Kara Sea some decades
back was not only incomplete, but also erroneous.   It was believed that its animal life was exceedingly scanty, and that algæ
were absolutely wanting ; no soundings had been taken elsewhere than close to the coast ; and much doubt was thrown, not
without reason, on the correctness of the maps.   Now all this is
changed to a great extent.   The coast line, bordering on the
sea, is settled on the maps ; the ice-conditions, currents and
depth of water in different parts of the sea are ascertained, and
we know that the old ideas of its poverty in animals and plants
are quite erroneous.

In respect to depth the Kara Sea is distinguished by a
special regularity, and by the absence of sudden changes.
Along the east coast of Novaya Zemlya and Vaygats Island
there runs a channel, up to 500 metres in depth, filled
with cold salt-water, which forms the haunt of a fauna
rich not only in individuals, but also in a large number
of remarkable and rare types, as Umbellula, Elpidia, Alecto,
asterids of many kinds, &c.   Towards the east the sea-bottom
rises gradually and then forms a plain lying 30 to 90 metres
below the surface of the sea, nearly as level as the surface of
the superincumbent water.   The bottom of the sea in the south
and west parts of it consists of clay, in the regions of Beli
Ostrov of·sand, farther north of gravel.   Shells of crustacea and
pebbles are here often surrounded by bog-ore formations,
resembling the figures on page 186.   These also occur over an
extensive area north-east of Port Dickson in such quantity that
they might be used for the manufacture of iron, if the region
were less inaccessible.

Even in the shallower parts of the Kara Sea the water at
the bottom is nearly as salt as in the Atlantic Ocean, and all
the year round cooled to a temperature of —2° to —2°·7.   The
surface-water, on the contrary, is very variable in its composition,
sometimes at certain places almost drinkable, and in summer
often strongly heated.   The remarkable circumstance takes
place here that the surface water in consequence of its limited
salinity freezes to ice if it be exposed to the temperature which
prevails in the salt stratum of water next the bottom, and that
it forms a deadly poison for many of the decapoda, worms,
mussels, crustacea and asterids which crawl in myriads among
the beds of clay or sand at the bottom.

At many places the loose nature of the bottom does not
permit the existence of any algæ, but in the neighbourhood of

Beli Ostrov, Johannesen discovered extensive banks covered with "sea-grass"
(algæ), and from the east coast of Novaya
Zemlya Dr. Kjellman in 1875 collected
no small number of algæ,[1] being thereby
enabled to take exception to the old
erroneous statements as to the nature of
the marine flora. He has drawn up for
this work a full account of the marine
vegetation in the Kara Sea, which will
be found further on.

I shall now return to the account of our
passage across this sea. On this subject my
journal contains the following notes:

August 2nd. Still glorious weather—
no ice. The *Lena* appears to wish to

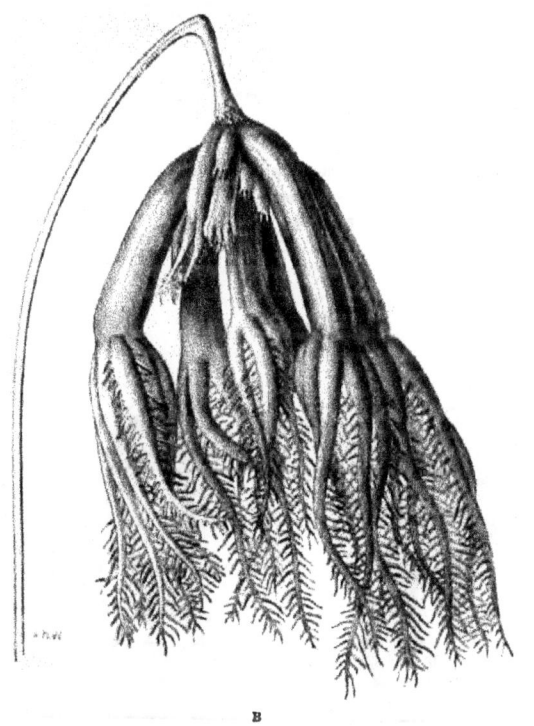

B

UMBELLULA FROM THE KARA SEA.

ᴀ. Polype stem entire, one-half the natural size.

ʙ. Polype stem, upper part, one-and-a-half times the natural size.

[1] Already in 1771 one of Pallas' companions, the student Sujeff, found
large algæ in the Kara Sea (Pallas, *Reise.* St. Petersburg, 1771—1776,
iii. p. 34).

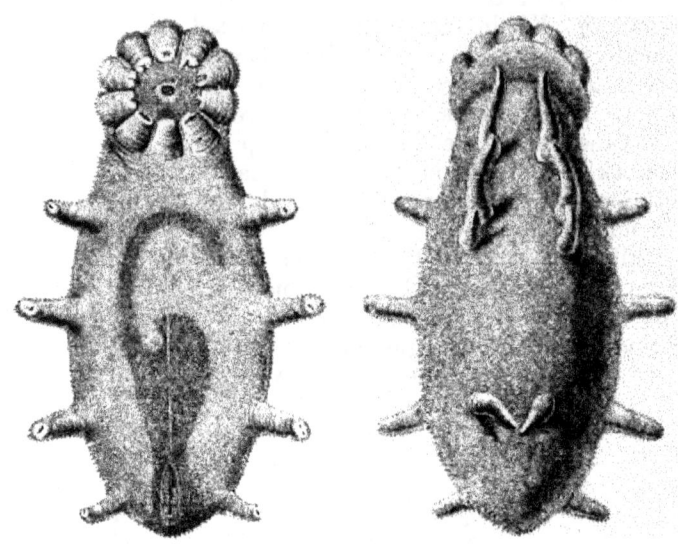

A   B

ELPIDIA GLACIALIS (THÉEL), FROM THE KARA SEA.

Magnified three times.

A. Belly. B. Back.

MANGANIFEROUS IRON-ORE FORMATIONS FROM THE KARA SEA.

Half the natural size.

get away from the other vessels, and does not observe the flag which was hoisted as the signal agreed upon beforehand that her Captain should come on board, or at least bring his little vessel within hail. The *Fraser* was therefore sent in pursuit, and succeeded in overtaking her towards night.

August 3rd. In the morning Captain Johannesen came on board the *Vega.* I gave him orders to take on board Dr. Almquist and Lieutenants Hovgaard and Nordquist, and go with them to Beli Ostrov, where they should have freedom for thirty-six hours to study the people, animals, and plants, as they pleased; the *Lena* was then, if possible, to pass through the Sound between the island and Yalmal to Port Dickson, where the three other vessels should be found. Almquist, Nordquist, and Hovgaard were already quite in order for the excursion; they went immediately on board the *Lena,* and were soon, thanks to the great power of the engine in proportion to the size of the vessel, far on their way.

In the course of the day we met with very open and rotten ice, which would only have been of use to us by its moderating effect on the sea, if it had not been accompanied by the usual attendant of the border of the ice, a thick fog, which, however, sometimes lightened. Towards evening we came in sight of Beli Ostrov. This island, as seen from the sea, forms a quite level plain, which rises little above the surface of the water. The sea off the island is of an even depth, but so shallow, that at a distance of twenty to thirty kilometres from the shore there is only from seven to nine metres of water. According to a communication from Captain Schwanenberg, there is, however, a depth of three to four metres close to the north shore. Such a state of things, that is, a uniform depth, amounting near the shore to from four to ten metres, but afterwards increasing only gradually and remaining unchanged over very extensive areas, is very common in the Arctic regions, and is caused by the ice-mud-work which goes on there nearly all the year round. Another remarkable effect of the action of the ice is that all the blocks of stone to be found in the sea next the beach are forced up on land. The beach itself is formed accordingly at many places, for instance at several points in Matotschkin Sound, of a nearly continuous stone rampart going to the sea level, while in front of it there is a quite even sea bottom without a fragment of stone.

August 4th. In the morning a gentle heaving indicated that the sea was again free of ice, at least over a considerable space to windward. Yesterday the salinity of the water was already diminished and the amount of clay increased; now the water after being filtered is almost drinkable. It has assumed a yellowish-grey colour and is nearly opaque, so that the vessel appears to sail in clay mud. We are evidently in the area of the Ob-Yenisej current. The ice we sailed through yesterday probably came, from the Gulf of Obi, Yenisej or Pjäsina. Its surface was dirty, not clean and white like the surface of glacier-ice or the sea-ice that has never come in contact with land or with muddy river-water. Off the large rivers the ice, when the snow has melted, is generally covered with a yellow layer of clay. This clay evidently consists of mud, which had been washed down by the river-water and been afterwards thrown up by the swell on the snow covered-ice. The layer of snow acts as a filter and separates the mud from the water. The former, therefore, after the melting of the snow may form upon true sea-ice a layer of dirt, containing a large number of minute organisms which live only in fresh water.

SECTION FROM THE SOUTH COAST OF MATOTSCHKIN SOUND,
Showing the origin of Stone-ramparts at the beach.

August 5th. Still under sail in the Kara Sea, in which a few pieces of ice are floating about. The ice completely disappeared when we came north-west of Beli Ostrov. We were several times in the course of the day in only nine metres of water, which, however, in consequence of the evenness of the bottom, is not dangerous. Fog, a heavy sea, and an intermittent but pretty fresh breeze delayed our progress.

August 6th. At three o'clock in the morning we had land in sight. In the fog we had gone a little way up the Gulf of Yenisej, and so had to turn in order to reach our destination, Port Dickson. The mast-tops of the *Express* were seen projecting over Islands to the north, and both vessels soon anchored south of an island which was supposed to be Dickson's Island, but when the *Fraser* soon after joined us we learned that this was a mistake. The shore, which, seen from our first anchorage, appeared to be that of the mainland, belonged in fact to the pretty extensive island, off which the haven itself is situated.

After an excursion on land, in the course of which a covey of partridges was seen, and Dr. Kjellman on the diorite rocks of the island made a pretty abundant collection of plants, belonging partly to species which he had not before met with in the Arctic regions, we again weighed anchor in order to remove to the proper harbour.

Captain Palander went before in a steam launch in order to examine the yet unsurveyed fairway. On the way he fell in with and killed a bear, an exceedingly fat and large male. Like the bear Dr. Théel shot here in 1875, he had only mosses and lichens in his stomach, and as it is scarcely probable that the bear in this region can catch a great many seals in summer, it is to be supposed that his food consists principally of vegetable substances, with the, addition perhaps of a reindeer or two when he can succeed in getting hold of them. In the year 1875 we saw here an old male bear that appeared to pasture quite peaceably in company with some reindeer, probably with a view to get near enough to spring upon them. Bears must besides be very common in that part of the north coast of Siberia, for during the few days we now remained there, two more were shot, both of them very fat.

The haven, which has now been surveyed by Lieutenant Bove, was discovered by me in 1875 and named Port Dickson. It is the best known haven on the whole north coast of Asia, and will certainly in the future be of great importance for the foreign commerce of Siberia. It is surrounded on all sides by rocky islands, and is thus completely sheltered. The anchorage is a good clay bottom. The haven may be entered both from the north and from the south-west; but in sailing in, caution should be used, because some rocky shoals may be met with which are not shown on Lieutenant Bove's sketch chart, which was made in the greatest haste. The water probably varies con-siderably as to its salinity with the season of the year and with ebb and flood tides, but is never, even at the surface, completely fresh. It can therefore be used in cooking only in case of the greatest necessity. But two streams on the mainland, one debouching north and the other south of the harbour, yield an abundant supply of good water, in case snow water cannot be obtained from any of the beds of snow which up to autumn are to be found at several places along the strand escarpments in the neighbourhood of the harbour.

At our arrival six wild reindeer were seen pasturing on Dick-son's Island ; one of them was killed by Palander, the others were

stalked unsuccessfully. Some bears, as has already been stated,
were also seen, and everywhere among the heaps of stones there
were numerous remains of the lemming and the fox. With
these exceptions there were few of the higher animals. Of
birds we thus saw only snow-buntings, which bred among the
stone heaps both on the mainland and on the islands, a
covey of ptarmigan, a large number of birds, principally
species of Tringa and Phalaropus, but not further determined, eiders, black guillemots and burgomasters in limited
numbers, and long-tailed ducks and loons in somewhat greater
abundance. There are no "down islands," and as there are no
precipitous shore cliffs neither are there any looneries. A shoal
of fish was seen in Lena Sound, and fish are probably exceedingly abundant. Seals and white whales also perhaps occur
here at certain seasons of the year in no small numbers. It
was doubtless with a view to hunt these animals that a hut
was occupied, the remains of which are visible on one of the small
rocky islands at the north entrance into the harbour. The ruin,
if we may apply the term to a wooden hut which has fallen in
pieces, showed that the building had consisted of a room with a
fireplace and a storehouse situated in front, and that it was only
intended as a summer dwelling for the hunters and fishers who
came hither during the hunting season from the now deserted
simovies [1] lying farther south.

I am convinced that the day will come when great warehouses
and many dwellings inhabited all the year round will be found
at Port Dickson. Now the region is entirely uninhabited as far
as Goltschicha, although, as the map reproduced here shows,
numerous dwelling-houses were to be found built along the river
bank and sea-shore beyond the mouth of the Yenisej and as far
as to the Pjäsina. They have long since been abandoned, in the
first place in consequence of the hunting falling off, but probably
also because even here, far away on the north coast of Siberia,
the old simple and unpretentious habits have given way to new
wants which were difficult to satisfy at the time when no
steamers carried on traffic on the river Yenisej. Thus, for
instance, the difficulty of procuring meal some decades back,
accordingly before the commencement of steam communication
on the Yenisej, led to the abandonment of a *simovie* situated on
the eastern bank of the river in latitude 72° 25' north.

The *simovies* at the mouth of the Yenisej formed in their
time the most northerly fixed dwelling-places of the European
races.[2] Situated as they were at the foot of the cold *tundra*,

---

[1] Dwellings intended both for winter and summer habitation.
[2] The most northerly fixed dwelling-place, which is at present inhabited
by Europeans, is the Danish commercial post Tasiusak, in north-western
Greenland, situated in 73° 24' N.L. How little is known, even in Russia,

MAP

)UTH OF THE YENISEJ

FROM

.S RUSSICUS CURA ET OPERE ACADEMIÆ
MPERIALIS SCIENTIARUM PETROPOLITANÆ.
ETROPOLI 1745.

Sjewerowostocznoi

Zim Ubeino
Zim. Bjeczeszno
Zim. Zwjerewo
Zim. Koskino
Zim. Morzewskoe
Z Zdorowskoe
Erszewo

Zim. Maloe
Zim. strelowo
Niz. Troickoe
Zim. Turuehan
skago Monustyrja
Zim. Wolyino
gdje Majak
Zim. Szadrino

Zim Topowo
Zim Spiridonowo
Niz Kulaszewo

Gu
sino
Ustotroicko
Z. Krestowsko
Zyrfakez
Koremo Sudisko Zim.
R. Gluboka
Sarjeko Zim.
R. Gribowka

Zwjerewo
Woiniszno
Z. Staro
zwjerewo
Z. Landino
Wyrupowo
Zwierewo
Oszmarino Zwjerewo
Wjatkino

Gribowsko Kolczcha
Waginsko
Golubinskie Magazeiny
Bakarewsko Zim
Zim. Priluszno
Zim. Korepowo
Z. Mezenkino
Z. Rybno
Z. Nazarowo
Z i Gostinoj nos
Korgowskoe Iakowlewa
z. Werch Troicko
Z Szestakowo
Z. Nasonowo
Z. Kozilkino
Z. Tarnaboszikowo
Z. Gubino
Z. Isanowo
Nikonowo
Muksuninsko
Tolstonosko
Suzinskoe
Kazanrowa
Mikiszki
no
Czosz
kino

Z Zwjere wo
Z Łoszino
Z Derjabino
Z Ipatowo
Zi
wo
Mjasniko
Z Koszelewo
Z Frotowo
Z Telenino
Komino
Bezuklabicyno
Letowo
Zaostrowo
szno
Ladiszino

R. Ozerna
R. Gydy
R. Iary
R. Polyolowy
R. Totoja
R. Ales
R. Gydy
R. Cheta
R. Cheta

exposed to continual snowstorms in winter and to close fogs
during the greater part of summer, which here is extremely
short, it seems as if they could not offer their inhabitants
many opportunities for enjoyment, and the reason why this tract
was chosen for a residence, especially in a country so rich in
fertile soil as Siberia, appears to be difficult to find. The
remains of an old *simovie* (Krestovskoj), which I saw in 1875
while travelling up the river along with Dr. Lundström and Dr.
Stuxberg, however, produced the impression that a true home
life had once been led there. Three houses with turf-covered

RUINS OF A SIMOVIE AT KRESTOVSKOJ.
After a drawing by A. Stuxberg.

roofs then still remained in such a state that one could form an
idea of their former arrangement and of the life which had
been carried on in them.   Each cabin contained a whole labyrinth of very small rooms ; dwelling-rooms with sleeping places
fixed to the walls, bake-rooms with immense fireplaces, bathing
houses with furnaces for vapour-baths, storehouses for train-oil
with large train-drenched blubber troughs hollowed out of

of the former dwellings at the mouth of the Yenisej may be seen from
*Neueste Nachrichten über die nördlichste Gegend von Sibirien zwischen den
Flüssen Pjässida und Chatanga in Fragen und Antworten abgefasst. Mit
Einleitung und Anmerkungen vom Herausgeber* (K. E. v. Baer und Gr. v.
Helmersen, *Beiträge zur Kenntniss des russischen Reiches,* vol. iv. p. 269.
St. Petersburg, 1841).

enormous tree-stems, blubber tanks with remains of the white whale, &c., all witnessing that the place had had a flourishing period, when prosperity was found there, when the home was regarded with loyalty, and formed in all its loneliness the central point of a life richer perhaps in peace and well-being than one is inclined beforehand to suppose.

In 1875 a "prikaschik" (foreman) and three Russian labourers lived all the year round at Goltschicha. Sverevo was inhabited by one man and Priluschnoj by an old man and his son. All were poor; they dwelt in small turf-covered cabins, consisting of a lobby and a dirty room, smoked and sooty, with a large fireplace, wooden benches along the walls, and a sleeping place fixed to the wall, high above the floor. Of household furniture only the implements of fishing and the chase were numerously represented. There were in addition pots and pans, and occasionally a tea-urn. The houses were all situated near the river-bank, so high up that they could not be reached by the spring inundations. A disorderly midden was always to be found in the near neighbourhood, with a number of draught dogs wandering about on it seeking something to eat. Only one of the Russian settlers here was married, and we were informed that there was no great supply of the material for Russian housewives for the inhabitants of these regions. At least the Cossack Feodor, who in 1875 and 1876 made several unsuccessful attempts to serve me as pilot, and who himself was a bachelor already grown old and wrinkled, complained that the fair or weaker sex was poorly represented among the Russians. He often talked of the advantages of mixed marriages, being of opinion, under the inspiration of memory or hope, I know not which, that a Dolgan woman was the most eligible *parti* for a man disposed to marry in that part of the world.

A little farther south, but still far north of the limit of trees, there are, however, very well-to-do peasants, who inhabit large *simovies*, consisting of a great number of houses and rooms, in which a certain luxury prevails, where one walks on floor-coverings of skins, where the windows are whole, the sacred pictures covered with plates of gold and silver, and the walls provided with mirrors and covered with finely coloured copper-plate portraits of Russian Czars and generals. This prosperity is won by traffic with the natives, who wander about as nomads on the *tundra* with their reindeer herds.

The cliffs around Port Dickson consist of diorite, hard and difficult to break in pieces, but weathering readily. The rocky hills are therefore so generally split up that they form enormous stone mounds. They were covered with a great abundance of lichens, and the plains between them yielded to Dr. Kjellman the following phanerogamous plants :

Cineraria frigida RICHARDS.
Erigeron uniflorus L.
Saussurea alpina DC.
Taraxacum phymatocarpum J. VAHL.
Gymnandra Stelleri CH. & SCHL.
Pedicularis sudetica WILLD.
  „   hirsuta L.
  „   Oederi VAHL.
Eritrichium villosum BUNGE.
Myosotis silvatica HOFFM.
Astragalus alpinus L.
Oxytropis campestris (L.) DC.
Dryas octopetala L.
Sieversia glacialis R. BR.
Potentilla emarginata PURSH.
Saxifraga oppositifolia L.
  „   bronchialis L.
  „   Hirculus L.   .
  „   stellaris L.
  „   nivalis L.
  „   hieraciifolia WALDST. & KIT.
  „   punctata L.
  „   cernua L.
  „   rivularis L.
  „   cæspitosa L.
Chrysosplenium alternifolium L.
Rhodiola rosea L.
Parrya macrocarpa R. BR.
Cardamine pratensis L.
  „   bellidifolia L.
Eutrema Edwardsii R. BR.
Cochlearia fenestrata R. BR.
Draba alpina L.
  „   oblongata (R. BR.) DC.
  „   corymbosa R. BR.
  „   Wahlenbergii HN.
  „   altaica (LEDEB.) BUNGE.
Papaver nudicaule L.
Ranunculus pygmæus WG.

Ranunculus hyperboreus ROTTB.
  „   lapponicus L.
  „   nivalis L.
  „   sulphureus SOL.
  „   affinis R. BR.
Caltha palustris L.
Wahlbergella apetala (L.) FR.
Stellaria Edwardsii R. BR.
Cerastium alpinum L.
Alsine arctica FENZL.
  „   macrocarpa FENZL.
  „   rubella WG.
Sagina nivalis FR.
Oxyria digyna (L.) HILL.
Rumex arcticus TRAUTV.
Polygonum viviparum L.
  „   Bistorta L.
Salix polaris WG.
Festuca rubra L.
Poa cenisea ALL.
  ,,   arctica R. BR.
Glyceria angustata R. BR.
Catabrosa algida (SOL.) FR.
  ,,   concinna TH. FR.
Colpodium latifolium R. BR.
Dupontia Fisheri R. BR.
Koeleria hirsuta GAUD.
Aira cæspitosa L.
Alopecurus alpinus SM.
Eriophorum angustifolium ROTH.
  „   vaginatum L.
  „   Scheuchzeri HOPPE.
Carex rigida GOOD.
  „   aquatilis WG.
Juncus biglumis L.
Luzula hyperborea R. BR.
  ,,   arctica BL.
Lloydia serotina (L.) REICHENB.

Our botanists thus made on land a not inconsiderable collection, considering the northerly position of the region. On the other hand no large algæ were met with in the sea, nor was it to be expected that there would, for the samples of water taken up with Ekman's instrument showed that the salinity at the bottom was as slight as at the surface, viz. only 0·3 per cent. The temperature of the water was also at the time of our visit about the same at the bottom as at the surface, viz. + 9° to + 10°. In spring, when the snow melts, the water here is probably quite fresh, in winter again cold, and as

salt as at the bottom of the Kara Sea. Under so variable
hydrographical conditions we might have expected an exceedingly scanty marine fauna, but this was by no means the
case. For the dredgings in the harbour gave Dr. Stuxberg a
not inconsiderable yield, consisting of the same types as those
which are found in the salt water at the bottom of the Kara Sea.

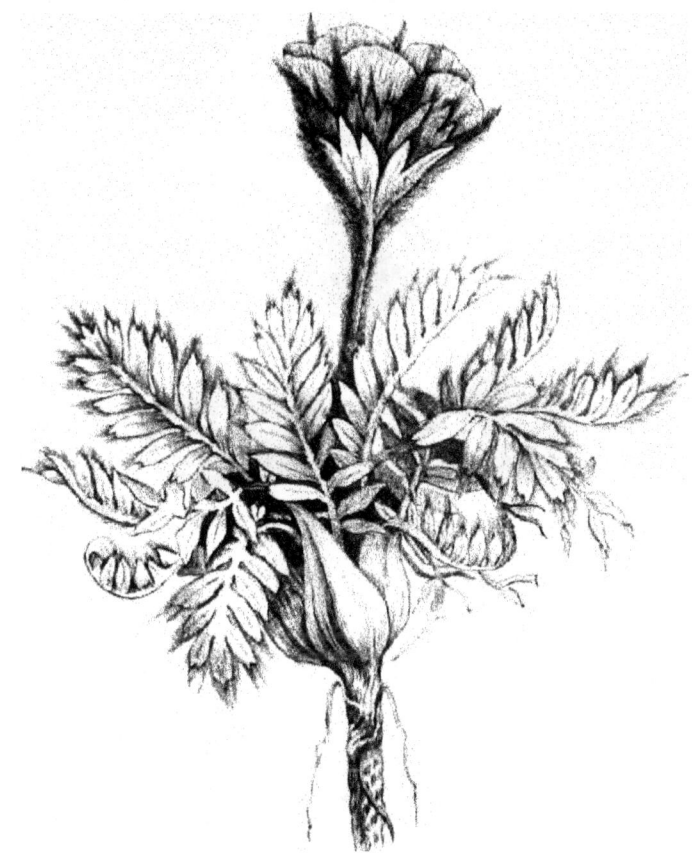

SIEVERSIA GLACIALIS R. BR.
From Port Dickson.

This circumstance appears to show that certain evertebrate
types can endure a much greater variation in the temperature
and salinity of the water than the algæ, and that there is a
number of species which, though as a rule they live in the
strongly cooled layer of salt water at the bottom of the
Kara Sea, can bear without injury a considerable diminution in
the salinity of the water and an increase of temperature of
about 12°.

For the science of our time, which so often places the origin
of a northern form in the south; and *vice versâ*, as the foundation
of very wide theoretical conclusions, a knowledge of the types
which can live by turns in nearly fresh water of a temperature
of + 10°, and in water cooled to − 2°·7 and of nearly the same
salinity as that of the Mediterranean, must have a certain
interest. The most remarkable were, according to Dr. Stuxberg,
the following: a species of Mysis, *Diastylis Rathkei* KR.,
Idothea entomon LIN., *Idothea Sabinei* KR., two species of
Lysianassida, *Pontoporeia setosa* STBRG., *Halimedon brevicalcar*
GOËS, an Annelid, a Molgula, *Yoldia intermedia* M. SARS,
Yoldia (?) *arctica* GRAY, and a Solecurtus.

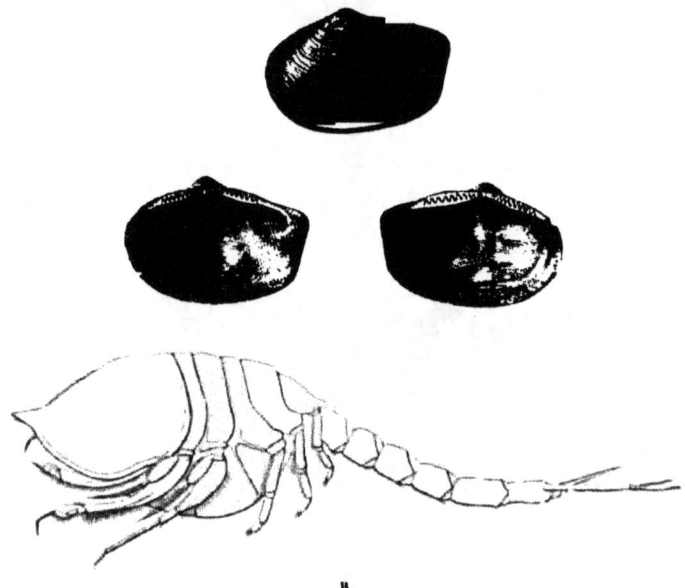

B

EVERTEBRATES FROM PORT DICKSON.

A. Yoldia arctica GRAY.   One and two-thirds of natural size.   B. Diastylis Rathkei KR
Magnified three times.

Driftwood in the form both of small branches and pieces of
roots, and of whole trees with adhering portions of branches
and roots, occurs in such quantities at the bottom of two well-
protected coves at Port Dickson, that the seafarer may without
difficulty provide himself with the necessary stock of fuel. The
great mass of the driftwood which the river bears along,
however, does not remain on its own banks, but floats
out to sea to drift about with the marine currents until
the wood has absorbed so much water that it sinks, or
until it is thrown up on the shores of Novaya Zemlya, the

north coast of Asia, Spitzbergen or perhaps Greenland. Another portion of the wood sinks, before it reaches the sea, often in such a way that the stems stand upright in the river bottom, with one end, so to say, rooted in the sand. They may thus be inconvenient for the navigation, at least at the shallower places of the river. A bay immediately off Port Dickson was almost barred by a natural palisade-work of driftwood stems.

August 7th. The *Vega* coaled from the *Express.* In the evening the *Lena* arrived, 36 hours after the *Vega* had anchored, that is to say, precisely at the appointed time. Concerning this excursion, Dr. Almquist reports:

" On the 2nd August we—Hovgaard, Nordquist and I—went on board the *Lena* to make an excursion to Beli Ostrov. We were to land on the south-western headland and there undertake botanical and zoological researches. Thereafter we were to direct some attention to the opposite shore of Yalmal and visit the Samoyeds living there.

"We left the *Vega* at eleven o'clock forenoon. In the course of the day we saw here and there in the south scattered ice, and at half-past ten at night we ran into a large belt, about 300 metres broad, of scattered ice, which lay stretched out from N.E. to S.W. It was passed without difficulty. In the course of the night we now and then fell in with a little scattered ice, and in the morning with a belt of masses of ice, of considerable dimensions; sounding constantly in 10 to $3\frac{1}{2}$ metres water we succeeded, notwithstanding the fog and rain, in finding the straits between Beli Ostrov and the mainland, and on the 3rd August at eleven o'clock forenoon we anchored a little to the east of the southern extremity of the island. The *Lena* lay in $3\frac{1}{4}$ metres water, about an English mile out to sea. The water was shallow for so great a distance from the beach that we had to leave our boat about 300 metres out to sea and wade to land.

" Beli Ostrov consists entirely of fine sand, and only on that part of the beach which is washed by the sea-water did we see any stones as large as walnuts; higher up we did not find a piece of stone even of the size of the nail. The highest point of the island appears to be scarcely three metres above the surface of the sea. That part of the island over which the sea water washes, that is, the beach and the deep bays which indent the land here and there, shows the fine sand bare, without trace of vegetation. Where the ground rises a little, it becomes covered with a black and white variegated covering of mosses and lichens; scattered among which at long intervals are small tufts of grass. First somewhat higher up and properly only round the marshy margins of the numerous small fresh-water lakes and in hollows and bogs, is the ground slightly green. The higher plants are represented by only 17 species, all small and stunted,[1] most of them rising only some few lines above the sand. Very few plants reached a height of 15 centimetres. No kind of willow was found, nor any flower seen of any other colour than green or white.

"The lichen-flora too was scanty. No species showed any great luxuriance, and seldom did the black and white lichen-crust produce any 'apothecium.' The lichen-vegetation was most abundant on the driftwood of the beach and on the tufts in the marshes. The larger lichens, as the reindeer and Iceland lichens, occurred very sparingly. About 80 species were found. The land evertebrates were so sparingly represented, that only three diptera, one species of hymenoptera, and some insect larvæ and spiders could be collected. Only poduræ were found in great abundance; they completely covered the whole ground at the beach.

"Several herds of reindeer were seen, but we did not succeed in getting within range of them. A little fish of the Cottus family was caught by Nordquist in a ditch which was in connection with the sea. Driftwood still fresh was found in great abundance, and farther up on land here and there lay a more rotten stem.

"Rain and fog rendered impossible any determination of position. During night we went across the sound and anchored about an English mile and a half from the shore of Yalmal, right opposite some Samoyed tents which we discovered a little inland. In the same unfavourable weather as that of the day before we attempted to land there, but found the water too shallow. First pretty far to the east we succeeded in reaching the beach at a place where the land rose out of the sea with a steep bank about nine metres high. Above the bank, which consisted of loose clay, we found a plain with the appearance of a rich watered *tundra*, full of marshes and streams, and therefore presenting a very green appearance. In order to meet with the Samoyeds we now went westwards, passing several rivulets which

---

[1] The collections made here were after our return determined by Dr. Kjellman, who has communicated the following list:

Saxifraga stellaris L.	Aira cæspitosa L.
„ cernua L.	Hierochloa pauciflora R. Br.
„ rivularis L.	Eriophorum russeolum Fr.
Cochlearia fenestrata R. Br.	„ Scheuchzeri Hoppe.
Stellaria humifusa Rottb.	Carex salina Wg.
Sagina nivalis Fr.	„ ursina Desv.
Arctophila pendulina (Læst.) Ands.	Luzula hyperborea R. Br.
Catabrosa algida (Sol.) Fr.	„ arctica Bl.
Dupontia Fisheri R. Br.	

cut deeply into the land and had high banks, until after half an ·
hour's walking we came to a broad but not very deep river, which
it was impossible to ford.   We therefore returned to our boat with
the view of seeking a landing-place ou the other side of the river ;
but as the *Lena's* distance from land was considerable · and the
breeze was freshening, the captain considered that the time at
our disposal did not permit us to undertake so long an excursion.

"So far as we may judge from our hasty visit, the vegetation
on this part of Yalmal struck us as being remarkably abundant.
The high banks especially were richly covered by phanerogamous
plants and lichens, and would have deserved a closer examination.
Our cursory observations of the plants here may however be
interesting for comparison with the flora of Beli Ostrov; we
collected and noted the higher plants [1] and about 40 species of
lichens.   Nordquist found that the fauna resembled that of the
neighbouring island, and collected besides two species of
Coleoptera.

"After lying 26 hours in the sound we weighed anchor again
and went westwards, following a channel with ten to sixteen
metres water.   We could not find its course farther to the east,
and were compelled, although we were near the eastern extremity
of Beli Ostrov, to turn in order to pass out through the western
entrance of the sound.   We saw a quantity of stranded ice on
the north coast of the island, which, seen from the sea, did not
present any dissimilarity to the part which we had visited.   On
the 7th August we arrived at Port Dickson."

From Lieutenant Hovgaard's report on this excursion, a map
is given here of Beli Ostrov and the neighbouring coast of
Yalmal, in which I have named the sound between the island
and the mainland after MALYGIN, one of the gallant Russian
seamen who first sailed through it nearly a century and a
half ago.

Yalmal has been visited by Europeans so seldom, and their
observations are scattered in printed papers so inaccessible, that
it may perhaps not be out of place here to collect the most

---

[1] These according to Dr. Kjellman's determination are :

Saxifraga cernua L.	Arctophila pendulina (LÆST.) AND.
„ cæspitosa L.	Catabrosa algida (Sol.) FR.
Cochlearia fenestrata R. BR.	„ concinna TH. FR.
Draba alpina L.	Dupontia Fisheri R. BR.
Ranunculus sulphureus SOL.	Calamagrostis lapponica L.
„ nivalis L.	Carex salina WG.
„ pygmæus WG.	„ rigida GOOD.
„ lapponicus L.	Eriophorum russeolum FR.
„ borealis TRAUTV.	Luzula arcuata SM. f. hyperborea
Stellaria Edwardsii R. BR.	R. BR.
Salix glauca L.	Lloydia serotina (L.) REICHENB.

important facts which are known regarding this peninsula, along with the necessary bibliographical references.

First as to its name, it is sometimes also written "Yelmert Land," [1] but this is quite incorrect.

"Yalmal" is of Samoyed origin, and has, according to a private communication from the well-known philologist Dr. E. D. EUROPÆUS, the distinctive meaning " land's-end." YELMERT again was a boatswain with the Dutch whale-fisher VLAMINGH, who in 1664 sailed round the northern extremity of Novaya Zemlya to Barents' winter haven, and thence farther to the south-east. Vlamingh himself at his turning-point saw no land, though all signs showed that land ought to be found in the neighbourhood; but several of the crew thought they saw land, and the report of this to a Dutch mapmaker, DICK REMBRANTSZ. VAN NIEROP, led to the introduction of the supposed land into a great many maps, commonly as a large island in the Kara Sea. This island was named Yelmert Land. The similarity between the names Yelmert Land and Yalmal, and the doubt as to the existence of the Yelmert Island first shown on the maps, have led to the transfer of the name Yelmert Land to the peninsula which separates the Gulf of Obi from the Kara Sea. It is to be remarked, however, that the name Yalmal is not found in the older accounts of voyages from the European waters to the Obi. The first time I met with it was in the narrative of Skuratov's journey in 1737, as the designation of the most north-easterly promontory of the peninsula which now bears that name.

Yalmal's grassy plains offer the Samoyeds during summer reindeer pastures which are highly valued, and the land is said to have a very numerous population in comparison with other regions along the shores of the Polar Sea, the greater portion, however, drawing southward towards winter with their large herds of reindeer. But the land is, notwithstanding this, among the most imperfectly known parts of the great Russian empire. Some information regarding it we may obtain from sketches of the following journeys :

SELIFONTOV, 1737. In the months of July and August the surveyor Selifontov travelled in a reindeer sledge along the coast of the Gulf of Obi as far as to Beli Ostrov. About this journey unfortunately nothing else has been published than is to be found in LITKE, *Viermalige Reise*, &c., Berlin, 1835, p. 66, and WRANGEL, *Sibirische Reise*, Berlin, 1839, p. 37.

---

[1] On the maps in Linschoten's work already quoted, printed in 1601, and in Blavii *Atlas Major* (1665, t. i. pp. 24, 25), this land is called " Nieu West Vrieslant" and " West Frisia Nova," names which indeed have priority *in print*, but yet cannot obtain a preference over the inhabitants' own beautiful name.

SUJEFF, in 1771, travelled under the direction of Pallas over the southern part of Yalmal from Obdorsk to the Kara Sea, and gives an instructive account of observations made during his journey in PALLAS, *Reise durch verschiedene Provinzen des russischen Reiches*, St. Petersburg, 1771—76, III. pp. 14—35.

KRUSENSTERN, 1862. `During his second voyage in the Kara Sea, which ended with the abandonment of the ship *Yermak* on the coast of Yalmal in about 69° 54′ N.L., Krusenstern junior escaped with his crew to the shore, reaching it in a completely destitute condition. He had lost all, and would certainly have perished if he had not near the landing-place fallen in with a rich Samoyed, the owner of two thousand reindeer, who received the shipwrecked men in a very friendly way, and conveyed them with his reindeer to Obdorsk, distant in a straight line 500, but, according to the Samoyed's reckoning, 1,000 versts. In the sketch of Krusenstern's travels, to which I have had access, there is unfortunately no information regarding the tribe with which he came in contact during this remarkable journey.[1]

WALDBURG-ZEIL and FINSCH, 1876. A very full and exceedingly interesting description of the natural conditions in the southernmost part of the peninsula is to be found in the accounts of Count Waldburg-Zeil and Dr. Finsch's journey in the year 1876.[2]

SCHWANENBERG, 1877. Captain Schwanenberg landed on the north part of Beli Ostrov during the remarkable voyage which he made in that year from the Yenisej to St. Petersburg. No traces of men, but some of reindeer and bears, were visible. The sea was sufficiently deep close to the shore for vessels of light draught, according to a private communication which I have received from Captain Schwanenberg.

THE SWEDISH EXPEDITION, 1875. During this voyage we landed about the middle of the west coast of Yalmal. In order to give an idea of the nature of the country, I make the following extract from my narrative of the voyage,[3] which has had but a limited circulation :

"In the afternoon of the 8th August I landed, along with

---

[1] Paul von Krusenstern, *Skizzen aus seinem Seemannsleben.* Hirschberg in Silesia. Farther on I intend to give a more detailed account of von Krusenstern's two voyages in the Kara Sea.

[2] *Deutsche Geogr. Blätter* von Lindemann Namens d. Geogr. Gesellsch., Bremen. I. 1877, II. 1878. O. Finsch, *Reise nach West-Sibirien im Jahre 1876.* Berlin, 1879. A bibliographical list has been drawn up by Count von Waldburg-Zeil under the title, *Litteratur-Nachweis für das Gebiet des unteren Ob.*

[3] Nordenskiöld, *Redogörelse för en expedition till mynningen af Jenisej och Sibirien år 1875*, Bih. till Kongl. Vet.-Ak. Handl, vol. iv., No. 1, p. 38–42.

Lundström and Stuxberg, on a headland projecting a little from
Yalmal, on the north side of the mouth of a pretty large river.
The landing place was situated in lat. 72° 18′, long. 68° 42′. The
land was bounded here by a low beach, from which at a distance
of one hundred paces a steep bank rose to a height of from six
to thirty metres.   Beyond this bank there is an extensive,
slightly undulating plain, covered with a vegetation which indeed
was exceedingly monotonous, but much more luxuriant than
that of Vaygats Island or Novaya Zemlya.   The uniformity of
the vegetation is perhaps caused, in a considerable degree, by

PLACE OF SACRIFICE ON YALMAL.
After a drawing by A. N. Lundström.

the uniform nature of the terrain.   There is no solid rock here.
The ground everywhere consists of sand and sandy clay, in which
I could not find a stone so large as a bullet or even 'as a pea,
though I searched for a distance of several kilometres along the
strand-bank.   Nor did the dredge bring up any stones from the
sea-bottom off the coast, a circumstance which, among other
things, is remarkable, because it appears to show that the strand-
ice from the Obi and Yenisej does not drift down to and melt
in this part of the Kara Sea.   Nor do the sand beds contain any
sub-fossil shells, as is the case with the sand beds of the Yenisej

tundra. ' Noah's wood ' also appears to be absent here. To judge from our observations at this place, the peninsula between the Gulf of Obi and the Kara Sea thus differs very essentially from the *tundra* lying east of the Yenisej.

"We saw no inhabitants, but everywhere along the beach numerous traces of men—some of them barefoot—of reindeer, dogs and Samoyed sleighs, were visible. On the top of the strand-bank was found a place of sacrifice, consisting of forty-five bears' skulls of various ages placed in a heap, a large number of reindeer skulls, the lower jaw of a walrus, &c. From most of the bears' skulls the canine teeth were broken out, and the lower jaw was frequently entirely wanting. Some of the bones were overgrown with moss and lay sunk in the earth; others had, as the adhering flesh showed, been placed there during the present year. In the middle of the heap of bones stood four erect pieces of wood. Two consisted of sticks a metre in length with notches cut in them, serving to bear up the reindeer and bears' skulls, which were partly placed on the points of the sticks or hung up by means of the notches, or spitted on the sticks by four-cornered holes cut in the skulls. The two others, which clearly were the proper idols of this place of sacrifice, consisted of driftwood roots, on which some carvings had been made to distinguish the eyes, mouth, and nose. The parts of the pieces of wood, intended to represent the eyes and mouth, had recently been besmeared with blood, and there still lay at the heap of bones the entrails of a newly-killed reindeer. Close beside were found the remains of a fireplace, and of a midden, consisting of reindeer bones of various kinds and the lower jaws of bears.

"As the sandy slopes of the beach offered no suitable breeding-place for looms, black guillemots, or other sea-fowl, and there were no islands along the coast which could serve as breeding-places for eiders and other species of geese which breed in colonies, the abundant bird-life of the Polar Sea was wanting here. At the mouth of the river, however, large flocks of eiders and long-tailed ducks flew about, and on the sandy banks along the shore, flocks of *Calidris arenaria* and a Tringa or two ran about restlessly seeking their food. The solitude of the *tundra* was broken only by a couple of larks and a pair of falcons (*Falco peregrinus*) with young. Traces of reindeer were also seen, and two fox-traps set on the strand-bank showed that foxes occur in these regions in sufficient numbers to be the object of capture.

"Later in the afternoon, when some solar altitudes had been taken, in order to determine the geographical position of the place, we rowed back to our vessel and sailed on, keeping at some distance from the coast, and at one place passing between the shore and a long series of blocks of ground-ice, which had

stranded along the coast in a depth of nine to sixteen metres.
During night we passed a place where five Samoyed tents were
pitched, in whose neighbourhood a large number of reindeer
pastured. The land was now quite low, and the sea had become
considerably shallower. The course was therefore shaped for the
N.W., in which direction deeper water was soon met with.
Notwithstanding the slight salinity and high temperature
($+ 7°·7$) of the surface water a *Clio borealis* and a large number
of Copepoda were taken at the surface."

The excursion now described and Almquist's and Hovgaard's
landing in 1878 were, as far as I am aware, the only occasions
on which naturalists have visited the northern part of that
peninsula which separates the Kara Sea from the Obi. The
Norwegian hunters also visit the place seldom, the main reasons
being the inaccessibility of the shallow east coast, and the want
of harbours. They now, however, land occasionally to take in
water, and perhaps to barter the tobacco they have saved from
their rations, knives they have no use for, and old-fashioned
guns, gunpowder, lead, &c., for the products of the Samoyeds'
reindeer husbandry, hunting and fishing. At first the natives
fled when they saw the Norwegians coming, and, when they
could not make their escape, they saluted them with great
humility, falling on their knees and bending their heads to the
earth, and were unwilling to enter into any traffic with them
or to show them their goods. But since the Samoyeds observed
that the Norwegians never did them any harm, the mistrust
and excessive humility have completely disappeared. Now a
visit of Europeans is very agreeable to them, partly for the
opportunity which it offers of obtaining by barter certain
articles of necessity, luxury, or show, partly perhaps also for
the interruption thereby caused in the monotony of the *tundra*
life. When the walrus-hunters row or sail along that open
coast, it often happens that natives run backwards and forwards
on the shore, and by signs eagerly invite the foreigners to land;
if they do so, and there are any wealthy Samoyeds in the
neighbourhood, there immediately begins a grand entertainment,
according to the customs of the people, with more than one
trait reminding us of the sketches from the traditional periods
of the civilised nations.

What I have stated here is about all that we know of Yalmal,
and we see from this that a very promising, yet untouched field
for researches in ethnography and natural history here lies
before future travellers to the Yenisej.

What sort of winter is there at the mouth of the Yenisej?
We have for the present no information on this point, as no scientific man has wintered there. But on the other hand we have a

very exciting narrative of the wintering of the Fin, NUMMELIN, at the Briochov Islands in the Yenisej in lat. 70° 48' north. I visited the place on the 27th August 1875. It consisted of a fishing post, occupied only in summer, and at that season of the year very attractive, surrounded as it is by luxuriant vegetation of grass and bushes. The houses were situated on a sound running between the Briochov Islands, which form the northernmost group of the labyrinth of islands which occupy the channel of the Yenisej between 69½° and 71° N. L. At the

"JORDGAMMOR" ON THE BRIOCHOV ISLANDS.
After a sketch by the Author.

time of our visit the fishing was over for the season and the place deserted. But two small houses and a number of earth-huts (*jordgammor*), all in good repair, stood on the river bank and gave evidence, along with a number of large boats drawn up on land, and wooden vessels intended for salting fish, of the industry which had been carried on there earlier in the summer. It was at this place that Nummelin passed one of the severest winters that Arctic literature has to record.[1]

[1] I give the particulars of this wintering partly after communications made to me in conversation by Nummelin, partly after *Göteborgs Handels-och Sjöfartstidning* for the 20th and 21st November, 1877. This *first* and, as far as I know, only detailed narrative of the voyage in question, was dictated to the editor of that journal, *reference being made to the log by*

M

In 1876 M. Sidoroff, well known for the lively interest which
he takes in navigation in the Siberian waters, had a ship *Severnoe
Sianie* (the *Aurora*) built and fitted out at Yeniseisk, in order to
carry goods from the Yenisej to Europe. The vessel was placed
under the command of a Russian sea-captain, Schwanenberg.
Under him Nummelin served as mate, and the vessel had a
crew of eighteen men, most of whom had been exiled to Siberia for
crime. In consequence of various mishaps the vessel could not
get farther the first year than to the neighbourhood of the
mouth of the Yenisej, where it was left in winter quarters
at the place which has been named above. Nummelin and
four exiles remained on board, while Schwanenberg and the
rest of the crew returned to Yeniseisk on the 28th September.
Frost had already commenced. During the two following weeks
the temperature kept in the neighbourhood of the freezing
point; clear weather alternating with snow and rain.

On the 5th of October the crew withdrew to their winter
quarters, having previously collected driftwood and placed it
in heaps in order that they might easily find it under the snow.

On the 16th October the thermometer at eight o'clock in the
morning showed − 4·5° and afterwards sank lower every day, until
after the 21st October the mercury for some days was constantly
under − 10°. On the 26th October the temperature was − 18°,
but in the beginning of November it rose again to − 2°. On the
6th November it sank again to − 17°, but rose on the 11th to
− 3·5°. On the 14th November the thermometer showed − 23·5°,
on the 21st − 29·5°. Next day in the morning it stocd at − 32°,
and in the evening at − 37°, but these figures were arrived at
by guess, the instrument not indicating so low temperatures.
This temperature of − 30° to − 32°, varying with frozen
mercury, continued till the end of November, when it rose again
to − 11·5°. At Christmas there was again a temperature of − 31°,
and the six following days the mercury was frozen, with which
the new year came in. The temperature then rose again to − 20°,
but soon sank so that from the 16th January the mercury was
frozen for five days. On the 22nd January the reading was − 9°.
On the 26th the mercury froze again, and on the 29th the temperature was − 6°. During the month of February the temperature
never rose above − 24°; the mercury was frozen on the 20th, 25th,
26th, and 28th. This was the case on the 1st, 3rd, 6th, 7th,
14th, 16th, and 18th March; on the 22nd March the reading
was − 7°, on the 30th − 29°. April began with − 31°, but the
temperature afterwards rose, so that on the 16th it reached − 11°
and varied between − 21° and − 6° (the 25th). On the 2nd May the
reading in the morning and evening was − 12°, at mid-day − 2° to

Schwanenberg and Nummelin. Schwanenberg had come to Gothenburg
some days before with his Yeniseisk-built vessel.

− 5°. On the 8th May it was +0, on the 17th − 10·5°, on the
31st + 0·5°. June began with + 1·5°. On the 8th the reading
at mid-day was + 11°, on the morning and evening of the same
day + 2° to + 3°. During the remainder of June and the month
of July the temperature varied between + 2° and + 21°.

It was in such circumstances that Nummelin and his four
companions lived in the ill-provided house of planks on the
Little Briochov Island. They removed to it, as has been already
said, on the 5th October; on the 20th the ice was so hard frozen
that they could walk upon it. On the 26th snowstorms
commenced, so that it was impossible to go out of the house.

The sun was visible for the last time on the 21st November,
and it reappeared on the 19th January. On the 15th May the
sun no longer set. The temperature was then under the
freezing-point of mercury. That the upper edge of the sun
should be visible on the 19th January we must assume a horizontal refraction of nearly 1°. The islands on the Yenisej are
so low that there was probably a pretty open horizon towards
the south.

Soon after Christmas scurvy began to show itself. Nummelin's companions were condemned and punished criminals, in
whom there was to be expected neither physical nor moral
power of resistance to this disease. They all died, three of
scurvy, and one in the attempt to cross from the Briochov
Islands to a *simovie* at Tolstoinos. In their stead Nummelin
succeeded in procuring two men from Tolstoinos, and later on
one from Goltschicha. On the 11th May a relief party arrived
from the south. It consisted of three men under the mate
Meyenwaldt, whom Sidoroff had sent to help to save the vessel.
They had first to shovel away the snow which weighed it down.
The snow lay nearly six metres deep on the river ice, which
was three metres thick. When they at last had got the vessel
nearly dug out, it was buried again by a new snowstorm.

In the middle of June the ice began to move, and the river
water rose so high that Nummelin, Meyenwaldt, and four men,
along with two dogs, were compelled to betake themselves to
the roof of the hut, where they had laid in a small stock of
provisions and fuel. Here they passed six days in constant
peril of their lives.

The river had now risen five metres ; the roof of the hut rose
but a quarter of a metre above the surface of the swollen river,
and was every instant in danger of being carried away by a
floating piece of ice. In such a case a small boat tied to the
roof was their only means of escape.

The whole landscape was overflowed. The other houses and
huts were carried away by the water and the drifting ice, which
also constantly threatened the only remaining building. The

men on its roof were compelled to work night and day to keep the pieces of ice at a distance with poles.

The great inundation had even taken the migrating birds at unawares. For long stretches there was not a dry spot for them to rest upon, and thus it happened that exhausted ptarmigan alighted among the men on the roof; once a ptarmigan settled on Meyenwaldt's head, and a pair on the dogs.

On the 23rd June the water began to fall, and by the 25th it had sunk so low that Nummelin and his companions could leave the roof and remove to the deserted interior of the house.

The narrative of Nummelin's return to Europe by sea, in company with Schwanenberg, belongs to a following chapter.

CHAPTER V.

The history of the North-East Passage from 1556 to 1878—Burrough, 1556 —Pet and Jackman, 1580—The first voyage of the Dutch, 1594—Oliver Brunel—The second voyage, 1595—The third voyage, 1596—Hudson, 1608 — Gourdon, 1611 — Bosman, 1625 — De la Martinière, 1653— Vlamingh, 1664—Snobberger, 1675—Roule reaches a land north of Novaya Zemlya—Wood and Flawes, 1676 -Discussion in England concerning the state of the ice in the Polar Sea—Views of the condition of the Polar Sea still divided—Payer and Weyprecht, 1872-74.

THE sea which washes the north coast of European Russia is named by King Alfred· (*Orosius*, Book I. Chaps. i. ii.) the Quaen Sea (in Anglo-Saxon *Cwen Sae*),[1] a distinctive name, which unquestionably has the priority, and well deserves to be retained. To the inhabitants of Western Europe the islands Novaya Zemlya and Vaygats, first became known through Stephen Burrough's voyage of discovery in 1556. Burrough therefore is often called the discoverer of Novaya Zemlya, but incorrectly. For when he came thither he found Russian vessels, manned by hunters well acquainted with the navigable waters and the land. It is clear from this that Novaya Zemlya had then already been known to the inhabitants of Northern Russia for such a length of time that a very actively prosecuted hunting could arise there. . It is even probable that in the same way as the northernmost part of Norway was already known for a thousand years back, not only to wandering Lapps, but also to Norwegians and Quaens, the lands round Yugor Schar and Vaygats were known several centuries before Burrough's time, not only to the nomad Samoyeds on the main-

[1] In Bosworth's translation this name is replaced by *White Sea*, an unnecessary modernising of the name, and incorrect besides, as the White Sea is only a bay of the ocean which bounds Europe on the north.

land, but also to various Beorma or Finnish tribes. Probably the Samoyeds then, as now, drove their reindeer herds up thither to pasture on the grassy plains along the coast of the Polar Sea, where they were less troubled by the mosquito and the reindeer fly than further to the south, and probably the wild nomads were accompanied then, as now, by merchants from the more civilised races settled in Northern Russia. The name Novaya Zemlya (New Land), indicates that it was discovered at a later period, probably by Russians, but we know neither when nor how.[1] The narrative of Stephen Burrough's voyage, which like so many others has been preserved from oblivion by Hakluyt's famous collection, thus not only forms a sketch of the first expedition of West-Europeans to Novaya Zemlya, but is also the principal source of our knowledge of the earliest Russian voyages to these regions. I shall on this account go into greater detail in the case of this voyage than in those of the other voyages that will be referred to here.

It is self-evident that the new important commercial treaties, to which Chancelor's discovery of the route from England to the White Sea led, would be hailed with great delight both in England and in Russia, and would give occasion to a number of new undertakings. At first, as early as 1555, there was formed in England a company of "merchant adventurers of England for the discoverie of landes, territories, isles, dominions, and seigniories unknowen," commonly called "the Muscovy Company." Sebastian Cabot, then almost an octogenarian, was appointed governor for the term of his natural life, and a number of privileges were conferred upon it by the rulers both of England and Russia. At the same time negotiators, merchants and inquirers were sent by different ways from England to Russia in order to confirm the amity with that country, and more thoroughly examine the, at least to England, new world, which had now been discovered in the East. But a detailed account of these journeys does not enter into the plan of this work.

With this, however, men were not content. They considered Chancelor's voyage as but the first step to something far more important, namely, the opening of the North-East Passage to China and India. While Chancelor himself the year after his return was sent along with several merchants to the White

---

[1] The Russian chronicles state that the land between the Dwina and the Petchora (Savolotskaja Tchud) was made tributary under the Slavs in Novgorod during the first half of the ninth century. A monastery is spoken of in the beginning of the twelfth century at the mouth of the Dwina, whence we may conclude that the land was even then partly peopled by Russians, but we want trustworthy information as to the time when the Russian-Finnish Arctic voyages began (compare F. Litke, *Vier-malige Reise durch das nördliche Eismeer*. Berlin, 1835, p. 3).

Sea, a further attempt was planned to reach the east coast of
Asia by the same route. A small vessel, the *Searchthrift*, was
fitted out for this purpose and placed under the command of
Stephen Burrough.[1] The most important occurrences during
the voyage were the following :—

On the $\frac{3rd\ May}{23rd\ April}$, 1556, the start was made from Ratcliffe to
Blackwall and Grays. Here Sebastian Cabot came on board,
together with some distinguished gentlemen and ladies. They
were first entertained on board the vessel and gave liberal
presents to the sailors, alms being given at the same time to a
number of poor people in order that they might pray for good
luck and a good voyage ; "then at the signe of the Christopher,
Master Cabot and his friends banketted, and made them that
were in the company great cheere ; and for very joy that he
had to see the towardness of our intended discovery, he entered
into the dance himselfe, amongst the rest of the young and
lusty company." At Orwell Burrough left his own vessel, in
order, at the wish of the merchants, to make the passage to
Vardoehus in the *Edward Bonaventure*. In the end of May
he was off the North Cape, which name Burrough says he
gave to this northernmost headland of Europe during his
first voyage.[2] When Burrough left the *Edward Bonaventure*
and went on board his own vessel is not stated, but on the $\frac{17th}{7th}$
June he replied on the *Searchthrift* to the parting salute of
the *Edward Bonaventure*. On the $\frac{20th}{10th}$ June Kola was reached,
and its latitude fixed at 65° 48'.[3]

"On Thursday the $\frac{21st}{11th}$ June at 6 of the clocke in the morning there came aboord of vs one of the Russe Lodiaes, rowing
with twentie oares, and there were foure and twentie men in
her. The master of the boate presented me with a great loafe
of bread, and six rings of bread, which they call Colaches,
and foure dryed pikes, and a peck of fine otemeale, and I gave

---

[1] The voyage is described in *Hakluyt*, 1st Edition, p. 311. It is inserted
in the list of contents in the following terms : " The voyage of Steven
Burrough towarde the River Ob, intending the discoverie of the north-east
passage. An. 1556." It appears from the introduction to Hakluyt's work
that the narrative was revised by Burrough himself. In the text Burrowe
is written instead of Burrough.

[2] As I have already mentioned, von Herbertstein states that the Russians
(Istoma and others) as early as 1496 sailed round the northern extremity
of Norway in boats, which when necessary could be carried over land.
North Cape, or rather Nordkyn, was called at that time Murmanski Nos (the
Norman Cape). When Hulsius in his collection of travels gives von
Herbertstein's account of Istoma's voyage, he considers Swjatoi Nos on
the Kola peninsula to be North Cape (Hamel, *Tradescant*, St. Petersburg,
1847, p. 40).

[3] This must be a slip of the pen or an error of the press ; it was probably
intended to be 68° 48'. Kola lies in 68° 51' N. L.

vnto the Master of the boate a combe, and a small glasse. He
declared vnto me that he was bound to Pechora, and after that
I made to drinke, the tide being somewhat broken, they gently
departed. The Master's name was Pheother (Feodor). . . .
Thursday (the ²⁰ᵗʰ⁄₁₉ᵗʰJune) we weyed our ankers in the Riuer Cola,
and went into the Sea seuen or eight leagues, where we met
with the winde farre Northerly, that of force it constrained vs
to goe againe backe into the sayd riuer, where came aboord of
vs sundry of their Boates, which declared unto me that they
were also bound to the northwards, a fishing for Morse and
Salmon and gave me liberally of their white and wheaten bread.

"As we roade in this riuer, wee saw dayly comming downe
the riuer many of the Lodias, and they that had least, had
foure and twentie men in them, and at the last they grew to
thirtie saile of them.; and amongst the rest, there was one of
them whose name was Gabriel, who shewed me very much
friendshippe, and he declared vnto mee that all they were
bound to Pechora, a fishing for salmons, and morses : insomuch
that hee shewed mee by demonstrations, that with a faire winde
we had seuen or eight dayes sailing to the riuer Pechora, so
that I was glad of their company. This Gabriel promised to
giue mee warning of shoales, as he did indeede. . . . Sunday
being the one and twentieth day [of June, 1st July new style],
Gabriel gaue mee a barrell of Meade, and one of his speciall
friends gaue me a barrell of beere, which was caryed upon
mens backs at least 2 miles.

"Munday we departed. from. the riuer Cola, with all the rest
of the said Lodias, but sailing before the wind they were all
too good for vs :¹ but according to promise, this Gabriel and his
friend did often strike their sayles, and taryed for us forsaking
their owne company. Tuesday at an Eastnortheast sunne we
were thwart of Cape St. John.² It is to be vnderstood, that
from the Cape S. John vnto the riuer or bay that goeth to
Mezen, it is all sunke land, and full of shoales and dangers,

¹ This statement is very remarkable. For it shows that the vessels,
that were then used by the Russians and Fins, were not very inferior as
compared with those of the West-Europeans, which is confirmed by the
fact, among others, that, nowhere in accounts of the voyages of the
English or Dutch in former times to Novaya Zemlya, do we find it stated
that in respect to navigation they were very superior to the Kola men.
As the Russian-Finnish *lodjas* of the time were probably beyond the
influence of the shipbuilding art of Western Europe, it is of importance to
collect all that is known about the way in which these vessels were built.
Several drawings of them occur in the accounts of the Dutch voyages, but
it is uncertain how far they are accurate. According to these the *lodja*
was klinker-built, with boards not riveted together but bound fast with
willows, as is still occasionally practised in these regions. The form of
the craft besides reminds us of that of the present walrus-hunting sloop.
² Cape Woronov, on the west side of the mouth of the river Mesen.

you shall haue scant two fadome water and see no land. And
this present day wee came to an anker thwart of a creeke,
which is 4 or 5 leagues to the northwards of the sayd Cape,
into which creeke Gabriel and his fellows rowed, but we could
not get in : and before night there were about 20 saile that
went into the sayd creeke, the wind being at the Northeast.
We had indifferent good landfang. This afternoone Gabriel
came aboord with his skiffe, and then I rewarded him for the
good company that he kept with vs ouer the Shoales, with two
small iuory combes, and a steele glasse with two or three trifles

RUSSIAN "LODJA."
After G. de Veer.

more, for which he was not ungratefull. But notwithstanding, his first company had gotten further to the Northwards.
Wednesday being Midsummer day we sent our skiffe aland to
sound the creeke, where they found it almost drie at a low
water. And all the Lodias within were on ground. (In consequence of the threatening appearance of the weather Burrough determined to go into the bay at high water. In
doing so he ran aground, but got help from his Russian
friends.) Gabriel came out with his skiffe, and so did sundry
others also, shewing their good will to help us, but all to no
purpose, for they were likely to have bene drowned for their

labour, insomuch that I desired Gabriel to lend me his
anker, because our owne ankers were too big for our skiffe
to lay out, who sent me his owne, and borrowed another also
and sent it vs."

After much trouble Burrough succeeded in getting his vessel
off the shoal, and then sought for a better anchorage on the
other side of Cape St. John.

"Friday ($\frac{\text{6th July}}{\text{26th June}}$) at afternoone we weyed, and departed from
thence, the wether being mostly faire, and the winde at East-
southeast, and plied for the place where we left our cable and
anker, and our hawser, and as soone as we were at an anker the
foresaid Gabriel came aboord of vs, with 3 or foure more of
their small boats, and brought with them of their Aquauitæ
and Meade, professing unto me very much friendship, and
reioiced to see vs againe, declaring that they earnestly thought
that we had bene lost. This Gabriel declared vnto me that
they had saued both the ankers and our hauser, and after we
had thus communed, I caused 4 or 5 of them to goe into
my cabbin, where I gaue them figs and made them such cheere
as I could. While I was banketing of them, there came
another of their Skiffes aboord with one who was a Kerill
(Karelian), whose name afterwards I learned, and that he
dwelt in Colmogro, and Gabriel dwelled in the towne of Cola,
which is not far from the river's mouth. This foresaid Keril
said vnto me that one of the ankers which I borrowed was his.
I gaue him thanks for the lone of it, thinking it had bene
sufficient. And as I continued in our accustomed maner, that
if the present which they brought were worth entertainment,
they had it accordingly, he brought nothing with him, and
therfore I regarded him but litle. And thus we ended, and
they took their leaue and went ashore. At their comming
ashore, Gabriel and Keril were at vnconvenient words, and by
the eares, as I vnderstand; the cause was because the one had
better enterteinment than the other; but you shal vnderstand
that Gabriel was not able to make his party good, because
there were 17 lodias of the Keril's company who tooke
his part, and but 2 of Gabriel's company. The next high
water Gabriel and his company departed from thence, and
rowed to their former company and neighbours, which were
in number 28 at the least, and all of them belonging to
the river Cola. And as I vnderstood Keril made reckoning
that the hauser which was fast in his anker should have bene
his owne, and at first would not deliver it to our boat, insomuch
that I sent him worde that I would complain vpon him, whereupon he deliuered the hauser to my company. The next day

being Saturday, I sent our boat on shore to fetch fresh water
and wood, and at their comming on shore this Keril welcomed
our men most gently, and also banketed them, and in the
meanetime caused some of his men to fill our baricoes with
water, and to help our men to beare wood into their boat; and
then he put on his best silke coate, and his collar of pearles
and came aboorde againe,, and brought his present with him :
and thus having more respect vnto his present than to his
person, because I perceiued him to be vain-glorious, I bade
him welcome and gaue him a dish of figs ; and then he
declared vnto me that his father was a gentleman, and that he
was able to shew me pleasure, and not. Gabriel, who was but a
priest's sonne."

After Burrough has given account of a storm, during which
he lost a jolly boat, which he had purchased at Vardoehus, and
by which they were detained some time in the neighbourhood
of Cape St. John (whose latitude was fixed at 66° 50') he
continues :—

"Saturday (the $\frac{14}{24}$th July) at a Northnorthwest sunne the
wind came at Eastnortheast, and then we weied, and plied to
the Northwards, and as we were two leagues shot past the
Cape, we saw a house standing in a valley, which is dainty to
be seene in those parts and by and by I saw three men on the
top of the hil. Then I iudged them, as it afterwards proued,
that they were men which came from some other place to set
traps to take vermin [1] for their furres, which traps we did
perceiue very thicke alongst the shore as we went."

The 14th to the 19th July, new style, were passed on the
coast of Kanin Nos.[2] On the 19th at noon Burrough was in
lat. 68° 40' north. On Friday, the $\frac{19}{20}$th July another storm
appeared to threaten.

" And as I was musing what was best to be done, I saw a sail
come out of a creeke under the foresayd Caninoz, which was
my friend Gabriel, who forsook his harborough and company,
and came as neere us as he might, and pointed vs to the
Eastwards, and then we weyed and followed him. Saturday we
went eastsoutheast and followed Gabriel, and he brought vs
into an harborough called Morgiouets, which is 30 leagues from
Caninoz. This morning Gabriel saw a smoke on ye way,
who rowed vnto it with his skiffe, which smoke was two leagues

---

[1] Probably mountain foxes. Remains of these fox-traps are still
frequently met with along the coast of the Polar Sea, where the Russians
have carried on hunting.
[2] Kanin Nos is in 68° 30' N. L.

from the place where we road; and at a Northwest sunne
he came aboord again, and brought with him a Samoed,[1] which
was but a young man; his apparell was then strange vnto vs,
and he presented me with three young wild geese, and one
young barnacle."

On the $\frac{24th}{14th}$ July Burrough sailed past Dolgoi Island, and the
following day entered the mouth of the Petchora, the latitude
of which was fixed at 69° 10'.[2] On the $\frac{30th}{20th}$ they sailed out
again over sandbanks in only five feet of water, and thanked
God that their vessel was of so light draught. The day after
ice was met with for the first time. On the $\frac{4th Aug.}{6th July}$ in lat.
70° 20' north, they had the meeting already described with an
enormous whale.[3] Somewhat later on the same day the
Searchthrift anchored in a good haven between two islands,
situated in 70° 42' N. L.[4] They were named by Burrough
St. James's Islands.

"Tuesday, the $\frac{7th Aug.}{28th July}$ we plyed to the Westwards alongst
the shoare, the wind being at Northwest, and as I was about
to come to anker, we saw a sail comming about the point
whereunder we thought to have ankered. Then I sent a skiffe
aboorde of him, and at their comming aboord, they tooke
acquaintance of them, and the chiefe man said hee had bene
in our company in the riuer Cola, and also declared vnto them
that we were past the way which should bring vs to the Ob.
This land, sayd he, is called Nova Zembla, that is to say, the
New Land; and then he came aboord himselfe with his skiffe he
told me the like . . . he made me also certaine demonstrations
of the way to the Ob. I gave him a steele glasse, two pewter
spoons, and a paire of veluet sheathed knives; and then he
seemed somewhat the more willing to tary and shewed me as
much as he knew for our purpose; he also gave me 17
wild geese: . . . This man's name was Loshak. Wednesday, as we plied to Eastwards, we espied another saile, which
was one of this Loshak's company, and we bare roome and
spake with him, who in like sort tolde us of the Ob, as the other
had done. . . . Friday (the $\frac{10th Aug.}{31st July}$) the gale of winde began to
increase, and came Westerly withall, so that by a Northwest
sunne we were at an anker among the Islands of Waigats,
where we saw two small lodias; the one of them came aboord
of us and presented me with a great loafe of bread; and they told

---

[1] This was the first meeting between West-Europeans and Samoyeds.
[2] The capes which bound the mouth of the Petchora—Cape Ruski
Savorot and Cape Medinski Savorot,—are very nearly in lat. 69°.
[3] See above, page 129.
[4] Evidently islands near the southern extremity of Novaya Zemlya.

me they were all of Colmogro, except one man that dwelt at
Pechora, who seemed to be the chiefest among them in killing
of the Morse.[1] There were some of their company on shoare
which did chase a white beare ouer the high clifs into the
water, which beare the lodia that was aboord of us killed in
our sight. This day there was a great gale of wind at North,
and we saw so much ice driving a seaboord that it was then no
going to sea."

During the first days of August the vessel lay for the most
part in company with or in the neighbourhood of Loshak,
who gave them information about the Samoyeds, after which
Burrough visited their sacrificial places.[2]

"Tuesday (the ¹⁴th) August we turned for the harborough
where Loshak's barke lay;[3] where, as before, we road vnder an
Island. And there he came aboord of vs and said vnto me : if
God send wind and weather to serve, I will go to the Ob with
you, because the Morses were scant at these Islands of Vaigats ;
but if he could not get to the riuer of Ob, then he sayd hee
would goe to the riuer of Narainzay,[4] where the people were not
altogether so savage as the Samoyds of the Ob are : hee
shewed me that they will shoot at all men to the vttermost of
their power, that cannot speake their speech."

On the ⁶th of August much ice was seen to drift towards the
haven where the vessel lay, wherefore Burrough removed back
to the place where he had lain a few days before, and whose
latitude he now found to be 70° 25'. Loshak left him unexpectedly the following day, while Burrough was taking solar
altitudes, and on the ⁶th Burrough too weighed anchor to sail
south along the coast of Vaygats. After sailing about in these
waters for a time, and being exposed to a severe storm with
an exceedingly heavy sea, Burrough, on the ³rd Sept./²³rd Aug., determined to
turn. On the ²¹st September he arrived at Colmogro, where
he wintered with a view to continue his voyage next year to
the Obi. This voyage, however, was abandoned, because he
instead went westwards in order to search for two of the ships

[1] Probably he was of Finnish race. The Quaens in North Norway are
still the most skilful harpooners. In recent times they have found rivals
in skill with the harpoon and gun in the Lapps.
[2] The information Burrough obtained regarding the Samoyeds is given
above at page 80.
[3] From the context, and the circumstance that "much ice was drifting
in the sea," we may conclude that this haven was situated on the north
side of the island at the entrance to the Kara Port.
[4] Probably the river which on Massa's map is called Narontza, and
debouches on the west coast of Yalmal.

which accompanied Chancelor, and which had been lost during the return voyage from Archangel.[1]

From this narrative we see that a highly developed Russian or Russian-Finnish navigation was carried on as early as the middle of the fifteenth century between the White Sea, the Petchora, Vaygats, and Novaya Zemlya, and that at that time the Russians or Finns even sailed to the Obi. The sketch, which Burrough gives of the Russian or Russian-Finnish hunters, shows, besides, that they were brave and skilful seamen, with vessels which for the time were very good, and even superior to the English in sailing before the wind. With very few alterations this sketch might also be applied to the present state of things in these regions, which shows that they continue to stand at a point which was then high, but is now low. Taking a general view of matters, it appears as if these lands had rather fallen behind than advanced in well-being during the last three hundred years.

To judge by a letter from the Russian Merchant Company, which was formed in London, it was at his own instance that Stephen Burrough in 1557 sailed from Colmogro, not to Obi,

[1] All the three vessels that were employed in the first English expedition to the North-east had an unfortunate fate, viz. :

The *Edward Bonaventure*, commanded by Chancelor and Burrough, sailed in 1553 from England to the White Sea, returned to England in 1554, and was on the way plundered by the Dutch (*Purchas*, iii. p. 250); started again with Chancelor for the Dwina in 1555, and returned the same year to England under Captain John Buckland ; accompanied Burrough in 1556 to the Kola peninsula; went thence to the Dwina to convey to England Chancelor and a Russian embassy, consisting of the ambassador Ossip Gregorjevitsch Nepeja and a suite of sixteen men ; the vessel besides being laden with goods to the value of 20,000*l.* It was wrecked in the neighbourhood of Aberdeen (Aberdour Bay) on the 20th (10th) November. Chancelor himself, his wife, and seven Russians were drowned, and most of the cargo lost.

The *Bona Esperanza,* admiral of the fleet during the expedition of 1553. Its commander and whole crew perished, as has been already stated, of disease at Arzina on the coast of Kola in the beginning of 1554. The vessel was saved and was to have been used in 1556 to carry to England the Russian embassy already mentioned. After having been driven by a storm into the North Sea, it reached a harbour in the neighbourhood of Trondhjem, but after leaving that harbour disappeared completely, nothing being known of its fate.

The *Bona Confidentia* was saved like the *Bona Esperanza* after the disastrous wintering at Arzina; was also used in conveying the Russian embassy from Archangel in 1556, but stranded on the Norwegian coast, every man on board perishing and the whole cargo being lost.

Of the four vessels that left the Dwina on the 2nd August, 1556, only the *Philip and Mary* succeeded, after wintering at Trondhjem, in reaching the Thames on the 28th (18th) April, 1557. (A letter of Master Henrie Lane to the worshipfull Master William Sanderson, containing a brief discourse of that which passed in the north-east discoverie, for the space of three and thirtie yeeres, *Purchas,* iii. p. 249.)

but to the coast of Russian Lapland to search for the lost
vessels.[1] The following year the English were so occupied with
their new commercial treaties with Russia and with the fitting
out of Frobisher's three expeditions to the north-west, that it
was long before a new attempt was made in the direction of the
north-east, namely, till ARTHUR PET'S voyage in 1580.[2] He was
the first who penetrated from Western Europe into the Kara
Sea, and thus brought the solution of the problem of the
North-east Passage to the Pacific a good way forward. The
principal incidents of this voyage too must therefore be briefly
stated here.

PET and JACKMAN, the former in the *George*, the latter in the
William, sailed from Harwich on the $\frac{9th June}{30th May}$ 1580. On the
$\frac{2nd July}{22nd June}$ they doubled the North Cape, and on the $\frac{12th}{2nd}$ July, Pet
was separated from Jackman after appointing to meet with him
at "Verove Ostrove or Waygats." On the $\frac{15}{5}$th land was in
sight, the latitude having the preceding day been ascertained
to be 71° 38'. Pet was thus at Gooseland, on the west coast
of Novaya Zemlya. He now sailed E.S.E., and fell in with ice
on the $\frac{16}{6}$th July. On the $\frac{20}{10}$th July, land was seen, and the
vessel anchored at an island, probably one of the many small
islands in the Kara Port, where wood and water were taken
on board.

On the $\frac{24}{14}$th July, Pet was in the neighbourhood of land in
70° 26'. At first he thought that the land was an island, and
endeavoured to sail round it, but as he did not succeed in doing
so, he supposed it to be Novaya Zemlya. Hence he sailed in
different directions between S.W. and S.E., and was on the
$\frac{26}{16}$th in 69° 40' N. L. Next day there was lightning with showers
of rain. Pet believed himself now to be in Petchora Bay, and
after sighting, on the $\frac{28}{18}$th July, the headland which bounds the
mouth of the river on the north-east, he sailed, it would seem,
between this headland and the Selenetz Island into the great
bay east of Medinski Savorot. Here he made soundings on
the supposition that the sound between Vaygats Island and the

---

[1] Hamel, *Tradescant der ältere*, p. 106. Hakluyt, 1st edition, p. 326.
The voiage of the foresaid M. Stephen Burrough An. 1557 *from Colmogro to
Wardhouse, &c.* This voyage of Burrough has attracted little attention;
from it however we learn that the Dutch even at that time carried on an
extensive commerce with Russian Lapland. In the same narrative there
is also a list of words with statements of prices and suitable goods for
trade with the inhabitants of the Kola peninsula.

[2] Two accounts of this voyage are to be found in Hakluyt's collection
(pp. 466 and 476). A copy of Pet's own journal was discovered some
years ago, along with other books, frozen in among the remains of
Barents' wintering on the north-east side of Novaya Zemlya. It has not
been published, but is in the possession of Consul Rein at Hammerfest.

mainland would open out at this place, but the water was found to be too shallow, even for a boat. Pet now sailed past Yugor Schar along the coast of Vaygats towards Novaya Zemlya, to a bay on the west coast of Vaygats Island, where he anchored between two small islands, which were supposed to be Woronski Ostrov. *The entrance to an excellent haven was indicated on both sides by two crosses.*[1] On the islands there was abundance of driftwood, and on one of them was found a cross, at the foot of which a man was buried. Pet inscribed his name on the cross, and likewise on a stone at the foot of the cross, "in order that Jackman, if he came thither, might know that Pet had been there." In the afternoon Pet again weighed anchor, doubled the western extremity of Vaygats Island, and continued his voyage, following all along the coast of Vaygats, first to the north and north-east, then to the south, between an ice-field and the land, until the ice came so close to the shore that the vessel could make no headway, when he anchored in a good haven by an island which lay on the east side of Vaygats in the neighbourhood of the mainland. It was perhaps the island which in recent maps is called Mestni island. Pet was thus now in the Kara Sea.[2] The latitude given— 69° 14'—shows even, if it is correct, that he went far into the bay at the mouth of the Kara river. Here Pet fell in with his comrade Jackman, from whom he had parted on the coast of Kola, and of whose voyage during the interval we know nothing. When the vessels met they were both damaged by ice. As in addition, the sea to the north and east was barred by compact masses of ice, the captains, after deliberating with the inferior officers, determined to return. They had, also, during the return voyage, to contend with formidable ice obstacles, until, on the $\frac{25}{15}$th August, in Lat. 69° 49' north, near the south-eastern extremity of Vaygats they met with open water. They sailed along the east coast of Vaygats through the Kara Port, which was passed on the $\frac{27}{17}$th August. Hence the course was shaped for Kolgujev Island, on whose sandbanks both vessels

---

[1] The Russians had thus landmarks on Novaya Zemlya 300 years ago.

[2] It is commonly assumed that Pet sailed into the Kara Sea through Yugor Schar, but that this was not the case is shown partly by the fact that he never speaks of sailing through a long and narrow sound, partly by the account of the many islands which he saw in his voyage, and partly by the statement that coming from the south he sailed round the western-most promontory of Vaygats Island. If we except small rocks near the shore, there are no islands off the southern part of Vaygats Island. In sailing east of Medinski Savorot, Pet took the land south of Yugor Schar for Vaygats, and the soundings on the 29th (19th) July were carried out undoubtedly in the mouth of some small river debouching there.

ran aground, but were soon got off again without loss. The latitude of the sandbanks was correctly fixed at 68° 48'.

On the $\frac{1st Sept.}{22nd Aug.}$ the *William* was again lost sight of.[1] On the $\frac{8th Sept.}{29th Aug.}$ the *George* anchored in Tana Fiord, on which there was a town named Hungon.[2] Two days afterwards the *George* doubled the North Cape, and on the $\frac{5th Nov.}{26th Oct.}$ again anchored at Ratcliffe.

Pet and Jackman were the first north-east explorers who ventured themselves in earnest amongst the drift-ice. In navigating among ice they showed good judgment and readiness of resource, and in the history of navigation the honour falls to them of having commanded the first vessels from Western Europe that forced their way into the Kara Sea. It is therefore without justification that BARROW says of them that they were but indifferent navigators.[3]

With Pet and Jackman's voyage the English North-East Passage expeditions were broken off for a long time. But the problem was, instead, taken up with great zeal in Holland. Through the fortunate issue of the war of freedom with Spain, and the incitement to enterprise which civil freedom always brings along with it, Holland, already a great industrial and commercial state, had begun, towards the close of the sixteenth century, to develop into a maritime power of the first rank. But navigation to India and China was then rendered impossible for the Dutch, as for the English, by the supremacy of Spain and Portugal at sea, and through the endeavours of these countries to retain the sole right to the commercial routes they had discovered. In order to become sharers in the great profits which commerce with the land of silks and perfumes brought with it, it therefore appeared to be indispensable to discover

---

[1] Of Jackman Hakluyt says (2nd Edition, i. p. 453): "William with Charles Jackman came to a haven in Norway between Tronden and Rostock in October, 1580, and wintered there. Thence the following February he went with a vessel, belonging to the king of Denmark, to Iceland, and since then nothing has been heard of him." About that time an English ship stranded at the Ob, and the crew were killed by the Samoyeds. It has been conjectured that it possibly was Jackman (compare *Purchas*, iii. p. 546; *Hamel*, p. 238). It is more probable that the vessel which suffered this fate was that which, two years before Pet and Jackman's voyage, appears to have been sent out by the Muscovy Company to penetrate eastwards from the Petchora. The members of this expedition were James Bassendine, James Woodcocke, and Richard Brown, but we know nothing concerning it except the very sensible and judicious rules that were drawn up for the expedition (*Hakluyt*, 1st Edition, p. 406).

[2] I have not been able to find any name resembling this on modern maps.

[3] *A Chronological History of Voyages into the Arctic Regions.* London. 1818, p. 99.

a new sea route north of Asia or America to the Eastern seas. If such a route had been actually found, it was clear that the position of Holland would have been specially favourable for undertaking this lucrative trade. In this state of things we have to seek for the reason of the delight with which the Dutch hailed the first proposal to force a passage by sea north of Asia to China or Japan. Three successive expeditions were at great expense fitted out for this purpose. These expeditions did not, indeed, attain the intended goal—the discovery of a north-eastern sea route to Eastern Asia, but they not only gained for themselves a prominent place in the history of geographical discovery, but also repaid a hundred fold the money that had been spent on them, in part directly through the whale-fishing to which they gave rise, and which was so profitable to Holland, and in part indirectly through the elevation they gave to the self-respect and national feeling of the people. They compared the achievements of their countrymen among the ice and snow of the Polar lands to the voyage of the Argonauts, to Hannibal's passage of the Alps, and to the campaign of the Macedonians in Asia and the deserts of Libya (see, for instance, BLAVIUS, *Atlas major*, Latin edition, t. i., pp. 24 and 31). As these voyages together present the grandest attempts to solve the problem that lay before the *Vega* expedition, I shall here give a somewhat detailed account of them.

NAVARCHVS
HOLLANDVS

DUTCH SKIPPER.
After G. de Veer.

THE FIRST DUTCH EXPEDITION, 1594.—This was fitted out at the expense of private persons, mainly by the merchants BALTHASAR MUCHERON, JACOB VALCKE, and FRANCISCUS MAELSON. The first intention was to send out only two vessels with the view of forcing a passage through the sound at Vaygats towards the east, but on the famous geographer PLANCIUS representing that the route north of Novaya Zemlya was that which would lead most certainly to the desired goal, other two were fitted out, so that no fewer than four vessels went out in the year 1594 on an exploratory expedition towards the north. Of these, two, viz. a large vessel, specially equipped,

N

it would appear, for the northern waters, called the *Mercurius*, and commanded by WILLEM BARENTS,[1] and a common fishing sloop, attempted the way past the northern extremity of Novaya Zemlya. The two others, viz. the *Swan* of Zeeland, commanded by CORNELIUS CORNELISZ. NAY, and the *Mercurius* of Enkhuizen, commanded by BRANDT YSBRANDTSZ. TETGALES, were to pass through the sound at Vaygats Island.

All the four vessels left the Texel on the ⅕th June, and eighteen days later arrived at Kilduin in Russian Lapland, a place where at that time vessels, bound for the White Sea, often called. Here the two divisions of the expedition parted company.

Barents sailed to Novaya Zemlya, which was reached on the ¹⁴⁄₇th July in 73° 25'; the latitude was determined by measuring the altitude of the midnight sun at an island which was called Willem's Island. Barents sailed on along the coast in a northerly direction, and two days afterwards reached the latitude of 75° 54' north. On the ¹⁹⁄₇th July there was a remarkable chase of a Polar bear. The bear was fallen in with on land and was pierced by a bullet, but notwithstanding this he threw himself into the water, and swam with a vigour "that surpassed all that had been heard of the lion or other wild animal." Some of the crew pursued him in a boat, and succeeded in casting a noose round his neck in order to catch him living, with a view to carry him to Holland. But when the bear knew that he was caught "he roared and threw himself about so violently that it can scarcely be described in words." In order to tire him they gave him a little longer line, rowing forward slowly the while, and Barents at intervals struck him with a rope. Enraged at this treatment, the bear swam to the boat, and caught it with one of his forepaws, on which Barents said: "he wishes to rest himself a little." But the bear had another object in view, for he cast himself into the boat with such violence that half his body was soon within it. The sailors were so frightened that they rushed to the fore and thought that their last hour was come. Fortunately the bear could make no further advance, because the noose that was

---

[1] His proper name was Willem Barentszoon; it was also written Barentz, Barendsz, Bernardsson, &c. Barents' three voyages formed the subject of a work by GERRIT DE VEER, which was published for the first time in 1598 at Amsterdam in a Dutch, a Latin, and a French edition. The last-mentioned has the following title: *Vray Description de Trois Voyages des Mer très admirables faicts . . . par les navires d'Hollande & Zelande au nord . . . vers les Royaumes de China & Catay, etc.* Afterwards this work was frequently reprinted in different languages, both singly and in DE BRY'S, PURCHAS', and other collections of travels. See on this point P. A. Tiele, *Mémoire bibliographique sur les journaux des navigateurs Néerlandais.* Amsterdam, 1867.

thrown round his neck had fastened in the rudder. A sailor taking courage, now went aft and killed the bear with the stroke of an axe. The skin was sent to Amsterdam. On account of this occurrence the place was called " Bear Cape."

Barents sailed on towards the north and north-east, past the place which he called Cruys Eylandt (Cross Island)[1] and Cape Nassau, a name which has been retained in recent maps, to the latitude of 77° 55', which was reached on the $\frac{23rd}{13th}$ July. Here from the mast-top an ice-field was seen, which it was impossible to see beyond, which compelled Barents to turn. However, he still remained in these northern regions, waiting for a better state of the ice, till the $\frac{8th\ August}{29th\ July}$, when the vessel was due west

CAPTURE OF A POLAR BEAR.
After G. de Veer.

of a promontory situated in latitude 77° north, which was named Ice Cape. Some gold-glittering stones were found here on the ground. Such *finds* have played a not inconsiderable *rôle* in the history of Arctic voyages, and shiploads of worthless ore have on several occasions been brought home. On the $\frac{10th\ August}{31st\ July}$, while sailing among the Orange Islands, they saw 200 walruses on land. The sailors attacked them with axes and lances, without killing a single walrus, but they succeeded during the attempt to kill them in striking out several tusks, which they carried home with them.

Convinced that he could not reach the intended goal by this

---

[1] From two large crosses which were found erected on the island. This shows that the Russians had also explored the north part of Novaya Zemlya before the West-Europeans.

N 2

northern route, Barents determined, after consulting with his
men, to turn south and sail to Vaygats. While sailing down,
Barents, in latitude 71° north, makes the remark that he was
now probably at a place where OLIVER BRUNEL [1] had been
before, and which had been named by him Costinsark, evidently
the present Kostin Schar, a Russian name still in use for the
sound which separates Meschduschar Island from the main
island. It ought to be observed, however, that on old maps

[1] The name Oliver Brunel occurs so often in accounts of the first voyages
to Novaya Zemlya, and the man who bore it appears to have exercised so
great an influence on the development of commercial communications with
Russia, and the sending out of exploratory expeditions to the North Polar
Sea, that I shall give a brief sketch of his life, mainly after S. Muller,
Geschiedenis der Noordsche Compagnie, Utrecht, 1874, p. 26.

Oliver Brunel was born in Brussels, and in 1565 went in a Russian
vessel from Kola to Kolmogor in order to learn the Russian language and
make himself acquainted with the trade of the region. But the English,
who of course eagerly endeavoured to prevent any intrusion on their
newly-discovered commercial territory, prevailed on the Russians to keep
him in prison for several years. In the end he was set at liberty, or rather
handed over to the rich merchants Jakov and Grigory Anikiev (Stroganov).
In consequence of this, Brunel came to take part in the commercial
expeditions sent out by this mercantile house (which by the conquest of
Siberia acquired a world-historical importance, both by land and sea), to
the parts of Asia bordering on Russia, whereby he became well acquainted
with the Polar Sea and the Gulf of Obi. Brunel afterwards brought about
direct communication between the Netherlands and the great commercial
house, almost sovereign *de facto* if not *de jure* in extensive countries. In
connection with this Brunel made strenuous exertions to open in earnest the
navigation of the Netherlands to the White Sea, and there found a
Netherlands factory, which was placed not on Rosen Island, which was
occupied by the English, but on the spot where the present Archangel is
situated. Brunel next took part in preparations for a Russian North-east
expedition, for which Swedish shipbuilders were received into Stroganov's
service. Brunel himself travelled by land to Holland to enlist men. A
number of particulars regarding these undertakings of Brunel are contained in a letter of JOHN BALAK to GERARD MERCATOR, dated "Arusburgi
ad Ossellam fluvium" the 20th February, 1581. The letter is printed in
the second edition of *Hakluyt*, 1598, i. p. 509. Scarcely however had
Brunel returned to his native country, before he altered his plan and
wished to procure for his own fatherland the honour and advantage of the
undertaking. The first attempt of the Dutch to reach China and Japan by
the north-east thus came about. Of this voyage we know only that Brunel
endeavoured without success to sail through Yugor Schar, and that his
vessel, heavily laden with furs, plates of mica, and rock-crystal, was
wrecked on the way home at the mouth of the Petchora (*Beschryvinghe
vander Samoyeden Landt in Tartarien, &c.* Amsterdam, 1612. S. Muller's
Photolithographic Reproduction, 1878). The mica and rock-crystal were
undoubtedly brought from the Ural, as no useful plates of mica or large
rock-crystals are found in the region of the Petchora. Brunel then entered
the Danish service. For we know that an Oliver Brunel during the reign
of King Fredrik II. in Denmark offered to explore Greenland, and for that
purpose in 1583 obtained the right to settle in Bergen and there enjoy six
years freedom from taxes (Cf. *Groenlands historiske Mindesmærker*, Copenhagen, 1838, vol. iii. p. 666).

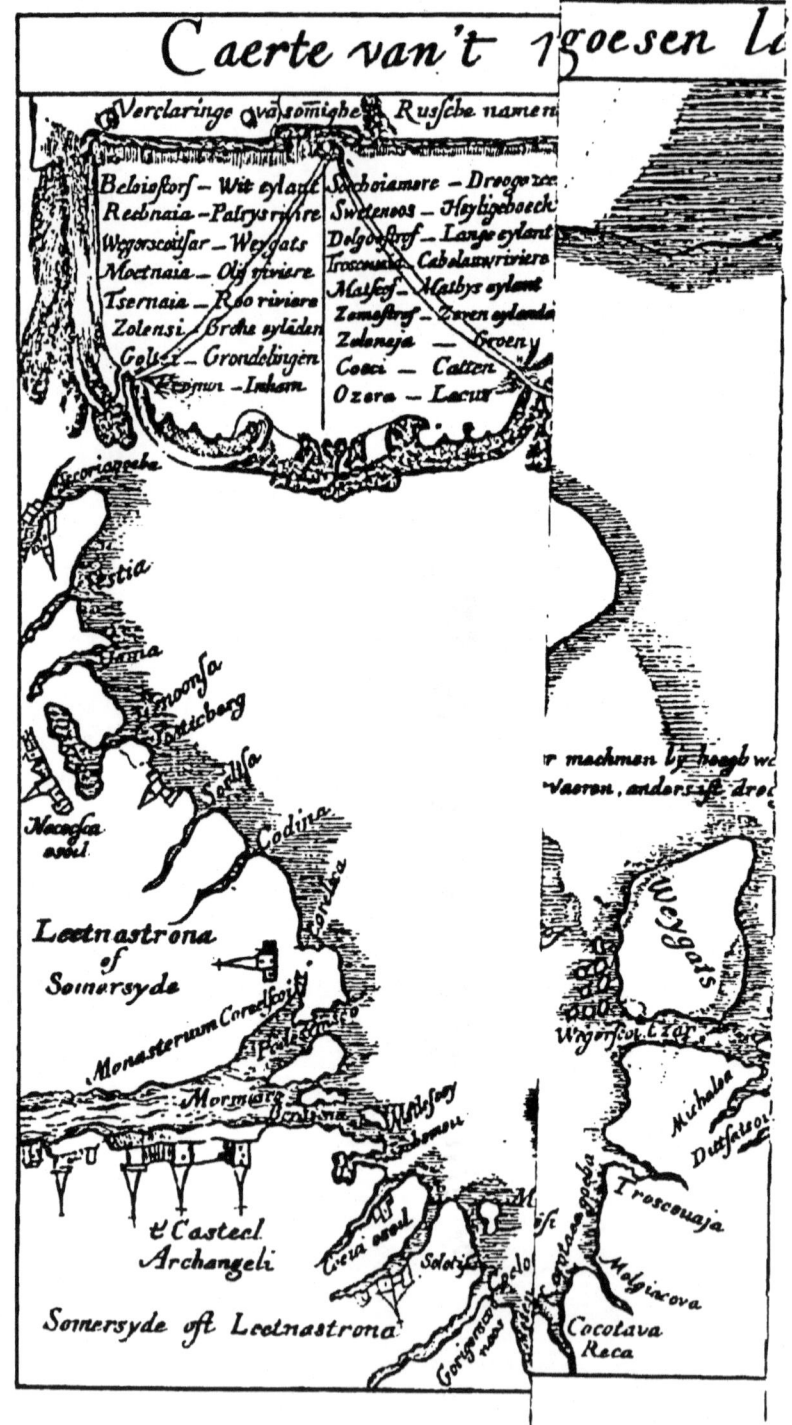

Caerte van 't goesen la

Verclaringe va somighe Russche namen

Beloiosforf — Wit eylant   Sucheiamere — Dreogeree
Reebnaia — Palrysrivire   Sweteneos — Heyligeboeck
Wegorscoiisar — Weygats   Dolgosforf — Lange eylant
Moetnaia — Olij riviere   Iroscena — Cabelaureriviere
Tsernaia — Roo riviere   Matseof — Mathys eylant
Zolensi — Broke eyladen   Zemaftrof — Zeven eylanden
Golsi — Grondelingen   Zolenaja — Groeny
Reynun — Inham   Cosci — Catten
                 Ozera — Lacus

Goriapeehe

stia

noonsa
icberg

Solsa

Codina

Necogsa
aeel

Leetnastrona
of
Somersyde

Monasterium Coredfoii

Mormere

t'Casteel
Archangeli

Somersyde oft Leetnastrona

machmen by hoogh wa
vaeren, anders de droe

Weygats

Wgorscoi.iqi

Michalea
Dufsateoi

Troscouaja

Melgicova

Cocotava
Reca

Zatotschkin Schar is often marked with some perversion of the word Kostin Schar.

South of "St. Laurens Bay,"[1] in 70⅘°, Barents, on the 21st/11th August, found upon a headland a cross erected, and in the neighbourhood of it three wooden buildings, the hull of a Russian vessel and several sacks of meal, and at the same place some graves, all clearly remains of some Russian salmon-fishers. On the 5th August he arrived at Dolgoi Island, where he fell in with the two other vessels from Zeeland and Enkhuizen that had come thither shortly before. All the four vessels sailed back thence to Holland, arriving there in the middle of September. The narrative of this voyage closes with the statement that Barents brought home with him a walrus, which had been fallen in with and killed on the drift-ice. Barents during this journey discovered and explored the northern part of Novaya Zemlya, never before visited by West-European seafarers.

The two other vessels, that left the Texel at the same time as Barents, also made a remarkable voyage, specially sketched by the distinguished voyager JAN HUYGHEN VAN LINSCHOTEN.[2]

The vessels were manned by fifty men, among them two interpreters—a Slav, CHRISTOFFEL SPLINDLER, and a Dutch merchant, who had lived long in Russia, FR. DE LA DALE. Provisions for eight months only were taken on board. At first Nay and Tetgales accompanied Barents to Kilduin, which island is delineated and described in considerable detail in Linschoten's work.

On the 12th/2nd July Nay and Tetgales sailed from Kilduin for Waygats Island. Three days afterwards they fell in with much drift-ice. On the 20th/10th they arrived at Toxar, according to Linschoten's map an island on the Timan coast, a little west of the entrance to Petchora. They there met with a Russian lodja whose captain stated that he believed, after hearsay, that the Vaygats Sound[3] was continually covered with ice, and that, when it was passed, men came to a sea which lay to the south of, and was warmer than, the Polar Sea. Some other Russians added, the following day, that it was quite possible to sail through Vaygats Sound, if the whales and walruses, that

---

[1] Probably the Sachanich Bay of the Russians.

[2] *Voyagie, ofte Schip Vaert, van Jan Huyghen van Linschoten, van by Noorden om langes Nooruvegen de Noortcaep, Laplant, Vinlant, Ruslandt . . . tot voorby de rerier Oby,* Franeker, 1601. Another edition at Amsterdam in 1624, and in abstract in Saeghman's collection of travels in 1665. The voyage is also described in Blavii *Atlas Major*, 1665. Linschoten was "commis" on board, a post which included both the employment of supercargo and that of owners' commissioner.

[3] That is Yugor Schar. This name also occurs, though in a somewhat altered form, as "Wegorscoi tzar," on Isaac Massa's map of 1612, which, according to the statement of the publisher, is a copy of a Russian chart.

destroy all vessels that seek to pass through, did not form an obstacle; that the great number of rocks and reefs scarcely permitted the passage of a vessel; and finally, that the Grand Duke had ordered three vessels to attempt the passage, but that they had all been crushed by ice.

JAN HUYGHEN VAN LINSCHOTEN,
Born in 1563 at Haarlem, died in 1611 at Enkhuizen.
After a portrait in his work, *Navigatio in Orientalem sive Lusitanorum Indiam*, Hagæ Comitis, 1599.

On the $\frac{22nd}{12th}$ July there came to Toxar hunters from the White Sea, who spoke another language than the Russians, and belonged to another race of men—they were evidently Finns or Karelians. A large number of whales were seen in the haven, which gave occasion to a remark by Linschoten that whale-fishing

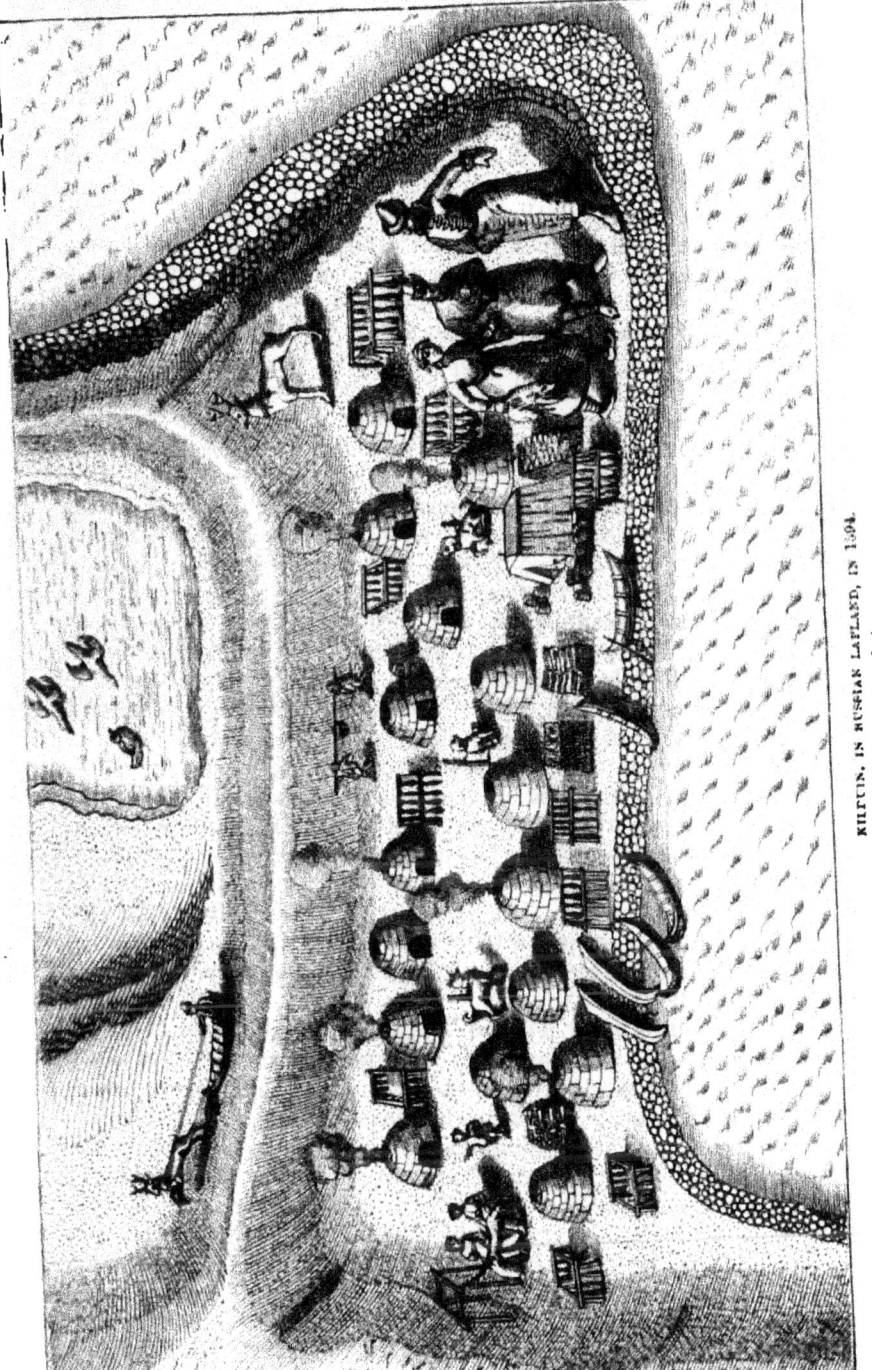

KILDUIN, IN RUSSIAN LAPLAND, IN 1594.
After Linschoten.

ought to be profitable there. After the ice had broken up, and
crosses with inscriptions giving information of their movements
had been erected on the shore, they sailed on. On the $\frac{11}{21}$st July
they sighted Vaygats. They landed at a headland marked with
two crosses, and there fell in with a native, clad in much the
same way as a Kilduin Lapp, who soon took to flight. Other
headlands marked with crosses were afterwards visited, and
places where idols were found set up by hundreds. Linschoten
also landed on that Idol Cape which was visited during the
voyage of the *Vega*. There were then from three to four
hundred wooden idols, which, according to Linschoten's description, were very similar in appearance to those we saw. They
were so ill made, says he, that one could scarcely guess that
they were intended to represent men. The visage was very
broad, the nose projecting, there were two holes in place of the
eyes, and another hole represented the mouth. Five, six, or
seven faces were often found carved on one and the same stock,
"perhaps intended to represent a whole family." Many Russian
crosses were also erected there. Some days later they found on
the south shore of the sound a small house filled with idols,
much better made than the former, with eyes and paps
of metal. While the Dutch were employed in examining this
collection of idols, a reindeer sledge was driven forward in which
sat a man armed with a bow. When he saw the foreigners he
called loudly, on which a number of sledges with about thirty
men drove out of a valley and endeavoured to surround the
Dutch. They now fled in haste to their boat, and when it had
left the beach the Samoyeds shot at it with their arrows, but
without hitting it. This bloodless conflict is, so far as we know,
the only one that took place between the natives and the
north-east voyagers. The latter are thus free from the great
bloodguiltiness which attaches to most of those, who in the
fifteenth and sixteenth centuries made voyages of discovery in
southern regions.

Some days later, on the $\frac{10th\ August}{31st\ July}$, the Dutch had a friendly
meeting with the Samoyeds, who gave them very correct in-
formation concerning the state of the land and the sea, telling
them that "after ten or twelve days they would meet with no
more ice, and that summer would last six or seven weeks
longer." After the Dutch had learned all they could from these
"barbarians, who had greater skill in managing their bow than
a nautical gnomon, and could give better information regarding
their hunting than about the navigable water," they took their
departure. When one of the sailors hereupon blew a horn, the
savages were so frightened, that they began to take to flight,
but, quieted by the assurance that the blast of the horn was
only a sign of friendship, they returned and on the beach

saluted the departing strangers, bowing themselves to the earth with uncovered heads and crossed hands.

On the $\frac{11\text{th}}{1\text{st}}$ August the Dutch, full of hope, sailed into the Kara Sea, or, as they called it, the "North Tartaric Ocean." They soon fell in with ice, on which account on the $\frac{12\text{th}}{2\text{nd}}$ they sought protection under Mestni Island (Staten Eiland). Here they found a sort of rock crystal resembling diamonds in all respects except hardness, a disappointing circumstance which was ascribed to the action of cold. Here also were seen images and sacrificial places, but no houses and no trees.

When Nay and Tetgales sailed on, they came to an extensive open sea, and on the $\frac{20}{10}$th August they believed that they were off the mouth of the Obi. Two of its principal mouth-arms they named, after the vessels, "Swan" and "Mercurius," names which have since been forgotten. It is quite evident that the river which the Dutch took for the Obi was the Kara, and that the mouth-arms, Swan and Mercurius, were two small coast rivers which debouch from Yalmal into the Kara Sea.

On the $\frac{21\text{st}}{11\text{th}}$ August they determined to return home, taking it for proved that, from the point which had been reached, it would be easy to double "Promontorium Tabin," and thus get to China by the north-east passage. A large number of whales were seen raising half their bodies out of the sea and spouting jets of water from their nostrils in the common way, which was considered a further sign that they had an extensive ocean before them.

On the $\frac{24}{14}$th August, Nay and Tetgales sailed again through Yugor Schar (Fretum Nassovicum), and the day after at three small islands, which were called Mauritius, Orange, and New Walcheren, they fell in with Barents, and all sailed home to Holland, fully convinced that the question of the possibility of a north-east passage to China was now solved. It was shown indeed, in the following year, that this supposition rested on quite too slight a foundation, but the voyages of Nay and Tetgales deserve in any case an honoured place in the history of navigation, for they extended considerably the know-ledge of the northern regions through the discovery, or at least through the first passage of, Yugor Schar, and, like Barents, these seafarers must get the credit of carrying out the task assigned to them with skill, insight, resolution, and resource.

THE SECOND DUTCH EXPEDITION, 1595.[1]—After the return of the first expedition a report of the discoveries which had been made was given in to Prince MAURICE of ORANGE, JAN VAN OLDENBARNEVELT, Advocate of Holland, and the other authorities at home. They were so convinced by this report

---

[1] Accounts of this expedition are given both by De Veer and Linschoten in the above-named works.

that the sea route to China was actually discovered, that they immediately made arrangements to send out the following year a flotilla of seven vessels, two from Amsterdam, two from Zeeland, two from Enkhuizen, and one from Rotterdam, with a view to open the new commercial communication.

The commanders of the vessels were CORNELIS NAY (Admiral), BRANDT TETGALES (Second in Command), BARENTS, LAMBERT GERRITSZ. OOM, THOMAS WILLEMSZ., HARMAN JANSZ., and HENDRIK HARTMAN. The lieutenants were LINSCHOTEN, JACOB HEEMSKERK, FRANÇOYS DE LA DALE, JAN CORNELISZ., RIJP,

South.

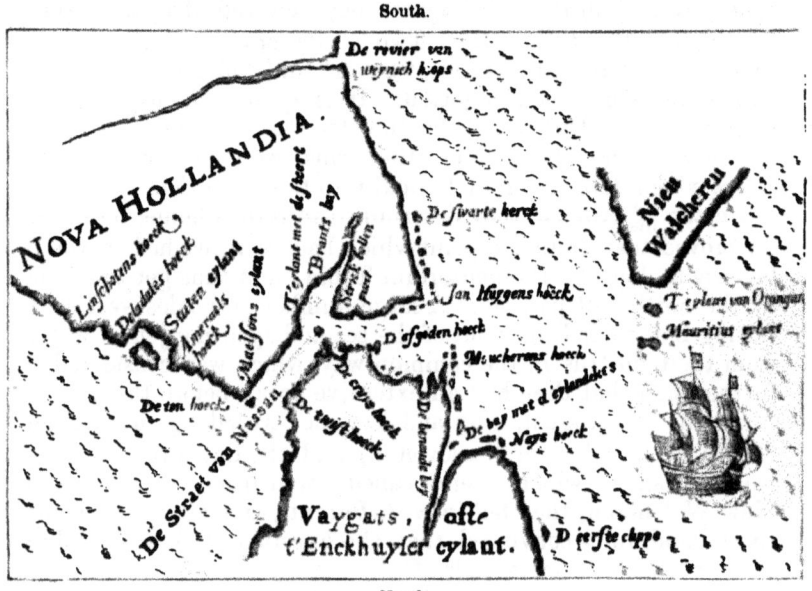

North.

MAP OF FRETUM NASSOVICUM OR YUGOR SCHAR.
After Linschoten.

and N. BUYS. Six of the vessels were laden with goods and coin ; the seventh was to return home with news when the fleet had sailed through Vaygats Sound. The great preparations, however, occupied so much time that it was not until the ${}^{12th}_{2nd}$ July that the voyage could be begun. On the ${}^{22nd}_{12th}$ August, Kegor on the Ribatschni peninsula was sighted, and on the ${}^{20}_{10}$th August the fleet arrived at the Sound between Vaygats and the mainland, and found a great deal of ice there.

On the ${}^{3rd Sep.}_{24th Aug.}$ the Dutch met with some Russians, who told them that the winter had been very severe, but that the ice would in a short time disappear, and that the summer would still

last six weeks. They also stated that the land to the northward, which was called Vaygats, was an island, separated on its
north side from Novaya Zemlya; that it was visited in summer
by natives, who towards winter returned to the mainland; that
Russian vessels, laden with goods, yearly sailed through Vaygats
Sound past the Obi to the river Gillissy (Yenisej), where they
passed the winter; that the dwellers on the Yenisej were of the
Greek-Christian religion, &c.

On the $\frac{10\text{th Sept.}}{31\text{st Aug.}}$ the Dutch came in contact with the Samoyeds
south of Vaygats Sound. Their " king " received the strangers
in a very hospitable and friendly manner, and informed them
that in three or four weeks the cold would begin, that in some
years the drift-ice did not disappear; that during winter the
whole sound and the bays and coves were frozen over, but that
the sea on both sides did not freeze; that beyond the mouth
of the river Ob there were the mouths of two other rivers,
of which the more remote was called the " Molconsay," the
nearer, which was often visited by Russian trading vessels, the
Gillissy; that the land continued beyond the Ob to a cape which
projected towards Novaya Zemlya, and that beyond this promontory there was a great sea, which extended along Tartary
to warm regions.[1]

When the Dutch sailed into the Kara Sea they fell in with
much ice, on which account they anchored at the island, Staten
Eiland, where during the preceding voyage rock crystal had
been found. Here two men were killed in the way that has
already been described.[2] Depressed by this unfortunate occurrence and afraid to expose their vessels, laden with valuable
goods, too late in the season, to the large quantity of ice which
drifted about in the Kara Sea, the commanders determined to
turn. The fleet returned to Holland without further adventure, passing through Vaygats Sound on the $\frac{28}{19}$th September.

This expedition did not yield any new contribution to the
knowledge of our globe. But it deserves to be noted that we
can state with certainty, with the knowledge we now possess of
the ice-conditions of the Kara Sea, that the Dutch during both
their first and second voyages had the way open to the Obi and
Yenisej. If they had availed themselves of this and continued
their voyage till they came to inhabited regions on either of
these rivers, a considerable commerce would certainly have
arisen between Middle Asia and Europe by this route as early
as the beginning of the seventeenth century.

---

[1] These remarkable statements are found in Linschoten's above-quoted
work printed in 1601, and cannot therefore be spurious. They thus show
that Taimur Land was inhabited by Samoyeds, and that the geography
of this region was then well known.

[2] See above, p. 110.

THE THIRD DUTCH EXPEDITION, 1596-97.[1]—After the
unfortunate issue of the expedition of 1595, which had been
fitted out at so great an expense, and which had raised so
great expectations, the States-General would not grant the
necessary funds for a third voyage, but they offered instead
a great prize to the states or merchants that at their own

UNSUCCESSFUL FIGHT WITH A POLAR BEAR,
During the Second Dutch Expedition. From De Veer.

expense should send out a vessel that should by the route north
of Asia force a passage to Asia and China.[2] Encouraged by

[1] The sketch of this voyage forms the main portion of the above mentioned work of De Veer. Undoubtedly the adventures during the wintering,
the first in so high a latitude, in the first place procured for De Veer's
work the enormous popularity it enjoyed, and led to its being translated
into so many languages.
[2] The resolution regarding the offer of this prize is given below :
Extract uit het Register der Resolutien van de Hoog Mogende Heeren
Staten Generael der Vereenigde Nederlanden.
          Folio 158 v[so]   13 April 1596.
De Gedeputeerde van de Heeren Staten van Holland verclaren dat heure
principalen geadviseert hebbende op de hervattinge van het voyagie naer
China en Japan, benoorden om, deselve voyage afgeslagen hebben, ten
aenzien van de groote costen die nu twee Jaren achter den anderen om de
reyse te verzoeken te vorgeefs angewent zijn, maer dat Hare E. goetge-
vonden ende geconsenteert hebben, mede tgevolgh van de andere provincien
bij zoeverre datter eenige coopluijden aventuriers bij compagnie ofte
anderssine de voerscreven reijse op heure costen ende risique, zonder te

this offer the merchants of Amsterdam sent out two vessels, one under the command of Willem Barents and Jacob van Heemskerk, the other under Jan Cornelisz. Rijp. The crew were chosen with care, unmarried men being preferred, with the idea that wife and children would detract from the bravery of the members of the expedition and lead them to return home prematurely.

On the $\frac{20}{10}$th May these vessels left Amsterdam. On the $\frac{14}{4}$th June they saw in lat. 71° North some beautiful parhelia, which are found delineated in De Veer's work, and Blavii *Atlas Major.*

On the $\frac{15}{5}$th June one of the crew cried out from the deck that he saw white swans, but on a closer examination it appeared that they consisted of large pieces of ice, which drifted along the edge of the pack.[1] On the $\frac{19}{9}$th they discovered, north of North Cape, a new island, situated in latitude 74° 30' North. A large bear was killed here, and on this account the island was called Bear Island. On the $\frac{20}{19}$th they came in the 80th degree of latitude to a another formerly unknown land, which they believed to be connected with Greenland. It was in fact the large group of islands, which afterwards obtained the name Spitzbergen. There were found here on a small island the eggs of a species of goose—*rotgansen,*[2] which comes yearly to Holland in great flocks, but whose breeding place was before unknown. With reference to this, De Veer says that it is finally proved that this goose is not, as has been hitherto supposed, propagated in Scotland by the goose laying her eggs from the branches of trees overhanging the water, the eggs

schepen ende tgelt van den lande, zonde begeren te verzoeken, dat men dezelve aventuriers de reijse gevonden ende gedaen hebbende, daervan brengende goet ende gelooofflijck beschijt, tot haer luijder wedercomste, zal vereeren mette somme van vijff en twintich duysent gulden eens. Item daar enboven accorderen den vrijdom voer twee jaren van convoyen der goederen die zij uit dese landen naer China off Japan zullen transporteren, ende noch vrijdom voer den tyd van acht jaren van te goederen die zij uit China ofte Japan in dese landen sullen bringen. Waerop geadviseert wesende hebben de Gedeputeerde van d'andere provincien hen daarmede geconformeert, die van Seelant opt welbehagen van heure principalen, maer die van Utrecht hebben verclart niet te consenteren ʼin de vereeringe van XXVᴹ £.

[1] Every Polar traveller has at one time or other made the same or a similar mistake. In 1861, for instance, a boat party, of whom I was one, thought that they saw clearly sailors in sou'-westers and with white shirt-sleeves building a cairn on a point which appeared to be at no great distance. But the cairn was found to be a very distant mountain, the shirt-sleeves were formed of snow-fields, the sou'-westers of pointed cliffs, and the motion arose from oscillatory changes in the atmospheric strata.

[2] Undoubtedly *Anser bernicla,* which is common on the west coast of Spitzbergen. The Dutch name ought neither to be translated *red goose,* as some Englishmen have done, nor confounded with *rotges.*

being broken in pieces against the surface of the water, and the newly hatched young immediately swimming about.

After an unsuccessful attempt had been made to sail to the north of Spitzbergen the vessels proceeded southwards along the west coast,[1] and on the $\frac{11\text{th}}{1\text{st}}$ July came again to Bear Island. Here the vessels parted company, Barents sailing eastwards towards Novaya Zemlya, Rijp northwards towards the east coast of Spitzbergen. On the $\frac{7}{17}$th July, Barents reached the west coast of Novaya Zemlya in latitude 73° 20′ North. On

BARENTS' AND RIJP'S VESSELS.
From De Veer.

the $\frac{20}{20}$th July, no further advance could be made for ice, which still lay close to the shore. During the stay here there were several adventures with bears, all of which came off successfully. In consequence of ice obstacles their progress was exceedingly slow, so that it was not until the $\frac{25}{15}$th August that they reached the Orange Islands. The following day several of the crew ascended a high mountain, from which they saw open water on the other side of an island. As glad at the sight of the

[1] See the copy of Barents' own map with his course laid down upon it, which is to be found in Pontanus, *Rerum et urbis Amstelodamensium Historia* (Amst. 1611), and is annexed to this work in photolithographic facsimile.

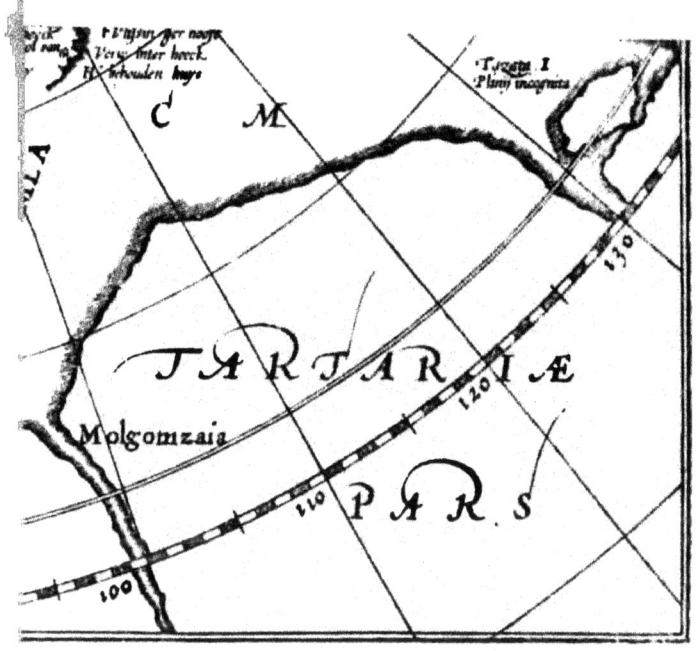

ⱯLA

C M

⁺ D'Insu_ler noort
Verw inter heeck.
H' Arhouden huge

·Tsjegia I
Plani incognita

ℐ𝒜ℛℐ𝒜ℛ ℐ Æ

Molgomzaia

ℙ𝒜ℛ S

130

120

110

100

A. AMST. 1611.

sea as the ten thousand under Xenophon, they rushed back
to the vessel to give Barents the important news. He now
did all he could to pass the north extremity of Novaya Zemlya.
He was successful in doing so, and on the $\frac{31}{21}$st a haven, situated
in about the latitude of 76° North, was reached with great
difficulty, but all attempts to sail eastwards from it were
unsuccessful. Finally, on the $\frac{4th\ Sept.}{25th\ Aug.}$ Barents determined to
return to Holland.

Now, however,.it was too late. The haven was blocked with
drift-ice, which was in constant motion, several times pressed
the vessel high up between the pieces of ice, and finally broke
the rudder in pieces. It was now evident that it would be
necessary to winter, and for this purpose the requisite tools,
household articles, and provisions were landed and men sent
out to examine the neighbourhood. Reindeer tracks were seen,
and, what was more important, there were found on the beach
large tree-stems with their roots still adhering, and other wood
which the marine currents had drifted to this otherwise completely woodless region. The drift-wood was collected in large
heaps that it might not be buried under the snow in winter.
A place was chosen for a house, and the Dutch began to draw
timber to the place. The openings in the drift-ice were on
the $\frac{25}{15}$th September covered with a crust of ice two inches thick,
but on the $\frac{5th\ Oct.}{25th\ Sept}$ the ice was again somewhat broken up which
however was of no advantage to the imprisoned, because their
vessel was forced up so high on a block of ground ice that
it could not be got off. Bears were hunted almost daily. They
were very bold and sometimes came on board the vessel. On
the $\frac{15}{5}$th October all ice was driven off as far as the eye could
see, but the vessel still lay motionless on the blocks of ground
ice. Round these the ice closed in again, to break up anew
at a greater or less distance from the beach. On the $\frac{4th\ March}{22nd\ Feb.}$ there
was still much open water visible from the beach, and on the
$\frac{16}{6}$th and $\frac{13}{3}$th March, the sea appears to have been in one
direction completely free of ice.

On the $\frac{31}{21}$st October, the crew began to remove into the house,
where they afterwards passed the winter 1596-97 with many
sufferings, dangers, difficulties, and privations which are described in De Veer's work. The crew, however, never lost
courage, which undoubtedly was a principal cause of most of
them being saved. The house was built on the north-east side
of Novaya Zemlya, on the shore of Barents' Ice Haven. It
was situated far to the north of any other place where men
had previously passed the winter. The land and its animal
life was unknown, the hard frozen, almost rock-fast and yet
continually moving ice-covering, with which the sea was

bound, was something quite novel, as also were the effects which
long continued and severe cold exerts on animate and inanimate
objects. Before the attempt was made it was not considered
at all certain that men could actually endure the severe cold
of the highest north and the winter night three or four months
long. No wonder therefore that the skill and undaunted
resolution of the Dutch Polar explorers aroused unmingled
admiration among all civilised nations, and that the narrative
of their wintering was received with unbounded interest and

BARENTS' HOUSE, OUTSIDE.
From De Voer.

formed the subject of innumerable writings and reproductions
both in prose and verse in almost all civilised languages. Only
a few facts from the journal of the wintering need therefore
be given here.

On the $\frac{14}{7}$th November the sun disappeared, and was again
visible on the $\frac{3rd\ Feb.}{24th\ Jan.}$. These dates have caused scientific men
much perplexity, because in latitude 76° North, the upper edge
of the sun ought to have ceased to be visible when the sun's
south declination in autumn became greater than 13°,[1] and
to have again become visible when the declination again became
less than that figure; that is to say, the sun ought to have
been seen for the last time at Barents' Ice Haven. on the $\frac{27}{17}$th

[1] On the assumption of a horizontal refraction of about 45'.

October, and it ought to have appeared again there on the $\frac{14}{7}$th February. It has been supposed that the deviation arose from some considerable error in counting the days, but this was unanimously denied by the crew who wintered.[1] The bears disappeared and reappeared with the sun. Instead, foxes came during winter to the building, and were caught for food in numbers, many on the roof of the house. In order to pass the time and keep up their courage, the Dutch sometimes had

BARENTS' HOUSE, INSIDE.
From De Bry.

entertainments, at which the cheerfulness of the partakers had to make up for the meagreness of the fare. After the return of the sun the bears again came very close, so that there was

---

[1] See on this point De Veer, leaf 25 and an unpaged leaf between pages 30 and 31 in Blavii *Atlas Major*, tom. i. That a mistake occurred in the date is not possible, because the latitude was determined by solar observations on the 29th (19th) February, the 21st (11th) and 31st (21st) March (see De Veer, l. 27). Besides, at the correct date, the 3rd February (24th January), a conjunction of Jupiter and the moon was observed, whereby the difference of longitude between Ice Haven and Venice was determined to be 75°. However erroneous this determination may be, it shows, however, that the date was correct.

a number of hunting adventures with them, all of which came
off successfully. Several bears made themselves at home in
the vessel abandoned by the crew, casting everything about,
and broke up the hatch of the kitchen, covered as it was with
deep snow. An attempt to eat bear's liver resulted in those
that ate of it becoming very ill, and after recovery renewing
their skin over the whole body. Once during severe cold,
when pitcoal was used to warm the building, all the men in
it were like to have died of the fumes. On one or two occasions, for instance on the $\frac{25}{11}$th February, so much snow had
collected outside the door, that it was necessary to go out by the
chimney. For the preservation of their health the Dutch often
took a vapour bath in a barrel fitted up for the purpose.

On the $\frac{7\text{th May}}{27\text{th April}}$ the first small birds were seen, and on the $\frac{25}{15}$th
May Barents declared that if the vessel were not got off before
the end of the month, they should return in boats, which were
therefore immediately got ready. This was, however, attended
with great difficulty, because most of the crew had during the
course of the winter become exceedingly weak, evidently from
scurvy. After the equipment of the boats had been completed
and they had been properly laden with provisions, the Dutch at
last started on the $\frac{23\text{rd}}{13\text{th}}$ June.

A man had died on the $\frac{6\text{th Feb.}}{27\text{th Jan.}}$. At the beginning of the boat
voyage Barents himself was very ill, and six days after, on the
$\frac{20}{30}$th June, he died, while resting with his companions on a
large floe, being compelled to do so by the drift-ice. On the
same day one of the crew died, and on the $\frac{15}{5}$th July another.

On the $\frac{7\text{th Aug.}}{28\text{th July}}$ the returning Arctic explorers at St. Lawrens'
Bay fell in with two vessels manned by Russian hunters,
whose acquaintance the Dutchmen had made the year before,
and who now received them with great friendliness and pity for
their sufferings. They continued their voyage in their small
open boats, and all arrived in good health and spirits at Kola,
where they were received with festivities by the inhabitants.
It gave them still greater joy to meet here Jan Cornelisz. Rijp,
from whom they had parted at Bear Island the preceding year,
and of whose voyage we know only that he intended to sail up
along the east coast of Spitzbergen, and that, when this was
found to be impossible, he returned home the same autumn.

After the two boats, in which Barents' companions had
travelled with so many dangers and difficulties from their winter
haven to Russian Lapland, had been left in the merchant's yard[1]

[1] Built along with a weigh-house intended for the Norwegians in 1582
by the first vojvode in Kola (*Hamel*, p. 66). In Pontanus (*Rerum et
urbis Amstelodamensium Historia*, Amsterodami, 1611, p. 142), there is
a drawing of the inner yard of this house, and of the reception of
shipwrecked men there.

at Kola, as a memorial˙of the journey—the first memorial of
a Polar expedition was thus raised at Kola!—they went on
board Rijp's vessel, and sailed in it to Holland, arriving there
the ⁸ᵗʰ Nᵒᵛᵉᵐᵇᵉʳ⁄₃₀ₜₕ October. Sixteen men had left Holland with Barents,
twelve men returned in safety to their native land, and among
them JACOB VAN HEEMSKERK, a man who during the whole
voyage had played a prominent part, and afterwards lived long
enough to see the time when the Dutch were a match at sea

JACOB VAN HEEMSKERK.
Born in 1567 at Amsterdam, died in 1607 at Gibraltar.
After a contemporary engraving by N. de Clerck.

for the Spaniards.   For he fell as commander of the Dutch fleet
which defeated the Spanish at Gibraltar on April 25, 1607.

During Barents' third voyage Bear Island and Spitzbergen
were discovered, and the natural conditions of the high northern
regions during winter first became known.   On the other
hand, the unfortunate issue of the maritime expeditions sent
out from Holland appears to have completely deterred from

further attempts to find a north-eastern commercial route to
China and Japan, and this route was also now less necessary,
as Houtman returned with the first Dutch fleet from the East
Indies the same year that Barents' companions came back from
their wintering. The problem was therefore seriously taken up
anew for the first time during the present century ; though
during the intervening period attempts to solve it were not
wholly wanting.

For the desire to extend the White Sea trade to Siberia,
and jealousy of the companies that had known how to procure
for themselves a monopoly of the lucrative commerce with
eastern Asia, still led various merchants now and then during
the seventeenth century to send out vessels to try whether it
was possible to penetrate beyond Novaya Zemlya. I shall
confine myself here to an enumeration of the most important
of these undertakings, with the necessary bibliographical
references.

1608. HENRY HUDSON, during his second voyage, landed on
Novaya Zemlya at Karmakul Bay and other places, but did not
succeed in his attempt to sail further to the east, north of this
island. He made the voyage on account of English merchants.
A narrative of it is to be found in *Purchas* (iii. p. 574), and an
excellent critical collection of all the original documents
relating to Hudson's life and voyages in G. M. Asher's
Henry Hudson the Navigator, London, 1860 (Works issued by
the Hakluyt Society, No. 26). It was west of the Atlantic
that Hudson earned the laurels which gave him for all time so
prominent a place in the history of navigation, and the sea
there also became his grave. Eastwards he did not penetrate
so far as his predecessors. I cannot therefore here find room
for any account of his voyage to Novaya Zemlya; it may
only be mentioned that two of his crew on the morning
of the $\frac{25}{15}$th of June, 1608, in 75° N.L., saw a mermaid. The
following statement is taken from his journal : "This morning
one of the crew, as he looked over the side, saw a mermaid.
Another of his comrades came up at his call. She was
close to the vessel's side, looking steadily at the men. Soon
after she was thrown down by a wave. From the middle
upwards her back and breast were like a woman's. Her body
was as large as a man's, her skin very white, and long dark
hair hung down her back. When she dived, they saw her
tail, which resembled that of a dolphin and was spotted like
a mackerel's. The names of the men who saw her were
Thomas Hiller and Robert Rayner." It was probably a curious
seal that gave occasion to this version of the old yarn.

1611. WILLIAM GOURDON, with the title "appointed chief
pilote for discoverie to Ob," brought this year a cargo of goods

to Pustosersk, and sailed thence to Novaya Zemlya. At the mouth of the Petchora he saw 24 *lodjas*, manned with ten to 16 men each, bound for "Mangansei" east of Ob (*Purchas*, iii. pp. 530, 534). While attempting to get further information regarding these voyages to Siberia, the Muscovy company's envoy learned that, at least as a rule, the question was only of carrying goods by sea to the bottom of Kara Bay, whence they were transported overland to Ob, advantage being taken of two small rivers and a lake (*Purchas*, iii. p. 539). But other accounts lead us to infer that the Russian *lodjas* actually sailed to Ob, even through Matotschkin Schar, as appears from statements in *Purchas* (iii. pp. 804, 805). At the same place we find the statement, already quoted, of a Russian, who in 1584 offered for fifty roubles to act as guide overland from the Petchora to the Ob, that a West-European ship was wrecked at the mouth of the Ob, and its crew killed by the Samoyeds who lived there. The Russian also said that it was an easy matter to sail from Vaygats to the mouth of the Ob.

1612. The whaling captain JAN CORNELISZ. VAN HOORN endeavoured to sail north of Novaya Zemlya towards the east, but met with ice in 77° N.L., which compelled him to return (*Witsen*, p. 906).

1625. CORNELIS BOSMAN, at the instance of the Northern Company of the Netherlands, with a vessel of 90 tons, manned by 24 men, and provisioned for two and a half years, passed through Yugor Schar eastwards, but fell in with so much ice in the Kara Sea that he was compelled to seek for a harbour in that sound. There he waited for more favourable conditions, but was finally compelled by storm and ice to return with his object unaccomplished. (S. Müller *Geschiedenis der Noordsche Compagnie*, Utrecht, 1874, p. 185.)

1653.[1] This year a Danish expedition was sent out to the North-east. An account of the voyage was given by DE LA MARTINIÈRE, surgeon to the expedition, in a work published for the first time at Paris in 1671, with the following title : *Voyage des Pais Septentrionaux. Dans lequel se void les mœurs, manière de vivre, & superstitions des Norweguiens, Lappons, Kiloppes, Borandiens, Syberiens, Samojedes, Zembliens, & Islandois, enrichi de plusieurs figures*.[2] This work afterwards attained a considerable

---

[1] The year is incorrectly given as 1647 by F. von Adelung (*Kritisch-Litterärische Uebersicht*, &c.).

[2] The following editions are enumerated : four French, Paris, 1671, 1672, 1676, and Amsterdam, 1708 ; six German, Hamburg. 1675, Leipzig, 1703, 1706, 1710, 1711, and 1718 ; one Latin, Glückstadt, 1675 ; two Dutch, Amsterdam, 1681 and 1685 ; one Italian, printed in Conte Aurelio degli Anzi's *Il Genio Vagante*, Parma, 1691 ; two English, one printed separately in 1706, the other in Harris, *Navigantium atque Itinerantium Bibl.*, 3rd edition. London, 1744-48, Vol. II. p. 457.

circulation, doubtless in consequence of Martinière's easy style,
contrasting so strongly with the common dry ship's-log manner,
and the large number of wonderful stories he narrates, without
the least regard to truth or probability. He is the Münchhausen
of the North-east voyages. The Norse peasants, for instance, are
said to be all slaves to the nobles, who have sovereign power
over their property, tyrannise over their inferiors, and are prone
to insurrection. The elks are said to be liable to falling sickness,
and therefore fall down in convulsions when they are hunted—
hence their name "eleend." Sailors are said to have purchased
on the north-west coast of Norway for ten crowns and a pound

DE LA MARTINIÈRE'S MAP.

of tobacco three knots of wind from the Lapps living there, who
were all magicians; when the first knot was loosed, a gentle
breeze arose, the second gave a strong gale, the third a storm,
during which the vessel was in danger of being wrecked.[1]
Novaya Zemlya is stated to be inhabited by a peculiar tribe,
" the Zembliens," of whom two were taken prisoners and carried
to Copenhagen. De la Martinière also got the head of a walrus,
which had been harpooned with great difficulty; the animal was
drawn as a fish with a long horn projecting from its head. As

---

[1] The story of the wind knots is taken from Olaus Magnus, *De gentibus
septentrionalibus*, Rome, 1555, p. 119. There a drawing of the appearance
of the knots is also given.

a specimen of the birds of Novaya Zemlya a penguin was drawn and described, and finally the work closed with the rectification of the map of the Polar Regions, which according to the author's ideas ought to be as represented on page 198. I refer to these absurdities, because the account of Martinière's voyage exerted no little influence on the older writings relating to the Arctic Regions.

1664 and 1668. A whaling captain, WILLEM DE VLAMINGH, sailed in 1664 round the northern extremity of Novaya Zemlya to Barents' winter quarters, and thence eastwards, where one of his men thought he saw land (" Jelmert-landt," *Witsen*, p. 902).[1] The same Vlamingh says that in 1668 he discovered, twenty-five miles N.N.E. of Kolgujev, a new island three to four miles in circumference. This island, which was described in great detail, and named by the discoverer " Witsen's Island," has not since been seen again (*Witsen*, p. 923).

1666. In this year some vessels were sent from the Netherlands to the north-east. There were Jews among the owners and the seafarers were furnished with letters in Hebrew, because it was believed that they would come in contact with some of the lost tribes of Israel. Nothing further appears to have been known of the voyage, which undoubtedly was without result. (*Witsen*, p. 962.)

1675. A Dutch whaling captain, CORNELIS PIERSZ. SNOB-BERGER, visited Novaya Zemlya, on whose coast he killed three whales and six hundred walruses. He would probably have got still more " fish," if he had not in $72\frac{1}{2}°$ found an ore, which appeared to contain silver, gold, and other metals. Instead of blubber the skipper now loaded ore, which in his opinion was precious, but afterwards on being tested at home was found to be valueless (*Witsen*, p. 918).

17th Century, year not stated. Shipmaster CORNELIS ROULE is said to have sailed in the longitude of Novaya Zemlya to $84\frac{1}{2}°$ or 85° N.L. and there discovered a fjord-land, along which he sailed ten miles. Beyond that a large open sea was seen. From a high mountain situated on a sound, in which he rode, it appeared that he might sail one or two watches further to the north. He found there large numbers of birds, which were exceedingly tame (*Witsen*, p. 920). If we take some degrees from the latitude stated, which is perhaps not very unreasonable in dealing with the narratives of old whalers, which have passed through two or three hands, Roule may, as far back as two hundred years ago, have reached Franz-Josef's Land, and sailed along its coast to a very high latitude for those regions.

1676. WOOD and FLAWES were sent out from England by

[1] Compare page 156.

Charles II. to sail by the north-east passage to the Pacific. For this purpose the English Admiralty fitted out a vessel, the *Speedwell*, while "as all exploratory voyages are exposed to the possibility of disaster," another small ship, the *Prosperous*, was purchased and handed over to the expedition by private gentlemen.[1] The command of the first vessel was given to Captain Wood, the chief promoter of the undertaking, and the other vessel was commanded by Captain Flawes. The voyage was completely without result, as Wood did not penetrate so far, either to the north or east, as his predecessors or as the whalers, who appear to have at that time frequently visited North Novaya Zemlya. Wood had previously accompanied Sir John Narborough during a voyage through the dangerous Magellan Straits, in the course of which he became known as a bold and skilful seaman, but he not only wanted experience in sailing amongst ice, but also the endurance and the coolness that are required for voyages in the high north. He thereby showed himself to be quite unfit for the command which he undertook. Before his departure he was unreasonably certain of success; with the first encounter with ice his self-reliance gave way entirely; and when his vessel was wrecked on the coast of Novaya Zemlya, he knew no other way to keep up the courage of his men and prevent mutiny than to send the brandy bottle round.[2] Finally after his return he made Barents and other distinguished seafarers in the Arctic Regions answerable for all the skipper tales collected from quite other quarters, which he before his departure held to be proved undoubtedly true. This voyage would therefore not have been referred to here, if it had not been preceded and followed by lively discussions regarding the fitness of the Polar Sea for navigation, during which at least a portion of the experience which Dutch and English whalers had gained of the state of the ice between Greenland and Novaya Zemlya was rescued from oblivion, though unfortunately almost exclusively in the form of unconfirmed statements of very high latitudes, which had been occasionally reached. Three papers mainly led to Wood's voyage. These were :—

1. A letter, inserted in the *Transactions* of the Royal Society,[3]

[1] These were James Duke of York, Lord Berkley, Sir John Williamson, Sir John Bankes, Mr. Samuel Peeps, Captain Herbert, Mr. Dupey, and Mr. Hoopgood (Harris, *Nav. Bibl.*, vol. ii. p. 453).

[2] "All I could do in this exigency was to let the brandy-bottle go round, which kept them allways fox'd, till the 8th July Captain Flawes came so seasonably to our relief" (Barrow, *A Chronological History of Voyages into the Arctic Regions*. London, 1818, p. 268).

[3] "A letter, not long since written to the Publisher by an Experienced person residing at Amsterdam," etc. (*Philosophical Transactions*, vol. ix. p. 3. London, 1674).

on the state of Novaya Zemlya, said to be founded on discoveries which had been made at the express command of the Czar. The letter was accompanied by a map, drawn by an artist named Panelapoetski, who sent it from Moscow as a present to the writer. The Kara Sea is said to be a freshwater inland lake which freezes strongly in winter, and it is stated that according to the unanimous accounts of the Samoyeds and Tartars it is quite possible to sail north of Novaya Zemlya to Japan.

2. Another letter was inserted in the *Transactions* of the Royal Society,[1] in which the statement in the former letter on the connection of Novaya Zemlya with the mainland is repeated, and the difficulties which Barents met with ascribed to the circumstance that he sailed too near the land, along which the sea is often frozen; some miles from the shore, on the other hand, it never freezes, even at the Pole, unless occasionally. It is also said that some Amsterdam merchants sailed more than a hundred leagues eastward of Novaya Zemlya, and on that account petitioned the States-General for privileges.[2] However, in consequence of opposition from the Dutch East India Company, their petition was not granted, on which the merchants turned to Denmark. Here their proposal was immediately received with favour. Two vessels were fitted out, but instead of sailing to Japan, they went to Spitzbergen to the whale-fishing. It is further stated in the letter that it would not be unadvisable to let some persons live for a time with the Samoyeds, in order to find out what they knew of the matter, and that, when a more complete knowledge of the navigable waters was acquired, the whole voyage from England to Japan might be accomplished in five or six weeks. Were a

[1] "A summary Relation of what hath been hitherto discovered in the matter of the North-East passage; communicated by a good Hand" (*Phil. Trans.*, vol. x. p. 417. London, 1675).

[2] The time when the voyage was made is not stated in the letter quoted. Harris says that he with great difficulty ascertained the year of the successful voyage to the eastward to be 1670. He says further that the persons who gave him this information also stated that, at the time when this petition was given in to the States-General, it was also asserted that there was no difficulty in sailing northwards from Spitzbergen (Greenland), and that many Dutch vessels had actually done it. To confirm this statement the merchants proposed that the logs of the Spitzbergen fleet for the year 1655 should be examined. This was done. In seven of them it was found recorded that the vessels had sailed to 79° N. L. Three other logs agreed in the point that on the 1st August, 1655, 88° 56' *was observed*. The sea here was open and the swell heavy (Harris, *Nav. Bibl.*, ii. p. 453). J. R. Forster (*Geschichte der Entdeckungen und Schiffsfahrten im Norden*, Frankfurt a. d. Oder, 1874) appears to place the voyage eastward of Novaya Zemlya in the period before 1614. It is, however, probable that the voyage in question is Vlamingh's remarkable one in 1664, or that in 1666, of which I have already given an account.

wintering necessary, it would not be attended with any danger,
if, instead of a house of thick planks standing by itself, earth
huts were used.

3. A pamphlet, whose contents are given in the long and
peculiar title: A brief Discourse of a Passage by the North-
Pole to Japan, China, etc. Pleaded by Three Experiments:
and Answers to all Objections that can be urged against a
Passage that way. As: 1. By a Navigation from Amsterdam
into the North-Pole, and two Degrees beyond it. 2. By a
Navigation from Japan towards the North-Pole. 3. By an
Experiment made by the Czar of Muscovy, whereby it appears,
that to the Northwards of Nova Zembla, is a free and open Sea
as far as Japan, China, etc. With a Map of all the Discovered
Lands neerest to the Pole. By Joseph Moxon, Hydrographer
to the King's most Exellent Majesty. London, 1674."

The most remarkable passage in this scarce little book is the
following :—

"Being about twenty-two years ago in Amsterdam, I
went into a drinking-house to drink a cup of beer for my thirst,
and sitting by the public fire, among several people, there
happened a seaman to come in, who, seeing a friend of his
there, whom he knew went in the Greenland voyage, wondered
to see him, because it was not yet time for the Greenland fleet
to come home, and asked him what accident brought him home
so soon; his friend (who was the steer-man aforsaid in a
Greenland ship that summer) told him, that their ship went
not out to fish that summer, but only to take in the lading of
the whole fleet, to bring it to an early market. But, said he,
before the fleet had caught fish enough to lade us, we, by order
of the Greenland Company, sailed unto the north pole and back
again. Whereupon (his relation being novel to me) I entered
into discourse with him, and seemed to question the truth of
what he said; but he did ensure me it was true, and that the
ship was then in Amsterdam, and many of the seamen
belonging to her to justify the truth of it; and told me, moreover,
that they had sailed two degrees beyond the pole. I asked him
if they found no land or islands about the pole ? He told me,
No, they saw no ice; I asked him what weather they had
there?   He told me fine warm weather, such as was at
Amsterdam in the summer time and as hot." [1]

[1] In more recent times the whalers have been more modest in their
statements about high northern latitudes reached. Thus a Dutchman
who had gone whale-fishing for twenty-two years, at an accidental
meeting with Tschitschagoff in Bell Sound in the year 1766, stated among
other things that he himself had once been in 81°, but that he heard that
other whalers had been in 83° and had seen land over the ice. He had
seen the east coast of Greenland (Spitzbergen) only once in 75° N. L.

In addition to these stories there were several contributions to a solution of the problem, which Wood himself collected, as a statement by Captain Goulden, who had made thirty voyages to Spitzbergen, that two Dutchmen had penetrated eastward of that group of islands to 89° N.L.; the observation that on the coast of Corea whales had been caught with European harpoons in them;[1] and that driftwood eaten to the heart by the sea-worm was found on the coasts of the Polar lands, &c.[2]

When Wood failed, he abandoned the views he had before maintained, declaring that the statements on which he had founded his plans were downright lies and delusions. But the belief in a polar sea that is occasionally navigable is not yet given up. It has since then been maintained by such men as DAINES BARRINGTON,[3] FERDINAND VON WRANGEL, AUGUSTUS PETERMANN,[4] and others. Along with nearly all Polar travellers of the present day, I had long been of an opposite opinion, believing the Polar Sea to be constantly covered with impenetrable masses of ice, continuous or broken up, but I have come to entertain other views since in the course of two

(Herrn von Tschitschagoff Russisch-kaiserlichen Admirals *Reise nach dem Eismeer*, St. Petersburg, 1793, p. 83). Dutch shipmasters too, who in the beginning of the seventeenth century penetrated north of Spitsbergen to 82°, said that they had thence seen land towards the north (Müller, *Geschiedenis der Noordsche Compagnie*, p. 180).

[1] Witsen states, p. 43, that he had conversed with a Dutch seaman, Benedictus Klerk, who had formerly served on board a whaler, and afterwards been a prisoner in Corea. He had asserted that in whales that were killed on the coast of that country he had found Dutch harpoons. The Dutch then carried on whale-fishing only in the north part of the Atlantic. The *find* thus shows that whales can swim from one ocean to the other. As we know that these colossal inhabitants of the Polar Sea do not swim from one ice-ocean to the other across the equator, this observation must be considered very important, especially at a time when the question whether Asia and America are connected across the Pole was yet unsettled. Witson also enumerates, at p. 900, several occasions on which stone harpoons were found in the skins of whales caught in the North Atlantic. These harpoons, however, may as well be derived from the wild races, unacquainted with iron, at Davis Strait, as from tribes living on the north part of the Pacific. At Kamschatka, too, long before whale-fishing by Europeans began in Behring's Sea, harpoons marked with Latin letters were found in whales (Steller, *Beschreibung von dem Lande Kamtschatka*, Frankfurt und Leipzig, 1774, p. 102).

[2] The account of Wood's voyage was printed in London in 1694 by Smith and Walford, printers to the Royal Society (according to a statement by Barrington, *The possibility of approaching the North Pole asserted*, 2nd Edition, London, 1818, p. 34). I have only had an opportunity of seeing extracts from the account of this voyage in *Harris* and others.

[3] Barrington published a number of papers on this question, which are collected in the work whose title is given above, of which there were two editions.

[4] At several places in his *Mittheilungen*, 1855-79.

winterings—the first in 79° 53', that is to say, nearer the Pole than any other has wintered in the old world, the second in the neighbourhood of the Asiatic Pole of cold—I have seen that the sea does not freeze completely, even in the immediate neighbourhood of land. From this I draw the conclusion that the sea scarcely anywhere permanently [1] freezes over where it is of any considerable depth, and far from land. If this be the case, there is nothing unreasonable in the old accounts, and what has happened once we may expect to happen another time.

However this may be, it is certain that the ignominious result of Wood's voyage exerted so great a deterring influence from all new undertakings in the same direction, that nearly two hundred years elapsed before an expedition was again sent out with the distinctly declared intention, which was afterwards disavowed, of achieving a north-east passage. This was the famous Austrian expedition of PAYER and WEYPRECHT in 1872-74, which failed indeed in penetrating far to the eastward, but which in any case formed an epoch in the history of Arctic exploration by the discovery of Franz-Josef's Land and by many valuable researches on the natural conditions of the Polar lands. Considered as a North-east voyage, this expedition was the immediate predecessor of that of the *Vega*. It is so well known through numerous works recently published, and above all by Payer's spirited narrative, that I need not go into further detail regarding it.

But if the North-east voyages proper thus almost entirely ceased during the long interval between Wood's and Payer's voyages, a large number of other journeys for the purpose of research and hunting were instead carried out during this period, through which we obtained the first knowledge founded

---

[1] That thin sheets of ice are formed in clear and calm weather, even in the open sea and over great depths, was observed several times during the expedition of 1868. But when we consider that salt water has no maximum of density situated above the freezing-point, that ice is a bad conductor of heat, and that the clear, newly-formed ice is soon covered by a layer of snow which hinders radiation, it appears to me to be improbable that the ice-covering at deep, open places can become so thick that it is not broken up even by a moderate storm. Even the shallow harbour at Mussel Bay first froze permanently in the beginning of February, and in the end of January the swell in the harbour was so heavy, that all the three vessels of the Swedish Expedition were in danger of being wrecked —*in consequence of the tremendous sea in 80° N.L. in the end of January!* The sea must then have been open very far to the north-west. On the west coast of Spitzbergen the sea in winter is seldom completely frozen within sight of land. Even at Barents' winter haven on the north-east coast of Novaya Zemlya, the sea during the coldest season of the year was often free of ice, and Hudson's statement, "that it is not surprising that the navigator falls in with so much ice in the North Atlantic, when there are so many sounds and bays on Spitzbergen," shows that even he did not believe in any ice being formed in the open sea.

on actual observations of the natural conditions of Novaya Zemlya and the Kara Sea. Of these voyages, mainly made by Russians and Scandinavians, I shall give an account in the next chapter. It was these that prepared the way for the success which we at last achieved.

CHAPTER VI.

The North-east Voyages of the Russians and Norwegians—Rodivan Ivanov, 1690—The great Northern Expedition, 1734-37—The supposed richness in metals of Novaya Zemlya—Juschkov, 1757—Savva Loschkin, 1760—Rossmuislov, 1768—Lasarev, 1819—Lütke, 1821-24—Ivanov, 1822-28—Pachtussov, 1832-35—Von Baer, 1837—Zivolka and Moissejev, 1838-39—Von Krusenstern, 1860-62—The Origin and History of the Polar Sea Hunting—Carlsen, 1868—Ed. Johannesen, 1869-70—Ulve, Mack, and Quale, 1870—Mack, 1871—Discovery of the Relics of Barents' wintering—Tobiesen's wintering, 1872-73—The Swedish Expeditions, 1875 and 1876—Wiggins, 1876—Later Voyages to and from the Yenisej.

FROM what I have stated above it follows that the coast population of North Russia carried on an active navigation on the Polar Sea long before the English and the Dutch, and that commercial expeditions were often undertaken from the White Sea and the Petchora to the Ob and the Yenisej, sometimes wholly by sea round Yalmal, but most frequently partly by sea and partly by land transport over that peninsula. In the latter case the Russians went to work in the following way; they first sailed through Yugor Straits, and over the southern part of the Kara Sea to the mouth of the Mutnaja, a river debouching on Yalmal; they then rowed or towed the boats up the river and over two lakes to a ridge about 350 metres broad, which forms the watershed on Yalmal between the rivers running west and those running east; over this ridge the boats and the goods were dragged to another lake, Selennoe, from which they were finally carried down the river Selennaja to the Gulf of Obi.[1]

These and similar accounts were collected with great difficulty, and not without danger, by the Muscovy Company's envoys; but

[1] Compare: "The names of the places that the Russes sayle by, from Pechorskoie Zauorot to Mongozey" (*Purchas,* iii. p. 539): "The voyage of Master Josias Logan to Pechora, and his wintering there with Master William Pursglove and Marmaduke Wilson, Anno 1611" (*loc. cit.* p. 541): "Extracts taken out of two letters of Josias Logan from Pechora, to Master Hakluyt, Prebend of Westminster" (*loc. cit.* p. 546): "Other obseruations of the sayd William Pursglove" (*loc. cit.* p. 550). The last paper contains good information regarding the Obi, Tas, Yenisej, Pjäsina, Chatanga, and Lena.

among the accounts that have been thus preserved we do not find a single sketch of any special voyage, on the ground of which we could place a Russian name beside that of Willoughby, Burrough, Pet and Barents in the older history of the North-East Passage. The historical sources of Russia too must be similarly incomplete in this respect, to judge from the otherwise instructive historical introduction to Lütke's voyage. Gallant seamen, but no Hakluyt, were born during the sixteenth and seventeenth century on the shores of the White Sea, and therefore the names of these seamen and the story of their voyages have long since fallen into complete obscurity, excepting some in comparatively recent times.

In the second edition of Witsen's great work we find, at page 913, an account of an unsuccessful hunting voyage to the Kara Sea, undertaken in 1690, that is to say, at a time when voyages between the White Sea and the Obi and Yenisej were on the point of ceasing completely. The account was drawn up by Witsen from an oral communication by one of the shipwrecked men, Rodivan Ivanov, who was for several years mate on a Russian vessel, employed in seal-fishing on the coast of Novaya Zemlya and Vaygats Island.

On the $\frac{11th}{1st}$ September this Rodivan Ivanov suffered ship-wreck with two vessels on Serapoa Koska (Serapov's Bank), probably situated in the southern part of the Kara Sea. The ice was thrown up here in winter into lofty ice-casts with such a crashing noise that "the world was believed to be coming to an end," and at high water with a strong breeze the whole island was submerged with the exception of some knolls. On one of these the winter house was erected. It was built of clay, which was kneaded with the blood and hair of the seal and walrus. This mixture hardened to a solid mass, of which the walls were built with the help of boards from the vessel. The house thus afforded good protection not only from cold and bad weather, but also from bears. A furnace was also built inside the house and fired with driftwood collected on the beach. Train oil from the captured animals was used for lighting. There wintered here fifteen men in all, of whom eleven died of scurvy. Want of exercise perhaps mainly conduced to bring on this disease. For most of them did not leave the house during the winter night, five weeks long. Those were most healthy who had most exercise, as, for instance, the mate, who was the youngest among the crew, and therefore had to go round the island to collect wood. Another cause of the great mortality was the total want of provisions brought from home. For the first eight days their food consisted of seaweed dredged up from the bottom of the sea, with which some meal was mixed. After-wards they ate the flesh of the seal and walrus, and of the Polar bear and the fox. The flesh of the bear and the walrus, however, was considered *unclean*,[1] on which account it was eaten only in case of necessity, and the flesh of the fox had an unpleasant flavour. Sometimes the want of food was so great that they were compelled to eat the leather of their boots and furs. The number of the seals and walruses which they caught was so great, "that the killed animals, laid together, would have formed a heap ninety fathoms in length, of the same breadth, and six feet high."[2] They found, besides, on the island a stranded whale.

In spring Samoyeds came from the mainland, and plundered the Russians of part of their catch. Probably for fear of the Samoyeds, the surviving hunters did not go over the ice to the mainland, but remained on the desert island until by a fortunate accident they were rescued by some of their countrymen engaged in a hunting expedition. In connection with the account of this voyage Witsen states that the previous year a Russian hunting vessel stranded *east of the Ob*.

It is probable that towards the close of the sixteenth century the Russian hunting voyages to Novaya Zemlya had already fallen off considerably. The commercial voyages perhaps had long before altogether ceased. It appears as if after the complete conquest of Siberia the land route over the Ural mountains, formerly regarded with such superstitious feelings, was preferred, to the unsafe sea route across the Kara Sea, and as if the Government even put obstacles in the way of the latter by setting

[1] The stringent regulations regarding fasting of the Russians, especially the Old Believers, if they be literally observed, form an insuperable obstacle to the colonisation of high-northern regions, in which, to avoid scurvy, man requires an abundant supply of fresh flesh. Thus, undoubtedly, religious prejudices against certain kinds of food caused the failure of the colony of Old Believers which was founded in 1767 on Kolgujev Island, in order that its members might undisturbed use their old church books and cross themselves in the way they considered most proper. The same cause also perhaps conduced to the failure of the attempts which are said to have been made after the destruction of Novgorod by Ivan the Terrible in 1570 by fugitives from that town to found a colony on Novaya Zemlya (*Historische Nachrichten von den Samojeden und den Lappländern*, Riga und Mietau, 1769, p. 28). This book was first printed in French at Königsberg in 1762. The author was Klingstedt, a Swede in the Russian service, who long lived at Archangel.

[2] The statement is incredible, and probably originated in some mistake. To form such a heap of walruses at least 50,000 animals would have been required, and it is certain that fifteen men could not have killed so many. If we assume that in the statement of the length and breadth, feet ought to stand in place of fathoms, we get the still excessive number of 1,500 to 3,000 killed animals. Probably instead of 90 we should have 9, in which case the heap would correspond to about 500 walruses and seals killed. The walrus tusks collected weighed 40 pood, which again indicates the capture of 150 to 200 animals.

watches at Matvejev Island and at Yugor Straits.[1] These were
to receive payments from the hunters and merchants, and the
regulations and exactions connected with this arrangement
deprived the Polar Sea voyages of just that charm which had
hitherto induced the bravest and hardiest of the population
to devote themselves to the dangerous traffic to the Ob, and
to the employment of hunting, in which they were exposed to
so many dangers, and subject to so great privations.

The circumstance to which we have referred may also be the
reason why we do not know of a single voyage in this part
of the Polar Sea during the period which elapsed from the
voyage of Rodivan Ivanov to "the great Northern Expedition."
It examined, among other parts of the widely extended north
coast of the Russian empire, the southern portion also of the
navigable waters here in question, in the years 1734, 35,
under Muravjev and Paulov, and in 1736, 37 under Malygin,
Skuratov, and Suchotin. Their main working field however did
not lie here, but in Siberia itself; and I shall give an account
of their voyages in the Kara Sea further on, when I come to
treat of the development of our knowledge of the north coast
of Asia. Here I will only state that they actually succeeded,
after untold exertions, in penetrating from the White Sea to the
Ob, and that the maps of the land between that river and the
Petchora, which are still in use, are mainly grounded on the
work of the great northern expedition, but that the bad repute
of the Kara Sea also arose from the difficulties to which these
explorers were exposed, difficulties owing in no small degree
to the defective nature of the vessels, and a number of mistakes
which were made in connection with their equipment, the choice
of the time of sailing, &c.

Like all distant unknown regions, Novaya Zemlya was of old
renowned for its richness in the noble metals. The report indeed
has never been confirmed, and probably was occasioned only by the
occurrence of traces of ore, and the beautiful gold-glancing film
of pyrites with which a number of the fossils found here are
covered; but it has, notwithstanding, given occasion to a number
of voyages to Novaya Zemlya, of which the first known is that
of the mate JUSCHKOV, in 1757. As the mate of a hunting-
vessel he had observed the stones glittering with gold and
silver, and he succeeded in convincing an Archangel tallow-
merchant that they indicated great riches in the interior of
the earth. In order to get possession of these treasures the

---

[1] *Witsen*, p. 915. Klingstedt states that fifty soldiers with their wives
and children were removed in 1648 to Pustosersk, and that the vojvode
there had so large an income that in three or four years he could ac-
cumulate 12,000 to 15,000 roubles (*Historische Nachrichten von den
Samojeden*, &c., p. 53).

tallow-merchant fitted out a vessel, promising Juschkov at the same time a reward of 250 roubles for the discovery. The whole undertaking, however, led to no result, because the discoverer of these treasures died during the passage to Novaya Zemlya (Lütke, p. 70).

Three years after, in 1760,[1] a hunting mate, SAVVA LOSCH-KIN, a native of Olonets, hit on the idea, which was certainly a correct one, that the east coast of Novaya Zemlya, which was never visited by hunters, ought to be richer in game than other parts of the island. Induced by this idea, and probably also by the wish to do something extraordinary, he undertook a hunting expedition thither. Of this expedition we know only that he actually succeeded in travelling round the whole island, thanks to the resolution which led him to spend on this self-imposed task two winters and three summers. It was proved by this journey that Novaya Zemlya is actually an island, a fact which in the middle of last century was still doubted by many geographers.[2]

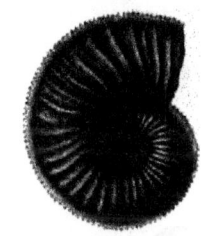

AMMONITE WITH GOLD LUSTRE
From Novaya Zemlya.
Ammonites alternans
v. BUCH.

Even after the failure of Juschkov's expedition the report of the richness of Novaya Zemlya in metals still maintained itself, and accordingly Lieutenant [3] Ross-MUISLOV was sent out with second mate GUBIN, the Polar Sea pilot TSCHIRAKIN, and eleven men, to search for the supposed treasures, and at the same time to survey the unknown portions of the island. The vessel that was used in this Polar Sea voyage must have been a very remarkable one. For shortly before the start, leaks, which had to be stopped, were discovered at many different places in it, and of its power of sailing Rossmuislov himself says: "So long as the wind came from the stern the large sail helped us exceedingly well, but, as soon as it turned and became a head wind, we were compelled to hoist another smaller sail, in consequence of which we were driven back to the point from which we came." Rossmuislov appears to have been a very skilful man in his profession. Without meeting with any obstacle from ice, but at all events with difficulty enough in consequence of the unsuitableness of the vessel, he arrived at Matotschkin Sound,

[1] According to Lütke, p. 70. Hamel, *Tradescant d. ältere*, gives the date 1742-44.

[2] Thus on the first map in an atlas published in 1737 by the St. Petersburg Academy, Novaya Zemlya is delineated as a peninsula projecting from Taimur Land north of the Pjäsina.

[3] Properly "Mate, with the rank of Lieutenant," from which we may conclude that Rossmuislov wanted the usual education of an officer.

P

which he carefully surveyed and took soundings in. From a
high mountain at its eastern mouth he saw on the ¹⁰ᵗʰ ˢᵉᵖᵗ ᐟ²⁹ᵗʰ ᴬᵘᵍ the
Kara Sea completely free of ice—and the way to the Yenisej
thus open ; but his vessel was useless for further sailing. He
therefore determined to winter at a bay named Tjulanaja Guba,
near the eastern entrance to Matotschkin Sound. To this place
he removed a house which some hunters had built on the sound
farther to the west, and erected another house, the materials
of which he had brought from home, on a headland jutting out
into the sound a little more to the east. The latter I visited
in 1876. The walls were then still standing, but the flat roof,

VIEW FROM MATOTSCHKIN SCHAR.
After a drawing by Hj. Thëel. 1875.

loaded with earth and stones, had fallen in, as is often the case
with deserted wooden houses in the Polar regions. The house
was small, and had consisted of a lobby and a room with an
immense fireplace, and sleeping places fixed to the walls.
   On the ¹ˢᵗ ᴼᶜᵗ ᐟ²⁰ᵗʰ ˢᵉᵖᵗ, Matotschkin Sound was frozen over, and some
days after the Kara Sea was covered with ice as far as the eye
could reach. Storms from the north-east, west, and north-west,
with drifting snow of such violence prevailed during the course
of the winter that one could scarcely go ten fathoms from the
house. In its neighbourhood a man was overtaken by such
a storm of drifting snow while hunting a reindeer. When he

did not return after two days' absence it was determined to note him in the journal as having "perished without burial."

On the $\frac{28}{17}$th April, 1769, there was a storm from the south-west, with mist, rain, and hail as large as half a bullet. On the $\frac{2nd\ June}{22nd\ May}$ a dreadful wind raged from the north-west, bringing from the high mountains a "sharp smoke-like air,"—it was certainly a *föhn* wind. The painful, depressing effect of this wind is generally known from Switzerland and from north-western Greenland. At the latter place it rushes right down with excessive violence from the ice-desert of the interior. But far from on that account bringing cold with it, the temperature suddenly rises above the freezing-point, the snow disappears as if by magic through melting and evaporation, and men and animals feel themselves suffering from the sudden change in the weather. Such winds besides occur everywhere in the Polar regions in the neighbourhood of high mountains, and it is probably on their account that a stay in the hill-enclosed kettle-valleys is in Greenland considered to be very unhealthy and to lead to attacks of scurvy among the inhabitants.

The crew remained during the winter whole days, indeed whole weeks in succession, in their confined dwellings, carefully made tight, without taking any regular exercise in the open air. We can easily understand from this that they could not escape scurvy, by which most of them appear to have been attacked, and of which seven died, among them Tschirakin. It is sur-prising that any one of them could survive with such a mode of life during the dark Polar night. The brewing of *quass*, the daily baking of bread, and perhaps even the vapour-baths, mainly contributed to this. ·

On the $\frac{29}{18}$th July the ice on Matotschkin Schar broke up, and on the $\frac{13th}{2nd}$ August the sound was completely free of ice. An attempt was now made to continue the voyage across the Kara Sea, and an endeavour was made for this purpose to put the vessel, defective from the first, and now still further damaged by ice, in repair, by stopping the leaks, as far as possible, with a mixture of clay and decayed seaweed. "Floating coffins" have often been used in Arctic voyages, and many times with greater success than the stateliest man-of-war. This time, however, Rossmuislov, after having sailed some few miles eastward from Matotsch-kin Sound, in order to avoid certain loss, had to return to his winter quarters, where he fortunately fell in with a Russian hunter, with whom he commenced his return to Archangel. No precious metals were found, nor "any pearl-mussels," but Tschirakin confided to Rossmuislov the secret that at a certain place on the south coast he had found a block of stone of such extraordinary beauty that in the light of day it shone with the most splendid fire. After Tschirakin's death

Rossmuislov sought for the stone, but without success, and he therefore broke out in violent reproaches of his deceased comrade. I can, however, free him from the blame of deception; for, during my voyage in 1875, I found in several of the blocks of schist in the region small veins of quartz, crossing the mass of stone. The walls of these veins were covered with hundreds of sharply-developed rock crystals with mirror-bright faces. Tschirakin's precious stone was doubtless nothing else than a druse of this shining but valueless mineral.

Once more, nearly fifty years after Rossmuislov's voyage, in the year 1807, a miner, LUDLOW, was sent out to investigate more thoroughly the supposed richness of the island in metals. He returned without having found any ore, but with the first accounts of the geological formation of the country ; and we have his companion POSPJELOV to thank for some careful surveys on the west coast of Novaya Zemlya.

The next expedition to the island was equipped and sent out from the naval dockyard at Archangel in 1819 under Lieutenant LASAREV, and had, in comparison with its predecessors, very abundant resources. But Lasarev was clearly unfit for the task he had undertaken, of commanding an Arctic exploratory expedition. In the middle of summer many of his crew were attacked by scurvy. Some few weeks after his departure from Archangel, at a time when pools of excellent drinking-water are to be found on nearly every large piece of drift-ice, and rapid torrents of melted snow empty themselves everywhere along the coast into the sea, he complains of the difficulty of procuring fresh water, &c. The expedition accordingly was altogether fruitless.

Of much greater importance were Captain-lieutenant (afterwards Admiral Count) LÜTKE'S voyages to Novaya Zemlya in the summers of 1821, 1822, 1823, and 1824, voyages conducted with special skill and scientific insight. The narrative of them forms one of the richest sources of our knowledge of this part of the Polar Sea. But as he did not penetrate in any direction farther than his predecessors, an account of these voyages does not enter into the plan of the historical part of this work.

Among Russian journeys the following may be noticed :—

Those of the mate IVANOV in 1822-28, during which he surveyed the coast between the Kara river and the Petchora by overland travelling in Samoyed sleighs.

PACHTUSSOV'S voyages in 1832-35.[1] W. BRANDT, merchant,

[1] These remarkable voyages were described for the first time, after the accounts of Zivolka, by the academician K. E. v. Baer in *Bulletin scientifique publ. par l'Acad. Imp. des Sciences de St. Petersburg*, t. ii. No. 9, 10, 11 (1837). Before this there does not appear to have been in St. Petersburg any knowledge of Pachtussov's voyages, the most remarkable which the history of Russian Polar Sea exploration has to show.

and KLOKOV, chief of the civil service, at Archangel, sent out in 1832 an expedition with very comprehensive aims from that town, for the purpose of re-establishing the sea-route to the Yenisej, of surveying the east coast of Novaya Zemlya, and of walrus-hunting there. Three vessels were employed, viz., a "carbasse" manned by ten men, including the Commander-lieutenant in the corps of mates Pachtussov, who in previous voyages with Ivanov had become well acquainted with land and people along

FRIEDRICH BENJAMIN VON LÜTKE.
Born in 1797 in St. Petersburg.

the coasts of the Polar Sea;[1] the schooner *Yenisej* under Lieutenant KROTOV with ten men; and a hunting *lodja* commanded by the hunting mate GWOSDAREV. Pachtussov was to undertake the east coast of Novaya Zemlya, Krotov to sail

---

[1] The carbasse was named, like the vessels of Lasarev and Lütke, the *Novaya Zemlya*. It was forty-two feet long, fourteen feet beam, and six feet deep, decked fore and aft, and with the open space between protected by canvas from breakers.

through Matotschkin Sound and across the Kara Sea to the Yenisej, and Gwosdarev to carry on hunting in order to cover part of the costs of the expedition.

Pachtussov could not penetrate into the Kara Sea, but wintered the first time on South Novaya Zemlya in 70° 36′ N. L. and 59° 32′ E L. (Greenwich), in an old house which he found there, and which according to an inscription on a cross in its neighbourhood had been built in 1759. This ruinous house was repaired with driftwood, which was found in great abundance in that region. A separate bath-house was built, and was connected with the dwelling-house by a passage formed of empty barrels and covered with canvas. Eleven days were spent in putting the old house into such repair that it could be occupied. It was afterwards kept so warm that the inmates could stay there in their shirt-sleeves without freezing. The Commander, clear-headed and specially fit for his post as he was, did not permit his crew to fall into habits of idleness, dirt, and laziness, but kept them to regular work, bathing and change of linen twice a week. Every second hour meteorological observations were taken. During the whole winter the crew remained in good health, but in spring (March) scurvy broke out, notwithstanding the precautions that were taken, and two men died of it in May. Many times during winter the ice broke up, and at a short distance from the land the Kara Sea was open as far as the eye could reach. A herd of reindeer numbering about 500 head were seen in the end of September; a number of foxes were taken in traps, and two Polar bears were killed. Geese were seen for the first time in spring on the $\frac{7}{15}$th of May.

Next summer Pachtussov rowed up along the east coast to 71° 38′ N. L. On the west bank of a river, called Savina, he found a very good harbour. He found there the remains of a hut, with a cross erected beside it, on which was the inscription "Savva Th——anov 9th June 1742," which he considered to belong to the time of Savva Loschkin's voyage. After his return from this boat journey Pachtussov went on board his vessel and sailed along the east coast north of Matotschkin Sound from the $\frac{2nd}{14th}$ July to the $\frac{25}{13}$th August without meeting with any obstacle from ice. During this voyage he passed a very good harbour in 72° 26′ N. L., in a bay, called Lütke's Bay. Pachtussov then returned through Matotschkin Sound to the Petchora. Even along the east coast of North Novaya Zemlya the sea was open, but the stock of provisions, intended at their departure from Archangel for fourteen months, was now so low, that the gallant Polar explorer could not avail himself of this opportunity of perhaps circumnavigating the whole of Novaya Zemlya.

Of the two other vessels that sailed from Archangel at the

same time as Pachtussov's, the *lodja* returned heavily laden
with the spoils of the chase, but on the other hand nothing
was ever heard of the *Yenisej*. A concern, not without
justification, for its fate, and the desire to acquire as good
knowledge of the east coast of the North Island as had been
obtained of that of the South, gave occasion to Pachtussov's
second voyage.

For this the Government fitted out two vessels, a schooner and
a "carbasse," which were named after the two officers of the
Yenisej, Krotov and Kasakov. The command of the former was
undertaken by Pachtussov, and of the latter by the mate
ZIVOLKA. This time they wintered in 1834-35 on the south
side of Matotschkin Sound at the mouth of the river Tschirakina,
in a house built for the purpose, for which they used, besides
materials brought with them, the remains of three old huts,
found in the neighbourhood, and the wreck of Rossmuislov's
vessel which still lay on the beach. The house was a palace in
comparison with that in which Pachtussov wintered before.
It consisted of two rooms, one 21 feet by 16 feet, intended
for the crew (fourteen men), the other 12 feet by 10 feet,
for the officers and surgeon, with a bath-house in addition.
Matotschkin Sound was frozen over for the first time on the $\frac{28}{16}$th
November. The thermometer never sank below the freezing-
point of mercury, and the cold of winter could be easily borne,
because the crew wore the Samoyed dress. But the snow-
storms were so severe, that sometimes it was impossible for eight
days at a time to leave the house, which was so snowed up that
the opening in the roof for smoke had several times to be used
as a door. The house had no true chimney, but was built like a
Lapp hut. Eleven of the bears, who came in large numbers
to the hut, were killed, one of them on the roof and another in
the porch. During winter the crew were kept in constant employment in killing foxes and at other work. Their state of
health was also very good for the circumstances of the time.
Only two men died. In spring Matotschkin Sound and part of
the east coast of the North Island were surveyed by means of
sledge journeys, after which an attempt was made during summer
to circumnavigate the North Island, but without success. Lightning accompanied by heavy rain was observed on the $\frac{24}{13}$th June.
On the $\frac{15}{3}$ September they sailed back to Archangel. Unfortunately soon after his arrival there Pachtussov fell ill of nervous
fever and died on the $\frac{19}{7}$th November, 1835. It was a great loss,
for by his devotion to the task he had undertaken, by judgment,
courage, and endurance, he takes one of the foremost places
among the Polar explorers of all countries. Besides, few of the
older Arctic expeditions have brought home such a series of
valuable astronomical determinations of position, geodetical

measurements, meteorological and tidal observations, &c., as
Pachtussov.[1]

In 1837 the famous naturalist K. E. VON BAER undertook a
voyage to Novaya Zemlya accompanied by Lieutenant ZIVOLKA,
LEHMANN the geologist, RÖDER the draughtsman, and PHILIPPOV
the conservator.[2] They visited Matotschkin Schar, penetrated
by boat to its eastern end and found the Kara Sea open, landing
afterwards at Besimannaja Bay, Nechvatova, and on an island
in Kostin Schar. The expedition thus nowhere penetrated so
far as its predecessors, but it is of importance as the first
examination of the natural history of the Polar Sea surrounding
Novaya Zemlya carried out by actual men of science. With all
the respect we must entertain for von Baer's great name as a
scientific man, it cannot be denied that, through his papers on
the natural history of the island, grounded on a cursory inspection, a number of erroneous ideas regarding the natural
conditions of the eastern Polar Sea obtained a footing in scientific literature.

In order to complete the survey of the island the Russian
Government sent out in 1838 a new expedition under Lieutenants Zivolka and MOISSEJEV. They wintered in 1838-39 in
Melkaja Guba on the west coast of Novaya Zemlya in 73° 57'
N. L.; but on this occasion Pachtussov's judgment and insight
were wanting, and the wintering was very unfortunate. Of the
twenty-five men belonging to the expedition most were attacked
during winter by scurvy; nine died, among them Zivolka himself. During spring, excursions for the purpose of surveying the
neighbouring coasts had to be broken off because they had not
brought snow-glasses with them—a thing that Pachtussov
did not neglect, being accustomed besides to blacken the under
eyelid as a protection against the blinding brightness of the
snow. By the expedition, however, considerable stretches of
the west coast of Novaya Zemlya were surveyed, and valuable
contributions to a knowledge of the climatic conditions of this
region obtained. These turned out to be less severe than had
been expected. During winter the thermometer never sank
below −33°; in July there were only two nights of frost, and on
two occasions + 18° was observed in the shade; in August there
were only three hours of frost. All this depends of course on

[1] The details of Pachtussov's voyages are taken partly from von Baer's
work already quoted, partly from Carl Svenske, *Noraya Zemlya*, &c., St.
Petersburg, 1866 (in Russian, published at the expense of M. K. Sidoroff),
and J. Spörer, *Nowaja Semlä in geographischer, naturhistorischer und
volkswirthschaftlicher Beziehung, nach den Quellen bearbeitet.* Ergänz-Heft.
No. 21 zu Peterm. *Geogr. Mittheilungen*, Gotha, 1867.
[2] *Bulletin scientifique publié par l'Académie Imp. de St. Petersburg*, t. ii.
(1837), p. 315 ; iii. (1839), p. 96, and other places.

the neighbourhood of warm marine currents and of a sea open all the year round at a short distance from the coast.

With this unfortunate and to all appearance ill-arranged expedition the Russian Novaya Zemlya voyages ceased for a long time. For before the beginning of the Norwegian hunting we have only two other Russian voyages to notice in our sketch of the history of the North East passage.

The first of these owed its origin to the desire of the captain of a Russian man-of-war, PAUL VON KRUSENSTERN, to undertake a voyage in the Polar Sea in a schooner, the *Yermak*, which belonged to him and which was for the time lying at the Petchora, in order to survey the coasts lying to the eastward. He intended himself to undertake the command, and to take

AUGUST KARLOVITZ ZIVOLKA.
Born in 1810 at Warsaw; died in 1839 on Novaya Zemlya.
After a pen-and-ink drawing communicated by Herr Paul Daschkoff.

with him as second in command his son PAUL VON KRUSENSTERN, lieutenant in the Russian marine. The latter was sent before to equip the *Yermak*, which he did with wonderful judgment and skill, in the best way possible, in a region where at that time nearly every requisite for the equipment of a vessel was wanting. The elder Krusenstern was unable to reach the place of sailing in time, on which account the command was given to the son.

He left the mouth of the Petchora on the $\frac{\text{10th Sept.}}{\text{29th Aug.}}$, 1860. Three days after he reached the Kara port, which was completely

free of ice, as was the sea to the eastward. But the late season
of the year, the defective equipment of the *Yermak*, and, it
would appear, the wording of the orders he had received,
compelled him to turn after he had penetrated some distance
into the Kara Sea. On the $\frac{19}{7}$th September accordingly he was
again at the Petchora, without having reached his goal. The
attempt to penetrate eastwards from this river was resumed at
the instance of MICHAEL SIDOROFF, afterwards so well known
as the restless promoter of sea-communication between Siberia
and Europe. The *Yermak* was repaired, along with a decked
Norwegian pilot-boat, which was named the *Embrio*. The

PAUL VON KRUSENSTERN, JUNIOR.
Born at Revel in 1834; died at Dorpat in 1871.

command was undertaken by P. von Krusenstern, junior. He
left the anchorage Kuya on the Petchora on the $\frac{19th}{1st}$ August.
On the $\frac{26}{14}$th August, the two small vessels sailed into Yugor
Schar, after having been long detained during their course by
storms and head-winds. Some huts erected by hunters were
seen on the right shore of the sound, and on both sides of it
Samoyed "chums" (tents of reindeer skin) and reindeer. The

inhabitants had climbed up on the roofs and indicated their astonishment by gesticulations. Both vessels anchored in the neighbourhood of Vaygats Island. But a couple of hours afterwards large masses of ice drove with an altered current into the harbour, forced the *Yermak* from its anchor and carried the vessel into the Kara Sea. It was only with great trouble that it was released from the ice and anchored in the eastern mouth of Yugor Schar.

On the $\frac{27}{15}$th von Krusenstern again weighed anchor, either

MICHAEL KONSTANTINOVITSCH SIDOROFF.
Born in 1823 at Archangel.

to sail to the eastward or to search for a more secure anchorage than that which he had been compelled for the time to make use of. But the wind was so light that he could not hold a course independent of the currents. It was, therefore, necessary to moor the vessel to a large ice-field, and with this the *Yermak* during the following days drifted farther and farther. Soon the vessel was completely enclosed by the ice, and thus rendered unmanageable. The weather was often fine, the thermometer showed + 4°, a strong aërial reflection elevated images of the pieces of ice at the horizon, and gave them the most wonderful and beautiful forms. Everywhere there were upon the ice fresh-water pools, some of which were of great extent and of no inconsiderable depth. Thus, on the ice-field lying nearest the vessel there were different "lakes," one of which was used for drinking, another for filling the water-casks, a third to supply washing-water to the crew, and a fourth for washing their clothes.

On the $\frac{3rd\ Sept.}{22nd\ Aug.}$ the ice began to be pressed together by a light W.S.W. wind. Convinced that the vessel would soon be nipped, the men on board began to save the stock of provisions and the boats, by placing them on the ice, but the pressure soon ceased. There fell a heavy rain, which afterwards, when the wind changed to north-west, passed into snow. On the $\frac{7th\ Sept.}{26th\ Aug.}$ the coast of Yalmal was sighted. A fathom-thick ice-floe shot under the vessel and caused it to heel over to starboard. The following day there was a storm from the S.S.W. with snow. The ice forcing itself forward shook the vessel several times so violently that the crew rushed up to save the provisions, &c., on the ice. They were now in the neighbourhood of 70° N.L. and 65° E.L. (Greenwich), almost right off the mouth of the Kara river. The crew worked the whole day with axes and iron bars hewing off the sharp projecting corners of the ice-blocks that were pressed against the vessel. On the $\frac{11th\ Sept.}{30th\ Aug.}$ there was warm weather with rain. The ice was in so violent motion that it was impossible to walk upon it. On the afternoon of the same day the *Yermak* sustained several violent concussions, and the hull was lifted one foot. On the $\frac{13th}{1st}$ September, a violent storm broke out, which drove the vessel to the north-east. It was expected every moment that the vessel would be nipped, and a tent was accordingly pitched on the ice, in order that part of the provisions from the hold might be placed in it. Wood even was carried to it. It was Russia's thousand-years' day, and it was celebrated with a festive ball and merry songs, although they every instant expected their vessel to be crushed by the masses of ice that were pressed together by the fearful storm. On the $\frac{14th}{2nd}$ September, the stem of the vessel was forced five feet above the water-line, and the whole night a continual cracking of timbers was heard in the hull. The water rose rapidly to a depth of two feet. Every man left the vessel and removed to the ice, but soon after the immense ice-field on which the tent was pitched went in pieces, while the leak in the vessel closed, and the crew in consequence went on board again. On the $\frac{15th}{3rd}$ September, the vessel was again pressed so, that the deck at times was bent to the form of a vault. On the $\frac{19th}{7th}$ September, von Krusenstern called the crew together that they might choose from their number three persons to advise with the commander on the best means of making their escape, and two days after the vessel was abandoned, after a meal at which the crew were literally offered all the house afforded. They then broke up for a journey to land, which was exceedingly difficult on account of the unevenness of the ice. They were soon obliged to leave the boat, which they had at first endeavoured to drag along with them over the ice, and take the most indispensable of the provisions on their own backs. On leaving the ship a sailor had secretly got possession of so much brandy, that during the first day's march he had the opportunity of drinking himself dead drunk. To carry him along was not possible, to wait was not advisable. He was left therefore to sleep off the drink ; and in order that he might do so as soon as possible they took off his clothes and left him lying upon the ice with only his shirt on. Next day, however, he got up with his comrades after following their track in the darkness the whole night. Open places were often met with, which the travellers had to cross on pieces of drift-ice rowed forward by boat-hooks. Once when the shipwrecked men were ferrying themselves over upon a piece of ice which was already fully loaded, six walruses were seen in the neighbourhood. They showed a disposition to accompany the .seafarers on the piece of ice, which in that case would certainly have sunk, and it was only after a ball had been sent through the leader's head that the animals gave up their plan for resting, which gave evidence of a gregariousness as great as their want of acquaintance with mankind. After Krusenstern and his companions had for several days in succession drifted backwards and forwards on a piece of ice in the neighbourhood of land, and traversed long stretches by jumping from one piece of ice to another, they at last reached the shore on the $\frac{28}{16}$th September. In the immediate neighbourhood they found an encampment, whose inhabitants (Samoyeds) gave the shipwrecked men a friendly reception, and entertained them with the luxuries of the reindeer herd—raw and cooked reindeer flesh, reindeer tongues, reindeer marrow—raw fish and goose-fat. After the meal was finished the exhausted wanderers lay down to sleep in the Samoyed tents on the soft reindeer skins ; " all sorrows and difficulties were forgotten ; we felt a boundless enjoyment, as if we had come to paradise." Thence they travelled in reindeer sledges to Obdorsk, everywhere received in a friendly and hospitable manner by the wild tribes on the way, although the hospitality sometimes became troublesome, as for instance when an Ostyak compelled von Krusenstern to drink tea six times a day, and six cups each time, and offered him as a special luxury an extract of tobacco in brandy.[1]

[1] Paul von Krusenstern, *Skizzen aus seinem Seemannsleben. Seinen Freunden gewidmet.* Hirschberg in Silesia, without date.

Krusenstern's adventurous journey across the Kara Sea is one
of the many proofs that a Polar navigator ought above everything to avoid being beset. The very circumstance that the
ice-field, in which he became fixed in the neighbourhood of
Yugor Schar, could drift across to the east coast of the Kara
Sea, shows that it was for the most part open, and that a
steamer or a good sailing-vessel that year, and probably also
the preceding, might very readily have reached the mouth of
the Ob or the Yenisej. The narrative of von Krusenstern's
journey is besides the first complete sketch we have of a passage
from west to east over the Kara Sea. Little idea could any one
then have that within a single decade a number of vessels
should sail free and unhindered along this route.

Soon after the two voyages I have described above, and
before they became generally known in the geographical literature of Western Europe, a new era began in the navigation of
the Kara Sea, which was brought about by the Norwegian
hunters being compelled to seek for new fields of sport on and
beyond Novaya Zemlya.

The history of the Spitzbergen hunting has not yet been
written in a satisfactory way, and is in many respects very
obscure. It is supposed that after the discovery of Spitzbergen
in 1596 by Barents, the hunting in the Polar Seas began during
BENNET'S first voyage in 1603, and that the whale-fishing was
introduced by JONAS POOLE in 1610. But already in the following year Poole, whose vessel was then wrecked on the west coast
of Spitzbergen, found in Horn Sound a ship from Hull, to
which he gave charge of saving his cargo, and two years after
the English were compelled, in order to keep foreigners from
the fishing field they wished to monopolise, to send out six
men-of-war, which found there eight Spanish, and a number of
Dutch and French vessels (*Purchas*, iii. pp. 462, 716, &c.).
Even in our days the accounts of new sources of wealth do not
spread so speedily as in this case, unless, along with the history
of the discovery which was written by Hakluyt, Purchas, De
Veer, &c., there had been an unknown history of discovery and
the whale-fishing, of which it may still be possible to collect
some particulars from the archives of San Sebastian, Dunkirk,
Hull, and other ports.

However this may be, it is certain that the English and
Dutch North-east voyages gave origin to a whale-fishery in the
sea round Spitzbergen, which increased by many millions the
national wealth of these rich commercial states. The fishing
went on at first immediately along the coasts, from which,
however, the whales were soon driven, so that the whale-fishers
had to seek new fishing-grounds, first farther out to sea between
Spitzbergen and Greenland, then in Davis' Strait, and finally in

the South Polar Sea, or in the sea on both sides of Behring's Straits.

Spitzbergen, when the whale-fishing ceased in its neighbourhood, was mostly abandoned, until the Russians began to settle there, principally for the hunting of the mountain fox and the reindeer. Of their hunting voyages we know very little, but that they had been widely prosecuted is shown by the remains

NORWEGIAN HUNTING SLOOP

The *Proven*, employed by the Swedish Expedition to the Yenisej in 1875.

of their dwellings or huts on nearly all the fjords of Spitzbergen. They seem to have often wintered, probably because the defective build of their vessels only permitted them to sail to and from Spitzbergen during the height of summer, and they could not thus take part without wintering in the autumn hunting, during which the fattest reindeer are got; nor could the thick and valuable fur of the winter-fox be obtained without

wintering.[1]   But the hunting voyages of the Russians to Spitzbergen have also long ceased.   The last voyage thither took
place in 1851-52, and had a very unfortunate issue for most of
those who took part in it, twelve men dying out of twenty.   On
the other hand, the Norwegian voyages to Spitzbergen for the
seal and walrus-hunting, begun in the end of last century, still
go on.   Their history, too, is, even here in the North, very
incompletely known, at least to 1858, when the Swedish scientific expeditions began regularly to visit those regions, and to
include in the narratives of their voyages more or less complete
accounts of the Norwegian hunting, an example that has since
been followed, though by no means very completely or systema-
tically, by the editors of Norwegian and foreign journals, in
the first place by Petermann's *Mittheilungen*.[2]

Between 1860 and 1870 the game (walrus, seal, bear, and
reindeer) began to diminish in such a degree that the hunters
were compelled to seek for themselves new hunting-grounds.
They turned to the north and east, the less accessible parts of
Spitzbergen, afterwards still farther eastwards towards Novaya
Zemlya, and beyond this island to the Kara Sea, and they
penetrated farther than all their predecessors.   In the history
of the North-East passage therefore some pages must always be
devoted to the bold voyages to Novaya Zemlya of these small
hunting sloops, provisioned only for the summer.

The Norwegian hunter who first visited Novaya Zemlya was
ELLING CARLSEN, afterwards known as a member of the
Austrian Polar expedition.   In 1868 he sailed in a sloop from
Hammerfest on a hunting voyage eastward, forced his way into
the Kara Sea through the Kara Port, but soon returned through
Yugor Schar, and then sailed northwards as far as Cape Nassau.
Induced by the abundance of game, he returned next year to the
same regions, and then succeeded in penetrating the Kara Sea
as far as the neighbourhood of Beli Ostrov, whence he returned
to Norway through Matotschkin Schar.   Carlsen's lead was

[1] Information regarding the mode of life of the Russian hunters on the
coasts of Spitzbergen is to be found in P. A. le Roy, *Relation des avantures
arrivées à quatre matelots Russes, &c.* 1766 ; Tschitschagov's *Reise nach dem
Eismeer*, St. Petersburg, 1793 ; John Bacstrom, *Account of a voyage to
Spitzbergen*, 1780, London, 1808 (as stated ; I have not seen this work);
B. M. Keilhau, *Reise i Öst og Vest Finmarken, samt til Beeren-Eiland og
Spetsbergen i Aarene 1827 og 1828*, Christiania, 1831 ; A. Erman, *Archiv
für wissenschaftliche Kunde von Russland*, Part 13 (1854), p. 260 ; K.
Chydenius, *Svenska expeditionen till Spetsbergen 1861* (p. 435) ; Dunér and
Nordenskiöld, *Svenska Expeditioner till Spetsbergen och Jan Mayen 1863 och
1864* (p. 101).

[2] Before 1858 there is to be found in Petermann's *Mittheilungen* only a
single notice of the Norwegian Spitzbergen hunting, the existence of
which was at the time probably known to no great number of European
geographers.

immediately followed by several Norwegian hunters, one of whom, EDWARD JOHANNESEN, made a very remarkable voyage, of which I will here give a brief account.

Johannesen anchored on the 31st May, 1869, at Meschdu-schar Island, without having seen any drift-ice in the course of his voyage. He then sailed up along the west coast of Novaya Zemlya in nearly open water past Matotschkin Sound to Cape Nassau, which was reached on the 19th June. Hence he returned, following the coast toward the south, until, on the 29th June, he sailed through the Kara Port into the Kara Sea.

ELLING CARLSEN.
Born at Tromsoe in 1819.

This was passed in very open water, and after coming to its eastern side he followed the coast of Yalmal towards the north to Beli Ostrov. This island was reached on the 7th August, and from it he steered south along the east coast of Novaya Zemlya to the Kara Port, through which he returned to Norway.[1]

The same year, the English sportsman, Mr. JOHN PALLISER [2] sailed across the Kara Sea, through Matotschkin Schar to Beli Ostrov. He returned through Yugor Schar with abundance

---

[1] The first account of this voyage was published in *Öfversigt af Svenska Vetenskaps-akademiens förhandlingar*, 1870, p. 111.
[2] *Athenæum*, 1869, p. 498. Petermann's *Mittheilungen*, 1869, p. 391.

of booty[1] from the hunting-grounds where formerly the
walruses tumbled undisturbed among the drift-ice, and where
the white bear has not yet met his superior.[2]

These voyages are amongst the most remarkable that the
history of Arctic navigation can show. They at once overturned
all the theories which, on the ground of an often superficial
study of preceding unsuccessful voyages, had been set up
regarding the state of the ice east of Novaya Zemlya, and they

EDWARD HOLM JOHANNESEN.
Born in 1844, at Balsfjord Parsonage.

thus form the starting-point of a new era in the history of the
North-East Passage.

After his return to Norway Johannesen sent to the Academy
of Sciences in Stockholm a paper on his voyage in 1869, and on
his hydrographical observations in the Kara Sea, for which he
received a silver medal. This I was commissioned to send him,
and in the correspondence which took place regarding it I on
one occasion said in jest that a circumnavigation of Novaya

[1] Palliser's game consisted of 49 walruses, 14 Polar bears and 25
seals ; that of the working hunters was many times greater. All the
vessels which went from Tromsoe that year captured 805 walruses, 2,302
seals, 53 bears, &c.

[2] Sidoroff too started in 1869 on a north-east voyage in a steamer of his
own, the *George*. However, he only reached the Petchora, and the statement
that went the round of the press, that the *George* actually reached the Ob,
is thus one of the many mistakes which so readily find their way into the
news of the day.

Zemlya would certainly entitle him to a gold medal from the same famous scientific institution that had given him the silver medal. I myself travelled the following summer, in 1870, to Greenland, and returned thence late in autumn. I then had the pleasure of receiving from Captain Johannesen a new paper, afterwards inserted in the *Öfversigt*, of the transactions of the Royal Academy of Sciences for the year 1871, p. 157, "Hydrografiske Iakttagelser under en Fangsttour 1870 rundt om Novaja Zemlja." Johannesen now as on the first occasion sailed backwards and forwards along the west coast of Novaya Zemlya, then through the Kara Port, which was passed on the 12th July. He then followed the east coast of Vaygats to Mestni Island, where he came in contact with Samoyeds, in connection with which he makes the remark, certainly quite unexpected by philologists, that in the language of the Samoyeds "certain Norwegian words were recognised." Their exterior was not at all attractive. They had flat noses, their eyes were dreadfully oblique, and many had also oblique mouths. The men received the foreigners drawn up in a row, with the women in the second rank. All were very friendly. On the 11th August he was on the coast of Yalmal in 71° 48' N.L., whence he sailed over to Novaya Zemlya in order to take on board wood and water. He anchored in the neighbourhood of Udde Bay in 73° 48' N.L., and saw there twenty wild reindeer. Then he sailed again over the Kara Sea to Yalmal.

During these cruisings in the Kara Sea the summer had passed. Johannesen's vessel was now full, but notwithstanding this he determined, at a season of the year when the walrus-hunters commonly return to Norway, to see whether the offered prize could not be won into the bargain. The course was shaped first to the north-east, then westward to the north coast of Novaya Zemlya, which was reached on the 3rd September. The whole sea here was open, which Johannesen, on the ground of finding Norwegian fishing-net floats among the driftwood, attributed to the action of the Gulf Stream. Hence he returned to Norway, after having completed a voyage which some years before all geographical authorities would have considered an impossibility. I need scarcely mention that the Academy in Stockholm redeemed the promise which one of its members had given without the necessary authority. Johannesen was then twenty-six years old. Son of a skilful hunter, he had from his childhood taken part in Arctic voyages, and thus grown up in the employment to which he had devoted himself.

The same year several other walrus-hunters also made remarkable voyages in the Kara Sea. Captain E. A. ULVE first sailed along the west coast of Novaya Zemlya to 76° 47' N. L., then back to Matotschkin Schar, through which he passed on the

7th and 8th August into the Kara Sea, which was completely
free of ice, with the exception of some few very scattered pieces.
After sailing backwards and forwards in different directions in
the Kara Sea, he returned through the Kara Port on the 24th
August. Captain F. E. MACK made a similar voyage. He
sailed from the 28th June to the 8th July northwards along the
west coast of Novaya Zemlya, which was free of ice between the
Petchora and the Admiralty Peninsula, where fast ice was
found, and fourteen sailing vessels and two steamers were now
assembled. On the 8th and 9th June thunder was heard here.
From the Admiralty Peninsula Mack sailed again, first to the
south, and then, on the 18th July, through Matotschkin Sound
into the Kara Sea, which was nearly free of ice. Captain P.
QUALE, again, and A. O. NEDREVAAG, sailing master, penetrated
through Yugor Sound into the Kara Sea, and sailed there to
75° 22′ N.L., and 74° 35′ E.L. (Greenwich).[1]

Also in 1871 a number of walrus-hunters made remarkable
voyages in the Kara Sea. Of these, however, only one, Mack,
in the schooner *Pole Star*, penetrated eastwards farther than all
his predecessors. On the 14th June he sailed into the Kara
Sea through the Kara Port, but found the sea still covered with
continuous fast ice, from 1·8 to 2 metres in thickness. He
therefore turned and sailed northwards along the west coast of
Novaya Zemlya to the Gulf Stream Islands (76° 10′ N.L.),
where he remained till the 3rd of August. The temperature
of the air rose here to + 10°·5. The name, which the Norwegian
walrus-hunters have given these islands, owes its origin to the
large number of objects from southern seas which the Gulf
Stream carries with it thither, as floats from the Norwegian
fisheries, with their owner's marks frequently recognisable by
the walrus-hunters—beans of *Entada gigalobium* from the West
Indies, pumice-stone from Iceland, fragments of wrecked vessels,
&c. On the 3rd of August Mack passed the northernmost
promontory of Novaya Zemlya. Hence he sailed into the Kara
Sea where at first he fell in with ice. Farther on, however, the
ice disappeared completely, and Mack on the 12th of September
reached 75° 25′ N.L. and 82° 30′ E.L. (Greenwich) according

---

[1] Petermann's *Mittheilungen*, 1871, p. 97. Along with Ulve's, Mack's,
and Quale's voyages, Petermann refers to a voyage round Novaya Zemlya
by T. Torkildsen. In this case, however, Petermann was exposed to a
possibly unintended deception. Torkildsen, who visited the Polar Sea for
the first time in 1870, indeed made the voyage round Novaya Zemlya, but
only as a rescued man on Johannesen's vessel. Torkildsen's own vessel, the
Alfa, had been wrecked on the 13th July at the bottom of Kara Bay, after
which the skipper and six men were saved by Johannesen, yet by no
means so that Torkildsen, as is stated by Petermann, had the least command of the vessel that saved him. (Cf. *Tromsoe Stiftstidende*, 1871,
No. 23.)

to Petermann, but 81° 11' Long. according to the *Tromsoe Stiftstidende.* He returned through Yugor Schar, which was passed on the 26th September.[1] The same year E. Johannesen after long endeavouring without success to make his way into the Kara Sea through the southern strait, sailed northwards along the west coast of Novaya Zemlya, and did not leave Cape Nassau until the 15th October.

From the same year too Petermann also publishes very remarkable journals of the Norwegian walrus-hunting captains, S. TOBIESEN, H. CH. JOHANNESEN, J. N. ISAKSEN, SÖREN JOHANNESEN, DOERMA, SIMONSEN, and E. CARLSEN; but as none of these gallant seamen that year penetrated to the north or east beyond the points which their predecessors had reached, I may be allowed with regard to their voyages to refer to *Mittheilungen* for 1872 (pp. 386—391 and 395), also to the maps which are inserted in the same volume of that journal (pl. 19 and 20), and which are grounded on the working out by Prof. H. MOHN, of Christiania, of his countrymen's observations. With respect to Captain E. Carlsen's voyage, however, it may be stated, that in the course of it a discovery was made, which has been represented as that of an Arctic Pompeii, remarkably well protected against the depredation of the tooth of Time, not indeed by lava and volcanic ashes, but by ice and snow. For when Carlsen on the 9th September landed on the north-east coast of Novaya Zemlya in 76° 7' N.L., he found there a house, 10 metres long and 6 metres wide, with the roof fallen in, long since abandoned and filled with gravel and ice. From this frozen gravel were dug up a large number of household articles, books, boxes, &c., which showed that they were relics of Barents' winter dwelling, which now, almost three hundred years after the place had been abandoned, came to the light of day, so well preserved that they gave a lively idea of the way in which the European passed his first winter in the true Polar regions. When Carlsen had erected a cairn in which he placed a tin canister containing an account of the discovery, he took on board the most important of the articles which he had found and returned to Norway. There he sold them at first for 10,800 crowns to an Englishman, Mr. Ellis C. Lister Kay, who afterwards made them over for the price he had paid for them to the Dutch Government. They are now to be found arranged at the Marine Department at the Hague in a model room, which is an exact reproduction of the interior of Barents' house on Novaya Zemlya.[2]

---

[1] *Tromsoe Stiftstidende,* 1871, No. 83; Petermann's *Mittheilungen,* 1872, p. 384.

[2] Cf. *The Three Voyages of William Barents,* by Gerrit de Veer, 2nd Edition, with an Introduction by Lieutenant Koolemans Beynen. London, 1876 (Works issued by the Hakluyt Society, No. 54).

After Carlsen, Barents' winter haven was visited in the year 1875 by the Norwegian walrus-hunter, M. GUNDERSEN, who among other things found there a broken chest containing two maps and a Dutch translation of the narrative of Pet's, and Jackman's voyages, and in the year 1876 by MR. CHARLES GARDINER, who through more systematic excavations succeeded in collecting a considerable additional number of remarkable things, among which were the ink-horn and the pens which the Polar travellers had used nearly three centuries ago, and a powder-horn, containing a short account, signed by Heemskerk and Barents, of the most important incidents of the expedition. Gundersen's *find* is still, as far as I know, at Hammerfest; Gardiner's has been handed over to the Dutch Government to be preserved along with the other Barents relics at the Hague.

In 1872 the state of the ice both north of Spitzbergen and round Novaya Zemlya was exceedingly unfavourable,[1] and several of the scientific expeditions and hunting vessels, which that year visited the Arctic Ocean, there underwent severe calamities and misfortunes. Five of the best hunting vessels from Tromsoe were lost in the ice; the Swedish expedition, which that year started for the north, could not, as was intended, erect its winter dwelling on the Seven Islands, but was compelled to winter at the more southerly Mussel Bay; and the Austrian expedition under the leadership of Payer and Weyprecht was beset by ice a few hours after its campaign had commenced in earnest. It is well known how this carefully equipped expedition afterwards for two winters in succession drifted about in the Polar Sea, until it finally came to a standstill at a previously unknown land lying north of Novaya Zemlya, which was named after the Austrian Emperor, Franz Josef. These two expeditions, however, did not touch the territory of the *Vega's* voyage, on which account I cannot here take any further notice of them.[2] But the same year a wintering took place on the west coast of Novaya Zemlya, of which I consider that I ought to give a somewhat more detailed account, both because in the course of it one of the most gallant Polar voyagers of Norway met his

---

[1] The sea in the neighbourhood of Spitzbergen on the east was on the other hand very open that year, so that it was possible at the same time to reach and circumnavigate the large island situated to the east of Spitzbergen, which had been seen in 1864 by Dunér and me from the top of White Mount in the interior of Stor Fjord.

[2] Nor does space permit me to give an account of various expeditions, which indeed concerned Novaya Zemlya, but did not penetrate farther eastward than their predecessors; for instance, the Rosenthal expedition of 1871, in which the well-known African traveller and Spitzbergen voyager Baron von Heuglin, and the Norwegian botanist Aage Aagaard, took part as naturalists; Payer and Weyprecht's voyage of reconnaissance in the sea between Spitzbergen and Novaya Zemlya in 1871 &c.

fate, and because it shows us various new, hitherto untouched sides of winter life in the High North.

SIVERT TOBIESEN was one of the oldest and boldest of the Norwegian walrus-hunting skippers; he had with life and soul devoted himself to his calling, and in it was exposed to many dangers and difficulties, which he knew how to escape through courage and skill. In 1864 he had sailed round the north-eastern part of North-east Land, and had been very successful in hunting; but as he was about to return home, his vessel was beset by ice near the southern entrance to Hinloopen Strait, where the same fate also overtook two other hunting sloops, one

SIVERT KRISTIAN TOBIESEN.
Born at Tromsoe in 1821, died on Novaya Zemlya in 1873.

of them commanded by the old hunting skipper MATTILAS, who in the winter of 1872-73 died in a tent at Grey Hook, the other by the skipper J. ÅSTRÖM. They were compelled to save themselves in boats, in which they rowed through Hinloopen Strait to the mouth of Ice Fjord, where the shipwrecked crews were met and saved by the Swedish expedition of 1864. He passed the winter of 1865-66 happily, in a house built for the purpose on Bear Island, and communicated to the Swedish Academy of Sciences a series of valuable meteorological observations, made during the wintering.[1]   After 1868 he had made

[1] Kongl. *Svenska Vetenskaps-akademiens handlingar*, 1869.

several successful voyages to Novaya Zemlya, some of which
were also remarkable from a geographical point of view, and in
1872 he was also on a hunting expedition to the same regions.
As he could not enter the Kara Sea, he sailed up along the west
coast, where in the middle of September he was beset in the
neighbourhood of the Cross Islands. Hence seven of the crew
travelled south in a boat to seek for a vessel, but Tobiesen himself, his son, and two men, remained on board. Their stock of
provisions consisted of only a small barrel of bread, a sack of
corners and fragments of ship biscuit, a small quantity of coffee,
tea, sugar, syrup, groats, salt meat, salt fish, a few pounds of
pork, a couple of tin canisters of preserved vegetables, a little

TOBIESEN'S WINTER HOUSE ON BEAR ISLAND.
After a sketch by the Author.

bad butter, &c. There was abundance of wood on board and
on the land. Notwithstanding the defective equipment they
went on bravely and hopefully with the preparations for wintering, gathered drift-wood in heaps on the beach, threw a tent of
sails over the vessel, threw up snow about its sides, covered the
deck with the hides of the seals and walruses that had been
captured during summer, did what could be done to bring
about good ventilation on board, &c. A large number of
bears came to the winter station at the commencement of
the wintering, affording an abundant supply of fresh bears'
flesh. So long as this lasted, the health of the party was

good, but when it came to an end at the new year, their food for three weeks consisted mainly of ill-smelling salt bears' flesh. Tobiesen and one of the men were now taken ill. The cold sank to – 39½° C.[1] On the 29th of April, 1873, Tobiesen died of scurvy. In the month of May his son was also attacked, and died on the 5th July. The two men also suffered from scurvy, but recovered. They rowed south in the month of August, and were rescued by a Russian hunting-vessel.

The seven men, the harpooner Henrik Nilsen, Ole Andreas Olsen, Axel Henriksen, Amandus Hansen, Nils Andreas Foxen, Johan Andersson and Lars Larsen, who rowed away in autumn had an exceedingly remarkable fate. When they left the vessel they could only take with them fourteen ship biscuits, six boxes of lucifers, two guns, with ammunition, a spy-glass, a coffee-pot and an iron pot, but no winter clothes to protect them from the cold. At first, in order to get to open water, they had to drag the boat about seven kilometres over the ice. They then steered southwards along the land. The journey was made under circumstances of great difficulty and privation. The darkness and cold increased, as did the storm, and what was worst of all their stock of provisions was very soon consumed. On the second day, however, they were fortunate enough to shoot a bear; afterwards they also succeeded in killing a pair of seals. Finally, after having partly rowed and partly sailed about three weeks (they had no almanac with them), and travelled nearly 400 kilometres, they came to two small hunting or store houses, which the Russians had built on the north side of Gooseland. In order to have at least a roof over their heads the exhausted men settled there, though in the house they found neither food, clothes, nor hunting implements. They were all much enfeebled by hunger, thirst, cold, and the long boat journey; their feet were swollen and partly frost-bitten.

They remained in the house three weeks, and during that time shot a seal, two white foxes, and four reindeer, with which they kept in their lives; but as it appeared that there were no more reindeer to be had, and there were no more opportunities of shooting seals or reindeer, they determined to leave the house and endeavour to get to Vaygats Island. When they broke up, Ole Andreas Olsen and Henrik Nilsen took the guns and ammunition, while the other five commenced the journey with some small sledges they had found at the house, on which they loaded what they had of clothes and other articles. The

---

[1] At Mussel Bay, too, during the winter of 1872-73, the greatest degree of cold was the same; that is to say, at neither place did it reach the freezing-point of mercury. At the *Vega's* winter station, on the contrary, it was considerably greater.

boat was left behind. Soon after they left the house Ole
Andreas Olsen and Henrik Nilsen were separated in a snow-
storm from the others who drew the sledges. The latter now
agreed to determine by lot whether they should return to the
house or continue their journey, and when the lot fell for the
latter they allowed it to settle the matter, and so went south.[1]

Their position was now desperate in the extreme. When
they left the house they had about half a pound of reindeer
flesh and a little blubber remaining. The weather was dreadful; they were badly clothed, and they wanted water. In consequence they could make only very short days' marches. At
night they buried themselves in the snow, and while the rest
slept, one man kept constant watch, to prevent the others from
being snowed up and to keep the bears at a distance. They all
held out till the sixth night. Then Amandus Hansen died.
The rest were compelled to leave him in the snow and continue
their journey as well as they could, but they had by degrees
become so weak and exhausted that, after having traversed
probably about 100 kilometres, for the most part along the
coast, they had to leave even the sledges and the most of what
they had with them. The seventh or eighth day they caught
sight of a little pile of fuel, and the track of a sledge in the
snow. By following this track for about ten kilometres they
found a small house, inhabited by Samoyeds, who immediately
gave them a friendly reception, and entertained them in the
most hospitable way. In particular they showed much kindness
to Nils Andreas Foxen, whose toes were frost-bitten, and who
was in other respects much enfeebled.

These Samoyeds, three men, three women, and a boy, spoke
Russian. They had settled for the winter on the south part of
Gooseland to shoot the seal and the walrus. They had with
them a large barge, besides some small Samoyed boats, and were
comparatively well provided with reindeer flesh, meal, tea,
sugar, &c. Their guns were old flint-lock fowling-pieces, but
they were good shots. With these Samoyeds the four shipwrecked men remained the whole winter, and were tolerably
well off. When the weather permitted they assisted the
Samoyeds in capturing seals, and when the weather was bad they
passed the time as well as they could, the Samoyeds generally
employing themselves in playing cards or draughts. In order
to avoid scurvy the Samoyeds often took exercise in the open
air, and ate reindeer flesh, partly cooked and partly raw, and
drank the blood. They lived in the house until March was well
advanced, when, for want of fuel they were obliged to hew it

---

[1] It is very common that the hunters in cases of importance and danger,
when it is difficult to settle what course ought to be taken, permit the
drawing of lots to determine the choice.

down. Instead they removed into a tent of reindeer skin. These Samoyeds appear to have been Christians in name, though they must have had strange ideas of their new God. When, for instance, they saw a seal and missed shooting it, they shot at the sun, because they believed that God was angry with them. They lived in a sort of marriage, but if the man became unfriendly to the woman, or tired of her, he could take another; they had no clocks, but, notwithstanding, had a tolerably good idea of time by the help of the stars and the sun ; instead of an almanac they used a piece of wood, in which for every day they cut a notch. Although they sometimes quarrelled with and threatened one another, they were, however, on the whole friendly, and reasonable, and showed much kindness to the four shipwrecked men, whom they provided with warm skin clothes, and during the whole time with food in abundance, according to their circumstances, so that they did not suffer any want.

Ole Andreas Olsen and Henrik Nilsen had, when they were separated in the snowstorm from the sledge party, half a pound of flesh and their guns, and nothing more. They did not succeed in finding any game, and though they were not very far from the house, they required three days and a half to get back to it. In the meantime, also, these two comrades in misfortune had been separated. Henrik Nilsen found the house first, lighted a fire, roasted and ate some pieces of fox flesh that he found remaining. Ole Andreas Olsen, who in desperation had endeavoured to quench his thirst with sea-water, was so weak that, when late at night he came to the boat, he could not crawl up to the house. He had kept himself in life by eating snow and devouring large pieces of his " pesk," which was made of the raw hides of reindeer he had previously shot. After having lain a while in the boat he crept up to the house, where he found Henrik sleeping by the fire, which was not yet quite extinguished. The following day they both began to make arrangements for a lengthened stay in the house. But here they found nothing, neither food, household furniture, nor aught else. Nor did they succeed at first in getting any game ; and for more than a fortnight they sustained life by boiling and gnawing the flesh from the bones of the reindeer, the seal, and the bear, that lay under the snow, remains from the Russian hunting excursions of the preceding year. Finally, before Christmas they succeeded in killing a reindeer. Their lucifers were now done, but they lighted a fire by loading their guns with a mixture of which gunpowder formed a part, and firing into old ropes, left behind by· the Russians, which they picked asunder and dried. One of the Russian huts they tore down and used as fuel. They had neither axe nor saw, but they split up the fuel by means of a piece of iron, which they took from the keel of the boat, and of which they made, by hammering with stones, a sort of knife. Of some nails, which they also took from the boat, they likewise forged needles by means of stones ; they used reindeer sinews for thread, and of the hides they sewed clothes for themselves. They lived in the hut until some time in April. During this time they shot eleven reindeer and a bear, so that they did not actually suffer·hunger ; but in the middle of April they had powder remaining for only three shots, and they now saw the impossibility of supporting themselves longer at that place, wherefore they determined to go farther south, in order, if possible, to reach Vaygats Island. They went by land along the sea-shore, leaving the boat behind. After the lapse of some days they came to the same Samoyeds with whom the other four of the crew were, and they now remained till the middle of June with the Samoyeds, who gave them the same hospitable treatment as their companions in misfortune. When at the time specified it was determined to · fetch the boat from the Russian hut, in order that they might make their way southwards, Johan Andersson, a Swede by birth, declared that he wished to remain with the Samoyeds, and was not willing to accompany the other five on their homeward journey.

The latter now dragged the boat for two days over the ice ; but when it became too heavy they had to cut it through the middle and leave a half behind. Of a large sealskin, which they got from the Samoyeds, they made a stern to the other half, which they continued to drag over the ice for three days, until they came to open water. Then they rowed in the truncated boat ten days, until they reached a fast ice-border at the Vaygats Island, where they again fell in with Samoyeds. Even by these, who could speak neither Russian nor Quaen, and by whom they could with difficulty make themselves understood, they were well received. They remained there eight days and got good entertainment. These Samoyeds had tame reindeer, with which they sent the shipwrecked men on their way southwards, till they fell in with a vessel, with which four returned to Norway. Lars Larsen now did not wish to go home, preferring to remain with the Samoyed family which he had last met with. Samoyed life, however, must not be so pleasant after all, for in a year or two both the men who had remained among the Samoyeds returned home. As a reward for the hospitality which the shipwrecked walrus-hunters had received from the Samoyeds on Gooseland, the Norwegian Government presented them with a number of gifts, consisting of clothes, pearls, breechloaders, with ammunition, &c., which were handed over to them with festive speeches and toasts on the 17th July, 1880. During the entertainment which took place on this occasion on the coast of Novaya Zemlya, toasts were drunk in champagne, and it is said that this liquor was very much relished by the Samoyeds.[1]

As little as Tobiesen could any other walrus-hunter make his way, either in 1872 or 1873, into the Kara Sea, the entrances of which were during these summers blocked by a compact belt of ice, which extended along the east coast of Novaya Zemlya and Vaygats Island to the mainland. In the belief of a large number of experienced walrus-hunters, with whom I have conversed on the subject, this belt of ice was only some few nautical miles broad, and it is therefore probable that even in those years there would have been no obstacle to prevent a passage eastwards by this route in autumn.

In 1874, on the contrary, the state of the ice became very favourable, and many walrus-hunters again as formerly sailed in all directions across the Kara Sea, which this year was also visited by an Englishman, Captain J. WIGGINS. None of them, however, penetrated farther to the east or north than Johannesen, Carlsen, Mack, and others had done during the years 1869-70.

It was not until the following year that the North-east voyages took a step forward, important both in a purely geographical as well as a practical point of view, when I succeeded in a walrus-hunting sloop, the *Proeven*, commanded by the walrus-hunting Captain Isaksen, in sailing through Yugor Straits, which were passed on 2nd August, and over the nearly ice-free Kara Sea as far as to the mouth of the Yenisej. The *Proeven* anchored there on the 15th August 1875, in, or more correctly immediately off, the same splendid haven where the *Vega* expedition lay at anchor from the 6th to the 10th August, 1878. Hence I sailed under various difficulties along with Dr. Stuxberg and Dr. Lundström and three men in a Nordland boat, up the river to Saostrovskoj, where we fell in with a steamer, in which we afterwards travelled to Yenisejsk. On leaving Port Dickson I handed over the command to Dr. Kjellman, who along with Dr. Thëel returned by sea to Europe across the Kara Sea and through Matotschkin Schar, which was passed during the return voyage on the 4th to the 11th September.

By this voyage of 1875 I was the first who succeeded in penetrating from the Atlantic Ocean in a vessel to the mouths of the great Siberian rivers. One of the objects which the old

[1] The statements made here regarding the wintering of Tobiesen and his companions are taken partly from a copy which I caused to be made of his journal, partly from an account of the adventures of the seven hunters, copied from *Finmarksposten* into *Aftonbladet* for 1873, No. 220. Finally, the account of the distribution of presents to the Samoyeds is copied from Norwegian journals into *Aftonbladet* for 1880, No. 197.

North-east voyagers had aimed at was thus at last accomplished, and that in a way that promised to be of immense practical importance for the whole of Siberia. The voyage was also regarded in that light by leading men in the great empire of the East, and our return journey from Yenisejsk by Krasnojarsk, Tomsk, Omsk, Yekaterineburg, Nischni-Novgorod, Moscow and St. Petersburg, became therefore a journey from *fête* to *fête*. But a number of voices were simultaneously raised, which asserted that the success of the *Proeven* depended on an accidental combination of fortunate circumstances, which would not soon occur again. In order to show that this was not the case, and that I might myself bring the first goods by sea to Siberia, I undertook my second voyage to the Yenisej in 1876, in which I penetrated with the steamer *Ymer*, not only to the mouth of the river, but also up the river to the neighbourhood of Yakovieva in 71° N. L. Hence I returned the same year by sea to Europe.[1] In the gulf of Yenisej a large island was discovered, which I named after Mr. Alexander Sibiriakoff, who defrayed the principal expenses of the expedition. Before starting on this voyage, I visited the Philadelphia Exhibition, and it may perhaps deserve to be mentioned, that leaving New York on the 1st July by one of the ordinary steamers, and going on board my own vessel in Norway, I reached the mouth of the Yenisej on the 15th August, that is to say, in forty-six days.

The same year Captain Wiggins also undertook a voyage to the Yenisej, in which he penetrated with a steamer up the river beyond the labyrinth of islands lying between 70° and 71° N. L. The vessel wintered there, but was lost the following spring at the breaking up of the ice.[2]

The voyages of the *Proeven* and the *Ymer* led to several purely commercial voyages to the Yenisej and the Ob, of which however I can here with the greatest brevity mention only the following :

The Swedish steamer *Fraser*, commanded by the German Captain DALLMANN, after having been fitted out at Gothenburg on Sibiriakoff's account, sailed in 1877 with a cargo from Bremen

---

[1] The dates of the *Ymer's* voyage are as follows :—Left the coast of Norway on the 26th July ; stay at Matotschkin Sound, through which I, on this occasion, steamed into the Kara Sea from the 30th July to the 5th August; arrival at the Yenisej on the 15th August ; arrival at the anchorage at Goltschicha on the 16th August; commenced the return voyage on the 1st September, in the course of it passed Matotschkin Schar on the 7th September.

[2] Of Captain Wiggins' voyage I know only that his original destination was the Ob, but that on account of currents and shoals which he encountered at the mouth of this river, he altered his plan, and reached the Yenisej in the beginning of September.

to the Yenisej and back. The vessel left Hammerfest on the 9th August, arrived at Goltschicha on the 21st August, commenced the return voyage on the 14th September, and on the 24th of the same month was back at Hammerfest.

The steamer *Louise* commanded by Captain DAHL, with a cargo of iron, olive oil, and sugar, the same year made the first voyage from England to Tobolsk, starting from Hull on the 18th July and arriving at Tobolsk on the 20th September.[1]

Captain SCHWANENBERG sailed in a half-decked sloop, the *Utrennaja Saria*, from the Yenisej to Europe. To what has

JOSEPH WIGGINS.

been already said of this voyage, I may here add a few words more.

During the inundation in the spring of 1877, which compelled the mate Nummelin to betake himself for eight days to the roof of the fragile dwelling in which he had passed the winter, the Yenisejsk-built vessel, the *Aurora* (or *Sewernoe Sianie*) was lost. Schwanenberg, who soon afterwards came to the neighbourhood, succeeded in purchasing from an Englishman, Mr. SEEBOHM, another little vessel, which was also built at

---

[1] *Deutsche Geographische Blätter*, Bremen, 1870, i. p. 216, and ii. p. 35.

Yenisejsk by Mr. Boiling for the purpose of transporting thither
the goods which I had carried in the *Ymer* to Korepovskoj, a
simovie on the bank of the Yenisej in 71° 19′ N.L. The
goods however had been taken up the river by a steamer, on
which account the vessel was sold by Boiling to Mr. Seebohm,
who made an excursion in it to the lower courses of the
Yenisej for ornithological researches. He named the vessel the
Ibis. When Mr. Seebohm no longer required it, there was at
first a proposal that it should be taken over by Captain Wiggins,
who, as has been already stated, had the year before come to

DAVID IVANOVITSCH SCHWANENBERG.
Born in Courland in 1831.

the Yenisej with a small steamer, which wintered at the islands
in the river, and had now stranded during the breaking up of
the ice. He wished to carry his men on the *Ibis* either home
or to the Ob, but the English seamen declared that they would
not for all the world's honour and riches sail in that vessel.
Schwanenberg had thus an opportunity of purchasing the
vessel, whose name he altered to the *Utrennaja Saria* (the
Dawn), and to the surprise of all experienced seamen he
actually made a successful passage to Norway. The vessel
was then towed along the coast to Gothenburg, and through

the Göta Canal to Stockholm, and finally crossed the Baltic to St. Petersburg.

On the 13th August Schwanenberg hoisted the Russian flag on his little vessel. During his outward passage he met, in the mouth of the Yenisej, Sibiriakoff's steamer the *Fraser*, Captain Dallmann, who in vain endeavoured to dissuade him from prosecuting the adventurous voyage. He anchored at Beli Ostrov on the 24th August, passed the Kara Port on the 30th August, and reached Vardoe on the 11th September. The *Utrennaja*

GUSTAF ADOLF NUMMELIN.
Born at Viborg in 1853.

Saria arrived at Christiania on the 31st October, at Gothenburg on the 15th November, passed Motala on the 20th, reached Stockholm on the 23rd November and St. Petersburg on the 3rd December. Everywhere in Scandinavia the gallant seamen met with the heartiest reception. Their vessel was the first that sailed from the town of Yenisejsk to Europe, and is still when this is being written, the only one.

The *Dawn* is 56 feet long, 14 feet beam, and draws 6 feet of water. Aft there is a little cabin in which there is scant space

R

for three men. Cooking is done in the fore. The cargo consisted of a small quantity of graphite, fish, furs, and other samples of the products of Siberia.

The vessel was manned by Captain Schwanenberg, the mates

THE SLOOP UTRENNAJA SARIA.

Nummelin and Meywaldt, and two exiled criminals, who in this unexpected way returned to their native country. I take it for granted that by the rare nautical exploit they took part in, they there won forgiveness for former offences.

Mag.

E

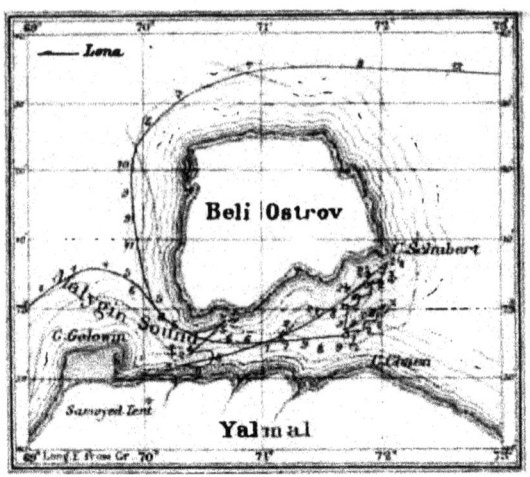

Map of **CAPE CHELYUSKIN** by G. Bove.

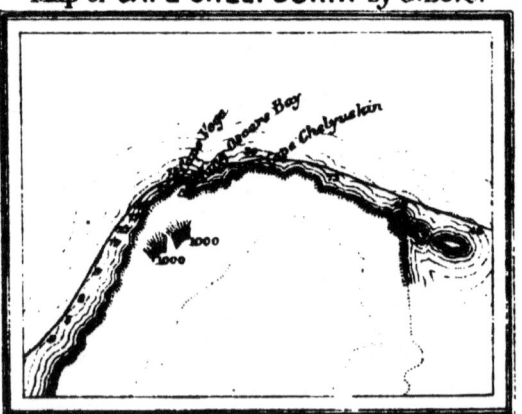

CHAPTER VII.

Departure from Port Dickson—Landing on a rocky island east of the Yenisej—Self-dead animals—Discovery of crystals on the surface of the drift-ice—Cosmic dust—Stay in Actinia Bay—Johannesen's discovery of the island Ensamheten—Arrival at Cape Chelyuskin—The natural state of the land and sea there—Attempt to penetrate right eastwards to the New Siberian Islands—The effect of the mist—Abundant dredging-yield—Preobraschenie Island—Separation from the *Lena* at the mouth of the river Lena.

WHEN on the morning of the 9th August the *Fraser* and *Express* sailed for the point higher up the river where their cargo was lying, the *Vega* and the *Lena* were also ready to sail. I, however, permitted the vessels to remain at Port Dickson a day longer, in order to allow Lieutenant Bove to finish his survey, and for the purpose of determining astronomically, if possible, the position of this important place. In consequence of a continuous fog, however, I had as little opportunity of doing so on this occasion as during the voyage of 1875, which serves to show of what sort the weather is during summer at the place where the warm water of the Yenisej is poured into the Arctic Ocean. It was thus not until the morning of the 10th August that the *Vega* and the *Lena* weighed anchor in order to continue their voyage. The course was shaped for the most westerly of the islands, which old maps place off the estuary-bay of the Pjäsina, and name Kammenni Ostrova (Stone Islands), a name which seems to indicate that in their natural state they correspond to the rocky islands about Port Dickson. The sky was hid by mist, the temperature of the air rose to + 10°·4 C. ; that of the water was at first + 10°, afterwards + 8° ; its salinity at the surface of the sea was inconsiderable. No ice was seen during the course of the day. Favoured by a fresh breeze from the south-east, the *Vega* could thus begin her voyage with all sail set. Small rocky islands, which are not to be found on the chart, soon reminded us of the untrustworthiness of the maps. This, together with the prevailing fog, compelled Captain Palander to sail forward with great caution, keeping a good outlook and sounding constantly. Warm weather and an open sea were also favourable for the next day's voyage. But the fog now became so dense, that the *Vega* had to lie-to in the morning at one of the many small islands which we still met with on our way.

Dr. Kjellman, Dr. Almquist, Lieutenant Nordquist, and I, landed here. The bare and utterly desolate island consisted of a low gneiss rock, rising here and there into cliffs, which were

R 2

shattered by the frost and rather richly clothed with lichens. On the more low-lying places the rock was covered with a layer of gravel, which, through drying and consequent contraction, had burst into six-sided figures, mostly from 0·3 to 0·5 metre in diameter. The interior of the figures was completely bare of vegetation, only in the cracks there was to be seen an exceedingly scanty growth of stunted mosses, lichens, and flowering plants. Of the last-named group there were found fifteen species,[1] which could with success, or more correctly without succumbing, survive the struggle for existence on the little poor archipelago, protected by no mountain heights, from the storms of the Polar Sea; but of these species, perhaps a couple seldom develop any flowers. The mosses, too, were in great part without fruit, with the exception of those which grew on the margin, formed of hard clay covered with mud, of a pool, filled with brackish water and lying close to the sea-margin. A large number of pieces of driftwood scattered round this pool showed that the place was occasionally overflowed with sea-water, which thus appears to have been favourable to the development of the mosses. Of lichens Dr. Almquist found a number of species, well developed, and occurring in comparative abundance. On the contrary, the sea, although the surrounding rocky islands indicated a good bottom for algæ, was so completely destitute of the higher algæ, that only a single microscopic species was found by Dr. Kjellman. No mammalia were seen, not even the usual inhabitant of the desolate rocky islands of the Polar Sea, the Polar bear, who, in regions where he has not made acquaintance with the hunter's ball or lance, in secure reliance on his hitherto unvanquished might, seldom neglects to scrutinise the newly arrived guests from the tops of high rocks or ice-blocks. We saw here only six species of birds. The first of these that attracted our attention was the snow-bunting, which had left the more fertile mountain heights of the south to choose this bare and desolate island in the Arctic Ocean for its breeding-place, and now fluttered round the stone mounds, where it had its nest, with unceasing twitter, as if to express its satisfaction with its choice. Further, two species of waders, *Tringa maritima* and *Phalaropus fulicarius*, were observed running restlessly about the beach to collect their food, which consists of insects.

---

[1] Namely, according to Dr. Kjellman's determination, the following :—

Saxifraga oppositifolia L.	Cerastium alpinum L.
,, rivularis L.	Alsine macrocarpa FENZL.
,, cæspitosa L.	Sagina nivalis FR.
Cardamine bellidifolia L.	Salix polaris WG.
Cochlearia fenestrata R. BR.	Glyceria vilfoidea (ANDS.) TH. FR.
Ranunculus hyperboreus ROTTB.	Catabrosa algida (SOL.) FR.
Stellaria Edwardsii R. BR.	Aira cæspitosa L.
	Juncus biglumis L.

The birds that were killed often had their crops full of the remains of insects, although living at a place where the naturalist has to search for hours to find a dozen gnats or their equals in size, a circumstance that tells very favourably for these birds' power of vision, of locomotion, and of apprehension. It is difficult in any case to understand what it is that attracts this insectivorous bird to one of the regions that is poorest in insect life in the whole world. The glaucous gulls' plunderer, the skua, and its chastiser the bold tern, were also observed, as were a few barnacle geese. On the other hand, no eiders were met with. All the birds named occurred only in inconsiderable numbers, and

THE VEGA AND LENA MOORED TO AN ICE-FLOE.
On the morning of the 12th August, 1878. After a drawing by O. Nordquist.

there was nothing found here resembling the life which prevails on a Spitzbergen fowl-island. Finally, it may be mentioned that Lieutenant Nordquist found under stones and pieces of drift-wood a few insects, among them a beetle (a *staphylinid*). Dr. Stuxberg afterwards found a specimen of the same insect species at Cape Chelyuskin itself. No beetle is found on Spitzbergen, though the greater portion of that group of islands is, in respect of climate, soil, and vegetation, much better favoured than the region now in question. This seems to me to show that the insect fauna of Spitzbergen, exceedingly inconsiderable and limited in numbers as it is, has migrated thither in comparatively recent times, and in how high a degree the migration

of beetles is rendered difficult by their inability to pass broad
expanses of water.

By afternoon the air had again cleared somewhat, so that we
could sail on. A piece of ice was seen here and there, and at
night the ice increased for a little to an unpleasant extent.
Now, however, it did not occur in such quantity as to prove an
obstacle to navigation in clear weather or in known waters.

On the 12th August we still sailed through considerable
fields of scattered drift-ice, consisting partly of old ice of large
dimensions, partly of very rotten year's ice. It formed, however, no serious obstacle to our advance, and nearer the shore
we would probably have had quite open water, but of course it
was not advisable to go too near land in the fog and unknown
waters without being obliged. A large number of fish (*Gadus
polaris*) were seen above the foot of a large block of ground ice,
near which we lay-to for some hours. Next day we saw near one
of the islands, where the water was very clear, the sea-bottom
bestrewed with innumerable fish of the same species. They
had probably perished from the same cause which often kills
fish in the river Ob in so great numbers that the water is in-
fected, namely, from a large shoal of fish having been enclosed
by ice in a small hole, where the water, when its surface has
frozen, could no longer by absorption from the air replace
the oxygen consumed, and where the fish have thus been
literally drowned. I mention this inconsiderable *find* of some
self-dead fish, because self-dead vertebrate animals, even fish,
are found exceedingly seldom. Such *finds* therefore deserve to
be noted with much greater care than, for instance, the occurrence of animal species in the neighbourhood of places where
they have been seen a thousand times before. During my nine
expeditions in the Arctic regions, where animal life during
summer is so exceedingly abundant, the case just mentioned
has been one of the few in which I have found remains of recent
vertebrate animals which could be proved to have died a natural
death. Near hunting-grounds there are to be seen often enough
the remains of reindeer, seals, foxes, or birds that have died
from gunshot wounds, but no self-dead Polar bear, seal, walrus,
white whale, fox, goose, auk, lemming or other vertebrate. The
Polar bear and the reindeer are found there in hundreds, the
seal, walrus, and white whale in thousands, and birds in millions.[1]
These animals must die a "natural" death in untold numbers.
What becomes of their bodies? Of this we have for the
present no idea, and yet we have here a problem of immense

[1] I can remember only one other instance of finding self-dead vertebrate
animals, viz. when in 1873, as has already been stated (p. 86), I found
a large number of dead rotges on the ice at the mouth of Hinloopen
Strait.

importance for the answering of a large number of questions
concerning the formation of fossiliferous strata. It is strange
in any case that on Spitzbergen it is easier to find vertebræ of
a gigantic lizard of the Trias, than bones of a self-dead seal,
walrus, or bird, and the same also holds good of more southerly
inhabited lands.

On the 13th August we again sailed past a large number of
small rocks or islands. The sea was at first pretty free of ice,
but was afterwards bestrewed with even, thin pieces of drift-ice,
which were not forced up on each other, and thus had not been
exposed in winter to any ice-pressure. This ice did not cause
any inconvenience to the navigation, but at the same time all
was wrapt in a very close mist, which soon compelled us to
anchor near the shore in a little bay. I endeavoured without
success to determine the position of the place by astronomical
observations. Along the shore there still remained nearly
everywhere a pretty high snow and ice-foot, which in the fog
presented the appearance of immense glaciers. The land besides was free of ice. In respect of its geological formation and
its animals and plants it resembled completely the island I have
just described. But the sea-water here was clear and salt, and
the dredging therefore yielded to Dr. Kjellman some large algæ,
and to Dr. Stuxberg a large number of marine evertebrates.

When the fog lightened, we immediately steamed on, but we
had scarcely got to sea before we were again wrapped in so close
a fog that we were compelled to lie-to for the night beside a
large piece of drift-ice. The hempen tangles were used, and
brought up a very abundant yield of large, beautiful animal
forms, a large number of asterids, Astrophyton, Antedon, &c.
There was besides made here an exceedingly remarkable, and
to me still, while I write, a very enigmatical *find*.

For several years back I have been zealous for the examination of all substances of the nature of dust which fall to the
surface of the earth with rain or snow, and I have proved that a
portion of them is of cosmic origin. This inconsiderable fall of
dust is thus of immense importance for the history of the development of our globe, and we regard it, besides, with the
intense interest which we inevitably cherish for all that brings
us an actual experience regarding the material world beyond
our globe. The inhabited countries of the earth, however, are
less suitable for such investigations, as the particles of cosmic
dust falling down here in very limited quantity can only with
difficulty be distinguished from the dust of civilization, arising
from human dwellings, from the offal of industry, from furnaces
and the chimneys of steam-engines. The case is quite different
on the snow and ice-fields of the High North, remote from
human habitations and the tracks of steamers. Every foreign

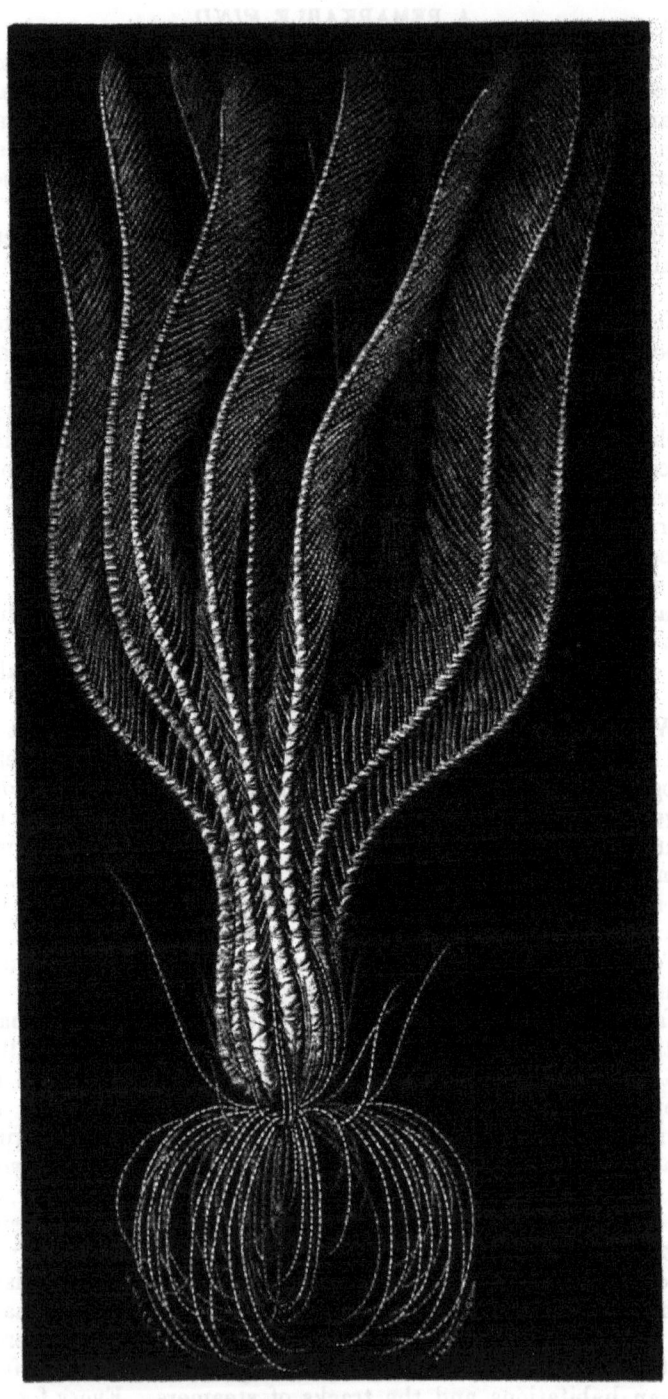

HAIRSTAR FROM THE TAIMUR COAST.
Antedon Eschrichtii, J. MÜLLER.
Three-fifths of the natural size.

grain of dust can here be easily distinguished and removed, and there is a strong probability that the offal of civilization is here nearly wholly wanting. It is self-evident from this that I would not be disposed to neglect the first opportunity for renewed investigations in the direction indicated, which our involuntary rest at the drift-ice field offered.

Immediately after the *Vega* lay-to, I therefore went down on the ice in order to see whether here too some such metalliferous dust, as I had before found north of Spitzbergen, was not to be found on the surface of the ice. Nothing of the kind, however, was to be seen. On the other hand, Lieutenant Nordquist observed small yellow specks in the snow, which I asked him to collect and hand over for investigation to Dr. Kjellman. For I supposed that the specks consisted of diatom ooze. After examining them Dr. Kjellman however declared that they did not consist of any organic substance, but of crystallised grains of sand. I too now examined them more closely, but unfortunately not until the morning after we had left the ice-field, and then found that the supposed ooze consisted of pale yellow crystals (not fragments of crystals) without mixture of foreign matter. The quantity of crystals, which were obtained from about three litres of snow, skimmed from the surface of the snow on an area of at most 10 square metres,

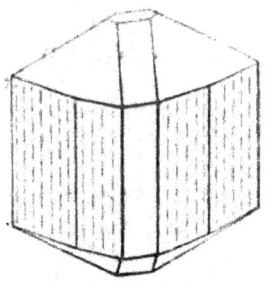

FORM OF THE CRYSTALS
Found on the ice off the Taimur coast.
Magnified thirty to forty times.

amounted to nearly 0·2 gram. The crystals were found only near the surface of the snow, not in the deeper layers. They were up to 1 mm. in diameter, had the appearance shown in the accompanying woodcut, and appeared to belong to the rhombic system, as they had one perfect cleavage and formed striated prisms terminated at either end by truncated pyramids. Unfortunately I could not make any actual measurements of them, because after being kept for some time in the air they weathered to a white non-crystalline powder. They lay, without being sensibly dissolved, for a whole night in the water formed by the melting of the snow. On being heated, too, they fell asunder into a tasteless white powder. The white powder, that was formed by the weathering of the crystals, was analysed after our return—21 months after the discovery of the crystals—and was found to contain only carbonate of lime.

The original composition and origin of this substance appears to me exceedingly enigmatical. It was not common carbonate of lime, for the crystals were rhombohedral and did not show the cleavage of calcite. Nor can there be a question of its being arragonite, because this mineral might indeed fall asunder of "itself," but in that case the newly-formed powder ought to be crystalline. Have the crystals originally been a new hydrated carbonate of lime, formed by crystallising out of the sea-water in intense cold, and then losing its water at a temperature of 10° or 20° above the freezing-point? In such a case they ought not to have been found on the surface of the *snow*, but lower down on the surface of the *ice*. Or have they fallen down from the inter-planetary spaces to the surface of the earth, and before crumbling down have had a composition differing from terrestrial substances in the same way as various chemical compounds found in recent times in meteoric stones? The occurrence of the crystals in the uppermost layer of snow and their falling asunder in the air, tell in favour of this view. Unfortunately there is now no possibility of settling these questions, but at all events this discovery is a further incitement to those who travel in the High North to collect with extreme care, from snow-fields lying far from the ordinary routes of communication, all foreign substances, though apparently of trifling importance.

As this question can be answered with the greatest ease and certainty by investigations in the Polar regions, I shall here, for the guidance of future travellers, enumerate some discoveries of a like nature which have been made by me, or at my instance.

1. In the beginning of December, 1871, there happened at Stockholm an exceedingly heavy fall of snow, perhaps the heaviest which has taken place in the memory of man. Several persons perished in the snow in the immediate neighbourhood of Stockholm. During the last days of the snowfall I had about a cubic metre of snow collected and melted in a vessel. It left a residue of black powder, which contained grains of metallic iron that were attracted by the magnet.

2. In the middle of March, 1872, a similar investigation was made by my brother, KARL NORDENSKIÖLD, in a remote forest settlement, Evois, in Finland. Here, too, was obtained, on the melting of the snow, a small residuum, consisting of a black powder containing metallic iron.

3. On the 8th August and 2nd September of the same year, I examined, north of Spitzbergen, in 80° N.L., and 13° to 15° E.L., the layer of snow that there covered the ice. The nature of this layer is shown by the accompanying woodcut, in which 1, is new-fallen snow; 2, a layer of hardened old snow, eight mm. in thickness; 3, a layer of snow conglomerated to a crystalline granular mass; and 4, common granular hardened snow. Layer 3 was full of small black grains, among which

were found numerous metallic particles that were attracted by the magnet, and were found to contain iron, cobalt, and possibly nickel also.

4. On the melting of 500 gram. hail, which fell in Stockholm in the autumn of 1873, similar metallic particles containing cobalt (nickel) were obtained, which, in this case, might possibly have come from the neighbouring roofs, because the hail was collected in a yard surrounded by houses roofed with sheet-iron painted red. The black colour of the metallic particles enclosed in the hail, their position in the hail, and finally, the cobalt they contained, however, indicate in this case too, a quite different origin.

5. In a dust (kryokonite), collected on the inland ice of Greenland in the month of July, 1870, there were also found mixed with it grains of metallic iron, containing cobalt. The main mass consisted of a crystalline, double-refracting silicate, drenched through with an ill-smelling organic substance. The dust was found in large quantities at the bottom of innumerable small holes in the surface of the inland ice. This dust could scarcely be of volcanic origin, because by its crystalline structure it differs completely from the glass-dust that is commonly thrown out of volcanoes, and is often carried by the wind to very remote regions, as also from the dust which, on the 30th March, 1875, fell at many places in the middle of Scandinavia, and which was proved to have been thrown out by volcanoes on Iceland. For, while kryokonite consists of small angular double-refracting crystal fragments without any mixture of particles of glass, the volcanic Haga-dust[1] consists almost wholly of small microscopic glass bubbles that have no action, on the polarisation-planes of the light that passes through them.

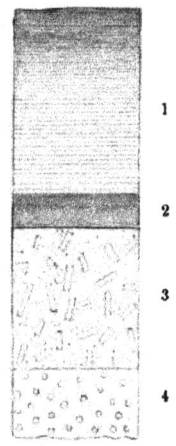

SECTION OF THE UPPER PART OF THE SNOW ON A DRIFT-ICE FIELD IN 80° N.L.

One-half the natural size.

---

[1] I use this name because the ash-rain of March 1875 was first observed at Haga palace near Stockholm, and thus at the outer limit of the known area of distribution of the dust. It was first through the request which in consequence of this observation was published in the newspapers, that communications regarding singular observations in other quarters should be sent to the Swedish Academy of Sciences, that it became known that a similar rain had about the same time taken place over a very large part of middle Sweden and Norway. The dust however did not fall evenly, but distributed in spots, and at several different times. The distance from Stockholm of the volcanoes, where the outbreak took place, is nearly 2000 kilometres.

Similar investigations have since been made, among others, by M. TISSANDIER in Paris, and during NARES' English Polar Expedition.

It may appear to many that it is below the dignity of science to concern one's self with so trifling an affair as the fall of a small quantity of dust. But this is by no means the case. For I estimate the quantity of the dust that was found on the ice north of Spitzbergen at from 0·1 to 1 milligram per square metre, and probably the whole fall of dust for the year far exceeded the latter figure. But a milligram on every square metre of the surface of the earth amounts for the whole globe to five hundred million kilograms (say half a million tons)! Such a mass collected year by year during the geological ages, of a duration probably incomprehensible by us, forms too important a factor to be neglected, when the fundamental facts of the geological history of our planet are enumerated. A continuation of these investigations will perhaps show, that our globe has increased gradually from a small beginning to the dimensions it now possesses; that a considerable quantity of the constituents of our sedimentary strata, especially of those that have been deposited in the open sea far from land, are of cosmic origin; and will throw an unexpected light on the origin of the fire-hearths of the volcanoes, and afford a simple explanation of the remarkable resemblance which unmistakably exists between plutonic rocks and meteoric stones.[1]

On the 14th August, when the fog had lightened a little, we got up steam, but were soon compelled to anchor again in a bay running into Taimur Island from the north side of Taimur Sound, which I named Actinia Bay from the large number of actinia which the dredge brought up there. It is, besides, not the only place in the Kara Sea which might be named from the evertebrate life prevailing there, so unexpectedly abundant.

Unfavourable weather detained us in Actinia Bay, which is a good and well-protected haven, till the 18th August, during which time excursions were made in various directions, among others farther into Taimur Sound, where a variable strong current was found to prevail. The Sound is too shallow to be passed through by large vessels. The rocks round Taimur Sound consist of gneiss strata, which form low ridges that have been so shattered by the frost that they have been converted into immense lichen-clad stone mounds. Between these stretch extensive valleys and plains, now free of snow, if we

[1] Namely, by showing that the principal material of the plutonic and volcanic rocks is of cosmic origin, and that the phenomena of heat, which occur in these layers, depend on chemical changes to which the cosmic sediment, after being covered by thick terrestrial formations, is subjected

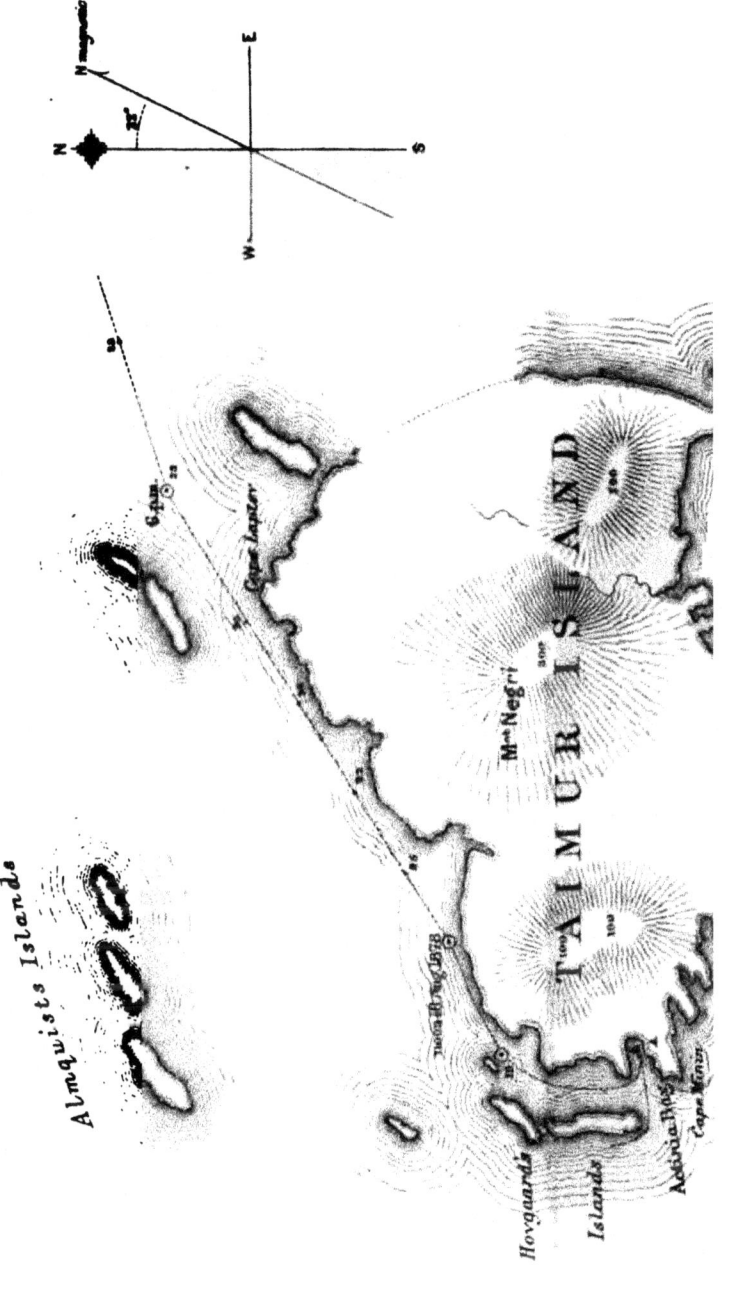

except a snow-drift remaining here and there in the hollows. The plains were all covered with a very green continuous vegetation, which however on a closer examination was found to be not a true turf, but a mixture of grasses, allied plants, and a large number of different kinds of mosses and lichens. Actual flowers were found here only sparingly.[1] In this respect the coast *tundra* shows a remarkable difference from the coast lands on Vaygats Island and Novaya Zemlya. On the other hand, the abundance of luxuriant lichens and mosses was striking. The mosses along the beach and the borders of the snow-drifts remaining here and there bore fruit in abundance. Animal life on land was scanty; some few reindeer were seen, a mountain fox was killed, and a lemming caught.

Only the following birds were seen : owls (*Strix nyctea*) rather numerous, of which one was killed ; a species of falcon, which was hunted unsuccessfully ; snow buntings, breeding very generally in the stone mounds ; a covey of snow ptarmigan, of which some young birds were shot ; six species of waders, the most common birds of the region, of which a large number were shot ; two kinds of gulls (*Larus glaucus* and *tridactylus*) ; *Lestris parasitica* and *Buffonii*, the latter the more common of the two ; *Anser bernicla*, very common ; and finally the long-tailed duck (*Harelda glacialis*) in great flocks swimming in the Sound. Bird life, viewed as a whole, was still scanty here, in comparison with that which we were accustomed to see in the northern regions west of Novaya Zemlya.

In the sea the higher animal life was somewhat more abundant. A walrus had been seen during the passage from the Yenisej, and on the ice drifting about in the Sound a number of seals, both *Phoca barbata* and *Phoca hispida*, were observed.

[1] Dr. Kjellman has given the following list of the flowering plants collected by him in this region :—

Cineraria frigida RICHARDS.
Potentilla emarginata PURSH.
Saxifraga stellaris L. f. comosa.
   ,,   nivalis L.
   ,,   cernua L.
   ,,   rivularis L.
Chrysosplenium alternifolium L.
Cardamine bellidifolia L.
Draba corymbosa R. BR.
Papaver nudicaule L.
Ranunculus pygmæus WG.
   ,,   hyperboreus ROTTB.
   ,,   sulphureus SOL.
Stellaria Edwardsii R. BR.
Cerastium alpinum L.
Alsine macrocarpa FENZL.
Salix polaris WG.

Poa arctica R. BR.
Arctophila pendulina (LÆST.) ANDJ.
Catabrosa algida (Sol.) FR.
Colpodium latifolium R. BR.
Dupontia Fisheri R. BR.
Pleuropogon Sabini R. BR.
Aira cæspitosa L.
Hierochloa pauciflora R. BR.
Calamagrostis lapponica (WG.) HN.
Alopecurus alpinus SM.
Eriophorum angustifolium ROTH.
   ,,   Scheuchzeri HOPPE.
Carex aquatilis WG.
   ,,   rigida GOOD.
Juncus biglumis L.
Luzula hyperborea R. BR.
   ,,   arctica BL.

This gave rise to the supposition that at the sea-bottom animal life was richer, which was also confirmed by the dredging-yield. Nowhere was seen on our arrival any trace of man, but a cairn now indicates the place, off which the *Vega* and the *Lena* were anchored.

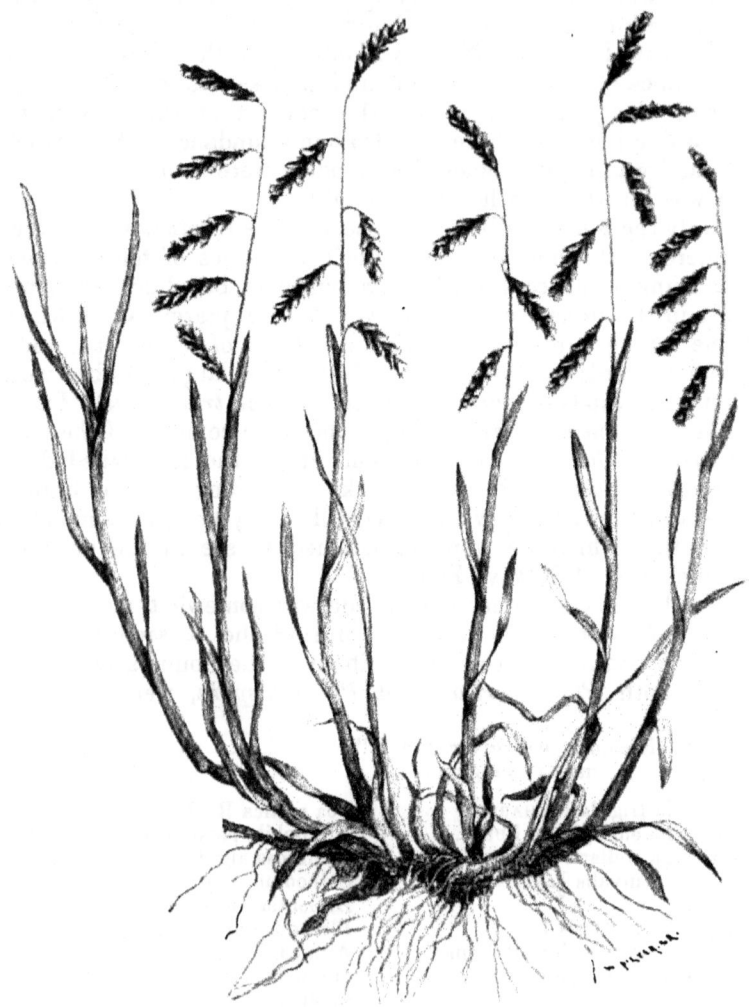

GRASS FROM ACTINIA BAY.
Pleuropogon Sabini, R. Br.

In this sea never before visited by any vessel, however, we were nearly coming in contact with a countryman. For while we lay at anchor in Taimur Sound, Captain Edward Johannesen came into the neighbourhood of the same place with his sailing

vessel *Nordland* from Tromsoe. He had left Norway on the 22nd
May 1878, had come to Gooseland in Novaya Zemlya on the 6th
June, and had reached the northernmost point of that island
on the 22nd July. Here loud thunder was heard on the 26th
July. On the 10th August he steered eastwards from Novaya
Zemlya across the Kara Sea between 76° and 77° N.L. in open
water. On the 16th he had the Taimur country in sight.
Here he turned, and steered first to the west, then to the north.
In 77° 31' N.L. and 86° E.L. from Greenwich he discovered and
circumnavigated a new island, which was named "Ensamheten"
(Solitude). The island was free of snow, but not overgrown with
grass. The animals that were seen were some bears and bearded
seals, terns, fulmars, ivory gulls, flocks of black guillemots, and
a " bird with a rounded tail and long bill," probably some wader.
On the north-east side of the island a strong northerly current
prevailed. The remote position and desolate appearance of the
island gave occasion to the name proposed by Johannesen.
Hence Johannesen sailed with a great bend to the north, which
brought him to 78° N.L., back to the northern extremity of
Novaya Zemlya, and thence on the 12th September to Norway.
During the return voyage across the Kara Sea also scarcely any
ice was met with.[1]

   An exceedingly persistent fog prevailed during the whole
of the time we remained here, but at last on the 18th it lightened a little. We immediately weighed anchor and steamed
along the western shore of Taimur Island. It is surrounded by
a large number of islands that are not given on the map, and
possibly Taimur Island itself is divided by sounds into several
parts. During our voyage, however, the fog that was still very
close hindered us from mapping, otherwise than in a very loose
way, the islands, large and small, between and past which the
Vega searched for a passage. So much we could in any case see,
that the northern extremity of Taimur Island does not run so
far north as the common maps show.

   Ice we met with only in small quantity, and what we saw was
very rotten fjord or river ice. I scarcely believe that in the
course of the day we met with a single piece of ice large enough
to flense a seal upon. We had as yet seen no true old drift-ice
such as is to be met with north of Spitzbergen. In respect
to the nature of the ice, there is a complete dissimilarity between
the Kara Sea and the sea north and east of Spitzbergen. Another
striking difference is the scarcity of warm-blooded animals
which prevails in this region, hitherto exempted from all hunting.
In the course of the day we had not seen a single bird—something

----

[1] *H. Mohn.* Die Insel Einsamkeit, &c., with a map (Petermann's *Mittheilungen*, 1879, p. 57).

which never before happened to me during a summer journey in
the Arctic Regions—and scarcely any seals.

On the 19th August we continued to sail and steam along
the coast, mostly in a very close fog, which only at intervals
dispersed so much that the lie of the coast could be made out.
In order that they might not be separated, both vessels had
often to signal to each other with the steam-whistle. The sea
was bright as a mirror. Drift ice was seen now and then, but
only in small quantity and very rotten; but in the course of the
day we steamed past an extensive unbroken ice field, fast to the
land, which occupied a bay on the west side of the Chelyuskin
peninsula. The ice, of which it consisted, appeared in the mist
immensely rough and high, although in fact it was nearly as
rotten as that of which the narrow belts of ice were formed
which we now and then met with out at sea.

The fog prevented all view far across the ice, and I already
feared that the northernmost promontory of Asia would be so
surrounded with ice that we could not land upon it. But soon a
dark ice-free cape peeped out of the mist in the north-east. A
bay open to the north here cuts into the land, and in this bay
both the vessels anchored on the 19th August at 6 o'clock p.m.

We had now reached a great goal, which for centuries had
been the object of unsuccessful struggles. For the first time a
vessel lay at anchor off the northernmost cape of the old world.
No wonder then that the occurrence was celebrated by a display
of flags and the firing of salutes, and, when we returned from our
excursion on land, by festivities on board, by wine and toasts.

As on our arrival at the Yenisej, we were received here too by
a large Polar bear, who, even before the vessel anchored, was
seen to go backwards and forwards on the beach, now and then
turning his glance and his nose uneasily out to sea in order to
investigate what remarkable guests had now for the first time
come to his kingdom. A boat was put off to kill him. Brusewitz was the chosen shot; but on this occasion the bear took care
not to form any closer acquaintance with our guns. The firing
of the salute put him so thoroughly to flight, that he did not, as
bears are wont, return the following day.

The north point of Asia forms a low promontory, which a bay
divides into two, the eastern arm projecting a little farther to
the north than the western. A ridge of hills with gently sloping sides runs into the land from the eastern point, and appears
within sight of the western to reach a height of 300 metres.
Like the plains lying below, the summits of this range were
nearly free of snow. Only on the hill-sides or in deep furrows
excavated by the streams of melted snow, and in dales in the
plains, were large white snow fields to be seen. A low ice-foot
still remained at most places along the shore. But no glacier

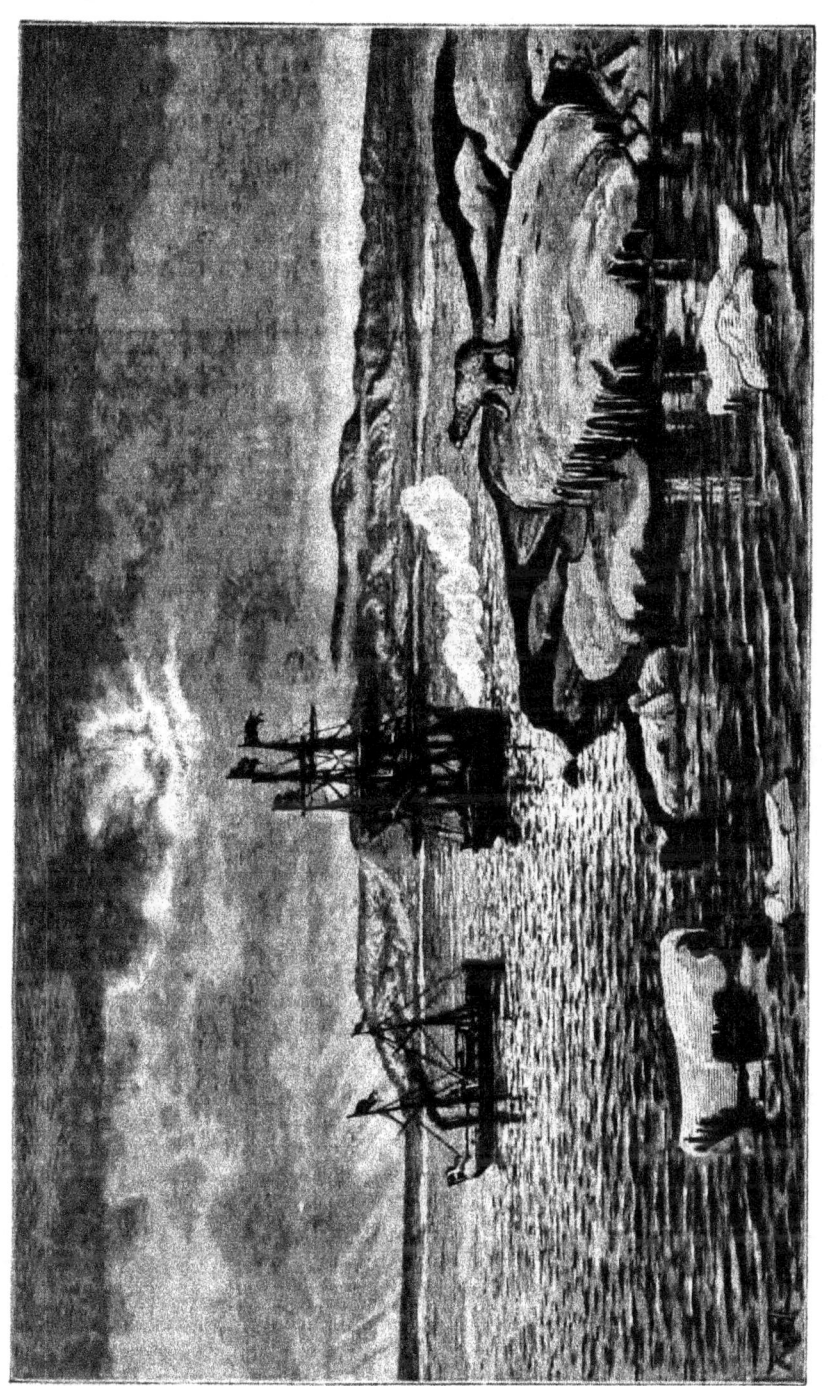

THE VEGA AND LENA SALUTING CAPE CHELYUSKIN.

After a drawing by A. Hovgaard

rolled its bluish-white ice-masses down the mountain sides, and
no inland lakes, no perpendicular cliffs, no high mountain
summits, gave any natural beauty to the landscape, which was
the most monotonous and the most desolate I have seen in the
High North.

As on the island off which we lay at anchor on the 11th
August, the ground was everywhere burst asunder into more or
less regular six-sided figures, the interior of which was usually
bare of vegetation, while stunted flowering-plants, lichens and

VIEW AT CAPE CHELYUSKIN DURING THE STAY OF THE EXPEDITION.
After a drawing by A. Hovgaard.

mosses, rose out of the cracks. At some few places, however
the ground was covered with a carpet of mosses, lichens, grasses
and allied plants, resembling that which I previously found at
Actinia Bay. Yet the flowering-plants were less numerous here,
and the mosses more stunted and bearing fruit less abundantly.
The lichen flora was also, according to Dr. Almquist's examination, monotonous, though very luxuriant. The plants were
most abundant on the farthest extremity of the Cape. It
almost appeared as if many of the plants of the Taimur country
had attempted to migrate hence farther to the north, but meeting the sea, had stood still, unable to go farther and unwilling

to turn.   For here Dr. Kjellman found on a very limited area nearly all the plants of the region.   The species which were distinctive of the vegetation here were the following: *Saxifraga oppositifolia* L., *Papaver nudicaule* L., *Draba alpina* L., *Cerastium alpinum* L., *Stellaria Edwardsii* R. BR., *Alsine macrocarpa* FENZL., *Aira cæspitosa* L., *Catabrosa algida* (SOL.) FR., and *Alopecurus alpinus* SM.   The following plants occurred less frequently: *Eritrichium villosum* BUNGE, *Saxifraga nivalis* L., *S. cernua* L., *S. rivularis* L., *S. stellaris* L., *S. cæspitosa* L., *S. flagellaris* WILLD., *S. serpyllifolia* PURSH., *Cardamine bellidifolia* L., *Cochlearia fenestrata* R. BR., *Oxyria digyna* (L.) HILL., *Salix polaris* WG., *Poa flexuosa* WG., and *Luzula hyperborea* R. BR. There were thus found in all only twenty-three species of inconsiderable flowering-plants, among them eight species belonging to the Saxifrage family, a sulphur-yellow poppy, commonly cultivated in our gardens, and the exceedingly beautiful, forget-me-not-like Eritrichium.   That the vegetation here on the northernmost point of Asia has to contend with a severe climate is shown, among other things, as Dr. Kjellman has pointed out, by most of the flowering-plants there having a special tendency to form exceedingly compact half-globular tufts.

†

THE BEETLE LIVING FARTHEST
TO THE NORTH.
Micralymma Dicksoni
MÄKL.
Magnified twelve times.

The only insects which occurred here in any large number were poduræ, but some flies were also seen, and even a beetle, the before-mentioned Staphylinid.   Of birds, there were seen a large number of sand-pipers, an exceedingly numerous flock of barnacle geese—evidently migrating to more southerly regions, perhaps from some Polar land lying to the north of Cape Chelyuskin—a loom, some kittiwakes and ivory gulls, and remains of owls.   Mammalia were represented by the bear already mentioned, and by the reindeer and the lemming, whose traces and dung were seen on the plains.   In the sea, a walrus, several rough seals (*Phoca hispida*), and two shoals of white whales were seen.

All rivers were now dried up, but wide, shallow river-beds indicated that during the snow-melting season there was an abundant flow of water.   The rush of snow-rivulets and the cry of birds then certainly cause an interruption in the desolation and silence which were now spread over the clay beds of the plains, nearly bare of all vegetation.   Probably, however, a little farther into the country, in some valley protected from the winds of the Polar Sea, we might find quite different natural conditions,

s 2

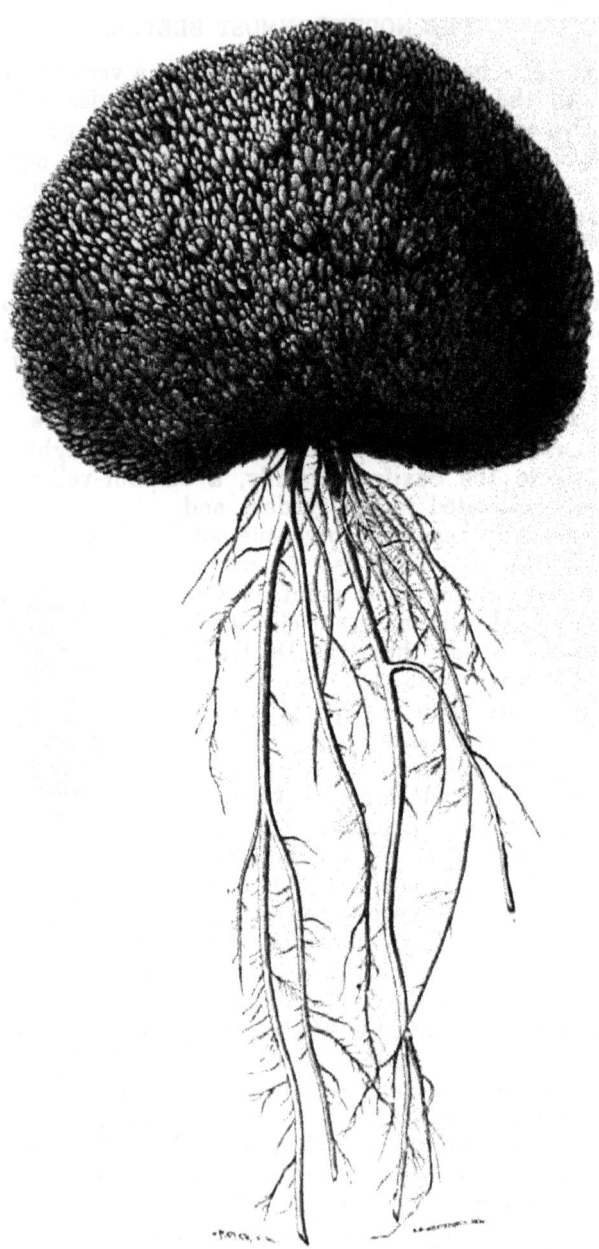

DRABA ALPINA L., FROM CAPE CHELYUSKIN.
Natural size.

a more abundant animal life, and a vegetable world, in summer, as rich in flowers as that which we meet with in the valleys of Ice Fjord or the "Nameless Bay" (Besimannaja Bay). We saw no trace of man here. The accounts, which were current as early as the sixteenth century, relating to the nature of the north point of Asia, however, make it probable that the Siberian nomads at one time drove their reindeer herds up hither. It is even not impossible that Russian hunters from Chatanga may have prosecuted the chase here, and that Chelyuskin actually was here, of which we have evidence in the very correct way in which the Cape, that now rightly bears his name, is laid down on the Russian maps.[1]

The rocks consist of a clay-slate, with crystals resembling chiastolite and crystals of sulphide of iron interspersed. At the Cape itself the clay-slate is crossed by a thick vein of pure white quartz. Here, according to an old custom of Polar travellers, a stately cairn was erected.

In order to get a good astronomical determination of the position of this important point I remained there until the 20th August at noon. The *Lena* was ordered to steam out to dredge during this time. Eight minutes north of the bay, where we lay at anchor, heavy and very close ice was met with. There the depth of the sea increased rapidly. Animal life at the sea-bottom was very abundant, among other things in large asterids and ophiurids.

According to the plan of the voyage I now wished to steam from this point right eastwards towards the New Siberian Islands, in order to see if we should fall in with land on the way. On the 20th and 21st we went forward in this direction among scattered drift-ice, which was heavier and less broken up than that which we had met with on the

---

[1] This has been doubted by Russian geographers. Von Baer for instance says: —

" Darüber ist gar kein Zweifel, dass dieses Vorgebirge nie umsegelt ist, und dass es auf einem Irrthum beruhte, wenn Laptew auf einer Seefahrt die Bucht, in welche der Taimur sich mündet, erreicht zu haben glaubte. Seine eigenen späteren Fahrten erwiesen diesen Irrthum. Die Vergleichung der Berichte und Verhältnisse lässt mich aber auch glauben, dass selbst zu Lande man das Ende dieses Vorgebirges nie erreicht habe; sondern Tscheljuskin, um dieser, man kann wohl sagen, grässlichen Versuche endlich überhoben zu seyn, sich zu der ungegründeten Behauptung entschloss, er habe das Ende gesehen, und sich überzeugt, Sibirien sei nach Norden überall vom Meere umgränzt," [statement by von Baer in *Neueste Nachrichten über die nördlichste Gegend von Sibirien;* von Baer and von Helmersen, *Beiträge zur Kenntniss des Russischen Reiches.* IV. St. Petersburg, 1841, p. 275]. In the following page in the same paper von Baer indeed says that he will not lay any special weight on Strahlenberg's statement that Siberia and Novaya Zemlya hang together, but he appears to believe that they are connected by a bridge of perpetual ice.

other side of Taimur Land, but without meeting with any
serious obstacles. We fell in also with some very large ice-
floes, but not with any icebergs. We were besides again
attended by so close a mist that we could only see ice-fields
and pieces of ice in the
immediate neighbourhood
of the vessel. Besides
species of Lestris [and
kittiwakes, we now [also
saw looms, birds that are
almost wanting in the Kara
Sea. Johannesen was of
opinion that the presence
of these birds showed that
the sea is not completely
frozen over in winter, because it is not probable
that the loom in autumn
and spring would fly across
the frozen Kara Sea to
seek in this distant region
their food and their breed-
ing-haunts.

The night before the
22nd we steamed through
pretty close ice. The whole
day so thick a fog still
prevailed that we could
not see the extent of the
ice-fields in the neigh-
bourhood of the vessel.
Towards noon we were,
therefore, compelled to take
a more southerly course.
When we found that we
could not advance in this
direction, we lay-to at a
large ice-floe, waiting for
clear weather, until in the

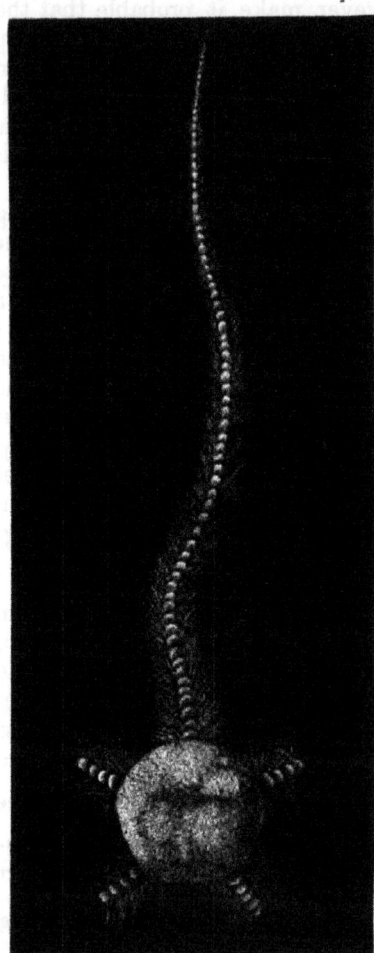

OPHIURID FROM THE SEA NORTH OF CAPE
CHELYUSKIN.
Ophiacantha bidentata, RETZ.
One and one-third of the natural size.

afternoon the fog again
lightened somewhat, so that
we could continue our
voyage. But it was not
long before the fog again became so thick that, as the sailors
say, you could cut it with a knife. There was now evidently a risk that the *Vega*, while thus continuing to " box
the compass" in the ice-labyrinth, in which we had entangled

ourselves, would meet with the same fate that befell the *Tegett-hoff*. In order to avoid this, it became necessary to abandon our attempt to sail from Cape Chelyuskin straight to the New Siberian Islands, and to endeavour to reach as soon as possible the open water at the coast.

When it cleared on the morning of the 23rd, we therefore began again to steam forward among the fields of drift-ice, but now not with the intention of advancing in a given direction, but only of getting to open water. The ice-fields we now met with were very much broken up, which was an indication that we could not be very far from the edge of the *pack*. But notwithstanding this, all our attempts to find penetrable ice in an easterly, westerly, or southerly direction were unsuccessful. We had thus to search in a northerly direction for the opening by which we had sailed in. This was so much the more unpleasant as the wind had changed to a pretty fresh N.W. breeze, on which account, with the *Vega's* weak steam-power, we could make way only slowly. It was not until 6.30 p.m. that we at last came to the sack-formed opening in the ice through which we had sailed in at noon of the previous day.

One can scarcely, without having experienced it, form any idea of the optical illusions, which are produced by mist, in regions where the size of the objects which are visible through the fog is not known beforehand, and thus does not give the spectator an idea of the distance. Our estimate of distance and size in such cases depends wholly on accident. The obscure contours of the fog-concealed objects themselves, besides, are often by the ignorance of the spectator converted into whimsical fantastic forms. During a boat-journey in Hinloopen Strait I once intended to row among drift-ice to an island at a distance of some few kilometres. When the boat started the air was clear, but while we were employed, as best we could, in shoot-ing sea-fowl for dinner, all was wrapt in a thick mist, and that so unexpectedly, that we had not time to take the bearings of the island. This led to a not altogether pleasant row by guess among the pieces of ice that were drifting about in rapid motion in the sound. All exerted themselves as much as possible to get sight of the island, whose beach would afford us a safe resting-place. While thus occupied, a dark border was seen through the mist at the horizon. It was taken for the island which we were bound for, and it was not at first considered remarkable that the dark border rose rapidly, for we thought that the mist was dispersing and in consequence of that more of the land was visible. Soon two white snow-fields, that we had not observed before, were seen on both sides of the land, and immediately after this was changed to a sea-monster, re-sembling a walrus-head, as large as a mountain. This got life

and motion, and finally sank all at once to the head of a common
walrus, which lay on a piece of ice in the neighbourhood of the
boat; the white tusks formed the snow-fields and the dark-brown
round head the mountain. Scarce was this illusion gone when
one of the men cried out "Land right ahead—high land!" We
now all saw before us a high Alpine region, with mountain peaks
and glaciers, but this too sank a moment afterwards all at once
to a common ice-border, blackened with earth. In the spring of
1873 Palander and I with nine men made a sledge journey round
North-east Land. In the course of this journey a great many
bears were seen and killed. When a bear was seen while we
were dragging our sledges forward, the train commonly stood
still, and, not to frighten the bear, all the men concealed themselves behind the sledges, with the exception of the marksman,
who, squatting down in some convenient place, waited till his
prey should come sufficiently within range to be killed with
certainty. It happened once during foggy weather on the ice at
Wahlenberg Bay that the bear that was expected and had been
clearly seen by all of us, instead of approaching with his usual
supple zigzag movements, and with his ordinary attempts to
nose himself to a sure insight into the fitness of the foreigners for
food, just as the marksman took aim, spread out gigantic wings
and flew away in the form of a small ivory gull. Another time
during the same sledge journey we heard from the tent in which
we rested, the cook, who was employed outside, cry out: "A bear!
A great bear! No! a reindeer, a very little reindeer!" The
same instant a well-directed shot was fired, and the bear-rein-
deer was found to be a very small fox, which thus paid with
its life for the honour of having for some moments played the
part of a big animal. From these accounts it may be seen
how difficult navigation among drift-ice must be in unknown
waters.

On the two occasions on which the vessel was anchored to
ice-floes the trawl-net was used, and the hempen tangles. The
net was drawn forward slowly with the ice which was drifting to
the north-west before a fresh S.E. breeze which was blowing
at the time. The yield of the trawling was extraordinarily
abundant; large asterids, crinoids, sponges, holothuria, a
gigantic sea-spider (Pycnogonid), masses of worms, crustacea,
&c. *It was the most abundant yield that the trawl-net at any
one time brought up during the whole of our voyage round the
coast of Asia*, and this from the sea off the northern extremity
of that continent.

Among the forms collected here we may specially refer to
the large sea-spider, of which a drawing is given (p. 265)
and three specimens of small stalked crinoids. The depth
varied between 60 and 100 metres. The temperature of the

water was at the surface + 0° to − 0°·6 ; at the bottom − 1°·4 to
1°·6 ; its salinity was considerable, both at the bottom, where it
was very nearly equal to that of the other great oceans, and at
the surface, where it was indeed about a fifth-part less, but

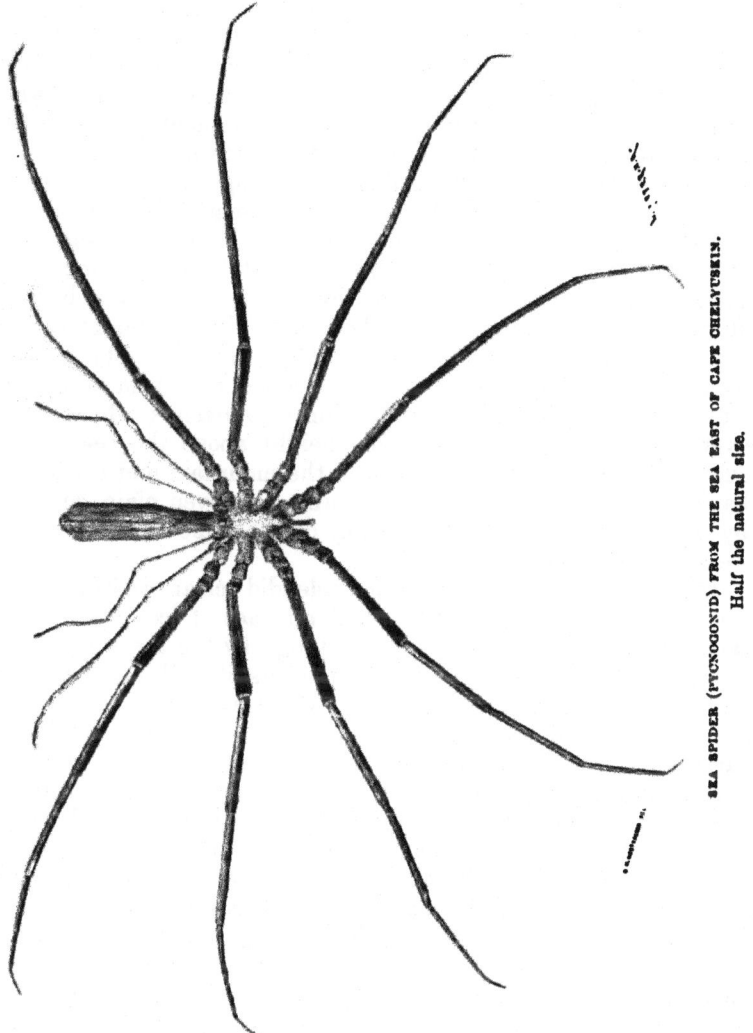

SEA SPIDER (PYCNOGONID) FROM THE SEA EAST OF CAPE CHELYUSKIN.
Half the natural size.

yet much greater than that of the surface-water in the Kara
Sea.

It is singular that a temperature under the freezing-point
of pure water should be advantageous for the development
of an animal life so extremely rich as that which is found here,

and that this animal life should not suffer any harm from the complete darkness, which during the greater portion of the year prevails at the bottom of the ice-covered sea.

When we got out of the ice we steamed towards the land, which was sighted on the 23rd at 8.45 p.m. The land was low and free from snow; the depth of the sea at a distance of ten kilometres from the coast varied between thirteen and fifteen metres. The coast here stretched from north to south. We followed it at a distance of seven to ten kilometres. A north-westerly breeze here carried the vessel, without the help of steam, rapidly forward over a completely smooth sea.

On the 24th August we still sailed along the land towards the south. The depth of the sea now increased to thirty-three metres at a distance of ten kilometres from land. The land rose gradually, and some distance from the coast beautiful mountain chains were seen, which, judging by the eye, rose to a height of from 600 to 900 metres. They were, like the plains along the coast, quite free from snow. Only in the clefts of the mountains there remained some few collections of snow or ice, which at two places appeared to form true glaciers, which however terminated at a considerable height above the sea. The snow-free slopes between the foot of the mountain and the shore bank, thirty to sixty metres high, formed an even plain, covered by a brownish-green turf, probably of the same nature as that we saw on Taimur Island.

During the forenoon we had splendid clear weather, and often we could see from the vessel no trace of ice. We saw a large number of walruses, and to judge by the fire which this sight kindled in the eyes of our hunters, it will not be long till the Norwegian hunting voyages are extended to the sea north and east of the north point of Asia. We saw besides a large number of looms and black guillemots, the former accompanied by young of the year, as large as rotges. About noon we sighted "land ahead to larboard." It was evidently Preobraschenie Island. I determined to land on it for a few hours to carry on researches in natural history, and to fix the position of the place by astronomical observations, if the weather should permit. The distance of this high-lying island was however greater than we expected. So that it was not until six o'clock in the evening that we could anchor off its south-west side, near the almost perpendicular face of cliffs abounding in sea-fowl.

During the last two days we had been sailing over a region, which on recent maps is marked as land. This shows that a considerable change must be made on the map of North Siberia, and I shall therefore quote here the observations on which the determination of our course is grounded.

	Observed	
	Latitude.	Longitude.
Cape Chelyuskin[1]	77° 36·8′	103° 17·2′
On board the *Vega*[2] at noon of the 21st Aug.	77° 25′	109° 12′
„ „ „ „ „ „ „ 22nd „	76° 53′	116° 9′
„ „ „ „ „ „ „ 23rd „	76° 48′	115° 0′
„ „ „ „ „ „ „ 24th „	75° 0′	113° 33′

At the last-mentioned point we had land to starboard of us at an estimated distance of 4′. Preobraschenie Island lay S. 21° W. 17·5′ off. It is on the ground of these data and of the courses recorded ·in the log, that the track of the *Vega* has been laid down on the map, and no doubt can arise that the position of the east coast of Taimur peninsula, as indicated by us, is in the main correct.

Preobraschenie Island forms a pretty even grassy plain, lying from thirty to sixty metres above the sea-level, which in the north-west terminates towards the sea with an almost perpendicular rocky wall, but to the south-east sinks gradually down to two sand-banks which run far out to sea. At the time of our visit the island was free of snow and covered with a carpet of mosses mixed with grass, which was exceedingly abundant, especially on the south-west slopes of the island, pro-.tected as they were from the north winds. Here we encountered anew the Arctic animal world in all its profusion. The ledges of the perpendicular shore-cliffs of the island formed the breeding-place of numberless looms and kittiwakes, to which a few black guillemots attached themselves. Along the farthest margin of the beach waders ran busily backwards and forwards in order to collect their food. At the summits of the cliffs a flock of glaucous gulls were breeding, and on the slopes of the low land the white mountain owl was seen lying in wait for its prey, quiet and motionless for hours, but as usual it was wary and shy, so that it was only with difficulty that the hunter could get within range of it. At some places there extended between the foot of the " loomery " and the sea a stone-bestrewn beach, which at high water was mostly covered by the sea, and at low water was full of shallow salt-water pools. Here had settled two Polar bears that were soon killed, one by Lieutenant Brusewitz, the other by Captain Johannesen. The bears had evidently been on the hunt for looms, which along with their young, large as rotges and already able to swim, were swimming in the pools of water at the foot of the " loomery," and above all perhaps they were lying in wait for birds which by some accident

[1] According to an observation with an artificial horizon on land.
[2] According to an observation on board. The observations for longitude that were made some hours before or after noon, are reduced to noon.

happened to fall down from the breeding-place. In the sea no small number of seals were seen, and but a few hours before our arrival at the island we had sailed past herds of walrus.

Vegetation was much more luxuriant and richer in species than at Cape Chelyuskin, and naturally bore a more southern stamp, not only in consequence of the more southerly position of the island, but also on account of its shores being washed

PREOBRASCHENIE ISLAND.
After a sketch by O. Nordquist.

by the water of the Chatanga river, which is warm during summer.[1]

[1] The following 65 species were collected here by Dr. Kjellman:—

Saussurea alpina DC.
Gymnandra Stelleri CHAM. & SCHLECHT.
Pedicularis hirsuta L.
Eritrichium villosum BUNGE.
Myosotis silvatica HOFFM.
Phaca frigida L.
Dryas octopetala L.
Sieversia glacialis R. BR.
Potentilla emarginata PURSH.
Saxifraga oppositifolia L.
  „   bronchialis L.
  „   flagellaris WILLD.
  „   Hirculus L.
  „   serpyllifolia PURSH.

Saxifraga stellaris L. f. comosa.
  „   nivalis L.
  „   hieraciifolia WALDST. & KIT.
  „   punctata L.
  „   cernua L.
  „   rivularis L.
  „   cæspitosa L.
Chrysosplenium alternifolium L.
Eutrema Edwardsii R. BR.
Parrya macrocarpa R. BR.
Cardamine bellidifolia L.
Cochlearia fenestrata R. BR.
Draba alpina L.
Papaver nudicaule L.

Unfortunately, on account of the advanced season of the year, I could only allow the *Vega* to remain a few hours off this interesting island, and at 10.30 p.m. accordingly the anchor was weighed and our voyage along the coast resumed.

On the 25th, 26th and 27th August we had for the most part calm, fine weather, and the sea was completely free of ice. The temperature of the water again rose to $+5°\!\cdot\!8$, and its salinity diminished considerably. But the depth now decreased so much, that, for instance, on the night before the 26th' we had great difficulty in getting past some shoals lying west of the delta of the Lena, off the mouth of the Olonek.

It had originally been my intention to let the *Vega* separate from the *Lena* at some anchorage in one of the mouth-arms of the Lena river. But on account of the shallowness of the water, the favourable wind and the ice-free sea, that now lay before us to the eastward, I determined to part from the *Lena* in the open sea off Tumat Island. This parting took place on the night between the 27th and 28th August, after Captain Johannesen had been signalled to come on board the *Vega*, to receive orders, passport,[1] and letters for home. As a parting salute to our trusty little attendant during our voyage round the north point of Asia some rockets were fired, on which we steamed or sailed on, each to his destination.

During our passage from Norway to the Lena we had been much troubled with fog, but it was only when we left the navigable water along the coast to the east of Cape Chelyuskin that we fell in with ice in such quantity that it was an obstacle

Ranunculus pygmæus WG.	Glyceria angustata R. BR.
,, hyperboreus ROTTB.	,, vilfoidea (ANDS.) TH. FR.
,, nivalis L.	Arctophila pendulina (LÆST.) AND.
,, sulphureus SOL.	Catabrosa algida (SOL.) FR.
Caltha palustris L.	Colpodium latifolium R. BR.
Wahlbergella apetala (L.) FR.	Dupontia Fisheri R. BR.
Stellaria humifusa ROTTB.	Aira cæspitosa L.
,, Edwardsii R. BR.	Hierochloa pauciflora R. BR.
Cerastium alpinum L.	Alopecurus alpinus SM.
Alsine macrocarpa FENZL.	Eriophorum angustifolium ROTH.
,, rubella WG.	,, russeolum FR.
Sagina nivalis FR.	,, Scheuchzeri HOPPE.
Oxyria digyna (L.) HILL.	Carex ursina DESV.
Polygonum viviparum L.	,, aquatilis WG.
Salix arctica PALL.	Juncus biglumis L.
,, reticulata L.	Luzula hyperborea R. BR.
,, polaris WG.	,, arctica BL.
Poa arctica R. BR.	Lloydia serotina (L.) REICHENB.
,, pratensis L.	

[1] Before our departure, I had through the Swedish Foreign Office obtained from the Russian Government letters patent in which the Russian authorities with whom we might come in contact were instructed to give us all the assistance that circumstances might call for.

to our voyage.   If the coast had been followed the whole time,
if the weather had been clear and the navigable water sufficiently surveyed, so that it had been possible to keep the course
of the vessel near the land, the voyage of the *Vega* to the mouth
of the Lena *would never have been obstructed by ice*, and I am
convinced that this will happen year after year during the close
of August, at least between the Yenisej and the Lena. For I
believe that the place where ice-obstacles will perhaps be met
with most frequently will not be the north point of Asia, but
the region east of the entrance to the Kara Sea.

CHAPTER VIII.

The voyage of the *Fraser* and the *Express* up the Yenisej and their return
to Norway—Contract for the piloting of the *Lena* up the Lena river—
The voyage of the *Lena* through the delta and up the river to Yakutsk
—The natural state of Siberia in general—The river territories—The
fitness of the land for cultivation and the necessity for improved communications—The great rivers, the future commercial highways of
Siberia—Voyage up the Yenisej in 1875—Sibiriakoff's Island—The
tundra—The primeval Siberian forest—The inhabitants of Western
Siberia : the Russians, the Exiles, the " Asiatics"—Ways of travelling
on the Yenisej : dog-boats, floating trading stores propelled by steam
—New prospects for Siberia.

I HAVE mentioned in the Introduction that the *Vega* during
the first part of the voyage was accompanied by three other
vessels, which together with the principal vessel of the Expedition stood at my disposal and under my orders, and I have stated
in passing that their voyages too deserve a place in the history
of navigation.   Now, when we were parted from the vessel
which had accompanied the *Vega* farthest in her route eastwards,
it may be the proper place to give a brief account of the close
of the voyages of the *Fraser*, the *Express*, and the *Lena*, and
give reasons for what I have said of the importance of these
voyages.
    On the 9th August at 10 a.m., after Mr. Serebrenikoff had
gone on board the *Express* to take command, as Sibiriakoff's
commissioner, of the two vessels bound for the Yenisej, the
Fraser, with the *Express* in tow, started from Port Dickson for
the river.   The voyage passed without other adventures than
that in consequence of unacquaintance with the navigable
waters the vessel sometimes gently grounded.   On the 11th
August Korepovskoj was reached, the same place where I laid up
in 1876 the goods which I had brought with me in the *Ymer*.
Here my old friend from my voyages of 1875 and 1876, the

Cossack Feodor, was taken on board. He however proved now as unskilful a pilot as before. Notwithstanding his experience in 1876, when he several times ran the *Ymer* aground, he had not yet got a clear idea of the difference between the build of an ocean vessel and of the common flat-bottomed Yenisej lighters, and his conception of the responsibility of a pilot was expressed by his seeking, when he was allowed to take his own course, to forget in the arms of sleep all dangers and difficulties. Mr. Serebrenikoff and the captains of the vessels were therefore themselves compelled by means of frequent soundings, which were commonly made from a steam launch in advance, to

THE STEAMER "FRASER."

endeavour to find out the proper course. The navigable water between the level islands covered with bushy thickets and rich grassy meadows was often very narrow, but appears to have been pretty deep, as, even when the vessels went forward without the guidance of a skilful pilot, there was a depth of from 5 to 30 metres; and after a fisher, who knew the river better than Feodor, had been taken on board, it was found possible to go at full speed between the more southerly of the Briochov Islands[1] in a depth of 30 to 50 metres. On 14th August the vessels reached Tolstojnos, where a very well preserved *simovie* is situated about 70° 10′ N.L., 370 kilometres south of Port

---

[1] With this name, for want of another, I denote all the innumerable islands which lie in the Yenisej between 69° 45′ and 71° N.L.

Dickson. On the 15th August they anchored in a good haven at Saostrovskoj, a *simovie* lying 100 kilometres farther up the river at the limit of trees, where the goods were to be discharged and another cargo taken on board. After a jetty had been constructed on the 16th, the landing of the goods began on the 17th, and was finished on the 20th. The *Fraser* went still farther up the river to Dudino, in order to load various goods laid up there—tallow, wheat, rye, and oats. On the 2nd September the steamer returned to Saostrovskoj, where in the meantime the *Express* had taken on board her cargo.

Dudino is a church village, situated at the point where the river Dudinka flows into the Yenisej. Here live two priests, a *smotritel* (a police official), a couple of exiles, some Russian workmen, and a number of natives, as well as the owner of the place, the influential merchant SOTNIKOFF. This active and able man is in an economical point of view ruler over the whole of the surrounding region, all whose inhabitants are in one way or other dependent upon him. He exchanges grain, brandy, sugar, tea, iron goods, powder and lead, cloth and leather, for furs, fish, mammoth-ivory, &c.; and these goods are sent by steamer to Yenisejsk to be forwarded from thence to China, Moscow, St. Petersburg, &c. Among other things he is also the owner of very thick coal-seams in the Noril Mountains lying about 60 kilometres from Dudino. This simple and unostentatious man has been very obliging to all the scientific men who have visited the region. His dwelling, situated in the neighbourhood of the limit of trees, is probably the stateliest palace of the Siberian *tundra*, admired by natives from far and near. It is built of large logs, consists of two stories, has a roof painted green, many windows with decorated frames painted white and blue ; the rooms are warm, provided with carpets of furs, pot-flowers in the windows, numerous sacred pictures, photographs, and copper engravings.

On the 7th September all was ready for departure. The *Fraser* and *Express* weighed anchor to commence the return voyage down the river. At Tolstojnos two days after they met the steamer *Moskwa*[1] of Bremen, Captain Dallmann, having on

[1] The *Moskwa* was the first steamer which penetrated from the Atlantic to the town of Yenisejsk. The principal dates of this voyage may therefore be quoted here.

Baron Knoop, along with several Russian merchants, had chartered in 1878 a steamer, the *Louise ;* but this vessel stranded on the coast of Norway. The *Zaritza*, another Norwegian steamer, was chartered instead to carry the *Louise's* goods to their destination. But this vessel too stranded at the mouth of the Yenisej, and was abandoned by the crew, who were rescued by a small steamer, the *Moskwa*, which accompanied the *Zaritza*. In this steamer Captain Dallmann, the Bremen merchant Helwig Schmidt, and Ehlertz, an official in the Russian finance office, now travelled up the river. The *Moskwa* had a successful voyage, arriving on the 4th September at

board the crew of the Norwegian steamer *Zaritza*, Captain Brun, which had stranded at the mouth of the Yenisej and been abandoned by the crew. In the case of this stranding, however, the damage done had not been greater than that, when the *Fraser* fell in with the stranded *Zaritza*, it could be pumped dry, taken off the shoal, and, the engine having first been put in order, carried back to Norway. On the 19th September all the three vessels arrived at Matotschkin Sound, where they lay some days in Beluga Bay in order to take in water and trim the cargo and coal ; after which on the 22nd of the same month they sailed through the sound to the west, and on the 26th anchored at Hammerfest in good condition and with full cargoes.[1] The goods, which now for the first time were carried from the Yenisej to Europe, consisted of about 600 tons—tallow, wheat, rye and oats. The goods imported into Siberia consisted mainly of 16 tons nails, 8 tons horseshoes, 4 tons horsenails, 16¼ tons bar iron, 33 tons tobacco, 60 tons salt, 24 casks petroleum, an iron lighter in pieces with the necessary adjuncts of anchors, &c.[2]

Before I begin to give an account of the voyage of the *Lena*, I must briefly mention the steps which Mr. Sibiriakoff took for her safety during her voyage from the mouth of the river, where she was to part from the *Vega*, to her proper destination, the town of Yakutsk. It is naturally very difficult for a vessel to seek her way without a pilot through an extensive delta completely unknown in a hydrographic respect, and crossed by a large number of deeper or shallower river arms. Mr. Sibiriakoff had therefore arranged that a river pilot should meet the *Lena* at the north point of the delta, and had through Mr. Kolesoff negoti-ated with him the following contract, which I reproduce here in full, because it gives in several respects a very graphic picture of various social relations in these remote regions. The copy of the contract which has been communicated to me when translated runs thus :—

At Yakutsk, in the year one thousand eight hundred and seventy-eight on the 18th February, I, the undersigned Yakut

Goltschicha, passing Turuchansk in consequence of a number of delays only on the 24th September, reaching Podkamenaja Tunguska on the 1st October, and on the 14th of the same month its destination, a winter harbour on the Tschorna river, some miles north of Yenisejsk. (Fahrt auf dem Yenissej von der Mündung bis Yenisejsk im Sommer 1878 ; Petermann's *Mittheilungen*, 1879, p. 81.)

[1] The particulars of the voyages of these vessels are taken from a copy which I have received of Captain Emil Nilsson's log.

[2] The goods carried by me and by Wiggins to the Yenisej in 1876, and those which Schwanenberg carried thence in 1877, were properly only samples on a somewhat large scale. I have no knowledge of the goods which the *Zaritza* had on board when she ran aground at the mouth of the Yenisej.

T

AFONASH FEODOROFF WINOKUROFF, have concluded the following contract with IVAN PLATONOWITSCH KOLESOFF, merchant of the second guild in the town of Yakutsk.

1. I, Winokuroff bind myself as pilot to carry the vessel of Professor Nordenskiöld's expedition up the river Lena from the village Tas-Ary, which lies about 150 versts below the village Bulun. From Tumat Island, which is situated in the north-eastern part of the Lena delta, I bind myself for the piloting of the same vessel to procure at my own cost among the inhabitants of the place a pilot who knows well the deepest channel of the Lena river as far as the village Tas-Ary. This pilot the chief of the expedition shall discharge at the village Tas-Ary.

2. As I am not master of the Russian language I bind myself to bring along with me a Yakut interpreter, who knows the Russian language and is able to write. In May of this year, I, Winokuroff, with the interpreter shall travel from the town of Yakutsk down the Lena river to Tumat Island and there along with the interpreter wait for the expedition.

3. During the passage down the river I am bound to hire among the inhabitants of the regions a competent guide, who shall accompany us in my own boats to the island by the deepest channel in the Lena delta. During the passage from the village Tas-Ary I shall take soundings and record the depth of the fairway.

4. Between the village Bulun and Tumat Island, I bind myself to seek for two places for the wintering of the vessel, which are quite suitable for the purpose, and protected from ice. I shall further lay before the commander of the expedition a journal containing everything which I can find that it would be advantageous to know for the safety of navigation and for the wintering of the vessels, also accounts of the places which are dangerous or unsuitable for navigation.

5. On my arrival at Tumat Island I shall make it my first duty to find a deep and convenient haven for the seagoing vessels on the western side of the island. For this purpose I bind myself to have with me two boats, which, if necessary, shall be given over to the expedition. At the haven when found I bind myself to erect on some eminence near the shore of the island, which can be seen from Cape Olonek, a signal tower of driftwood or earth, like a Cossack mound, not lower than seven feet. On this foundation I shall raise a pyramidal frame of three or more thick logs, on the top of which I shall fix a flagstaff with a pulley block for the flag. The flag is to be flown at least 42 feet from the ground. I shall guard the landmark thus erected until the river freezes. For this purpose Herr Kolesoff has provided me with a ready-made flag, a pulley block and a line. And when the nights become dark I shall light two or three

large fires or hang up lanterns on the landmark itself, so that these fires or lanterns may be seen from the sea.

6. From the village Tas-Ary I shall carry the vessel of the expedition to the town of Yakutsk, inasmuch as I shall show the proper fairway on the Lena river. The interpreter shall be at my side during the whole journey.

7. During the whole time from the day when I start from Yakutsk, up to the close of my time of service in Nordenskiöld's expedition we, I, Winokuroff, and my interpreter, must be always sober (never intoxicated), behave faithfully and courteously, and punctually comply with the captain's orders.

8. For all these obligations Herr Kolesoff has to pay me 900 roubles.

9. After the arrival of the expedition at Yakutsk I will not be allowed to leave the ship without the permission of the chief, but shall still remain on board. If the captain finds it necessary that I accompany him back to the mouth of the Lena, I shall conform to his wish in consideration of an extra fee of 300 roubles. During this latter passage I am not bound to have with me any interpreter.

10. If the arrival of the expedition at Tumat Island is delayed by any circumstance to the month of November, I have the right to betake myself along with my interpreter to Yakutsk, and here to produce to Herr Kolesoff an official certificate given by Commandant Baschleff or any other local official that I had erected a landmark on Tumat Island and remained there until the river was frozen over, and that I did not leave until the expedition was no longer to be expected. Then Herr Kolesoff on the ground of this contract must settle with me by paying me the whole sum of 900 roubles, together with 200 roubles for my return journey.

11. If the vessel of the expedition arrive at Tumat Island so late that the voyage becomes impossible, we, I and my interpreter, shall winter with the expedition until the river becomes open in 1879. And in this case we, I and my interpreter, shall live at our own expense, and serve the expedition as belonging to its crew. After the commencement of navigation in 1879 I shall conduct the vessel from the wintering station to the town of Yakutsk. On this account I have to receive, besides the 900 roubles coming to me, 800 roubles more. If during this voyage too it should be necessary to accompany the vessels from Yakutsk back to the mouth of the Lena, I shall do that, and receive on that account 300 roubles. But if the vessels winter at Yakutsk, I shall be free during winter, and only during next year's voyage, if so required, accompany them to the mouth of the Lena. In that case I have to receive 300 roubles.

12. Of this sum agreed upon Herr Kolesoff shall pay me in advance on the conclusion of this contract 300 roubles, in the month of May, at my departure 150 roubles, and at the village Bulun 250 roubles, for my payment to my companions and pilot and other expenses. The balance shall be paid to me after my return to Yakutsk.

13. In the month of May, at the time for starting, if I be prevented by illness from betaking myself to Tumat Island, I shall repay to Herr Kolesoff the sum paid to me at the conclusion of this contract, with the exception of the money I have paid to the interpreter as pocket-money and for the boats. Should I not be able to repay the sum, I, Winokuroff, shall work out the amount not repaid at Herr Sibiriakoff's gold mines.

14. All this are we, the two contracting parties, bound to observe in full and without infringement.

A note to the copy further informs us that to this contract the Yakut Afonasii Feodoroff Winokuroff had, in place of his signature, attached his own seal, which the Yakut Alexii Zassimoff Mironoff had engraved, and that the conditions had been approved by the merchant Ivan Kolesoff, and the whole registered at the police-office of the Yakutsk circle.

The contract had been entered into with the friendly co-operation of the Governor and Bishop of Yakutsk, who were much interested in the proposed voyage. The latter knew the coast of the Polar Sea from his own experience. But notwithstanding all this, the affair was attended with no better success than that the pilot celebrated the receipt of the large sum of money by getting thoroughly intoxicated, and while in that state he broke one of the bones of the fore-arm. He was thus unable ever to reach the appointed rendezvous, and Johannesen was allowed to manage by his own hand, as best he could, his little steamer.

After the _Lena_ had parted with the _Vega_ during the night between the 27th and 28th August, she steamed towards land, and came the same day to the northernmost cape of the Lena delta, situated in 73° 47′ N.L.[1] It was here that the pilot's landmark was to have been erected, but there was no pilot here, and no flagstaff was visible. In order to fall in with this landmark Johannesen sailed forty kilometres westward along the shore, but as his search in this direction was not attended with success, he turned back to the first-mentioned place and landed there. On the shore stood a very old hut, already completely filled with earth. It probably dated from some of the expeditions which visited the region in the beginning of the century.

[1] According to Johannesen's determination. On Wrangel's map the latitude of this cape is given as 73° 30′. Johannesen found the longitude to be 125° 31′ instead of 127°.

Wild reindeer were seen in large numbers. As according to the contract which has been quoted the landmark was to be visible from Cape Olonek, Johannesen steamed once more to the west, running as close to the land as possible. But as the water here became shallower and shallower without any signal-tower being visible, Johannesen had to find his way himself through the delta; and for this purpose he determined to search for the easternmost arm of the river, which, on the maps, is drawn as being very broad, and also appears to have been made use of by the vessels of "the great northern expeditions."[1]

THE STEAMER "LENA."

Forty kilometres east of the northern extremity of the Lena delta Johannesen encountered three sandbanks, which he sailed

[1] According to Latkin (Petermann's *Mittheilungen*, 1879, p. 92), the Lena delta is crossed by seven main arms, the westernmost of which is called Anatartisch. It debouches into the sea at a cape 58 feet high named Ice Cape (Ledjanoi). Next come the river arm Bjelkoj, then Tumat, at whose mouth a landmark erected by Laptev in 1739 is still in existence. Then come the other three main arms, Kychistach, Trofimov, and Kischlach, and finally the very broad eastmost arm, Bychov. Probably some of the smaller river arms are to be preferred for sailing up the river to this broad arm, which is fouled by shoals.

round.   After passing these the water became deeper, so that
he could advance at a distance of five kilometres from land.
On the 1st September Johannesen anchored in a bay on the
mainland in the neighbourhood of the Bychov mouth, whence
on the 3rd September, at 2.30 a.m., he continued his course up
the river, but by 10 o'clock the *Lena* was aground.   The water
was falling, and did not begin to rise until an hour after midnight.   It was not, therefore, until 8 a.m. the following day
that the *Lena* was got off, and that with great difficulty.   The
sailing through the delta was rendered difficult by the maps,
which were made 140 years ago, being now useless.   For the

HANS CHRISTIAN JOHANNESEN.
Captain of the "Lena." Born in 1846.

delta has undergone great alterations since then.   Where at
that time there were sandbanks, there are now large islands,
overgrown with wood and grass.   At other places again whole
islands have been washed away by the river.
     While the vessel was aground nine Tunguses came on board.
They rowed in small boats, which were made of a single tree
stem, hollowed out, and could just carry a man each.   Johannesen endeavoured in vain to induce some of the Tunguses to
pilot the steamer; he did not succeed in explaining his wish to
them, notwithstanding all the attempts of the Russian interpreter, a proof of the slight contact these Tunguses had had

with the rulers of Siberia, and also of the difficulty and unwillingness with which the savage learns the language of the
civilised nations.

It was not until the 7th September that the delta was finally
passed, and the *Lena* steamed in the river proper, where the
fairway became considerably better. Johannesen says in his
account of the voyage that it is improbable that any of the
western arms of the Lena are of importance, partly because the
mass of water which flows in an easterly direction is very
considerable in comparison with the whole quantity of water in
the river, partly because the western and northern arms which
Johannesen visited contained only salt water, while the water
in the eastern arm was completely free from any salt taste. On
the 8th, early in the morning, the first fixed dwelling-place on
the Lena, Tas-Ary, was reached. Here the voyagers landed to
get information about the fairway, but could not enter into
communication with the natives, because they were Tunguses.
In the afternoon of the same day they came to another river
village, Bulun. Impatient to proceed, and supposing that it
too was inhabited wholly by "Asiatics," [1] Johannesen intended
to pass it without stopping. But when the inhabitants saw the
steamer they welcomed it with a salute from all the guns that
could be got hold of in haste.[2] The *Lena* then anchored. Two
Crown officials and a priest came on board, and the latter
performed a thanksgiving service.

Even at that remote spot on the border of the *tundra* the
Asiatic comprehended very well the importance of vessels from
the great oceans being able to reach the large rivers of Siberia,
I too had a proof of this in the year 1875. While still rowing
up the river in my own Nordland boat with two scientific men
and three hunters, before we got up with the steamer *Alexander*
we landed, among others, at a place where a number of Dolgans
were collected. When they understood clearly that we had
come to them, not as brandy-sellers or fish-buyers from the
south, but from the north, *from the ocean,* they went into complete ecstasies. We were exposed to unpleasant embraces from
our skin-clad admirers, and finally one of us had the misfortune
to get a bath in the river in the course of an attempt which the
Dolgans in their excitement made to carry him almost with
violence to the boat, which was lying in the shallow water some
distance from the shore. At Dudino, also, the priests living
there held a thanksgiving service for our happy arrival thither.
Two of them said mass, while the clerk, clad in a sheepskin
caftan reaching to his feet, zealously and devoutly swung an

---

[1] A common name used in Siberia for all the native races.
[2] This has been incorrectly interpreted as if they shot at the vessel.

immense censer. The odour from it was at first not particularly pleasant, but it soon became so strong and disagreeable that I, who had my place in front of the audience, was like to choke, though the ceremony was performed in the open air. Soon the clerk was completely concealed in a dense cloud of smoke, and it was now observed that his skin cloak had been set fire to at the same time as the incense. The service, however, was not interrupted by this incident, but the fire was merely extinguished by a bucket of water being thrown, to the amusement of all, over the clerk.

At nine in the morning the *Lena* continued her voyage up the river with the priest and the Crown officials on board, but they had soon to be landed, because in their joy they had become dead drunk. On the 13th September Schigansk was reached, and samples of the coal found there were taken on board, but these proved unserviceable,[1] and on the, 21st September the *Lena* reached Yakutsk. The first vessel which, coming from the ocean, reached the heart of Siberia was received with great goodwill and hospitality, both by the authorities and the common people. But when Johannesen did not find here Sibiriakoff's representative Kolesoff, he continued his voyage up the river, until on the 8th October, he came to the village Njaskaja, 220 versts from Vitim, in about 60° N.L. Here he turned back to Yakutsk and laid up the steamer in winter quarters a little to the south of that town.

Both the *Fraser* and *Express* and the *Lena* had thus fully answered the purposes intended before the departure of the expedition, and their voyages will always form an important link in the chain of the attempts through which navigation in the Siberian Polar Sea has been opened.

In order to give an idea of the influence which this sea-route may have on the commerce of the world, and the new source of fortune and prosperity which thereby may be rendered accessible to millions, I shall in a few words give an account of the nature of the territory which by means of this sea-communication will be brought into contact with the old civilised countries of Europe.

If we take Siberia in its widest sense, that is to say, if we include under that name not only Siberia proper, but also the parts of High Asia which lie round the sources of the great Siberian rivers, this land may very well be compared in extent,

---

[1] A coal seam is often unfit for use near the surface, where for centuries it has been uncovered and exposed to the action of the atmosphere, while farther down it may yield very good coal. It is probable besides that the layers of shale, which often surround the coal seams, have in this case been mistaken for the true coal. For those who are inexperienced in coal-mining to make such a mistake is the rule and not the exception.

climate, fertility, and the possibility of supporting a dense population, with America north of 40° N.L. Like America, Siberia is occupied in the north by woodless plains. South of this region, where only the hunter, the fisher, and the reindeer nomad can find a scanty livelihood, there lies a widely extended forest territory, difficult of cultivation, and in its natural conditions, perhaps, somewhat resembling Sweden and Finland north of 60° or 61° N.L. South of this wooded belt, again, we have, both in Siberia and America, immeasurable stretches of an

YAKUTSK IN THE SEVENTEENTH CENTURY.
After Witsen.

exceedingly fertile soil, of whose power to repay the toil of the cultivator the grain exports during recent years from the frontier lands between the United States and Canada have afforded so striking evidence. There is, however, this dissimilarity between Siberia and America, that while the products of the soil in America may be carried easily and cheaply to the harbours of the Atlantic and the Pacific, the best part of Siberia, that which lies round the upper part of the courses of the Irtisch-Ob and the Yenisej, is shut out from the great oceans of the world by immense tracts lying in front of it, and the great rivers which in Siberia cross the country and appear to be intended by nature to form not only the arteries for its inner life, but also channels of communication with the rest of the world, all flow towards the north and fall into a sea which, down to the most recent times, has been considered completely inaccessible.

Of these rivers the double river, Ob-Irtisch, with its numerous affluents, occupies an area of more than 60,000 geographical

YAKUTSK IN OUR DAYS.
After a recent Russian drawing.

square miles, the Yenisej-Angara, not quite 50,000, and the Lena, somewhat over 40,000.[1] As the map of the river system

[1] In order not to write without due examination about figures which have been written about a thousand times before, I have, with the help of Petermann's map of North and Middle Asia in Stieler's Hand-Atlas, calculated the extent of the areas of the Siberian rivers, and found them to be :—

	Square kilometres.	Geographical square miles.
River area of the Ob (with the Tas)...	3,445,000	62,560
„ „ „ Yenisej	2,712,000	49,250
„ „ „ Lena	2,395,000	43,500

Of these areas 4,966,000 square kilometres, or about 90,000 geographical square miles, lie south of 60° N.L.

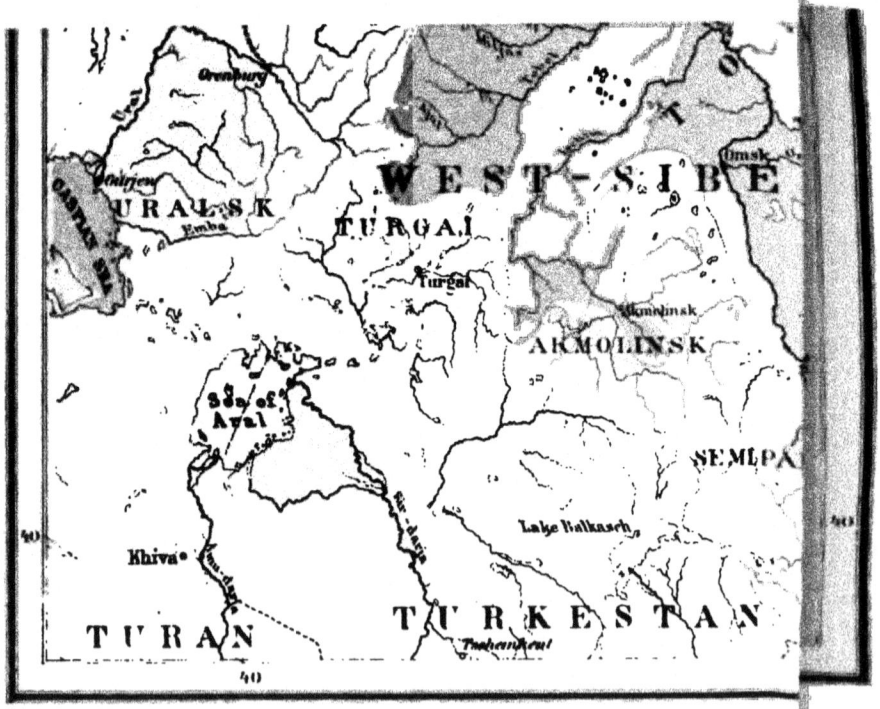

After A.Petermann's Map of North and Middle Asia in Stielers Hand-Atlas, 1880

of Siberia, which accompanies this work, shows, but a small part
of these enormous territories lies north of the Arctic Circle, and
y very inconsiderable portions of it are occupied by woodless
tundra, which is explained by the fact that the greater part of
the coast-land bordering on the Arctic Ocean is drained by
several rivers of its own, and therefore cannot be considered to
belong to the river territories now in question.   If we draw the
northern boundary of the land that may be cultivated with
advantage at 60° N.L., there remains a cultivable area of
600,000 geographical square miles.   Perhaps a third part of this
is occupied by rocky country which is wooded, and probably
capable of being cultivated only with considerable difficulty,
but the rest consists for the most part of easily cultivated
grassy plains, with little wood, and covered with the most
luxuriant vegetation.   The soil, in many places resembling
the black earth or *tscherno-sem* of Russia, recompenses with
abundant harvests even the slightest labour of cultivation.
Notwithstanding this, these regions now support only an exceedingly sparse population, but many, many millions may without
difficulty find their subsistence there when once cultivation has
developed the rich natural resources of the country.

It is a circumstance specially fortunate for the future development of Siberia that its three great rivers are already navigable
for the greater part of their course.   The Ob is navigable from
isk (52¼° N.L.), and the Irtisch at least from Semipalitinsk
(60° 18' N.L.).   The Yenisej, again, which, after leaving the
region of its sources in China, crosses with its two main arms
the whole of Siberia from north to south, from the forty-sixth to
the seventy-third degree of latitude, and thus traverses a territory which corresponds in length to the distance between Venice
and the North Cape, or between the mouth of the Mississippi
and the north part of Lake Winnipeg, and is already navigable
in nature from the sea to Yenisejsk.   To this town goods are
already transported *down* both the main arms from Minusinsk
and the region of Lake Baikal.   It is said that the Angara
might be made quite navigable during its whole course at an
expenditure trifling in comparison with the advantages that
could thus be gained, as well as its continuation, the Selenga,
and its lower part between the Chinese frontier and Lake Baikal.
In this way a river route would be opened for the conveyance of
the products of North China and South Siberia to a sea which
an ordinary steamer would cross in five or six days to the White
Sea or the North Cape.   A similar communication with the
Atlantic may be opened on the double river Ob-Irtisch with
Western Siberia and High Asia as far as to Chinese Dsungaria,
where the Irtisch begins its course as a small river, the Black
isch, which falls into Lake Saisan, and rises south of the

Altai Mountains in the neighbourhood of the Selenga, the source-river of the Yenisej. At several places the river territories of the Ob and the Yenisej nearly reach hands to one another through affluents, which rise so close to each other that the two river systems might easily be connected by canals. This is also the case with the affluents of the Yenisej and the Lena, which at many places almost meet, and the Lena itself is, according to Latkin's statement, navigable from the village of Kotschuga to the sea. We see from this how extraordinarily advantageous is the natural system of interior communication which Siberia possesses, and at the same time that a communication by sea between this country and the rest of the world is possible only by the Arctic Ocean. It is on this that the enormous importance of the navigation of the Siberian Polar Sea depends. If this can be brought about, Siberia, with an inconsiderable expenditure in making canals, will not only become one of the most fortunate countries of the globe in respect of the possibility of the cheap transport of goods, but the old proposal of a north-eastern commercial route to China may even become a reality. If, on the other hand, navigation on the Polar Sea be not brought about, Siberia will still long remain what it is at present—a land rich in raw materials, but poor in all that is required for the convenience and comfort with which the civilised man in our days can with difficulty dispense.

Many perhaps believe that the present want of commercial communication may be removed by a railway running across Russia and Southern Siberia. But this is by no means the case. On the contrary, communication by sea is an indispensable condition of such a railway being profitable. For it can never come in question to carry on a railway the products of the forest or the field over the stretch of three to five thousand kilometres which separates the fertile river territory of the Ob-Irtisch from the nearest European port. Even if we suppose that the railway freight, inclusive of all costs could be reduced to a farthing the kilometre-ton, it would in any case rise, from the grain regions of Siberia to a harbour on the Baltic, to from 4l. to nearly 7l. per ton. So high a freight, with the costs of loading in addition, none of the common products of agriculture or forestry can stand, as may easily be seen if we compare this amount with the prices current in the markets of the world for wheat, rye, oats, barley, timber, &c. But if the Siberian countryman cannot sell his raw products, the land will continue to be as thinly peopled as it is at present, nor can the sparse population which will be found there procure themselves means to purchase such products of the industry of the present day as are able to bear long railway carriage. In the absence of contemporaneous sea-communication the railway will therefore be without traffic, the land such as it is at present, and the unprosperous condition of the European population undiminished.

In order to give the reader an idea of the present natural conditions, and the present communication on a Siberian river I shall, before returning to the sketch of the voyage of the *Vega*, give some extracts from notes made during my journey up the Yenisej in 1875, reminding the reader, however, that the natural conditions of the Ob-Irtisch and the Lena differ considerably from those of the Yenisej, the Ob-Irtisch flowing through lower, more fertile, and more thickly peopled regions, the Lena again through a wilder, more beautiful, but less cultivated country.

When one travels up the river from Port Dickson, the broad sound between Sibiriakoff's Island and the mainland is first passed, but the island is so low that it is not visible from the eastern bank of the river arm which is usually followed in sailing up or down the river. The mainland, on the other hand, is at first high-lying, and in sailing along the coast it is possible to distinguish various spurs of the range of hills, estimated to be from 150 to 200 metres high, in the interior. These are free of snow in summer. A little south of Port Dickson they run to the river bank, where they form a low rock and rocky island projecting into the river, named after some otherwise unknown Siberian Polar trapper, Yefremov Kamen.

Sibiriakoff's Island has never, so far as we know, been visited by man, not even during the time when numerous *simovies* were found at the mouth of the Yenisej. For no indication of this island is found in the older maps of Siberia, although these, as appears from the fac-simile reproduced at page 147, give the names of a number of *simovies* at the mouth of the Yenisej, now abandoned. Nor is it mentioned in the accounts of the voyages of the great northern expeditions. The western strand of the island, the only one I have seen, completely bore the stamp of the *tundra* described below. Several reindeer were seen pasturing on the low grassy eminences of the island, giving promise of abundant sport to the hunter who first lands there.

Still at Yefremov Kamen we saw in 1875 three Polar bears who appeared to pasture in all peacefulness among the rocks, and did not allow themselves to be disturbed by the enormous log-fire of driftwood we lighted on the strand to make our coffee. Here were found for the last time during our journey up the river actual marine animals : Appendicularia, Clio, medusæ, large beroids, &c. Large bushy plants were still completely wanting, but the vegetable world already began to assume a stamp differing from the Arctic Ocean flora proper. A

short distance south of Yefremov Kamen begins the veritable
tundra, a woodless plain, interrupted by no mountain heights,
with small lakes scattered over it, and narrow valleys crossing
it, which often make an excursion on the apparently level plain
exceedingly tiresome.

As is the case with all the other Siberian rivers running from
south to north,[1] the western strand of the Yenisej, wherever it
is formed of loose, earthy layers, is also quite low and often
marshy, while on the other hand the eastern strand consists of
a steep bank, ten to twenty metres high, which north of the

RIVER VIEW ON THE YENISEJ.
From a drawing by A. N. Lundström.

limit of trees is distributed in a very remarkable way into
pyramidal pointed mounds.   Numerous shells of crustacea
found here, belonging to species which still live in the Polar
Sea, show that at least the upper earthy layer of the *tundra*

---

[1] For the northern hemisphere it is a general rule that where rivers
flow through loose, earthy strata in a direction deviating considerably
from that of the parallels of latitude, the right bank, when one stands
facing the mouth of the river, is high, and the left low. The cause
of this is the globular form of the earth and its rotation, which gives
rivers flowing north a tendency towards the east, and to rivers flowing
south a tendency to the west. This tendency is resisted by the bank,
but it is gradually eaten into and washed away by degrees, so that the
river bed, in the course of thousands of years, is shifted in the direction
indicated.

was deposited in a sea resembling that which now washes the north coast of Siberia.[1]

The *tundra* itself is in summer completely free of snow, but at a limited depth from the surface the ground is continually frozen. At some places the earthy strata alternate with strata of pure, clear ice. It is in these frozen strata that complete carcases of elephants and rhinoceroses have been found, which have been protected from putrefaction for hundreds of thousands of years. Such *finds*, however, are uncommon, but on the other hand single bones from this primeval animal world occur in rich abundance, and along with them masses of old drift-wood, originating from the Mammoth period, known by the Russian natives of Siberia under the distinctive name of "Noah's wood." Besides there are to be seen in the most recent layer of the Yenesej *tundra*, considerably north of the present limit of actual trees, large tree-stems with their roots fast in the soil, which show that the limit of trees in the Yenesej region, even during our geological period, went further north than now, perhaps as far as, in consequence of favourable local circumstances, it now goes on the Lena.

On the slopes of the steep *tundra* bank and in several of the *tundra* valleys there is an exceedingly rich vegetation, which already, only 100 kilometres south of Yefremov Kamen, forms actual thickets of flowering plants, while the *tundra* itself is overgrown with an exceedingly scanty carpet, consisting more of mosses than of grasses. Salices of little height go as far north as Port Dickson (73° 30′ N.L.), the dwarf birch (*Betula nana*, L.) is met with, though only as a bush creeping along the ground, at Cape Schaitanskoj (72° 8′ N.L.) ; and here in 1875, on the ice-mixed soil of the *tundra*, we gathered ripe cloudberries. Very luxuriant alders (*Alnaster fruticosus*, LEDEB.) occur already at Mesenkin (71° 28′ N.L.), and the Briochov Islands (70° to 71° N.L.), are in several places covered with rich and luxuriant thickets of bushes. But the limit of trees proper is considered to begin first at the great bend which the river makes in

---

[1] As specimens of the sub-fossil mollusc fauna of the *tundra* some of the common species are delineated on page 288. These are :—

1. *Mya arenaria*, Lin. ⅔ of natural size.
2. *Mya truncata*, Lin. var. *Uddevallensis*, Forbes. ⅔.
3. *Saxicava pholadis*, Lin. ⅔.
4. *Tellina lata*, Gmel. ⅔.
5. *Cardium ciliatum*, Fabr. ⅔.
6. *Leda pernula*, Müll. var. *buccata*, Steenstr. Natural size.
7. *Nucula expansa*, Reeve. Nat. size.
8. *Fusus Kröyeri*, Möll. ⅔.
9. *Fusus fornicatus*, Reeve. ⅔.
10. *Fusus tornatus*, Gould. ⅔.
11. *Margarita elegantissima*, Bean. Natural size.
12. *Pleurotoma plicifera*, Wood. Natural size.
13. *Pleurotoma pyramidalis*, Ström. 1½.
14. *Trichotropis borealis*, Brod. 1½.
15. *Natica helicoides*, Johnst. Nat. size.

SUB-FOSSIL MARINE CRUSTACEA FROM THE TUNDRA.

69° 40′ N.L., a little north of Dudino. Here the hills are covered with a sort of wood consisting of half-withered, grey, moss-grown larches (*Larix sibirica*), which seldom reach a height of more than seven to ten metres, and which much less deserve the name of trees than the luxuriant alder bushes which grow nearly 2° farther north. But some few miles south of this place, and still far north of the Arctic Circle, the pine forest becomes tall. Here begins a veritable forest, the greatest the earth has to show, extending with little interruption from the Ural to the neighbourhood of the Sea of Ochotsk, and from the fifty-eighth or fifty-ninth degree of latitude to far north of the Arctic Circle, that is to say, about one thousand kilometres from north to south, and perhaps four times as much from east to west. It is a primeval forest of enormous extent, nearly untouched by the axe of the cultivator, but at many places devastated by extensive forest fires.

On the high eastern bank of the Yenisej the forest begins immediately at the river bank. It consists principally of pines : the cembra pine (*Pinus Cembra*, L.), valued for its seeds, enormous larches, the nearly awl-formed Siberian pine (*Pinus sibirica*, LEDEB.), the fir (*Pinus obovata*, TURCZ.), and scattered trees of the common pine (*Pinus sylvestris*, L.). Most of these already north of the Arctic Circle reach a colossal size, but in such a case are often here, far from all forestry, grey and half-dried up with age. Between the trees the ground is so covered with fallen branches and stems, only some of which are fresh, the others converted into a mass of wood-mould held together only by the bark, that there one willingly avoids going forward on an unbroken path. If that must be done, the progress made is small, and there is constant danger of breaking one's bones in the labyrinth of stems. Nearly everywhere the fallen stems are covered, often concealed, by an exceedingly luxuriant bed of mosses, while on the other hand tree-lichens, probably in consequence of the dry inland climate of Siberia, occur sparingly. The pines, therefore, want the shaggy covering common in Sweden, and the bark of the birches which are seen here and there among the pines is distinguished by an uncommon blinding whiteness.

The western bank of the Yenisej consists, like the innumerable islands of the river, for the most part of lowlying and marshy stretches of land, which at the season of the spring floods are overflowed by the river and abundantly manured with its mud. In this way there is formed here a fertile tract of meadow covered partly with a grassy turf untouched by the scythe, partly with a very peculiar bush vegetation, rising to a height of eight metres, among which there are to be found a number of families of plants well known by us in Sweden, as

U

Impatiens, Urtica, Sonchus, Heracleum, &c., but in gigantic
forms unknown at home. Often a dense thicket of a willow
(*Salix vitellenia*, L.), whose straight, branchless stems resemble
at a distance the bamboo woods of the south, alternates with
level, grassy carpets of a lively green and small streams in such
a way as gives the whole the appearance of the most smiling
park carefully kept free of fallen branches and dry grass. It is
the river water which in spring has played the gardener's part
in these parks, seldom trodden by the foot of man and endlessly
rich in the most splendid greenery. Near the river there are
also to be found carpets of a uniform green, consisting of a
short kind of Equisetum, unmixed with any other plants, which
forms a " gazon," to which no nobleman's country seat can show
a match. The drawback is, that a stay in these regions during
summer is nearly rendered impossible by the enormous number
of mosquitoes with which the air is infested.

A table drawn up by DR. ARNELL, to be found in *Redogörelse
för de svenska expeditionerna till mynningen af Jenisej år 1876*,[1]
shows the distribution of the most important varieties of trees.
From it we see that on the Yenisej the birch (*Betula odorata*,
BECHST.), the fir (*Pinus obovata*, TURCZ.), the larch (*Pinus
larix*, L.), and the juniper (*Juniperus communis*, L.), go to
69° 35′ N.L. (that is to say to the latitude of Tromsoe); the
sallow (*Salix caprea*, L.) to 68° 55′; the bird's cherry (*Prunus
padus*, L.), and the Siberian pine (*Pinus sibirica*, LEDEB.), to
66° 30′; the aspen (*Populus tremula*, L.) to 65° 55′ (the latitude
of Haparanda); the pine (*Pinus sylvatica*, L.) to 65° 50′, &c.

In the middle of the forest belt the wood appears to cover
the whole land without interruption, there being, unless
exceptionally, no open places. But towards the north the forest
passes into the treeless *tundra* through bare spots occurring
here and there, which gradually increase, until trees grow only
in valleys and sheltered places, and finally disappear completely.
Similar is the passage of the forest to treeless regions (steppes),
which at first are here and there bestrewed with more or less
detached groups of broad-leaved trees, until they wholly disappear, and the land forms an endless plain, out of whose fertile
soil the warm summer sun calls forth a great variety of
luxuriant vegetable forms, whose many-hued flowers, often
large and splendid, clothe the fields with the richest splendour
of colour. Here is the true homeland of many of the show-
plants in the flower-gardens of Europe, as, for instance, the
peony, the Siberian robinia, the blue iris, &c.

If the Siberian wooded belt forms the most extensive forest
in the world. this flower-steppe forms the world's greatest
cultivable field, in all probability unequalled in extent and

[1] *Bihang till Vet. Akad. Handl.* Bd. iv. No. 11, p. 42.

fertility. Without manure and with an exceedingly small amount of labour expended on cultivation, man will year by year draw forth from its black soil the most abundant harvests. For the present, however, this land, with its splendid capabilities for cultivation, has an exceedingly scanty population; and this holds good in a yet higher degree of the forest belt, which is less susceptible of cultivation. At a considerable distance from the rivers it is for the most part an unknown land, where the European seldom or never sets his foot, and where only the native nomad or hunter wanders about. These forests, however, are by no means so rich in game as might be expected, perhaps because the mosquitoes in summer are unendurable by warm-blooded animals.

The main population in the forest belt consists of native nomad or hunting tribes, of which Samoyeds, Ostyaks, Tunguses, and Yakuts are the most numerous. Only along the rivers do we find Russian villages and peasant settlements, placed there for trading with the natives, for fishing, and at some places for washing gold. Not till we come to the middle of the country is the Russian population more numerous; here it spreads out in a broad belt over the whole of the immense expanse between the Ural and the Angara.

In the farthest north the Russian dwelling-places consist of single cabins built of logs or planks from broken-up lighters,[1] and having flat, turf-covered roofs. Such carvings and ornaments as are commonly found on the houses of the well-to-do Russian peasant, and whose artistic outlines indicate that the inhabitants have had time to think of something else than the satisfaction of the wants of the moment, are here completely wanting; but further south the villages are larger, and the houses finer, with raised roofs and high gables richly ornamented with wood-carvings. A church, painted in bright colours, generally shows that one of the inhabitants of the village has become rich enough to be at the expense of this ornament to his native place. The whole indicates a degree of prosperity, and the interiors of the houses, if we except the cockroaches, which swarm everywhere, are very clean. The walls are ornamented with numerous, if not very artistic, photographs and lithographs. Sacred pictures, richly ornamented, are placed in a corner, and before them hang several small oil-lamps, or small wax-lights, which are lighted on festive occasions. The sleeping

---

[1] Provisions and wares intended for trade with the natives are transported on the Yenisej, as on many other Siberian rivers, down the stream in colossal lighters, built of planks like logs. It does not pay to take them up the river again, on which account, after their lading has been taken out of them, they are either left on the bank to rot or broken up for the timber.

place is formed of a bedstead near the roof, so large that it
occupies a half or a third of the room, and at such a height
from the floor that one can stand upright under it.   There
a tropical heat commonly prevails, the occupant of the bed
accordingly enjoying an almost constant sweat-bath, which does
not prevent him from going out immediately into the open air
at a temperature at which mercury freezes.   Food is cooked in
large baking-ovens, which are fired daily for that purpose, and
at the same time heat the cabin.   Fresh bread is baked every
day, and even for the poor a large tea-urn (*samovar*) is an almost
indispensable household article.   The foreigner is certain to
receive a hearty and friendly welcome when he crosses the

SIBERIAN RIVER BOAT.
Used by the Norwegian traveller Chr. Hansteen on the river Angara.

threshold, and if he stays a short time in the cabin he will
generally, whatever time of the day it be, find himself drinking a glass of tea with his host.   The dress everywhere closely
resembles the Russian : for the rich, wide velvet trousers stuck
into the boots, a shirt showily embroidered with silver thread,
and a large caftan often lined with fur ; for the poor, if not too
ragged, the same cut, but the cloth inferior, dirty, and torn.
During winter, however, for going out of doors, the Samoyed
pesk is said to be common to high and low, Russian and native,
settled and nomad.

In my journey up the Yenisej in 1875 I met with only a

few persons in these regions who had been exiled thither for political reasons, but on the other hand very many exiled criminals of the deepest dye—murderers, thieves, forgers, incendiaries, &c. Among them were also some few Fins and even a Swede, or at least one who, according to his own statement in broken Swedish had formerly served in the King's Guard at Stockholm. Security of person and property was in any case complete, and it was remarkable that there did not appear to be any proper distinction of caste between the Russian-Siberian natives and those who had been exiled for crime. There appeared even to be little interest in ascertaining the crime—or, as the customary phrase appears to be here, the "misfortune"—which caused the exile. On making inquiry on this point I commonly got the answer, susceptible of many interpretations, "for bad behaviour." We found a peculiar sort of criminal colony at Selivaninskoj, a very large village situated on the eastern bank of the Yenisej in about the latitude of Aavasaksa. My journal of the expedition of 1875 contains the following notes of my visit to this colony.

The orthodox Russian church, as is well known, is tolerant towards the professors of foreign religions—Lutherans, Catholics, Jews, Mohammedans, Buddhists, Shamans, &c. ; but, on the other hand, in complete correspondence with what took place in former times within the Protestant world, persecutes sectaries within its own pale, with temporal punishments here upon earth and with threatenings of eternal in another world. Especially in former times a great many sectaries have been sent to Siberia, and therefore there are sometimes to be found there peculiar colonies enjoying great prosperity, exclusively inhabited by the members of a certain sect. Such is the Skopt colony at Selivaninskoj, in connection with which, however, it may be remarked that the nature of the religious delusion in this case accounts for the severity of the law or the authorities. For, on the ground of a text in the Gospel of Matthew interpreted in a very peculiar way, all Skoptzi subject themselves to a mutilation, in consequence of which the sect can only exist by new proselytes ; and remarkably enough, these madmen, notwithstanding all persecution, or perhaps just on that account, actually still gain followers. A large number of the Skoptzi were Fins from Ingermanland, with whom I could converse without difficulty. They had, through industry and perseverance, succeeded in creating for themselves a certain prosperity, were hospitable and friendly, and bore their hard fate with resignation. They would not themselves kill any warm-blooded animal, for it was "a sin to kill what God had created;" which did not hinder them from catching and eating fish, and from selling to us, who in any case were lost beings, a fine fat ox, on condition that our own

people should slaughter it. Their abstinence from some
kinds of animal food had besides the good result of inducing
them to devote themselves to the cultivation of the soil.
Round about their cabins accordingly there were patches of land
growing potatoes, turnips, and cabbage, which at least that year
yielded an abundant crop, though lying under the Arctic circle.
Farther south such plots increase in size, and yield rich crops,
at least of a very large potato. There is no proper cultivation of
grain till we come to Sykobatka, situated in 60° N.L., but in a
future, when forests and mosses are diminished, a profitable
agriculture will be carried on far to the northward.

OSTYAK TENT.
After a Photograph.

Along with the dwellings of the Russians, the tents of the
natives, or, as the Russians call them, "the Asiatics," are often
to be met with. They have the same shape as the Lapp "kota."
The Samoyed tent is commonly covered with reindeer skins, the
Ostyak tent with birch bark. In the neighbourhood of the
tent there are always large numbers of dogs, which during
winter are employed for general carrying purposes, and in
summer for towing boats up the river—a means of water transport which greatly astonished the Norwegian sailors with whom
I travelled up the river in 1875. To see people travelling in a
boat drawn by dogs appeared to them more remarkable than

TOWING WITH DOGS ON THE YENISEJ.

The Lent Lena with the Swedish Land Expedition of 1876 on board. After a drawing by Hj. Theel.

the Kremlin of Moscow, or the bells of Kiev. For such a journey a sufficient number of dogs are harnessed to a long line, one end of which is fastened to the stem of the boat. The dogs then go along the level bank, where they make actual foot-paths. The boat being of light draught is kept afloat at a sufficient distance from land partly by means of the rudder which is managed by a person sitting in the stern of the boat, and partly by poling from the fore. Small boats are often hollowed out of a single tree-stem, and may notwithstanding, thanks to the size which some of the pines attain in those

FISHING BOATS ON THE OB.
After a Photograph.

regions, be very roomy, and of a very beautiful shape. The dogs strongly resemble the Eskimo dogs in Greenland, which are also used as draught animals.

Most of the natives who have come into close contact with the Russians are said to profess the Christian religion. That many heathen customs, however, still adhere to them is shown, among other things, by the following incident : At a *simovie* where we landed for some hours on the 16th Sept. we found, as is common, a burying-place in the forest near the dwelling houses. The corpses were placed in large coffins above ground, at which

almost always a cross was erected. In one of the crosses a
sacred picture was inserted, which must be considered a further
proof that a Christian rested in the coffin. Notwithstanding
this, we found some clothes, which had belonged to the departed,
hanging on a bush beside the grave, together with a bundle containing food, principally dried fish. At the graves of the richer
natives the survivors are even said to place along with food
some rouble notes, in order that the departed may not be altogether without ready money on his entrance into the other
world.

GRAVES IN THE PRIMEVAL FOREST OF SIBERIA.
After a drawing by Hj. Theel.

Right opposite the village Nasimovskoj is a gold-digger's
deserted "residence," named Yermakova after the first conqueror of Siberia. The building owed its origin to the discovery
of sand-beds rich in gold, occupying a pretty extensive area
east of the Yenisej, which for a time had the repute of being
the richest gold territory in the world. Here in a short
time enormous fortunes were made; and accounts of the
hundreds of poods which one or another yearly reaped from
the sand-beds, and the fast reckless life led by those to whom
fortune dealt out the great prizes in the gold-digging lottery,
still form a favourite topic of conversation in the region. A

rise in the value of labour and a diminished production of the
noble metal have, however, since led to the abandonment of a
large number of the diggings that formerly were most productive ; others now scarcely pay the expense of the working.
Many of the gold-diggers who were formerly rich, in the
attempt to win more have been impoverished, and have disappeared ; others who have succeeded in retaining their "pood
of gold"—that is the mint unit which the gold-diggers prefer
to use in their conversation—have removed to Omsk, Krasnojarsk, Moscow, Petersburg, Paris, &c. The gold-diggers' resi-
dences stand, therefore, now deserted, and form on the eastern
bank of the river a row of half-decayed wooden ruins surrounded
by young trees, after which in no long time only the tradition
of the former period of prosperity will be found remaining. In
one respect indeed the gold-diggers have exerted a powerful
influence on the future of the country. For it was through
them that the first pioneers were scattered in the wilderness,
the first seed sown of the cultivation of the region.

In 1875 there were only two steamers on the Yenisej. These
were neither passenger nor cargo boats, but rather movable
commercial stores, propelled by steam. The fore-saloon formed
a shop provided with a desk, and shelves on which were to be
seen cloths, iron wares, guns, ammunition, tobacco, tea, matches,
sugar, brightly coloured copper engravings or lithographs, &c.
In the after-saloon was enthroned, among brandy casks, purchased furs, and other precious or delicate wares, he who had
the command on board, a kind and friendly merchant, who evidently did not concern himself much with the work of the
sailors, but rather with trade and the making of bargains, and
who was seldom called by the crew captain (kapitan), but generally master (hosain). After the steamer, or floating commercial
store, there was towed one or two lodjas, which served as magazines, in which meal and salt and other heavy goods were stored,
the purchased fish were salted and looked after, fresh bread baked
for the numerous crew, &c. And as there was not a single jetty
to be found the whole way between Yenisejsk and the sea, both
the steamer and the lodjas, in order to be able to load and deliver
goods at any point, had a large number of boats and lighters
in tow. No place was set apart for passengers, but travellers
were received in a friendly and hospitable manner when they
came on board, where they were then allowed to look out for
themselves as best they could. The nautical command was
held by two mates or pilots of a stately and original appearance,
who, clad in long caftans, sat each in his watch on a chair at
the wheel, generally without steering, mostly smoking a cigarette
made of coarse paper and, with the most careless appearance in
the world, exchanging jests with those who were going down the

river.   The prohibition of taking away the attention of the steersman from his work by conversation was thus not in force hereabouts.   A man stood constantly in the fore, uninterruptedly testing the depth with a long pole.   For in order to avoid the strong current of the main stream the course was always shaped as near the shore as possible, often so near that one could almost jump ashore, and my own Nordland boat, which was towed by the side of the steamer, was occasionally drawn over land.   It will be seen from this of how light draught the steamer was.

CHUKCH VILLAGE ON A SIBERIAN RIVER.
After a Photograph.

Siberia, especially the river territory of the Yenisej and the Lena, possesses rich coal seams, which probably extend under considerable portions of the Siberian plain, but are yet unworked and have attracted little attention.   The river steamers accordingly are fired, not with coal, but with wood, of which, if I remember right, 180 fathoms went to the voyage of the steamer *Alexander* up the river.   As the vessel could carry only a small portion of this quantity of wood at one time, frequent halts were necessary, not only for trading with the natives, but also for taking fuel on board.   In addition to this, the weak engine, *although the safety valves were overloaded when necessary with lead weights,* was sometimes unable to make head with all the vessels in tow against a current which at some places was very rapid, and often, in the attempt to find still water near the river bank, the steamer ran aground, notwithstanding the continual "ladno" cry of the poling pilot standing in the fore. It made so slow progress on this account that the passage from Saostrovskoj to Yenisejsk occupied a whole month.

The two main arms into which the Yenisej is divided south of Yenisejsk are too rapid for the present Yenisej steamers to ascend them, while, as has been already stated, there is no difficulty in descending these rivers from the Selenga and the Baikal Lake on the one hand, and from the Minusinsk region abounding in grain on the other. The banks here consist, in many places, of high rocky ridges covered with fine forests, with wonderfully beautiful valleys between them, covered with luxuriant vegetation.

What I have said regarding the mode of travelling up the Yenisej refers to the year 1875, in which I went up the river accompanied by two Swedish naturalists and three Norwegian seamen. It was then by no means unknown, for scientific men such as HANSTEEN (1829), CASTRÉN (1846), MIDDENDORFF (winter journeys in 1843 and 1844), and SCHMIDT (1866), had travelled hither and communicated their observations to the scientific world in valuable works on the nature and people of the region. But the visits of the West-European still formed rare exceptions; no West-European commercial traveller had yet wandered to those regions, and into the calculations of the friendly masters of the Yenisej river steamers no import of goods from, or export of goods to, Europe had ever entered. All at once a new period seemed to begin. If the change has not gone on so fast as many expected, life here, however, is more than it was at one time, and every year the change is more and more noticeable. It is on this account that I consider these notes from the journey of 1875 worthy of being preserved.

CHAPTER IX.

The New Siberian Islands—The Mammoth—Discovery of Mammoth and Rhinoceros mummies—Fossil Rhinoceros horns—Stolbovoj Island—Liachoff's Island—First discovery of this island—Passage through the sound between this island and the mainland—Animal life there—Formation of ice in water above the freezing point—The Bear Islands—The quantity and dimensions of the ice begin to increase—Different kinds of sea-ice—Renewed attempt to leave the open channel along the coast—Lighthouse Island—Voyage along the coast to Cape Schelagskoj—Advance delayed by ice, shoals, and fog—First meeting with the Chukches—Landing and visits to Chukch villages—Discovery of abandoned encampments—Trade with the natives rendered difficult by the want of means of exchange—Stay at Irkaipi—Onkilon graves—Information regarding the Onkilon race—Renewed contact with the Chukches—Kolyutschin Bay—American statements regarding the state of the ice north of Behring's Straits—The *Vega* beset.

AFTER the parting the *Lena*-shaped her course towards the land ; the *Vega* continued her voyage in a north-easterly direction towards the New Siberian Islands.

These have, from the time of their discovery, been renowned among the Russian ivory collectors for their extraordinary richness in tusks and portions of skeletons of the extinct northern species of elephant known by the name of *mammoth*.

We know by the careful researches of the academicians PALLAS, VON BAER, BRANDT, VON MIDDENDORFF, FR. SCHMIDT, &c., that the mammoth was a peculiar northern species of elephant with a covering of hair, which, at least during certain seasons of the year, lived under natural conditions closely resembling those which now prevail in middle and even in northern Siberia. The widely extended grassy plains and forests of North Asia were the proper homeland of this animal, and there it must at one time have wandered about in large herds.

The same, or a closely allied species of elephant, also occurred in North America, in England, France, Switzerland, Germany, and North Russia. Indeed, even in Sweden and Finland inconsiderable mammoth remains have sometimes been found.[1] But while in Europe only some more or less inconsiderable remains of bones are commonly to be found, in Siberia we meet not only with whole skeletons, but also whole animals frozen in the earth, with solidified blood, flesh, hide, and hair. Hence we may draw the conclusion that the mammoth died out, speaking geologically, not so very long ago. This is besides confirmed by

[1] Further information on this point is given by A. J. Malmgren in a paper on the occurrence and extent of mammoth-finds, and on the conditions of this animal's existence in former times (*Finska Vet.-Soc. Förhandl.* 1874—5).

a remarkable antiquarian discovery made in France. Along with a number of roughly worked flint flakes, pieces of ivory were found, on which, among other things, a mammoth with trunk, tusks, and hair was engraved in rough but unmistakable lineaments, and in a style resembling that which distinguishes the Chukch drawings, copies of which will be found further on in this work. This drawing, whose genuineness appears to be proved, surpasses in age, perhaps a hundredfold, the oldest monuments that Egypt has to show, and forms a remarkable proof that the mammoth, the original of the drawing, lived in Western Europe contemporaneously with man. The mammoth remains are thus derived from a gigantic animal form, living in former times in nearly all the lands now civilized, and whose carcase is not yet everywhere completely decomposed. Hence the great and intense interest which attaches to all that concerns this wonderful animal.

If the interpretation of an obscure passage in Pliny be correct, mammoth ivory has, from the most ancient times, formed a valued article of commerce, which, however, was often mistaken for the ivory of living elephants and of the walrus. But portions of the skeleton of the mammoth itself are first described in detail by WITSEN, who during his stay in Russia in 1686 collected a large number of statements regarding it, and at least in the second edition of his work gives good drawings of the under jaw of a mammoth and the cranium of a fossil species of ox, whose bones are found along with the remains of the mammoth (WITSEN, 2nd. edit. p. 746). But it appears to have escaped Witsen, who himself considered mammoth bones to be the remains of ancient elephants, and who well knew the walrus, that in a number of the accounts which he quotes, the mammoth and the walrus are clearly mixed up together, which is not so wonderful, as both are found on the coast of the Polar Sea, and both yielded ivory to the stocks of the Siberian merchants. In the same way all the statements which the French Jesuit, AVRIL, during his stay in Moscow in 1686, collected regarding the amphibious animal, Behemoth, occurring on the coast of the Tartarian Sea, (Polar Sea) refer not to the mammoth, as some writers, HOWORTH[1] for example, have supposed, but to the walrus. The name mammoth, which is probably of Tartar origin, Witsen appears to wish to derive from Behemoth, spoken of in the fortieth chapter of the Book of Job. The first mammoth tusk was brought to England in 1611, by JOSIAS LOGAN. It was purchased in the region of the Petchora, and attracted great

---

[1] Compare Ph. Avril, *Voyage en divers états d'Europe et d'Asie entrepris pour découvrir un nouveau chemin à la Chine*, etc., Paris, 1692, p. 209. Henry H. Howorth, "The Mammoth in Siberia" (*Geolog. Mag.* 1880, p. 408).

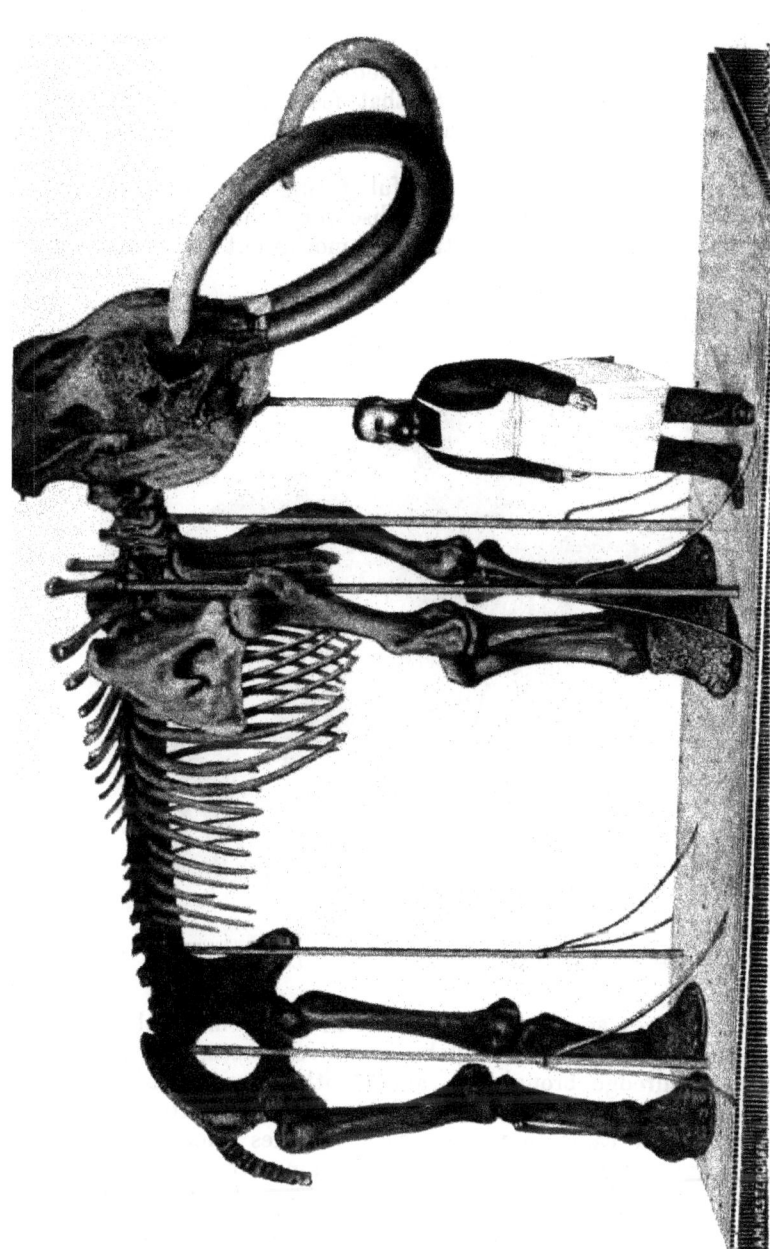

MAMMOTH SKELETON IN THE IMPERIAL MUSEUM OF THE ACADEMY OF SCIENCES IN ST. PETERSBURG.

After a Photograph communicated by the Academician Friedrich Schmidt in St Petersburg.

attention, as appears from Logan's remark in a letter to Hakluyt, that one would not have dreamed to find such wares in the region of the Petchora (*Purchas*, iii. p. 546). As Englishmen at that time visited Moscow frequently, and for long periods, this remark appears to indicate that fossil ivory first became known in the capital of Russia some time after the conquest of Siberia.

I have not, indeed, been successful during the voyage of the *Vega* in making any remarkable discovery that would throw light on the mode of life of the mammoth,[1] but as we now sail

RESTORED FORM OF THE MAMMOTH.

After JUKES, *The Student's Manual of Geology*, Edinburgh, 1862.

forward between shores probably richer in such remains than any other on the surface of the globe, and over a sea, from whose bottom our dredge brought up, along with pieces of driftwood, half-decayed portions of mammoth tusks, and as the savages with whom we came in contact, several times offered us very fine mammoth tusks or tools made of mammoth ivory, it may not perhaps be out of place here to give a brief account of some of the most important mammoth *finds* which have been

---

[1] As will be stated in detail further on, there were found during the *Vega* expedition very remarkable sub-fossil animal remains, not of the mammoth, however, but of various different species of the whale.

preserved for science. We can only refer to the discovery of mammoth *mummies*,[1] for the *finds* of mammoth tusks sufficiently well preserved to be used for carving are so frequent as to defy enumeration. Middendorff reckons the number of the tusks, which yearly come into the market, as at least a hundred pairs,[2] whence we may infer, that during the years that have elapsed since the conquest of Siberia useful tusks from more than 20,000 animals have been collected.

The discovery of a mammoth-*mummy* is mentioned for the first time in detail in the sketch of a journey which the Russian ambassador EVERT YSSBRANTS IDES, a Dutchman by birth, made in 1692 through Siberia to China. A person whom Yssbrants Ides had with him during his journey through Siberia, and who travelled every year to collect mammoth ivory, assured him that he had once found a head of this animal in a piece of frozen earth which had tumbled down. The flesh was putrefied, the neck-bone was still coloured by blood, and some distance from the head a frozen foot was found.[3] The foot was taken to Turuchansk, whence we may infer that the *find* was made on the Yenisej. Another time the same man found a pair of tusks weighing together twelve poods or nearly 200 kilogram. Ides' informant further stated, that while the heathen Yakuts, Tunguses, and Ostyaks, supposed that the mammoth always lived in the earth and went about in it, however hard the ground might be frozen, also that the large animal died when it came so far up that it saw or smelled the air; the old Russians living in Siberia were of opinion that the mammoth was an animal of the same kind as the elephant, though with tusks somewhat more bent and closer together; that before the Flood Siberia had been warmer than now, and elephants had then lived in numbers there; that they had been drowned in the Flood, and afterwards, when the climate became colder, had frozen in the river mud.[4]

The folk-lore of the natives regarding the mode of life of the mammoth under ground is given in still greater detail in J. B. MÜLLER'S *Leben und Gewonheiten der Ostiaken unter dem Polo*

---

[1] The word *mummies* is used by Von Middendorff to designate carcases of ancient animals found in the frozen soil of Siberia.

[2] The calculation is probably rather too low than too high. The steamer alone, in which I travelled up the Yenisej in 1875, carried over a hundred tusks, of which however the most were blackened, and many were so decayed that I cannot comprehend how the great expense of transport from the *tundra* of the Yenisej could be covered by the value of this article. According to the statement of the ivory dealers the whole parcel, good and bad together, was paid for at a common average price.

[3] Notices of yet other *finds* of mammoth carcases occur, according to Middendorff (*Sib. Reise*, IV. i. p. 274) in the scarce and to me inaccessible first edition of Witsen's *Noord en Oost Tartarye* (1692, Vol. II. p. 473).

[4] E. Yssbrants Ides, *Dreyjärige Reise nach China*, etc., Frankfort, 1707, p. 55. The first edition was published in Amsterdam, in Dutch, in 1704.

X

arctico wohnende, &c. Berlin, 1720 (in French in *Recueil de Voiages au Nord*, Amsterdam, 1731-38, Vol. VIII. p. 373). According to the accounts given by Müller, who lived in Siberia as a Swedish prisoner of war,[1] the tusks formed the animal's horns. With these, which were fastened above the eyes and were movable, the animal dug a way for itself through the clay and mud, but when it came to sandy soil, the sand ran together so that the mammoth stuck fast and perished. Müller further states, that many assured him that they themselves had seen such animals on the other side of Beresovsk in large grottos in the Ural mountains (*loc. cit.* p. 382).

KLAPROTH received a similar account of the mammoth's way of life from the Chinese in the Russo-Chinese frontier and trading town Kyachta. For mammoth ivory was considered to be tusks of the giant rat *tien-shu*, which is only found in the cold regions along the coast of the Polar Sea, avoids the light, and lives in dark holes in the interior of the earth. Its flesh is said to be cooling and wholesome. Some Chinese literati considered that the discovery of these immense earth rats might even explain the origin of earthquakes.[2]

It was not until the latter half of the last century that a European scientific man had an opportunity of examining a similar *find*. In the year 1771 a complete rhinoceros, with flesh and hide, was uncovered by a landslip on the river Wilui in 64° N.L. Its head and feet are still preserved at St. Petersburg. All the other parts were allowed to be destroyed for want of means of transport and preservation.[3] What was taken away showed that this primeval rhinoceros (*Rhinoceros antiquitatis* Blumenbach) had been covered with hair and differed from all now living species of the same family, though strongly resembling them in shape and size. Already, long before the horns of the fossil rhinoceros had attracted the attention of the natives, pieces of these horns were used for the same purposes for which the Chukches employ strips of whalebone, viz. to increase the elasticity of their bows. They were considered at

---

[1] Strahlenberg in *Das Nord- und Ostliche Theil von Europa und Asia*, Stockholm, 1730, p. 393, also gives a large number of statements regarding the fossil Siberian ivory, and mentions that the distinguished Siberian traveller Messerschmidt found a complete skeleton on the river Tom.

[2] Tilesius, *De skeleto mammonteo Sibirico* (*Mém. de l'Acad. de St. Pétersbourg, T. V. pour l'année 1812*, p. 409). Middendorff, *Sib. Reise*, IV. i. p. 274. Von Olfers, *Die Überreste vorweltlicher Riesenthiere in Beziehung zu Ostasiatischen Sagen und Chinesischen Schriften* (*Abhandl. der Akad. d. Wissensch. zü Berlin aus dem Jahre 1839*, p 51).

[3] P. S. Pallas, *De reliquiis animalium exoticorum per Asiam borealem repertis complementum* (*Novi commentarii Acad. Sc Petropolitanæ*, XVII. pro anno 1772, p. 576), and *Reise durch verschiedene Provinzen des Russischen Reichs*, Th. III. St. Petersburg, 1776, p. 97.

the same time to exert a like beneficial influence on the arrow, tending to make it hit the mark, as, according to the hunter's superstition among ourselves in former days, some cat's claws and owl's eyes placed in the bullet mould had on the ball. The natives believed that the crania and horns of the rhinoceros found along with the remains of the mammoth belonged to gigantic birds, regarding which there were told in the tents of the Yakut, the Ostyak and the Tunguse many tales resembling that of the bird Roc in the *Thousand and One Nights*.   Ermann

SIBERIAN RHINOCEROS HORN.
Preserved in the Museum at St. Petersburg.

and Middendorff even suppose that such *finds* two thousand years ago gave occasion to Herodotus' account of the Arimaspi and the gold-guarding dragons (*Herodotus*, Book IV. chap. 27). Certain it is that during the middle ages such "grip-claws" were preserved, as of great value, in the treasuries and art collections of that time, and that they gave rise to many a romantic story in the folk-lore both of the West and East.   Even in this century Hedenström, the otherwise sagacious traveller on the Siberian Polar Sea, believed that the fossil rhinoceros' horns

x 2

were actual "grip-claws." For he mentions in his oft-quoted
work, that he had seen such a claw 20 verschoks (0·9 metre) in
length, and when he visited St. Petersburg in 1830, the scientific
men there did not succeed in convincing him that his ideas on
this subject were incorrect.[1]

A new *find* of a mammoth *mummy* was made in 1787, when
the natives informed the Russian travellers SARYTSCHEV and
MERK, that about 100 versts below the village Alasejsk, situated
on the river Alasej running into the Polar Sea, a gigantic
animal had been washed out of the sand beds of the beach
in an upright posture, undamaged, with hide and hair. The
find, however, does not appear to have been thoroughly
examined.[2]

In 1799 a Tunguse found on the Tamut Peninsula, which juts
out into the sea immediately south-east of the river-arm by
which the *Lena* steamed up the river, another frozen-in mammoth. He waited patiently five years for the ground thawing
so much as that the precious tusks should be uncovered. The
softer parts of the animal accordingly were partly torn in pieces
and destroyed by beasts of prey and dogs, when the place was
closely examined in 1806 by ADAMS the Academician. Only
the head and two of the feet were then almost undamaged.
The skeleton, part of the hide, a large quantity of long hair and
woolly hair a foot and a half long were taken away. How fresh
the carcase was may be seen from the fact that parts of the eye
could still be clearly distinguished. Similar remains had been
found two years before, a little further beyond the mouth of the
Lena, but they were neither examined nor removed.[3]

A new *find* was made in 1839, when a complete mammoth
was uncovered by a landslip on the shore of a large lake to the
west of the mouth of the Yenisej, seventy versts from the Polar
Sea. It was originally almost entire, so that even the trunk
appears to have been preserved, to judge by the statement of
the natives that a black tongue as long as a month-old reindeer
calf was hanging out of the mouth; but it had, when it was
removed in 1842, by the care of the merchant TROFIMOV, been
already much destroyed.[4]

[1] Hedenström, *Otryoki o Sibiri*, St. Petersburg, 1830, p. 125. Ermann's
Archiv, Part 24, p. 140.

[2] Compare K. E. v. Baer's paper in *Mélanges Biologiques*, T. V. St. Péters-
bourg, 1866, p. 691; Middendorff, IV. i. p. 277; Gavrila Sarytschev's
Achtjährige Reise in nordöstlichen Sibirien, etc., translated by J. H. Busse,
Th. 1, Leipzig, 1805, p. 106.

[3] Adams' account is inserted at p. 431 in the work of Tilesius already
quoted. Von Baer gives a detailed account of this and other important
finds of the same nature in the above-quoted paper in Tome V. of *Mélanges
Biologiques*, St. Pétersbourg, pp. 645—740.

[4] Middendorff, IV. 1, p. 272.

Next after Trofimov's mammoth come the mammoth-*finds* of Middendorff and Schmidt. The former was made in 1843 on the bank of the river Tajmur, under 75° N.L.; the latter in 1866 on the Gyda *tundra*, west of the mouth of the Yenisej in 70° 13′ N.L. The soft parts of these *finds* were not so well preserved as those just mentioned. But the *finds* at all events had a greater importance for science, from the localities having been thoroughly examined by competent scientific men. Middendorff arrived at the result that the animal found by him had floated from more southerly regions to the place where it was found. Schmidt on the other hand found that the stratum which contained the mammoth rested on a bed of marine clay, containing shells of high northern species of crustacea which still live in the Polar Sea, and that it was covered with strata of sand alternating with beds, from a quarter to half a foot thick, of decayed remains of plants, which completely correspond with the turf beds which are still formed in the lakes of the *tundra*. Even the very beds of earth and clay in which the bones, pieces of hide, and hair of the mammoth *mummy* were enclosed, contained pieces of larch, branches and leaves of the dwarf birch (*Betula. nana*), and of two northern species of willow (*Salix glauca* and *herbacea*).[1] It appears from this that the climate of Siberia at the time when these mammoth-carcases were imbedded, was very nearly the same as the present, and as the stream in whose neighbourhood the find was made is a comparatively inconsiderable *tundra* river, lying wholly to the north of the limit of trees, there is no probability that the carcase drifted with the spring ice from the wooded region of Siberia towards the north. Schmidt, therefore, supposes that the Siberian elephant, if it did not always live in the northernmost parts of Asia, occasionally wandered thither, in the same way that the reindeer now betakes itself to the coast of the Polar Sea. VON BRANDT, VON SCHMALHAUSEN, and others, had besides already shown that the remains of food which were found in the hollows of the teeth of the Wilui rhinoceros consisted of portions of leaves and needles of species of trees which still grow in Siberia.[2]

Soon after the mammoth found on the Gyda *tundra* had been examined by Schmidt, similar *finds* were examined by GERHARD VON MAYDELL, at three different places between the rivers Kolyma and Indigirka, about a hundred kilometres from the Polar Sea. With respect to these *finds* I can only refer to a

---

[1] Friedrich Schmidt, *Wissenschaftliche Resultate der zur Aufsuchung eines Mammuthcadavers ausgesandten Expedition* (*Mém. de l'Acad. de St. Pétersbourg*, Ser. VII. T. XVIII. No. 1, 1872).

[2] Brandt, *Berichte der preussischen Akad. der Wissenchaften*, 1846, p. 224. Von Schmalhausen, *Bull. de l'Acad. de St. Pétersbourg*, T. XXII. p. 291.

paper by L. VON SCHRENCK in the *Bulletin* of the St. Petersburg Academy, T. XVI. 1871, p. 147.

Under the guidance of natives I collected in 1876 at the confluence of the river Mesenkin with the Yenisej, in 71° 28′ N.L., some fragments of bones and pieces of the hide of a mammoth. The hide was 20 to 25 millimetres thick and nearly tanned by age, which ought not to appear wonderful, when we consider that, though the mammoth lived in one of the latest periods of the history of our globe, hundreds of thousands, perhaps millions of years have, however, passed since the animal died to which these pieces of skin once belonged. It was clear that they had been washed by the neighbouring river Mesenkin out of the tundra-bank, but I endeavoured, without success, to discover the original locality, which was probably already concealed by river mud. In the neighbourhood was found a very fine cranium of the musk ox.

A new and important *find* was made in 1877 on a tributary of the Lena, in the circle Werchojansk, in 69° N.L. For there was found there an exceedingly well-preserved carcase of a rhinoceros (*Rhinoceros Merckii*, Jaeg.), a different species from the Wilui rhinoceros examined by Pallas. However, before the carcase was washed away by the river, there had only been removed the hair-covered head and one foot.[1] From the *find* Schrenck draws the conclusion that this rhinoceros belonged to a high-northern species, adapted to a cold climate, and living in, or at least occasionally wandering to, the regions where the carcase was found. There the mean temperature of the year is now very low,[2] the winter exceedingly cold (− 63°·2 has been registered) and the short summer exceedingly warm. Nowhere on earth does the temperature show extremes so widely separated as here. Although the trees in winter often split with tremendous noise, and the ground is rent with the cold, the wood is luxuriant and extends to the neighbourhood of the Polar Sea, where besides, the winter is much milder than farther in the interior. With respect to the possibility of these large animals finding sufficient pasture in the regions in question, it

[1] The *find* is described by Herr Czersky in the Transactions published by the East Siberian division of the St. Petersburg Geographical Society; and subsequently by Dr. Leopold von Schrenck in *Mém. de l'Acad. de St. Pétersbourg*, Ser. VII. T. XXVII. No. 7, 1880.

[2] The mean temperature of the different months is shown in the following table :—

JAN.	FEB.	MARCH	APRIL	MAY	JUNE	
−48°·9	−47°·2	−33°·9	−14°·0	−0°·40	+13°·4	Of the Year.
JULY	AUG.	SEPT.	OCT.	NOV.	DEC.	−16°·7
+15°·4	+11°·9	+2°·3	−13°·9	−39° 1	−45°·7	

ought not to be overlooked that in sheltered places overflowed
by the spring inundations there are found, still far north of the
limit of trees, luxuriant bushy thickets, whose newly-expanded
juicy leaves, burned up by no tropical sun, perhaps form a
special luxury for grass-eating animals, and that *even the bleakest
stretches of land in the high north are fertile in comparison with
many regions where at least the camel can find nourishment, for
instance the east coast of the Red Sea.*

The nearer we come to the coast of the Polar Sea, the more
common are the remains of the mammoth, especially at places
where there have been great landslips at the river banks when
the ice breaks up in spring.   Nowhere, however, are they found
in such numbers as on the New Siberian Islands.   Here Hedenström in the space of a verst saw ten tusks sticking out of the
ground, and from a single sandbank on the west side of Liachoff's Island the ivory collectors had, when this traveller visited
the spot, for eighty years made their best tusk harvest.   That
new *finds* may be made there year by year depends on the bones
and tusks being washed by the waves out of the sandbeds on
the shore, so that after an east wind which has lasted some time
they may be collected at low water on the banks then laid
dry.   The tusks which are found on the coast of the Polar
Sea are said to be smaller than those that are found farther
south, a circumstance which possibly may be explained by
supposing that, while the mammoth wandered about on the
plains of Siberia, animals of different ages pastured in company, and that the younger of them, as being more agile and
perhaps more troubled by flies than the older, went farther
north than these.

Along with bones of the mammoth there are found on the
New Siberian Islands, in not inconsiderable numbers, portions of
the skeletons of other animal forms, little known, but naturally
of immense importance for ascertaining the vertebrate fauna
which lived at the same time with the mammoth on the plains
of Siberia, and the New Siberian group of islands is not less
remarkable for the " wood-hills," highly enigmatical as to their
mode of formation, which Hedenström found on the south coast
of the northernmost island.   These hills are sixty-four metres
high, and consist of thick horizontal sandstone beds alternating
with strata of fissile bituminous tree stems, heaped on each
other to the top of the hill.   In the lower part of the hill the
tree stems lie horizontally, but in the upper strata they stand
upright, though perhaps not rootfast.[1]   The flora and fauna of
the island group besides are still completely unknown, and the
fossils, among them ammonites with exquisite pearly lustre,

[1] Hedenström, *loc. cit.* p. 128.   To find stranded driftwood in an upright
position is nothing uncommon.

which Hedenström brought home from the rock strata on
Kotelnoj Island, hold out inducement to further researches,
which ought to yield the geologist valuable information as to the
former climate and the former distribution of land and sea on
the surface of the globe. The knowledge of the hydrography
of this region is besides an indispensable condition for judging
of the state of the ice in the sea which washes the north coast
of Asia. Here lies the single available starting-point for the
exploration of the yet altogether unknown sea farther to the
north, and from hills on the two northernmost islands Hedenström
thought that across the sea to the north-west and north-east he

STOLBOVOJ ISLAND.
After a drawing by O. Nordquist.

saw obscure outlines of new land, on which no man had yet set
his foot. All these circumstances confer on this group of islands
an uncommon interest in a scientific and geographical respect,
and therefore no long time can elapse until a scientific expedition be sent to these regions. Just for this reason I now
desired, as a preparation for a future voyage, to wander about
here for a couple of days, partly on foot, partly by boat.

The air was calm, but for the most part clouded, the
temperature as high as + 4°, the sea clear of ice, the salinity of
the water 1·8 per cent. with a temperature of + 2° to + 3°. At
first we made rapid progress, but after having in the afternoon of the 28th August sighted ·the westernmost islands,

Semenoffskoj and Stolbovoj, the sea became so shallow that for
long stretches we were compelled to sail in six to seven metres
water. Some very rotten ice, or rather ice sludge, was also met
with, which compelled us to make tedious *détours*, and prevented
the *Vega* from going at full speed.

The animal life was among the scantiest I had seen during my
many travels in the Polar Seas. A few seals were visible. Of
birds we saw some terns and gulls, and even far out at sea
a pretty large number of phalaropes—the most common kind of
bird on the coast of the Asiatic Polar Sea, at least in autumn.
Stolbovoj Island was, especially on the north side, high with
precipitous shore-cliffs which afforded splendid breeding-places
for looms, black guillemots and gulls. At all such cliffs there
breed on Spitzbergen millions of sea fowl, which are met with
out on the surrounding sea in great flocks searching for their
food. Here not a single loom was seen, and even the number of
the gulls was small, which indeed in some degree was to be
accounted for by the late season of the year, but also by the
circumstance that no colony of birds had settled on the rocky
shores of the island.

The sea bottom consisted at certain places of hard-packed
sand, or rather, as I shall endeavour to show farther on, of
frozen sand, from which the trawl net brought up no animals.
At other places there was found a clay, exceedingly rich in
Idothea entomon and *Sabinei* and an extraordinary mass of
bryozoa, resembling collections of the eggs of mollusca.

It was not until the 30th of August that we were off the west
side of Ljachoff's Island, on which I intended to land. The
north coast, and, as it appeared the day after, the east coast was
clear of ice, but the winds recently prevailing had heaped a
mass of rotten ice on the west coast. The sea besides was so
shallow here, that already at a distance 15' from land we had
a depth of only eight metres. The ice heaped against the west
coast of the island did not indeed form any very serious obstacle
to the advance of the *Vega*, but in case we had attempted to
land there it might have been inconvenient enough, when the
considerable distance between the vessel and the land was to
be traversed in a boat or the steam launch, and it might even,
if a sudden frost had occurred, have become a fetter, which would
have confined us to that spot for the winter. Even a storm
arising hastily might in this shallow water have been actually
dangerous to the vessel anchored in an open road. The prospect
of wandering about for some days on the island did not appear
to me to outweigh the danger of the possible failure of the main
object of the expedition. I therefore gave up for the time
my intention of landing. The course was shaped southwards
towards the sound, of so bad repute in the history of the

Siberian Polar Sea, which separates Ljachoff's Island from the mainland.

So far as we could judge at a distance from the appearance of the rocks, Stolbovoj consisted of stratified rocks, Ljachoff's Island, on the contrary, like the mainland opposite, of high hills, much shattered, probably formed of Plutonic stone-masses.

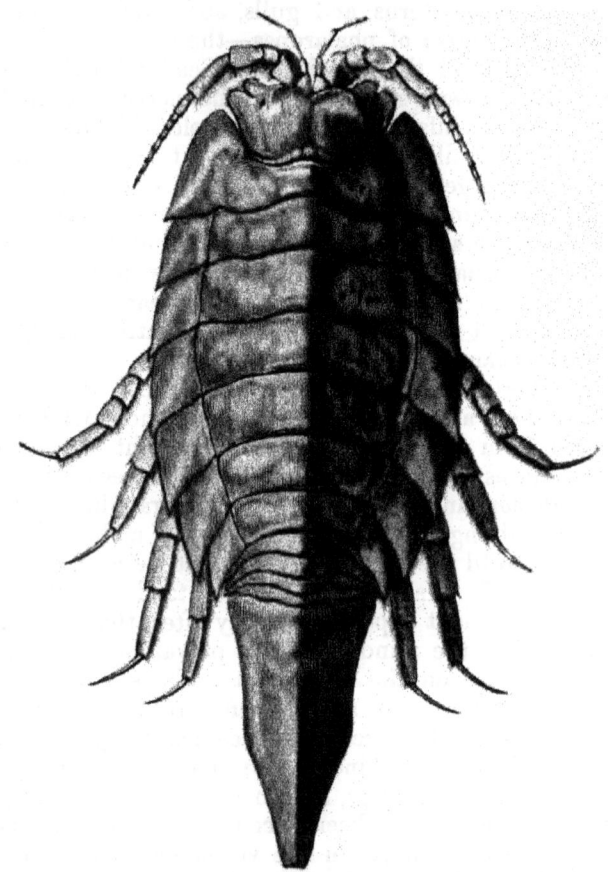

IDOTHEA ENTOMON, LIN.
From the sea north of the mouth of the Lena
Natural size.

Between these there are extensive plains, which, according to a statement by the land surveyor CHVOINOFF, who by order of the Czar visited the island in 1775, are formed of ice and sand, in which lie imbedded enormous masses of the bones and tusks of the mammoth, mixed with the horns and skulls of some kind of ox and with rhinoceros' horns. Bones of the whale and walrus are not mentioned as occurring there, but "long small screw-formed bones," by which are probably meant the tusks of the narwhal.[1]

All was now clear of snow, with the exception of a few of the deeper clefts between the mountains. No traces of glaciers were visible, not even such small collections of ice as are to be

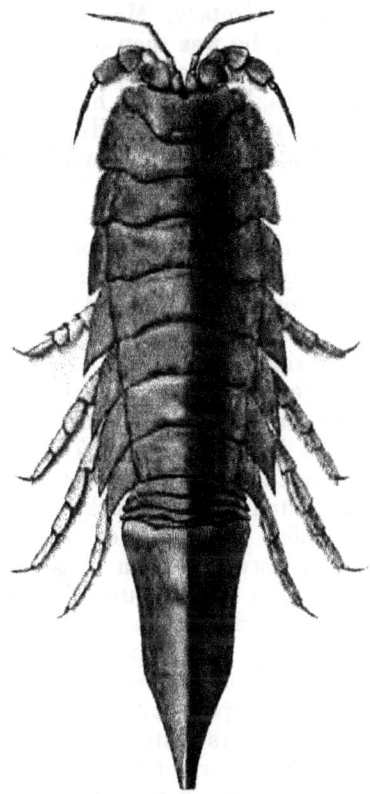

IDOTHEA SABINEI, KRÖYER.
From the sea off the mouth of the Lena
Natural size.

found everywhere on Spitzbergen where the land rises a few hundred feet above the surface of the sea. Nor, to judge by

[1] Martin Sauer, *An account of a Geographical and Astronomical Expedition to the Northern Parts of Russia by Commodore Joseph Billings*, London, 1802, p. 105. The walrus does not occur in the sea between the mouth of the Chatanga and Wrangel Land, and large whales are never seen at the New Siberian Islands, but during Hedenstiöm's stay in these regions three narwhals were enclosed in the ice near the shore at the mouth of the Yana (*Otrywki o Sibiri*, p. 131).

the appearance of the hills, have there been any glaciers in former times, and this is certainly the case on the mainland. The northernmost part of Asia in that case has never been covered by such an ice-sheet as is assumed by the supporters of a general ice age embracing the whole globe.

The large island right opposite to Svjatoinos was discovered in 1770 by LJACHOFF, whose name the island now bears. In 1788 Billings' private secretary, MARTIN SAUER, met with Ljachoff at Yakutsk, but he was then old and infirm, on which account, when Sauer requested information regarding the islands in the Polar Sea, he referred him to one of his companions, ZAITAI PROTODIAKONOFF. He informed him that the discovery was occasioned by an enormous herd of reindeer which Ljachoff, in the month of April 1770, saw going from Svjatoinos towards the south, and whose track came over the ice from the north. On the correct supposition that the reindeer came from some land lying to the north, Ljachoff followed the track in a dog-sledge, and thus discovered the two most southerly of the New Siberian Islands, a discovery which was rewarded by the Czarina Catherine II., with the exclusive right to hunt and collect ivory on them.[1]

Ljachoff states the breadth of the sound between the mainland and the nearest large island at 70 versts or 40'. On Wrangel's map again the breadth is not quite 30'. On the mainland side it is bounded by a rocky headland projecting far into the sea, which often formed the turning point in attempts to penetrate eastwards from the mouth of the river Lena, and perhaps just on that account, like many other headlands dangerous to the navigator on the north coast of Russia, was called *Svjatoinos* (the holy cape), a name which for the oldest Russian Polar Sea navigators appears to have had the same signification as " the cape that can be passed with difficulty." No one however now thinks with any apprehension of the two " holy capes," which in former times limited the voyages of the Russians and Fins living on the White Sea to the east and west, and this, I am quite convinced, will some time be the case with this and all other holy capes in the Siberian Polar Sea.

The sea water in the sound was much mixed with river water and had a comparatively high temperature, even at a depth of nine to eleven metres. The animal life at the sea bottom was poor in species but rich in individuals, consisting principally of

[1] Martin Sauer, *An account of a Geographical and Astronomical Expedition to the Northern Parts of Russia by Commodore Joseph Billings*, London, 1802, p. 103. A. Ermann, *Reise um die Erde*, Berlin, 1833—48, D. 1, B. 2, p. 258. Ermann's statement, that the knowledge of the existence of these islands was concealed from the government up to the year 1806, is clearly incorrect.

Idothea entomon, of which Dr. Stuxberg counted 800 specimens from a single sweep of the dredge. There were obtained at the same time, besides a few specimens of *Idothea Sabinei*, sponges and bryozoa in great abundance, and small mussels, crustacea, vermes, &c. Various fishes were also caught, and some small algæ collected. The trawl-net besides brought up from the bottom some fragments of mammoth tusks, and a large number of pieces of wood, for the most part sticks or branches, which appear to have stood upright in the clay, to judge from the fact that one of their ends was often covered with living bryozoa. These sticks often caused great inconvenience to the dredgers, by tearing the net that was being dragged along the bottom.

LJACHOFF'S ISLAND.
After a drawing by O. Nordquist.

On the night preceding the 31st of August, as we steamed past Svjatoinos, a peculiar phenomenon was observed. The sky was clear in the zenith and in the east; in the west, on the other hand, there was a bluish-grey bank of cloud. The temperature of the water near the surface varied between + 1° and + 1°·6, that of the air on the vessel between +1°·5 and +1°·8. Although thus both the air and the water had a temperature somewhat above the freezing-point, ice was seen to form on the calm, mirror-bright surface of the sea. This ice consisted partly of needles, partly of a thin sheet. I have previously on several occasions observed in the Arctic seas a similar phenomenon, that is to say, have observed the formation of ice when the temperature of the air was above the freezing-point. On this occasion, when the temperature of the uppermost stratum of water was also above the freezing-point, the formation of ice was clearly a sort of hoar-frost phenomenon, caused by radiation of heat, perhaps both upwards towards the. atmosphere and downwards towards the bottom layer of water, cooled below the freezing-point.

The whole day we continued our voyage eastwards with glorious weather over a smooth ice-free sea, and in the same way on the 1st September, with a gentle southerly wind, the temperature of the air at noon in the shade being + 5°·6. On the night before the 2nd September the wind became northerly and the temperature of the air sank to − 1°. Little land was seen, though we were still not very far from the coast. Near to it there was a broad ice-free, or nearly ice-free, channel, but farther out to sea ice commenced. The following night snow fell, so that the whole of the deck and the Bear Islands, which we reached on the 3rd September, were sprinkled with it.

Hitherto, during the whole time we sailed *along the coast*, we had scarcely met with any fields of drift-ice but such as were formed of rotten, even, thin and scattered pieces of ice, in many places almost converted into ice-sludge, without an "ice-foot" and often dirty on the surface. No iceberg had been seen, nor any large glacier ice-blocks, such as on the coasts of Spitzbergen replace the Greenland icebergs. But east of Svjatoinos the ice began to increase in size and assume the same appearance as the ice north of Spitzbergen. It was here, besides, less dirty, and rested on a hard ice-foot projecting deep under water and treacherous for the navigator.

The ice of the Polar Sea may be divided into the following varieties :—

1. *Icebergs.* The true icebergs have a height above the surface of the water rising to 100 metres. They often ground in a depth of 200 to 300 metres, and have thus sometimes a cross section of up to 400, perhaps 500 metres. Their area may amount to several square kilometres. Such enormous blocks of ice are projected into the North Polar Sea only from the glaciers of Greenland, and according to Payer's statement, from those of Franz-Josef Land also ; but not, as some authors (GEIKIE, BROWN, and others) appear to assume and have shown by incorrect ideal drawings, from glaciers which project into the sea and there terminate with a perpendicular evenly-cut border, but from very uneven glaciers which always enter the sea in the bottoms of deep fjords, and are split up into icebergs long before they reach it. It is desirable that those who write on the origin of icebergs, should take into consideration the fact that icebergs are only formed at places where a violent motion takes

place in the mass of the ice, which again within a comparatively short time results in the excavation of the deep ice-fjord. The largest iceberg, which, so far as I know, has been *measured* in that part of the Polar Sea which lies between Spitzbergen and Wrangel Land, is one which Barents saw at Cape Nassau on the $\frac{17}{7}$th August 1596. It was sixteen fathoms high, and had grounded in a depth of thirty-six fathoms. In the South Polar Sea icebergs occur in great numbers and of enormous size. If we may assume that they have an origin similar to those of Greenland, it is probable that round the South Pole there is an extensive continent indented by deep fjords.

2. *Glacier Ice-blocks.* These, which indeed have often been called icebergs, are distinguished from true icebergs not only by their size, but also by the way in which they are formed. They have seldom a cross section of more than thirty or forty metres, and it is only exceptionally that they are more than ten metres high above the surface of the water. They originate from the "calving" of glaciers which project into the sea with a straight and evenly high precipitous border. Such glaciers occur in large numbers on the coasts of Spitzbergen, and they are there of the same height as similar evenly-cut glaciers on Greenland. According to the statement of the Dane PETERSEN, who took part both in KANE's expedition in 1853-55 and in Torell's in 1861, the glaciers, for instance, at Hinloopen Strait in Spitzbergen, are fully equal, with respect to their size and the height of their borders above the sea-level, to the enormous and much bewritten Humboldt glacier in Greenland. In Spitzbergen too we find at two places miniatures of the Greenland ice-currents, for instance the glacier which filled the North Haven in Bell Sound, another glacier which filled an old Dutch whaling haven between Recherche Bay and Van Keulen Bay, a glacier on the north side of Wahlenberg Bay and perhaps at that part of the inland ice marked in my map of the expedition of 1872 as a bay on the east coast of North-east Land. It is even possible that small icebergs may be projected from the last-mentioned place, and thence drift out into the sea on the east coast of Spitzbergen.

Glacier-ice shows a great disposition to fall asunder into smaller pieces without any perceptible cause. It is full of cavities, containing compressed air, which, when the ice melts, bursts its attenuated envelope with a crackling sound like that of the electric spark. It thus behaves in this respect in the same way as some mineral salts which dissolve in water with slight explosions. Barents relates that on the $\frac{20}{10}$th August 1596 he anchored his vessel to a block of ice which was aground on the coast of Novaya Zemlya. Suddenly, and without any perceptible cause, the rock of ice burst asunder into hundreds of smaller pieces with a tremendous noise, and to the great terror of all the men on board. Similar occurrences on a smaller scale I have myself witnessed. The cause to which they are due appears to me to be the following. The ice-block while part of the glacier is exposed to very severe pressure, which ceases when it falls into the sea. The pressure now in most cases equalises itself without any bursting asunder, but it sometimes happens that the inner strongly compressed portions of the ice-block cannot, although the pressure has ceased, expand freely in consequence of the continuous ice-envelope by which they are still surrounded. A powerful internal tension must thereby arise in the whole mass, which finally leads to its bursting into a thousand pieces. We have here a Prince Rupert's drop, but one whose diameter may rise to fifty metres, and which consists not of glass but of ice.

Glacier ice-blocks occur abundantly on the coasts of Spitzbergen and north Novaya Zemlya, but appear to be wanting or exceedingly rare along the whole north coast of Asia, between Yugor Schar and Wrangel Land. East of this they again occur, but not in any great numbers. This appears to show that the Western Siberian Polar Sea is not surrounded by any glacial lands. The glacier ice is commonly of a blue colour. When melted it yields a pure water, free of salt. Sometimes however it gives traces of salt, which are derived from the spray which the storms have carried high up on the surface of the glacier.

3. Pieces of ice from the ice-foot formed along the sea beach or the banks of rivers. They rise sometimes five or six metres above the surface of the water. They consist commonly of dirty ice, mixed with earth.

4. *River Ice*, level, comparatively small ice fields, which, when they reach the sea, are already so rotten that they soon melt away and disappear.

5. The walrus-hunters' *Bay Ice*; by which we understand level ice-fields formed in fjords and bays along the coast, and which have there been exposed to a comparatively early summer heat. The bay ice therefore melts away completely during summer, and it is not commonly much pressed together. When all the snow upon it has disappeared, there is to be seen above the surface of the water a little ice of the same colour as the water, while under water very considerable portions of unmelted hard ice are still remaining. This has given rise to the walrus-hunters' statement, which has been warmly maintained, that the ice in autumn finally disappears by sinking. Nearly all the ice we met with in the course of our voyage belonged to this variety.

6. *Sea Ice*, or heavy ice, which often exhibits traces of having

been much pressed together, but has not been exposed to any early summer heat. The walrus-hunters call it sea ice, wishing, I imagine, to indicate thereby that it is formed in the sea farther up towards the north. That it has drifted down from the north is indeed correct, but that it has been formed far from land over a considerable depth in the open sea is perhaps uncertain, as the ice that is formed there cannot, we think, be very thick. It has rather perhaps drifted down from the neighbourhood of some yet unknown Polar continent. Of this ice are formed most of the ice-fields in the seas east of Greenland, north of Spitzbergen, between Spitzbergen and the north island of Novaya Zemlya, and north of Behring's Straits. In the northern seas it does not melt completely during the summer, and remains of sea ice therefore often enter as component parts into the bay ice formed during the following winter. The latter then becomes rough and uneven from remnants of old sea ice being frozen into the newly formed ice. Sea ice is often pressed together so as to form great *torosses* or ice-casts, formed of pieces of ice which at first are angular and piled loose on each other, but gradually become rounded, and freeze together into enormous blocks of ice, which, together with the glacier ice-blocks, form the principal mass of the ground ice found on the coasts of the Polar lands. The water which is obtained by melting sea-ice is not completely free from salt, but the older it is the less salt does it contain.

East of the Bear Islands heavy sea-ice in pretty compact masses had drifted down towards the coast, but still left an open ice-free channel along the land. Here the higher animal world was exceedingly poor, which, as far as the avi-fauna was concerned, must be in some degree ascribed to the late season of the year. For Wrangel mentions a cliff at the Bear Islands which was covered with numberless birds' nests. He saw besides, on the largest of these islands, traces of the bear, wolf, fox, lemming, and reindeer (Wrangel's *Reise*, i. pp. 304 and 327). Now the surrounding sea was completely deserted. No Polar bear saluted us from the ice-floes, no walruses, and only very few seals were visible. During many watches not a single natatory bird was seen. Only the phalarope was still met with in large numbers, even pretty far out at sea. Perhaps it was then migrating from the north. The lower animal world was more abundant. From the surface of the sea the drag-net brought up various small surface crustacea, inconsiderable in themselves, but important as food for larger animals ; and from the sea-bottom were obtained a large number of the same animal forms as from the sound at Svjatoinos, and in addition some beautiful asterids and a multitude of very large beaker sponges.

Y

On the 3rd September, after we had sailed past the Bear Islands, the course was shaped right for Cape Chelagskoj. This course, as will be seen by a glance at the map, carried us far from the coast, and thus out of the channel next the land, in which we had hitherto sailed. The ice was heavy and close, although at first so distributed that it was navigable. But with a north wind, which began to blow on the night before the 1st September, the temperature fell below the freezing-point, and the water between the pieces of drift-ice was covered with a very thick crust of ice, and the drift-ice came closer and closer together. It thus became impossible to continue the course which we had taken. We therefore turned towards the land, and at 6 o'clock P.M., after various bends in the ice and a few concussions against the pieces of ice that barred our way, again

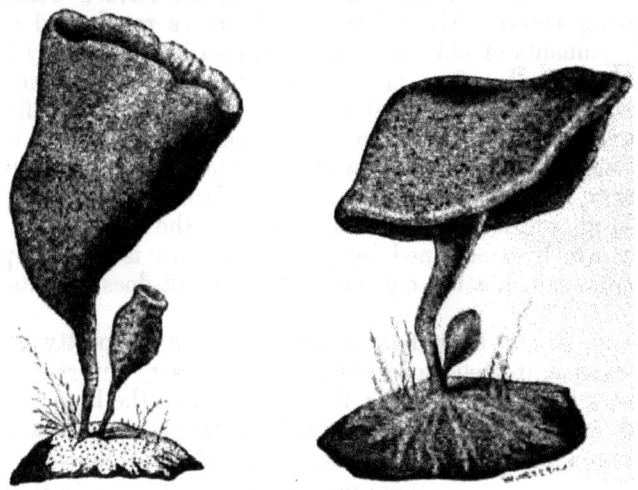

BEAKER SPONGES.
From the sea off the mouth of the Kolyma.

reached the ice-free channel, eight to twelve kilometres broad, next the land. While we lay a little way in among the drift-ice fields we could see no sign of open water, but it appeared as if the compact ice extended all the way to land, a circumstance which shows how careful the navigator ought to be in expressing an opinon as to the nature of the *pack* beyond the immediate neighbourhood of the vessel. The temperature of the air, which in the ice-field had sunk to $-3°$, now rose at once to $+4°·1$, while that of the water rose from $-1°·2$ to $+3°·5$, and its salinity fell from 2·4 to 1·3 per cent. All showed that we had now come into the current of the Kolyma, which from causes which have been already stated, runs from the mouth of the river along the land in an easterly direction.

The Bear Islands lying off the mouth of the Kolyma are, for the most part, formed of a plutonic rock, whose upper part has weathered away, leaving gigantic isolated pillars. Four such pillars have given to the easternmost of the islands the name Lighthouse Island (Fyrpelarön). Similar ruin-like formations are found not only on Cape Baranov, which lies right opposite, but also at a great number of other places in that portion of the north coast of Siberia which lies farther to the east. Generally these cliff ruins are collected together over considerable areas in groups or regular rows. They have thus, when seen from the sea, so bewildering a resemblance to the ruins of a gigantic city which had once been surrounded by strong walls and been full of temples and splendid buildings,

LIGHTHOUSE ISLAND.
After a drawing by O. Nordquist.

that one is almost tempted to see in them memorials of the exploits of a Tamerlane or a Chingis Khan up here in the high north.

The north side of the hill-tops was powdered with new-fallen snow, but the rest of the land was clear of snow. The distance between the south point of Ljachoff's Island and the Bear Islands is 360'. This distance we had traversed in three days, having thus made 120' in the twenty-four hours, or 5' per hour. If we consider the time lost in dredging, sounding, and determining the temperature and salinity of the water, and the caution which the navigator must observe during a voyage in quite unknown waters, this speed shows that during this part of our

Y 2

voyage we were hindered by ice only to a slight extent. Cape
Baranov was passed on the night before the 5th September, the
mouth of Chaun Bay on the night before the 6th September,
and Cape Chelagskoj was reached on the 6th at 4 o'clock P.M.
The distance in a right line between this headland and the Bear
Islands is 180'. In consequence of the many *détours* in the ice
we had required 2½ days to traverse this distance, which corresponds to 72' per day, or 3' per hour, a speed which in a
voyage in unknown, and for the most part ice-bestrewed waters,
must yet be considered very satisfactory. But after this our
progress began to be much slower. At midnight the sun was
already 12° to 13° below the horizon, and the nights were now
so dark that at that time of day we were compelled to lie still
anchored to some large ground-ice. A further loss of time was
caused by the dense fog which often prevailed by day, and which
in the unknown shallow water next the land compelled Captain
Palander to advance with extreme caution. The navigation
along the north coast of Asia began to get somewhat monotonous.
Even the most zealous Polar traveller may tire at last of mere
ice, shallow water, and fog ; and mere fog, shallow water and ice.

Now, however, a pleasant change began, by our coming at
last in contact with natives. In the whole stretch from Yugor
Schar to Cape Chelagskoj we had seen neither men nor human
habitations, if I except the old uninhabited hut between Cape
Chelyuskin and the Chatanga. But on the 6th September,
when we were a little way off Cape Chelagskoj, two boats were
sighted. Every man, with the exception of the cook, who
could be induced by no catastrophe to leave his pots and pans,
and who had circumnavigated Asia and Europe perhaps without
having been once on land, rushed on deck. The boats were of
skin, built in the same way as the "umiaks" or women's boats
of the Eskimo. They were fully laden with laughing and
chattering natives, men, women, and children, who indicated
by cries and gesticulations that they wished to come on board.
The engine was stopped, the boats lay to, and a large number
of skin-clad, bare-headed beings climbed up over the gunwale in
a way that clearly indicated that they had seen vessels before.
A lively talk began, but we soon became aware that none of the
crew of the boats or the vessel knew any language common to
both. It was an unfortunate circumstance, but signs were
employed as far as possible. This did not prevent the chatter
from going on, and great gladness soon came to prevail, especially
when some presents began to be distributed, mainly consisting
of tobacco and Dutch clay pipes. It was remarkable that none
of them could speak a single word of Russian, while a boy
could count tolerably well up to ten in English, which shows that
the natives here come into closer contact with American whalers

than with Russian traders.   They acknowledged the name
chukch or *chautchu.*

Many of them were tall, well-grown men.   They were clothed
in close fitting skin trousers and " pesks " of reindeer skin.   The
head was bare, the hair always clipped short, with the exception
of a small fringe in front, where the hair had a length of four
centimetres and was combed down over the brow.   Some had a
cap of the sort used by the Russians at Chabarova, stuck into
the belt behind, but they appeared to consider the weather still
too warm for the use of this head-covering.   The hair of most
of them was bluish-black and exceedingly thick.   The women
were tattooed with black or bluish-black lines on the brow and
nose, a number of similar lines on the chin, and finally some
embellishments on the cheeks.   The type of face did not strike

CHUKCH BOATS.

one as so unpleasant as that of the Samoyeds or Eskimo.   Some
of the young girls were even not absolutely ugly.   In comparison
with the Samoyeds they were even rather cleanly, and had a
beautiful, almost reddish-white complexion.   Two of the men
were quite fair.   Probably they were descendants of Russians,
who for some reason or other, as prisoners of war or fugitives,
had come to live among the Chukches and had been nationalised
by them.

In a little we continued our voyage, after the Chukches had
returned to their boats, evidently well pleased with the gifts
they had received and the leaf tobacco I had dealt out in
bundles,—along with the clay pipes, of which every one got as
many as he could carry between his fingers,—with the finery and

old clothes which my comrades and the crew strewed around them with generous hand.   For we were all convinced that after some days we should come to waters where winter clothes would be altogether unnecessary, where our want of any article could easily be supplied at the nearest port, and where the means of exchange would not consist of goods, but of stamped pieces of metal and slips of paper.

On the 7th September, we steamed the whole day along the

A CHUKCH IN SEAL-GUT GREAT COAT.
After a photograph by L. Palander.

coast in pretty open ice.   At night we lay to at a floe.   The hempen tangles and the trawl-net were put out and yielded a very rich harvest.   But in the morning we found ourselves again so surrounded by ice and fog, that, after several unsuccessful attempts to make an immediate advance, we were compelled to lie-to at a large piece of drift-ice near the shore.   When the fog had lightened so much that the vessel could be seen from the land, we were again visited by a large number of natives, whom as before we entertained as best we could.   They invited

us by evident signs to land and visit their tents. As it was in
any case impossible immediately to continue our voyage, I
accepted the invitation, ordered a boat to be put out, and landed
along with most of my comrades.

The beach here is formed of a low bank of sand which runs
between the sea and a small shallow lagoon or fresh-water lake,
whose surface is nearly on a level with that of the sea. Farther
into the interior the land rises gradually to bare hills, clear of
snow or only covered with a thin coating of powdered snow
from the fall of the last few days. Lagoon formations, with
either fresh or salt water, of the same kind as those which we
saw here for the first time, are distinctive of the north-eastern
coast of Siberia. It is these formations which gave rise to the
statement that on the north coast of Siberia it is difficult to
settle the boundaries between sea and land. In winter this may
be difficult enough, for the low bank which separates the lagoon
from the sea is not easily distinguished when it has become
covered with snow, and it may therefore readily happen in winter
journeys along the coast that one is far into the land while he
still believes himself to be out on the sea-ice. But when the
snow has melted, the boundary is sharp enough, and the sea by
no means shallow for such a distance as old accounts would
indicate. A continual ice-mud-work also goes on here during
the whole summer. Quite close to the beach accordingly the
depth of water is two metres, and a kilometre farther out ten to
eleven metres. Off the high rocky promontories the water is
commonly navigable even for vessels of considerable draught
close to the foot of the cliffs.

The villages of the Chukches commonly stand on the bank of
sand which separates the lagoon from the sea. The dwellings
consist of roomy skin tents, which inclose a sleeping chamber of
the form of a parallelopiped surrounded by warm well-prepared
reindeer skins, and lighted and warmed by one or more train-oil
lamps. It is here that the family sleep during summer, and
here most of them live day and night during winter. In summer, less frequently in winter, a fire is lighted besides in the
outer tent with wood, for which purpose a hole is opened in the
top of the raised tent roof. But to be compelled to use wood
for heating the inner tent the Chukches consider the extremity
of scarcity of fuel.

We were received everywhere in a very friendly way, and were
offered whatever the house afforded. At the time the supply
of food was abundant. In one tent reindeer beef was being
boiled in a large cast-iron pot. At another two recently shot
or slaughtered reindeer were being cut in pieces. At a third an
old woman was employed in taking out of the paunch of the
reindeer the green spinage-like contents and cramming them

into a sealskin bag, evidently to be preserved for green food
during winter. The hand was used in this case as a scoop, and
the naked arms were coloured high up with the certainly un-
appetising spinage, which however, according to the statements
of Danish colonists in Greenland, has no unpleasant taste. Other
skin sacks filled with train-oil stood in rows along the walls of
the tent.

The Chukches offered train-oil for sale, and appeared to be
surprised that we would not purchase any. In all the tents
were found seals cut in pieces, a proof that the catch of seals had
recently been abundant. At one tent lay two fresh walrus heads
with large beautiful tusks. I tried without success to purchase
these heads, but next day the tusks were offered to us. The

CHUKCH TENT.
After a photograph by L. Palander.

Chukches appear to have a prejudice against disposing of
the heads of slain animals. According to older travellers they
even pay the walrus-head a sort of worship.

Children were met with in great numbers, healthy and
thriving. In the inner tent the older children went nearly
naked, and I saw them go out from it without shoes or other
covering and run between the tents on the hoarfrost-covered
ground. The younger were carried on the shoulders both of
men and women, and were then so wrapped up that they
resembled balls of skin. The children were treated with marked
friendliness, and the older ones were never heard to utter an
angry word. I purchased here a large number of household
articles and dresses, which I shall describe further on.

On the morning of the 9th September we endeavoured to steam on, but were soon compelled by the dense fog to lie-to again at a ground-ice, which, when the fog lightened, was found to have stranded quite close to land. The depth here was eleven metres. At this place we lay till the morning of the 10th. The beach was formed of a sandbank,[1] which immediately above high-water mark was covered with a close grassy turf, a proof that the climate here, notwithstanding the neighbourhood of the pole of cold, is much more favourable to the development of vegetation than even the most favoured parts of the west coast of Spitzbergen. Farther inland was seen a very high, but snow-free, range of hills, and far beyond them some high snow-covered mountain summits. No glaciers were found here, though I consider it probable that small ones may be found in the valleys between the high fells in the interior. Nor were any erratic blocks found either in the interior of the coast country or along the strand bank. Thus it is probable that no such ice-covered land as Greenland for the present bounds the Siberian Polar Sea towards the north. At two places at the level of the sea in the neighbourhood of our anchorage the solid rock was bare. There it formed perpendicular shore cliffs, nine to twelve metres high, consisting of magnesian slate, limestone more or less mixed with quartz, and silicious slate. The strata were nearly perpendicular, ran from north to south, and did not contain any fossils. From a geological point of view therefore these rocks were of little interest. But they were abundantly covered with lichens, and yielded to Dr. Almquist important contributions to a knowledge of the previously quite unknown lichen flora of this region.

The harvest of the higher land plants on the other hand was, in consequence of the far advanced season of the year, inconsiderable, if also of great scientific interest, as coming from a region never before visited by any botanist. In the sea Dr. Kjellman dredged without success for algæ. Of the higher animals we saw only a walrus and some few seals, but no land mammalia. Lemmings must however occasionally occur in incredible numbers, to judge by the holes and passages, excavated by these animals, by which the ground is crossed in all directions. Of birds the phalarope was still the most common

---

[1] Of course the earth here at an inconsiderable depth under the surface is constantly frozen, but I have nowhere seen such alternating layers of earth and ice, crossed by veins of ice, as Hedenström in his oft-quoted work (*Otrywki o Sibiri*, p. 119) says he found at the sea-coast. Probably such a peculiar formation arises only at places where the spring floods bring down thick layers of mud, which cover the beds of ice formed during the winter and protect them for thousands of years from melting. I shall have an opportunity of returning to the interesting questions relating to this point.

s] ecies, especially at sea, where in flocks of six or seven it swam incessantly backwards and forwards between the pieces of ice.

No tents were met with in the neighbourhood of the vessel's anchorage, but at many places along the beach there were seen marks of old encampments, sooty rolled stones which had been used in the erection of the tents, broken household articles, and above all remains of the bones of the seal, reindeer, and walrus. At one place, a large number of walrus skulls lay in a ring, possibly remains from an entertainment following a large catch. Near the place where the tents had stood, at the mouth of a small stream not yet dried up or frozen, Dr. Stuxberg discovered some small mounds containing burnt bones. The cremation had been so complete that only one of the pieces of bone that were found could be determined by Dr. Almquist. It was a human tooth. After cremation the remains of the bones and the ash had been collected in an excavation, and covered first with turf and then with small flat stones. The encampments struck me as having

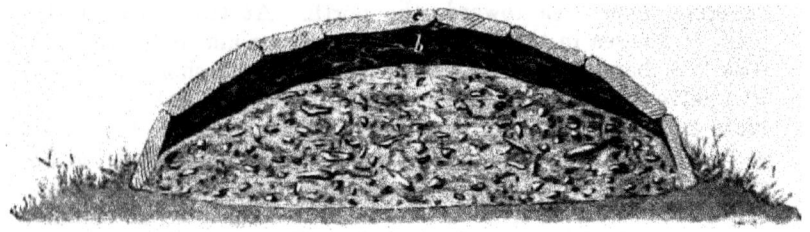

SECTION OF A CHUKCH GRAVE.[1]
After a drawing by A. Stuxberg.
a. Layer of burned bones, much weathered.   *b.* Layer of turf and twigs.   *c.* Stones.

been abandoned only a few years ago, and even the collections of bones did not appear to me to be old. But we ought to be very cautious when we endeavour in the Arctic regions to estimate the age of an old encampment, because in judging of the changes which the surface of the earth undergoes with time we are apt to be guided by our experience from more southerly regions. To how limited an extent this experience may be utilised in the high north is shown by RINK'S assertion that on Greenland at some of the huts of the Norwegian colonists, which have been deserted for centuries, footpaths can still be

[1] Since we discovered the Chukches also bury their dead by laying them out on the *tundra*, we have begun to entertain doubts whether the collection of bones delineated here was actually a grave. Possibly these mounds were only the remains of fireplaces, where the Chukches had used as fuel train-drenched bones, and which they had afterwards for some reason or other endeavoured to protect from the action of the atmosphere.

distinguished,[1] an observation to which I would scarcely give credence, until I had myself seen something similar at the site of a house in the bottom of Jacobshaven ice-fjord in north-western Greenland, which had been abandoned for one or two centuries. Here footpaths as sharply defined as if they had been trampled yesterday ran from the ruin in different directions. It may therefore very readily happen] that the encampments in the neighbourhood of our present anchorage were older than we would be inclined at first sight to suppose. No refuse heaps of any importance were seen here.

This was the first time that any vessel had lain-to on this coast. Our arrival was therefore evidently considered by the natives a very remarkable occurrence, and the report of it appears to have spread very rapidly. For though there were no tents in the neighbourhood, we had many visitors. I still availed myself of the opportunity of procuring by barter a large number of articles distinctive of the Chukches' mode of life. Eight years before I had collected and purchased a large number of ethnographical articles, and I was now surprised at the close correspondence there was between the household articles purchased from the Chukches, and those found in Greenland in old Eskimo graves.

My traffic with the natives was on this occasion attended with great difficulty. For I suffered from a sensible want of the first condition for the successful prosecution of a commercial under-taking, goods in demand. Because, during the expeditions of 1875 and 1876, I found myself unable to make use of the small wares I carried with me for barter with the natives, and found that Russian paper money was readily taken. I had, at the departure of the *Vega* from Sweden, taken with me only money, not wares intended for barter. But money was of little use here. A twenty-five rouble note was less valued by the Chukches than a showy soap-box, and a gold or silver coin less than tin or brass buttons. I could, indeed, get rid of a few fifty-öre pieces, but only after I had first adapted them by boring to take the place of earrings.

The only proper wares for barter I now had were tobacco and Dutch clay pipes. Of tobacco I had only some dozen bundles, taken from a parcel which Mr. Sibiriakoff intended to import into Siberia by the Yenisej. Certain as I was of reaching the Pacific this autumn, I scattered my stock of tobacco around me with so liberal a hand that it was soon exhausted, and my Chukch friends' wants satisfied for several weeks. I therefore, as far as this currency was concerned, already when the *Vega* was beset, suffered the prodigal's fate of being soon left with an empty

[1] H. Rink, *Grönland geographisk og statistisk beskrevet*, Bd. 2, Copenhagen, 1857, p. 344.

purse. Dutch clay pipes, again, I had in great abundance, from
the accident that two boxes of these pipes, which were to have
been imported into Siberia with the expedition of 1876, did not
reach Trondhjem until the *Ymer* had sailed from that town.
They were instead taken on the *Vega*, and now, though quite
too fragile for the hard fingers of Chukches, answered well for
smaller bargains, as gifts of welcome to a large number of
natives collected at the vessel, and as gifts to children in order
to gain the favour of their parents. I besides distributed a large
quantity of silver coin with King Oscar's effigy, in order, if any
misfortune overtook us, to afford a means of ascertaining the
places we had visited.

For the benefit of future travellers I may state that the wares
most in demand are large sewing and darning needles, pots,
knives (preferably large), axes, saws, boring tools and other iron
tools, linen and woollen shirts (preferably of bright colours, but
also white), neckerchiefs, tobacco and sugar. To these may be
added the spirits which are in so great request among all savages;
a currency of which, indeed, there was great abundance on the
Vega, but which I considered myself prevented from making
use of. In exchange for this it is possible to obtain, in short,
anything whatever from many of the natives, but by no means
from all, for even here there are men who will not taste spirits,
but with a gesture of disdain refuse the glass that is offered
them. The Chukches are otherwise shrewd and calculating
men of business, accustomed to study their own advantage.
They have been brought up to this from childhood through the
barter which they carry on between America and Siberia.
Many a beaver-skin that comes to the market at Irbit belongs to
an animal that has been caught in America, whose skin has passed
from hand to hand among the wild men of America and Siberia,
until it finally reaches the Russian merchant. For this barter a
sort of market is held on an island in Behring's Straits. At
the most remote markets in Polar America, a beaver-skin is
said some years ago to have been occasionally exchanged for a
leaf of tobacco.[1] An exceedingly beautiful black fox-skin was
offered to me by a Chukch for a pot. Unfortunately I had
none that I could dispense with. Here, too, prices have risen.
When the Russians first came to Kamchatka, they got eight
sable-skins for a knife, and eighteen for an axe, and yet the
Kamchadales laughed at the credulous foreigners who were
so easily deceived. At Yakutsk, when the Russians first
settled there, a pot was even sold for as many sable-skins as
it could hold.[2]

[1] C. von Dittmar, *Bulletin hist.-philolog. de l'Acad. de St. Pétersbourg.*
XIII. 1856, p. 130.
[2] Krascheninnikov, *Histoire et Description du Kamtschatka*, Amsterdam
1770, II. p. 95. A. Erman, *Reise um die Erde*, D. 1, B. 2, p. 255.

During the night before the 10th September, the surface of the sea was covered with a very thick sheet of newly-frozen ice, which was broken up again in the neighbourhood of the vessel by blocks of old ice drifting about. The *pack* itself appeared to have scattered a little. We therefore weighed anchor to continue our voyage. At first a *détour* towards the west was necessary to get round a field of drift-ice. Here too, however, our way was barred by a belt of old ice, which was bound together so firmly by the ice that had been formed in the course of the night, that a couple of hours' work with axes and ice-hatchets was required to open a channel through it. On the other side of this belt of ice we came again into pretty open

IRKAIPIJ.
After a drawing by O. Nordquist.

water, but the fog, instead, became so dense that we had again to lie-to at a ground-ice, lying farther out to the sea but more to the west than our former resting-place. On the night before the 11th there was a violent motion among the ice. Fortunately the air cleared in the morning, so that we could hold on our course among pretty open ice, until on the approach of night we were obliged as usual to lie-to at a ground-ice.

The following day, the 12th September, when we had passed Irkaipij, or Cape North, a good way, we fell in with so close ice that there was no possibility of penetrating farther. We were therefore compelled to return, and were able to make our way with great difficulty among the closely packed masses of drift ice. Here the vessel was anchored in the lee of a ground-ice, which had stranded near the northernmost spur of Irkaipij, until a strong tidal current began to carry large pieces of drift-ice past the vessel's anchorage. She was now removed and anchored anew in a little bay open to the north, which was formed by two rocky points jutting out from the mainland. Unfortunately we were detained here, waiting for a better state of the ice, until the 18th September. It was this involuntary delay which must be considered the main cause of our wintering.

Irkaipij is the northernmost promontory in that part of Asia, which was seen by Cook in 1778. It was, therefore, called by him Cape North, a name which has since been adopted in most

REMAINS OF AN ONKILON HOUSE.
a. Seen from the side.   *b.* From above.
After a drawing by O. Nordquist.

maps, although it is apt to lead to confusion from capes similarly named being found in most countries. It is also incorrect, because the cape does not form the northernmost promontory either of the whole of Siberia, or of any considerable portion of it. For the northernmost point of the mainland of Siberia is Cape Chelyuskin, the northernmost in the land east of the Lena Svjatoinos, the northernmost in the stretch of coast east of Chaun Bay, Cape Chelagskoj, and so on. Cape North ought, therefore, to be replaced by the original name Irkaipij, which is well known to all the natives between Chaun Bay and Behring's Straits.

On the neck of land which connects Irkaipij with the mainland, there was at the time of our visit a village consisting of sixteen tents. We saw here also *ruins*, viz. the remains of a large number of old house-sites, which belonged to a race called *Onkilon*,[1] who formerly inhabited these regions, and some centuries ago were driven by the Chukches, according to tradition, to some remote islands in the Polar Sea.   At these old house-sites Dr. Almquist and Lieutenant Nordquist set on foot excavations in order to collect contributions to the ethnography of this traditional race. The houses appear to have been built, at least partly, of the bones of the whale, and half sunk in the earth.   The refuse

IMPLEMENTS FOUND IN THE RUINS OF AN ONKILON HOUSE.

1. Stone chisel with bone handle, one-half the natural size.   2, 4. Knives of slate, one-third
3, 7. Spear-heads of slate, one-third.   5. Spear-head of bone, one-third.
6. Bone spoon, one-third.

heaps in the neighbourhood contained bones of several species of the whale, among them the white whale, and of the seal, walrus, reindeer, bear, dog, fox, and various kinds of birds. Besides these remains of the produce of the chase, there were found implements of stone and bone, among which were stone

[1] *Ankali* signifies in Chukch dwellers on the coast, and is now used to denote the Chukches living on the coast. A similar word, Onkilon, was formerly used as the name of the Eskimo tribe that lived on the coast of the Polar Sea when the Chukch migration reached that point.

axes, which, after lying 250 years in the earth, were still fixed
to their handles of wood or bone. Even the thongs with which
the axe had been bound fast to, or *wedged into*, the handle, were
still remaining. The tusks of the walrus[1] had to the former
inhabitants of the place, as to the Chukches of the present,
yielded a material which in many cases may be used with
greater advantage than flint for spear-heads, bird-arrows, fish-
hooks, ice-axes, &c. Walrus tusks, more or less worked, accordingly were found in the excavations in great abundance. The
bones of the whale had also been employed on a great scale, but
we did not find any large pieces of mammoth tusks, an indication
that the race was not in any intimate contact with the inhabitants of the regions to the westward, so rich in the remains of
the mammoth.[2] At many places the old Onkilon houses were
used by the Chukches as stores for blubber; and at others,
excavations had been made in the refuse heaps in search of
walrus tusks. Our researches were regarded by the Chukches
with mistrust. An old man who came, as it were by chance,
from the interior of the country past the place where we worked,
remained there a while, regarding our labours with apparent
indifference, until he convinced himself that from simplicity, or
some other reason unintelligible to him, we avoided touching the
blubber-stores, but instead rooted up in search of old fragments
of bone or stone-flakes.

Remains of old dwellings were found even at the highest
points among the stone mounds of Irkaipij, and here perhaps was
the last asylum of the Onkilon race. At many places on the
mountain slopes were seen large collections of bones, consisting
partly of a large number (at one place up to fifty) of bears'
skulls overgrown with lichens, laid in circles, with the nose
inwards, partly of the skulls of the reindeer, Polar bear,[3] and
walrus, mixed together in a less regular circle, in the midst of

[1] The walrus now appears to be very rare in the sea north of Behring's
Straits, but formerly it must have been found there in large numbers, and
made that region a veritable paradise for every hunting tribe. While we
during our long stay there saw only a few walruses, Cook, in 1778, saw an
enormous number, and an interesting drawing of walruses is to be found
in the account of his third voyage. *A Voyage to the Pacific Ocean, etc.*,
Vol. III. (by James King), London, 1784, p. 259, pl. 52.

[2] The greatest number of mammoth tusks is obtained from the stretches
of land and the islands between the Chatanga and Chaun Bay. Here the
walrus is wanting. The inhabitants of North Siberia therefore praise the
wisdom of the Creator, who lets the walrus live in the regions where the
mammoth is wanting, and has scattered mammoth ivory in the earthy layers
of the coasts where the walrus does not occur (A. Erman, *Reise um die
Erde*. Berlin, 1833—48, D. 1, B. 2, p. 264).

[3] Among the bears' skulls brought home from this place Lieut. Nordquist
found after his return home the skull of a sea-lion (*Otaria Stelleri*). It is
however, uncertain whether the animal was captured in the region, or
whether the cranium was brought hither from Kamchatka.

which reindeer horns were found set up. Along with the reindeer horns there was found the coronal bone of an elk with portions of the horns still attached. Beside the other bones lay innumerable temple-bones of the seal, for the most part fresh and not lichen-covered. Other seal bones were almost completely absent, which shows that temple-bones were not remains of weathered seal skulls, but had been gathered to the place for one reason or another in recent times. No portions of human skeletons were found in the neighbourhood. These places are sacrificial places, which the one race has inherited from the other.

WRANGEL gives the following account of the tribe which lived here in former times:—

" As is well known the sea-coast at Anadyr Bay is inhabited by a race of men, who, by their bodily formation, dress, language, differ manifestly from the Chukches, and call themselves Onkilon - seafolk. In the account of Captain BILLING'S journey through the country of the Chukches, he shows the near relationship the language of this coast tribe has to that of the Aleutians at Kadyak, who are of the same primitive stem as the Greenlanders. Tradition relates that upwards of two hundred years ago these Onkilon occupied the whole of the Chukch coast, from Cape Chelagskoj to Behring's Straits, and indeed we still find along the whole of this stretch remains of their earth huts, which must have been very unlike the present dwellings of the Chukches ; they have the form of small mounds, are half sunk in the ground and closed above with whale ribs, which are covered with a thick layer of earth. A violent quarrel between Krächoj, the chief of these North-Asiatic Eskimo, and an *errim* or chief of the reindeer Chukches, broke out into open feud. Krächoj drew the shorter straw, and found himself compelled to fly, and leave the country with his people ; since then the whole coast has been desolate and uninhabited. Of the emigration of these Onkilon, the inhabitants of the village Irkaipij, where Krächoj appears to have lived, narrated the following story. He had killed a Chukch *errim*, and was therefore eagerly pursued by the son of the murdered man, whose pursuit he for a considerable time escaped. Finally Krächoj believed that he had found a secure asylum on the rock at Irkaipij, where he fortified himself behind a sort of natural wall, which can still be seen. But the young Chukch *errim*, driven by desire to avenge his father's death, finds means to make his way within the fortification and kills Krächoj's son. Although the blood-revenge was now probably complete according to the prevailing ideas, Krächoj must have feared a further pursuit by his unrelenting enemy, for during night he lowers

z

himself with thongs from his lofty asylum, nearly overhanging
the sea, enters a boat, which waits for him at the foot of the cliff,
and, in order to lead his pursuers astray, steers first towards the
east, but at nightfall turns to the west, reaches Schalaurov
Island, and there fortifies himself in an earth hut, whose remains
we (Wrangel's expedition) have still seen. Here he then collected
·all the members of his tribe, and fled with them in 15 'baydars'
to the land whose mountains the Chukches assure themselves
they can in clear sunshine see from Cape Yakan. During the
following winter a Chukch related to Krächoj disappeared in
addition with his family and reindeer, and it is supposed that he
too betook himself to the land beyond the sea. With this
another tradition agrees, which was communicated to us by the
inhabitants of Kolyutschin Island. For an old man informed
me (Wrangel) that during his grandfather's lifetime a 'baydar'
with seven Chukches, among them a woman, had ventured too
far out to sea. After they had long been driven hither and
thither by the wind, they stranded on a country unknown to
them, whose inhabitants struck the Chukches themselves as
coarse and brutish. The shipwrecked men were all murdered.
Only the woman was saved, was very well treated, and taken
round the whole country, and shown to the natives as something
rare and remarkable. So she came at last to the Kargauts,
a race living on the American coast at Behring's Straits, whence
she found means to escape to her own tribe. This woman told
her countrymen much about her travels and adventures; among
other things she said that she had been in a great land which
lay north of Kolyutschin Island, stretched far to the *west*, and
was probably connected with America. This land was inhabited
by several races of men; those living in the west resembled the
Chukches in every respect, but those living in the east were so
wild and brutish, that they scarcely deserved to be called men.
The whole account, both of the woman herself and of the
narrators of the tradition, is mixed up with so many improbable
adventures, that it would scarcely be deserving of any attention
were it not remarkable for its correspondence with the history
of Krächoj." [1]

When Wrangel wrote that, he did not believe in the existence
of the land which is to be found set out on his map in 177° E. L.
and 71° N. L., and which, afterwards discovered by the Englishman KELLET, according to the saying, *lucus a non lucendo*,
obtained the name of Wrangel Land. Now we know that the
land spoken of by tradition actually exists, and therefore there
is much that even tells in favour of its extending as far as to
the archipelago on the north coast of America.

[1] Wrangel's *Reise*, Th. 2, Berlin, 1839, p. 220.

With this fresh light thrown upon it, the old Chukch woman's story ought to furnish a valuable hint for future exploratory voyages in the sea north of Behring's Straits, and an important contribution towards forming a judgment of the fate which has befallen the American *Jeannette* expedition, of which, while this is being written, accounts are still wanting.[1]

Between us and the inhabitants of the present Chukch village at Irkaipij there soon arose very friendly relations. A somewhat stout, well-grown, tall and handsome man named Chepurin, we took at first to be chief. He was therefore repeatedly entertained in the gunroom, on which occasions small gifts were given him to secure his friendship. Chepurin had clearly a weakness for gentility and grandeur, and could now, by means of the barter he carried on with us and the presents he received, gratify his love of show to a degree of which he probably had never before dreamed. When during the last days of our stay he paid a visit to the *Vega* he was clad in a red woollen shirt drawn over his " pesk," and from either ear hung a gilt watch-chain, to the lower end of which a perforated ten-öre piece was fastened. Already on our arrival he was better clothed than the others, his tent was larger and provided with two sleeping apartments, one for each of his wives. But notwithstanding all this we soon found that we had made a mistake, when, thinking that a society could not exist without government, we assigned to him so exalted a position. Here, as in all Chukch villages which we afterwards visited, absolute anarchy prevailed.

At the same time the greatest unanimity reigned in the little headless community. Children, healthy and thriving, tenderly cared for by the inhabitants, were found in large numbers. A good word to them was sufficient to pave the way for a friendly reception in the tent. The women were treated as the equals of the men, and the wife was always consulted by the husband when a more important bargain than usual was to be made ; many times it was carried through only after the giver of advice had been bribed with a neckerchief or a variegated handkerchief. The articles which the man purchased were immediately committed to the wife's keeping. One of the children had round his neck a band of pearls with a Chinese coin having a square hole in the middle,

---

[1] According to a paper in *Deutsche Geografische Blätter*, B. IV. p. 54, Captain E. Dallmann, in 1866, as commander of the Havai schooner *W. C. Talbot*, not only saw but landed on Wrangel Land. As Captain Dallmann of recent years has been in pretty close contact with a large number of geographers, and communications from him have been previously inserted in geographical journals, it appears strange that he has now for the first time made public this important voyage. At all events, Dallmann's statement that the musk-ox occurs on the coast of the Polar Sea and on Wrangel Land is erroneous. He has here confused the musk-ox with the reindeer.

suspended from it; another bore a perforated American cent piece. None knew a word of Russian, but here too a youngster could count ten in English. They also knew the word "ship." In all the tents, reindeer stomachs were seen with their contents, or sacks stuffed full of other green herbs. Several times we were offered in return for the bits of sugar and pieces of tobacco which we distributed, wrinkled root-bulbs somewhat larger than a hazel nut, which had an exceedingly pleasant taste, resembling that of fresh nuts. A seal caught in a net among the ice during our visit was cut up in the tent by the women. On this occasion they were surrounded by a large number of children, who were now and then treated to bloody strips of flesh. The youngsters carried on the work of cutting up *con amore*, coquetting a little with their bloody arms and faces.

The rock which prevails in this region consists mainly of gabbro, which in the interior forms several isolated, black, plateau-formed hills, 100 to 150 metres high, between which an even, grassy, but treeless plain extends. It probably rests on sedimentary strata. For on the western side of Irkaipij the plutonic rock is seen to rest on a black slate with traces of fossils, for the most part obscure vegetable impressions, probably belonging to the Permian Carboniferous formation.

Uneasy at the protracted delay here I made an excursion to a hill in the neighbourhood of our anchorage, which, according to a barometrical measurement, was 129 metres high, in order, from a considerable height, to get a better view of the ice than was possible by a boat reconnaisance. The hill was called by the Chukches Hammong-Ommang. From it we had an extensive view of the sea. It was everywhere covered with closely packed drift-ice. Only next the land was seen an open channel, which, however, was interrupted in an ominous way by belts of ice.

The plutonic rock, of which the hill was formed, was almost everywhere broken up by the action of the frost into angular blocks of stone, so that its surface was converted into an enormous stone mound. The stones were on the wind side covered with a translucent glassy ice-crust, which readily fell away, and added considerably to the difficulty of the ascent. I had previously observed the formation of such an ice-crust on the northernmost mountain summits of Spitzbergen.[1] It arises undoubtedly from the fall of super-cooled mist, that is to say of mist whose vesicles have been cooled considerably below the freezing-point without being changed to ice, which first takes place when, after falling, they come in contact with ice or snow, or some angular hard object. It is such a mist that causes the icing down of the rigging of vessels, a very unpleasant phenomenon

[1] Cf. *Redogörelse för den svenska polarexpeditionen år 1872-73* (Bihang till Vet. Ak. handl. Bd. 2, No. 18, p. 91).

for the navigator, which we experienced during the following days, when the tackling of the *Vega* was covered with pieces of ice so large, and layers so thick, that accidents might have happened by the falling of the ice on the deck.[1]

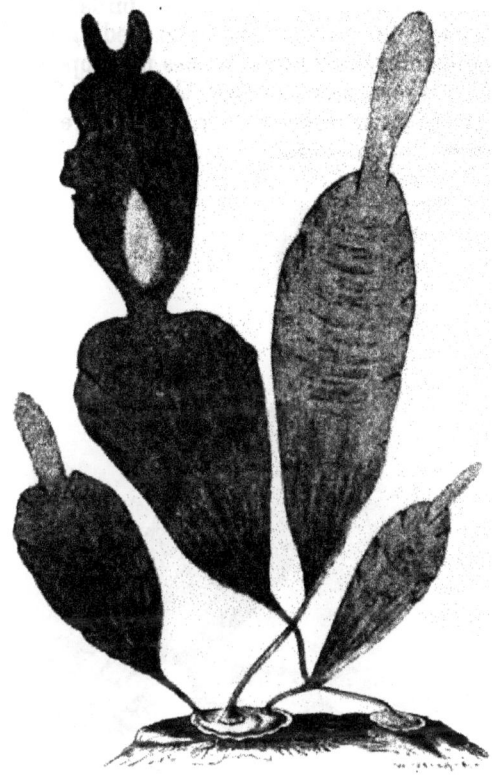

ALGA FROM IRKAIPJ.
Laminaria solidungula (J G Ag.)

The dredgings here yielded to Dr. Kjellman some algæ, and to Dr. Stuxberg masses of a species of cumacea, *Diastylis*

[1] A more dangerous kind of icing down threatens the navigator in severe weather not only in the Polar Seas but also in the Baltic and the North Sea. For it happens at that season that the sea-water at the surface is over-cooled, that is, cooled below the freezing-point without being frozen. Every wave which strikes the vessel is then converted by the concussion into ice-sludge, which increases and freezes together to hard ice so speedily that all attempts to remove it from the deck are in vain. In a few hours the vessel may be changed into an unmanageable floating block of ice which the sailors, exhausted by hard labour, must in despair abandon to its fate. Such an icing down, though with a fortunate issue, befell the steamer *Sofia* in the month of October off Bear Island, during the Swedish Polar Expedition of 1868.

Rathkei Kr., of *Acanthostephia Malmgreni* Goës, and *Liparis gelatinosus* Pallas, but little else. On the steep slopes of the north side of Irkaipij a species of cormorant had settled in so large numbers that the cliff there might be called a true fowl-fell. A large number of seals were visible among the ice, and along with the comorant a few other birds, principally phalaropes. Fish were now seen only in exceedingly small numbers. Even in the summer, fishing here does not appear to be specially abundant, to judge from the fact that the Chukches had not collected any stock for the winter. We were offered, however, a salmon or two of small size.

CORMORANT FROM IRKAIPIJ.
Graculus bicristatus (Pallas).

On the 18th September [1] the state of the ice was quite unchanged. If a wintering was to be avoided, it was, however,

---

[1] Irkaipij lies in 180° long. from Greenwich. To bring our day-reckoning into agreement with that of the New World, we ought thus to have here lessened our date by one day, and have written the 17th for the 18th September. But as, with the exception of the short excursion to Port Clarence and St. Edward Island, we always followed the coasts of the Old World, and during our stay in the new hemisphere did not visit any place inhabited by Europeans, we retained during the whole of our voyage our European day-reckoning unaltered. If we had met with an American whaler, we would have been before him one day, our 27th September would thus have corresponded to his 26th. The same would have been the case on our coming to an American port.

not advisable to remain longer here. It had besides appeared from the hill-top which I visited the day before that an open water channel, only interrupted at two places by ice, was still to be found along the coast. The anchor accordingly was weighed, and the *Vega* steamed on, but in a depth of only 6 to 8 metres. As the *Vega's* draught is from 4·8 to 5 metres, we had only a little water under the keel, and that among ice in quite unknown waters. About twenty kilometres from the anchorage, we met with a belt of ice through which we could make our way though only with great difficulty, thanks to the *Vega's* strong bow ena- · bling her to withstand the violent concussions. Our voyage was then continued, often in yet shallower water than before, until the vessel, at 8 o'clock in the morning, struck on a ground ice foot. The tide was falling, and on that account it was not until next morning that we could get off, after a considerable portion of the ground-ice, on whose foot the *Vega* had run up, had been hewn away with axes and ice-hatchets. Some attempts were made to blast the ice with gunpowder, but they were unsuccessful. For this purpose dynamite is much more efficacious, and this explosive ought therefore always to form part of the equipment in voyages in which belts of ice have to be broken through.

On the 19th we continued our voyage in the same way as before, in still and for the most part shallow water near the coast, between high masses of ground-ice, which frequently had the most picturesque forms. Later in the day we again fell in with very low ice formed in rivers and shut-in inlets of the sea, and came into slightly salt water having a temperature above the freezing-point.

After having been moored during the night to a large ground-ice, the *Vega* continued her course on the 20th September almost exclusively among low, dirty ice, which had not been much pressed together during the preceding winter. This ice was not so deep in the water as the blue ground-ice, and could therefore drift nearer the coast, a great inconvenience for our vessel, which drew so much water. We soon came to a place where the ice was packed so close to land that an open channel only 3½ to 4½ metres deep remained close to the shore. We were therefore compelled after some hours' sailing to lie-to at a ground-ice to await more favourable circumstances. The wind had now gone from west to north and north-west. Notwithstanding this the temperature became milder and the weather rainy, a sign that great open stretches of water lay to the north and north-west of us. During the night before the 21st it rained heavily, the wind being N.N.W. and the temperature + 2°. An attempt was made on that day to find some place where the belt of drift-ice that was pressed against the land could be broken through, but it was unsuccessful, probably in consequence of the exceedingly dense fog which prevailed.

Dredging gave but a scanty yield here, probably because the animal life in water so shallow as that in which we were anchored, is destroyed by the ground-ices, which drift about here for the greater part of the year. Excursions to the neighbouring coast on the other hand, notwithstanding the late season of the year, afforded to the botanists of the *Vega* valuable information regarding the flora of the region.

On the 22nd I made, along with Captain Palander, an excursion in the steam launch to take soundings farther to the east. We soon succeeded in discovering a channel of sufficient depth and not too much blocked with ice, and on the 23rd the *Vega* was

PIECES OF ICE FROM THE COAST OF THE CHUKCH PENINSULA.
After a drawing by O. Nordquist.

able to resume her voyage among very closely packed drift-ice, often so near the land that she had only a fourth of a metre of water under her keel. We went forward however, if slowly.

The land here formed a grassy plain, still clear of snow, rising inland to gently sloping hills or earthy heights. The beach was strewn with a not inconsiderable quantity of driftwood, and here and there were seen the remains of old dwelling-places. On the evening of the 23rd September we lay-to at a ground-ice in a pretty large opening of the ice-field. This opening closed in the course of the night, so that on the 24th and 25th we could make only very little progress, but on the 26th we continued our course, at first with difficulty, but afterwards

in pretty open water to the headland which on the maps is
called Cape Onman. The natives too, who came on board here,
gave the place that name. The ice we met with on that day
was heavier than before, and bluish-white, not dirty. It was
accordingly formed farther out at sea.

On the 27th we continued our course in somewhat open water
to Kolyutschin Bay. No large river debouches in the bottom
of this great fjord, the only one on the north coast of Asia which,
by its long narrow form, the configuration of the neighbouring
shores, and its division into two at the bottom, reminds us of the
Spitzbergen fjords which have been excavated by glaciers. The
mouth of the bay was filled with very closely packed drift-ice
that had gathered round the island situated there, which was
inhabited by a large number of Chukch families. In order to
avoid this ice the *Vega* made a considerable *détour* up the fjord.
The weather was calm and fine, but new ice was formed everywhere among the old drift-ice where it was closely packed.
Small seals swarmed by hundreds among the ice, following the
wake of the vessel with curiosity. Birds on the contrary were
seen in limited numbers. Most of them had evidently already
migrated to more southerly seas. At 4.45 P.M. the vessel was
anchored to an ice-floe near the eastern shore of the fjord. It
could be seen from this point that the ice at the headland, which
bounded the mouth of the fjord to the east, lay so near land
that there was a risk that the open water next the shore would
not be deep enough for the *Vega*.

Lieutenant Hovgaard was therefore sent with the steam
launch to take soundings. He returned with the report that
the water off the headland was sufficiently deep. At the same
time, accompanied by several of the naturalists, I made an
excursion on land. In the course of this excursion the hunter
Johnsen was sent to the top of the range of heights which
occupied the interior of the promontory, in order to get a view
of the state of the ice farther to the east. Johnsen too returned
with the very comforting news that a very broad open channel
extended beyond the headland along the coast to the south-east.
I was wandering about along with my comrades on the slopes
near the beach in order, so far as the falling darkness permitted,
to examine its natural conditions, when Johnsen came down;
he informed us that from the top of the height one could hear
bustle and noise and see fires at an encampment on the other
side of the headland. He supposed that the natives were
celebrating some festival. I had a strong inclination to go
thither in order, as I thought, "to take farewell of the Chukches,"
for I was quite certain that on some of the following days we
should sail into the Pacific. But it was already late in the
evening and dark, and we were not yet sufficiently acquainted

with the disposition of the Chukches to go by night, without any serious occasion, in small numbers and provided only with the weapons of the chase, to an encampment with which we were not acquainted. It was not until afterwards that we learned that such a visit was not attended with any danger. Instead of going to the encampment, as the vessel in any case could not weigh anchor this evening, we remained some hours longer on the beach and lighted there an immense log fire of drift-wood, round which we were soon all collected, chatting merrily about the remaining part of the voyage in seas where not cold but heat would trouble us, and where our progress at least would not be obstructed by ice, continual fog, and unknown shallows. None of us then had any idea that, instead of the heat of the tropics, we would for the next ten months be experiencing a winter at the pole of cold, frozen in on an unprotected road, under almost continual snow-storms, and with a temperature which often sank below the freezing-point of mercury.

The evening was glorious, the sky clear, and the air so calm that the flames and smoke of the log fire rose high against the sky. The dark surface of the water, covered as it was with a thin film of ice, reflected its light as a fire-way straight as a line, bounded far away at the horizon by a belt of ice, whose inequalities appeared in the darkness as the summits of a distant high mountain chain. The temperature in the quite draught-free air was felt to be mild, and the thermometer showed only 2° under the freezing-point. This slight degree of cold was however sufficient to cover the sea in the course of the night with a sheet of newly-frozen ice, which, as the following days' experience showed, at the opener places could indeed only delay, not obstruct the advance of the *Vega*, but which however bound together the fields of drift-ice collected off the coast so firmly that a vessel, even with the help of steam, could with difficulty force her way through.

When on the following day, the 28th September, we had sailed past the headland which bounds Kolyutschin Bay on the east, the channel next the coast, clear of drift-ice, but covered with newly formed ice, became suddenly shallow. The depth was too small for the *Vega*, for which we had now to seek a course among the blocks of ground-ice and fields of drift-ice in the offing. The night's frost had bound these so firmly together that the attempt failed. We were thus compelled to lie-to at a ground-ice so much the more certain of getting off with the first shift of the wind, and of being able to traverse the few miles that separated us from the open water at Behring's Straits, as whalers on several occasions had not left this region until the middle of October.

As American whalers had during the last decades extended their whale-fishing to the North Behring Sea, I applied before my departure from home both directly and through the Foreign Office to several American scientific men and authorities with a request for information as to the state of the ice in that sea. In all quarters my request was received with special good-will and best wishes for the projected journey. I thus obtained both a large quantity of printed matter otherwise difficult of access, and maps of the sea between North America and North Asia, and oral and written communications from several persons : among whom may be mentioned the distinguished naturalist, Prof. W. H. DALL of Washington, who lived for a long time in the Territory of Alaska and the north part of the Pacific; Admiral JOHN RODGERS, who was commander of the American man-of-war, *Vincennes*, when cruising north of Behring's Straits in 1855; and WASHBURN MAYNOD, Lieutenant in the American Navy. I had besides obtained important information from the German sea-captain E. DALLMANN, who for several years commanded a vessel in these waters for coast traffic with the natives. Space does not permit me to insert all these writings here. But to show that there were good grounds for not considering the season of navigation in the sea between Kolyutschin Bay and Behring's Straits closed at the end of September, I shall make some extracts from a letter sent to me, through the American Consul-General in Stockholm, N. A. ELVING, from Mr. MILLER, the president of the Alaska Commercial Company.

" The following is an epitome of the information we have received regarding the subject of your inquiry.

" The bark *Massachusetts*, Captain O. WILLIAMS, was in 74° 30' N.L. and 173° W.L. on the 21st Sept. 1867. No ice in sight in the north, but to the east saw ice. Saw high peaks bearing W.N.W. about 60'. Captain Williams is of opinion that Plover Island, so-called by Kellet, is a headland of Wrangel Land. Captain Williams says that he is of opinion from his observations, that usually after the middle of August there is no ice south of 70°—west of 175°, until the 1st of October. There is hardly a year but that you could go as far as Cape North (Irkaipij), which is 180°, during the month of September. If the winds through July and August have prevailed from the S.W., as is usual, the north shore will be found clear of ice. The season of 1877 was regarded as an ' icy season,' a good deal of ice to southward. 1876 was an open season; as was 1875. Our captain, GUSTAV NIEBAUM, states that the east side of Behring's Straits is open till November; he passed through the Straits as late as October 22nd two different seasons. The north shore was clear of all danger within reasonable distance.

In 1869 the bark *Navy* anchored under Kolyutschin Island from the 8th to the 10th October.   On the 10th October of that year there was no ice south and east of Wrangel Land."

These accounts show that I indeed might have reason to be uneasy at my ill luck in again losing some days at a place at whose bare coast, exposed to the winds of the Polar Sea, there was little of scientific interest to employ ourselves with, little at least in comparison with what one could do in a few days, for instance, at the Islands in Behring's Straits or in St. Lawrence Bay, lying as it does south of the easternmost promontory of Asia and therefore sheltered from the winds of the Arctic Ocean, but that there were no grounds for fearing that it would be necessary to winter there.   I also thought that I could come to the same conclusion from the experience gained in my wintering on Spitzbergen in 1872-73, when permanent ice was first formed in our haven, in the 80th degree of latitude, during the month of February.   Now, however, the case was quite different.   The fragile ice-sheet, which on the 28th September bound together the ground-ices and hindered our progress, increased daily in strength under the influence of severer and severer cold until it was melted by the summer heat of the following year.   Long after we were beset, however, there was still open water on the coast four or five kilometres from our winter haven, and after our return home I was informed that, on the day on which we were frozen in, an American whaler was anchored at that place.

Whether our sailing along the north coast of Asia to Kolyut-schin Bay was a fortunate accident or not, the future will show. I for my part believe that it was a fortunate accident, which will often happen.   Certain it is, in any case, that when we had 'come so far as to this point, our being frozen in was a quite accidental misfortune brought about by an unusual state of the ice in the autumn of 1878 in the North Behring Sea.

CHAPTER X.

Wintering becomes necessary—The position of the *Vega*—The ice round the vessel—American ship in the neighbourhood of the *Vega* when frozen in—The nature of the neighbouring country—The *Vega* is prepared for wintering—Provision-depôt and observatories established on land —The winter dress—Temperature on board—Health and dietary—Cold, wind, and snow—The Chukches on board—Menka's visit—Letters sent home—Nordquist and Hovgaard's excursion to Menka's encampment— Another visit of Menka—The fate of the letters—Nordquist's journey to Pidlin—*Find* of a Chukch grave—Hunting—Scientific work—Life on board—Christmas Eve.

ASSURED that a few hours' southerly wind would be sufficient to break up the belt of ice, scarcely a Swedish mile [1] in breadth, that barred our way, and rendered confident by the above-quoted communications from experts in America concerning the state of the ice in the sea north of Behring's Straits, I was not at first very uneasy at the delay, of which we took advantage by making short excursions on land and holding converse with the inhabitants. First, when day after day passed without any change taking place, it became clear to me that we must make preparations for wintering just on the threshold between the Arctic and the Pacific Oceans. It was an unexpected disappointment, which it was more difficult to bear with equanimity, as it was evident that we would have avoided it if we had come some hours earlier to the eastern side of Kolyutschin Bay. There were numerous occasions during the preceding part of our voyage on which these hours might have been saved: the *Vega* did not require to stay so long at Port Dickson, we might have saved a day at Taimur Island, have dredged somewhat less west of the New Siberian Islands, and so on ; and above all, our long stay at Irkaipij waiting for an improvement in the state of the ice, was fatal, because at least three days were lost there without any change for the better taking place.

The position of the vessel was by no means very secure. For the *Vega*, when frozen in, as appears from the sketch map to be found further on, did not lie at anchor in any haven, but was only, in the expectation of finding a favourable opportunity to steam on, anchored behind a ground-ice, which had stranded in a depth of $9\frac{1}{2}$ metres, 1,400 metres from land, in a road which was quite open from true N. 74° W. by north to east. The vessel had here no other protection against the violent ice-pressure which winter storms are wont to cause in the Polar seas, than a rock of ice stranded at high water, and therefore also at high water not very securely fixed. Fortunately the tide

[1] Equal to 6·64 English miles.

just on the occasion of our being frozen in, appears to have been higher than at any other time during the course of the winter. The ice-rocks, therefore, first floated again far into the summer of 1879, when their parts that projected above the water had diminished by melting. Little was wanting besides to make our winter haven still worse than it was in reality. For the *Vega* was anchored the first time on the 28th September at some small ice-blocks which had stranded 200 metres nearer the land, but was removed the following day from that place, because there were only a few inches of water under her keel. Had the vessel remained at her first anchorage, it had gone ill with us.

TOROSS.
From the neighbourhood of the *Vega's* winter quarters.

For the newly formed ice, during the furious autumn storms, especially during the night between the 14th and 15th December, was pressed over these ice-blocks. The sheet of ice about half a metre thick, was thereby broken up with loud noise into thousands of pieces, which were thrown up on the under-lying ground-ices so as to form an enormous *toross*, or rampart of loose, angular blocks of ice. A vessel anchored there would have been buried under pieces of ice, pressed aground, and crushed very early in the winter.

When the *Vega* was beset, the sea near the coast, as has been already stated, was covered with newly formed ice, too thin to carry a foot passenger, but thick enough to prevent the passage of a boat. In the offing lay, as far as the eye could see, closely packed drift-ice, which was bound together so firmly by the newly formed ice, that it was vain to endeavour to force a passage. Already, by the 2nd October, it was possible, by observing the necessary precautions, to walk upon the newly formed ice nearest the vessel, and on the 3rd October, the Chukches came on board on foot. On the 10th there were still weak places here and there between the vessel and the land, and a blue sky to the eastward indicated that there was still open water in that direction. That this " clearing " was at a considerable distance from the vessel was seen from an excursion which Dr. Almquist undertook in a north-easterly direction on the 13th October, when, after walking about twenty kilometres over closely packed drift-ice, he was compelled to turn without having reached the open water. It was clear that the *Vega* was surrounded by a band, at least thirty kilometres broad, of drift-ice fields, united by newly formed ice, which in the course of the winter reached a considerable thickness.[1]

In this immense ice-sheet there often arose in the course of the winter cracks of great length. They ran uninterruptedly across newly formed ice-fields, and old, high ground-ices. One of the largest of these cracks was formed on the night before the 15th December right under the bow of the vessel. It was nearly a metre broad, and very long. Commonly the cracks were only some centimetres broad, but, notwithstanding this, they were troublesome enough, because the sea-water forced itself up through them to the surface of the ice and drenched the snow lying next to it.

The causes of the formation of the cracks were twofold. Either they arose from a violent wind disturbing somewhat the position of the newly formed ice, or through the contraction of the ice in severe cold. The formation of the cracks took place with a more or less loud report, and, to judge from the number of these reports, more frequently than could be observed from the

---

[1] When it had become evident that we could make no further advance before next year, Lieut. Brusewitz occasionally measured the thickness of the newly formed ice, with the following results :—

THICKNESS OF THE ICE.

1 December,	56	centimetres.	1 May,	154	centimetres.
1 January,	92	,,	15	,, 162	,,
1 February,	108	,,	1 June,	154	,,
15 ,,	120	,,	15	,, 151	,,
1 March,	123	,,	1 July,	104	,,
1 April,	128	,,	15	,, 67	,, (full of holes).
15 ,,	139	,,	18	,, The ice broke up.	

appearance of the snow-covered ice. Thus even during severe cold
the apparently continuous ice-sheet was divided into innumerable
pieces lying in the close proximity of each other, which either
were completely loose or bound together only by the weak ice-
band which was gradually formed under the snow on the surface
of the water which had forced its way into the crack. Up to
a distance of about six kilometres from the shore the ice in any
case lay during the course of the whole winter nearly undisturbed, with the exception of the small cracks just mentioned.
Farther out to sea, on the other hand, it was in constant motion.
So-called *polynias* or open places probably occur here all the year
round, and when the weather was favourable we could therefore
nearly always see a blue water sky at the horizon from true N.W. to
E. A southerly wind after some days brought the open water
channel so near the vessel that it was possible to walk to it in a
few hours. It then swarmed with seals—an indication that it was
in connection with a sea that was constantly open. The neighbourhood of such a sea perhaps also accounts for the circumstance
that we did not see a single seal-hole in the ice-fields that
surrounded the vessel.

The ground-ice, to which the *Vega* was moored on the 29th
September, and under which she lay during the course of the
winter, was about forty metres long and twenty-five metres
broad; its highest point lay six metres above the surface of the
water. It was thus not very large, but gave the vessel good
shelter. This ground-ice, along with the vessel and the newly
formed ice-field lying between it and the shore, was indeed
moved considerably nearer land during the violent autumn
storms. A groan or two and a knocking sound in the hull of
the vessel indicated that it did not escape very severe pressure;
but the *Vega* did not during the course of the winter suffer any
damage, either from this or from the severe cold, during which
sharp reports often indicated that some crack in the wood-
work had widened through the freezing of the water that had
made its way into the vessel. "Cold so that the walls crack"
is a well-known expression, with which we inhabitants of the
North often connect memories from some stormy winter evening, passed by the home hearth; but here these reports heard in
our cabins, especially at night, were unpleasant enough, giving
rise to fears that the newly formed or widened cracks would
cause dangerous leaks in the vessel's hull. In consequence of
iron contracting more than wood under the influence of cold,
the heads of the iron bolts, with which the ship's timbers
were fastened together, in the course of the winter sank deep
into the outside planking. But no serious leak arose in this
way, perhaps because the cold only acted on that part of the
vessel which lay above the surface of the water.

Already during the first days of our wintering we interpreted various lively accounts of the natives, which they illustrated by signs, to mean that a whaler would be found at Serdze Kamen, in the neighbourhood of the *Vega's* winter haven. On this account Lieutenant Brusewitz was sent out on the 4th October with two men and the little boat, *Louise*, built in Copenhagen for the expedition of 1872-73, and intended for sledge-journeys, with instructions to ascertain, if possible, if such was the case. He returned late at night the same day without having got sight of any vessel. We now supposed that the whole depended on our having misunderstood the accounts of the Chukches. But a letter which I received after our return, from Mr. W. BARTLETT, dated New Bedford, 6th January, 1880, shows that this had not been the case. For he writes, among other things : —

" The writer's son, GIDEON W. BARTLETT, left San Francisco 1st June, 1878, in our freighter ship *Syren*, of 875 tons, for St. Lawrence Bay, arriving there July 8th, and, after loading 6,100 barrels of oil and 37,000 lbs. of bone from our whalers, she sailed for New Bedford direct, touching at Honolulu to land her bone, to come here *viâ* San Francisco, and he joined our whaler bark, *Rainbow*, at St. Lawrence Bay, and went on a tour of observation and pleasure, visiting Point Barrow and going as far east as Lion Reefs, near Camden Bay, and then returning to Point Barrow, and going over to Herald Island, and while there visiting our different whalers, seeing one " bowhead " caught and cut in, and September 25th he came down in the schooner *W. M. Meyer* to San Francisco, arriving there October 22nd. By a comparison of dates we find he passed near Cape Serdze September 29th, or one day after you anchored near Kolyutschin Bay."

The 29th September according to the American day-reckoning corresponds to the 30th according to that of the old world, which was still followed on board the *Vega*. The schooner *W. M. Meyer* thus lay at Serdze Kamen two days after we anchored in our winter haven. The distance between the two places is only about 70 kilometres.

The winter haven was situated in 67° 4' 49" north latitude, and 173° 23' 2" longitude west from Greenwich, 1·4 kilometres from land. The distance from East Cape was 120', and from Point Hope near Cape Lisburn on the American side, 180'.

The neighbouring land formed a plain rising gradually from the sea, slightly undulating and crossed by river valleys, which indeed when the *Vega* was frozen in was covered with hoarfrost

A A

and frozen, but still clear of snow, so that our botanists could
form an idea of the flora of the region, previously quite unknown.
Next the shore were found close beds of Elymus, alternating
with carpets of *Halianthus peploides,* and further up a poor, even,
gravelly soil, covered with water in spring, on which grew only
a slate-like lichen, *Gyrophora proboscidea,* and a few flowering
plants, of which *Armeria sibirica* was the most common.
Within the beach were extensive salt and fresh-water lagoons,
separated by low land, whose banks were covered with a pretty
luxuriant carpet, formed of mosses, grasses, and Carices. But
first on the neighbouring high land, where the weathered gneiss
strata yielded a more fertile soil than the sterile sand thrown
up out of the sea, did the vegetation assume a more variegated
stamp. No trace of trees[1] was indeed found there, but low
willow bushes, extensive carpets of *Empetrum nigrum* and
Andromeda tetragona were seen, along with large tufts of a
species of Artemisia. Between these shoot forth in summer, to
judge partly from the dried and frozen remains of plants which
Dr. Kjellman collected in autumn, partly from collections made
in spring, a limited number of flowering plants, some of which
are well known at home, as the red whortleberry, the cloudberry, and the dandelion.

Although experience from preceding Polar journeys and
specially from the Swedish expedition of 1872-73, showed that
even at the 80th degree of latitude the sea may suddenly break
up in the middle of winter, we however soon found, as has
been already stated, that we must make preparations for
wintering. The necessary arrangements were accordingly made.
The snow which collected on deck, and which at first was daily
swept away, was allowed to remain, so that it finally formed a
layer 30 centimetres thick, of hard tramped snow or ice, which
in no inconsiderable degree contributed to increase the resistance
of the deck to cold, and for the same purpose snowdrifts were
thrown up along the vessel's sides. A stately ice stair was
carried up from the ice to the starboard gunwale. A large tent
made for the purpose at Karlskrona was pitched from the bridge
to the fore, so that only the poop was open. Aft the tent was
quite open, the blast and drifting snow having also free entrance
from the sides and from an incompletely closed opening in the
fore. The protection it yielded against the cold was indeed
greatly diminished in this way, but instead it did not have the
least injurious action on the air on the vessel, a circumstance
specially deserving of attention for its influence on the state of
health on board. Often under this tent in the dark days of
winter there blazed a brisk smithy fire, round which the

[1] Low brush is probably to be met with in the interior of the Chukch
peninsula at places which are protected from the cold north winds.

THE "VEGA" IN WINTER QUARTERS.

After a photograph, taken in the spring of 1879 by L. Palander.

Chukches crowded in curious wonder at the skill with which the smith fashioned the glowing iron. Here the cook dealt out to the Chukches the soup and meat that were left over, and the loaves of bread which at every baking were baked for them. Here was our reception saloon, where tobacco and sugar were distributed to the women and children, and where sometimes, if seldom, a frozen hunter or fisherman was treated to a little spirits. Here pieces of wood and vertebræ of the whale were valued and purchased, and here tedious negotiations were carried on regarding journeys in dog-sledges in different directions.

The violent motion which took place in the ice during the night before the 15th December, gave us a sharp warning that our position in the open road was by no means so secure as was desirable, but that there was a possibility that the vessel might be nipped suddenly and without any previous warning. If such a misfortune had happened, the crew of the *Vega* would certainly have had no difficulty in getting to land over the ice. But the yield of hunting appeared to be so scanty, and the Chukches were, as almost always, so destitute of all stock of provisions— for they literally obey the command to take no thought for to-morrow—that there was every probability that we, having come safe ashore, would die of hunger, if no provisions were saved from the vessel. This again, as the principal part of the provisions was of course down in the hold, would have been attended with great difficulty, if the *Vega* had been suddenly in the night cut into by the ice at the water-line. In order as far as possible to secure ourselves against the consequences of such a misfortune, a depôt of provisions, guns, ammunition, &c., reckoned for 30 men and 100 days, was formed on land. Fortunately we did not require to depend upon it. The stores were laid up on the beach without the protection of lock or bolt, covered only with sails and oars, and no watch was kept at the place. Notwithstanding this, and the want of food which occasionally prevailed among the natives, it remained untouched both by the Chukches who lived in the neighbourhood, and by those who daily drove past the place from distant regions. All however knew very well the contents of the sail-covered heap, and they undoubtedly supposed that there were to be found there treasures of immense value, and provisions enough for the whole population of the Chukch peninsula for a whole year.

The Magnetical Observatory was erected, as will be told in greater detail further on, upon the beach a kilometre and a half from the vessel. To this house the observers had to walk to and fro at least four times in the twenty-four hours over an ice-field, covered with loose snow, as fine as dust, that was set in motion by the least puff of wind, and then in a few moments completely obliterated every footprint. When the moon did not shine, the winter nights were so dark, that it was impossible to distinguish the very nearest objects, and day after day during the course of the winter we had, besides, drifting snow so thick that the high dark hull of the vessel itself could be distinguished only when one was in its immediate neighbourhood! In walking from land during the darkness of the night and in drifting snow it would have been very difficult to find one's way to the vessel without guidance, and he would have been helplessly lost who went astray. To prevent such an accident, the precaution was taken of running a line over high ice-pillars between the Observatory and the vessel. Even with the help of the guideline it was often difficult enough to find our way.

The attempt to keep open a channel in the ice round the vessel during the whole winter had soon to be given up, but two holes were kept constantly open, one by the side of the vessel in case of fire, and the other for the tidal observations which Captain Palander set on foot during the winter. The latter hole was chosen by a little seal as its haunt for a long time, until one day we entertained ourselves by catching him with the necessary care, and making him pay an involuntary visit on board, where he was offered various delicacies, which however were disregarded. The seal was let loose again in his hole, but notwithstanding the friendliness we showed him, he never more returned.

From the meteorological observations it appears that the winter was not so cold as the winters in the Franklin archipelago or in the coldest parts of the mainland of Siberia.[1] On the other hand, it was exceedingly stormy at the *Vega's* winter station, and day after day, night after night, we have gone to and from the Observatory in a high wind and a cold of $-30°$ to $-46°$ C. In calm weather a cold of $-40°$ is scarcely very troublesome, but with only a slight draught a degree of cold of for instance $-35°$ is actually dangerous for one who goes against the wind, and without the necessary precautions exposes uncovered parts of the face, the hands, or the wrists, to the cold current of air. Without one's being warned by any severe pain frostbite arises, which, if it be not in time thawed by rubbing the injured part with the hand, or with melting snow, may readily become very serious. Most of those who for the first time took part

---

[1] According to H. Wild's newly-published large work, " *Die Temperatur Verhältnisse des Russischen Reiches*, 2e Hälfte, St. Petersburg, 1881," the Old World's cold-pole lies in the neighbourhood of the town Werchojansk (67° 34' N.L. 133° 51' E.L. from Greenwich). The mean temperature of the different months and of the whole year is given in the note at page 411. If the data on which these figures rest are correct, the winter at Werchojansk is immensely colder than at the *Vega's* winter station.

in a wintering in the high north, were, when the first cold occurred, more or less frostbitten, on several occasions so that there arose high frost-blisters filled with bloody water, several square centimetres in extent, but fortunately never to such a degree that any serious bad results followed. After we, new-

THE WINTER DRESS OF THE "VEGA" MEN.

comers to the Polar regions, warned by experience, became more careful, such frostbites occurred but seldom. Nor did there occur a single case of frostbite in the feet. To this conduced our clothing, which was adapted to the climate, and, besides good winter clothes of the sort commonly used in Sweden, consisted of the following articles of dress brought with us specially for use in the high north :—

1. An abundant stock of good *woollen under-clothing.*

2. A carefully made *blouse of sailcloth,* provided with many pockets, intended to be drawn over the ordinary seaman's dress as a protection against wind and drifting snow. This proved to be very suitable for the purpose for which it was intended, and was much liked by the crew.

3. A Lapp "*pesk*" *with leggings* was not so often used, because it was so warm that it was only with difficulty one could walk with it any considerable distance. On the other hand, in the case of winter journeys with dogs or reindeer it was indispensable.

4. A pair of very large *canvas boots* with leather soles. Inside these was put hay of *Carex vesicaria* L. The foot itself was covered with one or two pairs of stockings, above which there was a foot-strip of felt. Our boots were thus intermediate between the foot-covering introduced by Parry for Arctic journeys, and the hay-filled *komager* of the Lapps. All who used these canvas boots are unanimous in thinking that they left nothing to desire. Even in the case of extended excursions in wet snow they are to be preferred to leather shoes; for the latter become heavy and drenched with water, and can with difficulty be dried in the open air in the course of a night's rest. Canvas boots and the long hay in them on the other hand are easily dried in a single night. They are also light when wet, and in that state little prejudicial to health on account of the change of air which the hay under the foot renders possible. I therefore am of opinion that we are warranted in giving such boots the highest recommendation for winter journeys and winter hunting excursions, even in our own land.

5. An *Oresund cap* and a loose *felt hood* (baschlik) of the same sort as those which are used in the Russian army. I had bought the baschliks in St. Petersburg on account of the expedition.

6. *Fingerless gloves* of sealskin and chamois, with an inside lining of sheepskin and at the wrists bordered with long-haired fur. They were commonly carried with a band from the neck, as children are wont to carry their gloves. For outside work these thick gloves were too inconvenient; then fingerless woollen mittens were used.

7. *Coloured spectacles,* which were distributed to all the men in the beginning of February. One must himself have lived in the Polar regions during winter and spring, " after the return of the sun," to understand how indispensable is such a protection from the monotonous white light which then surrounds the eye in every direction. The inexperienced, though warned, seldom observe the necessary precautions, and commonly pay the penalty

by a more or less complete snowblindness, which indeed is not
very dangerous, but is always exceedingly painful, and which
lasts several days.

On board the vessel in our cabins and collection-rooms it was
besides by no means so cold as many would suppose. The sides
of the vessel in several places indeed, especially in the cabins,
were covered with a thick sheet of ice, and so was the skylight in
the gun-room. But in the inhabited parts of the vessel we had, a
little from the sides, commonly a temperature of+12° to+17°, that
is to say about the same as we in the north are wont to have in-
doors in winter, and certainly higher than the temperature of rooms
during the coldest days of the year in many cities in the south,
as for instance in Paris and Vienna. By night however the
temperature in the cabins sank sometimes to + 5° and + 10°, and
the boarding at the side of the berth became covered with ice.
In the work-room 'tweendecks the thermometer generally stood
about + 10°, and even in the underhold, which was not heated,
but lay under the water-line, the temperature was never under,
commonly 1° or 2° above, the freezing-point.

Much greater inconvenience than from cold did we in the
cabins suffer from the excessive heat and the fumes, which
firing in large cast-iron stoves is wont to cause in small close rooms.
When in the morning after a cold night the watch all too willingly
obeyed the direction, which sounded from different quarters, to fire
well, one had often his wish so thoroughly satisfied, that, in half an
hour after, every man lay bathed in perspiration. There was no
other help for it than to leave the cabin, take a cold bath and
a good rub down, dress rapidly, rush on deck for fresh air,
and cool in the temperature of −30° to −40° prevailing there.
Other opportunities for bathing were also given both to the officers
and crew, and the necessary care was taken to secure cleanliness,
a sanitary measure which ought never to be neglected in Arctic
winterings.

The state of health on board during the course of the winter
was exceedingly good. Dr. Almquist's report enumerates only
a few serious maladies, all successfully cured, among which may
be mentioned stomach colds and slight cases of inflammation of
the lungs, but not a single case of that insidious disease, scurvy,
which formerly raged in such a frightful way among the crews
in all long voyages, and which is still wont to gather so many
victims from among Polar travellers.

This good state of health depended in the first place on the
excellent spirit which inspired the scientific men, the officers
and the crew of the Expedition, but it ought also to be ascribed
to the suitable equipment of the *Vega*, arranged by Captain
Palander at Karlskrona, and above all to adjustment to the

climate of our dietary, which was settled on the ground of the experience gained in the expedition of 1872–73, and after taking the advice of its distinguished physician Dr. Envall. The dietary is shown in the following table :—

No. 1. SUNDAY.

Breakfast: butter 6 ort, coffee 10 ort, sugar 7·5 ort.[1]

Dinner: salt pork or dried fish 75 ort, sourkrout 75 ort, preserved or fresh potatoes 12 ort, preserved vegetables 5·5 ort, extract of meat 1·5 ort, raisins 5 ort, rice 50 ort, brandy or rum 2 cubic inches.

Supper: butter 6 ort, tea 1·5 ort, sugar 7·5 ort, barley-groats 10 cubic inches, cheese 12 ort.

No. 2. MONDAY, WEDNESDAY, and FRIDAY.

Breakfast same as No. 1.

Dinner: preserved meat or fish 1 portion, preserved potatoes 12 ort, preserved vegetables 5·5 ort, preserved leeks 1 portion, extract of meat 1·5 ort, brandy or rum 2 cubic inches.

Supper same as No. 1 without cheese.

No. 3. THURSDAY.

Breakfast same as No. 1.

Dinner: salt pork 1 lb., peas 10 cubic inches, extract of meat 1·5 ort, barley-groats 2 cubic inches, brandy or rum 2 cubic inches.

Supper same as No. 2.

No. 4. TUESDAY.

Breakfast: butter 6 ort, chocolate 10 ort, sugar 7·5 ort.

Dinner: salt meat 1 lb., maccaroni 15 ort (or brown beans 10 cubic inches or green peas 1 portion), fruit soup 1 portion, brandy or rum 2 cubic inches.

Supper same as No. 2.

No. 5. SATURDAY.

Breakfast same as No. 4.

Dinner: preserved beefsteak or stewed beef 1 portion, preserved or fresh potatoes 12 ort, preserved leeks 1 portion, fruit soup 1 portion, brandy or rum 2 cubic inches.

Supper same as No. 2.

Every man besides had served out to him daily 1¼ lb. dried bread or flour (⅔ wheat and ⅓ rye), 3 ort tobacco and 2 cubic inches vinegar ; and weekly 1 lb. wheat-flour, 30 ort butter, 21 ort salt, 7 ort mustard, 3 ort pepper, and two cubic inches vinegar.

[1] 1 lb. = 100 ort = 425·05 gram.   1 kanna = 100 cubic inches = 2·617 litres.

Besides what is included in the above list, "multegröt" (preserved cloudberries), mixed with rum, was served out twice a week from the 15th February to the 1st April. I would willingly have had a larger quantity of this, according to northern experience, excellent antidote to scurvy, but as the cloudberry harvest completely failed in 1877, I could not, at any price, procure for the expedition the quantity that was required. There was purchased in Finland instead, a large quantity of cranberry-juice, which was regularly served out to the crew and much liked by them. We carried with us besides a pair of living swine, which were slaughtered for the Christmas festivities.[1] All the men at that time had an opportunity of eating fresh pork twice a week, an invaluable interruption to the monotonous preserved provisions, which in its proportion conduced, during this festival, to which we inhabitants of the North are attached by so many memories, to enliven and cheer us.

COD FROM PITLEKAJ.
Gadus navaga, Kölreuter.
One-third of the natural size.

The produce of hunting was confined during the course of the winter to some ptarmigan and hares, and thus did not yield any contribution worth mentioning to the provisioning of the vessel. On the other hand, I was able by barter with the natives to procure fish in considerable abundance, so that at certain seasons the quantity was sufficient to allow of fresh fish being served out once a week. The kind of fish which was principally obtained during the winter, a sort of cod with greyish-green vertebræ, could however at first only be served in the gun-room, because the crew, on account of the colour of its bones, for a long time had an invincible dislike to it.

On many of the ground-ices in the neighbourhood of the vessel there were fresh-water collections of considerable depth which indeed were already hard frozen on the surface, but long

---

[1] To carry animals for slaughter on vessels during Polar expeditions cannot be sufficiently recommended. Their flesh acts beneficially by forming a change from the preserved provisions, which in course of time become exceedingly disagreeable, and their care a not less important interruption to the monotony of the winter life.

yielded us splendid water for drinking and washing. After the 14th of December, when all the smaller fresh-water collections were almost frozen to the bottom, and salt-water had made its way into the largest ones and those on which we most depended, it became necessary to procure water by melting ice.

The meteorological observations were made every fourth hour up to the 1st November; after that to the 1st April every hour ; after that again six times in the twenty-four hours. From the 27th November to the 1st April the thermometers were set up on land at the magnetical observatory ; before and after that time in the immediate neighbourhood of the vessel. During winter the charge of the meteorological observations was entrusted to Dr. Stuxberg, who at that season when all around us was covered with ice, was compelled to let his own zoological researches rest.

The state of the weather of course had a very sensible influence on our daily life, and formed the touchstone by which our equipment was tested. Space does not permit me to give in this work the detailed results of the meteorological observations. I shall therefore only state the following facts.

The greatest cold which was observed during the different months was in

October	the 24th	− 20°·8	March	the 29th	− 39°·8
November	the 30th	− 27°·2	April	the 15th	− 38°·0
December	the 23rd	− 37°·1	May	the 3rd	− 26°·8
January	the 25th	− 45°·7	June	the 3rd	− 14°·3
February	the 2nd	− 43°·8	July	the 2nd	− 1°·0

Twice we had the barometer uncommonly high, viz. :

On the 22nd December 6 A.M. 782·0 (0°) mm.
On the 17th February 6 A.M. 788·1 (0°) mm.

The lowest atmospheric pressure, 728·8 (0°) mm., occurred on the 31st December at two o'clock P.M.

The weather during the winter was very stormy, and the direction of the wind nearest the surface of the earth almost constantly between north-west and north-north-west. But already in atmospheric strata of inconsiderable height there prevailed, to judge by the direction of the clouds, a similar uninterrupted atmospheric current from the south-east, which when it occasionally sank to the surface of the earth brought with it air that was warmer and less saturated with moisture. The reason of this is easy to see, if we consider that Behring's Straits form a gate surrounded by pretty high mountains between the warm atmospheric area of the Pacific and the cold one of the Arctic Ocean. The winds must be arranged here approximately after the same laws as the draught in the door-opening between a warm and a cold room, that is to say, the cold current of air must go below from the cold room to the warm, the warm above from the warm room to the cold. The mountain heights which, according to the statement of the natives, are to be found in the interior of the Chukch peninsula besides conduce to the heat and dryness of the southerly and south-easterly winds. For they confer on the sea winds that pass over their summits the properties of the *föhn* winds. Our coldest winds have come from S.W. to W., that is to say, from the Old World's pole of cold, situated in the region of Werchojansk. On the existence of two currents of air, which at a certain height above the surface of the earth contend for the mastery, depends also the surprising rapidity with which the vault of heaven in the region of Behring's Straits becomes suddenly clouded over and again completely clear. Already the famous Behring's Straits' navigator, RODGERS, now Admiral in the American Navy, had noticed this circumstance, and likened it very strikingly to the drawing up and dropping of the curtain of a theatre.

In our notes on the weather a difference was always made between *snōyra* (fall of snow in wind) and *yrsnō* (snow-storm without snow-fall). The fall of snow was not very great, but as there was in the course of the winter no thaw of such continuance that the snow was at any time covered with a coherent melted crust, a considerable portion of the snow that fell remained so loose that with the least puff of wind it was whirled backwards and forwards. In a storm or strong breeze the snow was carried to higher strata of the atmosphere, which was speedily filled with so close and fine snow-dust, that objects at the distance of a few metres could no longer be distinguished. There was no possibility in such weather of keeping the way open, and the man that lost his way was helplessly lost, if he could not, like the Chukch snowed up in a drift, await the ceasing of the storm. But even when the wind was slight and the sky clear there ran a stream of snow some centimetres in height along the ground in the direction of the wind, and thus principally from N.W. to S.E. Even this shallow stream heaped snowdrifts everywhere where there was any protection from the wind, and buried more certainly, if less rapidly, than the drifting snow of the storm, exposed objects and trampled footpaths. The quantity of water, which in a frozen form is removed in this certainly not deep, but uninterrupted and rapid current over the north coast of Siberia to more southerly regions, must be equal to the mass of water in the giant rivers of our globe, and play a sufficiently great *rôle*, among others as a carrier of cold to the most northerly forest regions, to receive the attention of meteorologists.

The humidity of the air was observed both by August's

psychrometer and Saussure's hygrometer. But I do not believe that these instruments give trustworthy results at a temperature considerably under the freezing-point. Moreover the degree of humidity at the place where there can be a question of setting up a psychrometer and hygrometer during a wintering in the high north, has not the meteorological importance which has often been ascribed to it. For the instruments are as a rule set up in an isolated louvre case, standing at a height above the surface convenient for reading. While the snow is drifting almost uninterruptedly it is impossible to keep this case clear of snow. Even the air, which was originally quite dry, must here be saturated with moisture through evaporation from the surrounding layers of snow and from the snow dust which whirls about next the surface of the earth. In order to determine the true degree of humidity in the air, I would accordingly advise future travellers to these regions to weigh directly the water which a given measure of air contains by absorbing it in tubes with chloride of calcium, calcined sulphate of copper, or sulphuric acid. It would be easy to arrange an instrument for this purpose so that the whole work could be done under deck, the air from any stratum under the mast-top being examined at will. If I had had the means to make such an examination at the *Vega's* winter quarters, it would certainly have appeared that the relative humidity of the air at a height of some few metres above the surface of the earth was for the most part exceedingly small.

The sandy neck of land which on the side next the vessel divided the lagoons from the sea, was bestrewn with colossal bones of the whale, and with the refuse of the Chukches, who had lived and wandered about there for centuries, and besides with portions of the skeleton of the seal and walrus, with the excreta of men, dogs, birds, &c. The region was among the most disagreeable I have seen in any of the parts inhabited by fishing Lapps, Samoyeds, Chukches, or Eskimo. When the *Vega* was beset there were two Chukch villages on the neighbouring beach, of which the one that lay nearest our winter haven was called Pitlekaj. It consisted at first of seven tents, which in consequence of want of food their inhabitants removed gradually in the course of the winter to a region near Behring's Straits, where fish were more abundant. At the removal only the most indispensable articles were taken along, because there was an intention of returning at that season of the year when the chase again became more productive. The other encampment, Yinretlen, lay nearer the cape towards Kolyutschin Bay, and reckoned at the beginning of our wintering likewise seven tents, whose inhabitants appeared to be in better circumstances than those of Pitlekaj. They had during the autumn made a better catch and collected a greater stock. Only some of them accordingly removed during winter.

The following encampments lay at a somewhat greater distance from our winter quarters, but so near, however, that we were often visited by their inhabitants:

Pidlin, on the eastern shore of Kolyutschin Bay, four tents.

Kolyutschin, on the island of the same name, twenty-five tents. This village was not visited by any of the members of the *Vega* Expedition.

Rirajtinop, situated six kilometres east of Pitlekaj, three tents.

Irgunnuk, seven kilometres east of Pitlekaj, ten tents, of which, however, in February only four remained. The inhabitants of the others had for the winter sought a better fishing place farther eastward.

KAUTLJKAU, A CHUKCH GIRL FROM IRGUNNUK.
Front face and Profile.
After photographs by L. Palander.

The number of the persons who belonged to each tent was difficult to make out, because the Chukches were constantly visiting each other for the purpose of gossip and talk. On an average it may perhaps be put at five or six persons. Including the inhabitants of Kolyutschin Island, there thus lived about 300 natives in the neighbourhood of our winter quarters.

When we were beset, the ice next the shore, as has been already stated, was too weak to carry a foot passenger, and the difficulty of reaching the vessel from the land with the means which the Chukches had at their disposal was thus very great. When the natives observed us, there was in any case immediately a great commotion among them. Men, women, children, and dogs were seen running up and down the beach in eager confusion; some were seen driving in dog-sledges on the ice street next the sea. They evidently feared that the splendid opportunity which here lay before them of purchasing brandy and tobacco, would be lost. From the vessel we could see with glasses how several attempts were made to put out boats, but they were again given up, until at last a boat was got to a lane, clear of ice or only covered with a thin sheet, that ran from the shore to the neighbourhood of the vessel. In this a large skin boat was put out, which was filled brimful of men and women, regardless of the evident danger of navigating such a boat, heavily laden, through sharp newly formed ice. They rowed immediately to the vessel, and on reaching it most of them climbed without the least hesitation over the gunwale with jests and laughter, and the cry *anoaj anoaj* (good day, good day). Our first meeting with the inhabitants of this region, where we afterwards passed ten long months, was on both sides very hearty, and formed the starting-point of a very friendly relation between the Chukches and ourselves, which remained unaltered during the whole of our stay.

Regard for cleanliness compelled us to allow the Chukches to come below deck only exceptionally, which at first annoyed them much, so that one of them even showed a disposition to retaliate by keeping us out of the bedchamber in his tent. Our firmness on this point, however, combined with friendliness and generosity, soon calmed them, and it was not so easy for the men to exclude us from the inner tent, for in such visits we always had confections and tobacco with us, both for themselves and for the women and children. On board, the vessel's tent-covered deck soon became a veritable reception saloon for the whole population of the neighbourhood. Dog-team after dog-team stood all day in rows, or more correctly lay snowed up before the ice-built flight of steps to the deck of the *Vega*, patiently waiting for the return of the visitors, or for the pemmican I now and then from pity ordered to be given to the hungered animals. The report of the arrival of the remarkable foreigners must besides have spread with great rapidity. For we soon had visits even from distant settlements, and the *Vega* finally became a resting-place at which every passer-by stopped with his dog-team for some hours in order to satisfy his curiosity, or to obtain in exchange for good words or some more acceptable wares a little warm food, a bit of tobacco, and sometimes when the weather was very stormy, a little drop of spirits, by the Chukches called *ram*, a word whose origin is not to be sought for in the Swedish-Norwegian *dram*, but in the English word *rum*.

All who came on board were allowed to go about without let

or hindrance on our deck, which was encumbered with a great
many things. We had not however to lament the loss of the
merest trifle. Honesty was as much at home here as in the
huts of the reindeer Lapps. On the other hand, they soon
became very troublesome by their beggary, which was kept in
bounds by no feeling of self-respect. Nor did they fail to take
all possible advantage of what they doubtless considered the
great inexperience of the Europeans. Small deceptions in this
way were evidently not looked upon as blameworthy, but as
meritorious. Sometimes, for instance, they sold us the same
thing twice over, they were always liberal in promises which
they never intended to keep, and often gave deceptive accounts
of articles which were exposed for sale. Thus the carcases of
foxes were offered, after having been flayed and the head and
feet cut off, on several occasions as hares, and it was laughable
to see their astonishment at our immediately discovering the
fraud. The Chukches' complete want of acquaintance with
money and our small supply of articles for barter for which they
had a liking besides compelled even me to hold at least a portion
of our wares at a high price. Skins and blubber, the common
products of the Polar lands, to the great surprise of the natives,
were not purchased on the *Vega*. On the other hand a complete
collection of weapons, dresses, and household articles was procured by barter. All such purchases were made exclusively
on account of the Expedition, and in general the collection of
natural and ethnographical objects for private account was wholly
forbidden, a regulation which ought to be in force in every
scientific expedition to remote regions.

As the Chukches began to acquire a taste for our food, they
never neglected, especially during the time when their hunting
failed, to bring daily on board driftwood and the vertebræ and
other bones of the whale. They bartered these for bread. A
load of five bits of wood, from four to five inches in diameter
and six feet long, was commonly paid for with two or three ship
biscuits, that is to say with about 250 gram bread, the vertebra
of a whale with two ship biscuits, &c. By degrees two young
natives got into the habit of coming on board daily for the
purpose of performing, quite at their leisure, the office of
servant. The cook was their patron, and they obtained from
him in compensation for their services the larger share of the
left victuals. So considerable a quantity of food was distributed
partly as payment for services rendered or for goods purchased,
partly as gifts, that we contributed in a very great degree to
mitigate the famine which during midwinter threatened to
break out among the population.

None of the natives in the neighbourhood of the *Vega's*
winter station professed the Christian religion. None of them

spoke any European language, though one or two knew a couple
of English words and a Russian word of salutation. This was
a very unfortunate circumstance, which caused us much trouble.
But it was soon remedied by Lieut. Nordquist specially devoting
himself to the study of their language, and that with such zeal
and success that in a fortnight he could make himself pretty
well understood.   The natives stated to DE LONG in the autumn
of 1879 that a person on the "man of war" which wintered on
the north coast, spoke Chukch exceedingly well.   The difficulty
of studying the language was increased, to a not inconsiderable
degree, by the Chukches in their wish to co-operate with us in
finding a common speech being so courteous as not to correct,
but to adopt the mistakes, in the pronunciation or meaning of
words that were made on the *Vega*.   As a fruit of his studies
Lieut. Nordquist has drawn up an extensive vocabulary of this
little known language, and given a sketch of its grammatical
structure.[1]   The knowledge of the Chukch language, which

---

[1] I give here an extract from the Vocabulary, that the reader may form
some idea of the language of the north-east point of Asia :—

Tnáergin, heaven.
Tirkir, the sun.
Yédlin, the moon.
Angátlingan, a star.
Núttatschka, land.
Angka, sea.
Ljédljenki, winter.
Edljek, summer.
Edljéngat, day.
Nekita, night.
Ayguon, yesterday.
Íetkin, to-day.
Ergátti, to-morrow.
Gnúnian, north.
Emnungku, south.
Nikáyan, east.
Kayradljgin, west.
Tintin, ice.
Atljatlj, snow.
Yeetedli, the aurora.
Yengeen, mist.
Tédljgio, storm.
Éek, fire.
Kljautlj, a man, a human
    being.
Oráedlja, men.
Neáiren, a woman.
Nénena, a child.
Empenátschyo, father.
Émpengau, mother.
Ljéut, head.
Ljeutljka, face.
Dljedljádlin, eye.

Liljáptkóurgin, to see.
Huedljódlin, ear.
Huedljokodljáurgin, to
    hear.
Huádljomerkin, to un-
    derstand.
Huedljountákurgin, not
    to understand.
Yelá, nose.
Yekergin, mouth.
Kametkuaurgin, to eat.
Yedlinedljourgin,   to
    speak.
Mámmah,   a   woman's
    breast.
Mammatkóurgin,   to
    give suck.
Yéet, foot.
Retschaurgin, to stand.
Yetkatjergin, to lie.
Tschipiska, to sleep.
Kadljetschetuetjákurgin,
    to learn.
Pintekatkóurgin, to be
    born.
Kaertráljirgin, to die.
Kámakatan, to be sick.
Kámak, the Deity, a
    guardian Spirit.
Yáranga, tent.
Etschengeratlin, lamp.
Órguor, sledge.
Atkuát, boat.

Anetljkatlj,   fishing-
    hook.
Anedljourgin, to angle.
Uádlin, knife.
Tschúpak,   Kámeak
    dog.
Úmku, Polar bear.
Rérka, walrus.
Mémetlj, seal.
Kórang, reindeer.
Gátlje, bird.
Enne, fish.
Gúrgur, dwarf-birch.
Kukatkokcngadlin, wil-
    low-bush.
Gem, I.
Gemnin, mine.
Get, you.
Gemnin, yours.
Enkan, he.
Muri, we.
Turi, you.
Máyngin, much.
Pljúkin, little.
Konjpong, all.
I, yes.
Etlje, no.
Métschinka, thanks.
Énnen, one.
Nirak, two.
Nrok, three.
Nrak, four.
Metljingan, five.

B B

CHUKCHES ANGLING.

the other members of the Expedition acquired, was confined to a larger or smaller number of words; the natives also learned a word or two of our language, so that a *lingua franca* somewhat intelligible to both parties gradually arose, in which several of the crew soon became very much at home, and with which in case of necessity one could get along very well, although in this newly formed dialect all grammatical inflections were totally wanting. Besides, I set one of the crew, the walrus-hunter Johnsen, free for a considerable time from all work on board, in order that he might wander about the country daily, partly for hunting, partly for conversing with the natives. He succeeded in the beginning of winter in killing some ptarmigan and hares, got for me a great deal of important information regarding the mode of life of the Chukches, and procured several valuable ethnographical objects. But after a time, for what reason I could never make out, he took an invincible dislike to visit the Chuckch tents more, without however having come to any disagreement with their inhabitants.

On the 5th October the openings between the drift-ice fields next the vessel were covered with splendid skating ice, of which we availed ourselves by celebrating a gay and joyous skating festival. The Chukch women and children were now seen fishing for winter roach along the shore. In this sort of fishing a man, who always accompanies the fishing women, with an iron-shod lance cuts a hole in the ice so near the shore that the distance between the under corner of the hole and the bottom is only half a metre. Each hole is used only by one woman, and that only for a short time. Stooping down at the hole, in which the surface of the water is kept quite clear of pieces of ice by means of an ice-sieve, she endeavours to attract the fish by means of a peculiar wonderfully clattering cry. First when a fish is seen in the water an angling line, provided with a hook of bone, iron or copper, is thrown down, strips of the entrails of fish being employed as bait. A small metre-long staff with a single or double crook in the end was also used as a fishing implement. With this little leister the men cast up fish on the ice with incredible dexterity. When the ice became thicker, this fishing

ICE-SIEVE.
One-eighth of the natural size.

B B 2

was entirely given up, while during the whole winter a species
of cod and another of grayling were taken in great quantity
in a lagoon situated nearer Behring's Straits. The coregonus is
also caught in the inland lakes, although, at least at this season
of the year, only in limited quantity.

On the morning of the 6th October, we saw from the vessel
an extraordinary procession moving forward on the ice. A
number of Chukches drew a dog-sledge on which lay a man.
At first we supposed it was a man who was very ill, and who
came to seek the help of the physician, but when the procession reached the vessel's side, the supposed invalid climbed
very nimbly up the ice-covered rope-ladder (our ice-stair was
not yet in order), stepped immediately with a confident air,
giving evidence of high rank, upon the half-deck, crossed himself,
saluted graciously, and gave us to know in broken Russian that
he was a man of importance in that part of the country. It

SMELT FROM THE CHUKCH PENINSULA.
Osmerus eperlanus Lin.
One-third of the natural size.

now appeared that we were honoured with a visit from the
representative of the Russian empire, WASSILI MENKA, the
starost among the reindeer-Chukches. He was a little dark
man, with a pretty worn appearance, clad in a white variegated
"pesk" of reindeer skin, under which a blue flannel shirt was
visible. In order immediately on his arrival to inspire us with
respect, and perhaps also in order not to expose his precious
life to the false Ran's treachery, he came to the vessel over the
yet not quite trustworthy ice, riding in a sledge that was drawn
not by dogs but by his men. On his arrival he immediately
showed us credentials of his rank, and various evidences of the
payment of tribute (or market tolls), consisting of some few red
and some white fox-skins, reckoning the former at 1 rouble 80
copecks, the latter at 40 copecks each.

He was immediately invited down to the gun-room, entertained after the best of our ability, and bothered with a number

of questions which he evidently understood with difficulty, and answered in very unintelligible Russian. He was in any case the first with whom some of us could communicate, at least in a way. He could neither read nor write. On the other hand, he could quickly comprehend a map which was shown him, and point out with great accuracy a number of the more remarkable places in north-eastern Siberia. Of the existence of the Russian emperor the first official of the region had no idea; on the other hand, he knew that a very powerful person had his home at Irkutsk. On us he conferred the rank of "Ispravnik" in the neighbouring towns. At first he crossed himself with much

WASSILI MENKA.
Starost among the Reindeer Chukches
After a photograph by L. Palander.

zeal before some photographs and copper-plate engravings in the gun-room, but he soon ceased when he observed that we did not do likewise. Menka was accompanied by two badly-clad natives with very oblique eyes, whom we took at first for his servants or slaves. Afterwards we found that they were owners of reindeer, who considered themselves quite as good as Menka himself, and further on we even heard one of them speak of Menka's claim to be a chief with a compassionate smile. Now, however, they were exceedingly respectful, and it was by them that Menka's gift of welcome, two reindeer roasts, was carried forward with a certain stateliness. As a return

present we gave him a woollen shirt and some parcels of tobacco.
Menka said that he should travel in a few days to Markova, a
place inhabited by Russians on the river Anadyr, in the neighbourhood of the old Anadyrsk. Although I had not yet given
up hope of getting free before winter, I wished to endeavour
to utilize this opportunity of sending home accounts of the
Vega's position, the state of matters on board, &c. An open
letter was therefore written in Russian, and addressed to his
Excellency the Governor-General at Irkutsk, with the request
that he would communicate its contents to his Majesty, King
Oscar. This was placed, along with several private sealed
letters between a couple of pieces of board, and handed over to
Menka with a request to give them to the Russian authorities
at Markova. At first it appeared as if Menka understood the
letter as some sort of further credentials for himself. For when
he landed he assembled, in the presence of some of us, a circle
of Chukches round himself, placed himself with dignity in their
midst, opened out the paper, but so that he had it upside down,
and read from it long sentences in Chukch to an attentive
audience, astonished at his learning. Next forenoon we had
another visit of the great and learned chief. New presents
were exchanged, and he was entertained after our best ability.
Finally he danced to the chamber-organ, both alone and
together with some of his hosts, to the great entertainment of
the Europeans and Asiatics present.

As the state of the ice was still unaltered, I did not neglect
the opportunity that now offered of making acquaintance with
the interior of the country. With pleasure, accordingly, I gave
Lieutenants Nordquist and Hovgaard permission to pay a visit
to Menka's encampment. They started on the morning of the
8th October. Lieut. Nordquist has given me the following
account of their excursion :—

" On Tuesday, the 8th October at 10 o'clock A.M. Lieut.
Hovgaard and I travelled from Pitlekaj in dog-sledges into
the interior in a S.S.E. direction. Hovgaard and I had
each a Chukch as driver. Menka had with him a servant, who
almost all the time ran before as guide. My comrade's sledge
which was heaviest, was drawn by ten dogs, mine by eight, and
Menka's, which was the smallest and in which he sat alone, by
five. In general the Chukches appear to reckon four or five
dogs sufficient for a sledge with one person.

" The *tundra*, with marshes and streams scattered over it
was during the first part of our way only gently undulating
but the farther we went into the interior of the country the
more uneven it became, and when, at 8 o'clock next morning
we reached the goal of our journey—Menka's brother's camp—

we found ourselves in a valley, surrounded by hills, some of which rose about 300 metres above their bases. A portion of the vegetable covering the *tundra* could still be distinguished through the thin layer of snow. The most common plants on the drier places were *Aira alpina* and *Poa alpina*; on the more low-lying places there grew Glyceria, Pedicularis, and *Ledum palustre*; everywhere we found *Petasites frigida* and a species of Salix. The latter grew especially on the slopes in great masses, which covered spots having an area of twenty to thirty square metres. At some places this bush rose to a height of about a metre above the ground. The prevailing rock appeared to be granite. The bottoms of the valleys were formed of post-Tertiary formations, which most frequently consisted of sand and rolled stones, as, for instance, was the case in the great valley in which Menka's brother's camp was pitched.

"When, on the morning of the 9th, we came to the camp there met us some of the principal Chukches. They saluted Menka in the Russian way, by kissing him first on both cheeks

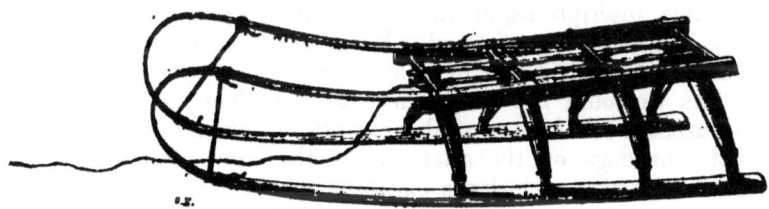

CHUKCH DOG-SLEDGE.

and then on the mouth. The Chukches, however, appear to be very averse to this ceremony, and scarcely ever touched each other with the mouth. Us they saluted in the common way, by stretching out the hand and bowing themselves. We then went into Menka's brother's tent, in front of which the whole inhabitants of the encampment were speedily assembled to look at us. The camp consisted of eighteen tents, pitched on both sides of a river which ran through the valley. The tents were inhabited by reindeer-Chukches, who carry on traffic between the Russians and a tribe living on the other side of Behring's Straits, whom they call *Yekargaules*. Between the tents we saw a great number of sledges, both empty and loaded. Some of these were light and low sledges for driving in, with runners bent upwards and backwards, others were heavier pack-sledges, made of stronger wood, with the runners not bent back. Some of the light sledges were provided with tilts of splints covered with reindeer-skins; others were completely covered, having an entrance only in front.

"The knives, axes, boring tools, &c., which I saw were of
iron and steel, and had evidently been obtained from Americans
or Russians. The household articles in Menka's brother's tent
consisted of some copper coffee-pots, which were used for
boiling water, a german-silver beaker with an English inscription, two teacups with saucers, flat wooden trays, and barrels.
The dress of the reindeer-Chukches is similar to that of the
coast-Chukches, only with this difference, that the former use
reindeer-skins exclusively, while the latter employ seal-skin in
addition. Some, on our arrival, put on blouses of variegated
cloth, probably of Russian manufacture. Among ornaments
may be mentioned glass-beads, strung on sinews, which were worn
in the ears or on the neck, chiefly by the women. These were
tattooed in the same way as those of the coast-Chukches. I saw
here, however, an old woman, who, besides the common tattooing
of the face, was tattooed on the shoulders, and another, who,
on the outside of the hands, had two parallel lines running
along the hand and an oblique line connecting them. The
men were not tattooed. Two of them carried crosses, with
Slavonic inscriptions, at the neck, others carried in the same
way forked pieces of wood. Whether these latter are to be
considered as their gods or as amulets I know not.

"As we could not obtain here the reindeer that we wished
to purchase on account of the expedition, we betook ourselves
with our dogs on the afternoon of the same day along with
Menka to his son-in-law's encampment, which we reached at
8 o'clock in the evening. We were received in a very friendly
way, and remained here over night. All the inhabitants of the
tent sleep together in the bedchamber of it, which is not
more than 2 to 2·4 metres long, 1·8 to 2 metres broad, and 1·2
to 1·5 metres high. Before they lie down they take supper.
Men and women wear during the night only a *cingulum pudicitiæ*, about fifteen centimetres broad, and are otherwise completely naked. In the morning the housewife rose first and
boiled a little flesh, which was then served in the bedchamber,
before its inmates had put on their clothes. She cut the meat
in slices in a tray, and distributed them afterwards. In the
morning we saw the Chukches catch and slaughter their reindeer.
Two men go into the herd, and when they have got sight of a
reindeer which they wish to have, they cast, at a distance of
nine or ten metres, a running noose over the animal's horns.
It now throws itself backwards and forwards in its attempts to
escape, and drags after it for some moments the man who holds
the noose. The other man in the meantime endeavours to
approach the reindeer, catches the animal by the horns and
throws it to the ground, killing it afterwards by a knife-stab
behind the shoulder. The reindeer is then handed over to the

women, who, by an incision in the side of the belly, take out
the entrails. The stomach is emptied of its contents, and is
then used to hold the blood. Finally the skin is taken off.
"About 10 o'clock A.M. we commenced our homeward journey.
At nightfall we sought to have a roof over our head in a
wretched Chukch tent on the shore of Lake Utschunutsch. It
was partly sunk in one of the small mounds which are found
here along the shore, and which are probably the remains of
old Onkilon dwellings. The present inhabitants, two old men
and an old woman, had their habitation arranged in the following way :—In the bottom of a cylindrical pit, one metre deep
and three and a half to four and a half metres in diameter, a
vertical pole was erected, against the upper end of which rested
a number of obliquely placed bars, rising from the edge of the
pit, which were covered with skins. The enclosure or bedchamber, peculiar to the Chukch tent, was not wanting here.
Otherwise the whole dwelling bore the stamp of poverty and
dirt. The food of the inmates appeared to be fish. Of this,
besides the fish we obtained here, the nets hanging in front of
the tent afforded evidence. Some clothes, an iron pot, two
wooden vessels, and a Shaman drum were the only things I
could discover in the tent.

"Next morning we continued our journey. On the other
side of Lake Utschunutsch we saw two dwellings, which
only consisted of boats turned upside down with some hides
drawn over them. The rest of the way we came past Najtskaj
and through Irgunnuk, where we were received in an exceedingly friendly fashion. By 7 o'clock in the evening of the 11th
October we were again on board the *Vega*."

From Lieutenant Hovgaard's report, which principally relates
to the topography of the region passed through, we make the
following extract relating to the endurance which the Chukches
and their dogs showed :—

"During our outward journey, which lasted twenty-one and a
half hours, Menka's attendant, the before-mentioned reindeer
owner, whom we at first took to be Menka's slave or servant,
ran without interruption before the sledges, and even when we
rested he was actively searching for the track, looking after the
dogs, &c. When we came to the camp he did not sleep, and,
notwithstanding, was as fresh during the following day's journey.
During the time he got no spirituous liquor, by express order of
Menka, who said that if he did he would not be able to continue
to run. Instead he chewed a surprising quantity of tobacco.
The dogs, during the whole time, were not an instant unyoked ;
in the mornings they lay half snowed up, and slept in front of
the sledges. We never saw the Chukches give them any food :

the only food they got was the frozen excrements of the fox and other animals, which they themselves snapped up in passing. Yet even on the last day no diminution in their power of draught was observable."

Nordquist brought with him, among other things, two reindeer, bought for a rouble and a half each. They were still very serviceable, though badly slaughtered. But the reindeer we purchased farther on in the winter were so poor that no one on board could persuade himself to eat them.

On the 18th October, by which time we believed that Menka would be already at Markova we were again visited by him and his son-in-law. He said he had no *akmimil* (fire-water) to keep holiday with, and now came to us to exchange three slaughtered reindeer for it. Our miscalculation with respect to the letters, which we hoped were long ago on their way to their destination, and my dislike to the mode of payment in question—I offered him, without success, half-imperials and metal rouble pieces instead of brandy—made his reception on this occasion less hearty, and he therefore left us soon. It was not until the 9th February, 1879, that we again got news from Menka by one of the Chukches, who had attended him the time before. The Chukch said that in ten days he had traversed the way between the *Vega's* winter haven and Markova, which would run to about ninety kilometres a day. According to his statement Menka had travelled with the letters to Yakutsk. The statement seemed very suspicious, and appeared afterwards to have been partly fabricated, or perhaps to have been misunderstood by us. But after our return to the world of newspapers we found that Menka had actually executed his commission. He, however, did not reach Anadyrsk until the $\frac{\text{7th March}}{\text{23rd February}}$. Thence the packet was sent to Irkutsk, arriving there on the $\frac{\text{10th May}}{\text{28th April}}$. The news reached Sweden by telegraph six days after, on the 16th May, just at a time when concern for the fate of the *Vega* was beginning to be very great, and the question of relief expeditions was seriously entertained.[1]

In order to relieve the apprehensions of our friends at home, it was, however, exceedingly important to give them some accounts of the position of the *Vega* during winter, and I therefore offered all the purchasing power which the treasures of guns, powder, ball, food, fine shirts, and even spirits, collected on board, could exert, in order to induce some natives to convey Lieutenants Nordquist and Bove to Markova or Nischni Kolymsk. The negotiations seemed at first to go on very well,

[1] The King of Sweden has since ordered a gold medal to be given to Wassili Menka in recognition of the fidelity with which he executed the commission of carrying our letters to a Russian post station.

an advance was demanded and given, but when the journey
should have commenced the Chukches always refused to start
on some pretext or other—now it was too cold, now too dark,
now there was no food for the dogs. The negotiations had thus
no other result than to make us acquainted with one of the
few less agreeable sides of the Chukches' disposition, namely,
the complete untrustworthiness of these otherwise excellent
savages, and their peculiar idea of the binding force of an
agreement.

The plans of travel just mentioned, however, led to Lieutenant Nordquist making an excursion with dog-sledges in order
to be even with one of the natives, who had received an advance
for driving him to Markova, but had not kept his promise.
Of this journey Lieutenant Nordquist gives the following
account :—

"On the 5th December, at 7.50 A.M., I started with a dog-
sledge for the village Pidlin, lying on Kolyutschin Bay. I was
driven by the Chukch Auango from Irgunnuk. He had a small,
light sledge, provided with runners of whalebone, drawn by six
dogs, of which the leader was harnessed before the other five,
which were fastened abreast in front of the sledge, each with its
draught belt. The dogs were weak and ill managed, and therefore went so slowly that I cannot estimate their speed at more
than two or three English miles an hour. As the journey both
thither and back lasted eight to nine hours, the distance between
Pitlekaj and Pidlin may be about twenty-five English miles.

"Pidlin and Kolyutschin Island are the only inhabited places
on Kolyutschin Bay. At the former place there are four tents,
pitched on the eastern shore of the bay, the number of the
inhabitants being a little over twenty persons. I was received
in front of the tents by the population of the village and
carried to the tent, which was inhabited by Chepcho, who now
promised to go with me in February to Anadyrsk. My host
had a wife and three children. At night the children were
completely undressed ; the adults had short trousers on, the
man of tanned skin, the woman of cloth. In the oppressive
heat, which was kept up by two train-oil lamps burning the
whole night, it was difficult to sleep even in the heavy reindeer-
skin dresses. Yet they covered themselves with reindeer skins.
Besides the heat there was a fearful stench—the Chukches
obeyed the calls of nature within the bedchamber—which I
could not stand without going out twice to get fresh air. When
we got up next morning our hostess served breakfast in a flat
tray, containing first seals' flesh and fat, with a sort of sourkrout of fermented willow-leaves, then seals' liver, and finally
seals' blood—all frozen.

"Among objects of ethnographical interest I saw, besides the Shaman drum which was found in every tent, and was not regarded with the superstitious dread which I have often observed elsewhere, a bundle of amulets fastened with a small thong, a wolf's skull, which was also hung up by a thong, the skin together with the whole cartilaginous portion of a wolf's nose and a flat stone. The amulets consisted of wooden forks, four to five centimetres long, of the sort which we often see the Chukches wear on the .breast. My host said that such an amulet worn round the neck was a powerful means of preventing disease. The wolf's skull which I had already got, he took back, because his four- or five-year-old son would need it in making choice of a wife. What part it played in this I did not however ascertain.

"While my driver harnessed the dogs for the journey home, I had an opportunity of seeing some little girls dance, which they did in the same way as that in which I had seen girls dance at Pitlekaj and Yinretlen. Two girls then place themselves either right opposite to or alongside of each other. In the former case they often lay their hands on each other's shoulders, bend by turns to either side, sometimes leap with the feet held together and wheel round, while they sing or rather grunt the measure.

"The journey home was commenced at eight o'clock in the morning. In the course of it my driver sang Chukch songs. These are often only imitations of the cries of animals or improvisations without any distinct metre or rhythm, and very little variation in the notes; only twice I thought I could distinguish a distinct melody. In the afternoon my driver told me the Chukch names of several stars. At five o'clock in the afternoon I reached the *Vega*."

On the 10th October, the new ice at many places in the neighbourhood of the vessel was still so weak that it was impossible to walk upon it, and blue-water skies at the horizon indicated that there were still considerable stretches of open water in the neighbourhood. But the drift-ice round about us lay so rock-fast, that I could already take solar altitudes from the deck of the vessel with a mercurial horizon. In order to ascertain the actual state of the case with reference to the open water, excursions were undertaken on the 13th October, in different directions. Dr. Kjellman could then, from the rocky promontory at Yinretlen, forty-two metres high, see large open spaces in the sea to the northward. Dr. Almquist went right out over the ice, following the track of Chukches, who had gone to catch seals. He travelled about twenty kilometres over closely packed drift-ice fields, without reaching open water, and found the newly frozen ice, with which the pieces of drift-ice were bound together, still everywhere unbroken. The Chukches, who visited the vessel in dog-sledges on the 28th October, informed us, however, that the sea a little to the east of us was still completely open.

On the 15th October, the hunter Johnsen returned from a hunting expedition quite terrified. He informed us that during his wanderings on the *tundra*, he had found a murdered man and brought with him, with the idea that, away here in the land of the Chukches, similar steps ought to be taken as in those lands which are blessed by a well-ordered judiciary, as *species facti*, some implements lying beside the dead man, among which was a very beautiful lance, on whose blade traces of having been inlaid in gold could still be discovered. Fortunately he had come with these things through the Chukch camp unobserved. From the description which was given me, however, I was able immediately to come to the conclusion that the question here was not of any murder, but of a dead man laid out on the *tundra*. I requested Dr. Almquist to visit the place, in order that he might make a more detailed examination. He confirmed my conjecture. As wolves, foxes, and ravens had already torn the corpse to pieces, the doctor considered that he, too, might take his share, and therefore brought home with him from his excursion, an object carefully wrapped up and concealed among the hunting equipment, namely, the Chukch's head. It was immediately sunk to the sea-bottom, where it remained for a couple of weeks to be skeletonised by the crustacea swarming there, and it now has its number in the collections brought home by the *Vega*. This sacrilege was never detected by the Chukches, and probably the wolves got the blame of it, as nearly every spring it was seen that the corpse, which had been laid out during autumn, lost its head during winter. It was, perhaps, more difficult to explain the disappearance of the lance, but of this, too, the maws of the wolves might well bear the blame.

Our hunters now made hunting excursions in different directions, but the supply of game was scanty. The openings in the ice probably swarmed with seals, but they were too distant, and without a boat it was impossible to carry on any hunting there. Not a single Polar bear now appeared to be visible in the neighbourhood, although bears' skulls are found at several places on the beach, and this animal appears to play a great part in the imagination of the natives, to judge of the many figures of bears among the bone carvings I purchased from the Chukches. The natives often have a small strip of bear's skin on the seat of their sledges, but I have not seen any whole bear's skin here ; perhaps the animal is being exterminated on the north coast of Siberia. Our wintering, therefore,

will not enrich Arctic literature with any new bear stories—
a very sensible difficulty for the writer himself. Wolves, on the
other hand, occur on the *tundra* in sufficient abundance, even if
one or other of the wolves found in mist and drifting snow,
and saluted with shot, turned out, on a critical determination of
species, to be our own dogs. At least, this was the case with the
"wolf," that inveigled one of the crew into shooting a ball one
dark night right through the thermometer case, fortunately
without injuring the instruments, and with no other result than
that he had afterwards to bear an endless number of jokes from

CHUKCH BONE-CARVINGS.
The two largest figures represent bears.

his comrades on account of his wolf-hunt. Foxes, white, red,
and black, also occurred here in great numbers, but they were
at that season difficult to get at, and besides they had perhaps
withdrawn from the coast. Hares, on the other hand, maintained
themselves during the whole winter at Yinretlen, by day partly
out on the ice, partly on the cape, by night in the neighbourhood
of the tents. Sweepings and offal from the proceeds of the
chase had there produced a vegetation, which, though concealed
by snow, yielded to the hares in winter a more abundant supply

of food than the barren *tundra.* It was remarkable that the
hares were allowed to live between the tents and in their neighbourhood without being disturbed by the score of lean and
hungry dogs belonging to the village. When farther into the
winter for the sake of facilitating the hare-hunting I had a hut
erected for Johnsen the hunter, he chose as the place for it
the immediate neighbourhood of the village, declaring that the
richest hunting-ground in the whole neighbourhood was just
there. The shooters stated that part of the hares became
snow-blind in spring. The hares here are larger than with us,
and have exceedingly delicious flesh.

HARES FROM CHUKCH LAND.

On our arrival most of the birds had already left these
regions, so inhospitable in winter, or were seen high up in the
air in collected flocks, flying towards the south entrance of
Behring's Straits. Still on the 19th October an endless procession of birds was seen drawing towards this region, but by
the 3rd November it was noted, as something uncommon, that
a gull settled on the refuse heaps in the neighbourhood of the
vessel. It resembled the ivory gull, but had a black head.
Perhaps it was the rare *Larus Sabinii,* of which a drawing has
been given above.[1] All the birds which passed us came from
the north-west, that is, from the north coast of Siberia, the
New Siberian Islands or Wrangel Land. Only the mountain

[1] See p. 93.

owl, a species of raven and the ptarmigan wintered in the region, the last named being occasionally snowed up.

The ptarmigan here is not indeed so plump and good as the Spitzbergen ptarmigan during winter, but in any case provided us with an always welcome, if scanty change from the tiresome preserved meat. When some ptarmigan were shot, they were therefore willingly saved up by the cook, along with the hares, for festivals. For in order to break the monotony on board an opportunity was seldom neglected that offered itself for holding festivities. Away there on the coast of the Chukch peninsula there were thus celebrated with great conscientiousness during the winter of 1878-9, not only our own birthdays but also those of King Oscar, King Christian and King Humbert, and of the Emperor Alexander. Every day a newspaper was distributed, for the day indeed, but for a past year. In addition we numbered among our diversions constant intercourse with the natives, and frequent visits to the neighbouring villages, driving in dog-sledges, a sport which would have been very enjoyable if the dogs of the natives had not been so exceedingly poor and bad, and finally industrious reading and zealous studies, for which I had provided the expedition with an extensive library, intended both for the scientific men and officers, and for the crew, numbering with the private stock of books nearly a thousand volumes.

All this time of course the purely scientific work was not neglected. In the first rank among these stood the meteorological and magnetical observations, which from the 1st November were made on land every hour. However fast the ice lay around the vessel it was impossible to get on it a sufficiently stable base for the magnetical variation instrument. The magnetical observatory was therefore erected on land of the finest building material any architect has had at his disposal, namely, large parallelopipeds of beautiful blue-coloured ice-blocks. The building was therefore called by the Chukches *Tintinyaranga* (the ice-house), a name which was soon adopted by the *Vega* men too. As mortar, the builder, Palander, used snow mixed with water, and the whole was covered with a roof of boards. But as after a time it appeared that the storm made its way through the joints and that these were gradually growing larger in consequence of the evaporation of the ice so that the drifting snow could find an entrance, the whole house had a sail drawn over it. As supports of the three variation instruments large blocks of wood were used, whose lower ends were sunk in pits, which, with great trouble, were excavated in the frozen ground, and then, when the block supports were placed, were filled with sand mixed with water. The ice-house was a spacious observatory, well-fitted for its

purpose in every respect. It had but one defect, the temperature was always at an uncomfortably low point. As no iron
could be used in the building, and we had no copper-stove with
us, we could not have any fireplace there. We endeavoured,
indeed, to use a copper fireplace, that had been intended for
sledge journeys, for heating, but only with the result that the
observatory was like to have gone to pieces. We succeeded
little better when we discovered farther on in the winter, while
trimming the hold, a forgotten cask of bear's oil. We considered this *find* a clear indication that instead of a stove fired
with wood we should, according to the custom of the Polar
races, use oil-lamps to mitigate the severe cold which deprived

THE OBSERVATORY AT PITLEKAJ.
After a drawing by O. Nordquist.

our stay in Tintinyaranga of part of its pleasure. But this mode
of firing proved altogether impracticable. The fumes of the
oil smelled worse than those of the charcoal, and the result of
this experiment was none other than that the splendid crystals
of ice, with which the roof and walls of the ice-house were
gradually clothed, were covered with black soot. Firing with
oil was abandoned, and the oil presented to our friends at
Yinretlen, who just then were complaining loudly that they
had no other fuel than wood.

Besides the nine scientific men and officers of the *Vega*, the

c c

engineer Nordström and the seaman Lundgren took part in the magnetical and meteorological observations. Every one had his watch of six hours, five of which were commonly passed in the ice-house. To walk from the vessel to the observatory, distant a kilometre and a half, with the temperature under the freezing point of mercury, or, what was much worse, during storm, with the temperature at − 36°, remain in the observatory for five hours in a temperature of − 17°, and then return to the vessel, commonly against the wind—for it came nearly always from the north or north-west—was dismal enough. None of us, however, suffered any harm from it. On the contrary, it struck me as if this compulsory interruption to our monotonous life on board and the long-continued stay in the open air had a refreshing influence both on body and soul.

In the neighbourhood of the ice-house the thermometer case was erected, and farther on in the winter there were built in the surrounding snowdrifts, two other observatories, not however of ice, but of snow, in the Greenland snow-building style. Our depôt of provisions was also placed in the neighbourhood, and at a sufficient distance from the magnetical observatory there was a large wooden chest, in which the Remington guns, which were carried for safety in excursions from the vessel, and other iron articles which the observer had with him, were placed before he entered the observatory.

The building of Tintinyaranga was followed by the Chukches with great interest. When they saw that we did not intend to live there, but that rare, glancing metal instruments were set up in it, and that a wonderfully abundant flood of light in comparison with their tent illumination was constantly maintained inside with a kind of light quite unknown to them (stearine candles and photogen lamps) a curious uneasiness began to prevail among them, which we could not quiet with the language of signs mixed with a Chukch word or two, to which our communications with the natives were at that time confined. Even farther on in the year, when an efficient though word-poor international language had gradually been formed between us, they made inquiries on this point, yet with considerable indifference. All sensible people among them had evidently already come to the conclusion that it was profitless trouble to seek a reasonable explanation of all the follies which the strange foreigners, richly provided with many earthly gifts but by no means with practical sense, perpetrated. In any case it was with a certain amazement and awe that they, when they exceptionally obtained permission, entered one by one through the doors in order to see the lamps burn and to peep into the tubes. Many times even a dog-team that had come a long way stopped for a few moments at the ice-house to satisfy the owner's curiosity, and on two occasions in very bad drifting weather we were compelled to give shelter to a wanderer who had gone astray.

When this ice-house was ready and hourly observations began in it, life on board took the stamp which it afterwards retained in the course of the winter. In order to give the reader an idea of our every-day life, I shall reproduce here the spirited sketch of a day on the *Vega*, which Dr. Kjellman gave in one of his home letters:—

" It is about half-past eight in the morning. He whose watch has expired has returned after five hours' stay in the ice-house, where the temperature during the night has been about −16°. His account of the weather is good enough. There are only thirty-two degrees of cold, it is half-clear, and, to be out of the ordinary, there is no wind. Breakfast is over. Cigars, cigarettes, and pipes are lighted, and the gun-room *personnel* go up on deck for a little exercise and fresh air, for below it is confined and close. The eye rests on the desolate, still faintly-lighted land-scape, which is exactly the same as it was yesterday; a white plain in all directions, across which a low, likewise white, chain of hillocks or *torosses* here and there raises itself, and over which some ravens, with feeble wing-strokes, fly forward, searching for something to support life with. ' Metschinko Orpist,' ' mets-chinko Okerpist,' ' metschinko Kellman,' &c., now sounds every-where on the vessel and from the ice in its neighbourhood. ' Orpist ' represents Nordquist, ' Okerpist ' again Stuxberg. It is the Chukches' morning salutation to us. To-day the com-paratively fine weather has drawn out a larger crowd than usual, thirty to forty human beings, from tender sucking babes to grey old folks, men as well as women; the latter in the word of salutation replacing the *tsch*-sound with an exceedingly soft caressing *ts* sound. That most of them have come driving is shown by the equipages standing in the neighbourhood of the vessel. They consist of small, low, narrow, light sledges, drawn by four to ten or twelve dogs. The sledges are made of small pieces of wood and bits of reindeer horn, held together by seal-skin straps. As runner-shoes thin plates of the ribs of the whale are used. The dogs, sharp-nosed, long-backed, and exces-sively dirty, have laid themselves to rest, curled together in the snow.

" The salutation is followed almost immediately to-day as on preceding days by some other words : ' Ouinga mouri kauka,' which may be translated thus : ' I am so hungry ; I have no food ; give me a little bread ! ' They suffer hunger now, the poor beings. Seal flesh, their main food, they cannot with the best will procure for the time. The only food they can get consists of fish (two kinds of cod), but this is quite too poor diet for them they have fallen off since we first met with them.

"Soon we are all surrounded by our Chukch acquaintances. The daily market begins. They have various things to offer, which they know to be of value to us, as weapons, furs, ornaments, playthings, fish, bones of the whale, algæ, vegetables, &c. For all this only 'kauka' is now asked. To-day the supply of whales' bones is large, in consequence of our desire, expressed on previous days, to obtain them. One has come with two vertebræ, one with a rib or some fragments of it, one with a shoulder-blade. They are not shy in laying heavy loads on their dogs.

"After the close of the promenade and the traffic with the natives, the gun-room *personnel* have begun their labours. Some keep in their cabins, others in the gun-room itself. The magnetical and meteorological observations made the day before are transcribed and subjected to a preliminary working-out, the natural history collections are examined and looked over, studies and authorship are prosecuted. The work is now and then interrupted by conversation partly serious, partly jocular. From the engine-room in the neighbourhood we hear the blows of hammers and the rasping of files. In the 'tweendecks, pretty well heated, but not very well lighted, some of the crew are employed at ordinary ship's work ; and in the region of the kitchen the cook is just in the midst of his preparations for dinner. He is in good humour as usual, but perhaps grumbles a little at the "mosucks"(a common name on board for the Chukches), who will not give him any peace by their continual cries for ' mimil' (water).

" The forenoon passes in all quietness and stillness. Immediately after noon nearly all the gun-room people are again on deck, promenading backwards and forwards. It is now very lively. It is the crew's meal-time. The whole crowd of Chukches are collected at the descent to their apartment, the lower deck. One soup basin after the other comes up ; they are immediately emptied of their contents by those who in the crowd and confusion are fortunate enough to get at them. Bread and pieces of meat and bits of sugar are distributed assiduously, and disappear with equal speed. Finally, the cook himself appears with a large kettle, containing a very large quantity of meat soup, which the Chukches like starving animals throw themselves upon, baling into them with spoons, empty preserve tins, and above all with the hands. Notwithstanding the exceedingly severe cold a woman here and there has uncovered one arm and half her breast in order not to be embarrassed by the wide reindeer-skin sleeve in her attempts to get at the contents of the kettle. The spectacle is by no means a pleasant one.

AN EVENING IN THE GUN-ROOM OF THE "VEGA" DURING THE WINTERING.

"By three o'clock it begins to grow dark, and one after the other of our guests depart, to return, the most of them, in the morning. Now it is quiet and still. About six the crew have finished their labours and dispose of the rest of the day as they please. Most of them are occupied with reading during the evening hours. When supper has been served at half-past seven in the gun-room, he who has the watch in the ice-house from nine to two next morning prepares for the performance of his disagreeable duty; the rest of the gun-room *personnel* are assembled there, and pass the evening in conversation, play, light reading, &c. At ten every one retires, and the lamps are extinguished. In many cabins, however, lights burn till after midnight.

"Such was in general our life on the *Vega*. One day was very like another. When the storm howled, the snow drifted, and the cold became too severe, we kept more below deck; when the weather was finer we lived more in the open air, often paying visits to the observatory in the ice-house, and among the Chukches living in the neighbourhood, or wandering about to come upon, if possible, some game."

The snow which fell during winter consisted more generally of small simple snow-crystals or ice-needles, than of the beautiful snow-flakes whose grand kaleidoscopic forms the inhabitants of the north so often have an opportunity of admiring. Already with a gentle wind and with a pretty clear atmosphere the lower strata of the atmosphere were full of these regular ice-needles, which refracted the rays of the sun, so as to produce parhelia and halos. Unfortunately however these were never so completely developed as the halos which I saw in 1873 during the sledge-journey round North-east Land on Spitzbergen; but I believed that even now I could confirm the correctness of the observation I then made, that the representation which is generally given of this beautiful phenomenon, in which the halo is delineated as a collection of regular circles, is not correct, but that it forms a very involved system of lines, extended over the whole vault of heaven, for the most part coloured on the sun-side and uncoloured on the opposite side, of the sort shown in the accompanying drawings taken from the account of the Spitzbergen Expedition of 1872-73.

Another very beautiful phenomenon, produced by the refraction of the solar rays by the ice-needles, which during winter were constantly mixed with the atmospheric strata lying nearest the surface of the earth, was that the mountain heights to the south of the *Vega* in a certain light appeared as if feathered with fire-clouds. In clear sunshine and a high wind we frequently saw, as it were, a glowing pillar of vapour arise obliquely from the summits of the mountains, giving them the appearance of volcanos, which throw out enormous columns of smoke, flame-coloured by the reflection from the glowing lava streams in the depths of the crater.

A blue water-sky was still visible out to sea, indicating that open water was to be found there. I therefore sent Johnsen the hunter over the ice on the 18th December to see how it was. In three-quarters of an hour's walking from the vessel he found an extensive opening, recently covered with thin, blue, newly frozen ice. A fresh northerly breeze blew at the time, and by it the drift-ice fields were forced together with such speed, that

REFRACTION-HALO.
Seen on Spitzbergen in May 1873, simultaneously with the Reflection-halo delineated on the following page.

Johnsen supposed that in a couple of hours the whole lead would be completely closed.

In such openings in Greenland white whales and other small whales are often enclosed by hundreds, the natives thus having an opportunity of making in a few hours a catch which would be sufficient for their support during the whole winter, indeed for years, if the idea of *saving* ever entered into the imagination of the savage. But here in a region where the pursuit of the whale is more productive than in any other sea, no such occurrence has happened. During the whole of our stay on the coast of the Chukch country we did not see a single whale. On the

other hand, masses of whales' bones were found thrown up on
the beach. At first I did not bestow much attention upon
them, thinking they were the bones of whales that had been
killed during the recent whale-fishing period. I soon found
however that this could not have been the case. For the bones
had evidently been washed out of the sandy dune running along
the beach, which had been deposited at a time when the present
coast lay ten to twenty metres below the surface of the sea,
thus hundreds or thousands of years ago, undoubtedly before
the time when the north coast of Asia was first inhabited by
man. The dune sand is, as recently exposed profiles show, quite
free from other kitchen-midden remains than those which occur

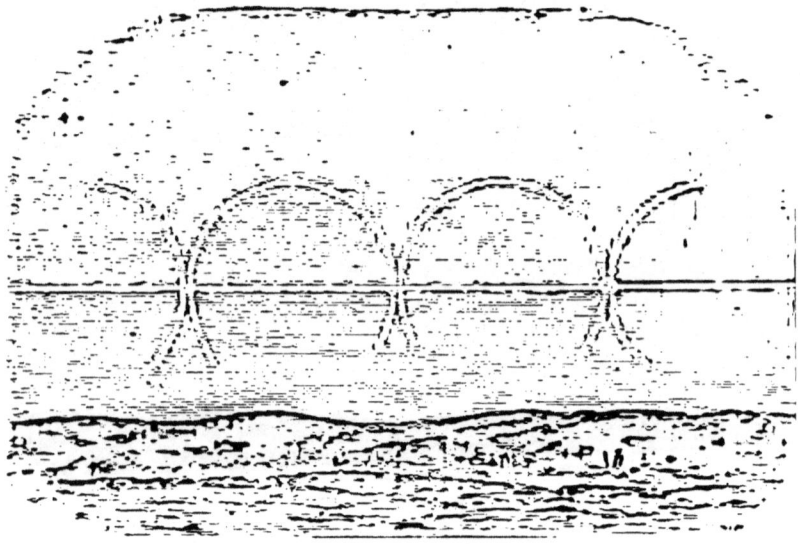

REFLECTION-HALO.

Seen simultaneously with the Refraction-halo delineated on the preceding page, in the part
of the sky opposite the sun.

upon its surface. The whales' bones in question were thus
subfossil. Their number was so great, that in the systematic
examination of the beach in the immediate neighbourhood of
the vessel, which I undertook during spring with the assistance
of Dr. Kjellman and half a dozen of the sailors, thirty neck-
bones and innumerable other bones of the whale were found in
a stretch of from four to five kilometres. Of course masses of
bones are still concealed in the sand; and a large number of
lower jaw-bones, ribs, shoulder-blades, and vertebræ had been
used for runner-shoes, tent-frames, spades, picks and other
implements. A portion, after being exposed for several years to

the action of the air, had undergone decay.   The bones are therefore found in greatest number at those places where the sand of
the dune has been recently carried away by the spring floods or
by the furious winds which prevail here, and which easily gain
the ascendency over the dry sand, bound together only by
widely scattered Elymus-stalks.   The largest crania belonged to
a species nearly allied to the *Balæna mysticetus.*   Crania of a
species of Rachianectes are also found along with some bones of .
smaller varieties of the whale.   No complete skeleton however
has been found, but we brought home with us so large a quantity
of the loose bones that the collection of whales' bones alone
would have formed a full cargo for a small vessel.   These bones
will be delineated and described by Professor A. W. MALM in
The Scientific Work of the Vega Expedition.   Special attention
was drawn to a skeleton, belonging to the *Balæna mysticetus,* by
its being still partially covered with skin, and by deep red,
almost fresh, flesh adhering to those parts of it which were
frozen fast in the ground.   This skeleton lay at a place where
the dune sand had recently been washed away and the coarse

SECTION OF THE BEACH STRATA AT PITLEKAJ.
1. Hard frozen coarse sand. 2. The sea. 3. Beach of fine dry sand with masses of bones of the
whale. 4. Coast-lagoon.

underlying sand uncovered, the whale-*mummy* also I suppose
coming to light at the same time.   That the whale in question
had not stranded in the memory of man the Chukches assured
me unanimously.   In such a case we have here a proof that
even portions of the flesh of gigantic sea-animals have been
protected against putrefaction in the frozen soil of Siberia—a
parallel to the mammoth-*mummies,* though from a considerably
more recent period.
     Christmas Eve was celebrated in the usual northern fashion.
We had indeed, neglected, as in the Expedition of 1872-73, to
take with us any Christmas tree.   But instead of it Dr. Kjellman
prevailed on our Chukch friends to bring with dog-sledges
willow-bushes from the valleys lying beyond the mountains to
the south.   By means of these a bare driftwood stem was
converted into a luxuriant, branchy tree which, to replace the
verdure, was clothed with variegated strips of paper, and planted
in the 'tweendecks, which after our enclosure in the ice had
been arranged as a working-room, and was now set in order for

the Christmas festivities, and richly and tastefully ornamented with flags. A large number of small wax-lights, which we had brought with us for the special purpose, were fixed in the Christmas tree, together with about two hundred Christmas boxes purchased or presented to us before our departure. At six o'clock in the afternoon all the officers and crew assembled in the 'tweendecks, and the drawing of lots began, now and then interrupted by a thundering polka round the peculiar Christmas tree. At supper neither Christmas ale nor ham was wanting. And later in the evening there made their appearance in the 'tweendecks five punchbowls, which were emptied with songs and toasts for King and Fatherland, for the objects of the Expedition, for its officers and men, for the families at home, for relatives and friends, and finally for those who decked and arranged the Christmas tree, who were the sailors C. Lundgren, and O. Hansson, and the firemen O. Ingelsson and C. Carlström. The other festivals were also celebrated in the best way, and at midnight before New Year's Day the new year was shot in with sharp explosive-shell firing from the rifled cannon of the Vega, and a number of rockets thrown up from the deck.

CHAPTER XI.

Hope of release at the new year—Bove's excursion to the open water—Mild weather and renewed severe cold—Mercury frozen—Popular lectures—Brusewitz's excursion to Najtskaj—Another despatch of letters home—The natives' accounts of the state of the ice on the coast of Chukch Land—The Chukches carry on traffic between Arctic America and Siberia—Excursions in the neighbourhood of winter quarters—The weather during spring—The melting of the snow—The aurora—The arrival of the migratory birds—The animal world of Chukch Land —Noah Elisej's relief expedition—A remarkable fish—The country clear of snow—Release—The North-East Passage achieved.

THE new year came in with a faint hope of release. For since the north and north-west winds that had prevailed almost constantly towards the close of December had given place to winds from the east and south, considerable " clearings " were again formed out at sea, and the Chukches again began to say that the ice would drift away, so that the vessel would be able to continue her voyage; a prediction which they always ended with a declaration, expressed both by words and gestures, that they would then bitterly lament, which they would also have had sufficient reason to do, considering the very friendly way in which they were treated by all on board the Vega, both officers and men.

On New Year's Day, in order to see the state of the ice farther out to sea, Lieut. Bove, accompanied by the hunter Johnsen, again made an excursion to the open water. Of this he gave the following account:—

" I left the vessel on the forenoon of 1st January and reached the open water after four hours' steady walking. The deep loose snow made walking very fatiguing, and three rows of *torosses* also contributed to this, mainly in consequence of the often snow-covered cracks, which crossed the ice-sheet in their neighbourhood. One of the *torosses* was ten metres high. The size of the blocks of ice, which were here heaped on each other, showed how powerful the forces were which had caused the formation of the *torosses*. These ice ramparts now afford a much needed protection to the *Vega's* winter haven. About halfway between the open water and the vessel the way was crossed by cracks running from east to west, and clearly indicating that the opening in the ice would have extended to the distance of a kilometre from the vessel, if the violent storm in December had lasted twelve hours longer. The *Vega* would thereby have been in great danger. The edge of the ice towards the open water was evenly cut, as with an immense knife, and was so strong that one could walk along it as on a rock. Even from the top of a five-metre-high ice-rampart no boundary of the open water could be seen to the north-east or north. Partly from this, partly from the extension of the water-sky in this direction, I draw the conclusion that the breadth of the open water was at least thirty-five kilometres. The 'clearing' was bounded on the east by an ice-rampart running north, which at a distance of nine or ten kilometres appeared to bend to the east. Possibly farther to the east beyond this ice-rampart there was another open water basin. The depth at the edge of the ice was twenty-one metres, the temperature of the water 2° C. The water ran at a considerable speed right out from the coast (*i.e.* from S S.E.). As it ran here nearly in a straight line, the current may have been a tidal one. The open water swarmed with seals, according to Johnsen both bearded and rough. Neither Polar bears, walruses, nor birds were seen."

Lieut. Bove's report confirmed me in my supposition that the open water, as towards the end of January 1873 at Mussel Bay might possibly extend as far as our anchorage and open for us the way to Behring's Straits, in which case we could not refrain from continuing our voyage, however unpleasant and dangerous it might be at this season of the year. The Chukches also declared repeatedly that the open water in January would continue for a considerable time, and in expectation of this got their simple fishing implements ready. But both they and we were disappointed in our expectation. The *Vega's* ice-fetters remained undisturbed, and the blue border at the horizon grew less and again disappeared. This caused so great a want of food, and above all of train oil, among the natives, that all the inhabitants of Pitlekaj, the village nearest to us, were compelled to remove to the eastward, notwithstanding that in order to mitigate the scarcity a considerable quantity of food was served out daily at the vessel.

It appears, however, as if an actual experience from the preceding year had been the ground of the Chukches' weather

THE OPEN WATER.

prediction. For on the 6th February a south-east wind began to blow, and the severe cold at once ceased. The temperature rose for a few hours to and even above the freezing-point. A water-sky was again formed along the horizon of the ice from north-east to north, and from the heights at the coast there was seen an extensive opening in the ice-fields, which a little east of Irgunnuk nearly reached the shore. Some kilometres farther east even the shore itself was free of ice, and from the hills our sailors thought they saw a heavy sea in the blue water border which bounded the circle of vision. If this was not an illusion caused by the unequal heating and oscillatory motion of the lower stratum of the atmosphere, the open water may have been of great extent. Perhaps the statement of the natives was correct, that it extended as far as Behring's Straits. But we could not now place complete reliance on their statements, since we had rewarded with extra treating some predictions, relating to ice and weather, that were favourable to us. Even between the vessel's anchorage and the land various cracks` had been formed, through which the sea-water had forced its way under the snow, and in which some of us got cold foot or leg baths during our walks to and from the land.

The Chukches at Irgunnuk were now successful in killing a Polar bear and seventy seals, of which some were ostentatiously set up in rows, along with frozen slices of blubber, along the outer walls of the tents, and others were laid down in the blubber cellars, which were soon filled to overflowing. At

THE ENCAMPMENT PITLEKAJ ABANDONED BY ITS INHABITANTS ON THE 18TH FEBRUARY, 1879.
After a drawing by O. Nordquist.

Yinretlen, the encampment nearer us, the hunters on the other hand had obtained only eight seals. Gladness and want of care for the morrow at all events prevailed here also, and our skin-clad friends availed themselves of the opportunity to exhibit a self-satisfied disdain of the simple provisions from the *Vega*, which the day before they had begged for with gestures so pitiful, and on which they must, in a day or two, again depend. The children, who had fallen off during recent weeks, if not in comparison with European children, at least with well-fed Chukch ones, began speedily to regain their former condition, and likewise the older people. Begging ceased for some days, but the vessel's deck still formed a favourite rendezvous for crowds of men, women, and children. Many passed here the greater part of the day, cheerful and gay in a temperature of −40° C., gossiped, helped a little, but always only a little, at the work on board, and so on. The mild weather, the prospect of our getting free, and of an abundant fishing for the Chukches, however, soon ceased. The temperature again sank below the freezing-point, that is *of mercury*, and the sea froze so far out from the shore that the Chukches could no longer carry on any fishing. Instead we saw them one morning come marching, like prisoners on an Egyptian or Assyrian monument, in goose-march over the ice toward the vessel, each with a burden on his shoulder, of whose true nature, while they were at a distance, we endeavoured in vain to form a guess. It was pieces of ice, not particularly large, which they, self-satisfied, cheerful and happy at their new hit, handed over to the cook to get from him in return some of the *kauka* (food) they some days before had despised.

The first time the temperature of the air sank under the freezing-point of mercury, was in January. It now became necessary to use instead of the mercury the spirit thermometers, which in expectation of the severe cold had been long ago hung up in the thermometer case. When mercury freezes in a common thermometer, it contracts so much that the column of mercury suddenly sinks in the tube, or if it is short, goes wholly into the ball. The position of the column is therefore no measure of the actual degree of cold when the freezing takes place. The reading of −89°, or even of −150°, which' at a time when it was not yet known that mercury could at a low temperature assume the solid form, was made on a mercurial thermometer in the north of Sweden,[1] and which at the time occasioned various discussions and doubts as to the trustworthiness of the observer, was certainly quite correct, and may be repeated at any time by cooling mercury under its freezing-point in a thermometer of sufficient length divided into degrees under 0°. The freezing of mercury[2] takes place from below upwards,

---

[1] And. Hellant, *Anmärkningar om en helt ovanlig köld i Torne* (*Remarks on a Quite Unusual Cold in Torne*), Vet.-akad. Handl. 1759, p. 314, and 1760, p. 312. In the latter paper Hellant himself shows that the column of mercury in a strongly cooled thermometer for a few moments *sinks farther* when the ball is rapidly heated. This is caused by the expansion of the glass when it is warmed before the heat has had time to communicate itself to the quicksilver in the ball, and therefore of course can happen only at a temperature above the freezing-point of mercury.

[2] That mercury solidifies in cold was discovered by some academicians in St. Petersburg on the 25th December, 1759, and caused at the time a great sensation, because by this discovery various erroneous ideas were rooted out which the chemists had inherited from the alchemists, and which were based on the supposed property of mercury of being at the same time a metal and a fluid.

the frozen metal as being heavier sinking down in that portion which is still fluid. If when it is half frozen the fluid be poured away from the frozen portion, we obtain groups of crystals, composed of small octohedrons, grouped together by the edges of the cube. None of our mercurial thermometers suffered any damage, nor was there any alteration of the position of the freezing-point in them from the mercury having frozen in them and again become fluid.

During the severe cold the ice naturally became thicker and thicker; and by the continual northerly winds still higher *torosses* were heaped up round the vessel, and larger and larger snow masses were collected between it and the land, and on the heights along the coast. All hopes or fears of an early release were again given up, and a perceptible dulness began to make itself felt after the bustle and festivities of the Christmas holidays. Instead there was now arranged a series of popular lectures which were held in the lower deck, and treated of the history of the North-East Passage, the first circumnavigations of the globe, the Austrian-Hungarian Expedition, the changes of the earth's surface, the origin of man, the importance of the leaf to the plants, &c. It became both for the officers and scientific men and the crew a little interruption to the monotony of the Arctic winter life, and the lecturer could always be certain of finding his little auditory all present and highly interested. Some slight attempts at musical evening entertainments were also made, but these failed for want of musical instruments and musical gifts among the *Vega* men. We had among us no suitable director of theatrical representations after the English-Arctic pattern, and even if we had had, I fear that the director would have found it very difficult to gather together the dramatic talents requisite for his entertainment.

On the 17th February Lieutenant Brusewitz made an excursion to Najtskaj, of which he gives the following account:—

"I and Notti left the vessel in the afternoon, and after two hours came to Rirajtinop, Notti's home; where we passed the night, together with his three younger brothers and an invalid sister, who all lived in the same tent-chamber. Immediately after our arrival one of the brothers began to get the dog-harness and sleigh ready for the following day's journey, while the rest of us went into the interior of the tent, where the invalid sister lay with her clothes off, but wrapt in reindeer skins. She took charge of two train-oil lamps, over which hung two cooking vessels, one formerly a preserve tin, and the other a bucket of tinned iron. One of the brothers came in with a tray, on which was placed a piece of seal blubber, together with frozen vegetables, principally willow leaves. The blubber was cut into small square pieces about the size of the thumb, after which cne of the brothers gave the sister a large portion both of the blubber and vegetables. The food was then served out to the others. Every piece of blubber was carefully imbedded in vegetables before it was eaten. When the vegetables were finished there was still some blubber, which was given to the dogs that lay in the outer tent. After this the boiled spare-ribs of a seal were partaken of, and finally a sort of soup, probably made from seal's blood. The sister had a first and special helping of these dishes. I also got an offer of every dish, and it did not appear to cause any offence that I did not accept the offer. After the close of the meal the cooking vessels were set down,

NOTTI AND HIS WIFE AITANGA.
After photographs by L. Palander.

the 'pesks' taken off, and some reindeer skins taken down from the roof and spread out. The older brothers lighted their pipes, and the younger lay down to sleep. I was shown to one of the side places in the tent, evidently Notti's own. One of the lamps was extinguished, after which all slept. During the night the girl complained several times, when one of the brothers always rose and attended to her. At six in the morning I wakened the party and reminded them of our journey. All rose immediately. Dressing proceeded slowly, because much attention was given to the foot covering. No food was produced, but all appeared quite pleased when I gave them of my stock, which consisted of bread and some preserved beef-steaks. Immediately after breakfast four dogs were harnessed to the sleigh, with

D D

which Notti and I continued our journey to Najtskaj, I riding
and he running alongside the sleigh. At Irgunnuk, a Chukch
village about an English mile east of Rirajtinop, a short
stay was made in order to try to borrow some dogs, but without
success. We continued our journey along the shore, and at
12 o'clock A.M. arrived at Najtskaj, which is from fifteen to eighteen kilometres E.S.E. from Irgunnuk. Here we were received
by most of our former neighbours, the inhabitants of Pitlekaj.
Of the thirteen tents of the village the five westernmost were occupied by the former population of Pitlekaj,
while the eight lying more to the eastward were inhabited by
other Chukches. The Pitlekaj people had not . pitched their
common large tents, but such as were of inconsiderable size or
small ones fastened close together. In all the tents here, as at
Rirajtinop and Irgunnuk, there was much blubber laid up; we
saw pieces of seal and whole seals piled up before the tents,
and on the way to Najtskaj we met several sledges loaded with
seals on their way to Pidlin. At Najtskaj I went out hunting
accompanied by a Chukch. We started eight hares, but did
not succeed in getting within range of them. A red fox was
seen at a great distance, but neither ptarmigan nor traces of
them could be discovered. At two in the afternoon I returned
to Irgunnuk and there got another sleigh drawn by ten dogs,
with which I soon reached the vessel."

On the 20th February three large Chukch sledges laden with
goods and drawn by sixteen to twenty dogs stopped at the *Vega*.
They said they came from the eastward, and were on
their way to the market in the neighbourhood of Nischni
Kolymsk. I again by way of experiment sent with them home-
letters, for which, as they declined to take money, I gave them as
postage three bottles of rum and abundant entertainment for
men and dogs. In consideration of this payment they bound
themselves faithfully to execute their commission and promised
to return in May. And they kept their word. For on the 8th
and 9th of May a large number of sledges heavily laden with reindeer skins and drawn by many dogs, passed along the coast from
west to east. Of course all rested at the *Vega*, the only house
of entertainment on the coast of the Asiatic Polar Sea, considering it as a matter of indisputable right, that they should in
return for a little talk and gossip obtain food and " ram." Very
eagerly they now informed us that a letter would come with
another dog train that might be expected in a few hours. This
was for us a very great piece of news, the importance of which
none can understand who has never hungered for months for
news from home, from the home-land and the home-world.
Eager to know if we had actually to expect *a post*.from Europe,

we asked them how large the packet was. "Very large" was
the answer, and the "ram" was of course measured accordingly.
But when at last the letter came it was found to be only an
exceedingly short note from some of the Russian officials at
Kolyma, informing me that our letters had reached him on the
₈ₜₕ April and had been immediately sent by express to Yakutsk.
Thence they were sent on by post, reaching Irkutsk on the ₂₀ₜₕ
May, and Sweden on the 2nd August.

During autumn and midwinter the sunshine was not of
course strong and continuous enough to be painful to the eyes,
but in February the light from the snow-clouds and the snowdrifts began to be troublesome enough. On the 22nd February
accordingly snow-spectacles were distributed to all the men, an
indispensable precaution, as I have before stated, in Arctic
journeys. Many of the Chukches were also attacked with snow-
blindness somewhat later in the season, and were very desirous
of obtaining from us blue-coloured spectacles. Johnsen even
stated that one of the hares he shot was evidently snow-blind.

On the evening of the 22nd February there burst upon us
a storm with drifting snow and a cold of − 36°. To be out in
such weather is not good even for a Chukch dog. Of this we
had confirmation the next day, when a Chukch who had lost his
way came on board, carrying a dog, frozen stiff, by the backbone,
like a dead hare. He had with his dog gone astray on the ice
and lain out, without eating anything, in a snow-drift for· the
night. The master himself had suffered nothing, he was only
hungry, the dog on the other hand scarcely showed any sign of
life. Both were naturally treated on board the *Vega* with great
commiseration and kindness. They were taken to the 'tweendecks, where neither Chukches nor Chukch dogs were otherwise
admitted; for the man an abundant meal was served of what we
believed he would relish best, and he was then allowed, probably for the first time in his life, to sleep if not under a sooty,
at least under a wooden roof. The dog was for hours carefully
subjected to massage, with the result that he came to life again,
which struck us, and, as it appeared, not least the Chukch
himself, as something wonderful.

In the beginning of March there passed us a large number of
sledges laden with reindeer skins, and drawn by eight to ten
dogs each. Every sledge had a driver, and as usual the women
took no part in the journey. These trains were on a commercial
journey from Irkaipij to Pük at Behring's Straits. We found
among the foremen many of our acquaintances from the preceding autumn, and I need not say that this gave occasion to a
special entertainment, for the people, bread, a little spirits, soup,
some sugar, and tobacco, for the dogs, pemmican. Conversation
during such visits became very lively, and went on with little

hindrance, since two of us were now somewhat at home in the
Chukch language. For if I except two men, Menka and Noak
Elisej, who could talk exceedingly defective Russian, there way
not one of the reindeer or dog-foremen travelling past who could
speak any European language, and notwithstanding this they
all carry on an active commerce with the Russians. But the
Chukch is proud enough to require that his own language shall
prevail in all international commerce in the north-east of Asia
and his neighbours find their advantage in this.

During the course of the winter, Lieutenant Nordquist
collected from the Chukch foremen coming from a distance who
travelled past, information regarding the state of the ice between
Chaun Bay and Behring's Straits at different seasons of the year
Considering the immense importance of the question, even in
a purely practical point of view, I shall quote verbatim the
statements which he thus collected.

*Statements regarding the state of the ice on the coast between
Cape Yakan and Behring's Straits by Chukches living there.*

" 1. A Chukch from Yekanenmitschikan, near Cape Yakan
said that it is usual for open water to be there the whole
summer.

" 2. A Chukch from Kinmankau, which lies a little to the west
of Cape Yakan, said the same.

" 3. A Chukch from Yakan stated that the sea there becomes
free of ice in the end of May or beginning of June. On the
other hand it is never open in winter.

" 4. Tatan from Yakan stated that the sea there is open from
the end of May or beginning of June to the latter part of
September or beginning of October, when the ice begins to drift
towards the land.

" 5. Rikkion from Vankarema said that the sea there is covered
with ice in winter but open in summer.

" 6. A reindeer Chukch, Rotschitlen, who lives about twelve
English miles from the *Vega's* winter quarters, said that
Kolyutschin Bay, by the Chukches called Pidlin, is clear of ice
the whole summer.

" 7. Urtridlin from Kolyutschin said that neither at that island
nor in Kolyutschin Bay is there any ice in summer.

" 8. Ranau, from Yinretlen, also said that Kolyutschin Bay is
always open in summer.

" 9. Ettiu, from the village Nettej, between Irgunnuk and
Behring's Straits, stated that the sea at Nettej is open in
summer, independently of the wind, in winter only when the
wind is southerly.

" 10. Vankatte, from Nettej, stated that the sea there become
open during the month " Tautinyadlin," that is, the latter part

of May and the beginning of June, and is again covered with ice during the month " Kutscshkau," or October and November.
" 11. Kepljeplja, from the village Irgunnuk, lying five English miles east of the *Vega's* winter quarters at Pitlekaj, said that the sea off these villages is open all summer, except when northerly winds prevail. On the other hand, he said that farther westward, as at Irkaipij, ice could nearly always be seen from the land.

" 12. Kapatljin, from Kingetschkun, a village between Irgunnuk and Behring's Straits, stated on the 11th January that there was then open water at that village. He said further, that Behring's Straits in winter are filled with ice when the wind is southerly, but open when the wind is northerly. The same day a Chukch from Nettej-Kengitschkau, also between Irgunnuk and Behring's Straits, stated that ice then lay off that village. He confirmed Kapatljin's statement regarding Behring's Straits.

" 13. Kvano, from Uedlje, near Behring's Straits, said that there the sea is always open from May to the end of September."

On the 13th March we came to know that spirits, too, form an article of commerce here. For, without having obtained any liquor from the *Vega*, the Chukches at Yinretlen had the means of indulging in a general fuddle, and that even their friendly disposition gives way under the effects of the intoxication we had a manifest proof, when the day after they came on board with blue and yellow eyes, not a little seedy and ashamed. In autumn a tall and stout Chukch giantess, who then paid us a visit, informed us that her husband had been murdered in a drunken quarrel.

Sledges of considerable size, drawn by reindeer, began after the middle of March to pass the *Vega* in pretty large numbers. They were laden with reindeer skins and goods bought at the Russian market-places, and intended for barter at Behring's Straits.

The reindeer Chukches are better clothed, and appear to be in better circumstances and more independent than the coast Chukches, or, as they ought to be called in correspondence with the former name, the dog Chukches. As every one owns a reindeer herd, all must follow the nomad mode of living, but at the same time they carried on traffic between the savages in the northernmost parts of America and the Russian fur-dealers in Siberia, and many pass their whole lives in commercial journeys. The principal market is held annually during the month of March, on an island in the river Little Anjui, 250 versts from Nischni Kolymsk. The barter goes on in accordance with a

normal price-list, mutually agreed upon by the Russian merchants and the oldest of the Chukches. The market is inaugurated on the part of the Russians by a mass performed by
the priest,[1] who always accompanies the Russian crown commissioner, and in the Chukches' camp with buffoonery by one of
the Chukch Shamans. At such a market there is said to be
considerable confusion, to judge by the spirited description which
Wrangel gives of it (*Reise*, i. p. 269). We ought, however, to
remember that this description refers to the customs that prevailed sixty years ago. Now, perhaps, there is a great change
there. In the commercial relations in north-eastern Asia in the
beginning of this century, we have probably a faithful picture
of the commerce of the Beormas in former days in north-
eastern Europe. Even the goods were probably of the same
sort at both places, perhaps, also, the stand-points of the culture
of the two races.

Besides the traders, a large number of Chukches from Kolyutschin Island and other villages to the west, travelled past us
with empty sledges, to which were harnessed only a few dogs.
They returned in the course of a few days with their sledges
fully laden with fish, which they said they had caught in a
lagoon situated to the eastward. They also sometimes sold a
delicious variety of the Coregonus taken in a lake in the
interior some distance from the coast.

Further on in winter a number of excursions were undertaken in different directions, partly to find out these fishing
places, partly to get an idea of the mode of life of the reindeer
Chukches. I, however, never ventured to give permission for
any long absence from the vessel, because I was quite convinced
that the sea round the *Vega* after a few days' constant southerly
storm might become open under circumstances which would not

[1] During the market the Russian priest endeavours to make proselytes;
he succeeds, too, by distributing tobacco to induce one or two to subject
themselves to the ceremony of baptism. No true conversion, however,
can scarcely come in question on account of the difference of language.
As an example of how this goes on, the following story of Wrangel's may
be quoted. At the market a young Chukch had been prevailed upon, by a
gift of some pounds of tobacco, to allow himself to be baptised. The ceremony began in presence of a number of spectators. The new convert
stood quiet and pretty decent in his place till he should step down into the
baptismal font, a large wooden tub filled with ice-cold water. In this,
according to the baptismal ritual, he ought to dip three times. But to
this he would consent on no condition. He shook his head constantly, and
brought forward a large number of reasons against it, which none understood. After long exhortations by the interpreter, in which promises of
tobacco probably again played the principal part, he finally gave way and
sprang courageously down into the ice-cold water, but immediately jumped
up again trembling with cold, crying, "My tobacco! my tobacco!" All
attempts to induce him to renew the bath were fruitless, the ceremony
was incomplete, and the Chukch only half baptised.

permit us to remain in the open road where we lay moored; my comrades' desire to penetrate far into the Chukch peninsula could not on that account be satisfied. But short as these excursions were, they give us, however, much information regarding our winter life, and our contact with the little-known tribe, on the coast of whose homeland the *Vega* had been beset, and on that account, perhaps, there may be reasons for making extracts from some of the reports given in to me with reference, to these journeys.

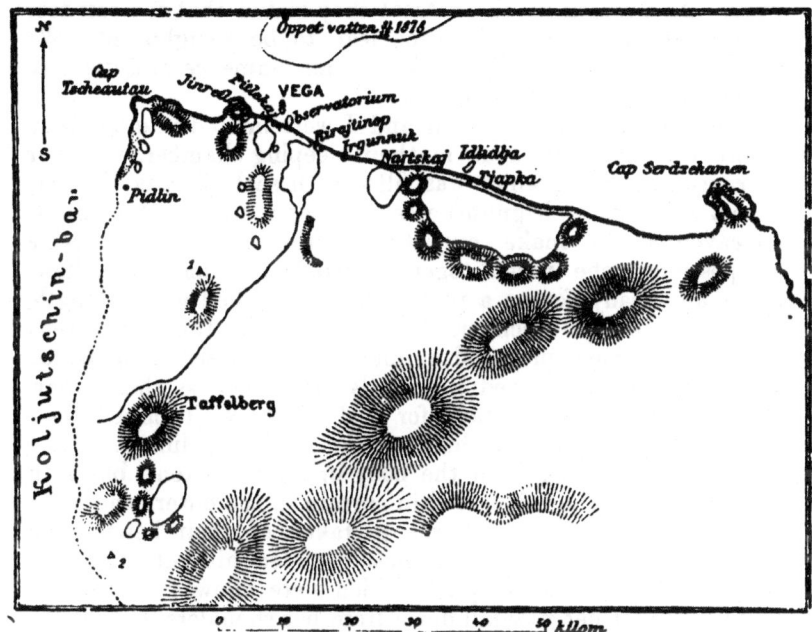

MAP OF THE REGION ROUND THE "VEGA'S" WINTER QUARTERS.
Mainly after G. Bove.
1. Rotschitlen's tent.   2. Yettugin's tent.

Palander's and Kjellman's excursion to a reindeer Chukch camp south-west of Pitlekaj, is sketched by the former thus :—

" On the 17th March, 1879, accompanied by Dr. Kjellman, I went out with a sledge and five men, among them a native as guide, to the reindeer Chukch camp in the neighbourhood of Taffelberg (Table Mountain), with a view to obtain fresh reindeer flesh. The expedition was fitted out with two days' provisions, tent, mattresses, and *pesks*. The reindeer Chukches were met with eleven English miles from the vessel. On an eminence here were found two tents, of which one at the time was uninhabited. The other was occupied by the Chukch, Rotschitlen, his young wife, and another young pair, the latter, if I understood them right, being on a visit, and properly having their home at Irgunnuk.

" Round the tent, which was considerably smaller than those we daily saw at the coast, lay a number of sledges piled up on one another.   These sledges differed from the common dog-sledges in being considerably larger and wider in the gauge.   The runners were clumsy and axed from large wood.

" Our proposal to purchase reindeer was immediately declined, although we offered in exchange bread, tobacco, rum, and even guns.   As a reason for this refusal they stated that the reindeer at this season of the year are too lean to be slaughtered.   We saw about fifty reindeer pasturing on an eminence at a distance of several thousand feet from us.

" In the afternoon Kjellman and I were invited into the tent, where we passed an hour in their sleeping chamber.   On our entrance the lamp, which was filled with seal oil, was lighted; a sort of moss (sphagnum) was used as a wick.   Our hostess endeavoured to make our stay in the tent as agreeable as possible; she rolled together reindeer skins for pillows and made ready for us a place where, stretched at full length, we might enjoy much needed repose.   In the outer tent the other women prepared supper, which consisted of boiled seal's-flesh.   We received a friendly invitation to share their meal, but as we had no taste for seal's-flesh, we declined their offer under the pretext that we had just had dinner.   They took their meal lying with the body in the inner tent, but with the head under the reindeer-skin curtain in the outer, where the food was.   After the meal was partaken of, their heads were drawn within the curtain ; our host divested himself of all his clothes, the trousers excepted, which were allowed to remain. Our hostess let her *pesk* fall down from her shoulders, so that the whole upper part of the body thus became bare.   The reindeer-skin boots were taken off, and turned outside in; they were carefully dried and hung up in the roof over the lamp to dry during the night.   We treated the women to some sugar, which, in consequence of their want of acquaintance with it, they at first examined with a certain caution, finding afterwards that it tasted exceeding well.   After the meal our host appeared to become sleepy ; we accordingly said good-night, and went to our own tent, where it was quite otherwise than warm, the temperature during the night being about − 11° C.

" After for the most part a sleepless night, we rose at half-past six next morning.   When we came out of the tent we saw all the reindeer advancing in a compact troop.   At the head was an old reindeer with large horns, that went forward to his master, who had in the meantime gone to meet the herd, and bade him good-morning by gently rubbing his nose against his master's hands. While this was going on the other reindeer stood drawn up in well-ordered ranks, like the crew in divisions on board a man-of-war. The owner then went forward and saluted every reindeer; they were allowed to stroke his hands with their noses. He on his part took every reindeer by the horn and examined it in the most careful way. After the inspection was ended at a sign given by the master the whole herd wheeled round and returned in closed ranks, with the old reindeer in front, to the previous day's pasture.

"The whole scene made a very favourable impression on us; it was not the grim hard savage showing in a coarse and barbarous way his superiority over the animals, but the good master treating his inferiors kindly; and having a friendly word for each of them. Here good relations prevailed between man and the animals. Rotschitlen himself was a stately young man, with an intelligent appearance and a supple handsome figure. His dress, of exceedingly good cut and of uncommonly fine reindeer skin, sat close to his well-grown frame, and gave us an opportunity of seeing his graceful and noble bearing, which was most observable when he was in motion.

"On our repeating our proposal to purchase reindeer we again met with a refusal, on which we struck our tent and commenced our return journey. We came on board on the 18th March at 3 o'clock P.M., after a march of four hours and three-quarters.

"The way to the reindeer camp rose and fell gently. The snow was hard and even, so that we could go forward rapidly. On the way out four foxes and some ravens were seen. At one place we found a large number of lemming passages excavated through the snow in an oblique direction towards the ground. Most of them were scratched up by foxes. The descent to an untouched lemming nest was cylindrical, and four and a half centimetres in diameter. During both days we had snow, and a thick and foggy atmosphere, so that we could see only a short distance before us; we did not however go astray, thanks to the good eyes and strongly developed sense of locality of our guide, the native."

Brusewitz's and Nordquist's Excursion to Nutschoitjin.

Of this Nordquist gives the following account:—

"On the 20th March, at 9 o'clock A.M. Lieut. Brusewitz, boatswain Lustig, the Norwegian hunters Johnsen and Sievertsen, the Chukch Notti, and I, left the *Vega*. Our equipment, which consisted of provisions for eight days, cooking apparatus, canvas tent, india-rubber mattresses, reindeer-skin *pesks*, &c., we drew after us on a sledge, At 2.45 P.M. we came to Nutschoitjin (Coregonus Lake). During our journey we passed a river which flows between Nutschoitjin and the mountain Hotschkeanranga, about ten English miles south of this lake, and falls into the great lagoon south of Pitlekaj. Farther into the interior this river, according to Notti's statement, flows through several lakes: he also informed us that in summer it abounds very much in salmon (*lienne*). Some sandy hills formed the watershed between it and Nutschoitjin. The only animal we saw during our outward journey was a fox. On the other hand we found traces of hares, ptarmigan, and a couple of lemmings. After we had found a suitable camping-place, we began to build a snow-house, which, however, we could not get ready till next day.

"On the 21st Brusewitz and I went out to view our nearest surroundings. On a hill north of the lake, where Potentilla, Carex, and Poa stuck up through the snow-covering, we saw a large number of traces of the fox, the hare, and the ptarmigan. We employed the 22nd in cutting some holes in the ice, which was about one and a half metres thick, and in setting a net. For I wished to ascertain what species of Coregonus it is which, according to Notti's statement, occurs in abundance in this lake. At the place where the net was set there was something more than a metre of water under the ice. The bottom consisted of mud. When we cut a hole in the middle of the lake in order to get deeper water we found that the ice, one and a half metres thick there, reached to the bottom.

"Next morning we got in the net eleven Coregoni, of which the largest were about thirty-five centimetres long. Although the weather was grey and we could not see very far, we went the same day to the hill Hotschkeanranga; partly to determine its height, and partly from its summit, which is visible for a great distance, to get a view of the appearance of the surrounding country. After crossing the river which flows between Nutschoitjin and Hotschkeanranga, we began to ascend the long slope on whose summit Hotschkanrakenljeut (Hotschkeanranga's head) rises with steep sides above the surrounding country. Over the slope were scattered loose blocks of stone of an eruptive rock. The crest of "the head" was also closely covered with loose stones. On the north or wind side these stones were covered with a hard beaten crust of snow nearly two feet thick; on the south side most of them were bare. According to Brusewitz the southern slopes are still steeper than the northern. South of the hill he saw a large valley—probably a lake—through which flows the river which we crossed.

"As on the outward journey I went with Notti, he advised me to offer a little food and brandy to the Spirit of the Lake,

itjaken kamak, in order to get good net fishing. On my inquiring
what appearance he had, Notti replied, "*uinga lilapen,*" "I have
never seen him." Besides this spirit there are in his view others
also in streams, in the earth, and in some mountains. The
Chukches also sacrifice to the sun and moon. On the other
hand they do not appear, as some other races, to pay any sort of
worship to their departed friends. When I gave him a biscuit
and bade him offer it, he made with the heel a little depression
in the snow on Nutschoitjin, crumbled a little bit of the biscuit
in pieces, and threw the crumbs into the hollow. The rest of
the biscuit he gave back, declaring that *kamak* did not require
more, and that we should now have more fish in the net than
the first time. Notti said also that the Chukches are wont to
sacrifice something for every catch. Thus have probably arisen
all the collections of bear and seal skulls and reindeer horns,
which we often saw on the Chukch coast, especially on
eminences.

"After we had read off the aneroid, we speedily made our way
to the snow-house, because during the interval a violent storm of
drifting snow had arisen, so that we could not see more than
half a score of paces before us. On the slope below "the head"
we had already on our way thither seen traces of two wild
reindeer. Notti said that there are a few of them on the hill
the whole winter. The greater number, however, draw farther
southward, and approach the coast only during summer. Johnsen
had wounded an owl (*Strix nyctea*), which however made its
escape. On the 24th snow fell and drifted during the whole
day, so that we could not go out to shoot. On the 25th we
came on board again.

"According to the aneroid observations made during the
journey, the highest summit we visited had a height of 197
metres."

*Lieutenant Bove's Account of an Excursion to Najtskaj and
Tjapka.*

"On the 19th April, at 4 o'clock A.M., the hunter Johnsen
and I started on a short excursion eastward along the coast,
with a view to pay a visit to the much frequented fishing
station Najtskaj, where our old friends from Pitlekaj had settled.
We had a little sledge which we ourselves drew, and which was
laden with provisions for three days and some meteorological
and hydrographical instruments.

"At 6 o'clock A.M. we reached Rirajtinop, where we found
Notti, a serviceable, talented, and agreeable youth. The village
Rirajtinop, which formerly consisted of a great many tents, now
had only one tent, Notti's, and it was poor enough. It gave the
inhabitants only a slight protection against wind and cold.

Among household articles in the tent I noticed a face-mask of wood, less shapeless than those which according to Whymper's drawings are found among the natives along the river Youcon, in the territory of Alaska, and according to Dr. Simpson among the West-Eskimo. I learned afterwards that this mask came from Päk, Behring's Straits, whither it was probably carried from the opposite American shore.

" The village Irgunnuk lies from three to four hundred metres from Rirajtinop, and consists of five tents, one of which two days before had been removed from Yinretlen. The tents are as usual placed on earthy eminences, and have if possible the entrance a couple of paces from some steep escarpment, manifestly in order that the door-opening may not be too much obstructed with snow. I reckon the population of Irgunnuk at forty persons.

" Off this village the ice is broken up even close to the land into *torosses*, five to six metres high, which form a chain which

THE SLEEPING CHAMBER IN A CHUKCH TENT.
After a drawing by the seaman Hansson.

closely follows the shore for a distance of five to six hundred metres to the eastward. The coast from Irgunnuk to Najtskaj runs in a straight line, is low, and only now and then interrupted by small earthy eminences, which all bear traces of old dwellings. Each of these heights has its special name : first Uelkantinop, then Tiumgatti, and lastly Tiungo, two miles west of Najtskaj. In the neighbourhood of Uelkantinop we were overtaken by a reindeer-Chukch, who accompanied us to Najtskaj in order there to purchase fish and seal-blubber. At noon we reached Najtskaj, where our arrival had been announced by a native, who, with his dog-team, had driven past us on the way. Accordingly on our entrance we were surrounded by the youth of the village, who deafened us with their unceasing cries [for bread (*kauka*), tobacco, *ram*, &c. After some moments the begging urchins were joined both by women and full-grown men.

We entered a tent, which belonged to a friend or perhaps relation of Notti. There we were very well received. In the same tent the reindeer-Chukch also lodged who had given us his company on the way. He went into the sleeping chamber, threw himself down there, took part in the family's evening meal, all almost without uttering a word to the hostess, and the next morning he started without having saluted the host. Hospitality is here of a peculiar kind. It may perhaps be expressed thus : *To-day I eat and sleep in your tent, to-morrow you eat and sleep in mine ;* and accordingly, as far as I saw, all, both rich and poor, both those who travelled with large sledges, and those who walked on foot, were received in the same way. All are sure to find a corner in the tent-chamber.

" The tent-chamber, or *yaranga,* as this part of the tent is called by the natives, takes up fully a third-part of the whole tent, and is at the same time work-room, dining-room, and sleeping chamber. Its form is that of a parallelopiped ; and a

a.   b.

CHUKCH LAMPS.

a. Wooden cup to place under the lamp. b. Lamp of burned clay.

One-fifth of the natural size.

moderately large sleeping chamber has a height of 1·80 metre, a length of 3·50, and a breadth of 2·20 metres. The walls are formed of reindeer-skin with the hair inwards, which are supported by a framework of posts and cross-bars. The floor consists of a layer of grass undermost, on which a walrus skin is spread. The grass and the skin do not form a very soft bed, yet one on which even a tired European wanderer may find rest. The interior of the sleeping-chamber is lighted and warmed by lamps, whose number varies according to the size of the room. A moderately large chamber has three lamps, the largest right opposite the entrance, the two others on the cross walls. The lamps are often made of a sort of stone, which is called by the natives *ukulschi.* They have the form of a large ladle. The fuel consists of train-oil, and moss is used for the wick. The lamps besides require constant attention, because half-an-hour's neglect is sufficient to make them smoke or go out. The flame is at one corner of the lamp, whose moss wick is trimmed with a piece of wood of the shape shown in the drawing. The lamp rests on a foot, and it in its turn in a basin. In this way every drop of oil that may be possibly spilled is collected. If there is anything that this people ought to save, it is certainly oil, for this signifies to them both light and heat. In the roof of the bedchamber some bars are fixed over the lamps on which clothes and shoes are hung to dry. The lamps are kept alight the whole day; during night they are commonly extinguished, as otherwise they would require continual attention. Some clothes and fishing implements, two or three reindeer skins to rest upon—these are the whole furniture of a Chukch tent.

"Every tent is besides provided with some drums (*yárar*). These are made of a wooden ring, about seventy centimetres in diameter, on which is stretched a skin of seal or walrus gut. The drum is beaten with a light stick of whalebone. The sound thus produced is melancholy, and is so in a yet higher

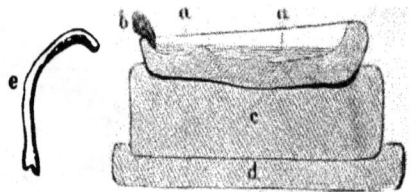

SECTION OF A CHUKCH LAMP.
After a drawing by G. Bove.
a a. The oil. *b.* The wick. *c.* The foot. *d.* The basin under it.
e. Stick for trimming the wick.

degree when it is accompanied by the natives' monotonous, commonly rhythmical songs, which appear to me to have a strong resemblance to those we hear in Japan and China. A still greater resemblance I thought I observed in the dances of these peoples. Notti is a splendid *yárar*-player. After some pressing he played several of their songs with a feeling for which I had not given him credit. The auditors were numerous, and by their smiles and merry eyes one could see that they were transported by the sounds which Notti knew how to call from the drum. Notti was also listened to in deep silence, with an admiration like that with which in a large room we listen to a distinguished pianist. I saw in the tent no other musical instrument than that just mentioned.

" The day we arrived at Najtskaj we employed in viewing the neighbourhood of the village. We accordingly ascended a hill about thirty metres high in the south of the village in order to get a clear idea of the region. From the summit of the hill we had a view of the two lagoons west and east of Najtskaj. The western appeared, with the exception of some earthy heights, to embrace the whole stretch of coast between Najtskaj, the hill at Yinretlen, and the mountains which are visible in the south from the Observatory. The lagoon east of Najtskaj is separated from the sea by a high rampart of sand, and extends about thirty kilometres into the interior, to the foot of the chain of hills which runs along there. To the eastward the lagoon extends along the coast to the neighbourhood of Serdze Kamen. This cape was clearly seen and, according to an estimate which I do not think was far from the truth, was situated at a distance of from twenty-five to twenty-six kilometres from Najtskaj. It sinks terracewise towards the sea, and its sides are covered with stone pillars, like those we saw in the neighbourhood of Cape Great Baranoff. Serdze Kamen to the south is connected with mountain heights which are the higher the farther they are from the sea. Some of these have a conical form, others are table-shaped, reminding us of the Ambas of Abyssinia. Ten or twelve miles into the interior they appear to reach a height of six hundred to nine hundred metres.

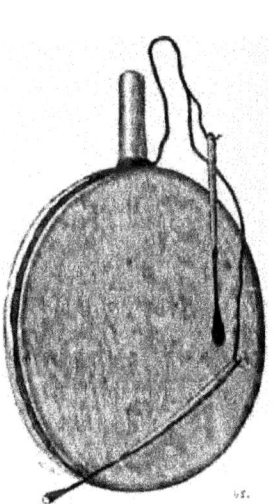

CHUKCH SHAMAN DRUM.
One-eighth the natural size

"The fishing in the eastern lagoon takes place mainly in the neighbourhood of Najtskaj, at a distance of about five kilometres from the village. Hooks are exclusively used, and no nets or other fishing implements. In a few minutes I saw twenty cod (*urokadlin*) caught, and about as many small fish, called by the natives *nukio-nukio*. For the fishing the natives make a hole in the ice, a decimetre in diameter. Round the hole they build, as a protection against wind and drifting snow, a snow wall eighty centimetres high, forming a circle with an inner diameter of a metre and a half. The fish-hooks are of iron and are not barbed. The line is about five metres long, and is fixed to a rod nearly a metre in length. At the end of the angling line hangs a weight of bone, and beside it the hook. It is generally the women who fish, yet there are generally two or three men about to open the holes, build the walls, and keep the fishing-places clear. All the holes with their shelter-walls lie in an arc, about a kilometre in length, whose convex side is turned to the east. The ice in the lagoon was 1·7 metre thick

the water 3·2 metres deep, and the thickness of snow on the
ice 0·3 metre.

"The day after our arrival at Najtskaj we visited the village
Tjapka, which lies at a distance of six kilometres. This village
contains thirteen tents, some of which are more roomy and
better built than any Chukch tent I have previously seen.
We lodged in a tent which belonged to Erere, a friendly man
with a face that was always cheerful. His sleeping-chamber
was so large that it could hold more than one family. We
found the inmates there completely naked, Erere's wife,
Kedlanga, not excepted. Kedlanga was well formed, her
bosom full, her stomach somewhat projecting, the thighs poor,
the legs slender, the feet small. The men appeared to have

THE COAST BETWEEN PADLJONNA AND ENJURMI.
To the west Idlidlja Island, in the background the village Tjapka, to the right the great lagoon.
After a drawing by O. Nordquist.

a greater disposition to stoutness than the women. Some of the
children had disproportionately large stomachs. Both men and
women wore copper rings on the legs, the wrists, and the upper
arms. On festivals they decorate themselves with iron rings,
with which some reminiscence appears to be connected, to judge
by the fact that they will not part with them.

"Erere's family was very numerous, according to the prevailing
state of matters here. He had five children, whose names,
according to their age, were, Hatanga, Etughi, Vedlat, Uai, and
Umodga. In all the tents which I visited I have inquired
the number of children. Only two or three wives had more
than three; the average may be estimated at two.

"The children are from their tenderest years set apart for

each other; thus Etughi, Erere's second son, who was little more than eight, was set apart for Keipteka, a girl of six or seven. Etughi and Keipteka slept under the same roof, though apart. " When they grow bigger," said Erere to me, " their sleeping-places will be put alongside each other." At what age this takes place I have not ascertained, but I suppose that it is very early, as is common with all Oriental races.

" Right opposite Tjapka lies a small island, by the natives called Idlidlja, which is about 800 metres in circumference. Its shores rise perpendicularly on all sides except that which is opposite Tjapka, in which direction it sinks with a steep slope. On the north end of it we found three or four whales' bones and some pieces of driftwood, but nothing to indicate that there had been any Onkilon dwellings there. The island swarmed with hares, which the inhabitants of Tjapka hunt with the bow. For this hunting they are accustomed to build circular walls of snow, pierced with loopholes, through which they shoot the unsuspecting animals.

" Regarding life in the tent I have still the following notes: The most troublesome work is given to the older women. They rise early to light and attend to the lamps, yoke the dogs, and go fishing. The young women, on the other hand, sleep far into the day. The housewives return at noon ; their work is then finished, if we do not consider as work the constant motion of the

BRACELET OF COPPER.
Half the natural size.

tongue in talk and gossip. The younger people have it assigned to them to sew clothes, arrange the fishing-lines and nets, prepare skins, &c. Sewing thread is made from the back sinews of the reindeer, which they procure by barter from the reindeer Chukches, giving for them fish and seal-blubber.

" One cannot, without having seen it, form any idea of the large quantity of food they can consume. One evening I saw eight persons, including one child, eat about 30 lbs. of food. The bill of fare was : 1, raw fish ; 2, soup ; 3, boiled fish ; 4, seal-blubber ; 5, seal-flesh. The raw fish commonly consists of frozen cod. The soup is made partly of vegetables, partly of seal-blood ; I saw both kinds. Vegetable soup was prepared by boiling equal quantities of water and vegetables, till the mixture formed a thick pap. The blood soup is cooked by boiling the blood together with water, fish, and fat. They are very fond of this soup. The seal-blubber they eat by stuffing into the mouth the piece which has been served to them, and then cutting a suitable mouthful with the knife, which they bring close to the lips. In the same way they do with the flesh.

E E

"With the exception of the old women's gossip the greatest quietness prevails in the sleeping-chamber. It is not common for men to visit each other. Thus the first night we spent at Najtskaj the tent where we lodged was full of people, but without the least disturbance arising. If one had anything to say he talked in quite a low tone, as if he were shy. He was listened to attentively, without any interruption. First when he had finished another began.

" Affection between spouses and parents and children is particularly strong. I have seen fathers kiss and caress their children before they went to rest, and what I found most remarkable was

THE NORTH END OF IDLIDLJA ISLAND.
After a drawing by O. Nordquist.

that the children never abused this tender treatment. Whatever one gave them, it was their first thought to divide it with their parents. In this respect and in many others they were far in advance of a large number of European children."

Lieutenant Bove's Report on an Excursion along with Dr. Almquist to the Interior of the Chukch Peninsula, from the 13th to the 17th June, 1879.

"We started from the vessel on the morning of the 13th June with a view to penetrate as far as possible into the interior of the Chukch peninsula. For the journey we had hired, for a liberal payment, two sledges drawn by dogs, from Rotschitlen, a Chukch at Irgunnuk. The dogs and sledges surpassed our expectation. In fourteen hours we traversed a distance of nearly forty minutes, including bends, which corresponds to a speed of three, perhaps four, English miles an hour, if we deduct the rests which were caused by the objects of the journey—scientific researches. This speed strikes me as not inconsiderable, if we consider the weight which the dogs must draw, and the badness and unevenness of the way. For the ground was undulating, like a sea agitated by a storm. But pleased as we were with our sledges and dogs, we were as dissatisfied with Rotschitlen, a fainted-hearted youth, without activity or experience. With another driver we might have been able in a few days to penetrate as far as the bottom of Kolyutschin Bay, which differs greatly in its form from that which Russian, English, and German maps give to it. It is not improbable that it is almost connected by lakes, lagoons, and rivers with St. Lawrence Bay or Metschigme Bay, whose inner parts are not yet investigated.

" After we left the lagoons at Pitlekaj and Yinretlen, the coast began gradually to rise by escarpments, each about five metres in height. The plains between the escarpments are full of lagoons or marshes. Such a terrain continued until, about five hours' way from the vessel, we came to a height of twenty-seven metres. From this point the terrace-formations cease, and the terrain then consists of a large number of ranges of heights, intersected by rivulets, which during the snow-melting season must be very much flooded. Seven or eight hours' way from the vessel we met with such a rivulet, which farther to the S.S.E. unites with another which runs between two rocky escarpments twenty metres high. On one of these we pitched our tent, in order to draw and examine some hills which were already divested of the winter dress they had worn for nine long months. On the top of one of the hills we found marks of two recently-struck tents, which probably belonged to a reindeer Chukch, who had now settled halfway between Pitlekaj and Table Mount upon a chain of heights which appears to separate the Irgunnuk lagoon from the rocky eastern shore of Kolyutschin Bay. At our resting-place we found a large number of reindeer horns and a heap of broken bones.

" After resuming our journey we came in a short time to the foot of Table Mount, whose height I reckoned at 180 metres. It slopes gently to the west and south (about 10°), but more steeply to the east and north (about 15°). The animal world there showed great activity. In less than an hour we saw more than a dozen foxes that ran up and down the hills and circled round us, as if they ran with a line. Fortunately for them they kept at a respectful distance from our doctor's sure gun.

" On the other side of Table Mount the ground sinks regular
towards Kolyutschin Bay. Here for a while we sought in vai
for Yettugin's tent, in which we intended to pass the night, an
which had been fixed upon as the starting-point of futur
excursions, till at last reindeer traces and afterwards the sight
some of these friendly animals brought us to the right way,
that about 9 o'clock P.M. we got sight of the longed-for dwellin
in the middle of a snow-desert. At the word *yaranga* (ten
the dogs pointed their ears, uttered a bark of joy, and ran at fu
speed towards the goal. We arrived at 10.30 P.M. In the ten
we were hospitably received by its mistress, who immediatel y
made the necessary preparations for our obtaining food and
rest. Yettugin himself was not at home, but he soon returned
with a sledge drawn by reindeer. These animals had scarcely
been unharnessed when they ran back to the herd, which
according to Yettugin's statement was six kilometres east of
the tent.

" I have never seen a family so afflicted with ailments as
Yettugin's. The sexagenarian father united in himself almost
all the bodily ailments which could fall to the lot of a mortal.
He was blind, leprous (?), and had no use of the left hand, the
right side of the face, and probably of the legs. His body was
nearly everywhere covered with the scars of old sores from four
to five centimetres in diameter. As Dr. Almquist and I were
compelled to pass the night in the same confined sleeping-
chamber with him, it was therefore not to be wondered at that
we drew ourselves as much as possible into our corner. The
sleeping-chamber or inner tent of a reindeer-Chukch is besides
much more habitable than that of a coast-Chukch; the air, if
not exactly pure, may at least be breathed, and the thick layer
of reindeer skins which covers the tent floor may well compare
in softness with our beds on board. Yettugin, his wife
Tengaech, and his brother Keuto, slept out of doors in order
to give us more room and not to disturb us when rising.
Keuto had inherited no small portion of his father's calamity.
He was deaf, half idiotic, and on his body there were already
traces of such spots as on the old man's. Keuto was however an
obliging youth, who during our stay in the tent did all that he
could to be of use to us, and constantly wandered about to get
birds and plants for us. He was a skilful archer ; I saw him at a
distance of twenty or twenty-five paces kill a small bird with a
blunt arrow, and when I placed myself as a target he hit me right
in the middle of the breast at a distance of perhaps thirty metres.

" The 14th was employed by me in astronomical and
geodetical observations, and by Dr. Almquist in excursions in
the neighbourhood of Yettugin's tent in order to investigate the
fauna and flora of the neighbourhood. About 10 o'clock P.M.

he returned, quite exhausted after eight hours' walking in deep
water-drenched snow under a perceptible solar heat. The
results of the excursion were in all respects exceedingly good,
not only in consequence of a number of *finds* in natural history,
but also through the discovery that the shore of Kolyutschin
Bay runs three-quarters of a mile south-west of Yettugin's tent,
which was situated in 66° 42′ 4″ North Lat., and 186° 24′ 0″
Long., east from Greenwich. Dr. Almquist had walked four or five
miles along the eastern shore of the bay, which at most places is
perpendicular with a height of fifteen metres. In consequence
of this discovery we determined to continue our hydrographical
observations as far as the bottom of the bay, which, according to
Yettugin's account, was two days' march from the tent. But we
could not carry out our plan in consequence of our guide's
laziness, for he declared that on no conditions would he
accompany us farther. Neither entreaties nor threats availed
to disturb this his resolution. I endeavoured myself to drive the
sledges, but the dogs would not move out of the spot, though,
following Rotschitlen's system, I thrashed them very soundly.

" The place where Yettugin's tent was pitched offered us a
view of an extensive snow-plain, which was inclosed on all sides
by high hills. In the north and north-east Table Mount and
the Tenen hill keep off the north winds, and to the south the
encampment is protected by a long and high mountain chain
from the winds coming from that quarter. I calculated the
height of some of the mountains at from 1200 to 1500 metres,
and their azure-blue colour furrowed by dark lines appears to
me to indicate the presence of ice on the slopes. One of the
summits of this mountain chain was easily recognisable. It was
a truncated cone, perhaps 1500 metres high. Kolyutschin Bay
lies between these mountains and Yettugin's tent. Its western
shore also appears to rise perpendicularly from the sea, and it is
higher than the eastern. The bay, which appears to be much
larger than it is represented on the maps, was covered with leve
ice ; only here and there a piece of ice covered with snow was
seen sticking up.

" As we were forced to desist from visiting the interior of Kolyutschin Bay, we determined to go to the ground where Yettugin's
reindeer pastured. We therefore left the tent on the evening
of the 15th and travelled E.N.E. The warmth, which had now
commenced, began to make travelling over snow fields difficult;
the dogs sank to the stomach, and not unfrequently we had to
alight in order to help the poor animals to climb the hills we were
obliged to ascend. Scarcely however had they come to the
reindeer tracks before even the most exhausted of them rushed
along at the top of their speed, which might be pleasant
enough uphill, but when they were coming down it was very

dangerous, because the slope nearly always ends with a steep escarpment. We came once, without observing it, to the edge of such a precipice, and if we had not succeeded in time in slackening our speed a nice confused mass of men, dogs, and sledges would have tumbled over it. In order to excite their draught animals the Chukches avail themselves of their dogs' inclination to run after the reindeer, and during their journeys they endeavour to spur them on yet more by now and then imitating the reindeer cry. After two or three hours' travelling we fell in with the first reindeer, and then by degrees with more and more, until finally about 11 o'clock P.M. we came to a numerous herd tended by Yettugin. I applied to him, asking him to barter a reindeer in good condition for a gun which I had brought along with me. After various evasions Yettugin at length promised to give us next day the reindeer for the gun. He would not however himself, or with his own knife, kill the reindeer; on which account I requested Dr. Almquist to give it the *coup de grâce.*

" In consequence of the soft state of the snow we were obliged to defer the commencement of our return journey to the evening of the 16th. We now travelled over the chain of hills which unites Table Mount with Tenen, and descended their northern steep slope towards an extensive plain, studded for the most part with bogs and marshes. The 17th came in with mist and considerable warmth. The mist limited the circle of vision to a distance of some few metres, and the high temperature in a short time destroyed the crust which had been formed in the course of the preceding night on the surface of the snow, and melted the layers of snow which still covered the northern slopes of these two hills. The southern slopes on the other hand were almost quite bare, and the valleys began to be filled with water. Four or five days as warm as these and I believe there scarcely would be any snow remaining round Kolyutschin Bay. The illusions caused by the white fog illuminated by the sunlight were very astonishing. Every small spot of ground appeared as an extensive snow-free field, every tuft of grass as a bush, and a fox in our immediate neighbourhood was for a moment taken for a gigantic bear. Besides, during such a fog the action of the sunlight on the eyes was exceedingly painful even in the case of those who carried preservers. During the return Rotschitlen lost his way in consequence of the numerous different tracks. Fortunately I had observed how we travelled, and could with the help of the compass pilot our two small craft to a good haven. On the 17th of June at 1.30 P.M. we were again in good condition on board the *Vega.*"

In the society on board the prospects of an alteration in the constant north winds, the perpetual snow-storms and the unceasing cold, and the hope of a speedy release from the fetters of the ice, were naturally constantly recurring topics of conversation. During this time many lively word-battles were fought between the weather prophets in the gunroom, and many bets made in jest between the optimists and pessimists. The former won a great victory, when at noon on the 8th February the temperature rose to $+ 0°\cdot1$ C., but with the exception of this success fortune always went against them. The north wind, the drifting snow and the cold, would never cease. A blue watersky indeed was often visible at the horizon to the north and north-east, but the "clearing" first reached our vessel a couple of hours before we left our winter haven for ever, and up to the 15th June the thickness of the ice was almost undiminished ($1\frac{1}{2}$ metre). The sun rose higher and higher, but without forming any crust upon the snow, although upon the black hull of the *Vega*, perhaps with the help of the heat in the interior, it had by the 14th March melted so much snow that small icicles were formed at the gunwale. It was one of the many deceptive prognostications of spring which were hailed with delight. However, immediately after severe cold recommenced and continued during the whole of the month of April, during which the temperature of the air never rose above $- 4°\cdot6$, the mean temperature being $- 18°\cdot9$.

May began with a temperature of $- 20°\cdot1$. On the 3rd the thermometer showed $- 26°\cdot8$, and in the "flower-month" we had only for a few hours mild weather with an air temperature $+ 1°\cdot8$. Even the beginning of June was very cold; on the 3rd we had $- 14°\cdot3$, with a mean temperature for the twenty-four hours of $- 9°\cdot4$. Still on the 13th the thermometer at midnight showed $- 8°\cdot0$, but the same day at noon with a gentle southerly wind a sudden change took place, and after that date it was only exceptionally that the thermometer in the open air sank below the freezing-point. The melting and evaporation of snow now began, and went on so rapidly that the land in the end of the month was almost free of snow.

Under what circumstances this took place is shown by the following abstract of the observations of temperature at Pitlekaj from the 13th June to the 13th July, 1879 :—

	Max.	Min.	Mean.		Max.	Min.	Mean.
June 13	$+ 3\cdot6°$	$- 8\cdot0°$	$- 1\cdot95°$	June 22	$+ 3\cdot0°$	$+ 1\cdot5°$	$+ 2\cdot28°$
14	$+ 2\cdot6$	$+ 0\cdot2$	$+ 1\cdot47$	23	$+ 4\cdot1$	$+ 1\cdot8$	$+ 3\cdot00$
15	$+ 3\cdot1$	$+ 1\cdot7$	$+ 2\cdot28$	24	$+ 6\cdot8$	$+ 0\cdot9$	$+ 3\cdot18$
16	$+ 1\cdot6$	$- 0\cdot6$	$+ 0\cdot90$	25	$+ 4\cdot4$	$+ 0\cdot4$	$+ 2\cdot30$
17	$+ 3\cdot0$	$+ 0\cdot2$	$+ 1\cdot22$	26	$+ 3\cdot8$	$+ 0\cdot6$	$+ 1\cdot77$
18	$+ 2\cdot4$	$- 0\cdot6$	$+ 1\cdot23$	27	$+ 1\cdot4$	$+ 0\cdot7$	$+ 1\cdot02$
19	$+ 3\cdot6$	$+ 1\cdot4$	$+ 2\cdot43$	28	$+ 2\cdot1$	$+ 0\cdot2$	$+ 0\cdot92$
20	$+ 3\cdot5$	$+ 1\cdot7$	$+ 2\cdot50$	29	$+ 0\cdot9$	$- 1\cdot0$	$- 0\cdot12$
21	$+ 2\cdot6$	$+ 1\cdot5$	$+ 2\cdot07$	30	$+ 1\cdot0$	$- 1\cdot8$	$- 0\cdot27$

	Max.	Min.	Mean.		Max.	Min.	Mean.
July 1	+ 0 8°	− 0·6°	+ 0·07°	July 10	+ 1·4°	+ 0·5°	+ 0·90°
2	+ 1·1	− 1·0	+ 0·40	11	+ 1·4	+ 0·6	+ 1·00
3	+ 5·0	+ 1·0	+ 2·28	12	+ 9·0	+ 0·5	+ 4·73
4	+ 3 8	+ 1·4	+ 2·68	13	+ 6·5	+ 3·7	+ 5·03
5	+ 5·2	+ 2·0	+ 3·60	14	+ 5·4	+ 1·8	+ 3·63
6	+ 3·3	+ 1·0	+ 2·28	15	+ 1·6	+ 0·6	+ 1·13
7	+ 5·0	+ 1·4	+ 2·68	16	+ 3·0	+ 0·6	+ 1·52
8	+ 8 6	+ 0·6	+ 4·82	17	+11·5	+ 3·8	+ 7·80
9	+ 1·8	+ 0·4	+ 0·97	18	+ 9·2	+ 6·2	+ 7·52

The figures in the maximum column, it will be seen, are by no means very high. That the enormous covering of snow which the north winds had heaped on the beach, could disappear so rapidly notwithstanding this low temperature probably depends on this, that a large portion of the heat which the solar rays bring with them acts directly in melting the snow without sun-warmed air being used as an intermediate agent or heat-carrier, partly also on the circumstance that the winds prevailing in spring come from the sea to the southward, and before they reach the north coast pass over considerable mountain heights in the interior of the country. They have therefore the nature of *föhn* winds, that is to say, the whole mass of air, which the wind carries with it, is heated, and its relative humidity is slight, because a large portion of the water which it originally contained has been condensed in passing over the mountain heights. Accordingly when the dry *föhn* winds prevail, a considerable evaporation of the snow takes place. The slight content of watery vapour in the atmosphere diminishes its power of absorbing the solar heat, and instead increases that portion of it which is found remaining when the sun's rays penetrate to the snowdrifts, and there conduce, not to raise the temperature, but to convert the snow into water.[1]

[1] In Lapland, too, the melting of the snow in spring is brought about in no inconsiderable degree by similar causes, i.e. by dry warm winds which come from the fells. On this point the governor of Norbotten län, H. A. Widmark, has sent me the following interesting letter:—
"However warm easterly and southerly winds may be in the parts of Swedish Lapland lying next the Kölen mountains, they are not able in any noteworthy degree to melt the masses of snow which fall in those regions during the winter months. On the other hand there comes every year, if we may rely on the statements of the Lapps, in the end of April or beginning of May, from the west (i.e. from the fells), a wind so strong and at the same time so warm, that in quite a short time—six to ten hours—it breaks up the snow-masses, makes them shrink together, forces the mountain sides from their snow covering, and changes the snow which lies on the ice of the great fell lakes to water. I have myself been out on the fells making measurements on two occasions when this wind came. On one occasion I was on the Great Lule water in the neighbourhood of the so-called Great Lake Fall. The night had been cold but the day became warm. Up to 1 o'clock P.M. it was calm, but immediately after the warm westerly wind began to blow, and by 6 o'clock P.M. all the snow on the ice was changed to

The aurora is, as is well known, a phenomenon at the same time cosmic and terrestrial, which on the one hand is confined within the atmosphere of our globe and stands in close connection with terrestrial magnetism, and on the other side is dependent on certain changes in the envelope of the sun, the nature of which is as yet little known, and which are indicated by the formation of spots on the sun; the distinguished Dutch physicist, VON BAUMHAUER, has even placed the occurrence of the aurora in connection with cosmic substances which fall in the form of dust from the interstellar spaces to the surface of the earth. This splendid natural phenomenon besides plays, though unjustifiably, a great *rôle* in imaginative sketches of winter life in the high north, and it is in the popular idea so connected with the ice and snow of the Polar lands, that most of the readers of sketches of Arctic travel would certainly consider it an indefensible omission if the author did not give an account of the aurora as seen from his winter station. The scientific man indeed knows that this neglect has, in most cases, been occasioned by the great infrequency of the strongly luminous aurora just in the Franklin archipelago on the north coast of America, where most of the Arctic winterings of this century have taken place ; but scarcely any journey of exploration has at all events been undertaken to the uninhabited regions of the high north, which has not in its working plan included the collection of new contributions towards clearing up the true nature of the aurora and its position in the heavens. But the scientific results have seldom corresponded to the expectations which had been entertained. Of purely Arctic expeditions, so far as I know, only two, the Austrian-Hungarian to Franz Josef Land (1872-74) and the Swedish to Mussel Bay (1872-73), have returned with full and instructive lists of auroras.[1] ROSS, PARRY, KANE, McCLINTOCK, HAYES, NARES, and others, have on the other hand only had opportunities of registering single auroras; the phenomenon in the case of their winterings has not formed any distinctive trait of the Polar winter night. It was the less to be expected that the *Vega* expedition would form an exception in this respect, as its voyage happened during one of the

water, in which we went wading to the knees. The Lapps in general await these warm westerly winds before they go to the fells in spring. Until these winds begin there is no pasture there for their reindeer herds."

[1] I do not include *La Recherche's* wintering in 1838 39 at Bosekop, in the northernmost part of Norway, as it took place in a region which is all the year round inhabited by hundreds of Europeans. During this expedition very splendid auroras were seen, and the studies of them by LOTTIN, BRAVAIS, LILLIEHÖÖK, and SILJESTRÖM, are among the most important contributions to a knowledge of the aurora we possess, while we have to thank the draughtsmen of the expedition for exceedingly faithful and masterly representations of the phenomenon.

AURORA AT THE "VEGA'S" WINTER QUARTERS, 3RD MARCH, 1879, AT 9 P.M.

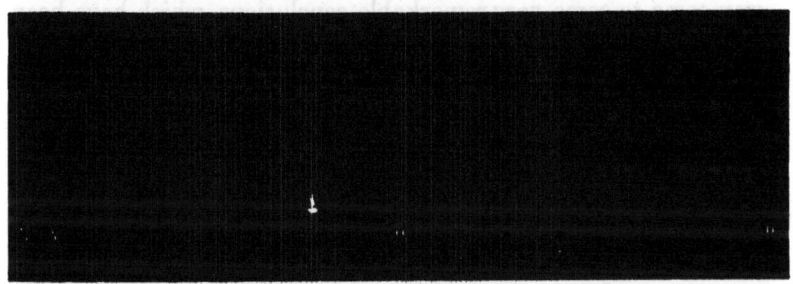

DOUBLE AURORA-ARCS SEEN 20TH MARCH, 1879, AT 9.30 P.M.

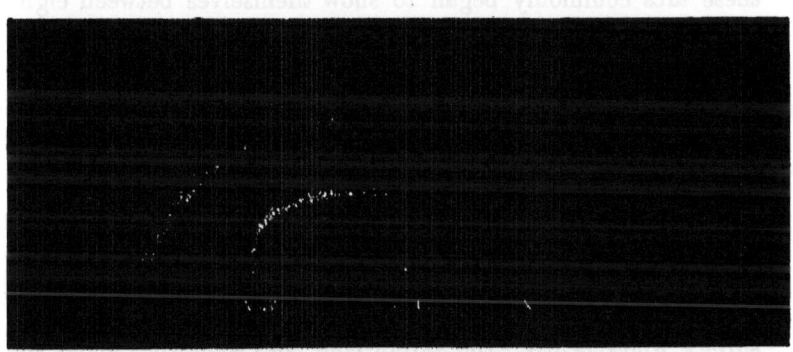

ELLIPTIC AURORA SEEN 21ST MARCH, 1879, AT 2.15 A.M.

ELLIPTIC AURORA SEEN 21ST MARCH, 1879, AT 3 A.M.

years of which we knew beforehand that it would be a minimum aurora year. It was just this circumstance, however,
which permitted me to study, in a region admirably suited for
the purpose, a portion of this natural phenomenon under uncommonly favourable circumstances. For the luminous arcs,
which even in Scandinavia generally form starting-points for the
radiant auroras, have here exhibited themselves undimmed by
the more splendid forms of the aurora. I have thus, undisturbed
by subsidiary phenomena, been able to devote myself to the
collection of contributions towards the ascertaining of the position of these luminous arcs, and I believe that I have in this
way come to some very remarkable conclusions, which have been
developed in detail in a separate paper printed in *The Scientific Work of the Vega Expedition* (Part I. p. 400). Here
space permits me only to make the following statement.

The appearance of the aurora at Behring's Straits in 1878-79
is shown in the accompanying woodcuts. We never saw here
the magnificent bands or draperies of rays which we are so
accustomed to in Scandinavia, but only halo-like luminous arcs,
which hour after hour, day after day, were unaltered in position.
When the sky was not clouded over and the faint light of the
aurora was not dimmed by the rays of the sun or the full moon,
these arcs commonly began to show themselves between eight
and nine o'clock P.M., and were then seen without interruption
during midwinter till six, and farther on in the year to three
o'clock in the morning. It follows from this that the aurora
even during a minimum year is a permanent natural
phenomenon. The nearly unalterable position of the arcs has
further rendered possible a number of measurements of its
height, extent, and position from which I believe I may draw the
following inferences; that our globe even during a minimum
aurora year is adorned with an almost constant, single, double, or
multiple luminous crown, whose inner edge is situated at a height
of about 200 kilometres or 0·03 radius of the earth above its
surface, whose centre, "the aurora-pole," lies somewhat under the
earth's surface, a little north of the magnetic-pole, and which,
with a diameter of 2,000 kilometres or 0·3 radius of the earth,
extends in a plane perpendicular to the radius of the earth, which
touches the centre of the circle.

I have named this luminous crown *the aurora glory* on account
of its form and its resemblance to the crown of rays round the
head of a saint. It stands in the same relation to the ray and
drapery auroras of Scandinavia as the trade and monsoon winds
in the south to the irregular winds and storms of the north. The
light of the crown itself is never distributed into rays, but resembles the light which passes through obscured glass. When
the aurora is stronger, the extent of the light-crown is altered :

double or multiple arcs are seen, generally lying in about the same plane and with a common centre, and rays are cast between the different arcs. Arcs are seldom seen which lie irregularly to or cross each other.

The area in which the common arc is visible is bounded by two circles drawn upon the earth's surface, with the aurora-pole for a centre and radii of 8° and 28° measured on the circumference of the globe. It touches only to a limited extent countries inhabited by races of European origin (the northernmost part of Scandinavia, Iceland, Danish Greenland), and even in the middle of this area there is a belt passing over middle Greenland, South Spitzbergen, and Franz Josef Land, where *the common arc* forms only a faint, very widely extended, luminous veil in the zenith, which perhaps is only perceptible by the winter darkness being there considerably diminished. This belt divides the regions where these luminous arcs are seen principally to the south from those in which they mainly appear on the northern horizon. In the area next the aurora-pole only the smaller, in middle Scandinavia only the larger, more irregularly formed luminous crowns are seen. But in the latter region, as in southern British America, aurora storms and ray and drapery auroras are instead common, and these appear to lie nearer the surface of the earth than the arc aurora. Most of the Polar expeditions have wintered so near the aurora-pole that *the common aurora arc* there lay under or quite near the horizon, and as the ray aurora appears to occur seldom within this circle, the reason is easily explained why the winter night was so seldom illuminated by the aurora at the winter quarters of these expeditions, and why the description of this phenomenon plays so small a part in their sketches of travels.

Long before the ground became bare and mild weather commenced, migratory birds began to arrive: first the snow-bunting on the 23rd April, then large flocks of geese, eiders, long-tailed ducks, gulls, and several kinds of waders and song-birds. First among the latter was the little elegant *Sylvia Eversmanni*, which in the middle of June settled in great flocks on the only dark spot which was yet to be seen in the quarter —the black deck of the *Vega*. All were evidently much exhausted, and the first the poor things did was to look out convenient sleeping places, of which there is abundance in the rigging of a vessel when small birds are concerned. I need scarcely add that our new guests, the forerunners of spring, were disturbed on board as little as possible.

We now began industriously to collect material for a knowledge of the avi- and mammal-fauna of the region. The collections, when this is being written, are not yet worked out, and I can therefore only make the following statement on this point:

From the acquaintance I had made during my own preceding journeys and the study of others', with the bird-world of the high north, I had got the erroneous idea that about the same species of birds are to be met with everywhere in the Polar lands of Europe, Asia, and America. Experience gained during the expedition of the *Vega* shows that this is by no means the case, but that the north-eastern promontory of Asia, the Chukch peninsula, forms in this respect a complete exception. Birds occur here in much fewer numbers, but with a very much greater variety of types than on Novaya Zemlya, Spitzbergen, and Greenland; in con-

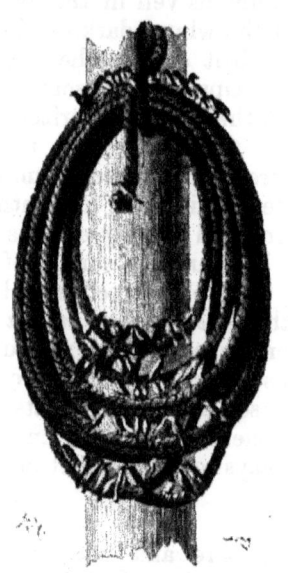

SONG-BIRDS IN THE RIGGING OF THE "VEGA."
June 1879.

sequence of which the bird-world on the Chukch peninsula has in its entirety a character differing wholly from that of the Atlantic Polar lands. We indeed meet here with types closely allied to the glaucous gull (*Larus glaucus*, Brünn.), the ivory gull (*L. eburneus*, Gmel.), the kittiwake (*L. tridactylus*, L.), the long-tailed duck (*Harelda glacialis*, L.), the king duck (*Somateria spectabilis*, L.),[1] the phalarope (*Phalaropus fulicarius*, Bonap.), the purple sandpiper (*Tringa maritima*, Brünn.), &c., of Spitzbergen and Novaya Zemlya; but along with these are found here many peculiar species, for instance the American eider (*Somateria V.-nigrum*, Gray), & swanlike goose, wholly white with black wing points (*Anser hyperboreus*, Pall.), a greyish-brown goose with bushy yellowish-white feather-covering on the head (*Anser pictus*, Pall.), a species of Fuligula, elegantly coloured on the head in velvet-black, white, and green (*Fuligula Stelleri*, Pall.), the beautifully marked, scarce *Larus Rossii*, Richards, of which Dr. Almquist on the 1st July, 1879, shot a specimen from the vessel, a little brown sandpiper with a spoonlike widened bill-point (*Eurynorhynchus pygmæus*, L.), and various song-birds not found in Sweden, &c. Besides, a number of the Scandinavian types living here also, according to Lieutenant Nordquist, are distinguished by less considerable differences in colour-marking and size. The

[1] The common eider (*S. mollissima*, L.) is absent here, or at least exceedingly rare.

singular spoon-billed sandpiper was at one time in spring so common
that it was twice served at the gunroom table, for which after
our return home we had to endure severe reproaches from animal
collectors. This bird is found only in some few museums. It
was first described by LINNÆUS in *Museum Adolphi Friderici,
Tomi secundi prodromus*, Holmiæ 1764, and then by C. P.
THUNBERG in the *Transactions* of the Swedish Academy of
Sciences for 1816 (P. 194), where it is stated that the homeland
of this bird is tropical America. It has since been caught a few
times in south-eastern Asia. Probably, like *Sylvia Ewersmanni*,
it passes the winter in the Philippine group of islands, but in
summer visits the high north. Like several other birds which
appeared in spring with the first bare spots it disappeared in
July. Perhaps it retired to the interior to breed in the bush, or,

Eurynorhynchus pygmæus, L.
At the side the bird's bill seen from above, of the natural size.

which is more probable, went farther north to the islands or
continents not yet discovered by Europeans, which in all probability connect Wrangel Land with the Franklin Archipelago.

The higher animal forms which, along with the Polar traveller.
dare to brave the cold and darkness of the Arctic night, exert
on him a peculiar attraction. Regarding these, Lieutenant
Nordquist has given me the following notes :—

" The mammal most common in winter on the north coast of
the Chukch peninsula is the *hare*. It differs from the fell hare
(*Lepus borealis*, Lillj.) by its larger size, and by the bones of its
nose not tapering so rapidly. It is generally met with in flocks
of five or six on the hills in the neighbourhood of the tents,
which are covered only with a thin layer of snow, notwith-

standing the large number of hungry dogs which wander abo¯
there.

"The *Arctic foxes* (*Vulpes lagopus*, L.) are very numerou▩
The common *fox* (*Vulpes vulgaris*, Gray) appears also to ⊏
common. A red fox, which Lieutenant Brusewitz shot from th▢
vessel in October, differed considerably from the common fo═
and approached the mountain fox. The food of the fox appea▩
in winter to consist of hares, ptarmigan, and lemmings. I hav◄
twice seen holes in the snow about a metre deep, and at th◄
mouth not more than thirty centimetres wide, which the
Chukches said were excavated by foxes searching for lemminga.

"Of the *lemming* I have seen three varieties, viz. *Myodes*
obensis, M. torquatus, and *Arvicola obscurus*. There is found
here also, according to the statements of the Chukches, a little
mouse, in all probability a Sorex. *Myodes torquatus* were got
the first time on the 12th January, *Myodes obensis* on the 13th
February. Both species were afterwards frequently brought on
board by Chukches, and during the winter lemmings were seen
not unfrequently running on the snow. *Myodes obensis* appeared
to be more numerous than the other species. It is singular that
all the nine specimens of *Myodes torquatus* I obtained during the
winter were males. Differing from both these species, *Arvicola*
obscurus does not appear to show itself above the snow during
winter. Of the latter I got eight specimens from the village
Tjapka, lying between Yinretlen and Behring's Straits. I afterwards got another from the village Irgunnuk, situated five
English miles east of Yinretlen.

"The more uncommon land mammals wintering in these
regions are the *wolf* and the *wild reindeer*. Footprints of the
latter were seen on the 23rd March, in the mountain region,
fifteen to twenty miles south of Yinretlen. According to the
Chukches' account some few reindeer remain on the hills along
the coast, while the greater number migrate southwards towards
winter. Besides these, two other mammals live here during
winter, though they are only seen during summer and autumn
because they hibernate the rest of the time. These are the
land bear and the *marmot* (*Arctomys sp.*). We saw no land
bear, but on the 8th October Lieutenant Hovgaard and I found
traces of this animal two or three English miles from the coast.
The Chukches say that the land bear is not uncommon .in
summer. The marmot occurs in large numbers. It was brought.
on board for the first time by a Chukch, and the following day
I myself saw it sitting on the top of a little hill, where it had
its dwelling.

"Besides the animals enumerated above, the natives talked of
another, which is called by them *nennet*, and is said to live by
the banks of rivers. According to their description it appears

to be the common *otter*.   As at most places where the lemming
is common, the *weasel* (*Mustela vulgaris*, Briss.) is also found
here.   I got from the Chukches two skins of this animal.
Whether the beaver occurs in the part of Chukch Land which
we visited I cannot say with certainty.   It is probable, because
the Chukches informed me that there was found here a weasel
which has the point of the tail black.

"Only two sea mammals have been seen in this region in the
course of the winter, viz. the *rough* or *bristled seal* and the
Polar bear.   On two occasions traces of the latter have been
observed in the neighbourhood of land.   They appear, however,

MARMOTS FROM CHUKCH LAND.

for the most part to keep by openings in the ice farther out to
sea, where during our stay two of them were killed by Chukches
from the neighbouring villages.   The rough seal is probably the
only species that occurs near the coast during winter.   It is
caught in great numbers, and forms, along with fish and various
vegetable substances, the main food of the Chukches.

"Of land birds there winter in the region only three species,
viz. an *owl* (*Strix nyctea*, L.), a *raven* (*Corvus sp.*), and a *ptarmigan* (*Lagopus subalpina*, Nilss.) ; the last-named is the most
common.   On the 14th December, during a sledge journey into
the country, I saw, about ten or twelve English miles from the

F F

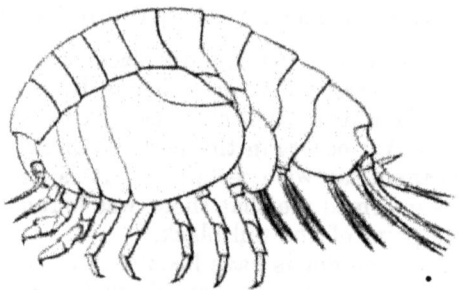

STEGOCEPHALUS KESSLERI (STUXB.).
Natural size.

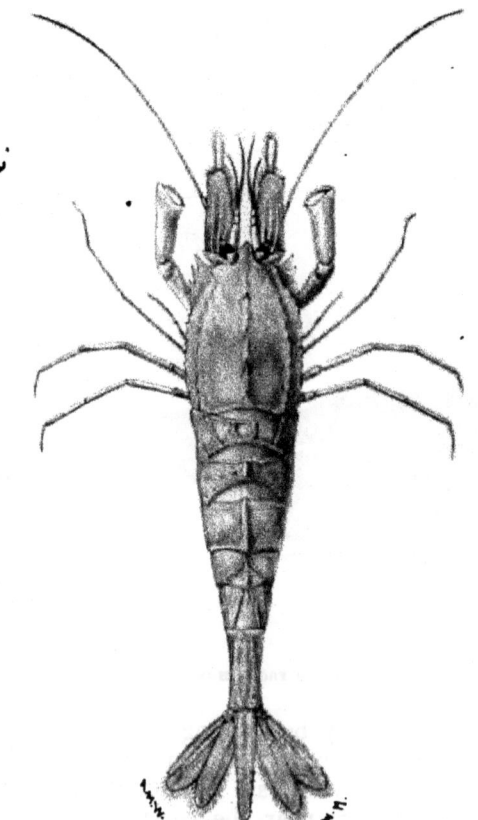

SABINEA SEPTEMCARINATA (SABINE).
Natural size.

EVERTEBRATES FROM THE SEA AT THE " VEGA'S " WINTER QUARTERS.

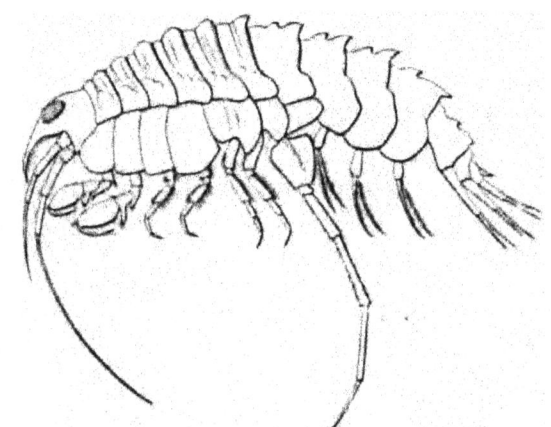

ACANTHOSTEPHIA MALMGRENI (GOËS).
Magnified twice.

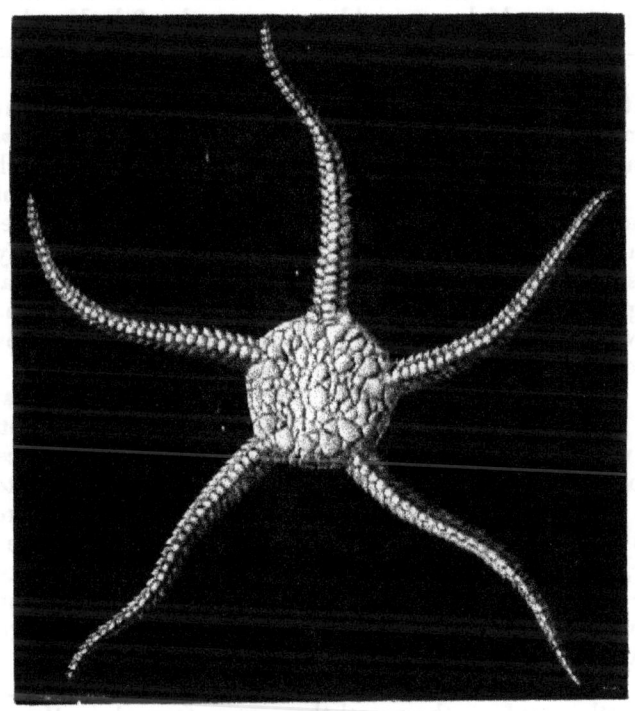

OPHIOGLYPHA NODOSA (LÜTKEN).
Magnified twice.

INVERTEBRATES FROM THE SEA AT THE "VEGA'S" WINTER QUARTERS.

F F 2

coast, two large coveys of ptarmigan, one of which probably
numbered over fifty. Nearer the coast, on the other hand, there
were found, especially during spring, for the most part only sing
birds. The raven is common at the Chukch villages, and builc
its nest in the neighbouring cliffs. The first egg was got on the
31st May. The mountain owl was seen for the first time on the
11th March, but, according to the statements of the Chukche
it is to be met with during the whole winter. In April and Ma
we also saw some mountain owls; on the 21st May I saw two.

"At open places in the sea there are found here in winter, the
Chukches say, two swimming birds, the *loom* (*Uria Brünnich*
Sabine) and the *black guillemot* (*Uria grylle*, L.). Of the
former we obtained two specimens for the first time on the
1st May, of the latter on the 19th of the same mont
Possibly there winter in open places of the sea besides these
birds a species of Mergulus, one of which came to the wint
quarters of the *Vega* on the 3rd November, and a Fuligula,
specimen of which was sold to us on the 9th March by
Chukch, who said he had killed it at a clearing off the coast."

After the arrival of the migratory birds hunting excursions
began to form a welcome interruption in our monotonous winter
life, and the produce of the hunting a no less agreeable change
from the preserved provisions. The Chukches besides offered
us daily a large number of different kinds of birds, especially
when they observed that we paid a higher price for many rare
kinds of birds, though small and of little use for food, than for
a big, fat goose. The Chukches killed small birds either by
throwing stones, or by shooting them with bow and arrows, in
connection with which it may be observed that most of them
were very poor archers. They also caught them with whalebone snares set on bare spots on the beach, generally between
two vertebræ of the whale. For pebbles are very scarce, but
the bones of the whale are found, as has been already stated, at
most places in large numbers on the strand-banks where the
tents are pitched. In June we began to get eggs of the gull,
eider, long-tailed duck, goose, and loom, in sufficient number for
table use. The supply, however, was by no means so abundant
as during the hatching season on Greenland, Spitzbergen, or
Novaya Zemlya.

A little way from the vessel there were formed, in the end of
May, two " leads," a few fathoms in breadth. On the 31st May
I sent some men to dredge at these places. They returned
with an abundant yield, but unfortunately the openings closed
again the next day, and when I and Lieutenant Bove visited
the place there was a large, newly-formed *toross* thrown up along

the edge of the former channel. Another "lead" was formed some days after, but closed again through a new disturbance of the position of the ice, a high ice-rampart, formed of loose blocks, heaped one over another, indicating the position of the former opening. Even the strongest vessel would have been crushed in such a channel by the forcing together of the ice. Of a different sort from both these occasional leads was an extensive opening which showed itself a kilometre or two north of the vessel. It is probable that with few interruptions, which, however, might have been difficult to pass, it extended as far as Behring's Straits, where, according to the statements of the Chukches, several whalers had already made their appearance. Round the vessel itself, however, the ice still lay fast and unbroken. Nor did the Chukches appear to expect that it would break up very soon, to judge by the number of vehicles drawn by dogs or reindeer which still passed us, both to the east and west. One of these travellers must here be specially mentioned, as his journey has been talked about as an expedition sent to our relief.

It was on the 19th June. A large number of Chukches travelling past us as usual came on board, partly to receive the tribute of hospitality to which they considered themselves entitled, partly to satisfy an easily understood curiosity and gossip a little about the most important occurrences of the preceding day. One of them, a middle-aged man, whom we had not seen before, with a friendly and self-satisfied bearing, whose face was a mere collection of wrinkles, and over whose *pesk* was drawn an old velvet shirt, presented himself with a certain pretentiousness as the chief NOAH ELISEJ. Since the mistake with the stately Chepurin, and since even Menka's supposed slave declared himself to be at least as good as Menka, we had begun to be rather indifferent to the rank of chief among the Chukches. Noah Elisej however, notwithstanding he thus brought forward his pretensions, was received like a common man, at which he appeared to be a little offended. But our behaviour soon changed, when Notti, or some other of our daily guests, who had become quite familiar with our fancies, tastes and weaknesses, informed us that Noah Elisej had with him a large, a very large letter. Old Noah thus carried a mail, perhaps a European mail. At once he became in our eyes a man of importance. After being stormed for a time with questions, he took from a bag which hung from his neck the ordinary pieces of board fastened together, which here serve as a postbag. They were found however to contain only a letter of a couple of lines from a Russian official at Nischni Kolymsk, without any news from Europe, but informing us that chief Noah Elisej was sent to us to assist us, if necessary. Noah first patted his stomach

to indicate that he was hungry and wanted food, and hawked
and pointed with his finger at his throat to let us know that a
ram would taste well. He then told us something which we did
not then exactly understand, but which we now have reason to
interpret as a statement that Noah was the leader of an expedition sent by the Siberian authorities to our relief, and that he was
therefore willing in return for suitable compensation to give us
some reindeer. I availed myself of the offer, and purchased three
animals for sugar, tea, and a little tobacco. Noah besides was
a friendly and easy-going man, who, Christian though he was,
travelled about with two wives and a large number of children,

NOAH ELISEJ.
After a photograph by L. Palander.

who all of course would see the vessel and get their treat of
tobacco, clay pipes, sugar, *ram*, &c.

So much flood water had now begun to collect on the ice,
especially near the land, that it was exceedingly difficult to walk
from the vessel to the shore and back. Many a proposed land
excursion was broken off by somebody, immediately after leaving
the vessel, sinking into some deep hole in the ice and thus getting
a cold bath. Excursions on land however began to be exceedingly
interesting to the botanists and zoologists; and therefore to avoid
the inconveniences mentioned I caused a tent to be pitched by
the side of the large lagoon between Pitlekaj and Yinretlen, and

a light boat to be carried thither. The bottom of the lagoon was still filled with ice, above which however the water stood so high that the boat floated in it. The naturalists settled by turns in the tent, and from it made excursions in different directions, as I hope with the result that the neighbourhood of Pitlekaj is now the best known tract on the north of Asia, which after all is not saying much. The first plant in flower (*Cochlearia fenestrata,* R. Br.) was seen on the 23rd June.[1] A week after the ground began to grow green and flowers of different kinds to show themselves in greater and greater numbers.[2] Some flies were

[1] During the expedition of 1861, when we were shut up by ice in Treurenberg Bay on Spitzbergen (79° 57′ N.L.) the first flower (*Saxifraga oppositifolia*, L.), was pulled on the 22nd June. After the wintering in 1872-73, Palander and I during our journey round North-east Land, saw the first flower on the same species of saxifrage as early as the 15th June, in the bottom of Wahlenberg Bay (79° 46′ N.L.).

[2] For the sake of completeness, I shall here also enumerate the plants which Dr. Kjellman found at Pitlekaj. Those marked with an * either themselves occur in Scandinavia or are represented by nearly allied forms.

Leucanthemum arcticum (L.) DC.
Artemisia arctica LESS.
    ,, vulgaris L. f. Tilesii LEDEB.
Cineraria frigida RICHARDS.
    ,, palustris L. f. congesta HOOK.
Antennaria alpina (L.) R. BR. f. Friesiana TRAUTV.
Petasites frigida.
Saussurea alpina (L.) DC. f. angustifolia (DC.)
Taraxacum officinale WEB.
Valeriana capitata PALL.
Gentiana glauca PALL.
Pedicularis sudetica WILLD.
    ,, Langsdorffii FISCH.
    ,, lanata WILLD. f. leiantha TRAUTV.
    ,, capitata ADAMS.
Polemonium cœruleum L.
Diapensia lapponica L.
Armeria sibirica TURCZ.
Primula nivalis PALL. f. pygmæa LEDEB.
    ,, borealis DUBY.
Loiseleuria procumbens (L.) DESV.
Ledum palustre L. f. decumbens AIT.
Vaccinium vitis idæa L.
Arctostaphylos alpina (L.) SPRENG.
Cassiope tetragona (L.) DON.
Hedysarum obscurum L.
Oxytropis nigrescens(PALL.)FISCH. f. pygmæa CHAM. species?

* Rubus Chamæmorus L.
* Comarum palustre L.
Potentilla fragiformis L.
    f. parviflora TRAUTV.
    f. villosa (PALL.)
* Sibbaldia procumbens L.
* Dryas octopetala L.
Spiræa betulæfolia PALL. f. typica MAXIM.
* Hippuris vulgaris L.
* Saxifraga stellaris L. f. comosa POIR.
    ,, punctata L.
*   ,, cernua L.
*   ,, rivularis L.
* Rhodiola rosea L.
* Empetrum nigrum L.
* Cardamine bellidifolia L.
Cochlearia fenestrata R. BR.
    f. typica MALMGR.
    f. prostata MALMGR.
Ranunculus Pallasii SEHLECHT.
*   ,, nivalis L.
*   ,, pygmæus WG.
*   ,, hyperboreus ROTTB.
* Aconitum Napellus L. f. delphinifolia REICHENB.
Claytonia acutifolia WILLD.
* Wahlbergella apetala (L.) FR.
* Stellaria longipes GOLDIE. f. humilis FENZL.
*   ,, humifusa ROTTB.
Cerastium maximum L.
*   ,, alpinum L. f. hirsuta KOCH.

seen on a sunshiny day in May (the 27th) in motion on the
surface of the snow, but it was not until the end of June that
insects began to show themselves in any large numbers, among
them many Harpalids, two large species of Carabus, and a large
Curculionid. The insects occurring here however are not very
numerous either in respect of species or individuals, which is not
strange when we consider that the earth at a limited depth from
the surface is constantly frozen. As even the shallow layer,
which thaws in summer, is hard frozen in winter, all the insects
which occur here must in one or other phase of their development endure being frozen solid for some time. But it may be
remarked with reason with reference to this, that if life in an
organism may so to speak be suspended for months by freezing
stiff without being destroyed, what is there to prevent this
suspension being extended over years, decades, or centuries?

The common idea, that all animal life ceases when the interior
animal heat sinks under the freezing-point of water, is besides
not quite correct. This is proved by the abundant evertebrate
life which is found at the bottom of the Polar Sea, even where
the water all the year round has a temperature of $-2°$ to $-2°·7$
C., and by the remarkable observation made during the wintering
at Mussel Bay in 1872–73, that small crustacea can live by
millions in water-drenched snow at a temperature of from $-2°$
to $-10°·2$ C. On this point I say in my account of the expedition
of 1872–73 :—[1]

* Halianthus peploides (L.) Fr.
    Alsine arctica (STEV.) FENZL.
* Sagina nivalis (LINDBL.) Fr.
* Polygonum Bistorta L.
*   „   viviparum L.
            „   polymorphum   L.   f.
                    frigida CHAM.
    Rumex arcticus TRAUTV.
* Oxyria digyna (L.) HILL.
    Salix boganidensis TRAUTV. f. lati-
        folia.
        „   Chamissonis ANDERS.
        „   arctica PALL.
        „   cuneata TURCZ.
*   „   reticulata L.
        „   species?
    Betula glandulosa MICHX. f. rotun-
        difolia REGEL.
    Elymus mollis TRIN.
* Festuca rubra L. f. arenaria
        OSB.
* Poa flexuosa WG.
    Arctophila effusa J. LGE.
    Glyceria vilfoidea (ANDS.) TH. FR.

Glyceria vaginata J. LGE. f. con-
        tracta J. LGE.
* Catabrosa algida (SOL.) Fr.
* Colpodium latifolium R. BR.
    Dupontia Fischeri R. BR.
* Trisetum subspicatum (L.) P. B.
* Aira cæspitosa · L. f. borealis
        TRAUTV.
    Alopecurus alpinus SM.
* Hierochloa alpina (LILJEBL.) ROEM.
        and SCH.
* Carex rariflora (WG.) SM.
*   „   aqvatilis f. epijegos LÆST.
*   „   glareosa WG.
*   „   lagopina WG.
* Eriophorum angustifolium ROTH.
*   „   vaginatum L.
*   „   russeolum FR.
* Luzula parviflora (EHRH.) DESV.
*   „   Wahlenbergii RUPR.
*   „   arcuata (WG.) Sw. f. con-
                fusa LINDEB.
* Juncus biglumis L.
    Lloydia serotina (L.) REICHENB.

[1] *Redogörelse för den svenska polarexpeditionen år* 1872-73. Bihang till
Vet.-Akad. Handl. Bd. 2, No. 18, p. 52.

If during winter one walks along the beach on the snow
1 at ebb is dry, but at flood tide is more or less drenched
through by sea-water, there rises at every step one takes, an
exceedingly intense, beautiful, bluish-white flash of light, which
the spectroscope gives a one-coloured labrador-blue spectrum.
A beautiful flash of light arises from the snow, before completely dark, when it is touched.   The flash lasts only a few
moments after the snow is left untouched, and is so intense, that
it appears as if a sea of fire would open at every step a man
takes.   It produces indeed a peculiar impression on a dark and
clear y winter day (the temperature of the air was sometimes in
the neighbourhood of the freezing-point of mercury) to walk
in this mixture of snow and flame, which at every step one
takes splashes about in all directions, shining with a light so
intense that one is ready to fear that his shoes or clothes will
catch fire."

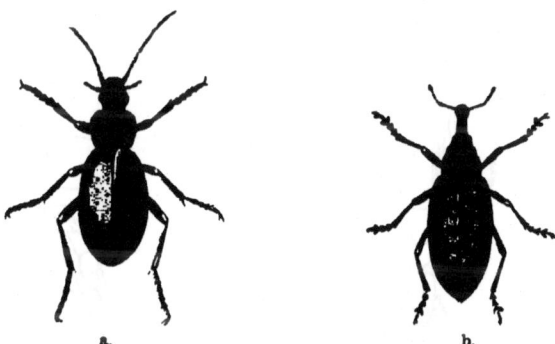

a.   b.
BEETLES FROM PITLEKAJ.
a. *Carabus truncaticollis* ESCHSCHOLTZ.   One and a half the natural size.
b. *Alophus sp*.   One and two-thirds the natural size.

a closer examination it appeared that this light-pheno-
menon proceeded from a minute crustacean, which according to
determination of Prof. W. LILLJEBORG belongs to the species
lia armata, A. Boeck, and whose proper element appears
snow-sludge drenched with salt water cooled considerably
0° C.   First when the temperature sinks below − 10°
the power of this small animal to emit light appear to cease.
As the element in which they live, the surface of the snow
at the beach, is in the course of the winter innumerable
times cooled twenty degrees more, it appears improbable that
minute animals suffer any harm by being exposed to a cold
from − 20° to − 30°, a very remarkable circumstance, as they
mostly do not possess in their organism any means of raising
internal animal heat in any noteworthy degree above the
temperature of the surrounding medium.

We did not see these animals at Pitlekaj, but a similar phenomenon, though on a smaller scale, was observed by Lieut. BELLOT[1] during a sledge-journey in Polar America. He believed that the light arose from decaying organic matter.

After the Chukches had told us that an exceedingly delicious black fish was to be found in the fresh-water lagoon at Yinretlen, which is wholly shut off from the sea and in winter freezes to the bottom, we made an excursion thither on the 8th July. Our friends at the encampment were immediately ready to help us, especially the women, Aitanga, and the twelve-year-old, somewhat spoiled *Vega*-favourite Reitinacka. They ran hither and thither

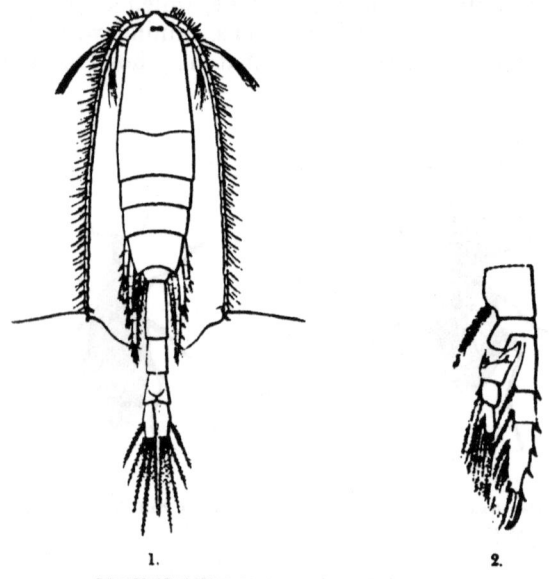

1.   2.

PHOSPHORESCENT CRUSTACEAN FROM MUSSEL BAY.

Metridia armata, A. Boeck.

1. A male magnified twelve times. 2. A foot of the second pair.

like light-hearted and playful children, to put the net in order and procure all that was needed for the fishing. We had carried with us from the vessel a net nine metres long and one deep. Along its upper border floats were fixed; to the lower was bound a long pole, to which were fastened five sticks, by which the pole was sunk to the bottom of the lagoon, a little way from the shore. Some natives wading in the cold water then pushed the net towards the land with sticks and the pole, which glided easily forward over the bottom of the lake, overgrown as it was

[1] *Journal d'un Voyage aux Mers Polaires.* Paris, 1854. Pp. 177 and 223.

with grass. In order to keep the fish from swimming away, the women waded at the sides of the net with their *pesks* much tucked up, screaming and making a noise, and now and then standing in order to indicate by a violent shaking that the water was very cold. The catch was abundant. We caught by hundreds a sort of fish altogether new to us, of a type which we should rather have expected to find in the marshes of the Equatorial regions than up here in the north. The fish were transported in a dog sledge to the vessel, where part of them was

REITINACKA
After a photograph by L. Palander.

placed in spirits for the zoologists and the rest fried, not without a protest from our old cook, who thought that the black slimy fish looked remarkably nasty and ugly. But the Chukches were right: it was a veritable delicacy, in taste somewhat resembling eel, but finer and more fleshy. These fish were besides as tough to kill as eels, for after lying an hour and a half in the air they swam, if replaced in the water, about as fast as before. How this species of fish passes the winter is still more enigmatical than the winter life of the insects. For the lagoon has no outlet and appears to freeze completely to the bottom. The mass of water which was found in autumn in the lagoon therefore still lay there as an unmelted layer of ice not yet broken up, which was covered with a stratum of flood water several feet deep, by which the neighbouring grassy plains were inundated. It was in this flood water that the fishing took place.

After our return home the Yinretlen fish was examined by Professor F. A. SMITT in Stockholm, who stated, in an address which he gave on it before the Swedish Academy of Sciences, that it belongs to a new species, to which Professor Smitt gave the name *Dallia delicatissima*. A closely allied form occurs in Alaska, and has been named *Dallia pectoralis*, Bean. These fishes are besides nearly allied to the dog-fish (*Umbra Krameri*, Fitzing), which is found in the Neusidler and Platten Lakes, and in grottos and other water-filled subterranean cavities in southern Europe. It is remarkable that the European species are considered uneatable, and even regarded with such loathing that

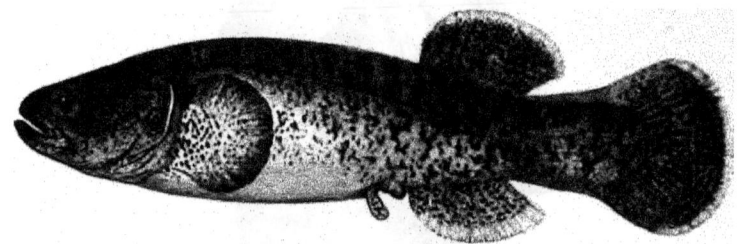

DOG-FISH FROM THE CHUKCH PENINSULA.
Dallia delicatissima, Smitt.
Half the natural size.

the fishermen throw them away as soon as caught because they consider them poisonous, and fear that their other fish would be destroyed by contact with it. They also consider it an affront if one asks them for dog-fish.[1] If we had known this we should not now have been able to certify that *Dallia delicatissima*, SMITT, truly deserves its name.

In the beginning of July the ground became free of snow and we could now form an idea of how the region looked in summer in which we had passed the winter. It was not just attractive. Far away in the south the land rose with terrace-formed escarpments to a hill, called by us Table Mount, which indeed was pretty high, but did not by any steep or bold cliffs yield any contribution to such a picturesque landscape border as is seldom wanting on the portions of Spitzbergen, Greenland, and the north part of Novaya Zemlya which I have visited; south

[1] Heckel and Kner, *Die Süsswasserfische Oesterreichs*, p. 295.

Novaya Zemlya has at least at most places bold picturesque shore-cliffs. If I except the rocky promontory at Yinretlen, where a cliff inhabited by ravens rises boldly out of the sea, and some cliffs situated farther in along the beach of Kolyutschin Bay, the shore in the immediate neighbourhood of our wintering station consisted everywhere only of a low beach formed of coarse sand. Upon this sand, which was always frozen, there ran parallel with the shore a broad bank or dune, 50 to 100 metres broad, of fine sand, not water-drenched in summer, and accordingly not bound together by ice in winter. It is upon this dune that the Chukches erect their tents. Marks of them are therefore met with nearly everywhere, and the dune accordingly is everywhere bestrewed with broken implements or refuse from the chase. Indeed it may be said without exaggeration that the whole north-eastern coast of the Siberian Polar Sea is bordered with a belt of sweepings and refuse of various kinds.

The coarse sand which underlies the dune is, as has been stated, continually frozen, excepting the shallow layer which is thawed in summer. It is here that the "frost formation" of Siberia begins, that is to say, the continually frozen layer of earth, which, with certain interruptions, extends from the Polar Sea far to the south, not only under the treeless *tundra*, but also under splendid forests and cultivated corn-fields.[1] To speak correctly, however, the frozen earth begins a little from the shore *under the sea*.[2] For on the coast the bottom often consists of hard frozen sand—"rock-hard sand," as the dredgers were accustomed to report. The frost formation in Siberia thus embraces not only terrestrial but also marine deposits, together with pure clear layers of ice, these last being formed in the mouths of rivers or small lakes by the ice of the river or lake frozen to the bottom being in spring covered with a layer of mud sufficiently thick to protect the ice from melting during summer. The frozen sea-bottom again appears to have been formed by the sand washed down by the rivers having carried

---

[1] Even pretty far south, in Scandinavia, there occur places with frozen earth which seldom thaws. Thus in Egyptinkorpi mosses in Nurmi and Pjeli parishes in Finland pinewoods are found growing over layers or "tufts" of frozen sand; but also, in other places in Eastern Finland, we find layers containing stumps, roots, &c., of different generations of trees, alternating with layers of frozen mould, according to a communication from the agronome Axel Asplund. A contribution to the knowledge of the way, or one of the ways, in which such formations arise, we obtain from the known fact that mines with an opening to the air, so far south as the middle of Sweden, are filled in a few years with a coherent mass of ice if the opening is allowed to remain open. If it is shut the ice melts again, but for this decades are required.

[2] Middendorff already states that the bottom of the sea of Okotsk is frozen. (*Sibirische Reise*, Bd. 4, 1, p. 502.)

with it when it sank some adhering water from the war
and almost fresh surface strata. At the sea-bottom the sa*
surrounded by *fresh* water freezing at 0° C. thus met a stratu
of *salt* water whose temperature was two or three degrees und
0°, in consequence of which the grains of sand froze fast 1
gether. That it may go on thus we had a direct proof wh*
in spring we sank from the *Vega* the bodies of animals to :
skeletonised by the crustacea that swarmed at the sea-botto*
If the sack, pierced at several places, in which the skeleton w
sunk was first allowed to fill with the slightly salt water fro
the surface and then sink rapidly to the bottom, it was found to 1
so filled with ice, when it was taken up a day or two afterward
that the crustacea were prevented from getting at the fles
We had already determined to abandon the convenient cleansir
process, when I succeeded in finding means to avoid the ii
convenience; this was attained by drawing the sack, whi
some distance under the surface, violently hither and thithe
so that the surface water carried down with it was got rid o
Frozen clay and ooze do not appear to occur at the bottom (
the Polar Sea. Animal life on the frozen sand was rathe
scanty, but algæ were met with there though in limited number

From the shore a plain commences, which is studded wit
extensive lagoons and a large number of small lakes. In sprin
this plain is so water-drenched and so crossed by deep rapi
snow-rivulets, that it is difficult, often impossible, to traverse it
Immediately after the disappearance of the snow a large numbe
of birds at all events had settled there. The Lapp sparrow ha
chosen a tuft projecting from the marshy ground on which to plac
its beautiful roofed dwelling, the waders in the neighbourhood ha
laid their eggs in most cases directly on the water-drenched mos
without trace of a nest, and on tufts completely surrounded b
the spring floods we met with the eggs of the loom, the long
tailed duck, the eider and the goose. Already during our sta*
the water ran away so rapidly, that places, which one day wer
covered with a watery mirror, over which a boat of light draugh
could be rowed forward, were changed the next day to we
marshy ground, covered with yellow grass-straws from the pre
ceding year. At many places the grassy sward had been tor
up by the ice and carried away, leaving openings sharply define
by right lines in the meadows, resembling a newly worked o:
place in a peat moss.

In summer there must be found here green meadows covere
with pretty tall grass, but at the time of our departure vegetatio
had not attained any great development, and the flowers that coul
be discovered were few. I presume however that a beautifu
Arctic flower-world grows up here, although, in consequence o
the exposure of the coast-country to the north winds, poor i*

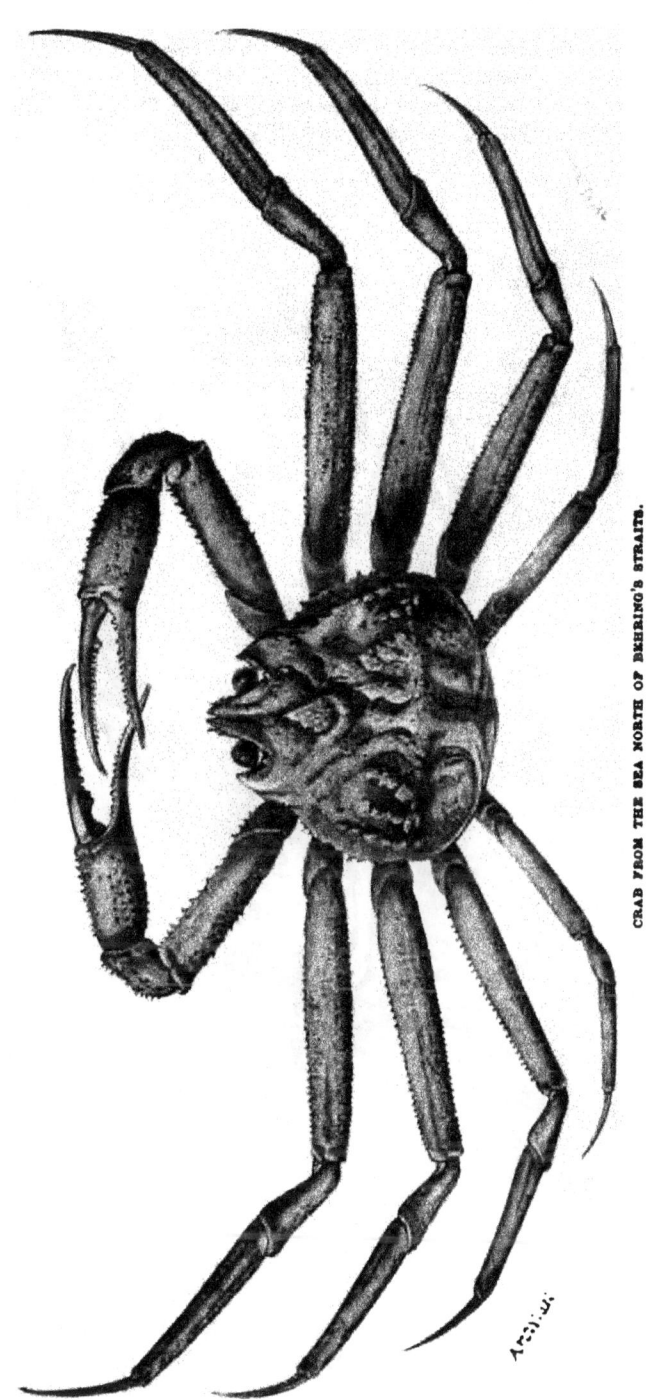

comparison with the vegetation in sheltered valleys in the interior of the country. There are found there too pretty high bushes, but on the other hand trees are represented at Pitlekaj only by a low species of willow which creeps along the ground.

TREE FROM PITLEKAJ.
Salix arctica, PALLAS   Natural size.

We did not, however, see even this "wood" in full leaf. For in order that full summer heat may begin it is necessary, even here, that the ice break up, and this longed-for

nent appeared to be yet far distant. The ice indeed
ime clear of snow in the beginning of July, and thus the
h and the flood water were lessened, which during the pre-
ng weeks had collected on its surface and made it very
cult to walk from the vessel to land. Now, again pretty
·shod and on a hard blue ice-surface, we could make ex-
ions in the neighbourhood of ·the vessel. We had however
ɔe cautious. The former cracks had in many places been
ened to greater or smaller openings by the flood water
ning down, and where a thin black object—a little gravel,
ece of tin from the preserved provision-cases, &c.—had lain
ihe ice there were formed round holes, resembling the seal-
ɛs which I saw in spring laid bare after the melting of the
w on the ice in the fjords of Spitzbergen. The strength
ihe ice besides was nearly unaltered, and on the 16th July
eavily loaded double sledge could still be driven from the
sel to the shore.
)n the 17th the " year's ice" next the land at last broke up,
that an extensive land clearing arose. But the ground-
· were still undisturbed, and between these the " year's ice"
n lay so fast, that all were agreed that at least fourteen
s must still pass before there was any prospect of getting

Vhen on the 16th the reindeer-Chukch Yettugin came on
rd, and, talking of the collection of whale-bones in which
had been engaged some days before, informed us that
·e was a mammoth bone at his tent, and that a mammoth
; stuck out at a place where the spring floods had cut into
bank of a river which flows from Table Mount to Riraitinop,
erefore did not hesitate to undertake an excursion to the
e. Our absence from the vessel was reckoned at five or six
;. It was my intention to go up the river in a skin boat
nging to Notti to the place where the mammoth tusk was,
thence to proceed on foot to Yettugin's tent. Yettugin
red us that the river was sufficiently deep for the flat-
omed boat. But when we had travelled a little way into
country it appeared that the river had fallen considerably
ug the day that Yettugin passed on the vessel. So certain
I however that the ice-barrier would not yet for a long
: be broken up, that I immediately after my return from the
rsion, which had thus been rendered unsuccessful, made
ngements for a new journey in order with other means of
sport to reach the goal.
'hile we were thus employed the forenoon of the 18th passed.
sat down to dinner at the usual time, without any suspicion
the time of our release was now at hand. During dinner
as suddenly observed that the vessel was moving slightly.

Palander rushed on deck, saw that the ice was in motion, ordered the boiler fires to be lighted, the engine having long ago been put in order in expectation of this moment, and in two hours, by 3.30 P.M. on the 18th July, the *Vega*, decked with flags, was under steam and sail again on the way to her destination.

We now found that a quite ice-free " lead " had arisen between the vessel and the open water next the shore, the ice-fields west of our ground-ices having at the same time drifted farther out to sea, so that the clearing along the shore had widened enough to give the *Vega* a sufficient depth of water. The course was shaped at first for the N.W. in order to make a *détour* round the drift-ice fields lying nearest us, then along the coast for Behring's Straits. On the height at Yinretlen there stood as we passed, the men, women and children of the village all assembled, looking out to sea at the fire-horse—the Chukches would perhaps say fire-dog or fire-reindeer—which carried their friends of the long winter months for ever away from their cold, bleak shores. Whether they shed tears, as they often said they would, we could not see from the distance which now parted us from them. But it may readily have happened that the easily moved disposition of the savage led them to do this. Certain it is that in many of us the sadness of separation mingled with the feelings of tempestuous joy which now rushed through the breast of every *Vega* man.

The *Vega* met no more ice-obstacles on her course to the Pacific. Serdze Kamen was passed at 1.30 A.M. of the 19th, but the fog was so dense that we could not clearly distinguish the contours of the land. Above the bank of mist at the horizon we could only see that this cape, so famous in the history of the navigation of the Siberian Polar Sea, is occupied by high mountains, split up, like those east of the Bear Islands, into ruin-like gigantic walls or columns. The sea was mirror-bright and nearly clear of ice, a walrus or two stuck up his head strangely magnified by the fog in our neighbourhood, seals swam round us in large numbers, and flocks of birds, which probably breed on the steep cliffs of Serdze Kamen, swarmed round the vessel. The trawl net repeatedly brought up from the sea-bottom a very abundant yield of worms, molluscs, crustacea, &c. A zoologist would here have had a rich working-field.

The fog continued, so that on the other side of Serdze Kamen we lost all sight of land, until on the morning of the 20th dark heights again began to peep out. These were the mountain summits of the easternmost promontory of Asia, East Cape, an unsuitable name, for which I have substituted on the map that of Cape Deschnev after the gallant Cossack who for the first time 230 years ago circumnavigated it.

By 11 A.M. we were in the middle of the sound which unites

J. L. ZALANDOR

he North Polar Sea with the Pacific, and from this point the *Vega* greeted the old and new worlds by a display of flags and he firing of a Swedish salute.

Thus finally was reached the goal towards which so many lations had struggled, all along from the time when Sir Hugh Willoughby, with the firing of salutes from cannon and with iurrahs from the festive-clad seamen, in the presence of an nnumerable crowd of jubilant men certain of success, ushered n the long series of North-East voyages. But, as 1 have before elated, their hopes were grimly disappointed. Sir Hugh and all iis men perished as pioneers of England's navigation and of 'oyages to the ice-encumbered sea which bounds Europe and Asia n the north. Innumerable other marine expeditions have since hen trodden the same path, always without success, and generally with the sacrifice of the vessel and of the life and health of nany brave seamen. Now for the first time, after the lapse of 336 years, and when most men experienced in sea matters had leclared the undertaking impossible, was the North-East Passage at last achieved. This has taken place, thanks to the discipline, zeal, and ability of our man-of-war's-men and their officers, without the sacrifice of a single human life, without sickness among those who took part in the undertaking, without the slightest damage to the vessel, and under circumstances which show that the same thing may be done again in most, perhaps in all years, in the course of a few weeks. It may be permitted us to say, that under such circumstances it was with pride we saw the blue-yellow flag rise to the mast-head and heard the Swedish salute, in the sound where the old and the new worlds reach hands to each other. The course along which we sailed is indeed no longer required as a commercial route between Europe and China. But it has been granted to this and the preceding Swedish expeditions to open a sea to navigation, and to confer on half a continent the possibility of communicating by sea with the oceans of the world.

CHAPTER XII.

The history, physique, disposition, and manners of the Chukches.

THE north coast of Siberia is now, with the exception of its westernmost and easternmost parts, literally a desert. In the west there projects between the mouth of the Ob and the southern portion of the Kara Sea the peninsula of Yalmal, which by its remote position, its grassy plains, and rivers abounding in fish, appears to form the earthly paradise of the Samoyed of the present day. Some hundred families belonging to this race wander about here with their numerous reindeer herds. During winter they withdraw to the interior of the country or southwards, and the coast is said then to be uninhabited. This is the case both summer and winter, not only with Beli Ostrov and the farthest portion of the peninsula between the Ob and the Yenisej (Mattesol), but also with the long stretch of coast between the mouth of the Yenisej and Chaun Bay. During the voyage of the *Vega* in 1878 we did not see a single native. No trace of man could be discovered at the places where we landed, and though for a long time we sailed quite near land, we saw from the sea only a single house on the shore, viz., the before-mentioned wooden hut on the east side of Chelyuskin peninsula. Russian *simovies* and native encampments are indeed still found on the rivers some distance from their mouths, but the former coast population has withdrawn to the interior of the country or died out,[1] and the north coast of Asia first begins again to be inhabited at Chaun Bay, namely, by the tribe with whom we came in contact during the latter part of the coast voyage of the *Vega* in 1878 and during the wintering.

I have already, it is true, given an account of various traits

[1] The north coast of America still forms the haunt of a not inconsiderable Eskimo population which, for a couple of centuries, has extended to the 80th degree of latitude. As the climate in the north part of the Old World differs little from that which prevails in corresponding regions of the New, as at both places there is an abundant supply of fish, and as the seal and walrus hunting—at least between the Yenisej and the Chatanga— ought to be as productive as on the north coast of America, this difference, which has arisen only recently, is very striking. It appears to me to be capable of explanation in the following way. Down to our days a large number of small savage tribes in America have carried on war with each other, the weaker, to escape extermination by the more powerful races, being compelled to flee to the ice deserts of the north, deeming themselves fortunate if they could there, in peace from their enemies, earn a living by adopting the mode of life of the Polar races, suitable as it is to the climate and resources of the land. The case was once the same in Siberia, and there are many indications that fragments of conquered tribes have been in former times driven up from the south, not only to the north coast of the mainland, but also beyond it to the islands lying off it. In Siberia, however, for the last 250 years, the case has been completely changed by the Russian conquest of the country. The pressure of the new government has, notwithstanding many single acts of violence, been on the whole less destructive to the original population than the influence which the Europeans have exerted in America. The Russian power has at least had a wholly beneficial influence, inasmuch as it has prevented the continual feuds between the native races. The tribes driven to the inhospitable North have been enabled to return to milder regions, and where this has not taken place they have, in the absence of new migrations from the South, succumbed in the fight with cold, hunger, and small-pox, or other diseases introduced by their new masters.

of the Chukches' disposition and mode of life, but I believe at
all events that a more exhaustive statement of what the *Vega*
men experienced in this region will be interesting to my readers,
even if in the course of it I am sometimes compelled to return
to subjects of which I have already treated.

In West-European writings the race, which inhabits the
north-easternmost portion of Asia, is mentioned for the first
time, so far as I know, by WITSEN, who in the second edition of
his work (1705, p. 671) quotes a statement by VOLODOMIR
ATLASSOV, that the inhabitants of the northernmost portions of
Siberia are called *Tsjuktsi*, without, however, giving any detailed
description of the people themselves. In maps from the end of
the seventeenth century names are still inscribed on this portion
of land which were borrowed from the history of High Asia, as
" Tenduc," " Quinsai," " Catacora," &c., but these are left out in
VAN KEULEN'S atlas of 1709, and instead there stands here
Zuczari. From about the same time we fall in with some
accounts of the Chukches in the narrative of the distinguished
painter CORNELIS DE BRUIN'S travels in Russia. A Russian
merchant, MICHAEL OSTATIOF, who passed fourteen years in
travelling in Siberia, gave de Bruin some information regarding
the countries he had travelled through ; among others he spoke
of *Korakie* and *Soegtsie*. The latter were sketched as a godless
pack, who worship the devil and carry with them their fathers'
bones to be used in their magical arts. The same Russian who
made these statements had also come in contact with " stationary"
(settled) Soegtsi, so called "because they pass the whole winter
hibernating, lying or sitting in their tents." [1] I have found the
first somewhat detailed accounts of the race in the note on page
10 of the under-quoted work, *Histoire généalogique des Tartares*,
Leyden, 1726. They are founded on the statements of Swedish
prisoners of war in Siberia.

The Russians, however, had made a much earlier acquaintance
with the Chukches ; for during their conquest of Siberia they
came in contact with this race before the middle of the seventeenth century. A company of hunters in 1646 sailed down the
Kolyma river to the Polar Sea. East of the Kolyma they fell
in with the Chukches, with whom they dealt in this way : they
laid down their goods on the beach and then retired, on which
the Chukches came thither, took the goods, and laid furs, walrus
tusks, or carvings in walrus ivory, in their place.[2] How such

[1] Cornelis de Bruin, *Reizen over Moskovie, door Persie en Indie*, &c.,
Amsterdam, 1711, p. 12. The author's name is also written De Bruyn
and Le Brun.

[2] Herodotus already states in book iv. chapter 196, that the Cartha-
ginians bartered goods in the same way with a tribe living on the coast of
Africa beyond the Gates of Hercules. The same mode of barter was still
in use nearly two thousand years later, when the west coast of Africa

journeys were repeated and finally led to the circumnavigation of the north-easternmost promontory of Asia belongs to a following chapter.

During these journeys the Russians often came in contact with the tribe which inhabited the north-eastern part of Asia, a contact which in general was not of a friendly nature. The bold hunters who contributed powerfully to the conquest of Siberia, and who even at their own hand entered into conflicts with whole armies from the heavenly empire, appear not to have behaved well when confronted with the warriors of the Chukch race. Even the attempts that were made with professional soldiers to conquer the land of the Chukches were without result, less however, perhaps, on account of the armed opposition which the Chukches made than from the nature of the country and the impossibility of even a small body of troops supportin; themselves. The following may be quoted as examples of these campaigns which throw light upon the former disposition and mode of life of this tribe.

In 1701 some Yukagires, who were tributary to Russia determined to make an attack on the Chukches, and requested from the commandant at Anadyrsk assistance against these enemies. A body of troops numbering twenty-four Russians and 110 Yukagires, was accordingly sent on a campaign along the coast from Anadyrsk to Chukotskojnos. By the way they fell in with thirteen tents, inhabited by Chukches who owned no reindeer. The inhabitants were required to submit and pay tribute. This the Chukches refused to do, on which the Russians killed most of the men and took the women and children prisoners. The men who were not cut down killed one another, preferring death to the loss of freedom. Some days after there was another fight with 300 Chukches, which, however, was so unfortunate for the latter that 200 are said to have fallen. The rest fled, but returned next day with a force ten times as strong, which finally compelled the Russo-Yukagirean troop to return with their object unaccomplished.

A similar campaign on a small scale was undertaken in 1711, but with the same issue. On a demand for tribute the Chukches answered : "The Russians have before come to us to demand tribute and hostages, but this we have refused to give, and thus we also intend to do in future." [1]

About fifteen years after this resultless campaign the Cossack colonel AFFANASSEJ SCHESTAKOV proposed to the Government

was visited by the Venetian Cadamosto. in 1454 (*Ramusio*, i., 1588, leaf 100).

[1] As security for the subjection of the conquered races, the Russians were accustomed to take a number of men and women from their principal families as hostages. These persons were called *amanates*, and were kept in a sort of slavery at the fixed winter dwellings of the Russians.

again to subdue this obstinate race, intending also to go over to
the American side, yet known only by report, in order to render
the races living there tributary to the Russians. The proposal
was accepted. A mate, JACOB HENS, a land-measurer, MICHAEL
GVOSDEV, an ore-tester, HERDEBOL, and ten sailors were
ordered by the Admiralty to accompany the expedition. At
Yekaterinenburg Schestakov was provided with some small
cannon and mortars with ammunition, and at Tobolsk with 400
Cossacks. In consequence of a great number of misfortunes,
among them shipwreck in the sea of Okotsk, there stood however but a small portion of this force at his disposal when he
began his campaign by marching into the country from the
bottom of Penschina Bay. This campaign too was exceedingly
unfortunate. After only a few days' march he came unexpectedly on a large body of Chukches, who themselves had gone to
war with the Koryäks. A fight took place on the $\frac{25}{14}$th March,
1730, in which Schestakov himself fell, hit by an arrow, and his
followers were killed or put to flight.

Among those who were ordered to accompany Schestakov in
this unfortunate campaign was Captain DMITRI PAULUTSKI.
Under his command a new campaign was undertaken against
the Chukches. With a force of 215 Russians, 160 Cossacks and
60 Yukagires, Paulutski left Anadyrsk on the $\frac{2rd}{12th}$ March, 1731,
and marched east of the sources of the Anadyr to the Polar Sea,
which was only reached after two months' march. Then he
went along the coast, partly by land, partly on the ice, to the
eastward. After fourteen days he fell in with a large Chukch
army, and having in vain summoned it to surrender, he
delivered a blow on the $\frac{19}{7}$th June, and obtained a complete
victory over the enemy. During the continuation of the
campaign along the coast he was compelled to fight on two
other occasions, one on the $\frac{11th\ July}{30th\ June}$ and the other on the $\frac{26}{14}$th July,
at Chukotskojnos itself, over which promontory he wished to
march to the mouth of the Anadyr. In both cases the victory
lay with the Russians, who, according to Müller's account based
on the official documents, in all three engagements lost only
three Cossacks, one Yukagire and five Koryäks. But notwithstanding all these defeats the Chukches refused to submit and
pay tribute to the Russians, on which account the only gain of
the campaign was the honour of avenging Schestakov's defeat
and of marching in triumph over Chukotskojnos. For this, ten
days were required. On the promontory, hills of considerable
height had to be passed. It appears as if Paulutski followed the
shore of Kolyutschin Bay to the south, and then marched over
the tongue of land which separates this bay from Anadyr Bay,
or to express it otherwise, which unites the Chukch peninsula
to the mainland of Siberia.

Many mistakes in comprehending the accounts of old travels to these regions have arisen from our ignorance of the great southern extension of Kolyutschin Bay, and from the same name being frequently used to distinguish different places on the coasts of Siberia. Thus we find on the map by A. ARROW-SMITH annexed to Sauer's account of Billing's travels a Serdze Kamen on the south side of Chukch peninsula, and it was perhaps just this Serdze Kamen, known and so named by the dwellers on the Anadyr, that is mentioned in Müller's account of Paulutski's campaign.

On the $\frac{\text{1st Nov.}}{\text{21st Oct.}}$ Paulutski returned to Anadyrsk, crowned with victory indeed, but without having brought his adversaries to lasting submission. No new attempt was made to induce the Chukches to submit, perhaps because Paulutski's campaign had rendered it evident that it was easier to win victories over the Chukches than to subdue them, and that the whole treasures of walrus tusks and skins belonging to the tribe would scarcely suffice to pay the expenses of the most inconsiderable campaign.

Perhaps too the accounts of Paulutski's victories may not be quite correct, at least the old repute of Chukches as a brave and savage race remained undiminished. Thus we read in a note already quoted at page 110 of the *Histoire généalogique des Tartares:*[1] "The north-eastern part of Asia is inhabited by two allied races, *Tzuktzchi* and *Tzchalatzki*, and south of them on the Eastern Ocean by a third, called *Olutorski.* They are the most savage tribe in the whole north of Asia, and will have nothing to do with the Russians, whom they inhumanly kill when they fall in with them, and when any of them fall into the hands of the Russians they kill themselves." On the map of LOTTERUS (1765) the Chukch Peninsula is coloured in a way differing from Russian Siberia; and there is the following inscription : *Tjuktzchi natio ferocissima et bellicosa Russorum inimica, qui capti se invicem interficiunt.* In 1777 GEORGIUS says in his *Beschreibung aller Nationen des Russischen Reichs* (part ii., p. 350) of the Chukches: "They are more savage, coarse, proud, refractory, thievish, false, and revengeful, than the neighbouring nomads the Koryäks. They are as bad and dangerous as the Tunguses are friendly. Twenty Chukches will beat fifty Koryäks. The *Ostrogs* (fortified places) lying in th neighbourhood of their country are even in continual fear o

---

[1] The work is a translation made at Tobolsk by Swedish officers, prisoners of war from the battle of Pultava, from a Tartar manuscript by Abulgasi Bayadur Chan. The original manuscript (?) is in the library at Upsala, to which it was presented in 1772 by Lieutenant-Colonel Schön-ström. The translation has notes by Bentinck, a Dutchman by birth, who was also taken prisoner in the Swedish service at Pultava.

them, and cost so much that the Government has recently withdrawn the oldest Russian settlement in those regions, Anadyrsk." Other statements to the same effect might be quoted, and even in our day the Chukches are, with or without justification, known in Siberia for stubbornness, courage, and love of freedom.

But what violence could not effect has been completely accomplished in a peaceful way.[1] The Chukches indeed do not pay any other taxes than some small market tolls, but a very active traffic is now carried on between them and the Russians, and many travellers have without inconvenience traversed their country, or have sailed along its pretty thickly inhabited coast.

Among former travellers on the Chukch peninsula, who visited the encampments of the coast Chukches, besides Behring, Cook, and other seafarers, the following may be mentioned:—

The Cossack, PETER ILIIN SIN POPOV, was sent in 1711 with two interpreters to examine the country of the Chukches, and has left some interesting accounts of his observations there (MÜLLER, Sammlung Russischer Geschichten, iii. p. 56).[2]

BILLINGS, with his companions SAUER, SARYTSCHEV, &c., visited Chukch-land in 1791. Among other things, accompanied by Dr. MERK, two interpreters and eight men, he made a journey from Metschigme Bay over the interior of Chukch-land to Yakutsk. Unfortunately the account we have of this remarkable journey is exceedingly incomplete.[3]

FERDINAND VON WRANGEL during his famous Siberian travels was much in contact with the Chukches, and among his other journeys travelled in the winter of 1823 in dog sledges along the coast of the Polar Sea from the Kolyma to Kolyutschin Island (Wrangel, Reise, ii. pp. 176-231). There are besides

---

[1] Lütke says (Erman's Archiv, iii. p. 464) that the peaceful relations with the Chukches began after the conclusion of a peace which was brought about ten years after the abandonment of Anadyrsk, where for thirty-six years there had been a garrison of 600 men, costing over a million roubles. This peace this formerly so quarrelsome people has kept conscientiously down to our days with the exception of some market brawls, which induced Treskin, Governor-General of Eastern Siberia, to conclude with them, in 1817, a commercial treaty which appears to have been faithfully adhered to, to the satisfaction and advantage of both parties (Dittmar, p. 128).

[2] Müller has likewise saved from oblivion some other accounts regarding the Chukches, collected soon after at Anadyrsk. When we now read these accounts, we find not only that the Chukches knew the Eskimo on the American side, but also stories regarding the Indians of Western America penetrated to them, and further, through the authorities in Siberia, came to Europe, a circumstance which deserves to be kept in mind in judging of the writings of Herodotus and Marco Polo.

[3] Sauer, An Account, &c., pp. 255 and 319. Sarytschev, Reise, übersetzt von Busse, ii. p. 102.

many notices of the Chukches at other places in the same
work (i. pp. 267-293 ; ii. pp. 156, 168, &c.).

FRIEDRICH VON LÜTKE in the course of his circumnavigation
of the globe in 1826-29, came in contact with the population
of the Chukch peninsula, whom he described in detail in
Erman's *Archiv* (iii. pp. 446-464). Here it ought to be noted
that, while the population on the North coast consists of true
Chukches, the coast population of the region which Lütke visited,
the stretch between the Anadyr and Cape Deschnev consists of
a tribe, *Namollo*, which differs from the Chukches, and is
nearly allied to the Eskimo on the American side of
Behring's Straits.

The English Franklin Expedition in the *Plover*, commanded
by Captain MOORE, wintered in 1848-49 at Chukotskojnos, and,
both at the winter station and in the course of extensive
excursions with dogs along the coast and to the interior of the
country, came much in contact with the natives. The observations made during the wintering were published in a work
of great importance for a knowledge of the tribes in question
by Lieutenant W. H. HOOPER, *Ten Months among the Tents of
the Tuski*, London 1853.

C. VON DITTMAR [1] travelled in 1853 in the north part of
Kamchatka, and there came in contact with the reindeer
nomads, especially with the Koryäks. The information he
gives us about the Chukches (p. 126) he had obtained from the
Nischni-Kolymsk merchant, TRIFONOV, who had traded with
them for twenty-eight years, and had repeatedly travelled in the
interior of the country.

Interesting contributions to a knowledge of the mode of living
of the reindeer-Chukches were also collected by Baron G. VON
MAYDELL, who, in 1868 and 1869, along with Dr. CARL VON
NEUMANN and others, made a journey from Yakutsk by Sredni-
Kolymsk and Anjui to Kolyutschin Bay. Unfortunately, with
regard to this expedition, I have only had access to some notices
in the *Proceedings of the Royal Geographical Society* (vol. 21,
London 1877, p. 213), and *Das Ausland* (1880, p. 861). The
proper sketch of the journey is to be found in *Isvestija*, published
by the Siberian division of the Russian Geographical Society,
parts 1 and 2.

With reference to the other travellers whose writings are
usually quoted as sources for a knowledge of the Chukches, it
may be mentioned that STELLER and KRASCHENINNIKOV only
touch in passing on the true Chukches, but instead give very
instructive and detailed accounts of the Koryäks, who are as

---

[1] *Über die Koriäken und die ihnen sehr nahe verwandten Tschuktschen*
(Bulletin historico-philologique de l'Académie de St. Pétersbourg, t. xiii.,
1856, p. 126).

nearly allied to the Chukches as the Spaniards to the Portuguese, but yet differ considerably in their mode of life; also that a part of these authors' statements regarding the Chukches do not at all refer to that tribe, but to the Eskimo. It appears indeed that recently, after the former national enmity had ceased, mixed races have arisen among these tribes. But it ought not to be forgotten that they differ widely in origin, although the Chukches as coming at a later date to the coast of the Polar Sea have adopted almost completely the hunting implements and household furniture of the Eskimo; and the Eskimo again, in the districts where they come in contact with the Chukches, have adopted various things from their language.

Like the Lapps and most other European and Asiatic Polar races, the Chukches fall into two divisions speaking the same language and belonging to the same race, but differing considerably in their mode of life. One division consists of reindeer nomads, who, with their often very numerous reindeer herds, wander about between Behring's Straits, and the Indigirka and the Penschina Bays. They live by tending reindeer and by trade, and consider themselves the chief part of the Chukch tribe. The other division of the race are the coast Chukches, who do not own any reindeer, but live in fixed but easily movable and frequently moved tents along the coast between Chaun Bay and Behring's Straits. But beyond East Cape there is found along the coast of Behring's Sea another tribe, nearly allied to the Eskimo. This is Wrangel's *Onkilon*, Lütke's *Namollo*. Now, however, Chukches also have settled at several points on this line of coast, and a portion of the Eskimo have adopted the language of the superior Chukch race. Thus the inhabitants at St. Lawrence Bay spoke Chukch, with little mixture of foreign words, and differed in their mode of life and appearance only inconsiderably from the Chukches, whom during the course of the winter we learned to know from nearly all parts of the Chukch peninsula. The same was the case with the natives who came on board the *Vega* while we sailed past East Cape, and with the two families we visited in Konyam Bay. But the natives in the north-west part of St. Lawrence Island talked an Eskimo dialect, quite different from Chukch. There were, however, many Chukch words incorporated with it. At Port Clarence on the contrary there lived pure Eskimo. Among them we found a Chukch woman who informed us that there were Chukch villages also on the American side of Behring's Strait, north of Prince of Wales Cape. These cannot, however, be very numerous or populous, as they are not mentioned in the accounts of the various English expeditions to those regions; they are not noticed for instance in Dr. JOHN SIMPSON'S instructive memoir on the Eskimo at Behring's Straits.

We were unable during the voyage of the *Vega* to obtain any data for estimating the number of the reindeer-Chukches. But the number of the coast Chukches may be arrived at in the following way. Lieutenant Nordquist collected from the numerous foremen who rested at the *Vega* information as to the names of the encampments which are to be found at present on the coast between Chaun Bay and Behring's Straits, and the number of tents at each village. He thus ascertained that the number of the tents in the coast villages amounts to about 400. The number of inhabitants in every tent may be, according to our experience, averaged at five. The population on the line of coast in question may thus amount to about 2,000, at most to 2,500, men, women, and children. The number of the reindeer-Chukches appears to be about the same. The whole population of Chukch-land may thus now amount to 4,000 or 5,000 persons. The Cossack Popov already mentioned, reckoned in 1711 that all the Chukches, both reindeer-owning and those with fixed dwellings, numbered 2,000 persons. Thus during the last two centuries, if these estimates are correct, this Polar race has doubled its numbers.

In order to give the reader an idea of the language of the Chukches, I have in a preceding chapter given an extract from the large vocabulary which Nordquist has collected. There appear to be no dialects differing very much from each other. Whether foreign words borrowed from other Asiatic languages have been adopted in Chukch we have not been able to make out. It is certain that no Russian words are used. The language strikes me as articulate and euphonious. It is nearly allied to the Koryäk, but so different from other, both East-Asiatic and American, tongues, that philologists have not yet succeeded in clearing up the relationship of the Chukches to other races.

Like most other Polar tribes, the Chukches now do not belong to any unmixed race. This one is soon convinced of, if he considers attentively the inhabitants of a large tent-village. Some are tall, with tallowlike, raven-black hair, brown complexion, high aquiline nose—in short, with an exterior that reminds us of the descriptions we read of the North American Indians. Others again by their dark hair, slight beard, sunk nose or rather projecting cheek-bones and oblique eyes, remind u. distinctly of the Mongolian race; and finally we meet among them with very fair faces, with features and complexion wh ic lead us to suspect that they are descendants of runaways c prisoners of war of purely Russian origin. The most commo t type is—straight, coarse, black hair of moderate length; t brow tapering upwards; the nose finely formed, but with a root often flattened : eyes by no means small; well-develop black eyebrows; projecting cheeks often swollen by frostbi

·hich is specially observable when the face is looked at from the
ide ; light, slightly brown complexion, which in the young women
s often nearly as red and white as in Europeans. The beard is
lways scanty. Nearly all are stout and well-grown; we saw no
ripples among them. The young women often strike one as
ery pretty if one can rid oneself of the unpleasant impression of
he dirt, which is never washed away but by the drifting snow of
/inter, and of the nauseous train-oil odour which in winter they
arry with them from the close tent-chamber. The children
early always make a pleasant impression by their healthy
ppearance, and their friendly and becoming behaviour.

The Chukches are a hardy race, but exceedingly indolent
vhen want of food does not force them to exertion. The men
luring their hunting excursions pass whole days in a cold of
- 30° to - 40° out upon the ice, without protection and without
arrying with them food or fuel. In such cases they slake their
hirst with snow, and assuage their hunger, if they have been suc-
essful in hunting, with the blood and flesh of the animals they
ave killed. Women nearly naked often during severe cold leave
)r a while the inner tent, or tent-chamber, where the train-oil
imp maintains a heat that is at times oppressive. A foreigner's
isit induces the completely naked children to half creep out from
nder the curtain of reindeer skin which separates the sleeping
iamber from the exterior tent, in which as it is not heated, the
imperature is generally little higher than that of the air outside.
n this temperature the mothers do not hesitate to show their
aked children, one or two years of age, to visitors for some
ioments.

Diseases are notwithstanding uncommon, with the exception
iat in autumn, before the severe cold commences, nearly all
iffer from a cough and cold. Very bad skin eruptions and
)res also occur so frequently that a stay in the inner tent is
hereby commonly rendered disgusting to Europeans. Some of
he sores however are merely frostbites, which most Chukches
ring on themselves by the carelessness with which during
igh winds they expose the bare neck, breasts, and wrists to
he lowest temperature. When frostbite has happened it is
reated, even though of considerable extent, with extreme care-
essness. They endeavour merely to thaw the frozen place as fast
s possible partly by chafing, partly by heating. On the other
iand we never saw any one who had had a deep frostbite on the
iands or feet, a circumstance which must be ascribed to the
erviceable nature of their shoes and gloves. From the beginning
if October 1878 to the middle of July 1879 no death appears
o have happened at any of the encampments near us. During
he same time the number of the inhabitants was increased by
wo or three births. During the wife's pregnancy the husband

TYPICAL CHUKCH FACES.

1. Manschetsko, a man from Pit'ekaj. 2. Young man from Irgunnuk. 3 Chajlrellin, a man from
Irgunnuk. 4. Reindeer-Cl ukch. 5. Old man from Irgunnuk. 6. Man from Yinretlen.

After photographs by L. Palander.

TYPICAL CHUKCH FACES.

1. 2. Nautsing, a woman from Pitlekaj.   3, 4. Rotschitlen.   5. Young man from Vankarema.
6. Young man from Irgunnuk.

After photographs by L. Palander.

was very affectionate to her, gave her his constant company in the tent, kissed and fondled her frequently in the presence strangers, and appeared to take a pride in showing her visitors.

We had no opportunity of witnessing any burial or marriag It appears as if the Chukches sometimes burn their dead, som times expose them on the *tundra* as food for beasts of prey, wi weapons, sledges, and household articles. They have perha begun to abandon the old custom of burning the dead, since t hunting has fallen off so that the supply of blubber for burni has diminished. I have before described the pits filled wi burned bones which Dr. Stuxberg found on the 9th Septemb 1878, by the bank of a dried-up rivulet. We took them for graves, but not having seen any more at our winter station, began to entertain doubts as to the correctness of our obser tion.[1] It is at least certain that the inhabitants of Pitleh exclusively bury their dead by laying them out on the *tundra*

SV   NO

PLAN OF A CHUKCH GRAVE.,
After a drawing by A. Stuxberg.

Regarding the man, buried or exposed in this way, wh Johnsen found on the 15th October, Dr. Almquist, who hims visited the place the next day, makes the following statement

"The place was situated five to seven kilometres from village Yinretlen, near the bottom of the little valley whi runs from this village in a southerly direction into the interi The body was exposed on a little low knoll only two fatho across. It was covered with loose snow, and was not frozen v hard. When it was loosened there was no proper pit to be seen the underlying snow and ice. The corpse lay from true N.N. to S.S.E., with the head to the former quarter. Under the he lay two black rounded stones, such as the Chukches use

[1] That the Chukches burn their dead with various ceremonies is sta by Sarytschev on the ground of communications by the interpreter Daur who lived among the reindeer-Chukches from 1787 to 1791, in order learn their language and customs, and to announce the arrival of Billin expedition (Sarytschev's *Reise*, ii. p. 108). The statement is thus certai quite trustworthy. The coast population with whom Hooper came contact, on the other hand, laid out their dead on special stages, wh the corpses were allowed to be eaten up by ravens or to decay (*loc.* p. 88).

housekeeping. Besides these there was no trace of anything
underlying or covering the corpse. The clothes had been torn
by beasts of prey from the body; the back was quite untouched,
but the face and breast were much wasted, and the arms and
legs almost wholly eaten up. On the knoll evident traces of
the wolf, the fox, and the raven were visible. Close to the
right side of the corpse had lain the weapons which Johnsen had
brought home the day before. Near the feet was found a sledge
completely broken in pieces, evidently new and smashed on the
spot. Not far off, we found lying on the snow pieces of a *pesk*
and of foot-coverings, both new and of the finest quality.
Beasts of prey had undoubtedly torn them off and pulled them
about. On the knoll there were found besides five or six other
graves, distinguished by small stones or a wooden block lying on
the even ground. Two of the graves were ornamented by a
collection of reindeer horns. The severe cold prevented me
from ascertaining whether these stones concealed the remains
of buried corpses. I considered that I might take the Chukch's
head, as otherwise the wolves would doubtless have eaten it up.
It was taken on board and skeletonised."

In the spring of 1879, after the snow was melted, we had
further opportunities of seeing a large number of burying-
places, or more correctly of places were dead Chukches had
been laid out. They were marked by stones placed in a peculiar
way, and were measured and examined in detail by Dr. Stuxberg,
who gives the following description of them :—

" The Chukch graves on the heights south of Pitlekaj and
Yinretlen, which were examined by me on the 4th and 7th
July, 1879, were nearly fifty in number. Every grave consisted
of an oval formed of large lying stones. At one end there was
generally a large stone raised on its edge, and from the opposite
end there went out one or two pieces of wood lying on the
ground. The area within the stone circle was sometimes overlaid with small stones, sometimes free and overgrown with grass.
At all the graves, at a distance of four to seven paces from the
stone standing on its edge in the longitudinal axis of the grave
or a little to the side of it, there was another smaller circle of
stones inclosing a heap of reindeer horns, commonly containing
also broken seals' skulls and other fragments of bones. Only
in one grave were found pieces of human bones. The graves
were evidently very old, for the bits of wood at the ends were
generally much decayed and almost wholly covered with earth,
and the stones were completely overgrown with lichens on the
upper side. I estimate the age of these graves at about two
hundred years."

H H

The Chukches do not dwell in snow huts, nor in wood⬛⬛n houses, because wood for building is not to be found in t⬛⬛e country of the coast Chukches, and because wooden houses a⬛⬛e unsuitable for the reindeer nomad. They live summer a⬛⬛d winter in tents of a peculiar construction, not used by any oth⬛⬛er race. For in order to afford protection from the cold the tent is double; the outer envelope inclosing an inner tent or sleepi⬛⬛g chamber. This has the form of a parallelopiped, about 3·5 metres long, 2·2 metres broad, and 1·8 metre high. It is su r-rounded by thick, warm, reindeer skins, and is further cover⬛⬛d with a layer of grass. The floor consists of a walrus sk⬛⬛n stretched over a foundation of twigs and straw. At night t⬛⬛e floor is covered with a carpet of reindeer skins, which is tak⬛⬛n away during the day. The rooms at the sides of the inner te⬛⬛t

TENT FRAME AT PITLEKAJ.
After a drawing by G. Bove.

are also shut off by curtains, and serve as pantries. The inner ten t is warmed by three train-oil lamps, which together with the hea t given off by the numerous human beings packed together in the tent, raise the temperature to such a height that the inhabitants even during the severest winter cold may be completely naked. The work of the women and the cooking are carried on in winter in this tent-chamber, very often also the calls of nature are obeyed in it. All this conduces to make the atmosphere prevailing there unendurable. There are also, however, cleanlier families, in whose sleeping chamber the air is not so disgusting.

In summer they live during the day, and cook and work, in the outer tent. This consists of seal and walrus skins sewed together, which however are generally so old, hairless, and full of holes, that they appear to have been used by several genera-tions. The skins of the outer tent are stretched over wooden

ribs, which are carefully bound together by thongs of skin.
The ribs rest partly on posts, partly on tripods of driftwood.
The posts are driven into the ground, and the tripods get the
necessary steadiness by a heavy stone or a seal-skin sack filled
with sand being suspended from the middle of them. In order
further to steady the tent a yet heavier stone is in the same
way suspended by a strap from the top of the tent-roof, or the
summit of the roof is made fast to the ground by thick
thongs. At one place a tackle from a wrecked vessel was
used for this purpose, being tightened with a block between
the top of the roof and an iron hook frozen into the ground.
The ribs in every tent are besides supported by T-formed
cross stays.

The entrance consists of a low door, which, when necessary,
may be closed with a reindeer skin. The floor of the outer
tent consists of the bare ground. This is kept very clean, and
the few household articles are hung up carefully and in an
orderly manner along the walls on the inner and outer sides of
the tent. Near the tent are some posts, as high as a man,
driven into the ground, with cross pieces on which skin boats,
oars, javelins, &c., are laid, and from which fishing and seal nets
are suspended.

In the neighbourhood of the dwellings the storehouse is placed.
It consists of a cellar excavated at some suitable place. The
sites of old Onkilon dwellings are often used for this purpose.
The descent is commonly covered with pieces of driftwood which
are loaded with stones; at one place the door, or rather the
hatch, of the cellar consisted of a whale's shoulder-blade. In
consequence of the unlimited confidence which otherwise was
wont to prevail between the natives and us, we were surprised
to find them unwilling to give the *Vega* men admittance to
their storehouses. Possibly the report of our excavations for
old implements at the sites of Onkilon dwellings at Irkaipij had
spread to Kolyutschin, and been interpreted as attempts at
plunder.

The tents were always situated on the sea shore, generally on
the small neck of land which separates the strand lagoons from
the sea. They are erected and taken down in a few hours. A
Chukch family can therefore easily change its place of residence,
and does remove very often from one village to another. Sometimes it appears to own the wooden frame of a tent at several
places, and in such cases at removal there are taken along
only the tent covering, the dogs, and the most necessary skin
and household articles. The others are left without inclosure,
lock, or watch, at the former dwelling-place, and one is certain
to find all untouched on his return. During short stays at
a place there are used, even when the temperature of the air

is considerably under the freezing-point, exceedingly defective tents or huts made with the skin boats that may happen to be available. Thus a young couple who returned in spring to Pitlekaj lived happy and content in a single thin and ragged tent or conical skin hut which below where it was broadest was only two and a half metres across. An accurate inventory, which I took during the absence of the newly married pair, showed that their whole household furniture consisted of a bad

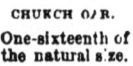

lamp, a good American axe, some reindeer skins, a small piece of mirror, a great many empty preserve tins from the *Vega*, which among other things were used for cooking, a fire-drill, a comb, leather for a pair of moccasins, some sewing implements, and some very incomplete and defective tools.

The boats are made of walrus skin, sewed together and stretched over a light frame-work of wood and pieces of bone. The different parts of the framework are bound together with thongs of skin or strings of whalebone. In form and size the Chukches' large boat, *atkuat* called by the Russians *baydar*, corresponds completely with the Greenlander's *umiak* or woman's boat. It is so light that four men can take it upon their shoulders, and yet so roomy that thirty men can be conveyed in it. One seldom sees *anatkuat* or boats intended for only one man; they are much worse built and uglier than the Greenlander's *kayak*. The large boats are rowed with broad-bladed oars, of which every man or woman manages only one. By means of these oars a sufficient number of rowers can for a little raise the speed of the boat to ten kilometres per hour. Like the Greenlanders, however, they often cease rowing in order to rest, laugh, and chatter, then row furiously for some minutes, rest themselves again, row rapidly, and so on. When the sea is covered with thin newly formed ice they put two men in the fore of the boat with one leg over in order to trample the ice in pieces.

CHUKCH OAR.
One-sixteenth of the natural size.

During winter the boats are laid up, and instead the dog-sledges are put in order. These are of a different construction from the Greenland sledges, commonly very light and narrow, made of some flexible kind of wood, and shod with plates of whales' jawbones, whales' ribs, or whalebone. In order to improve the running, the runners before the start are carefully covered with a layer of ice from two or three millimetres in thickness by repeatedly pouring water over them.[1] The different parts of the sledge are not fastened together by nails, but are bound together by strips of skin or strings of whalebone. On the low uncomfortable seat there commonly lies a piece of skin, generally of the Polar bear. The number of dogs that are harnessed to each sledge is variable. I have seen a Chukch riding behind two small lean dogs, who however appeared to draw their heavy load over even hard snow without any extraordinary exertion. At other sledges I have seen ten or twelve dogs, and a sledge laden with goods was drawn by a team of twenty-eight. The dogs are generally harnessed one pair before another to a long line common to all,[2] sometimes in the case of short excursions more than two abreast, or so irregularly that their position in relation to the sledge appears to have depended merely on the accidental length of the draught-line and the caprice of the driver. The dogs are guided not by reins but by continual crying and shouting, accompanied by lashes from a long whip. There is, besides, in every properly equipped sledge a short and thick staff mounted with iron, with a number of iron rings attached to the upper end. When nothing else will do, this staff is thrown at the offending animal. The staff is so heavy that the animal may readily get its death by such a throw. The dogs know this, and in consequence are so afraid of this grim implement that the rattling of the rings is sufficient to induce them to put forth extreme efforts. During rests the team is tied to the staff, which is driven into the snow.

The dog harness is made of inch-wide straps of skin, forming a neck or shoulder band, united on both sides by a strap to a girth, to one side of which the draught strap is fastened. Thanks to the excellent protection against the harness galling which the bushy coat of the dogs affords, little attention is needed for the harness, and I have never seen a single dog that was idle in consequence of sores from the harness. On the other hand, their feet are often hurt by the sharp snow. On this account the equipment of every sledge embraces a number

---

[1] If the runners are not shod with ice in this way the friction between them and the hard snow is very great during severe cold, and the draught accordingly exceedingly heavy.

[2] Nearly all the travellers from a great distance who passed the *Vega* had their dogs harnessed in this way. On the other hand, Sarytschev says that at St. Lawrence Bay all the dogs were harnessed abreast, and that this was the practice at Moore's winter quarters at Chukotskojnos is shown by the drawing at p. 71 of Hooper's work, already quoted. We ought to remember that at both these places the population were Eskimos who had adopted the Chukch language. The Greenland Eskimo have their dogs harnessed abreast, the Kamchadales in a long row. Naturally dogs harnessed abreast are unsuitable for wooded regions. The different methods of harnessing dogs mentioned here, therefore, indicate that the Eskimo have lived longer than the Chukches north of the limit of trees.

of dog shoes of the appearance shown in the accompanying
woodcut. They are used only in case of need.

The Chukch dogs are of the same breed, but smaller, than
the Eskimo dogs in Danish Greenland. They resemble wolves,
are long-legged, long-haired, and shaggy. The ears are short,
commonly upright; their colour very variable, from black or
white, and black or white spotted, to grey or yellowish-brown.
For innumerable generations they have been used as draught
animals, while as watch dogs they have not been required in a
country where theft or robbery appears never to take place.
The power of barking they have therefore completely lost, or
perhaps they never possessed it. Even a European may come
into the outer tent without any of the dogs there informing
their owner's sleeping in the inner tent by a sound of the
foreigner's arrival.

DOG SHOE.
One-third of the
natural size.

On the other hand, they are good though slow draught
animals, being capable of long-continued exertion. They are as dirty and as peaceable
as their owners. There are no fights made
between dog-teams belonging to different
tents, and they are rare between the dogs of
an encampment and those of strangers. In
Europe dogs are the friends of their masters
and the enemies of each other; here they
are the friends of each other and the slaves
of their masters. In winter they appear
in case of necessity to get along with very
little food; they are then exceedingly lean,
and for the most part lie motionless in some
snow-drift. They seldom leave the neighbourhood of the tent alone, not even to search for
food or hunt at their own hand and for their own account.
This appears to me so much the more remarkable, as they
are often several days, I am inclined to say weeks, in succession without getting any food from their masters. A
piece of a whale, with the skin and part of the flesh
adhering, washed out of frozen sandy strata thus lay untouched some thousand paces from Pitlekaj; and the neigh
bourhood of the tents, where the hungry dogs were constantly
wandering about, formed, as has been already stated, a favoui
haunt for ptarmigan and hares during winter. Young d
some months old are already harnessed along with the team
order that they may in time become accustomed to the draug
tackle. During the cold season the dogs are permitted to l
in the outer tent, the females with their young even in the
inner. We had two Scotch collies with us on the Vega. Th
at first frightened the natives very much with their ba

ɔ dogs of Chukches they soon took the same superior
ɪg as the European claims for himself in relation to the
. The dog was distinctly preferred by the female Chukch
population, and that too without the fights to which
ɪvour on the part of the fair commonly gives rise. A
ɔus canine progeny of mixed Scotch-Chukch breed has
risen at Pitlekaj. The young dogs had a complete
ɪlance to their father, and the natives were quite charmed
ɪem.

ɪn a dog is to be killed the Chukch stabs it with his
ɪnd then lets it bleed to death. Even when the scarcity
great that the natives at Pitlekaj and Yinretlen lived
on the food we gave them, they did not eat the dogs
ɪlled. On the other hand they had no objection to eating
crow.

ɪn the Chukch goes out on the ice to hunt seals he takes
ɪs with him, and it is these which take home the catch,
ɪnly with the draught-line fastened directly to the head
killed seal, which is then turned on its back and dragged
ɪe ice without anything under it. One of the inhabi-
f Yinretlen returned from the open water off the coast
successful hunting expedition with five seals, of which
ɪallest was laid on the sledge, the others being fastened
hind the other in a long row. After the last was drawn
pole, which was used in setting the net.

dress of the Chukches is made of reindeer or seal skin.
rmer, because it is warmer, is preferred as material for
ɪter dress. The men in winter are clad in two *pesks;*
ɪich is worn next the body is of thin skin with the hair
ɪ, the outer is of thick skin with the hair outwards.
ɪ, they wear, when it rains or wet snow falls, a great-coat
or of cotton cloth, which they call *calico.* On one oc-
I saw such an overcoat made of a kind of reindeer-
ɪ leather, which was of excellent quality and evidently
e manufacture. It had been originally white, but was or-
ɪed with broad brown painted borders. Some red and blue
ɪ shirts which we gave them were also worn above the
ɪthes, and by their showy colours awakened great satisfac-
the owners. The Chukch *pesk* is shorter than the Lapp
ɪt does not reach quite to the knees, and is confined at
ist with a belt. Under the *pesk* are worn two pairs of
ɪ, the inner pair with the hair inwards, and the outer with
r outwards. The trousers are well made, close fitting, and
ɪte above the foot. The foot-covering consists of reindeer
skin moccasins, which above the foot are fastened to
users in the way common among the Lapps. The soles
valrus-skin or bear-skin, and have the hair side inwards.

On the other parts of the moccasin the hair is outwards. Within the shoes are seal-skin stockings and hay. The head covering consists of a hood embroidered with beads, over which in severe cold is drawn an outer hood bordered with dog-skin. The outer hood is often quite close under the chin, and extends in a very well-fitting way over the shoulders. To a complete dress there also belong a skin neckerchief or boa, and a neck covering of multiple reindeer-skins, or of different kinds of skins sewn together in chess-board-like squares. In summer and far into the autumn the men go bareheaded, although they clip the hair on the crown of the head close to the root.

During the warm season of the year a number of the winter wraps are laid off in proportion to the increase of the heat, so

CHUKCH FACE-TATTOOING.
After a drawing by A. Stuxberg.

that the dress finally consists merely of a *pesk*, an overcoat, a pair of trousers. The summer moccasins are often as long the leg as our sea-boots. In the tent the men wear only sh trousers reaching to the hip, together with leather belts (heal belts) at the waist and on the arms. The man's dress is much ornamented. On the other hand, the men often we strings of beads in the ears, or a skin band set with lar tastefully arranged beads or a leather band with some lar beads on the brow. The leather band they will not willing part with, and a woman told us that the beads in it indica the number of enemies the wearer has killed. I am, howev quite certain that this was only an empty boast. Probably o

ormant referred to a tradition handed down from former war-
e periods to the present time, and thus we have here only a
ɩukch form of the boasting about martial feats common even
ɩong civilised nations.

To the dress of the men there belongs further a screen for the
es, which is often beautifully ornamented with beads and
ver mounting. This screen is worn especially in spring as a
ɔtection from the strong sunlight reflected from the snow-
ɩins. At this season of the year snow-blindness is very
ɩmmon, but notwithstanding this snow-spectacles of the kind
ɩich the Eskimo and even the Samoyeds use are unknown
ɾe.

a   b
CHUKCH CHILDREN.
Jirl from Irgunnuk. After a photograph by L. Palander. b. Boy from Pitlekaj, with his
mother's hood on. After a drawing by the seaman Hansson.

The men are not tattooed, but have sometimes a black or red
ɩss painted on the cheek. They wear the hair cut close to
ɞ root with the exception of a short tuft right on the crown
the head and a short fringe above the brow. The women
ve long hair, parted right in the middle, and plaited along
th strings of beads into plaits which hang down by the
ɾs. They are generally tattooed on the face, sometimes also
the arms and other parts of the body. The tattooing is done
degrees; possibly certain lines are first made at marriage.

The dress of the women, like that of the men, is double
ring winter. The outer *pesk*, which is longer and wider than

the man's, passes downwards into a sort of very wide trousers.
The sleeves too are exceedingly wide, so that the arm may easily
be drawn in and stuck out. Under the outer *pesk* there is an
inner *pesk*, or skin-shirt, and under them a pair of very short
trousers is worn. Where the outer *pesk* ends the moccasins
begin. At the neck the *pesk* is much cut away, so that a part
of the back is bare. I have seen girls go with the upper part
of the back exposed in this way even in a cold of − 30° or − 40°.
The stockings have the hair inwards, they are bordered with
dog-skin and go to the knees. The moccasins, chin-covers,
hoods, and neckerchiefs differ little from the corresponding
articles of men's dress. The woman's dress is in general more
ornamented than the man's, and the skins used for it appear to
be more carefully chosen and prepared. In the inner tent the
women go nearly naked, only with quite short under-trousers of
skin or *calico* or a narrow *cingulum pudicitiæ*. On the naked

b

SNOW-SHOES.

a. The common kind. *b*. Intended to be used in the way shown in the drawing on the
opposite page.

One-thirteenth of the natural size.

body there are worn besides one or two leather bands on on
arm, a leather band on the throat, another round the waist, and
some bracelets of iron or less frequently of copper on the wrists.
The younger women however do not like to show themselves in
this dress to foreigners, and they therefore hasten at their
entrance to cover the lower part of their body with the *pesk*, or
some other piece of dress that may be at hand.

When the children are some years old they get the same
dress as their parents, different for boys and girls. While small
they are put into a wide skin covering with the legs and arms
sewed together downwards. Behind there is a four-cornered
opening through which moss (the white, dead part of
Sphagnum), intended to absorb the excreta, is put in and
changed. At the ends of the arms two loops are fastened,
through which the child's legs are passed when the mother

wishes to put it away in some corner of the tent. The dress
itself appears not to be changed until it has become too small.
In the inner tent the children go completely naked.

Both men and women use snow-shoes during winter. Without them they will not willingly undertake any long walk in
loose snow. They consider such a walk so tiresome, that they
loudly commiserated one of my crew, who had to walk without
snow-shoes after drifting weather from the village Yinretlen to
the vessel, about three kilometres distant. Finally a woman's
compassion went so far that she presented him with a pair; an
instance of generosity on the part of our Chukch friends which
otherwise was exceedingly rare. The frame of the snow-shoes
is made of wood, the cross-pieces are of strong and well-stretched
thongs. This snow-shoe corresponds completely with that of
the Indians, and is exceedingly serviceable and easy to get

AN AINO 'MAN SKATING AFTER A REINDEER
Japanese drawing.

customed to. Another implement for travelling over snow
as offered by a Chukch who drove past the vessel in the
beginning of February. In consisted of a pair of immensely
wide skates of thin wood, covered with seal-skin, and raised at
both sides. I had difficulty in understanding how these broad
shapeless articles could be used with advantage until I learned
from the accompanying drawing that they may be employed as
a sort of sledges. The drawing is taken from a Japanese work,
whose title when translated runs thus: A Journey to the
north part of Japan (Yezo), 1804 (No. 565 of the Japanese
library I brought home with me).

In consequence of the difficulty which the Chukch has during
winter in procuring water by melting snow over the train-oil
lamp, there can be no washing of the body at that season of the
year. Faces are however whipped clean by the drifting snow,

but at the same time are generally swollen or sore from frost-bite. On the whole, the disposition of the Chukches to clean-liness is slight, and above all, their ideas of what is clean or unclean differs considerably from ours. Thus the women use urine as a wash for the face. At a common meal the hand is often used as a spoon, and after it is finished, a bowl filled with newly-passed urine instead of water is handed round the company for washing the hands. Change of clothes takes place seldom, and even when the outer dress is clean, new and well cut, of carefully-chosen beautiful skins, the under-dress is very dirty, and vermin numerous enough, though less so than might have been expected. Food is often eaten in a way which we consider disgusting, a titbit, for instance, is passed from mouth to mouth. The vessels in which food is served are used in many ways and seldom cleaned. On the other hand it may be stated that, in order not to make a stay in the confined tent-chamber too uncomfortable, certain rules are strictly observed. Thus, for instance, it is not per-mitted in the interior of the tent to spit on the floor, but this must be done into a vessel which in case of necessity is used as a night-utensil. In every outer tent there lies a specially carved reindeer horn, with which snow is removed from the clothes ; the outer *pesk* is usually put off before one goes into the inner tent and the shoes are carefully freed from snow. The carpet of walrus-skin, which covers the floor of the inner tent, is accordingly dry and clean. Even the outer tent is swept clean and free from loose snow, and the snow is daily shovelled away from the tent doors with a spade of whalebone. Every article both in the outer and inner tent is laid in its proper place, and so on.

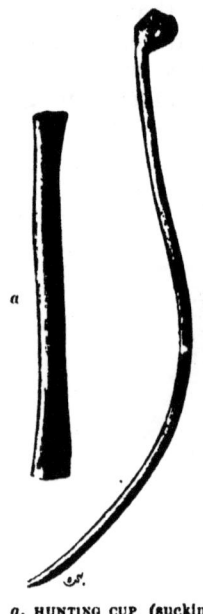

a. HUNTING CUP (sucking tube). One-fourth of the natural size.

b. SNOW - SCRAPER. One-eighth of the natural size.

As ornaments glass beads are principally used, some of them being suspended from the neck and ears, others sewed upon the hood and other articles of dress, or plaited into the hair. Embroidery of very pleasing patterns is also employed. In order to embellish the *pesks* strips of skin or marmots' and squirrels' tails, &c., are sewed upon them. Often a variega-ted artificial tail of different skins is fixed to the hood be-hind, or the skin of the hood is so chosen that the ears of the animal project on both sides of the head. Along with

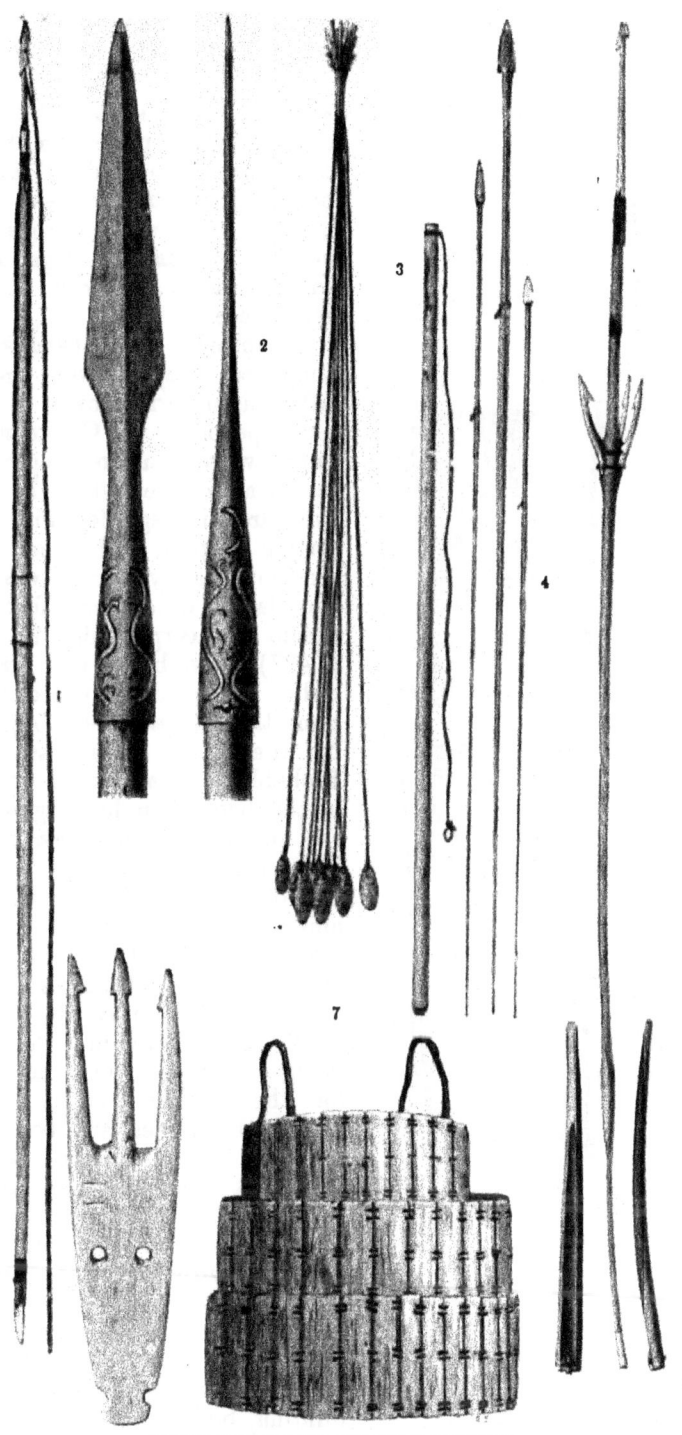

CHUKCH WEAPONS AND HUNTING IMPLEMENTS.

)oon, one-fifteenth of the natural size. 2. Spear found at a grave, one-fourth. 3. Bird
g. one-eighth. 4. Darts with whip-sling for casting them, one-seventh. 5. Bird-dart
h wooden handle for throwing, one-twelfth. 6. Leister of bone, one-fourth. 7. Ivory
t of mail, one-ninth.

the beads are fixed amulets, wooden tongs, small bone heads or bone figures, pieces of metal, coins, &c. One child had suspended from its neck an old Chinese coin with a square hole in the middle, together with a new American five-cent piece.

In former times beautiful and good weapons were probably highly prized by so warlike a people as the Chukches, but now weapons are properly scarce antiquities, which, however, are still regarded with a certain respect, and therefore are not readily parted with. The lance which was found beside the corpse (fig. 2 on p. 477) shows by its still partially preserved gold decorations that it had been forged by the hand of an artist. Probably it has formed part of the booty won long ago in the fights with the Cossacks. I procured by barter an ivory coat of mail (fig. 7 on p. 477), and remains of another. The ivory plates of the coat of mail are twelve centimetres in length, four in breadth, and nearly one in thickness, holes being bored at their edges for the leather thongs by which the plates are bound together. This binding has been so arranged that the whole coat of mail, when not in use, may be rolled together.

Along with the spear and the coat of mail the old Chukches used the bow for martial purposes. Now this weapon is employed only for hunting, but it appears as if even for this purpose it would

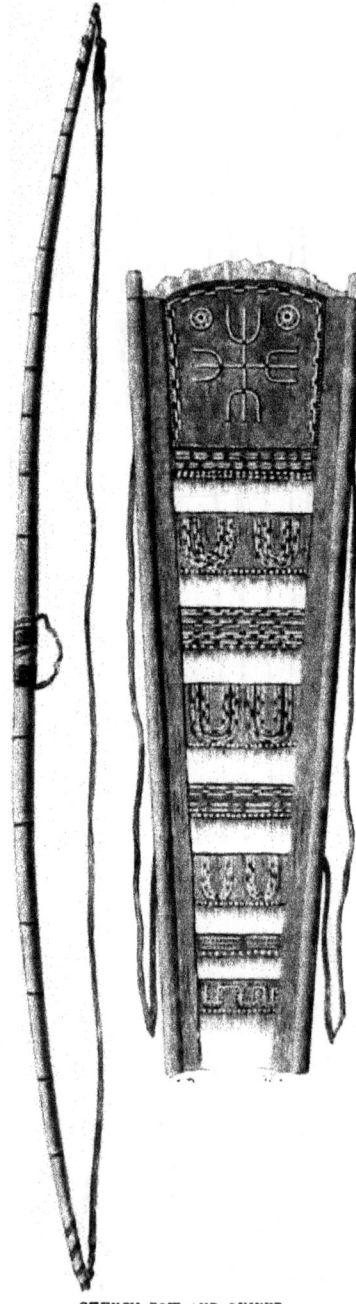

CHUKCH BOW AND QUIVER.
One-eighth of the natural size.

out of use.   Some of the natives, however, use
with great accuracy of aim. . The bows which I
commonly consisted of a badly worked, slightly
;tic piece of wood, with the ends drawn together by
ong.   Only some old bows had a finer form.   They
;er, and made with care ; for instance, they were
vith birch-bark, and strengthened by an artistic
if sinews on the outer side.   The arrows are of many

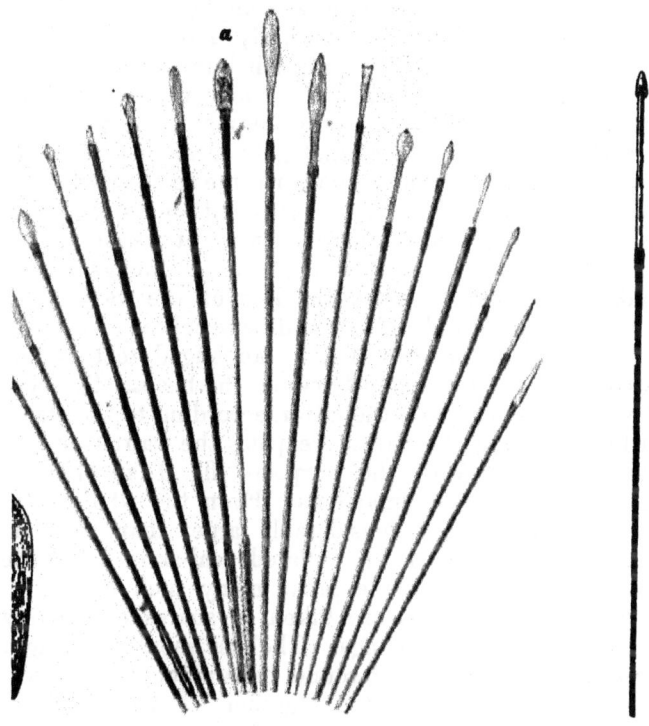

CHUKCH ARROWS.
iinth of the natural size. a. An arrowhead, one-half the natural size.

tly with bone or wooden, and partly with iron, points.
are generally wanting.   The shaft is a clumsily worked
wood.   Crossbows are occasionally used.   We have
bows for playthings, with carefully made, iron-pointed
At the encampments near the winter station we found
of percussion-lock guns, with caps, powder and lead.
e evidently little used, and my attempt to induce the
; to undertake long journeys by promises of a gun.
necessary supply of powder and lead completely
Vhen the Chukch, who carried our letters to Nischni

Kolymsk, was after his return rewarded with a red shirt,
gun, caps, powder and ball, he wished to exchange the gun and
ammunition for an axe.

The principal livelihood of the Chukches is derived from
hunting and fishing. Both are very abundant at certain seasons
of the year, but are less productive during the cold season, in
which case, in consequence of the little forethought of the
savage, there arises great scarcity both of food and fuel and
the means of melting snow. Of their hunting and fishing
implements I cannot give so complete accounts as I should
wish, because they very carefully avoided taking any of the
Vega's hunters with them on their hunting excursions.

The rough seal is taken with nets, made of strong seal-skin
thongs. The nets are set in summer among the ground-ices
along the shore. The animal gets entangled in the net and is
suffocated, as it can no longer come to the surface to breathe.
In winter the seal is taken partly with nets in "leads" among
the ice, partly with the harpoon when it crawls out of its hole;
it is also taken by means of a noose of thongs placed over its
hole. In order to avoid the loss of the valuable seal-blood,
which is considered an extraordinary delicacy by the Chukches,
the animal is never killed by an edged tool, if that can be
avoided, but by repeated blows on the head. The bear is killed
by the lance or knife, the latter, according to the statement of a
Chukch, being the surest weapon; the walrus and the largest
kind of seals with the harpoon (fig. 1, p. 477), or a lance
resembling the Greenlander's. Even the whale is harpooned,
but with a harpoon considerably larger than the common, and
to which as many as six inflated seal-skins are fastened. In
order to kill a whale a great many such harpoons must be
struck into it. Birds are taken in snares, or killed with bird-
javelins, arrows, and slings. The last mentioned (fig. 3, p. 477)
consist of a number of round balls of bone fastened to leather
thongs, which are knotted together. Some feathers are often
fixed to the knot in order to increase the resistance of the air to
this part of the sling. When the sling is thrown the bone balls
are thereby scattered in all directions, and the probability of
hitting becomes greater. Every man and boy in summer carries
with him such a sling, often bound round his head, and is immediately prepared to cast it at flocks of birds flying past.
Common slings are also used, consisting of two thongs and a
piece of skin fastened to them. The bird-dart (fig. 5. p. 477)
completely resembles that used by the Eskimo. A kind of
snare was used by the boys at Yinretlen to catch small birds
for our zoologist. They were made of whalebone fibres.

Fish are caught partly with nets, partly with the hook or
with a sort of leister (fig. 6, p. 477). The nets are made of

w-thread. I procured several of these, and was surprised at
small value which the natives set upon them, notwithstand-
the hard labour which must have been required for preparing
thread and making the net. The nets are also sometimes
as drift-nets. The fishing-rod consists of a shaft only
·y centimetres long, to which is fixed a short line made of
ws. The extreme end of the line passes though a large
er of ivory, to which are attached two or three tufts each
its hook of bone only, or of bone and copper, or bone and
The hook has three or four points projecting in different
:tions. I have before described how the hook is used in
mn in fishing for roach, also how the productive fishing
on in the neighbourhood of Tjapka.
ven for the coast Chukch reindeer flesh appears to form an
ortant article of food. He probably purchases his stock of
om the reindeer-Chukches for train-oil, skin straps, walrus
s, and perhaps fish. I suppose that part of the frozen
deer blood, which the inhabitants of the villages at our
er station used for soup, had been obtained in the same
. Wild reindeer, or reindeer that had run wild, were
ked with the lasso. Such animals, however, do not appear
to be found in any large numbers on the Chukch peninsula.
esides fish and flesh the Chukches consume immense quanti-
of herbs and other substances from the vegetable kingdom.[1]
most important of these are the leaves and young branches
great many different plants (for instance Salix, Rhodiola,
which are collected and after being cleaned are preserved
:al-skin sacks. Intentionally or unintentionally the contents
ie sacks sour during the course of the summer. In autumn
·freeze together to a lump of the form of the stretched
·skin. The frozen mass is cut in pieces and used with flesh,
h in the same way as we eat bread. Occasionally a vegetable
i is made from the pieces along with water, and is eaten
n. In the same way the contents of the reindeer stomach
ed. Algæ and different kinds of roots are also eaten, among
latter a kind of wrinkled tubers, which, as already stated
340, have a very agreeable taste.
i summer the Chukches eat cloud-berries, red bilberries, and
r berries, which are said to be found in great abundance in
interior of the country. The quantity of vegetable matter
:h is collected for food at that season of the year is very
iderable, and the natives do not appear to be very particular
ieir choice, if the leaves are only green, juicy, and free from

In exhaustive treatise on the food-substances which the Chukches
:r from the vegetable kingdom, written by Dr. Kjellman, is to be
1 in *The Scientific Work of the Vega Expedition*. Popov already states
the Chukches eat many berries, roots, and herbs (*Müller*, iii. p. 59).

I I

any bitter taste. When the inhabitants, in consequence of
scarcity of food, removed in the beginning of February from
Pitlekaj, they carried with them several sacks of frozen vegetables, and there were still some left in the cellars to be taken
away as required. In the tents at St. Lawrence Bay there la
heaps of leaf-clad willow-twigs and sacks filled with leaves an
stalks of Rhodiola. The writers who quote the Chukches a
an example of a race living exclusively on substances deriv
from the animal kingdom thus commit a complete mistake. On
the contrary, they appear at certain seasons of the year to be more
"graminivorous" than any other people I know, and with respect
to this their taste appears to me to give the anthropologist a hint
of certain traits of the mode of life of the people of the Stone Age
which have been completely overlooked. To judge from the
Chukches our primitive ancestors by no means so much resembled beasts of prey as they are commonly imagined to have
done, and it may, perhaps, have been the case that "bellum
omnium inter omnes" was first brought in with the higher
culture of the Bronze or Iron Age.

The cooking of the Chukches, like that of most wild races,
is very simple. After a successful catch all the dwellers in the
tent gormandise on the killed animal, and appear to find a
special pleasure in making their faces and hands as bloody as
possible. Alternately with the raw flesh are eaten pieces of
blubber and marrow, and bits of the intestines which have been
freed from their contents merely by pressing between the fingers.
Fish is eaten not only in a raw state, but also frozen so hard
that it can be broken in pieces. When opportunity offers the
Chukches do not, however, neglect to boil their food, or to roast
pieces of flesh over the train-oil lamp—the word *roast* ought
however in this case to be exchanged for *soot*. At a visit which
Lieutenant Hovgaard made at Najtskaj, the natives in the tent
where he was a guest ate for supper first seal-flesh soup, then
boiled fish, and lastly, boiled seal-flesh. They thus observed
completely the order of eating approved in Europe. The
Chukches are unacquainted with other forks than their fingers,
and even the use of the spoon is not common. Many carry
about with them a spoon of copper, tinned iron, or bone (fig. 8,
p. 486). The soup is often drunk directly out of the cooking
vessel, or sucked up through hollow bones (see the figure on
.p. 476). These are used as drinking cups, and like the spoons
are worn in the belt. As examples of Chukch dishes I may
further mention, vegetable soup, boiled seal-flesh, boiled fish,
blood soup, soup of seal-blood and blubber. To these we may
add soup from finely crushed bones, or from seal-flesh, blubber,
and bones. For crushing the bones there is in every tent a
hammer, consisting of an oval stone with a hollow round it for

a skin thong, with which the stone is fastened to the short shaft of wood or bone. The bones which are used for food are finely crushed with this implement against a stone anvil or a whale's vertebra, and then boiled with water and blood, before being eaten. At first we believed that this dish was intended for the dogs, but afterwards I had an opportunity of convincing myself that the natives themselves ate it; and that long before the time when they suffered from scarcity of provisions. The hammer is further of interest as forming one of the stone implements which are most frequently found in graves from the Stone Age. That the hammer was mainly intended for kitchen purposes appears from the circumstance that the women alone had it at their disposal, and were consulted when it was parted with. Along with such hammers there was to be found in every

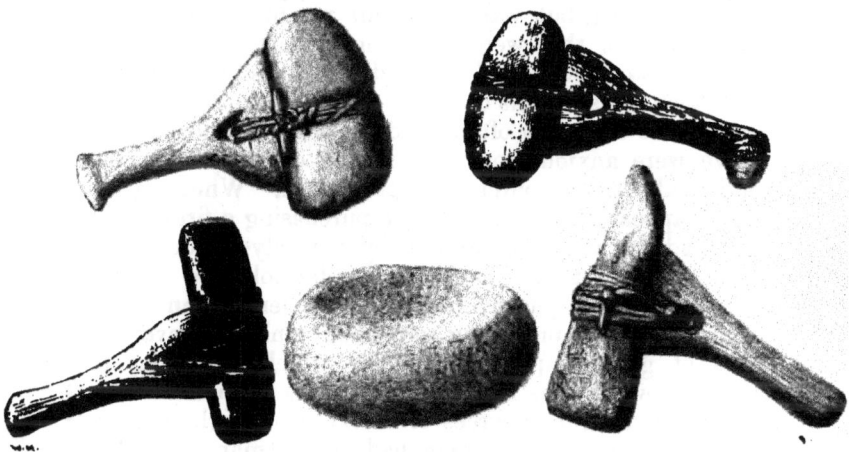

STONE HAMMERS AND ANVIL FOR CRUSHING BONES.
One-sixth of the natural size.

tent an anvil, consisting of a whale's vertebra or a large round stone with a bowl-formed depression worn or cut out in the middle of it.

During winter a great portion of the inhabitants of Yinretlen, Pitlekaj, and as far as from Irgunnuk, came daily on board to beg or buy themselves provisions, and during this period they were fed mainly by us. They soon accustomed themselves to our food. They appeared specially fond of pea-soup and porridge. The latter they generally laid out on a snow-drift to freeze, and then took it in the frozen form to the tents. Coffee they did not care for unless it was well sugared. Salt they did not use, but with sugar they were all highly delighted. They also drank tea with pleasure. Otherwise water forms their principal drink. They were, however, often compelled in winter, in consequence of the difficulty of melting over the train-oil lamps a sufficient quantity of snow, to quench their thirst with snow. On board they often asked for water, and drank at once large quantities of it.

Spirits, to which they are exceedingly addicted, they call, as has been already stated, in conversation with Europeans, "ram," the pronouncing of the word being often accompanied by a hawking noise, a happy expression, and a distinctive gesture, which consisted in carrying the open right hand from the mouth to the waist, or in counterfeiting the unintelligible talk of a drunken man. Among themselves they call it fire-water (*akmimil*). The promise of it was the most efficient means of getting an obstinate Chukch to comply with one's wishes. In case they undertook to drive us with their dog-teams, they were never desirous of finding out whether any stock of provisions was taken along, but warned by our parsimony in dealing out spirituous liquor, they were unwilling to start until they had examined the stock of "ram." That drunkenness, not the satisfying of the taste, was in this case the main object, is shown by the circumstance that they often fixed, as price for the articles they saw we were anxious to have, such a quantity of brandy as would make them completely intoxicated. When on one occasion I appeared very desirous of purchasing a fire-drill, which was found in a tent inhabited by a newly-wedded pair, the young and very pretty housewife undertook the negotiation, and immediately began by declaring that her husband could not part with the fire-producing implement unless I gave him the means of getting quite drunk, for which, according to her statement, which was illustrated by lively gesticulations representing the different degrees of intoxication, eight glasses were required. Not until the man had got so many would he be content, that is, dead drunk. I have myself observed, however, on several occasions that two small glasses are sufficient to make them unsteady on the legs. Under the influence of liquor they are cheerful, merry, and friendly, but troublesome by their excessive caressing. When in the company of intoxicated natives one must take good care that he does not unexpectedly get a kiss from some old greasy seal-hunter. Even the women readily took a glass, though evidently less addicted to intoxicants than the men. They however got their share, as did even the youngest of the children. When, as happened twice in the course of the winter, an encampment was fortunate enough to get a large stock of brandy sent it from Behring's Straits, the intoxication was general, and, as I have already stated, the bluish-yellow eyes the next day showed that quarrelsomeness had been called forth even among this peace-loving people by their dear *akmimil*. During our stay at the villages nearer

Behring's Straits two murders even took place, of which one at
east was committed by an intoxicated man.

However slight the contact the Chukches have with the
world that has reached the standpoint of the brandy industry is,
his means of enjoyment, however, appears to be the object of
egular barter. Many of the Chukches who travelled past us
were intoxicated, and shook with pride a not quite empty keg
r seal-skin sack, to let us hear by the dashing that it con-
ained liquid. One of the crew, whom I asked to ascertain
what sort of spirit it was, made friends with the owner, and
nduced him at last to part with about a thimbleful of it; more
ould not be given. According to the sailor's statement it was
without colour and flavour, clear as crystal, but weak. It was
thus probably Russian corn brandy, not gin.

During a visit which Lieutenants Hovgaard and Nordquist
made in the autumn of 1878 to the reindeer-Chukches in the
interior of the country, much diluted American gin was on the
contrary presented, and the tent owner showed his guests a
tin drinking-cup with the inscription, " Capt. Ravens, Brig
Timandra, 1878." Some of the natives stated distinctly that
they could purchase brandy at Behring's Straits all the year
round. All the men in the tent village, and most of the
women, but not the children, had at the time got completely
intoxicated in order to celebrate the arrival of the foreigners, or
perhaps rather that of the stock of brandy. As there are no
Europeans settled at Behring's Straits, at least on the Asiatic
side, we learn from the traffic in brandy that there are actually
natives abstemious enough to be able to deal in it.

Tobacco is in common use, both for smoking and chewing.[1]
Every native carries with him a pipe resembling that of the
Tunguse, and a tobacco-pouch (fig. 7, p. 486). The tobacco
is of many kinds, both Russian and American, and when the
stock of it is finished native substitutes are used. Preference
is given to the sweet, strong chewing tobacco, which sailors
generally use. In order to make the tobacco sweet which has
not before been drenched with molasses, the men are accustomed, when they get a piece of sugar, to break it down and
place it in the tobacco-pouch. The tobacco is often first chewed,
then dried behind the ear, and kept in a separate pouch suspended from the neck, to be afterwards smoked. The pipes are
so small that, like those of the Japanese, they may be smoked
out with a few strong whiffs. The smoke is swallowed.
Even the women and children smoke and chew, and they begin
to do so at so tender an age that we have seen a child, who

---

[1] Already, in the beginning of the eighteenth century, all the Siberian
tribes, men and women, old and young, smoked passionately (*Hist.
Généalog. des Tartares*, p. 66).

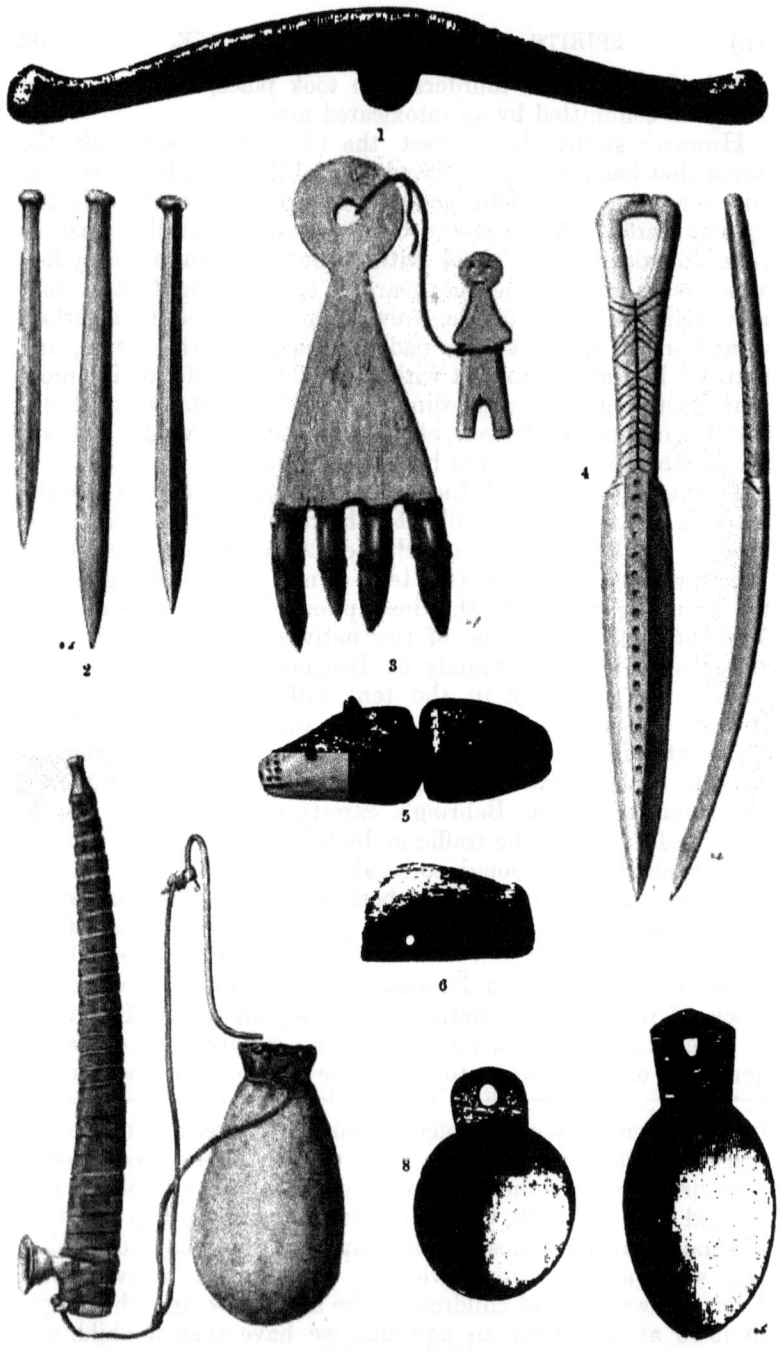

CHUKCH IMPLEMENTS.

1. Scraper for currying, one-seventh of the natural size. 2. Awls, one-half. 3. Ice-scraper intended for decoying the seal from its hole, with bone amulet affixed, one-half. 4. Bone knife, one-half. 5, 6. Amulets of bone, natural size. 7. Pipe and tobacco-pouch, one-third. 8. Metal spoons, one-third.

could indeed walk, but still sucked his mother, both chew tobacco, smoke, and take a "ram."

Some bundles of Ukraine tobacco, which I took with me for barter with the natives, put it into my power to procure a large number of contributions to the ethnological collection, which in the absence of other wares for barter I would otherwise have been unable to obtain. For the Chukches do not understand money. This is so much the more remarkable as they carry on a very extensive trade, and evidently are good mercantile men. According to von Dittmar (*loc. cit.* p. 129) there exists, or still existed in 1856, a steady, slow, but regular transport of goods along the whole north coast of Asia and America, by which Russian goods were conveyed to the innermost parts of Polar America, and furs instead found their way to the bazaars of Moscow and St. Petersburg. This traffic is carried on at five market places, of which three are situated in America, one on the islands at Behring's Straits, and one at Anjui near Kolyma. The last-mentioned is called by the Chukches "the fifth beaver market." [1]

The Chukches' principal articles of commerce consist of seal-skin, train-oil, fox-skins and other furs, walrus tusks, whalebone, &c. Instead they purchase tobacco, articles of iron, reindeer skin and reindeer flesh, and, when it can be had, spirit. A bargain is concluded very cautiously after long-continued consultation in a whispering tone between those present. I employed spirit as an article for barter only in the last necessity, but they soon observed that the desire to become owner of an uncommon article of art or antiquity overcame my determination, and they soon learned to avail themselves of this, especially as in all cases I made full payment for the article and gave the fire-water in the bargain.

The lamp (see the figures at pp. 413, 414), with which light is maintained in the tent, consists of a flat trough of wood, bone of the whale, soap-stone or burned clay, broader behind than before, and divided by an isolated toothed comb into two divisions. In the front division wicks of moss (Sphagnum sp.) are laid in a long thin row along the whole edge. Under the

---

[1] Dr. John Simpson gives good information regarding the American markets in his *Observations on the Western Esquimaux.* He enumerates three market places in America besides that at Behring's Straits. At the markets people are occupied also with dancing and games, which are carried on in such a lively manner that the market people scarcely sleep during the whole time. Matiuschin gives a very lively sketch of the market at Anjui, to which, in 1821, the Chukches still went fully armed with spears, bows, and arrows (Wrangel's *Reise,* i. p. 270), and a visit to it in 1868 is described by C. von Neumann, who took part as Astronomer in von Maydell's expedition to Chukch Land (*Eine Messe im Hochnorden; Das Ausland,* 1880, p. 861).

lamp there is always another vessel intended to receive the train-oil which may possibly be spilled.

In summer the natives also cook witk wood in the open air or in the outer tent, in winter only in the greatest necessity in the latter. For they find the smoke, which the wood gives off in the close tent, uncndurable. Although driftwood is to be found in great abundance on the beach, scarcity of train-oil was evidently considered by the natives as great a misfortune as scarcity of food. *Uinga eek*, no fuel (properly, no fire), was the constant cry even of those who drew loads of driftwood on board to earn bread for themselves. The circumstance that their fuel does not give off any smoke has the advantage that the eyes of the Chukches are not usually nearly so much attacked as those of the Lapps.

In the tent the women have always a watchful eye over the trimming of the lamp and the keeping up of the fire. The wooden pins she uses to trim the wick, and which naturally are drenched with train-oil, are used when required as a light or torch in the outer tent, to light pipes, &c. In the same way other pins dipped in train-oil are used.[1] Clay lamps are made by the Chukches themselves, the clay being well kneaded and moistened with urine. The burning is incomplete, and is indeed often wholly omitted.

Train-oil and other liquid wares are often kept in sacks of seal-skin, consisting of whole hides, out of which the body has been taken through the opening made by cutting off the head, and in which all holes, either natural or caused by the killing of the animal, have been firmly closed. In one of the forepaws there is then inserted with great skill a wooden air- and water-tight cock with spigot and faucet. In sacks intended for dry wares the paws are also cut off, and the opening through which the contents are put in and taken out is made right across the breast immediately below the forepaws.

Fire is lighted partly in the way common in Sweden some decades ago by means of flint and steel, partly by means of a drill implement. In the former case the steel generally consists of a piece of a file or some other old steel tool, or of pieces of iron or steel which have been especially forged for the purpose. Commonly the form of this tool indicates a European or Russian-Siberian origin, but I also acquired clumsily hammered pieces of iron, which appeared to form specimens of native skill in forging. A Chukch showed me a large fire-steel of the last mentioned kind, provided with a special handle of copper beautifully polished by long-continued use. He evidently

---

[1] I have seen such pins, also oblong stones, sooty at one end, which, after having been dipped in train-oil, have been used as torches, laid by the side of corpses in old Eskimo graves in north-western Greenland.

regarded it as a very precious thing, and I could not persuade him to part with it. On the supposition that the metal of the clumsily hammered pieces of iron might possibly be of meteoric origin I purchased as many of them as I could. But the examination, to which they were subjected after our return, showed that they contain no traces of nickel. The iron was thus not meteoric.

The flint consists of a beautiful chalcedony or agate, which has been formed in cavities in the volcanic rocks which occur so abundantly in north-eastern Asia, and which probably are also found here and there as pebbles in the beds of the *tundra* rivers. As tinder, are used partly the woolly hair of various animals, partly dry fragments of different kinds of plants. The steel and a large number of pieces of flint are kept in a skin pouch suspended from the neck. Within this pouch there is a smaller one, containing the tinder. It is thus kept warm by

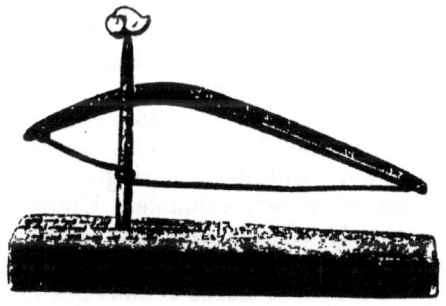

FIRE-DRILL.
One-eighth of the natural size.

the heat of the body, and protected from wet by its double envelope. Along with it the men often carry on their persons a sort of match of white, well-dried, and crushed willows, which are plaited together and placed in even rolls. This match burns slowly, evenly and well.

The other sort of fire-implement consists of a dry wooden pin, which by a common bow-drill is made to rub against a block of dry half-blackened wood. The upper part of this pin runs in a drill block of wood or bone. In one of the tools which I purchased the astragalus of a reindeer was used for this purpose. In the light-stock holes have been made to give support to the pin, and perhaps to facilitate the formation of the half-carbonised wood-meal which the drilling loosens from the light-stock and in which the red heat arises. When fire is to be lighted by means of this implement, the lower part of the drill pin is daubed over with a little train-oil, one foot holds the light-stock firm against the ground, the bowstring is put round the drill pin, the left hand presses the pin with the drill block against the light-stock, and the bow is carried backwards and forwards, not very rapidly, but evenly, steadily, and uninterruptedly, until fire appears. A couple of minutes are generally required to complete the process. The women appear to be more accustomed than the men to the use of this implement. An improved form of it consisted of a wooden pin on whose lower part a lense-formed and perforated block of wood was fixed. This block served as fly-wheel and weight. Across the wooden pin ran a perforated cross-bar which was fastened with two sinews to its upper end. By carrying this cross-bar backwards and forwards the pin could be turned round with great rapidity. The implement appears to me the more remarkable as it shows a new way of using the stone or brick lenses, which are often found in graves or old house-sites from the Stone Age.

Among the Chukches, as among many other wild races, lucifer matches have obtained the honour of being the first of the inventions of the civilized races that have been recognized as indisputably superior to their own. A request for lucifer matches was therefore one of the most common of those with which our friends at Behring's Straits tormented us during winter, and they were willing for a single box to offer things that in comparison were very valuable. Unfortunately we had no superfluous supply of this necessary article, or perhaps I ought to say fortunately, for if the Chukches for some years were able to get a couple of boxes of matches for a walrus tusk, I believe that with their usual carelessness they would soon completely forget the use of their own fire-implements.

Among household articles I may further mention the following :—

The *hide-scraper* (fig. 1, p. 486) is of stone or iron and fastened to a wooden handle. With this tool the moistened hide is cleaned very particularly, and is then rubbed, stretched and kneaded so carefully that several days go to the preparation of a single reindeer skin. That this is hard work is also shown by the woman who is employed at it in the tent dripping with perspiration. While thus employed she sits on a part of the skin and stretches out the other part with the united help of the hands and the bare feet. When the skin has been sufficiently worked, she fills a vessel with her own urine, mixes this with comminuted willow bark, which has been dried over the lamp, and rubs the blood-warm liquid into the reindeer skin. In order to give this a red colour on one side, the bark of a species of Pinus (?) is mixed with the tanning liquid. The skins are made very soft by this process, and on the inner side

semble chamois leather. Sometimes too the reindeer
inned to real chamois of very excellent quality.
rts of *ice mattocks;* the shaft is of wood, the blade of
e-formed one of whalebone, of the others of a walrus
is fixed to the shaft by skin thongs with great skill.
es both the shaft and blade are of bone, fastened
in a somewhat different way.
of native clay-slate. These are often perforated at one
carried along with the knife, the spoon, and the sucking
tened with an ivory tongs in the belt.

ICE MATTOCKS.
One-ninth of the natural size.

made *vessels of wood, bone of the whale, whalebone, and*
ifferent kinds.
, *boring tools, axes and pots* of European, American, or
origin, and in addition casks, pieces of cable, iron
eserved-meat tins, glasses, bottles, &c., obtained from
ich have anchored along the coast. Vessels have
visited the sea north of Behring's Straits only during
decades, and the contact between the sailors and the
s has not yet exerted any considerable influence on the

mode of life of the latter. The natives, however, complain that
the whalers destroy the walrus-hunting, while on the other
hand they see with pleasure trading vessels occasionally visiting
their coasts.

During our stay off the considerable encampment, Irkaipij,
we believed, as I have already stated, that we had found a chief
in a native named Chepurin, who, to judge by his dress, appeared
to be somewhat better off than the others, had two wives and a
stately exterior. He was accordingly entertained in the gun-
room, got the finest presents, and was in many ways the object
of special attention. Chepurin took his elevation easily, and
showed himself worthy of it by a grave and serious, perhaps
somewhat condescending behaviour, which further confirmed our
supposition and naturally increased the number of our presents.
Afterwards, however, we were quite convinced that we had
in this case committed a complete mistake, and that now there
are to be found among the Chukches living at the coast neither
any recognised chiefs nor any trace of social organisation.
During the former martial period of the history of the race
the state of things here was perhaps different, but now the
most complete anarchy prevails here, if by that word we
may denote a state of society in which disputes, crimes,
and punishments are unknown, or at least exceedingly rare.[1]
A sort of chieftainship appears, at all events, to be found among
the reindeer-Chukches living in the interior of the country.
At least there are among them men who can show commissions
from the Russian authorities. Such a man was the starost
Menka, of whose visit I have already given an account. Everything, however, indicated that his influence was exceedingly
small. He could neither read, write, nor speak Russian, and he
had no idea of the existence of a Russian Czar. All the tribute
he had delivered for several years, according to receipts which he
showed to us, consisted of some few fox-skins, which he had
probably received as market-tolls at Anjui and Markova. Menka
was attended on his visit to the vessel by two ill-clad men with a
type of face differing considerably from that common among the

[1] In the accounts which were collected regarding the Chukches at
Anadyrsk in the beginning of the eighteenth century, it is also stated that
they lived without any government. On the contrary, in M. von Krusenstern's *Voyage autour du monde, 1803-1806* (Paris, 1821, ii. p. 151), a report
of Governor Koscheleff is given on some negotiations which he had with
a "chief of the whole Chukch nation." I take it for granted that the
chiefship was of little account, and Koscheleff's whole sketch of his
meeting with the supposed chief bears an altogether too lively European
romantic stamp to be in any degree true to nature. At the same place it is
also said that a brother of Governor Koscheleff, in the winter of 1805-1806,
made a journey among the Chukches, on which, after his return, he sent a
report, accompanied by a Chukch vocabulary, to von Krusenstern.

Chukches. Their standing appeared to be so inferior that we took them for slaves, although mistakenly, at least with respect to one of them—Yettugin. He afterwards boasted that he owned a much larger reindeer-herd than Menka's, and talked readily, with a certain scorn, of Menka's chieftain pretensions. According to Russian authors there are actual slaves, probably the descendants of former prisoners of war, among the Chukches in the interior of the country. Among the dwellers on the coast, on the contrary, there is the most complete equality. We could never discover the smallest trace of any man exercising the least authority beyond his own family or his own tent.

The coast Chukches are not only heathens, but are also, so far as we could observe, devoid of every conception of higher beings. There are, however, superstitions. Thus most of them wear round the neck leather straps, to which small wooden tongs, or wooden carvings, are fixed. These are not parted with, and are not readily shown to foreigners. A boy had a band of beads sewed to his hood, and in front there was fastened an ivory carving, probably intended to represent a bear's head (fig. 6, on p. 486). It was so small, and so inartistically cut, that a man could undoubtedly make a dozen of them in a day. I, however, offered the father unsuccessfully a clasp-knife and tobacco for it, but the boy himself, having heard our bargaining, exchanged it soon after for a piece of sugar. When the father knew this he laughed good-naturedly, without making any attempt to get the bargain undone.

To certain tools small wooden images are affixed, as to the scraper figured above (fig. 3, p. 486), and similar images are found in large numbers in the lumber-room of the tent, where pieces of ivory, bits of agate and scrap-iron, are preserved. A selection from the large collection of such images which I made is here reproduced in woodcuts. If, also, these carvings may, in fact, be considered as representations of higher beings, the religious ideas which are connected with them, even judged from the Shaman standpoint, are exceedingly indistinct, less a consciousness, which still lives among the people, than a re-miniscence from former times. Most of the figures bear an evident stamp of the present dress and mode of life of the people. It appears to me to be remarkable, that in all the bone or wood carvings I have met with, the face has been cut flatter than it is in reality in this race of men. Some of the carvings appear to remind me of an ancient Buddhist image.

The drum, or more correctly, tambourine, so common among most of the Polar peoples, European, Asiatic, and American; among the Lapps, the Samoyeds, the Tunguses, and the Eskimo (see drawing on p. 415), is found in every Chukch tent. A certain superstition is also attached to it. They did not willingly

HUMAN FIGURES.

Nos. 1, 3, and 5, represent women with tattooed faces. No. 4 is of wood. No. 6 of wood with of tin ; the rest are of ivory.

play it in our presence, and they were unwilling to part with it.
If time permitted it was concealed on our entrance into the
tent. The drum consists of the peritoneum of a seal, stretched
over a narrow wooden ring fixed to a short handle. The drum-
stick consists of a splinter of whalebone 300 to 400 millimetres
long, which towards the end runs into a point so fine and flexible,
that it forms a sort of whipcord. When the thicker part of the
piece of whalebone is struck against the edge of the drum-skin,
the other end whips against the middle, and the skin is thus struck
twice at the same time. The drum is commonly played by the
man, and the playing is accompanied by a very monotonous
song. We have not seen it accompanied by dancing, twisting of
the countenance, or any other Shaman trick.

We did not see among the Chukches we met with any
Shamans. They are described by Wrangel, Hooper, and other
travellers. Wrangel states (vol. i. p. 284) that the Shamans in
the year 1814, when a severe epidemic broke out among the
Chukches and their reindeer at Anjui, declared that in order to
propitiate the spirits they must sacrifice Kotschen, one of the
most highly esteemed men of the tribe. He was so much
respected that no one would execute the sentence, but attempts
were made to get it altered, first by presents to the prophets,
and then by flogging them. But when this did not succeed,
as the disease continued to ravage, and no one would execute the
doom, Kotschen ordered his own son to do it. He was thus
compelled to stab his own father to death and give up the corpse
to the Shamans. The whole narrative conflicts absolutely with
the disposition and manners of the people with whom we
made acquaintance at Behring's Straits sixty-five years after
this occurrence, and I would be disposed to dispute entirely
the truthfulness of the statement, had not the history of our
own part of the world taught us that blood has flowed in
streams for dogmatic hair-splittings, which no one now troubles
himself about. Perhaps the breath of indifferentism has reached
even the ice deserts of the Polar lands.

The drum has besides also another use, which appears to have
little connection with its property of Shaman psychograph or
church bell. When the ladies unravel and comb their long
black hair, this is done carefully over the drum, on whose
bottom the numerous beings which the comb brings with it
from the warm hearth of home out into the cold wide world, are
collected and cracked—in case they are not eaten up. They
taste well according to the Chukch opinion, and are exceedingly
good for the breast. Even *gorm* (the large, fully developed, fat
larva of the reindeer fly, *Oestrus tarandi*) is pressed out of
the skin of the reindeer and eaten; as well as the full-grown
reindeer fly.

Some more of the superstitious traits which we observed among the Chukches may here be stated. After the good hunting in February we endeavoured without success to induce the Chukches to give us a head or skull of some of the seals they had killed. Even brandy was unsuccessfully offered for it, and it was only in the greatest secrecy that Notti, one of our best friends from Irgunnuk, dared to give us the fœtus of a seal. A raven was once shot in the neighbourhood of the ice-huose. The shot then went to the magnetical observatory, but before he entered, laid down the shot bird, the gun, and other articles in the before-mentioned implement chest placed in front of the observatory. A short time after there was great excitement before the tent. Some men, women, and children among the natives crowded round the chest, screaming and shouting. For the Chukches had observed that the raven, having been only stunned by the shot, had begun to scream and flutter in the chest, and they now indicated by word and gesture that a great misfortune was about to happen. Pity is not, as is well known, one of the good qualities of the savage. It was clear that in this case too it was not this feeling, but fear of the evil which the wounded crow could bring about, that caused this scene, and when a sailor immediately after twisted the neck of the bird, the Chukches had no objection to receive and eat it.

The winter of 1878-1879 appears to have been uncommonly severe, and hunting less productive than usual. This was ascribed to our presence. The Chukches asked us anxiously several times whether we intended to raise the water so high that the sea would reach their tents. When on the 11th February, after the hunting had failed for a long time, they succeeded at last in catching a number of seals, they threw water in their mouths before they were carried into the tents. This was done, they said, in order that the open "leads" in the ice should not close too soon.

Besides the drum the Chukches also use as a musical instrument a piece of wood, cloven into two halves, and again united after the crack has been somewhat widened in the middle, with a piece of whalebone inserted between the two halves. They also during the course of the winter made several attempts to make violins after patterns seen on board, and actually succeeded in making a better sounding-box than could have been expected beforehand. On the draught strap of the dog sledge there was often a small bell bought from the Russians, and the reindeer-Chukches are said sometimes to wear bells in the belt.

The dance I saw consisted in two women or children taking each other by the shoulders, and then hopping now on the one foot now on the other. When many took part in the dance, they

nselves in rows, sang a monotonous, meaningless song,
time, turned the eyes out and in, and threw them-
h spasmodic movements, clearly denoting pleasure
now to the right, now to the left. "La saison" for
song, the time of slaughtering reindeer, however, did
a during our stay, on which account our experience of
:hes' abilities in this way is exceedingly limited.
t they entered into with special delight; for instance,
shooting which Palander set on foot on New Year's Day
with a small rifled
1 the *Vega.* At
romen sat aft with
:en, far from the
shooting weapon,
ited their feelings
the same gestures
ich occasions are
distinguish the
nd fairer sex of
race. But soon
took the upper
ey pressed forward
:y could see best,
e out in a loud
ho!" when the
ired and the shells
in the air.
t sort is the art-
ie Chukches? As
almost belong to
Age, and as their
th Europeans has
inited that it has
ips conduced to
taste and skill in
question appears
iave a great inter-
for the historian
ho here obtains

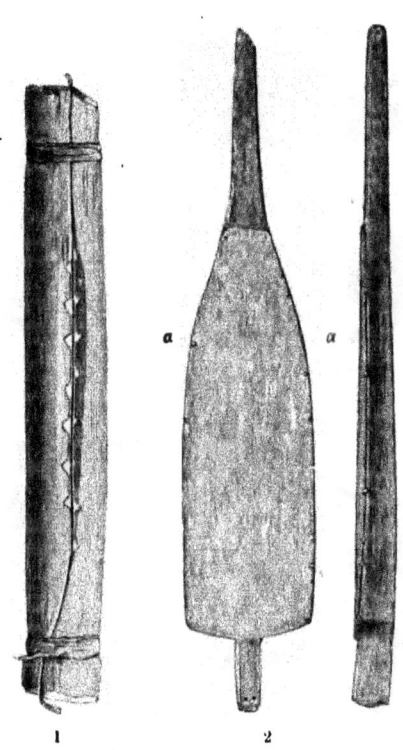

MUSICAL INSTRUMENTS.

1 Whistle-pipe, natural size. 2. Whistle-instru
ment, one-eighth of natural size; *a* mouth-hole.

n as to the nature of the seed from which at last the
e master has been developed in the course of ages and
ns, and for the archæologist, who finds here a starting
forming a judgment both of the Scandinavian rock-
nd the palæolithic drawings, which, in recent times
ed so great a part in enabling us to understand
, history of the human race. We have therefore
collected all that we could of Chukch carvings,

K K

DRAWINGS MADE BY CHUKCHES.

DRAWINGS MADE BY CHUKCHES.

drawings and patterns.   The most remarkable of these in one respect or another are to be found delineated in the woodcuts on the preceding pages.[1]

Many of the ivory carvings are old and worn, showing that they have been long in use, probably as amulets. Various of the animal images are the fruit of the imagination, and as such may be instructive.   In general the carvings are clumsy, though showing a distinctive style.   If we compare them with the Samoyed images we brought home with us, it appears that the genius of the Chukches for art has reached an incomparably higher development than that of the Polar race which inhabits the western portion of the north coast of Asia; on the other hand, they are in this respect evidently inferior to the Eskimo at Port Clarence.   The Chukch drawings too are roughly and clumsily executed, but many of them exhibit a certain power of hitting off the object.   These figures appear to me to show that the objections which have been raised to the genuineness of various palæolithic etchings, just on the ground of the artist's comparatively sure hand, are not justified.   Even patterns and ivory buckles show a certain taste.   Embroidery is done commonly on red-coloured strips of skin partly with white reindeer hair, partly with red and black wool, obtained in small quantity by barter from Behring's Straits.   The supply of colouring material is not particularly abundant.   It is obtained partly from the mineral kingdom (limonite of different colours, and graphite), partly from the vegetable kingdom (bark of various trees).   The mineral colours are ground with water between flat stones.   Bark is probably treated with urine.   Red is the Chukches' favourite colour.

In order to make a contribution towards an answer to the disputed question, in what degree is the colour-sense developed among savages, Dr. Almquist during the course of the winter instituted comprehensive researches according to the method worked out by Professor FR. HOLMGREN. A detailed account of these is to be found in The Scientific Work of the Vega Expedition, and in various scientific journals.   Here I shall only state that Dr. Almquist gives the following as the final result

[1] The originals of the drawings reproduced in the woodcuts are made paper, part with the lead pencil, part with red ochre. The different grou represent on the first page—1, a dog-team; 2, 3, whales; 4, hunting the Polar bear and the walrus ; 5, bullhead and cod; 6, man fishing; 7, hare hunting; 8, birds; 9, wood-chopper; 10, man leading a reindeer; walrus hunt—7 and 9 represent Europeans. On the second page- 1, a rein deer train ; 2, a reindeer taken with a lasso by two men ; 3, a man throw ing a harpoon ; 4, seal hunt fr m boat; 5, bear hunt; 6, the man in the moon ; 7, man leading a reindeer ; 8, reindeer ; 9, Chukch with staff and an archer ; 10, reindeer with herd; 11, reindeer; 12, two tents, man riding on a dog sledge, &c.

of his investigation : " That the Chukches in general possess as
good an organ for distinguishing colours as we Swedes. On the
other hand, they appear not to be accustomed to observe colours,
and to distinguish sharply any other colour than red. They
bring together all reds as something special, but consider that
green of a moderate brightness corresponds less with a green of
less brightness than with a blue of the same brightness. In
order to bring all greens together the Chukches thus require to
learn a new abstraction." Of 300 persons who were examined,
273 had a fully developed colour-sense, nine were completely
colour-blind, and eighteen incompletely colour-blind, or gave
uncertain indications.

From what has been stated above it appears that the coast
Chukches are without noteworthy religion, social organisation
or government. Had not experience from the Polar races of
America taught us differently we should have believed that with
such a literally anarchic and godless crew there would be no
security for life and property, immorality would be boundless,
and the weaker without any protection from the violence of the
stronger sex. This, however, is so far from being the case that
criminal statistics have been rendered impossible for want of
crimes, if we except acts of violence committed under the
influence of liquor.

During the winter the *Vega* was visited daily, as has been
stated in the account of the wintering, by the people from the
neighbouring villages, while our vessel at the same time formed
a resting-place for all the equipages which travelled from the
western tent-villages to the islands in Behring's Straits, and
vice versâ. Not only our neighbours, but people from a distance
whom we had never seen before, and probably would not see
again, came and went without hindrance among a great number
of objects which in their hands would have been precious
indeed. We had never any cause to regret the confidence we
placed in them. Even during the very hard time, when hunting completely failed, and when most of them lived on the food
which was served out on board, the large *dépôt* of provisions,
which we had placed on land without special watch, in case any
misfortune should befall our vessel, was untouched. On the
other hand, there were two instances in which they secretly
repossessed themselves of fish they had already sold, and which
were kept in a place on deck accessible to them. And with
the most innocent countenance in the world they then sold
them over again. This sort of dishonesty they evidently did
not regard as theft but as a permissible commercial trick.

This was not the only proof that the Chukches consider
deception in trade not only quite justifiable, but almost

creditable. While their own things were always made with the greatest care, all that they did specially for us was done with extreme carelessness, and they were seldom pleased with the price that was offered, until they became convinced that they could not get more. When they saw that we were anxious to get ptarmigan, they offered us from their winter stock under this name the young of *Larus eburneus*, which is marked in the same way, but of little use as food. When I with delight purchased this bird, which in its youthful dress is rare, and therefore valuable to the ornithologist, a self-satisfied smile passed over the countenance of the seller. He was evidently proud of

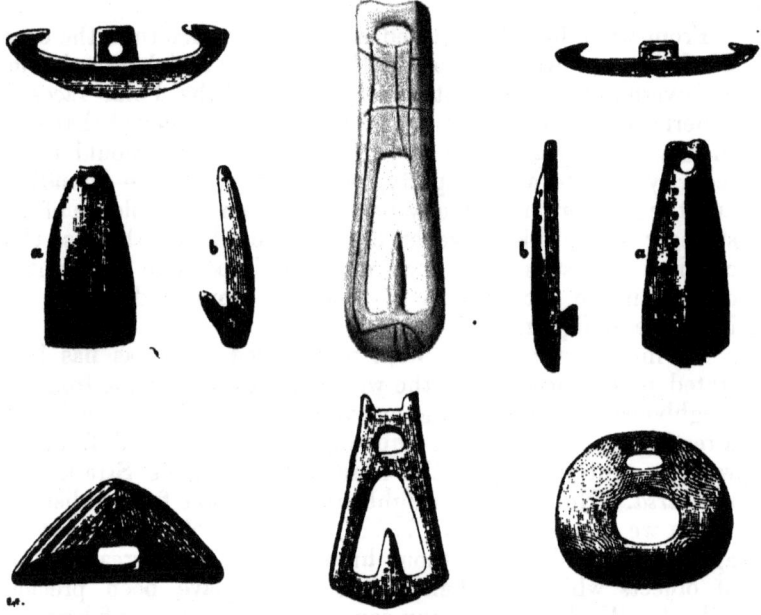

CHUKCH BUCKLES AND HOOKS OF IVORY.
Half the natural size.

his successful trick. Some prejudice, as has been already stated, prevented the Chukches from parting with the heads of the seal, though, in order to ascertain the species existing here, we offered a high price for them. "Irgatti" (to-morrow), or "Isgatti" if the promise was given by a woman, was the usual answer. But the promise was never kept. At last a boy came and gave us a skull, which he said belonged to a seal. On a more minute examination, however, it was found not to have belonged to a seal, but to an old dog, whose head it was evidently thought might, without any damage to the hunting, be handed over to the white magicians. This time it went worse with the

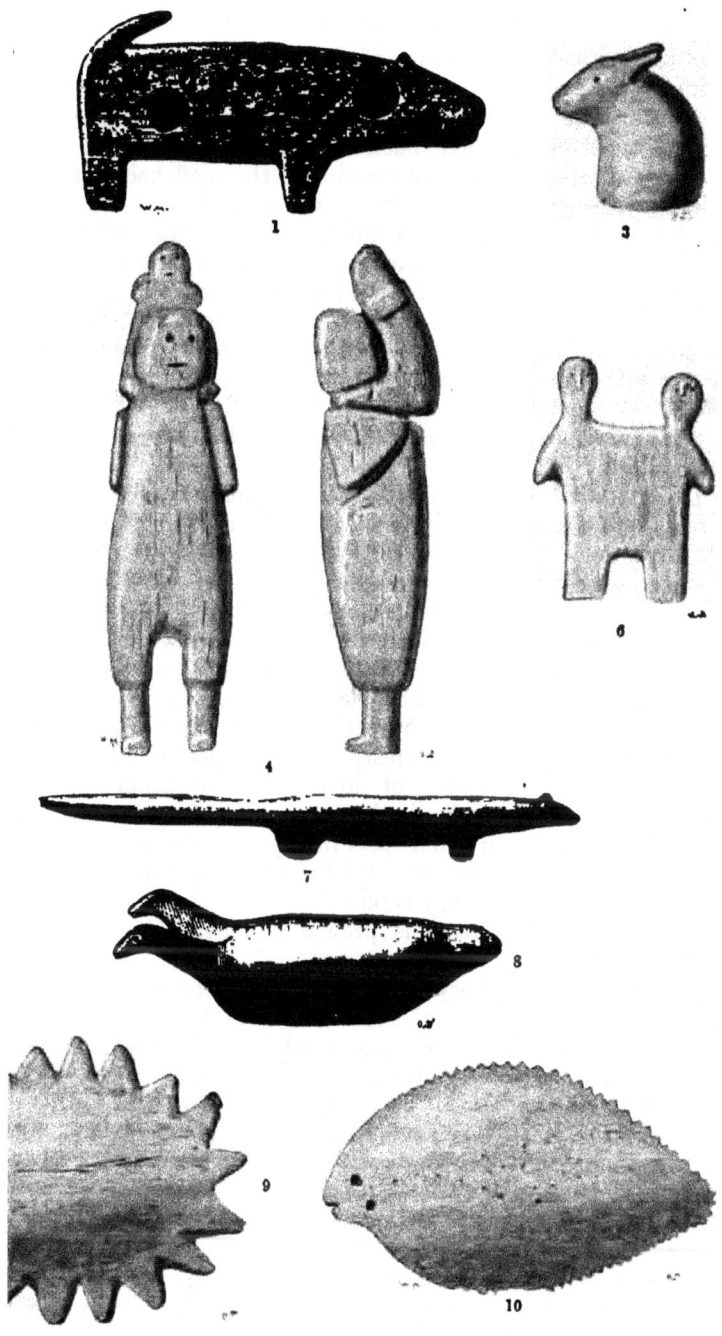

CHUKCH BONE CARVINGS.

al size. 2, 3. Hares, natural size. 4. Woman carrying her child on her shoulders, two-
Mollusc from the inland lakes (Branchypus?), natural size. 6. Monster, natural size
tural size. 8. Animal with three heads, two-thirds. 9. Asterid, natural size. 10. Fish
ze.

counterfeiter than in the case of the ptarmigan bargain. For a
couple of my comrades undertook to make the boy ashamed in
the presence of the other Chukches, saying with a laugh "that
he, a Chukch, must have been very stupid to commit such a
mistake," and it actually appeared as if the scoff had in this case
fallen into good ground. Another time, while I was in my
watch in the ice-house, there came a native to me and informed
me that he had driven a man from Irgunnuk to the vessel, but
that the man had not paid him, and asked me on that account
to give him a box of matches. When I replied that he must
have been already well paid on the vessel for his drive, he said
in a whining tone, "only a very little piece of bread." He was
not the least embarrassed, when I only laughed at the, as I
well knew, untruthful statement, and did not give him what
he asked.

The Chukches commonly live in monogamy; it is only
exceptionally that they have two wives, as was the case with
Chepurin, who has been already mentioned. It appeared as if
the wives were faithful to their husbands. It was only seldom
that cases occurred in which women, either in jest or earnest,
gave out that they wished a white man as a lover. A woman
not exactly eminent for beauty or cleanliness said, for instance,
on one occasion, that she had had two children by Chukches,
and now she wished to have a third by one of the ship's folk.
The young women were modest, often very pretty, and evidently
felt the same necessity of attracting attention by small
coquettish artifices as Eve's daughters of European race. We
may also understand their peculiar pronunciation of the language as an expression of feminine coquetry. For when they
wish to be attractive they replace the man's r-sound with a soft
s; thus, korang (reindeer) is pronounced by the women kosang,
tirkir (the sun) tiskis, and so on.

The women work very hard. Not only the management of
the children, the cooking, the melting of the ice, the putting
the tent in order, the sewing, and other "woman's work," lie to
their hand, but they receive the catch, in winter in the tent, in
summer at the beach, cut it in pieces, help with the fishing, at
least when it is in the neighbourhood of the tent, and carry out
the exceedingly laboriously tanning of the hides, and prepare
thread from sinews. In summer they collect green plants
in the meadows and hill-slopes in the neighbourhood of the
tents. They are therefore generally at home, and always busy.
The men have it for their share to procure for their family food
from the animal kingdom by hunting and fishing. With this purpose in view they are often out on long excursions. In the tent
the man is for the most part without occupation, sleeps, eats,
gossips, chats with his children, and so on, if he does not pass

in putting his hunting implements in order in a quite manner.

n the family the most remarkable unanimity prevails, ve never heard a hard word exchanged, either between l wife, parents and children, or between the married Ɪ own the tent and the unmarried who occasionally live in power of the woman appears to be very great. In the more important bargains, even about weapons and implements, she is, as a rule, consulted, and her advice . A number of things which form women's tools she ter away on her own responsibility, or in any other ꞁloy as she pleases. When the man has by barter pro-piece of cloth, tobacco, sugar, or such like, he generally over to his wife to keep.

ꞁhildren are neither chastised ded ; they are, however, the aved I have ever seen. Their ꞁr in the tent is equal to that ꞁst-brought-up European chil-ꞁhe parlour. They are not, per-wild as ours, but are addicted ꞁ which closely resemble those among us in the country. ꞁgs are also in use, for instance, ꞁws, windmills with two sails, the parents get any delicacy ꞁays give each of their chil-bit, and there is never any as to the size of each child's

If a piece of sugar is given of the children in a crowd it m mouth to mouth round the ꞁmpany. In the same way the child offers its father and a taste of the bit of sugar or piece of bread it has ven in childhood the Chukches are exceedingly patient. who fell down from the ship's stair, head foremost, ꞁs got so violent a blow that she was almost deprived ng, scarcely uttered a cry. A boy, three or four years much rolled up in furs, who fell down into a ditch the ice on the ship's deck, and in consequence of nvenient dress could not get up, lay quietly still until ꞁbserved and helped up by one of the crew.

Chukches' most troublesome fault is a disposition to that is limited by no feeling of self-respect. This is ꞁ counterbalanced by their unbounded hospitality and ꞁndness to each other, and is, perhaps, often caused by necessity. But they thus became veritable torments,

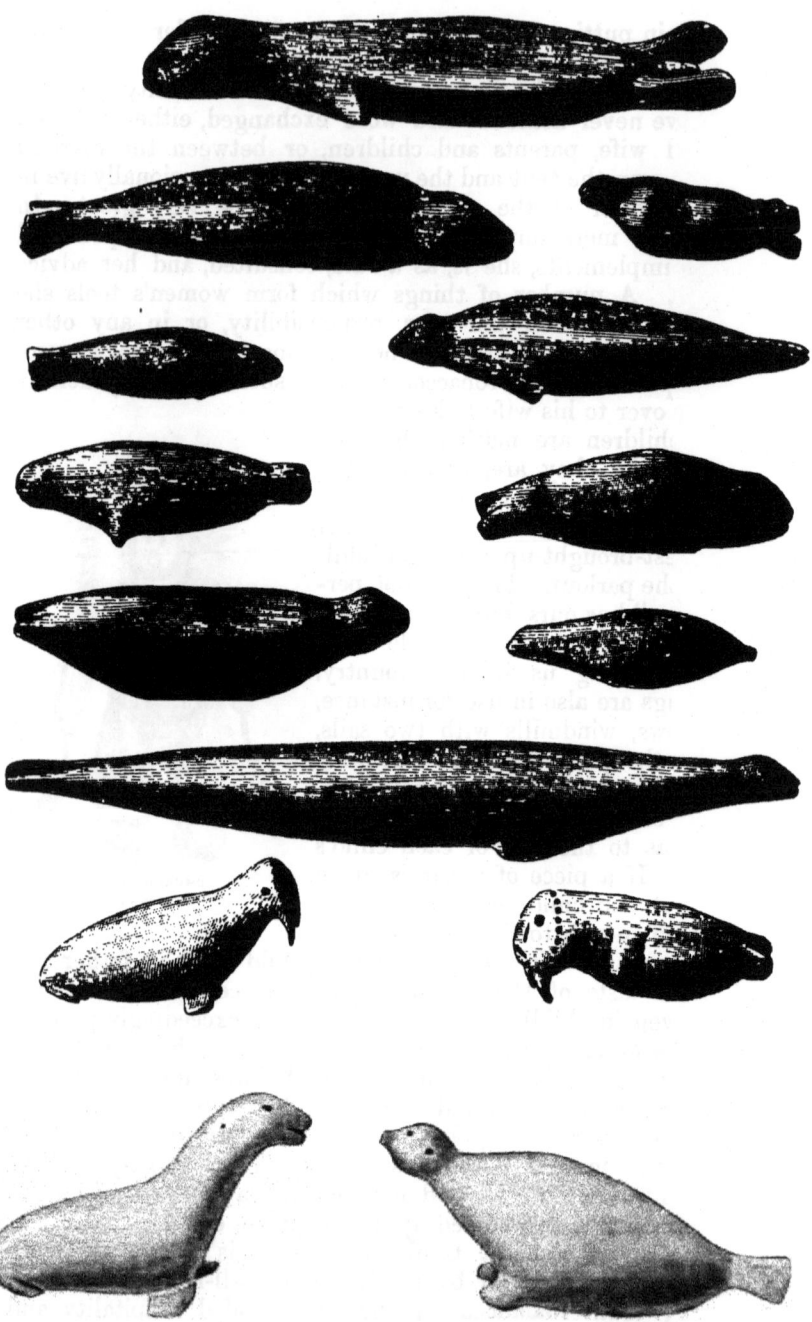

CHUKCH BONE CARVINGS.

Seals, walrusses, a sea-bear (the lowest figure to the left). The four lowest are of the natural size, the others two-thirds of the natural size.

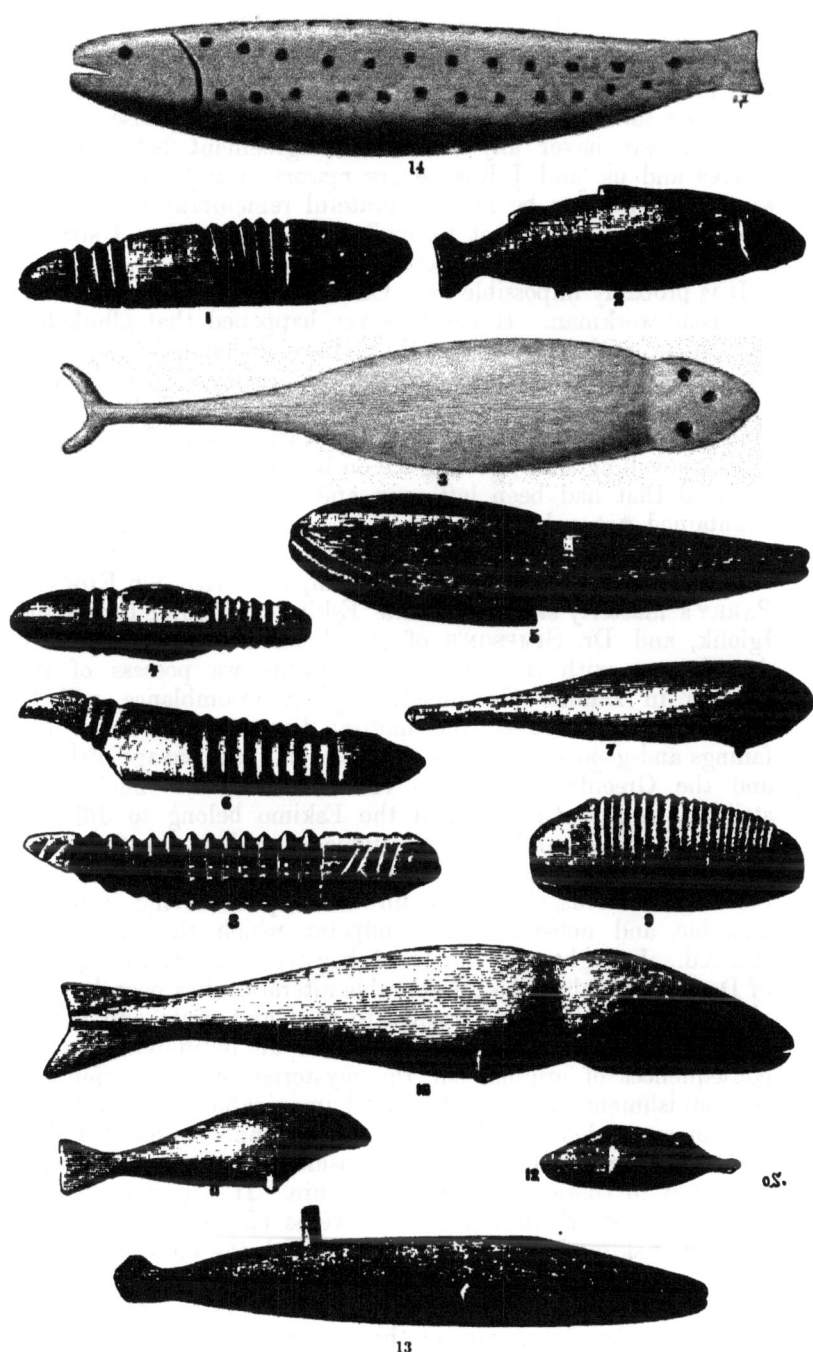

CHUKCH BONE CARVINGS.

Fishes, larvæ of flies (*gorm*), molluscs, and whales. Nos. 1 to 9 and 14, natural size. Nos. 10 to 13, two-thirds of the natural size.

putting to a hard test the patience, not only of the scientific men and officers, but also of the crew. The good nature with which our sailors met their demands was above all praise.

There was never any trace of disagreement between the natives and us, and I have every reason to suppose that our wintering will long be held in grateful remembrance by them, especially as, in order not to spoil their seal-hunting, I strictly forbade all unnecessary interference with it.

It is probably impossible for a Chukch to take the place of a European workman. It has, however, happened that Chukches have gone with whalers to the Sandwich Islands, and have become serviceable seamen. During our wintering two young men got accustomed to come on board and there to take a hand, in quite a leisurely way, at work of various kinds, as sawing wood, shovelling snow, getting ice on board, &c. In return they got food that had been left over, and thus, for the most part, maintained not only themselves, but also their families, during the time we remained in their neighbourhood.

If what I have here stated be compared with Sir EDWARD PARRY's masterly sketches of the Eskimo at Winter Island and Iglolik, and Dr. SIMPSON's of the Eskimo in North-western America, or with the numerous accounts we possess of the Eskimo in Danish Greenland, a great resemblance will be found to exist between the natural disposition, mode of life, failings and good qualities of the Chukches, the savage Eskimo, and the Greenlanders. This resemblance is so much more striking, as the Chukch and the Eskimo belong to different races, and speak quite different languages, and, as the former, to judge by old accounts of this people, did not, until the most recent generations, sink to the unwarlike, peace-loving, harmless, anarchic, and non-religious standpoint which they have now reached. It ought to be observed, however, that in the Eskimo of Danish Greenland no considerable alteration has been brought about by their all having learned to read and write and profess the Christian religion—although with an indifference to the consequences of original sin, the mysteries of redemption, and the punishments of hell, which all imaginable missionary zeal has not succeeded in overcoming. Their innocent natural state has not been altered in any considerable degree by being subjected to these conditions of culture. It is certain besides, that the blood which flows in the veins of the Greenlander is not pure Eskimo blood, but is mingled with the blood of some of the proudest martial races in the world. When we consider how rapidly, even now, when Greenland is in constant communication with the European mother-country, all descendants of mixed blood become complete Eskimo in language and mode of life, how difficult it often is, even for parents of pure European

to get their children to speak any other language than
the natives, and how they, on their part, seldom borrow
from the Europeans, how common mixed marriages and
of mixed blood are even now—in view of all this it
to me much more probable that Erik the Red's
s were quietly and peacefully converted into Eskimo,
at they were killed by the Eskimo.   A single century's
e separation from Europe would be sufficient to

CHUKCH BONE CARVINGS OF BIRDS.
Size of the originals

it thoroughly this alteration of the present European
ion of Greenland, and by the end of that period the
is of Danish rule would be very obscure in that land.
; some trifling quarrel between a ruler of the colony and
2 would take the foremost place among the surviving
is, and be interpreted as a reminiscence from a war or
nation
the present Chukches form, without doubt, a mixture of

several races, formerly savage and warlike, who have been
driven by foreign invaders from south to north, where they have
adopted a common language, and on whom the food-conditions
of the shore of the Polar Sea, the cold, snow, and darkness of
the Arctic night, the pure, light atmosphere of the Polar
summer, have impressed their ineffaceable stamp, a stamp which
meets us with little variation, not only among the people now
in question, but also—with the necessary allowance for the
changes, not always favourable, caused by constant intercourse
with Europeans—among the Lapps of Scandinavia and the
Samoyeds of Russia.

It would be of great psychological interest to ascertain
whether the change which has taken place in a peaceful
direction is progress or decadence. Notwithstanding all the
interest which the honesty, peaceableness, and innocent friendliness of the Polar tribes have for us, it is my belief that the
answer must be—*decadence.* For it strikes us as if we witness
here the conversion of a savage, coarse, and cruel man into a
being, nobler, indeed, but one in whom just those qualities
which distinguish man from the animals, and to which at once
the great deeds and the crimes of humanity have been due,
have been more and more effaced, and who, if special protection
or specially favourable circumstances be absent, will not be able
to maintain the struggle for existence with new races that may
seek to force their way into the country.

CHAPTER XIII.

The development of our knowledge of the north coast of Asia—Herodotus—Strabo—Pliny—Marco Polo—Herberstein's map—The conquest
of Siberia by the Russians—Deschnev's voyages—Coast navigation
between the Lena and the Kolyma—Accounts of islands in the Polar
Sea and old voyages to them—The discovery of Kamchatka—The
navigation of the Sea of Okotsk is opened by Swedish prisoners-of-
war—The Great Northern Expedition—Behring—Schalaurov—Andre-
yev's Land—The New Siberian islands—Hedenström's expeditions—
Anjou and Wrangel—Voyages from Behring's Straits westward—
Fictitious Polar voyages.

Now that the north-eastern promontory of Asia has been at last
circumnavigated, and vessels have thus sailed along all the
coasts of the old world, I shall before proceeding farther in my
sketch of the voyage of the *Vega*, give a short account of the
development of our knowledge of the north coast of Asia.

Already in primitive times the Greeks assumed that all the

ies of the earth were surrounded by the ocean. STRABO,
ı first century before Christ, after having shown that
R favoured this view, brings together in the first chapter
ı First Book of his geography reasons in support of it in
lowing terms:—

all directions in which man has penetrated to the utter-
boundary of the earth, he has met the sea, that is, the
He has sailed round the east coast towards India, the
oast towards Iberia and Mauritia, and a great part of the
and north coast. The remaining portion which has not
en sailed round in consequence of the voyages which have
ındertaken from both sides, not having been connected is
iderable. For those who have attempted to circumnavi-
he earth and have turned, declare that their undertaking
ıt fail in consequence of their having met with land, but
sequence of want of provisions and of complete timidity
At sea they could always have gone further. . . . This
that the earth is surrounded by water) also accords better
he phenomena of the tides, for as the ebb and flow are
vhere the same, or at least do not vary much, the cause of
ıotion is to be sought for in a single ocean." [1]

ı if men were thus agreed that the north coast of Asia and
ıe was bounded by the sea, there was for sixteen hundred
after the birth of Christ no actual knowledge of the nature
Asiatic portion of this line of coast. Obscure statements
ling it, however, were current at an early period.
ıle HERODOTUS, in the forty-fifth chapter of his Fourth
expressly says that no man, so far as was then known, had
ered whether the eastern and northern countries of Europe
ırrounded by the sea, he gives in the twenty-third and
y-fourth chapters of the same book the following account
countries lying to the north-east:—

s far as the territory of the Scythians all the land which
ave described is an uninterrupted plain, with cultivable
ıut beyond that the ground is stony and rugged. And on
ther side of this extensive stone-bound tract there live at
ıot of a high mountain-chain men who are bald from their
both men and women; they are also flat-nosed and have
chins. They speak a peculiar language, wear the Scythian
and live on the fruit of a tree. The tree on which they
s called *Ponticon*, is about as large as the wild fig-tree,
bears fruit which resembles a bean, but has a kernel.

juote this because the movement of the tides is still, in our own time,
use of to determine whether certain parts of the Polar seas are
:ted with each other or not.

When this fruit is ripe, they strain it through a cloth, and the juice which flows from it is thick and black and called *aschy*. This juice they suck or drink mixed with milk, and of the pressed fruits they make cakes which they eat; for they have not many cattle because the pasture is poor. . . . As far as to these bald people the land is now sufficiently well known, also the races on this side of them, because they are visited by Scythians. From them it is not difficult to collect information, which is also to be had from the Greeks at the port of the Borysthenes and other ports in Pontus. The Scythians who travel thither do business with the assistance of seven interpreters in seven languages. So far our knowledge extends. But of the land on the other side of the bald men none can give any trustworthy account because it is shut off by a separating wall of lofty trackless mountains, which no man can cross. But these bald men say—which, however, I do not believe—that men with goat's feet live on the mountains, and on the other side of them other men who sleep six months at a time. The latter statement, however, I cannot at all admit. On the other hand, the land east of the bald men, in which the Issedones live, is well known, but what is farther to the north, both on the other side of the bald men and of the Issedones, is only known by the statements of these tribes. . . . Above the Issedones live the one-eyed men, and the gold-guarding griffins. This information the Scythians have got from the Issedones and we from the Scythians, and we call the one-eyed race by the Scythian name Arimaspi, for in the Scythian language *arima* signifies one and *spou* the eye. The whole of the country which I have been speaking of has so hard and severe a winter, that there prevails there for eight months an altogether insupportable cold, so that if you pour water on the ground you will not make mud, but if you light a fire you will make mud. Even the sea freezes, and the whole Cimmerian Bosphorus, and the Scythians who live within the trench travel on the ice and drive over it in waggons. . . . Again, with reference to the feathers with which the Scythians say the air is filled, and which prevent the whole land lying beyond from being seen or travelled through, I entertain the following opinion. In the upper parts of this country it snows continually, but, as is natural, less in summer than in winter. And whoever has seen snow falling thick near him will know what I mean. For snow resembles feathers, and on account of the winter being so severe the northern parts of this continent cannot be inhabited. I believe then that the Scythians and their neighbours called snow feathers, on account of the resemblance between them. This is what is stated regarding the most remote regions."

These and other similar statements, notwithstanding the

rdities mixed up with them, are founded in the first
nce on the accounts of eye-witnesses, which have passed
mouth to mouth, from tribe to tribe, before they were
d down. Still several centuries after the time of Herodotus,
a the Roman power had reached its highest point, little
was known of the more remote parts of North Asia. While
dotus, in the two hundred and third chapter of his First

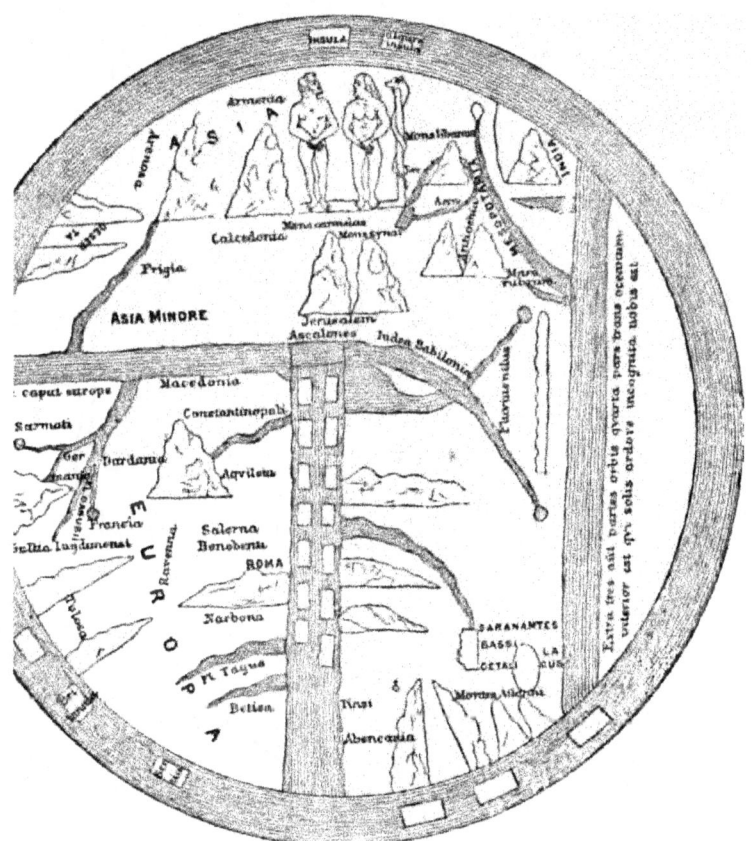

MAP OF THE WORLD, SAID TO BE OF THE TENTH CENTURY.
Found in a manuscript of the twelfth century in the Library at Turin.
From Santarem's Atlas.

, says that "the Caspian is a sea by itself having no
munication with any other sea," Strabo, induced by evidence
ished by the commander of a Greek fleet in that sea, states
k II. chapters i. and iv.) that the Caspian is a gulf of the
hern ocean, from which it is possible to sail to India.
IY THE ELDER (*Historia Naturalis*, Book VI. chapters xiii.

L L

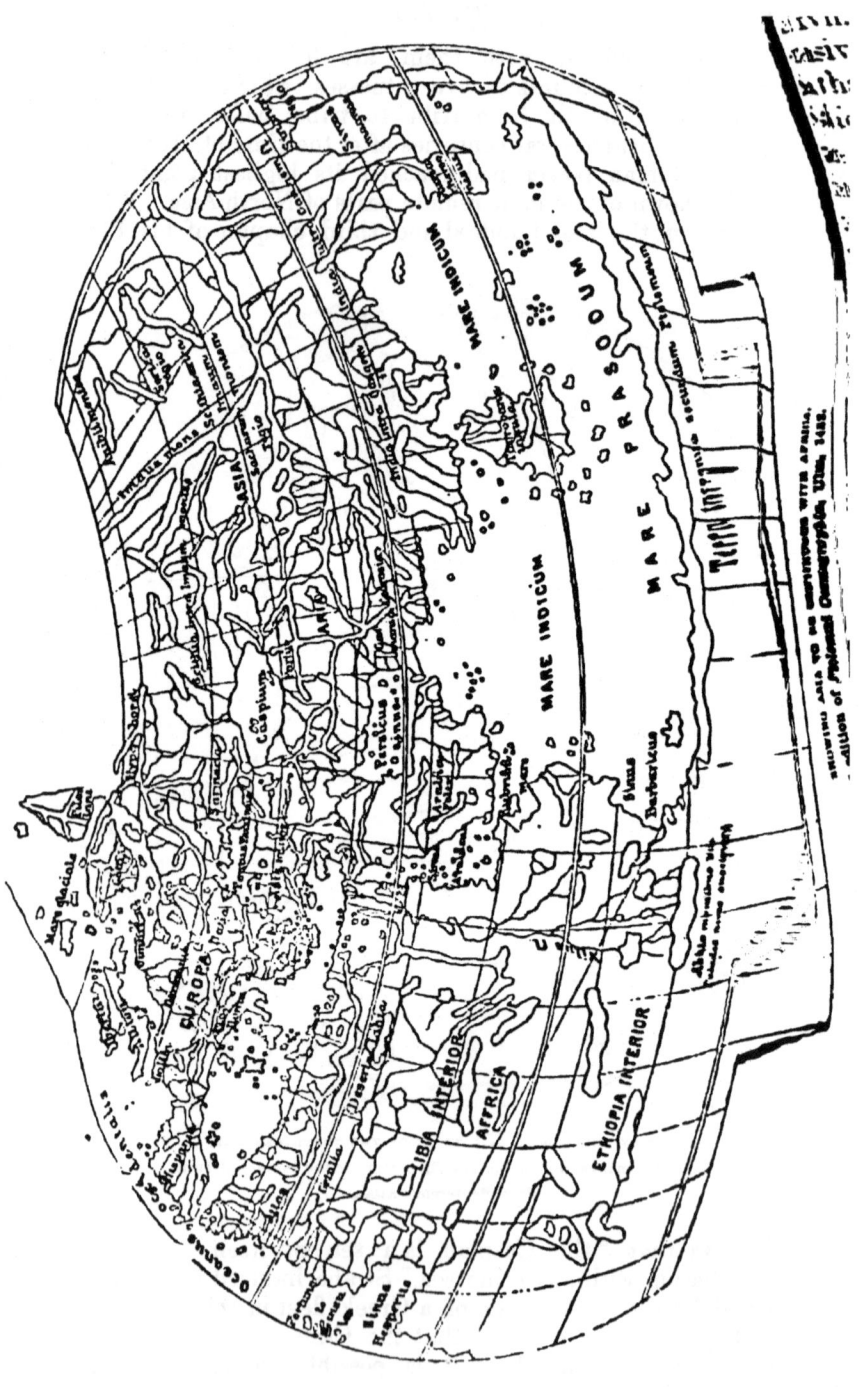

xvii.) states that the north part of Asia is occupied by
ᵣnsive deserts bounded on the north by the Scythian
, that these deserts run out to a headland, *Promontorium
hicum*, which is uninhabitable on account of snow. Then
ᵣe is a land inhabited by man-eating Scythians, then deserts,
ᵣ Scythians again, then deserts with wild animals to a
.ntain ridge rising out of the sea, which is called *Tabin*. The
people that are known beyond this are the Seri. PTOLEMY
his successors again supposed, though perhaps not ignorant
ᵣhe old statement that Africa had been circumnavigated
er Pharaoh Necho, that the Indian Ocean was an inland
everywhere surrounded by land, which united southern
.ca with the eastern part of Asia, an idea which was first
ᵣpletely abandoned by the chartographers of the fifteenth
ᵣury after the circumnavigation of Africa by VASCO DA
ᵣA.

ᵣhe knowledge of the geography of North Asia remained at
. point until MARCO POLO,[1] in the narrative of his remarkable
ᵣneys among the peoples of Middle Asia, gave some in-
ᵣnation regarding the most northerly lands of this quarter
the world also. The chapters which treat of this subject·
ᵣr the distinctive titles : " On the land of the Tartars living
the north," " On another region to which merchants only
ᵣel in waggons drawn by dogs," and " On the region where
ᵣkness prevails " (*De regione tenebrarum*). From the state-
ᵣts in these chapters it follows that hunters and traders

Marco Polo, in 1271, at the age of seventeen or eighteen, accompanied
father Nicolo, and his uncle Maffeo Polo, to High Asia. He remained
e until 1295, and during that time came into great favour with Kublai
n, who employed him, among other things, in a great number of
ortant public commissions, whereby he became well acquainted with
widely extended lands which lay under the sceptre of that ruler. After
ᵣeturn home he caused a great sensation by the riches he brought with
, which procured him the name *il Millione*, a name however which,
ᵣrding to others, was an expression of the doubts that were long enter-
ᵣd regarding the truthfulness of his, as we now know, mainly true
ᵣunts of the number of the people and the abundance of wealth in
lai Khan's lands. " Il Millione," in the meantime, became a popular
ival character, whose cue was to relate as many and as wonderful
rns " as possible, and in his narratives to deal preferably with millions.
ᵣpossible that the predecessor of Columbus might have descended to
erity merely as the original of this character if he had not, soon after
ᵣeturn home, taken part in a war against Genoa, in the course of which
ᵣas taken prisoner, and, during his imprisonment, related his recol-
ᵣons of his travels to a fellow-prisoner, who committed them to writing,
ᵣhat language is still uncertain. The work attracted great attention and
ᵣsoon spread, first in written copies, then by the press in a large number
ᵣifferent languages. It has not been translated into Swedish, but in the
ᵣal Library in Stockholm there is a very important and hitherto little
ᵣvn manuscript of it from the middle of the fourteenth century, of
ᵣh an edition is in course of publication in photo-lithographic facsimile.

already inhabited or wandered about in the present Siberia, and brought thence valuable furs of the black fox, sable, beaver, &c. The northernmost living men were said to be handsome, tall and stout but very pale for want of the sun. They obeyed no king or chief, but were coarse and uncivilised and lived as beasts.[1] Among the products of the northern countries white bears are mentioned, from which it appears that at that time the hunters

MAP OF THE WORLD AFTER FRA MAURO FROM THE MIDDLE OF THE FIFTEENTH CENTURY.
From Il mappamondo di Fra Mauro Camaldolese descritto ed illustrato da D. Placido Znria, Venezia, 1806.

had already reached the coast of the Polar Sea. But Marco Polo nowhere says expressly that Asia is bounded on the north by the sea.

All the maps of North Asia which have been published down

1 Homines illius regionis sunt pulchri, magni, et corpulenti, sed sunt multum pallidi . . . . et sunt homines inculti, et immorigerati et bestialiter viventes.

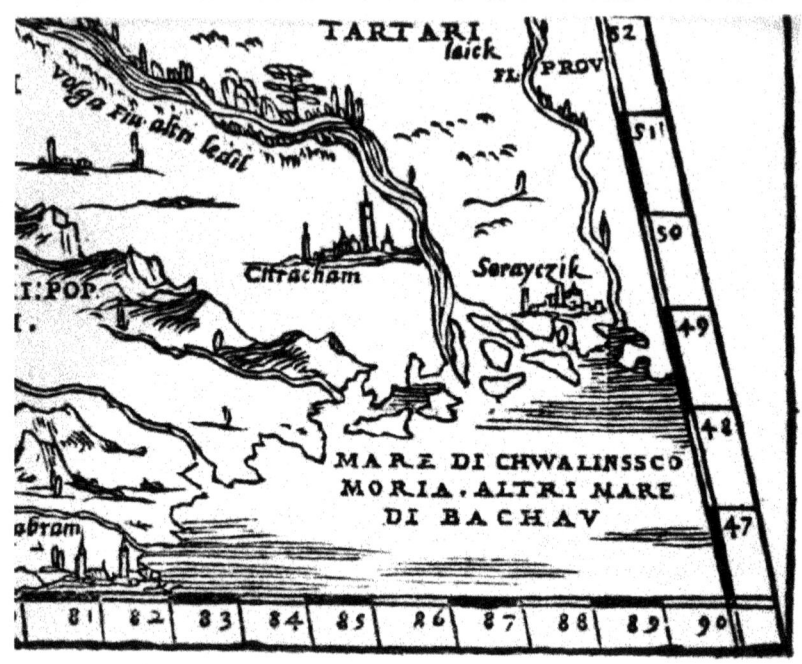

A. VENICE, 1550.

to the middle of the sixteenth century, are based to a greater or
less extent on interpretations of the accounts of Herodotus,
Pliny, and Marco Polo.   When they do not surround the whole
Indian Ocean with land, they give to Asia a much less extent
in the north and east than it actually possesses, make the land
in this direction completely bounded by sea, and delineate two
headlands projecting towards the north from the mainland.   To
these they give the names *Promontorium Scythicum* and *Tabin*,
and they besides place in the neighbourhood of the north coast
a large island to which they give the name that already occurs
in Pliny, *Insula Tazata*, which · reminds us, perhaps by an
accidental resemblance of sound, of the name of the river and
bay, Tas, between the Ob and the Yenisej.   Finally, the borders
of the maps are often adorned with pictures of wonderfully
formed men, whose dwellings the hunters placed in those
regions, the names being at the same time given of a larger
or smaller number of peoples and cities mentioned by Marco
Polo.

On the whole, the voyages of the Portuguese to India and
the Eastern archipelago, the discovery of America and the
first circumnavigation of the globe, exerted little influence on the
current ideas regarding the geography of North Asia.   A new
period in respect of our knowledge of this part of the old world
first began with the publication of HERBERSTEIN's *Rerum
Moscoviticarum Commentarii*, Vindobonæ 1549.[1]   This work has
annexed to it a map with the title " Moscovia Sigismundi
liberi baronis in Herberstein Neiperg et Gutnhag.   Anno
MDXLIX.   Hanc tabulam absolvit AUG. HIRSFOGEL Viennæ
Austriæ cum gra. et privi. imp.," [2] which indeed embraces only
a small part of Siberia, but shows that a knowledge of North
Russia now began to be based on actual observations.   A large
gulf, marked with the name Mare Glaciale (the present White
Sea) here projects into the north coast of Russia ; from the

---

[1] See note at page 45, for an account of von Herberstein and his
works.

[2] As the copy of the original map to which I have had access, being
coloured, is unsuitable for photo-lithographing, I give here instead a photo-
lithographic reproduction of the map in the Italian edition printed in 1550.
The map itself is unchanged in any essential particular, but the drawing
and engraving are better.   There is, besides, a still older map of Russia in
the first edition of Sebastian Münster's *Cosmographia Universalis*.   I have
not had access to this edition, but have had to the third edition of the same
work printed at Basel in 1550.   A very incomplete map of Russia engraved
on wood, on which, however, the Obi and the " Sybir " are to be found, is
inserted in this work at page 910.   The Dwina here falls not into the White
Sea but into the Gulf of Finland, through a lake to which the name Ladoga
is now given ; places like Astracan, Asof, Viborg, Calmahori (Kolmogor),
Solowki (Solovets), &c., are indicated pretty correctly, and in the White Sea
there is to be seen a very faithful representation of a walrus swimming.

south there falls into it a large river, called the Dwina. On
the banks of the Dwina there are forts or towns with the
names Solovoka (Solovets), Pinega, Colmogor, &c. There are
to be found on the map besides, the names Mesen, Peczora,
Oby,[1] Tumen, &c. Oby runs out of a large lake named Kythay
lacus. In the text, mention is made of Irtisch and Papingorod,
of walruses and white bears[2] by the coast of the Polar Sea, of
the Siberian cedar-tree, of the word Samoyed signifying self-
eaters, &c.[3] The walrus is described in great detail. It is
mentioned further that the Russian Grand Duke sent out two
men, SIMEON THEODOROVITSCH KURBSKI and Knes PIETRO
UCHATOI, to explore the lands east of the Petchora, &c.

Herberstein's work, where the narrative of Istoma's circumnavigation of the northern extremity of Europe, which has been
already quoted, is to be found, was published only a few years
before the first north-east voyages of the English and the Dutch,
of which I have before given a detailed account. Through
these the northernmost part of European Russia and the
westernmost part of the Asiatic Polar Sea were mapped, but an
actual knowledge of the north coast of Asia in its entirety
was obtained through the conquest of Siberia by the Russians.
It is impossible here to give an account of the campaigns, by
which the whole of this enormous territory was brought under
the sceptre of the Czar of Moscow, or of the private journeys for
sport, trade, and the collecting of tribute, by which this conquest
was facilitated. But as nearly every step which the Russian
invaders took forward also extended the knowledge of
regions previously quite unknown, I shall mention the years in
which during this conquest the most important occurrences in a
geographical point of view took place, and give a rather more
detailed account of the exploratory or military expeditions which
led directly to important results affecting the extension of our
knowledge of the geography of the region now in question.

The way was prepared for the conquest of Siberia through
peaceful commercial treaties[4] which a rich Russian peasant

---

[1] The river Ob is mentioned the first time in 1492, in the negotiations
which the Austrian ambassador, Michael Snups, carried on in Moscow in
order to obtain permission to travel in the interior of Russia (Adelung,
Uebersicht der Reisenden in Russland, p. 157).

[2] As before stated, Marco Polo mentions Polar bears but not walruses.

[3] Herodotus places Andropagi in nearly the same regions which are
now inhabited by the Samoyeds. Pliny also speaks of man-eating
Scythians.

[4] Arctic literature contains a nearly contemporaneous sketch of the first
Russian-Siberian commercial undertakings, *Beschryvinghe vander Samoyeden
Landt in Tartarien, nieulijcks onder't ghebiedt der Moscoviten gebracht. Wt
de Russche tale overgheset,* Anno 1609. Amsterdam, Hessel Gerritsz, 1612;
inserted in Latin, in 1613, in the same publisher's *Descriptio ac Delineatio*

A, ancestor of the STROGANOV family, entered into with
ild races settled in Western Siberia, whom he even partially
ed to pay a yearly tribute to the Czar of Moscow. In con-
·n with this he and his sons, in the middle of the sixteenth
ry, obtained large grants of land on the rivers Kama and
·vaja and their tributaries, with the right to build towns
rts there, whereby their riches, previously very considerable,
much increased. The family's extensive possessions, how-
were threatened in 1577 by a great danger, when a host of
ck freebooters, six to seven thousand strong, under the
-ship of YERMAK TIMOFEJEV, took flight to the country
. Chusovaja in order to avoid the troops which the Czar
·o subdue them and punish them for all the depredations
had committed on the Don, the Caspian Sea and the Volga.
·der to get rid of the freebooters, MAXIM STROGANOV,
·'s grandson, not only provided Yermak and his men with
·ecessary sustenance, but supported in every way the bold
·turer's plan of entering on a campaign for the conquest of
·a. This was begun in 1579. In 1580 Yermak passed the
and after several engagements marched in particular
st the Tartars living in Western Siberia, along the rivers
and Tura to Tjumen, and thence in 1581 farther along
Tobol and Irtisch to Kutschum Khan's residence Sibir,
ted in the neighbourhood of the present Tobolsk. It was
fortress, long since destroyed, which gave its name to the
e north part of Asia.
om this point the Russians, mainly following the great
s, and passing from one river territory to another at the
s where the tributaries almost met, spread out rapidly in
rections. Yermak himself indeed was drowned on the $\frac{16}{5}$th
st, 1584, in the river Irtisch, but the adventurers who
npanied him overran in a few decades the whole of the
nous territory lying north of the deserts of Central Asia
Ural to the Pacific, everywhere strengthening their
nion by building Ostrogs, or small fortresses, at suitable
s. It was the noble fur-yielding animals of the extensive
s of Siberia which played the same part with the Russian
yschleni, as gold with the Spanish adventurers in South
·ica.
the close of the sixteenth century the Cossacks had
ly possessed themselves of the greater part of the river
ory of the Irtisch-Ob, and sable-hunters had already gone

aphica Detectionis Freti (Photo-lithographic reproduction, by Fre-
Muller, Amsterdam, 1878). The same work, or more correctly,
tion of small geographical pamphlets, contains also Isak Massa's
·f the coast of the Polar Sea between the Kola peninsula and the
a, which I have reproduced.

as far north-east [1] as the river Tas, where the sable-hunting
was at one time very productive and occasioned the founding of
a town, Mangasej, which however was soon abandoned. In 1610
the Russian fur-hunters went from the river territory of the
Tas to the Yenisej, where the town Turuchansk was soon after
founded on the Turuchan, a tributary of the Yenisej. The
attempt to row down in boats from this point to the Polar Sea,
with the view of penetrating farther along the sea coast, failed
in consequence of ice obstacles, but led to the discovery of the
river Pjäsina and to the levying of tribute from the Samoyeds
living there. To get farther eastward the tributaries of
the Yenisej were made use of instead of the sea route.
Following these the Russians on the upper course of the
Tunguska met with the mountain ridge which separates the
river territory of the Yenisej from that of the Lena. This ridge
was crossed, and on the other side of it a new stream was met
with, which in the year 1627 led the adventurers to the Lena,
over whose river territory the Cossacks and fur-hunters, faithful to
their customs, immediately spread themselves in order to hunt,
purchase furs, and above all to impose "jassak" upon the tribes
living thereabouts. But they were 'not satisfied with this.
Already in 1636 the Cossack ELISEJ BUSA was sent out with an
express commission to explore the rivers beyond, falling into the
Polar Sea, and to render tributary the natives living on their
banks. He was accompanied by ten Cossacks, to whose
company forty fur-hunters afterwards attached themselves. In
1637 he came to the western mouth-arm of the Lena, from
which he went along the coast to the river Olenek, where he
passed the winter. Next year he returned by land to the Lena,
and built there two "kotsches," [2] in which he descended the
river to the Polar Sea. After five days' successful rowing along
the coast to the eastward he discovered the mouth of the Yana.
After three days' march up the river he fell in with a Yakut
tribe, from whom he got a rich booty of sable and other furs.
Here he passed the winter of 1638-39, here too he built
himself a new craft, and again started for the Polar Sea, he

[1] It is a peculiar circumstance that the vanguard of the Russian stream
of emigration which spread over Siberia, advanced along the northernmost
part of the country by the Tas, Turuchansk, Yakutsk, Kolyma, and Anadyrsk. This depended in the first place upon the races living there
having less power of resistance against the invaders, who were often very
few in number, than the tribes in the south, but also on the fact that the most
precious and most transportable treasures of Siberia—sable, beaver, and fox-
skins—were obtained in greatest quantity from these northern regions.

[2] Flat-bottomed, half-decked boats, twelve fathoms· in length. The
planks were fastened by wooden pins, the anchors were pieces of wood
with large stones bound to them, the rigging of thongs, and the sails often
of tanned reindeer hides (J. E. Fischer, *Sibirische Geschichte*, St. Petersburg, 1768, i. p. 517).

came to another river falling into the eastern mouth-arm of the Yana, where he found a Yukagir tribe, living in earth huts, with whom he passed two years more, collecting tribute from the tribes living in the neighbourhood.

At the same time IVANOV POSTNIK discovered by land the river Indigirka. As usual, tribute was collected from the neighbouring Yukagir tribes, yet not without fights in which the natives at first directed their weapons against the horses the Cossacks had along with them, thinking that the horses were more dangerous than the men. They had not seen horses before. A *simovie* was established, at which sixteen Cossacks were left behind. They built boats, sailed down the river to the Polar Sea to collect tribute, and discovered the river Alasej.

Some years after the river Kolyma appears to have been discovered, and in 1644 the Cossack, MICHAILO STADUCHIN, founded on that river a *simovie*, which afterwards increased to a small town, Nischni Kolymsk. Here Staduchin got three pieces of information which exerted considerable influence on later exploratory expeditions, for he acquired knowledge of the Chukches, at that time a military race, who possessed the part of North Asia which lay a little further to the east. Further, the natives and the Russian hunters, who swarmed in the region before Staduchiu, informed him that in the Polar Sea off the mouths of the Yana and the Indigirka there was a large island, which in clear weather could be seen from land, and which the Chukches reached in winter with reindeer sledges in one day from Chukotska, a river debouching in the Polar Sea east of the Kolyma. They brought home walrus tusks from the island, which was of considerable size, and the hunters supposed " that it was a continuation of Novaya Zemlya, which is visited by people from Mesen." Wrangel is of opinion that this account refers to no other than Krestovski Island, one of the Bear Islands. This, however, appears to me to be improbable. It is much more likely that it refers partly to the New Siberian Islands. partly to Wrangel Land, and perhaps even to America. That the Russians themselves had not then discovered Ljachoff's, or as it was then also called, Blischni Island, which lies so near the mainland, and is so high that it is impossible to avoid seeing it when one in clear weather sails past Svjatoinos, which lies east of the Yana, is a proof that at that time they had not sailed along the coast between the mouths of the Yana and the Indigirka. Finally, a great river, the Pogytscha, was spoken of, which could be reached in three or four days' sailing eastward from the mouth of the Kolyma. This was the first account which reached the conquerors of Siberia of the great river Anadyr which falls into the Pacific.

These accounts were sufficient to incite the Cossacks and
hunters to new expeditions. The beginning was made by ISAI
IGNATIEV from Mesen, who, along with several hunters, travelled down the Kolyma in 1646 to the Polar Sea, and then
along the coast eastwards. The sea was full of ice, but next
the land there was an open channel, in which the explorers
sailed two days. They then came to a bay, near whose shore
they anchored. Here the Russians had their first meeting with
the Chukches, to which reference has already been made.
Hence Ignatiev returned to the Kolyma ; and the booty was
considered so rich and his account of his journey so promising,
that preparations were immediately made in order next year
to send off a new maritime expedition fitted out on a larger
scale to the coast of the Polar Sea.

This time FEODOT ALEXEJEV from Kolmogor was chief of
the expedition, but along with him was sent, at the request of
the hunters, a Cossack in the Russian service in order to guard
the rights of the crown. His name was SIMEON IVANOV SIN
DESCHNEV ; in geographical writings he is commonly known
under the name of DESCHNEV. It was intended to search for
the mouth of the great river lying towards the east, regarding
which some information had been obtained from the natives,
and which was believed to fall into the Polar Sea. The first
voyage in 1647, with four vessels was unsuccessful, it is said,
because the sea was blocked with ice. But that this was not
the real reason is shown by the fact that, a new and larger
expedition was fitted out the following year with full expectation of success. The crews of the four boats had more probably
been considered too weak a force to venture among the
Chukches and the ice had to bear the blame of the retreat.
What man could not reproach the conquerors of Siberia with,
was pusillanimity and want of perseverance in carrying out a
plan which had once been sketched. Resistance always increased their power of action ; so also now. Seven boats were
fitted out the following year, 1648, all which were to sail down
to the Polar Sea, and then along the coast eastwards. The
object was to examine closely the unknown land and people
there, and to their own advantage and the extension of the
Russian power, to collect tribute from the tribes met with
during the expedition. Müller states that every boat was
manned with about thirty men—a number which appears to
me somewhat exaggerated, if we consider the nature of the
Siberian craft and the difficulty of feeding so large a number
either with provisions carried along with them or obtained
by hunting.

Four of the boats are not mentioned further in the narrative ;
they appear to have returned at an early period. The three

:rs, on the contrary, made a highly remarkable journey.
commanders of them were the Cossacks, GERASIM
:UDINOV and SIMEON DESCHNEV, and the hunter FEODOT
XEJEV. Deschnev entertained such hopes of success that
re his departure he promised to collect a tribute of seven
:s forty sable skins. The Siberian archives, according to
Ler, contain the following details.[1]

n ⅖th June, 1648, a start was made from the Kolyma. The
was open ; at least the boats came without any adventure
:h Deschnev thought worth the trouble of noting in his
ative to Great Chukotskojnos. Of this cape Deschnev
that it is quite different from the cape at the river
kotskaja. For it lies between north and north-east, and
ls with a rounding towards the Anadyr. On the Russian
a rivulet runs into the sea, at which the Chukches had
:d a heap of whales' bones. Right off the cape lie two
ids, on which people of Chukch race with perforated lips
ɜ seen. From this cape it is possible with a favourable
d to sail to the Anadyr in three days, and the way is not
;er by land, because the Anadyr falls into a gulf of the
At Chukotskojnos or, according to Wrangel, at a "holy
nontory," Svjatoinos (Serdze Kamen ?) previously reached,
cudinov's craft was shipwrecked. The crew were saved,
distributed on Deschnev's and Alexejev's boats. On the
September the Russians had a fight with the Chukches
ıg on the coast, in which fight Alexejev was wounded.
n after Deschnev's and Alexejev's "kotsches" were parted
er to meet again.
)eschnev was driven about by storms and head-winds until
; the beginning of October. Finally his vessel stranded near
mouth of the Olutorsk, in 61° N.L. Hence he marched
ı his twenty-five men to the Anadyr. He had expected
neet with some natives in its lower course, but the region
uninhabited, which caused the invaders much trouble,
ɪuse they suffered from want of provisions. Although

Ɉ. P. Müller, *Sammlung Russischer Geschichte*, St. Petersburg, 1758. Müller
rts in this work that it was he who, in 1736, first drew from the repositories
ιe Yakutsk archives the account of Deschnev's voyage, which before
time was known neither at the court of the Czar nor in the remotest
ɜ of Siberia. This, however, is not quite correct, for long before
er, the Swedish prisoner-of-war, Strahlenberg, knew that the Russians
elled by sea from the Kolyma to Kamchatka, which appears from his
of Asia, constructed during his stay in Siberia, and published in *Das*
ɹ- *und Ostliche Theil von Europa und Asia*, Stockholm, 1730. On this
there is the following inscription in the sea north of the Kolyma :—
ic Rutheni ab initio per Moles glaciales, quæ flante Borea ad Littora,
æque Austro versus Mare iterum pulsantur, magno Labore et Vitæ
·rimine transvecti sunt ad Regionem Kamtszatkam."

Deschnev could not obtain from the natives any augmentation
of the certainly very small supply of food which he carried
with him, he succeeded nevertheless in passing the winter in
that region. First in the course of the following summer did
he fall in with natives, from whom a large tribute was collected,
but not without fierce conflicts. A *simovie* was built at the
place where afterwards Anadyrski Ostrog was founded. While
Deschnev remained here, at a loss as to how, when the boats
were broken up, he would be able to return to the Kolyma,
or find a way thither by land, there came suddenly on the
6th May.
29th April. 1650, a new party of hunters to his winter hut.

For the accounts of islands in the Polar Sea, and of the river
Pogytscha, which was said to fall into the sea three or four days'
journey beyond the Kolyma, had led to the sending out of another
expedition under the Cossack STADUCHIN. He started from
Yakutsk in boats on the ¹⁸⁄₅th June, 1647, wintered on the Yana,
travelled thence in sledges to Indigirka, and there again built
boats in which he rowed to the Kolyma. It is to be observed
that Staduchin, just because he preferred the land-route to the
sea-route between the Yana and the Indigirka, missed discovering the large island in the Polar Sea, of which so much has
been said. Next summer (1649) Staduchin again sailed down
the river Kolyma to the sea, and then for seven days along its
coast eastwards, without finding the mouth of the river sought for
by him. He therefore returned with his object unaccomplished,
carrying with him a heap of walrus-tusks, which were sent
to Yakutsk as an appendix to a proposal to send out hunters
to the Polar Sea to hunt for these animals. In the meantime a true idea of the course of the Anadyr had been obtained
through statements collected from the natives, and a land-route
had become known between its territory and that of the Kolyma.
Several Cossacks and hunters now petitioned for the right to
settle on the Anadyr, and collect tribute from the tribes in that
neighbourhood. This was granted. Some natives were forced
to act as guides. The party started under the command of
SIMEON MOTORA, and came finally to Deschnev's *simovie* on the
Anadyr. Staduchin followed, and traversed the way in seven
weeks. He however soon quarrelled with Deschnev and Motora,
and parting from them on that account, betook himself to the
river Penschina. Deschnev and Motora built themselves boats
on the Anadyr in order to prosecute exploratory voyages, but
the latter was killed in 1651 in a fight with natives called
Anauls. They had been the first of all the natives of the
Pacific coast of North Asia to pay " jassak " to Deschnev, and
he had already at that time come into collision with them
and extirpated one of their tribes.

In 1652 Deschnev travelled down the Anadyr to the river

'uth, where he discovered a walrus-bank, whence he brought
me walrus-tusks. There afterwards arose a dispute between
Schnev and Selivestrov[1] regarding the rights founded on the
covery of this walrus-bank, which came before the authorities
Yakutsk, and it was from the documents relating to it that
ler obtained the information that enabled him to give a
rative of Deschnev's expedition. Only in this way have
particulars of this remarkable voyage been rescued from
mplete oblivion.[2]

In 1653 Deschnev gave orders to collect wood to build craft
which he intended to carry home by sea the tribute he
collected to the Kolyma, but he was cempelled to desist
m want of the necessary materials for the building and equip-
nt of the boats, comforting himself with the statement of
natives that the sea was not always so open as during
first voyage. Compelled by necessity, he remained a year
ger at the Anadyr, and in 1654 undertook a new hunting
yage to the walrus-bank, where he met with the before-
entioned Selivestrov. He here came in contact with the
atives (Koryäks), and found among them a Yakut woman, who
had belonged to Ankudinov. On asking her where her master
had gone to, she answered that Feodot and Gerasim (Ankudinov)
had died of scurvy, and that their companions had been killed
with the-exception of some few, who had saved themselves in
boats. It appears as if the latter had penetrated along the
coast as far as to the river Kamchatka. For when Kamchatka
was conquered by Atlassov in 1697 the natives stated that a
long time before one FEODOTOV (probably a son of Feodot
Alexejev) had lived among them along with some companions,
and had married their women. They were venerated almost
as gods. They were believed to be invulnerable until they
struck another, when the Kamchadals saw their mistake and
killed them.[3]

By the expeditions of Deschnev, Staduchin, and their
companions, the Russians had by degrees become acquainted
with the course of the Anadyr and with the tribes living on
its banks. But it still remained for them to acquire a more

---

[1] Selivestrov had accompanied Staduchin during his Polar Sea voyage,
and had, at his instance, been sent out to collect walrus-tusks on account of
the State. He appears to have come to the Anadyr by land.

[2] Strahlenberg must have collected the main details of this voyage by
oral communications from Russian hunters and traders.

[3] According to Müller. Krascheninnikov (*Histoire et description du
Kamtschatka*, Amsterdam, 1770, ii. p. 292) states, evidently from information obtained in Kamchatka, that the river Nikul is called Feodot-
ovchina after Feodot Alexejev, who not only penetrated thither, but also
sailed round the southern promontory of Kamchatka to the River Tigil,
where he and his followers perished in the way described by Müller.

complete knowledge of the islands which were said to be situated in the Polar Sea, and one must be surprised at the extreme difficulties which were encountered in attempting the solution of this apparently very simple geographical problem. The reason indeed was that the Siberian seamen never ventured to leave the immediate neighbourhood of the coast, a precaution which besides is very easily explained when the bad construction of their craft is considered. Along the shore of the Polar Sea on the other hand, a very active communication appears to have taken place between the Lena and the Kolyma, though of those voyages we only know such as in one way or another gave rise to actions before the courts or were characterised by specially remarkable dangers or losses.

In 1650 ANDREJ GORELOJ was sent by sea from Yakutsk to impose tribute on the tribes that lived at the sources of the Indigirka, and on the Moma, a tributary of the Indigirka. He passed Svjatoinos successfully and reached the mouth of the Kroma, but was there beset by ice, with which he drifted out to sea. After drifting about ten days he was compelled to abandon the vessel, which was soon after nipped, and go on foot over the ice to land. On the $\frac{2nd}{13th}$ November he came to the *simovie* Ujandino, where famine prevailed during the winter, *because the vessels, that should have brought provisions to the place, had either been lost or been compelled to turn ;* a statement which proves that at that time a regular navigation took place between certain parts of the coast of the Polar Sea.

The same year, the Cossack, TIMOFEJ BULDAKOV travelled by sea from the Lena to the Kolyma to take over the command of the neighbouring region. He reached the Kroma successfully, but was beset there and drifted out to sea. He then determined to endeavour to get to land over the ice. But this was no easy matter. The ice, which already was three feet thick, went suddenly into a thousand pieces, while the vessel drove before a furious gale farther and farther from the shore. This was repeated several times. When the sea at last froze over, the vessel was abandoned, and the party finally succeeded, worn out as they were by hunger, scurvy, work, and cold, in reaching land at the mouth of the Indigirka. The narrative of Buldakov's voyage is, besides, exceedingly remarkable, because a meeting is there spoken of with twelve " kotsches," filled with Cossacks, traders, and hunters, bound partly from the Lena to the rivers lying to the eastward, partly from the Kolyma and Indigirka to the Lena, a circumstance which shows how active the communication then was in the part of the Siberian Polar Sea in question. This is further confirmed by a narrative of NIKIFOR MALGIN. While Knes IVAN PETROVITSCH BARJATIN-

[Y was *vojvode* at Yakutsk (1667-75), Malgin travelled along
th a trader, ANDREJ WORIPAJEV, by sea from the Lena to the
)lyma. During this voyage the pilot directed the attention of
on board to an island, lying far out at sea, west of the mouth
the Kolyma. In course of a conversation regarding it, after
Lgin had succeeded in reaching the Kolyma, another trader,
KOB WIÄTKA, stated that on one occasion when he was sailing
h nine "kotsches" between the Lena and the Kolyma, three
them had been driven by wind to this island, and that
> men who had been sent ashore there, found traces of
known animals, but no inhabitants. All these narratives, however, do not appear to have met with
1 credence. In the beginning of the eighteenth century,
cordingly, new explorations and new expeditions were under-
ken. A Cossack, JAKOB PERMAKOV, stated that during a
>yage between the Lena and the Kolyma, he had seen off
Vjatoinos an island, of which he knew not whether it was
whabited or not, and likewise, that off the mouth of the Kolyma
here was an island which could be seen from land. In order to
make sure of the correctness of this statement, a Cossack,
MERCUREJ WAGIN, was sent out. He travelled along with
Permakov, in the month of May, in dog-sledges over the
ce from Svjatoinos to the island lying off it, that Permakov
had seen. They landed there, found it uninhabited and treeless,
and fixed its circumference at nine to twelve days' journey.
Beyond this island Wagin saw another, which, however, he could
not reach for want of provisions. He therefore determined to
urn, in order to undertake the journey the following year in a
)etter state of preparation. During the return journey the
)arty suffered severely from hunger, and in order to avoid
a renewal of the dangerous and difficult journey of exploration,
the men at last murdered Permakov, Wagin, and his son. The
crime was discovered, and the knowledge we possess of this
expedition is founded on the confused information obtained
during the examination of the murderers. Müller even throws
doubts on the truth of the whole narrative.

The attempts which were afterwards made to reach those
islands, partly by sea in 1712, by WASILEJ STADUCHIN, partly
by dog-sledges in 1714 by ALEXEJ MARKOV and GRIGOREJ
KUSAKOV, yielded no result. Ten years afterwards, "the old
saga" of the islands in the Polar Sea, induced one SIN BAJORSKI
FEODOT AMOSSOV to undertake an expedition with a view to
impose tribute on their inhabitants, but he was prevented by
ice from reaching his goal. On the way he met with a hunter,
IVAN WILLEGIN, who said, that along with another hunter,
GRIGOREJ SANKIN, he had travelled over the ice to these islands
from the mouth of the river Chukotskaja. He had seen neither

men nor trees, but some abandoned huts. "Probably this land extends all the way from the mouth of the Yana, past the Indigirka and Kolyma to the region which is inhabited by the Schelags, a Chukch tribe." He had learned this from a Schelag named Kopai, at whose home he had been the preceding year. In order to reach this land by sea it was necessary to start from the coast which the Schelags inhabited, because the sea was less covered by ice there.

As Amossov could not reach his goal by sea he travelled thither the same year, in November, 1724, over the ice, but his description of the land differs widely from that of his predecessor, and Müller appears to entertain great doubts of the truthfulness of the narrative.[1] On the ground of a map constructed by the Cossack, Colonel SCHESTAKOV, who, however, according to Müller, could neither read nor write, this new land was introduced into DELISLE and BUACHE'S map, with the addition that the Schelag Kopai lived there, and had there been taken prisoner by the Russians. This is so far incorrect, as Kopai did not live on any island, but on the mainland, and never was prisoner with the Russians, although after having paid tribute to them, he tired of doing so, and killed some of Amossov's people, after which no more was heard of him. Müller complains loudly of the incorrect statement regarding Kopai, but the learned academician commits a much greater mistake, inasmuch as he considers that he ought to leave the numerous accounts of hunters and Cossacks about land and islands in the Siberian Polar Sea completely out of account. All these lands are therefore left out of the map published by the Petersburg Academy in the year 1758.[2] It is in this respect much more incomplete than the map which accompanies Strahlenberg's book.[3]

Before I begin to sketch the explorations of the great

[1] But we ought to remember that the oldest accounts of islands in the Polar Sea relate to no fewer than four different lands, viz., 1. The New Siberian Islands lying off the mouth of the Lena and Svjatoinos; The Bear Islands; 3. Wrangel Land; 4. The north-western part America. Contradictions in accounts of the islands in the Polar probably depend on the uninhabited and treeless New Siberian islands being confused with America, which, in comparison with North Siberia, thickly peopled and well wooded, with the small Bear Islands, wi Wrangel Land, &c.

[2] *Nouvelle carte des découvertes faites par des vaisseaux russiens aux côtes inconnues de l'Amérique Septentrionale avec les pais adiacentes, dressée sur des mémoires authentiques des ceux qui ont assisté à ces découvertes et sur d'autres connoissances dont on rend raison dans un mémoire separé.* St. Petersbourg, l'Académie Impériale des Sciences, 1758.

[3] In this sketch of the discovery and conquest of Siberia I have followed J. E. Fischer, *Sibirische Geschichte*, St. Petersburg, 1768, and G. P. Müller, *Sammlung Russischer Geschichte*, St. Petersburg, 1758.

,hern expeditions, some account remains to be given of the
overy of Kamchatka. It appears from the preceding that
ıchatka was already reached by some of Deschnev's fol-
ırs, but their important discovery was completely unknown
[oscow. Kamchatka is, however, already mentioned in the
ative of Evert Ysbrants Ides' embassy to China in 1693-95 ;[1]
unts of it had probably been obtained from the Siberian
ves, who are accustomed to wander far and near. These
unts, however, are exceedingly incomplete, and therefore,
ODOMIR ATLASSOV, *piätidesätnik* (*i.e.*, commander of fifty
) at Anadyrsk, is considered the proper discoverer of
ıchatka.

ʳhile Atlassov was commander at Anadyrsk, he sent out in
5, the Cossack LUCAS SEMENOV SIN MOROSKO with sixteen
to bring the tribe living to the south under tribute. The
mission was executed, and on his return Morosko stated that
ıot only was among the Koryäks, but had also penetrated to
neighbourhood of the river Kamchatka, and that he took
amchadal " ostrog," and found in it some manuscripts in an
nown language, which, according to information afterwards
ıined, had belonged to some Japanese who had stranded on
coast of Kamchatka.[2] It was the first hint the conquerors
Siberia obtained of their being in the neighbourhood of
an.

'he year after Atlassov, with a larger force, followed the way
ch Morosko had opened up, and penetrated to the river
nchatka, where as a sign that he had taken possession of the
l, he erected a cross with an inscription, which when trans-
d runs thus : *In the year* 7205 (i.e. 1697) *on the 13th July
cross was erected by the piätidcsätnik Volodomir Atlassov and
followers,* 55 *men.* Atlassov then built on the Kamchatka
r a *simovie,* which was afterwards fortified and named Verchni
ntschatskoj Ostrog. Hence the Russians extended their
·er over the land, yet not without resistance, which was
; completely broken by the cruel suppression of the rebellion
730.

n 1700 Atlassov travelled to Moscow, carrying with him

In the twentieth chapter of *Dreyjührige Reise nach China,* &c., Frank-
1707. The first edition came out at Hamburg in 1698.
Müller, iii. p. 19. An account of Atlassov's conquest of Kamchatka
richt gedaen door zeker Moskovisch krygs-bediende Wolodimer Otlasofd,
t-man over vyftig, &c.) is besides to be found in Witsen (1705, *Nieuwe
ıaf,* 1785, p. 670). An account, written from oral communication by
.ssov himself, is to be found inserted in Strahlenperg's *Travels,* p. 431.
hlenberg considers Kamchatka and Yezo to be the same land. A
ɔry of the conquest of Kamchatka, evidently written according to
itions current in the country, is to be found in *Krascheninnikov* (French
ion of 1770, ii. p. 291). In this account 1698 and 1699 are given as the
ʳs of Morosko's and Atlassov's expeditions.

M M

a Japanese, who had been taken prisoner after being shipwrecked on the coast of Kamchatka, and the collected tribute
which consisted of the skins of 3,200 sables, 10 sea-otters,
7 beavers, 4 otters, 10 grey foxes and 191 red foxes. He was
received graciously, and sent back as commander of the Cossacks
in Yakutsk with orders to complete the conquest of Kamchatka.
An interruption however happened for some time in the path
of Atlassov as a warrior and discoverer, in consequence of his
having during his return journey to Yakutsk plundered a
Russian vessel laden with Chinese goods, an accessory circumstance which deserves to be mentioned for the light which it
throws on the character of this Pizarro of Kamchatka. He
was not set free until the year 1706, and then recovered his
command in Kamchatka, with strict orders to desist from all
arbitrary proceedings and acts of violence, and to do his best
for the discovery of new lands. The first part of this order he
however complied with only to a limited extent, which gave
occasion to repeated complaints [1] and revolts among the already
unbridled Cossacks. Finally, in 1711, Atlassov and several
other officers were murdered by their own countrymen. In
order to atone for this crime, and perhaps to get a little farther
from the arm of justice, their murderers, ANZIPHOROV and IVAN
KOSIREVSKOJ,[2] undertook to subdue the not yet conquered part
of Kamchatka, and the two northernmost of the Kurile
Islands. Further information about the countries lying farther
south was obtained from some Japanese who were shipwrecked
in 1710 on Kamchatka.

At first in order to get to Kamchatka the difficult detour by
Anadyrsk was taken. But in the year 1711 the commander at
Okotsk, SIN BOJARSKI PETER GUTUROV, was ordered, by the
energetic promoter of exploratory expeditions in Eastern Siberia,
the Yakutsk *voivode*, DOROFEJ TRAUERNICHT, to proceed by sea
from Okotsk to Kamchatka. But this voyage could not come

[1] Complaints were made, among other things, that in order to obtain
metal for making a still, he ordered all the copper belonging to the crown
which he carried with him, to be melted down. When the Cossacks first
came to Kamchatka and were, almost without a contest, acknowledged as
masters of the country, they found life there singularly agreeable, with one
drawback—there were no means of getting drunk. Finally, necessity
compelled the wild adventurers to betake themselves to what we should
now call chemico-technical experiments, which are described in considerable detail by Krascheninnikov (*loc. cit.* ii. p. 369). After many
failures they finally succeeded in distilling spirits from a sugar-bearing
plant growing in the country, and from that time this drink, or *raka*,
as they themselves call it, has been found in great abundance in that
country.

[2] He afterwards became a monk under the name of Ignatiev, came to
St. Petersburg in 1730, and himself wrote a narrative of his adventures,
discoveries, and services, which was printed first in the St. Petersburg
journals of the 26th March, 1730, and likewise abroad (*Müller*, iii. p. 82).

off because at that time there were at Okotsk neither seagoing boats, seamen, nor even men accustomed to the use of the compass. Some years after the governor Priuce GAGARIN sent to that town IVAN SOROKAUMOV with twelve Cossacks to make arrangements for this voyage. For want of ships and seamen however, this could not now be undertaken, and after Sorokaumov had created great confusion he was imprisoned by the authorities of the place, and sent back to the Governor. Peter I. now commanded *that men acquainted with navigation should be sought for among the Swedish prisoners of war and sent to Okotsk; that they should build a boat there and, provided with a compass, go by sea along with some Cossacks to Kamchatka and return.*[1] Thus navigation began on the Sea of Okotsk. Among the Swedes who opened it, is mentioned HENRY BUSCH,[2] according to Strahlenberg a Swedish corporal, who had previously been a ship-carpenter. According to Müller, who met with him at Yakutsk as late as 1736, he was born at Hoorn in Holland, had served at several places as a seaman, and finally among the Swedes as a trooper, until he was taken prisoner at Viborg in 1706. He gave Müller the following account of his first voyage across the Sea of Okotsk.

After arriving at Okotsk they had built a vessel, resembling the *lodjas* used at Archangel and Mesen for sailing on the White Sea and to Novaya Zemlya. The vessel was strong; its length was eight and a half fathoms, its breadth three fathoms, the freeboard, when the vessel was loaded, three and a half feet. The first voyage took place in June 1716. The voyagers began to sail along the coast towards the north-east, but an unfavourable wind drove the vessel, almost against the will of the seafarers, right across the sea to Kamchatka. The first land sighted was a cape which juts out north of the river Tigil. Being unacquainted with the coast the seafarers hesitated to land. During the delay a change of wind took place, whereby the vessel was driven back towards the coast of Okotsk. The wind again becoming favourable, the vessel was put about and anchored successfully in the Tigil. The men who were sent ashore found the houses deserted. For the Kamchadales being terrified at the

---

[1] Von Baer, *Beiträge zur Kentniss des Russischen Reiches*, xvi. p. 33.

[2] Ambjörn Molin, lieutenant in the Scanian cavalry regiment, who was taken prisoner at the Dnieper in 1709, also took part in these journeys. Compare *Berättelse om de i Stora Tartariet boende tartarer, som träffats längst nordost i Asien, på ärkebiskop E. Benzelii begäran upsatt af Ambjörn Molin* (*Account of the Tartars dwelling in Great Tartary who were met with at the north-east extremity of Asia, written at the request of Archbishop E. Benzelius by Ambjörn Molin*), published in Stockholm in 1880 by Aug. Strindberg, after a manuscript in the Linköping library.

large ship had made their escape to the woods. The seafarers
sailed on along the coast and landed at several places in order
that they might meet with the inhabitants, but for a long time
without success, until at last they fell in with a Kamchadal
girl, who was collecting edible roots. With her as a guide they
soon found dwellings, and even Cossacks, who had been sent out
to collect tribute. They wintered at the river Kompakova.
During the winter the sea cast up a whale, which had in its
carcase a harpoon of European manufacture and with Latin
letters. The vessel left the winter haven in the middle of
May (new style) 1717, but meeting with ice-fields was beset
in them for five and a half weeks. This occasioned great
scarcity of provisions. In the end of July the seafarers were
again back at Okotsk. From this time there has been regular
communication by sea between this town and Kamchatka.
The master of the vessel during the first voyage across the
Sea of Okotsk was the Cossack SOKOLOV.[1]

From what I have stated it follows that, thanks to the
fondness of the hunters and Cossacks for adventurous exploratory expeditions, the current ideas regarding the distribution
of the land and the courses of the rivers in north-eastern Asia
were in the main correct. But, in consequence of want of
knowledge of, or of doubts regarding, Deschnev's discoveries,
there prevailed an uncertainty whether Asia at its north-east
extremity was connected with America by a small neck of land,
in the same way as it is with Africa, or as North and South
America are connected with each other, a view which, in
consequence of the unscientific necessity of generalising
inherent in man, and the wish to have an explanation of
how the population extended from the old to the new world,
was long zealously defended.[2]   No one, either European or
native, had yet, so far as we know, extended his hunting
journeys to the northernmost promontory of Asia, in consequence of which the position which it was assumed to occupy
only depended on loose suppositions. It was possible for

[1] Müller, iii. p. 102. According to an oral communication by Busch,
Strahlenberg's account (p. 17) of this voyage appears to contain several
mistakes. The year is stated as 1713, the return voyage is said to have
occupied six days.
[2] As late as 1819, James Burney, first lieutenant on one of Captain
Cook's vessels during his voyage north of Behring's Straits, afterwards
captain and member of the Royal Society, considered it not proved that
Asia and America are separated by a sound. For he doubted the correctness of the accounts of Deschnev's voyage. Compare James Burney, A
Chronological History of North-eastern Voyages of Discovery. London, 1819,
p. 298 ; and a paper by Burney in the Transactions of the Royal Society,
1817. Burney was violently attacked for the views there expressed] by
Captain John Dundas Cochrane. Narrative of a Pedestrian Journey through
Russia and Siberian Tartary, 2nd ed. London, 1824, Appendix.

stance that Asia stretched with a cape as far as to the
ighbourhood of the Pole, or that a broad isthmus between the
äsina and the Olenek connected the known portion of this
arter of the world with an Asiatic Polar continent. Nor had
ographers a single actual determination of position or
ographical measurement from the whole of the immense
etch between the mouth of the Ob and Japan, and there was
mplete uncertainty as to the relative position of the eastern-
st possessions of the Russians on the one side and of Japan

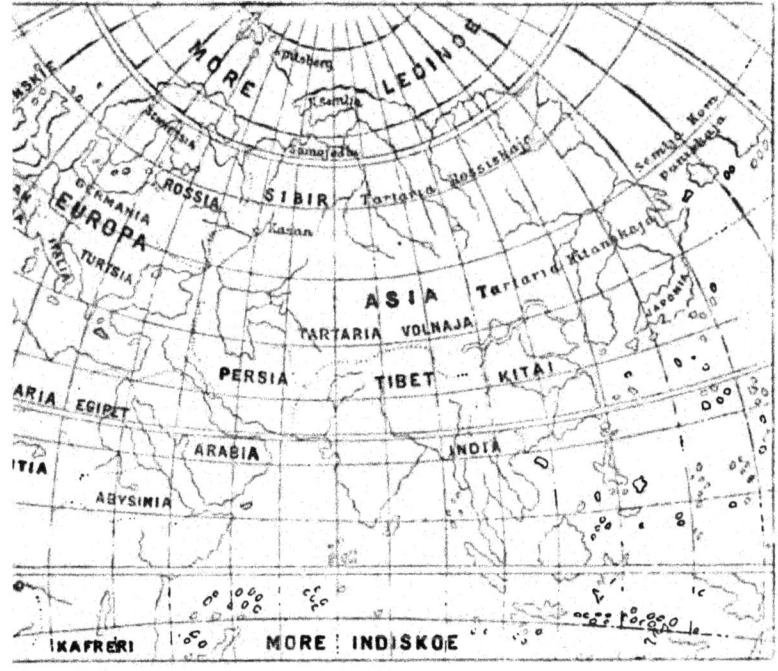

MAP OF ASIA
From an Atlas published by the Russian Academy of Sciences in 1737.

the other.[1] It was difficult to get the maps of the Russians
correspond with those of the Portuguese and the Dutch, at
e point where the discoveries of the different nations touched
ch other; which also was exceedingly natural, as at that time
ɔ limited an extent east and west by 1,700 kilometres was
mmonly assigned to Siberia. In order to investigate this
int, in order to fill up the great blank which still existed in

[1] The first astronomical determinations of position in Siberia were, per-
pɛ, made by Swedish prisoners of war; the first in China by Jesuits
Ł. Strahlenberg, p. 14).

the knowledge of the quarter of the world first inhabited by
man, and perhaps above all for the purpose of forming new
commercial treaties and of discovering new commercial routes,
Peter the Great during the latest years of his life arranged one
of the greatest geographical expeditions which the history of
the world can show. It was not until after his death, however,
that it was carried out, and then it went on for a series of years
on so large a scale that whole tribes are said to have been
impoverished through the severe exactions of transport that
were on its account imposed on the inhabitants of the Siberian
deserts. Its many different divisions are now comprehended
under the name—*the Great Northern Expedition.* Through the
writings of Behring, Müller, Gmelin, Steller, Krascheninnikov
and others, this expedition has acquired an important place for
all time in the history not only of geography but also of
ethnography, zoology, and botany ; and even now the inquirer,
when the natural conditions of North Asia are in question,
must return to these works. I shall therefore, before drawing
this chapter to a close, give a brief account of its principal
features.

The Great Northern Expedition was ushered in by " the first
expedition to Kamchatka." The commander of this expedition
was the Dane VITUS BEHRING, who was accompanied by
Lieutenant MORTON SPANGBERG, also a Dane by birth, and
ALEXEI CHIRIKOV. They left St. Petersburg in February 1725,
and took the land route across Siberia, carrying with them the
necessary materials with which in Kamchatka to build and
equip the vessel with which they should make their voyage of
exploration. More than three years were required for this
voyage, or rather for this geographico-scientific campaign ; in
which for the transport of the stores and the shipbuilding material
that had to be taken from Europe the rivers Irtisch, Ob, Ket,
Yenisej, Tunguska, Ilim, Aldan, Maja, Yudoma, and Urak were
taken advantage of. It was not until the $\frac{15}{7}$th April that a beginning could be made at Nischni Kamchatskoj Ostrog of the
building of the vessel, which was launched on the $\frac{21st}{10th}$ July ;
and on the $\frac{31st}{20th}$ of the same month Behring began his voyage.

He sailed in a north-easterly direction along the coast of
Kamchatka, which he surveyed. On the $\frac{19}{5}$th August in 64° 30′
N.L. he fell in with Chukches, who had still a reputation among
the Russians for invincible courage and ferocity. First one of
them came to the vessel, swimming on two inflated seal-skins,
" to inquire what was intended by the vessel's coming thither,"
after which their skin-boat lay to. Conversation was carried on
with them by means of a Koryäk interpreter. On the $\frac{21st}{1/th}$
August St. Lawrence Island was discovered, and on the $\frac{26}{15}$th of
the same month the explorers sailed past the north-eastern

romontory of Asia in 67° 18′ and observed that the coast trends
 the west from that point, as the Chukches had before informed
em. Behring on this account considered that he had fulfilled
is commission to ascertain whether Asia and America were
parated, and he now determined to turn, "partly because if the
oyage were continued along the coast ice might be met with,
om which it might not be so easy to get clear, partly on account
: the fogs, which had already begun to prevail, and partly
ecause it would be impossible, if a longer stay were made
ı these regions, to get back the same summer to Kamchatka.
here could be no question of passing the winter off the coast
: the Chukch Peninsula, because that would have been to expose
ıe expedition to certain destruction, either by being wrecked on
ıe jagged rocks of the open, unknown coast, or by perishing from
ant of fuel, or finally by dying under the hands of the fierce
nconquered Chukches." On the $\frac{1st Oct.}{20th Sept}$ the vessel returned to
[ischni Kamchatskoj Ostrog.[1] It was during this voyage that
ıe sound, which has since obtained the name of Behring's
straits, is considered to have been discovered. But it is now
nown that this discovery properly belongs to the gallant
unter Deschnev, who sailed through these straits eighty years
efore. I suppose therefore that the geographical world will
rith pleasure embrace the proposal to attach the name of
)eschnev along with that of Behring to this part of our globe ;
rhich may be done by substituting Cape Deschnev, as the name
f the easternmost promontory of Asia, for that of East Cape, an
ppellation which is misleading and unsuitable in many respects,
ieveral statements by Kamchadales regarding a great country
owards the east on the other side of the sea, induced Behring
he following year to sail away in order to ascertain whether
his was the case. In consequence of unfavourable weather he
id not succeed in reaching the coast of America, but returned
rith his object unaccomplished, after which he sailed to Okotsk,
rhere he arrived on the $\frac{3rd Aug.}{23rd July}$ 1729. Hence he betook himself
mmediately to St. Petersburg, which he reached after a journey
f six months and nine days.

In maps published during Behring's absence, partly by Swedish
fficers who had returned from imprisonment in Siberia,[2] Kam-
hatka had been delineated with so long an extension towards

---

[1] A short, but instructive account of Behring's first voyage, based on an
fficial communication from the Russian Government to the King of Poland,
s inserted in t. iv. p. 561 of *Description géographique de l'Empire de la
Chine, par le P. J. B. Du Halde*, La Haye, 1736. The same official report
ras probably the source of Müller's brief sketch of the voyage (*Müller*,
ii. p. 112). A map of it is inserted in the 1735 Paris edition of Du Halde's
rork, and in *Nouvel Atlas de la Chine, par M. D'Anville*, La Haye, 1737.

[2] *Histoire généalogique des Tartares* (note, p. 107), and Strahlenberg's oft-
juoted work (map, text, pp. 31 and 384).

the south that this peninsula was connected with Yezo, the northernmost of the large Japanese islands. The distance between Kamchatka and Japan, rich in wares, would thus have been quite inconsiderable. This nearness was believed to be further confirmed by another Japanese ship, manned by seventeen men and laden with silk, rice, and paper, having stranded in July 1729 on Kamchatka, south of Avatscha Bay. In this neighbourhood there was, along with a number of natives, a small party of Cossacks under the command of ANDREAS SCHTINNIKOV. He at first accepted several presents from the shipwrecked men, but afterwards withdrew from the place where the wreck took place. When the Japanese on this account rowed on in their boats along the coast, Schtinnikov gave orders to follow them in a *baydar* and kill them all but two. The cruel deed was carried into execution, on which the malefactors took possession of the goods, and broke in pieces the boats in order to obtain the iron with which the boards were fastened together. The two Japanese who were saved were carried to Nischni Kamchatskoj Ostrog. Here Schtinnikov was imprisoned and hanged for his crime. The Japanese were sent to St. Petersburg, where they learned the Russian language and were converted to Christianity, while some Russians in their turn learned Japanese. The Japanese died between 1736 and 1739. Both were from Smatsua; the elder, SOSA, had been a merchant, and the younger, GONSA, was a pilot's son. Their vessel had been bound for Osaka, but having been carried out of its course by a storm, had drifted about at sea for six months, stranding at last with so unfortunate a result for the greater part of the crew.

This sad occurrence further reminds us that much still remained unaccomplished with respect to the geography of north-eastern Asia. Behring's Kamchatka expedition had besides yielded no information regarding the position of the northern extremity of Asia, or of the part of America lying opposite to Kamchatka. A number of grave doubts appear besides to have been started as to the correctness of the observations during Behring's first voyage. All this induced him to make proposals for a continuation of his explorations, offering, along with his former companions, Spangberg and Chirikov, to take the command of the maritime expedition which was to start from Kamchatka to solve the questions proposed, both eastwards to ascertain the position of the east coast of Asia in relation to the west coast of America, and southwards to connect the areas which the West-Europeans and the Russians were exploring.

The Russian senate, the Board of Admiralty, and the Academy of Sciences were commissioned to develop this plan and to carry it into execution. With respect to the way in which the com-

ssion was executed I may be allowed to refer to Müller's oft-
oted work, and to a paper by VON BAER: *Peters des Grossen
rdienste um die Erweiterung der geographischen Kenntnisse
niträge zur Kenntniss des Russischen Reiches*, B. 16, St. Peters-
rg, 1872). Here I can only mention that it was principally
ough the untiring interest which KIRILOV, the secretary of
ι senate, took in the undertaking, that it attained such a
relopment that it may be said to have been perhaps the
atest scientific expedition which has ever been sent out by
r country. It was determined at the same time not only to
ertain the extent of Siberia to the north and east, but also to
amine its hitherto almost unknown ethnographical and natural
nditions. For this purpose the Great Northern Expedition was
ided into the following divisions :—

l. *An expedition to start from Archangel for the Ob.*[1]—For this
pedition two *kotsches* were employed, the *Ob* and the *Expedition*,
j feet long, 14 feet broad, and 8 feet deep, each manned with
men. The vessels, which were under the command of
eutenants PAULOV and MURAVJEV, left Archangel on the $\frac{15}{4}$th
ly, 1734. The first summer they only reached Mutnoi Saliv
the Kara Sea, whence they returned to the Petchora and
ntered at Pustosersk. The following year they broke up in
ne, but did not penetrate farther than in 1734. The unfavour-
e issue was ascribed to the vessels' unserviceableness for
rages in the Polar Sea, in consequence of which the Board
Admiralty ordered two other boats, 50 to 60 feet long, to be
ilt for the expedition, which were placed under the command
SKURATOV and SUCHOTIN, Muravjev being besides replaced
MALYGIN who sailed with the old vessels on the $\frac{7\text{th June}}{27\text{th May}}$, 1736,
vn the Petchora river, at whose mouth the *Expedition* was
ecked. Without permitting himself to be frightened by this,
lygin ordered his men to go on board the other vessel, in
ich with great dangers and difficulties they penetrated through
drift-ice to Dolgoj Island. Here on the $\frac{18}{7}$th August they
in with the new vessels sent from Archangel. Suchotin was
v sent back to Archangel on board the *Ob;* Malygin and
uratov sailed in the new vessels to the Kara river and
ntered there. During the winter 1736–1737 the men suffered
y slightly from scurvy, which was cured by anti-scorbutic

This expedition was under the command of the Admiralty; the others
er that of Behring. In my account I have followed partly Müller and
tly Wrangel, of whom the latter, in his book of travels, gives a his-
cal review of previous voyages along the coasts of the Asiatic Polar
The accounts of the voyages between the White Sea and the Yenisej
perly belong to a foregoing chapter in this work, but I quote them first
ι in order that I may treat of the different divisions of the Great
thern Expedition in the same connection.

plants growing in the region. The ice in the Kara river did not break up until the $\frac{12\text{th}}{1\text{st}}$ June, but so much ice still drifted about in the sea that a start could not be made until the $\frac{14\text{th}}{3\text{rd}}$ July. On the $\frac{4\text{th Aug.}}{24\text{th July}}$ the vessels anchored in the sound which I have named Malygin Sound. Here they were detained by head winds 25 days. Then they sailed on round a cape, which the Samoyeds call Yalmal, up the Gulf of Ob to the mouth of the river, which was reached on the $\frac{22\text{nd}}{11\text{th}}$ September, 1737, and then up the river to Soswa, where the vessels were laid up in winter quarters. The crews were taken to Beresov. Malygin returned to Petersburg, after having given Lieut. Skuratov and the second mate Golovin a commission to carry the vessels back to the Dwina the following year. They did not get back until August 1739. The return voyage thus also occupied two years, and was attended with much difficulty and danger.

Six years in all had thus gone to the voyage from Archangel to the Ob and back, which now can be accomplished without difficulty in a single summer. By means of Malygin's and Skuratov's voyages, and of a land journey which the land-measurer Selifontov undertook during July and August 1736 with reindeer along the west coast of Yalmal and then by boat to Beli Ostrov, Yalmal and the south coast of this large island were mapped, it would appear in the main correctly.[1]

2. *An expedition to sail from the Ob to the Yenisej.*—For this Behring ordered a double sloop, the *Tobol*, 70 feet long, 15 feet broad, and 8 feet deep, to be built at Tobolsk. The vessel had two masts, was armed with two small cannon, and was manned with 53 men, among whom were a land-measurer and a priest. The commander was Lieut. OWZYN. They sailed in company with some small craft carrying provisions from Tobolsk on the $\frac{26}{15}$th May, 1734, and came to the Gulf of Ob through the easternmost mouth-arm of the river on the $\frac{20}{9}$th June. There a storm damaged the tender-vessels. Of the timber of those which had sustained most damage, a storehouse was erected in 66° 36′ N.L., in which the provisions landed from the unserviceable craft were placed. When this was done they sailed on, but slowly in consequence of unfavourable winds and shallow water, so that it was not until the $\frac{17}{6}$th August that they reached 70° 4′ N.L. Hence they returned to Obdorsk, arriving there on the $\frac{15}{4}$th September. Seven days afterwards the Ob was covered with ice.

The following spring the voyage was resumed. On the $\frac{17}{6}$th June they came to the depôt formed the preceding year. At first ice formed an obstacle, but on the $\frac{31\text{st}}{20\text{th}}$ July it broke up, and the navigable water became clear. The crew had now begun to

[1] Wrangel, i. p. 36.

uffer so severely from scurvy, that of 53 only 17 were in good
iealth ; Owzyn therefore turned, that he might bring his sick
nen to Tobolsk. He reached this town on the $\frac{17}{6}$th October, and
he river froze over soon after. Owzyn now travelled to St.
'etersburg in order to give in, in person, reports of his unsuc-
essful voyages and to make suggestions as to the measures
hat ought to be taken to ensure better success to next year's
undertaking. His proposals on this point were mainly in the
lirection of building at Tobolsk a new vessel, which should
ccompany the *Tobol* during the dangerous voyage, and confer
ipon it greater safety. This was approved by the Board of
Admiralty, but the vessel could not be got ready till the summer
if 1736, on which account that year's voyage was undertaken in
.he same way as that of the preceding year, and with the same
iuccess. The new vessel was not ready until 1737. It came
with the shipbuilder KOSCHELEV and the mate MININ on the
$\frac{5}{16}$th June to Obdorsk, where Owzyn took command of it, handing
)ver the old one to Koschelev, and beginning his fourth voyage
lown the Gulf of Ob. This time he had better success. After
iailing pass Gyda Bay, he came, without meeting with any
ierious obstacles from ice, on the $\frac{27}{16}$th August to Cape Mattesol,
ind on the $\frac{12\text{th}}{1\text{st}}$ September to a storehouse erected for the expe-
lition by the care of the authorities on the bank of the Yenisej
n 71° 33′ N. L. The Yenisej froze over on the $\frac{21\text{st}}{10\text{th}}$ October.

Four years had thus gone to the accomplishment of Owzyn's
)urpose, but it can scarcely be doubted that if he had not turned
io early in the season, and if he had had steam, or a sailing
/essel of the present day at his disposal he would have been able
.o sail from the Ob to the Yenisej in a few weeks. It is at all
:vents Owzyn's perseverance to which we are in great measure
ndebted for the mapping of the Gulf of Ob, and the Bays of Tas
ind Gyda.[1]

3. *Voyages from the Yenisej towards Cape Taimur.*—In the
vinter of 1738 Owzyn and Koschelev were called to St. Peters-
)urg to answer for themselves with reference to a complaint
odged against them by the men under their command.[2] In

---

[1] Wrangel, i. p. 38.
[2] According to P. von Haven (*Nye og forbedrede Efterretningar om det
Russiske Rige*, Kjöbenhavn, 1747, ii. p. 20), "it was the custom in Peters-
)urg to send away those whose presence was inconvenient to help Behring
:o make new discoveries." It also went very ill with many of the gallant
Russian Polar travellers, and many of them were repaid with ingratitude.
Behring was received on his return from his first voyage, so rich in results,
with unjustified mistrust. Steller was exposed to continual trouble, was
.ong prevented from returning from Siberia, and finally perished during
nis journey home, broken down in body and soul. Prontschischev and
Lassinius succumbed to hardships and sufferings during their voyages in
the Polar Sea. Owzyn was degraded, among other things, because he used

their room Minin got the command of the expedition which was
to endeavour to penetrate farther eastwards along the coast of
the Polar Sea. The two first summers, 1738 and 1739, Minin
could not get further than to the northernmost *simovies* on the
Yenisej. But in 1740 he succeeded, as it appears in pretty open
water, in reaching on the west coast of the Taimur Peninsula the
latitude of 75° 15'. Here he turned on the $\frac{1st Sept.}{21st Aug.}$ on account of
"impenetrable" ice, but mainly in consequence of the late season
of the year. The preceding winter Minin had sent his mate
STERLEGOV in sledges to examine the coast. On the $\frac{25}{14}$th April
he reached 75° 26' N.L., and there erected a stone cairn on a rock
jutting out into the sea. Many open places appear to have been
seen in the offing. Minin and his party returned on account of
snow-blindness, and during the return voyage rested for a time
at a *simovie* on the river Pjäsina, whose existence there shows
how far the Russian hunters had extended their journeys.[1]

4. *Voyage from the Lena Westward.*—On the $\frac{30th July.}{11th June.}$ 1735, two
expeditions started from Yakutsk, each with its double sloop,
accompanied by a number of boats carrying provisions. One of
these double sloops was to go in an easterly direction under the
command of Lieut. LASSINIUS. I shall give an account of his
voyage farther on. The other was commanded by Lieut.
PRONTSCHISCHEV, whose object was to go from the Lena westwards, if possible to the Yenisej. The voyage down the river
was successful and pleasant. The river was from four to nine
fathoms deep, and on its banks, overgrown with birch and pine,
there were numerous tents and dwelling-houses whose inhabitants were engaged in fishing, which gave the neighbourhood of the river a lively and pleasant appearance.[2] On the
$\frac{14th}{3rd}$ August the explorers came to the mouth of the river, which
here divides into five arms, of which the easternmost was chosen
for sailing down to the Polar Sea. Here the two seafarers
were to part. Prontschischev staid at the river-mouth till
the $\frac{25}{14}$th August. He then sailed in 1½ to 2½ fathoms water
along the shore of the islands which are formed by the mouth-
arms of the Lena. On the $\frac{6th Sept.}{26th Aug.}$ he anchored in the mouth

to be too intimate at Obdorsk with exiles formerly of distinction. A few
years before the voyage of the *Vega*, Chelyuskin's trustworthiness was still
doubted. All the accounts of discoveries of islands and land in the Polar
Sea by persons connected with Siberia, have till the most recent times, been
considered more or less fictitious ; yet they are clearly in the main true.

[1] Wrangel, i. p. 46.
[2] According to Wrangel (i., note at p. 38 and 48), probably after a quotation from Prontschischev's journal. The Lena must be a splendid river, for
it has since made the same powerful impression, as on the seamen of the
Great Northern Expedition, on all others who have traversed its forest-
crowned river channel.

f the Olenek. A little way up the river some dwelling-ouses were met with, which hunters had built for use during immer. These were put in order for winter, which passed appily. On the $\frac{2\text{nd July}}{31\text{st June}}$ the ice broke up at the winter quar-ırs, but in the sea it lay still until the $\frac{14\text{th}}{3\text{rd}}$ August, and it ·as only then that Prontschischev could go to sea. The course ·as shaped for the north-east. The Chatanga was reached on ıe $\frac{24\text{th}}{13}$ August. On the beach, in 74° 48′ N.L., a hut was ıet with in which were found newly baked bread and some ogs, and which therefore appeared to belong to some Russian unters absent at the time. While sailing on along the coast ıe explorers, after having' passed two bays projecting into ıe land, came to an inlet which they erroneously took for ɦe mouth of the Taimur river. Among the reasons for his supposition is mentioned the immense number of gulls' ɾhich swarmed round the vessel in that region. The bay was ɒvered with fast ice, " which probably never breaks up," and ɾoad ice-fields stretched out to sea from the coast, on which 'olar bears were seen.

On the $\frac{21\text{st}}{20\text{th}}$ August, in 77° 29′ N.L., the vessel was suddenly urrounded with so large masses of ice that it could make no urther progress, and was every instant in danger of being ɨpped. Prontschischev therefore determined to turn, but this ɹt first was rendered impossible by a complete calm, a crust of ɒe being formed at the same time in open places between the ɹieces of drift-ice. If the latitude stated is correct, the turning ɹoint lay quite close to the northernmost promontory of Asia. Ⅴith a better vessel, and above all with the help of steam, ʔrontschischev would certainly have rounded it. The unbroken ɒe which he mentioned several times in his narrative, ought ɾrobably to be interpreted as belts of pretty closely packed rift-ice. Many times during my Arctic voyages have I sailed ɦrough belts of ice which, when observed from a boat some undred yards from their borders, have been reported as nmense unbroken ice-fields. On the $\frac{8\text{th Sept.}}{26\text{th Aug.}}$ a high north wind egan to blow which drove the vessel, with the surrounding ɟe-fields, towards the south. The voyagers had doubts as to ɦeir being saved, but the gusts of wind broke up the ice so ɦat the vessel got free and could sail to the mouth of the ȷhatanga, which, however, was already frozen over. The ex-ɹlorers were therefore compelled to continue their voyage ɒwards the Olenek, whose mouth was reached on the $\frac{8\text{th Sept}}{26\text{th Aug.}}$ ɪn the neighbourhood of the haven which they intended to nake, they were driven about by contrary winds and drift-ice ɪbout six days more, exposed to cold and wet, and worn out by ɘxertions and privations of every description. Prontschischev, ⱳho before had been sick, died of his illness on the $\frac{10\text{th Sept.}}{30\text{th Aug.}}$

to the great sorrow of his men, by whom he was held in great regard. The mate CHELYUSKIN, now took the command. On the ¹⁴ᵗʰ⁄₃ᵣ₄ Sept. he succeeded in carrying his vessel into the river Olenek. On its bank Prontschischev was buried with all the solemnities which circumstances permitted. To Prontschischev's melancholy fate there attaches an interest which is quite unique in the history of the Arctic exploratory voyages. He was newly married when he started. His young wife accompanied him on his journey, took part in his dangers and sufferings, survived him only two days, and now rests by his side in the grave on the desolate shore of the Polar Sea.

On the ⁹ᵗʰ ᴼᶜᵗ·⁄₂₈ₜₕ ₛₑₚₜ. the Olenek was frozen over and the winter became very severe for Chelyuskin and his companions. The following summer they returned to Yakutsk convinced of the impossibility of sailing round the north point of Asia, and as Behring was no longer to be found in that town, Chelyuskin started for St. Petersburg in order to give an oral account of Prontschischev's voyages. The Board of Admiralty, however, did not favour Chelyuskin's views, but considered that another attempt ought to be made by land, but if this, too, was unsuccessful, that the coast should be surveyed by land journeys. Lieut. CHARITON LAPTEV was appointed to carry out this last attempt to reach the Yenisej by sea from the Lena.

Laptev, accompanied by a number of small craft carrying provisions, left Yakutsk on the ²⁹th July, 1739, and on the ³¹ˢᵗ of the same month reached the mouth-arm of the Lena called Krestovskoj, on which he built, on a point jutting out into the sea, a high signal tower, one of the few · monuments that are to be found on the north coast of Asia, and which is on that account mentioned by succeeding travellers in those regions. He sailed hence along the coast past the mouth of the Olenek and passed a large bay to which, for what reason I know not, he gave the purely Swedish name of Nordvik. This bay was still covered with unbroken ice. After having been beset for several days Chatanga Bay, the voyagers on the ³¹ˢᵗ⁄₂₀ₜₕ August reached Cape Thaddeus, where the vessel was anchored the following day 76° 47′ N.L. A signal tower was built on the extremity of the cape, and the land-measurer CHEKIN was sent to examine the neighbouring territory, and Chelyuskin to search for the mouth of the river Taimur. Chekin could carry out no geodetic work on account of mist. Chelyuskin again reported that the whole bay and the sea in the offing were, as far as the eye could reach, covered with unbroken ice. This induced Laptev to turn. After many difficulties among the ice, he came, on the ⁷ᵗʰ ˢᵉᵖᵗ·⁄₂₇ₜₕ ᴬᵘᵍ· to the confluence of the river Bludnaya with the Chatanga. Here the winter was passed among a tribe of Tunguses living on the spot who owned no reindeer, and were therefore settled. They use

ogs as draught animals, and appear to have carried on a mode
f life resembling that of the coast Chukches.

In spring Chekin was sent to map the coast between the
'aimur and the Pjäsina. With thirty dog-sledges and accompanied
y a nomad Tunguse with eighteen reindeer,[1] he travelled over
and to the Taimur river, followed its course to the sea, and then
he coast towards the west of a distance of 100 versts. Scarcity
f provisions and food for his dogs compelled him to turn.
Laptev himself, convinced as he was of the impossibility of
ounding the north point of Asia, now wished to carry back his
'essel and the most of his stores to the Lena. After having with
great danger and difficulty sailed down the river to the Polar Sea,
eaching it on the $\frac{10th \; Aug.}{30th \; July.}$ the vessel on the $\frac{24}{13}$th was beset and
1ipped between pieces of ice, according to a statement on a
Russian map published in 1876 by the Hydrographical Depart-
nent in St. Petersburg, on the east coast of the Taimur Peninsula
n 75° 30′ N.L. Six days after there was a strong frost, so that
;hin ice was formed between the blocks of drift-ice. Some
foolhardy fellows went over the weakly frozen together pieces of
ice to land. Three days after Laptev himself and the rest of the
men could leave the vessel. Several streams, still unfrozen, lying
between them and their old winter station, however, prevented
them from going further. They endeavoured to get protection
from the cold by digging pits in the frozen earth and lying down
in them by turns one after the other. The men were sent daily
to the vessel to fetch as much as possible of the provisions left
behind, but on the $\frac{10th \; Sept.}{30th \; Aug.}$ the ice again broke up, and carried the
abandoned vessel out to sea.

By the $\frac{2nd \; Oct.}{21st \; Sept.}$ the streams at last had frozen so much that the
return journey could be begun to the former year's winter
station distant more than 500 kilometres. The journey through
the desolate *tundra*, perhaps never before trodden by the foot
of man, was attended with extreme difficulties, and it was
twenty-five days before Laptev and his men could again rest
in a warmed hut and get hot food. Twelve men perished
of cold and exhaustion. Laptev now determined to remain here
during the winter and to go the following spring over the *tundra*
to the Yenisej, where he hoped to find depôts with provisions and
ammunition. Nor did he now remain inactive. For he did not
wish to return until the surveys were complete. For want of
vessels these were to be made by land. Such of the men as

---

[1] These all perished "for want of fodder." This, however, is improbable. For, in 1878, we saw numerous traces of these animals as far to
the northward as Cape Chelyuskin, and very fat reindeer were shot both in
1861 and 1873, on the Seven Islands, the northernmost of all the islands of
the Old World, where vegetation is much poorer than in the regions now
in question.

were not required were therefore sent in spring over the *tundra*
to the Yenisej and the rest divided into three parties under
Laptev himself, Chekin, and Chelyuskin, who were to survey
each his portion of the coast between the Chatanga and the
Pjäsina and then meet at the Yenisej. These journeys were
successfully accomplished; the explorers travelled several times
without, it would appear, excessive difficulty, over the desolate
tundra between the Chatanga and the Taimur rivers, discovered
Lake Taimur, and surveyed considerable stretches of the coast.
But when they were all again assembled at Dudino, it was found
that the north point of Asia had not yet been travelled round and
surveyed. This was done in 1742 by Chelyuskin in the
course of a new sledge journey, of which the particulars
are only incompletely known, evidently because Chelyuskin's
statement, that he had reached the northernmost point of
Asia, was doubted down to the most recent times. After the
voyage of the *Vega*, however, there can be no more doubt on
this point.[1]

5. *Voyages from the Lena Eastward.*—During these Lieutenant
Lassinius and after his death Lieutenant DMITRI LAPTEV had the
command. A double sloop was built at Yakutsk for the voyage
of Lassinius. As I have already mentioned, he left this town,
accompanied by several cargo-boats, at the same time as Prontschischev, and both sailed together down the Lena to its mouth.
Lassinius was able to sail to the eastward as early as the $\frac{20}{7}$th
August. Four days after he came upon so much drift-ice that
he was compelled to lie to at the mouth of the river, 120 versts
to the east of the easternmost mouth-arm of the Lena. Here
abundance of driftwood was met with, and the stock of provisions appears also to have been large, but notwithstanding this,
scurvy broke out during the winter. Lassinius himself and most
of his men died. On being informèd of this, Behring sent a
relieving party, consisting of Lieutenant CHERBININ and fourteen
men to Lassinius' winter quarters. On their arrival on the $\frac{15}{4}$th
June they found only the priest, the mate, and seven sailors
alive of the fifty-three men who had started with Lassinius the
foregoing year from Yakutsk. These too were so ill that some
of them died during the return journey to Yakutsk. Dmitri
Laptev and a sufficient number of men, were sent at the same
time to take possession of the ship and renew the attempt to sail

---

[1] Wrangel, i. pp. 48 and 72. Of the journey round the northernmost
point of Asia, Wrangel says :—"Von der Tajmur-Mündung bis an das Kap
des heiligen Faddej konnte die Küste nicht beschifft werden, und die
Aufnahme, die der Steuermann Tschemokssin (Chelyuskin) auf dem Eise
in Narten vornahm, ist so oberflächlich und unbestimmt, dass die eigent-
liche Lage des nordöstlichen oder Tajmur-Kaps, welches die nördlichste
Spitse Asiens ausmacht, noch gar nicht ausgemittelt ist."

istwards.   He went to sea on the $\frac{10\text{th Aug.}}{30\text{th July.}}$ At first he had to
intend with serious obstacles from ice, and when at last he
reached open water he thought himself compelled to turn on
account of the advanced season of the year.   On the $\frac{2\text{nd Sept.}}{22\text{nd Aug.}}$ he
ime again to the Bychov mouth-arm of the Lena, up which he
und it difficult to make his way on account of the many
nknown shoals.   On the $\frac{19}{8}$th September the river was frozen
rer.   He wintered a little distance from the mouth ; and now
;ain scurvy made its appearance, but was cured by constant
tercise in the open air and by a decoction of cedar cones.   In
report sent from this place, Dmitri Laptev declared that it was
ite impossible to round the two projecting promontories
tween the Lena and the Indigirka, Capes Borchaja and
vjatoinos, because, according to the unanimous statement of
veral Yakuts living in the region, the ice there never melts or
ven loosens from the beach.   With Behring's permission he
avelled to St. Petersburg to lay the necessary information
fore the Board of Admiralty.   The Board determined that
nother attempt should be made by sea, and, if that was
nsuccessful, that the coast should be surveyed by means of
nd journeys.

It is now easy to see what was the cause of the unfortunate
sue of these two attempts to sail to the eastward.   The explorers
id vessels which were unsuitable for cruising, they turned too
irly in the season, and in consequence of their unwillingness to
far from land they sailed into the great bays east of the Lena,
im which no large river carries away the masses of ice that
ive been formed there during the winter, or that have been
ifted thither from the sea.   Dmitri Laptev and his companions
sides appear to have had a certain dislike to the commission
trusted to them, and, differing from Deschnev, they thus
nted the first condition of success—the fixed conviction of
e possibility of attaining their object.

By order of the Board of Admiralty Dmitri Laptev at all
ents began his second voyage, and now falsified his own
ediction, by rounding the two capes which he believed to be
vays surrounded by unbroken ice.   After he had passed them
; vessel was frozen in on the $\frac{20}{9}$th September.   Laptev had no
ea at what point of the coast he was, or how far he was from
id.   He remained in this unpleasant state for eleven days, at
e close of which one of the mates who had been sent out from
e vessel in a boat on the $\frac{11\text{th Sept.}}{31\text{st Aug.}}$ returned on foot over the ice
d reported that they were not far from the mouth of the
digirka.   Several Yakuts had settled on the neighbouring
ist, where was also a Russian *simovie*.   Laptev and his men
ntered there, and examined the surrounding country.   The
rveyor KINDÄKOV was sent out to map the coast to the Kolyma.

Among other things he observed that the sea here was very shallow near the shore, and that driftwood was wanting at the mouth of the Indigirka, but was found in large masses in the interior, 30 versts from the coast.

The following year, 1740, Laptev repaired as well as he could his vessel, which had been injured during the voyage of the preceding year, and then went again to sea on the $\frac{11th\ Aug.}{31st\ July.}$ On the $\frac{14th}{3rd}$ August he passed one of the Bear Islands, fixing its latitude at 71° 0′. On the $\frac{28th}{15}$th August, when Great Cape Baranov was reached, the progress of the vessel was arrested by masses of ice that extended as far as the eye could reach. Laptev now turned and sought for winter quarters on the Kolyma. On the $\frac{19}{8}$th July, 1741, this river became open, and Laptev went to sea to continue his voyage eastwards, but did not now succeed in rounding Great Cape Baranov. He was now fully convinced of the impossibility of reaching the Anadyr by sea, on which account he determined to penetrate to that river by land in order to survey it. This he did in the years 1741 and 1742. Thus ended the voyages of Dmitri Laptev, giving evidence if not of distinguished seamanship, of great perseverance, undaunted resolution, and fidelity to the trust committed to him.[1]

6. *Voyage for the purpose of exploring and surveying the coast of America.*—For this purpose Behring fitted out at Okotsk two vessels, of which he himself took the command of one, *St. Paul*, while the other, *St. Peter*, was placed under CHIRIKOV. They left Okotsk in 1740, and being prevented by shoal water from entering Bolschaja Reka, they both wintered in Avatscha Bay, whose excellent haven was called, from the names of the ships, Port Peter-Paul. On the $\frac{15}{4}$th June they left this haven, the naturalist GEORG WILHELM STELLER having first gone on board Behring's and the astronomer LOUIS DE L'ISLE DE LA CROYÈRE Chirikov's vessel. The course was shaped at first for the S.S.E., but afterwards, when no land could be discovered in this direction, for the N.E. and E. During a storm on the $\frac{1st\ July}{20th\ June}$ the vessels were separated. On the $\frac{2}{8}$th July Behring reached the coast of America in 58° to 59° N.L. A short distance from the shore Steller discovered here a splendid volcano, which was named St. Elias. The coast was inhabited, but the inhabitants

[1] Wrangel, i. p. 62. I have sketched the voyages between the White Sea and the Kolyma, principally after Engelhardt's German translation of Wrangel's Travels. It is, unfortunately, in many respects defective and confused, especially with respect to the sketch of Chariton Laptev and his followers, sledge journeys, undertaken in order to survey the coast between the Chatanga and the Pjäsina. Müller mentions these journeys only in passing. Wrangel gives as sources for his sketch (i. note at p. 38) *Memoirs of the Russian Admiralty*, als) the original journals of the journeys. Chelyuskin he calls Chemokssin.

fled when the vessel approached. From this point Behring wished to sail in a north-westerly direction to that promontory of Asia which formed the turning-point of his first voyage. It was however only with difficulty that in the almost constant fog the peninsula of Alaska could be rounded and the vessel could sail forward among the Aleutian island groups. Scurvy now broke out among the crew, and the commander himself suffered severely from it, on which account the command was mainly in the hands of Lieut. WAXEL. At an island the explorers came into contact with the natives, who at first were quite friendly, until one of them was offered brandy. He tasted the liquor, and was thereby so terrified that no gifts could calm his uneasiness. On this account those of the crew who were on land were ordered to come on board, but the savages wished to detain their guests. At last the Russians were set free, but a Koryäk whom they had taken with them as an interpreter was kept behind. In order to get him set at liberty, Waxel ordered two musket salvos to be fired over the heads of the natives, with the result that they all fell flat down from fright, and the Koryäk had an opportunity of making his escape. Now the fire-water is a liquor in great request among these savages, and they are not frightened at the firing of salvos of musketry.

During the following months Behring's vessel drifted about without any distinct plan, in the sea between Alaska and Kamchatka, in nearly constant fog, and in danger of stranding on some of the many unknown rocks and islands which were passed. On the 5th November the vessel was anchored at an island afterwards called Behring Island. Soon however a great wave arose which threw the vessel on land and crushed it against the rocky coast of the island. Of the wintering there, which, through Steller's taking part in it, became of so great importance for natural history, I shall give an account further on in connection with the narrative of our visit to Behring Island. Here I shall only remind the reader that Behring died of scurvy on the ⁸⁄₉th December, and that in the course of the voyage great part of his crew fell a sacrifice to the same disease. In spring the survivors built a new vessel out of the fragments of the old, and on the ₄th of August they sailed away from the island where they had undergone so many sufferings, and came eleven days after to a haven on Kamchatka.

After parting from Behring, Chirikov on the ⁴⁄₁₅th July sighted the coast of America in 56° N.L. The mate ABRAHAM DEMENTIEV was then sent ashore in the longboat, which was armed with a cannon and manned by ten well-armed men. When he did not return, another boat was sent after him. But this boat too did not come back. Probably the boats' crews were taken prisoners and killed by the Indians. After making another attempt to find his lost men, Chirikov determined to return to Kamchatka. He first sailed some distance northwards along the coast of America without being able to land, as both the vessel's boats were lost. Great scarcity of drinking-water was thus occasioned, which was felt the more severely as the return voyage was very protracted on account of head-winds and fog. During the voyage twenty-one men perished, among them de l'Isle de la Croyère, who died, as is said often to be the case with scurvy patients on board ship, while he was being carried from his bed up on deck to be put on land.[1]

The voyages of Behring and Chirikov, attended as they were by the sacrifice of so many human lives, gave us a knowledge of the position of North-western America in relation to that of North-eastern Asia, and led to the discovery of the long volcanic chain of islands between the Alaska peninsula and Kamchatka.

7. *Voyages to Japan.*—For these Captain SPANGBERG ordered a *hucker*, the *Erkeengeln Michael*, and a double sloop, the *Nadeschda*, to be built at Okotsk, the old vessel *Gabriel* being at the same time repaired for the same purpose. Spangberg himself took command of the *Michael*, that of the double sloop was given to Lieutenant WALTON, and of the *Gabriel* to Midshipman CHELTINGA. Drift-ice prevented a start until midsummer, and on that account nothing more could be done the first year (1738) than to examine the Kurile Islands to the 46th degree of latitude. From this point the vessels returned to Kamchatka, where they wintered at Bolschaja Reka. On the 2nd June, 22nd May, 1739, Spangberg with his little fleet again left this haven. All the vessels kept together at first, until in a violent storm attended with fog Spangberg and Cheltinga were parted from Walton. Both made a successful voyage to Japan and landed at several places, being always well received by the natives, who appeared to be very willing to have dealings with the foreigners. During the return voyage Spangberg landed in 43° 50′ N.L. on a large island north of Nippon. Here he saw the Aino race, enigmatical as to its origin, distinguished by an exceedingly abundant growth of hair and beard which sometimes extends over the greater part of the body. Spangberg returned to Okotsk on the 9th Nov. Walton sailed along the coast in a southerly direction to 33° N.L. Here was a town with 1,500 houses, where the Russian seafarers were received in a very friendly way even in private houses. Walton subsequently landed at two other places on the coast, returning afterwards to Okotsk, where he anchored on the 1st September, 21st August.

The very splendid results of Spangberg's and Walton's voyage

---

[1] In this account of Behring's and Chirikov's voyages, I have followed Müller (iii. pp. 187-268). More complete original accounts of Behring's voyage are quoted further on in the sketch of our visit to Behring Island.
[2] Müller, iii. p. 164.

r no means corresponded with the maps of Asia constructed
r the men who were at that time leaders of the Petersburg
cademy. Spangberg therefore during his return journey through
beria got orders to travel again to the same regions in order
settle the doubts that had arisen. A new vessel had to
: built, and with this he started in 1741 from Okotsk to
s former winter haven in Kamchatka. Hence he sailed in
'42 in a southerly direction, but he had scarcely passed the
st of the Kurile Islands when the vessel became so leaky
at he was compelled to turn. The second expedition of
)angberg to Japan was thus completely without result, a
rcumstance evidently brought about by the unjustified and
fensive doubts which led to it, and the arbitrary way in
hich it was arranged in St. Petersburg.

8. *Journeys in the interior of Siberia* by Gmelin, Müller,
eller, Krascheninnikov, de l'Isle de la Croyère, &c.—The
yages of these *savants* have indeed formed an epoch in our
lowledge of the ethnography and natural history of North Asia,
it the north coast itself they did not touch. An account of
em therefore lies beyond the limits of the history which I
ive undertaken to relate here.

The Great Northern Expedition by these journeys both by
a and land had gained a knowledge of the natural conditions
North Asia based on actual researches, had yielded pretty
mplete information regarding the boundary of that quarter
the globe towards the north, and of the relative position
the east coast of Asia and the west coast of America, had
scovered the Aleutian Islands, and had connected the Russian
scoveries in the east with those of the West-Europeans in
ipan and China.[1] The results were thus very grand and
)och-making. But these undertakings had also required very
nsiderable sacrifices, and long before they were finished they
ere looked upon in no favourable light by the Siberian
ithorities, on account of the heavy burden which the transport
provisions and other equipment through desolate regions
iposed upon the country. Nearly twenty years now elapsed
fore there was a new exploratory expedition in the Siberian
)lar Sea worthy of being registered in the history of geography.
ais time it was a private person, a Yakutsk merchant,
:HALAUROV, who proposed to repeat Deschnev's famous voyage,
id to gain this end sacrificed the whole of his means and

[1] It deserves to be noted as a literary curiosity that the famous French
vant and geographer, Vivien de Saint Martin, in his work, *Histoire de la
'ographie et des Découvertes géographiques*, Paris, 1873, does not say a single
rd regarding all those expeditions which form an epoch in our knowledge
the Old World.

his life itself. Accompanied by an exiled midshipman, IVAN
BACHOFF, and with a crew of deserters and deported men, he
sailed in 1760 from the Lena out into the Polar Sea, but
came the first year only to the Yana, where he wintered.
On the $\frac{9th August}{29th July}$, 1761, he continued his voyage towards the east,
always keeping near the coast. On the $\frac{17}{7}$th September he
rounded the dreaded Svjatoinos, sighting on the other side of
the sound a high-lying land, Ljachoff's Island. At the Bear
Islands, whither he was carried by a favourable wind over an
open sea, he first met with drift-ice, although, it appears, not
in any considerable quantity. But the season was already far
advanced, and he therefore considered it most advisable to
seek winter quarters at the mouth of the neighbouring Kolyma
river. Here he built a spacious winter dwelling, which was
surrounded by snow ramparts armed with cannon from the
vessel; probably the whole house was not so large as a peasant's
cabin at home, but it was at all events the grandest palace
on the north coast of Asia, often spoken of by later travellers,
and regarded by the natives with amazed admiration. In the
neighbourhood there was good reindeer hunting and abundant
fishing, on which account the winter passed so happily, that
only one man died of scurvy, an exceedingly favourable state
of things for that period.

The following year Schalaurov started on the $\frac{1st August}{21st July}$ but
calms and constant head-winds prevented him from passing
Cape Schelagskoj, until he was compelled by the late season
of the year to seek for winter quarters. For this he considered
the neighbouring coast unsuitable on account of the scarcity
of forests and driftwood; he therefore sailed back to the westward until after a great many mishaps he came again at last
on the $\frac{23rd}{13th}$ September to the house which he had built the
year before on the Kolyma.

He proposed immediately to make a renewed attempt the
following spring to reach his goal. But now his stores were
exhausted, and the wearied crew refused to accompany him.
In order to obtain funds for a new voyage he travelled to
Moscow, and by means of the assistance he succeeded in
procuring there, he commenced in 1766 a voyage from which
neither he nor any of his followers returned. COXE mentions
several things which tell in favour of his having actually rounded
Cape Deschnev and reached the Anadyr. But Wrangel believes
that he perished in the neighbourhood of Cape Schelagskoj.
For in 1823 the inhabitants of that cape showed Wrangel's
companion Matiuschkin a little ruinous house, built east of the
river Werkon on the coast of the Polar Sea. For many years
back the Chukches travelling past had found there human bones
gnawed by beasts of prey, and various household articles, which

ndicated that shipwrecked men had wintered there, and Wrangel
ccordingly supposes that it was there that Schalaurov perished
. sacrifice to the determination with which he prosecuted his
elf-imposed task of sailing round the north-eastern promontory
f Asia.[1]   \

In order to ascertain whether any truth lay at the bottom
f the view, generally adopted in Siberia, that the continent of
\merica extended along the north coast of Asia to the neigh-
ourhood of the islands situated there, CHICHERIN, Governor of
Siberia, in the winter of 1763 sent a sergeant, ANDREJEV, with
og-sledges on an ice journey towards the north. He succeeded
\\ reaching some islands of considerable extent, which Wrangel,
/ho always shows himself very sceptical with respect to the
xistence of new lands and islands in the Polar Sea, considers to
\ave been the Bear Islands. Now it appears to be pretty certain
hat Andrejev visited a south-westerly continuation of the land
\amed on recent maps " Wrangel Land," which in that case, like
he corresponding part of America, forms a collection of many
\\rge and small islands. Andrejev found everywhere numerous
)roofs that the islands which he visited had been formerly
nhabited. Among other things he saw a large hut built of
vood without the help of iron tools. The logs were as it were
\nawed with teeth (hewed with stone axes), and bound together
\vith thongs.[2] Its position and construction indicated that the
\ouse had been built for defence ; it had thus been found im-
)ossible in the desolate regions of the Polar Sea to avoid the
liscord and the strife which prevail in more southerly lands.
To the east and north-east Andrejev thought he saw a distant
and ; he is also clearly the true European discoverer of Wrangel
\\and, provided we do not consider that even he had a pre-
lecessor in the Cossack, FEODOR TATARINOV, who according to
he concluding words of Andrejev's journal appears to have
)reviously visited the same islands. It is highly desirable that
his journal, if still in existence, be published *in a completely
\naltered form*. How important this is appears from the fol-
owing paragraph in the instructions given to Billings :—" One
Sergeant Andrejev saw from the last of the Bear Islands a large
sland to which they (Andrejev and his companions) travelled in
log-sledges. But they turned when they had gone twenty
'ersts from the coast, because they saw fresh traces of a large

---

[1] An account of Schalaurov is given by Coxe (*Russian Discoveries*, &c.,
780, p. 323) and Wrangel (i. p. 73). That the hut seen by Matiuschkin
\ctually belonged to Schalaurov appears to me highly improbable, for
he traditions of the Siberian savages seldom extend sixty years back.

[2] Wrangel, i. p. 79.

number of men, who had travelled in sledges drawn by reindeer." [1]

In order to visit the large land in the north-east seen by Andrejev, there was sent out in the years 1769, 1770, and 1771 another expedition, consisting of the three surveyors, LEONTIEV, LUSSOV, and PUSCHKAREV, with dog-sledges over the ice to the north-east, but they succeeded neither in reaching the land in question, nor even ascertaining with certainty whether it actually existed or not. Among the natives, however, the belief in it was maintained very persistently, and they even knew how to give names to the tribes inhabiting it.

The New Siberian Islands, which previously had often been seen by travellers along the coast, were visited the first time in 1770 by LJACHOFF, who besides Ljachoff's island lying nearest the coast, also discovered the islands Maloj and Kotelnoj. On this account he obtained an exclusive right to collect mammoth tusks there, a branch of industry which since that time appears to have been carried on in these remote regions with no inconsiderable profit. The importance of the discovery led the government some years after to send thither a land surveyor, CHVOINOV,[2] by whom the islands were surveyed, and some further information obtained regarding the remarkable natural conditions in that region. According to Chvoinov the ground there consists at many places of a mixture of ice and sand with mammoth tusks, bones of a fossil species of ox, of the rhinoceros, &c. At many places one can literally roll off the carpet-like bed of moss from the ground, when it is found that the close, green vegetable covering has clear ice underlying it, a circumstance which I have also observed at several places in the Polar regions. The new islands were rich not only in ivory, but also in foxes with valuable skins, and other spoils of the chase of various kinds. They therefore formed for a time the goal of various hunters' expeditions. Among these hunters may be named SANNIKOV, who in 1805 discovered the islands Stolbovoj and Faddejev, SIROVATSKOJ, who in 1806 discovered Novaya Sibir, and BJELKOV, who in 1808 discovered the small islands named after him. In the meantime disputes arose about the hunting monopoly, especially after Bjelkov and others petitioned for permission to establish on Kotelnoj Island a hunting and trading station. (?)[3] This induced ROMANZOV, the Chancellor of Russia, to order once more these distant territory to be explored by HEDENSTRÖM,[4] a Siberian exile, who

[1] Sauer, An Account, &c., Appendix, p. 48.
[2] Sauer, loc. cit. p. 103, according to an oral communication by Ljachoff's follower Protodiakonov.
[3] Compare Wrangel, i. p. 98.
[4] Matthias Hedenström, Aulic Councillor, whose name indicates that he was of Swedish birth, died at the village Hajdukovo, seven versts from

ormerly been secretary to some eminent man in St. Petersburg. He started in dog-sledges on the $\frac{19}{7}$th March, 1809, from Ustjansk going over the ice to Ljachoff's Island, and thence to Faddejev Island, where the expedition was divided into two parts. Hedenström continued his course to Novaya Sibir, the south coast of which he surveyed. Here he discovered among other things the remarkable "tree mountain," which I have before mentioned. His companions KOSCHEVIN and SANNIKOV explored Faddejev, Maloj and Ljachoff's Islands. On Faddejev, Sannikov found a Yukagir sledge, stone skin-scrapers, and an axe made of mammoth ivory, whence he drew the conclusion that the island was inhabited before the Russians introduced iron among the savage tribes of Siberia.

The explorations thus commenced were continued in 1810. The explorers started on the $\frac{14\text{th}}{2\text{nd}}$ March from the mouth of the Indigirka, and after eleven days' journey came to Novaya Sibir. It had been Hedenström's original intention to employ reindeer and horses in exploring the islands, but he afterwards abandoned this plan, fearing that he would not find pasture for his draught animals. Both Hedenström and Sannikov believed that they saw from the north coast of the island bluish mountains on the horizon in the north-east. In order to reach this new land the former undertook a journey over the ice. It was so uneven, however, that in four days he could only penetrate about seventy versts. Here on the $\frac{9\text{th April}}{28\text{th March}}$ he met with quite open water, which appeared to extend to the Bear Islands, *i.e.* for a distance of about 500 versts. He therefore turned southward, and reached the mainland after forty-three days' very difficult travelling over the ice. During the journey Hedenström was saved from famine by his success in killing eleven Polar bears. A new attempt, which he made the same spring to reach with dog-sledges the unknown land in the north-east, was also without result in consequence of his meeting with broad, impassable 'leads" and openings in the ice, but even on this occasion he believed that he found many indications of the existence of an extensive land in the direction named. It was only with great difficulty that on the $\frac{20}{8}$th May he succeeded in reaching the mainland at Cape Baranov over very weak ice.

The same year Sannikov explored Kotelnoj Island, where he fell in with Bjelkov and several hunters, who had settled for the summer on the west coast of the island to collect mammoth tusks and hunt foxes there. He found also a Greek cross erected on

Tomsk, on the 2nd October (20th September), 1845, at the age of sixty-five. Biographical notes regarding Hedenström are to be found in the Calendar for the Irkutsh government for the year 1865, pp. 57-60 ; I have not, however, succeeded in procuring this work, or in finding any other notices of Hedenström's birthplace and life.

the beach and the remains of a vessel, which, to judge from its construction and the hunting implements scattered about in the neighbourhood, appeared to have belonged to an Archangel hunter, who had been driven by wind or ice from Spitzbergen cr Novaya Zemlya.

Next summer "the Hedenström expeditions" were concluded with the survey of the north coast of Novaya Sibir by CHENIZYN, and by a repetition of the attempt to penetrate from Cape Kamennoj over the ice in a north-easterly direction, this time

PETER FEODOROVITSCH ANJOU.
Born in 1795 in Russia, died in 1869 in St. Petersburg.

carried out by the Cossack TATARINOV, and finally by a renewed exploration of Faddejev Island by Sannikov. Tatarinov found the ice, probably in the end of March, so thin, that he did not dare to proceed farther, and beyond the thin ice the sea was seen to be quite open. Sannikov first explored Faddejev Island. He thought he saw from the hills of the island a high land in the north-east, but when he attempted to reach it over the ice, he came upon open water twenty-five versts from land. He therefore returned the same spring to Ustjansk in order there to

ip a caravan consisting of twenty-three reindeer, which
ted on the 14th May to go over the ice to Kotelnoj Island,
ch could be reached only with great difficulty in consequence
'leads" in the ice and the large quantity of salt water which
l accumulated upon it. The reindeer were exceedingly
eebled, but recovered rapidly on reaching land, so that
mikov was able under specially favourable circumstances to
ke a large number of interesting excursions, among others one

FERDINAND VON WRANGEL.
Born in 1796 at Pskov, died in 1870 at Dorpat.

ss the island. He stated that on the heights in the interior
t there were found skulls and bones of horses, oxen,
ffaloes" (Ovibos?) and sheep in so large numbers, that
as evident that whole herds of graminivora had lived there
)rmer times. Mammoth bones were also found everywhere
the island, whence Sannikov drew the conclusions, that all
e animals had lived at the same time, and that since then the
tate had considerably deteriorated. These suppositions he

considered to be further confirmed by the fact that large, partially petrified tree-stems were found scattered about on the island in still greater numbers than on Novaya Sibir.[1] Besides he found here everywhere remains of old " Yukagir dwellings "; the island had thus once been inhabited. After Sannikov had fetched Chenitzyn from Faddejev Island, where he had passed the summer in great want of provisions, and ordered him, who was probably a greater adept at the pen, to draw up a report of his own interesting researches, he commenced his return journey on the $\frac{8\text{th Nov.}}{27\text{th Oct.}}$, and arrived at Ustjansk on the $\frac{24}{13}$th November.

It may be said that through Hedenström's and Sannikov's exceedingly remarkable Polar journeys, the titles have been written of many important chapters in the history of the former and recent condition of our globe. But the inquirer has hitherto waited in vain for these chapters being completed through new researches carried out with improved appliances. For since then the New Siberian Islands have not been visited by any scientific expedition. Only in 1823 ANJOU, lieutenant in the Russian Navy, with the surgeon FIGURIN, and the mate ILGIN, made a new attempt to penetrate over the ice to the supposed lands in the north and north-east, but without success. Similar attempts were made at the same time from the Siberian mainland by another Russian naval officer, FERDINAND VON WRANGEL, accompanied by Dr. KÜBER, midshipman MATIUSCHKIN, and mate KOSMIN. They too were unsuccessful in penetrating over the ice far from the coast. Wrangel returned fully convinced that all the accounts which were current in Siberia of the land he wished to visit, and which now bears the name of Wrangel Land, were based on legends, mistake, and intentional untruths. But Anjou and Wrangel did an important service to Polar research by showing that the sea, even in the neighbourhood of the pole of cold, is not covered with any strong and continuous sheet of ice, even at that season of the year when cold reaches its maximum. By the attempts made nearly at the same time by Wrangel and Parry to penetrate farther northwards, the one from the north coasts of Siberia, and the other from those of Spitzbergen, Polar travellers for the first time got a correct idea how uneven and impassable ice is on a frozen sea, how little the

___

[1] A very remarkable geological fact is the number of tree-stems in all stages of decay and petrifaction, which are embedded in the rocks and earthy strata of Siberia, having their origin all along from the Jurassic age till now. It appears as if Siberia, during the whole of this immense period of time, has not been subjected to any great changes in a purely geographical respect, whereas in Europe there have been innumerable alternations of sea and land, and alps have been formed and disappeared. The Siberians call the tree-stems found on the *tundra* far from the sea and rivers *Adam's wood*, to distinguish them from more recent sub-fossil trees, which they call *Noah's wood,*

way over such a sea resembles the even polished surface of a frozen lake, over which we dwellers in the north are accustomed to speed along almost with the velocity of the wind. Wrangel's narrative at the same time forms an important source of knowledge both of preceding journeys and of the recent natural conditions on the north coast of Asia, as is only too evident from the frequent occasions on which I have quoted his work in my sketch of the voyage of the *Vega*.

It remains for me now to enumerate some voyages from Behring's Straits westward into the Siberian Polar Sea.

1778 and 1779.—During the third of his famous circumnavigations of the globe JAMES COOK penetrated through Behring's Straits into the Polar Sea, and then along the northeast coast of Asia westwards to Irkaipij, called by him Cape North. Thus the honour of having carried the first seagoing vessel to this sea also belongs to the great navigator. He besides confirmed Behring's determination of the position of the East Cape of Asia, and himself determined the position of the opposite coast of America.[1] The same voyage was approximately repeated the year after Cook's death by his successor CHARLES CLARKE, but without any new discoveries being made in the region in question.

1785-94.—The success which attended Cook in his exploratory voyages and the information, unlooked for even by the Russian government, which Coxe's work gave concerning the voyages of the Russian hunters in the North Pacific, led to the equipment of a grand new expedition, having for its object the further

---

[1] The first European who visited the part of America lying right opposite to Asia was Schestakov's companion, the surveyor Gvosdev. He crossed Behring's Straits to the American side as early as 1730 (*Müller*, iii. p. 131), and therefore ought properly to be considered as the discoverer of this sound. The north-westernmost part of America, Behring's Straits and the islands situated in it, are besides shown in Strahlenberg's map, which was made at least a decade before Gvosdev's voyage. There north-western America is delineated as a large island, inhabited by a tribe, the *Puchochotski*, who lived in a constant state of warfare with the *Giuchieghi*, who inhabited the islands in the sound. Wrangel Land is also shown in this remarkable map. In 1767, eleven years before Cook's voyage in the Polar Sea, the American side of Behring's Straits was also visited by Lieut. SYND with a Russian expedition, that started from Okotsk in 1764. In the short account of the voyage which is to be found in William Coxe's *Account of the Russian Discoveries*, &c., London, 1780, p. 300, it is said expressly that Synd considered the coast on which he landed to belong to America. On Synd's map, published by Coxe, the north part of the Behring Sea is enriched with a number of fictitious islands (St. Agaphonis, St. Myronis, St. Titi, St. Samuelis, and St. Andreæ). As Synd, according to Sarytchev in the work quoted below, p. 11, made the voyage in a boat, it is probable that by these names islands were indicated which lay quite close to the coast and were not so far from land as shown in the map; besides, the mountain-summits on St. Lawrence Island, which are separated by extensive low lands may perhaps have been taken for separate islands.

exploration of the sea which bounds the great Russian Empire
on the north and east. The plan was drawn up by Pallas and
Coxe, and the carrying out of it was entrusted to an English
naval officer in the Russian service, J. BILLINGS, who had taken
part in Cook's last voyage. Among the many others who were
members of the expedition may be mentioned Dr. MERK,
Dr. ROBECK, the secretary MARTIN SAUER, and the Captains
HALL, SARYTCHEV, and BEHRING the younger, in all more
than a hundred persons. The expedition was fitted out on a
very large scale, but in consequence of Billings' unfitness for
having the command of such an expedition the result by no
means corresponded to what might reasonably have been expected.
The expedition made an inconsiderable excursion into the Polar
Sea from the $\frac{9th}{19}$th June to the $\frac{9th Aug.}{29th July}$. 1787, and in 1791 Billings
sailed up to St. Lawrence Bay, from which he went over land
with eleven men to Yakutsk. The rest of this lengthened
expedition does not concern the regions now in question.[1]

Among voyages during the century it remains to give account
of those which have been made by OTTO VON KOTZEBUE, who
during his famous circumnavigation of the globe in 1815-18,
among other things also passed through Behring's Straits and
discovered the strata, remarkable in a geological point of view,
at Eschscholz Bay ; LÜTKE, who during his circumnavigation of
the globe in 1826-29, visited the islands and sound in the
neighbourhood of Chukotskoj-nos; MOORE, who wintered at
Chukotskoj-nos in 1848-49, and gave us much interesting
information as to the mode of life of the Namollos and
Chukches; KELLET, who in 1849 discovered Kellet Land and
Herald Island on the coast of Wrangel Land ; JOHN RODGERS,
who in 1855 carried out for the American government much
important hydrographical work in the seas on both sides of
Behring's Straits; DALLMANN, who during a trading voyage in
the Behring Sea landed at various points on Wrangel Land; LONG,
who in 1867, as captain of the whaling barque *Nile*, discovered the
sound between Wrangel Land and the mainland (Long Sound)
and penetrated from Behring's Straits westwards farther than

---

[1] Billings' voyage is described in Martin Sauer's *Account of a Geographical and Astronomical Expedition to the Northern Parts of Asia, &c.*, by
Commodore Joseph Billings, London, 1802, and Gavrila Sarytchev's
*Achtjährige Reise im nördlichen Sibirien, auf dem Eismeere und dem nord-
östlichen Ocean. Aus dem Russischen übersetzt von J. H. Busse*, Leipzig,
1805-1806. As interesting to our Swedish readers it may be mentioned
that the Russian hunter Prybilov informed Sauer that a Swedish brigantine,
Merkur, coppered, carrying sixteen cannon, commanded by J. H. Coxe, in
1788, cruised in the Behring Sea in order to destroy the Russian settlements
there. They however, according to Prybilov's statement to Sauer, "did
no damage, because they saw that we had nothing worth taking away.
They instead gave us gifts, because they were ashamed to offer violence
to such poor fellows as we " (Sauer, p. 213).

ny of his predecessors; DALL, who, at the same time that we are indebted to him for many important contributions to the knowledge of the natural conditions of the Behring Sea, also new examined the ice-strata at Eschscholz Bay, and many others—but as the historical part of the sketch of the voyage of the *Vega* has already occupied more space than was calculated upon, I consider myself compelled with respect to the voyages of these explorers to refer to the numerous and for the most part accessible writings which have already been published regarding them.[1]

Was the *Vega* actually the first, and is she at the moment when this is being written, the only vessel that has sailed from the Atlantic by the north to the Pacific? As follows from the above narrative, this question may perhaps be answered with considerable certainty in the affirmative, as it may also with truth be maintained that no vessel has gone the opposite way from the Pacific to the Atlantic.[2] But the fictitious literature of geography at all events comprehends accounts of various voyages between those seas by the north passage, and I consider myself obliged briefly to enumerate them.

The first is said to have been made as early as 1555 by a Portuguese, MARTIN CHACKE, who affirmed that he had been parted from his companions by a west wind, and had been driven

[1] Otto von Kotzebue, *Entdeckungs-Reise in die Süd-See und nach der Behrings Strasse*, Weimar, 1821 (Part III., Contributions in Natural History, by Adelbert von Chamisso).—Louis Choris, *Voyage pittoresque autour du monde*. Paris, 1822.

Frédérik Lütké, *Voyage autour du monde*, Paris, 1835-36.—F. H. von Kittlitz, *Denkwürdigkeiten einer Reise nach dem russischen Amerika, nach Mikronesien und durch Kamtschatka*, Gotha, 1858.

Kellet, *Voyage of H.M.S. "Herald,"* 1845-51. London, 1853 (Discovery of Herald Island and the east coast of Wrangel Land).

W. H. Hooper, *Ten Months among the Tents of the Tuski*, London, 1853 (Moore's wintering at Chukotskoj-nos).

John Rodgers, Behring's Sea and Arctic Ocean, from Surveys of the North Pacific Surveying Expedition, 1855 (only charts).—W. Heine, *Die Expedition in die Seen von China, Japan und Ochotsk, unter Commando von Commodore Colin Ringgold und Commodore John Rodgers*, Leipzig, 1858 (the expedition arrived at the result that Wrangel Land did not exist).

(Lindemann) *Wrangels Land im Jahre 1866, durch Kapiten Dallmann besucht (Deutsche Geograph. Blätter*, B. iv. p. 54, 1881).

Petermann, *Entdeckung eines neuen Polar-Landes durch den amerikan, Capt. Long*, 1867 (Mittheil. 1868, p. 1).—*Das neu-entdeckte Polar-Land,* &c. (Mittheil. 1869, p. 26).

[2] It ought to be remembered that the voyage of the distinguished Arctic explorer, McClure, carried out with so much gallantry and admirable perseverance, from the Pacific to the Atlantic along the north coast of America, took place to no inconsiderable extent *by sledge journeys over the ice*, and that no English vessel has ever sailed by this route from the one sea to the other. The North-west Passage has thus never been accomplished by a vessel.

forward between various islands to the entrance of a sound which ran north of America in 59° N.L.; finally that he had come S.W. of Iceland, and thence sailed to Lisbon, arriving there before his companions, who took the "common way," *i.e.* south of Africa. In 1579 an English pilot certified that he had read in Lisbon in 1567 a printed account of this voyage, which however he could not procure afterwards because all the copies had been destroyed by order of the king, who considered that such a discovery would have an injurious effect on the Indian trade of Portugal (*Purchas*, iii. p. 849). We now know that there is land where Chacke's channel was said to be situated, and it is also certain that the sound between the continent of America and the Franklin archipelago lying much farther to the north was already in the sixteenth century too much filled with ice for its being possible that an account of meeting with ice could be omitted from a true sketch of a voyage along the north coast of America.

In 1588 a still more remarkable voyage was said to have been made by the Portuguese, LORENZO FERRER MALDONADO. He is believed to have been a cosmographer who among other things concerned himself with the still unsolved problem of making a compass free from variation, and with the question, very difficult in his time, of finding a method of determining the longitude at sea (see the work of AMORETTI quoted below, p. 38). Of his imaginary voyage he has written a long narrative, of which a *Spanish* copy with some drawings and maps was found in a library at Milan. The narrative was published in Italian and French translations by the superintendent of the library, Chevalier CARLO AMORETTI,[1] who besides added to the work a number of his own learned notes, which however do not give evidence of experience in Arctic waters. The same narrative has since been published in English by J. BARROW (*A Chronological History of Voyages into the Arctic Regions*, &c., London, 1818. App. p. 24). The greater part of Maldonado's report consists of a detailed plan as to the way in which the new sea route would be used and fortified by the Spanish-Portuguese government.[2] The voyage itself is referred to merely in passing. Maldonado says that in the beginning of March he sailed from Newfoundland along the north coast of America in a westward direction. Cold, storm, and darkness, were at first very inconvenient for navigation, but at all events he reached without difficulty "Anian Sound," which separates Asia from America. This is described in detail. Here various ships were met with prepared to sail through the sound,

---

[1] Amoretti, *Viaggio del mare Atlantico al Pasifico per la via del Nord-Ovest*, &c. *Fatto del capitano Lorenzo Ferrer Maldonado, l'anno* MDLXXXVIII. Milano, 1811.

[2] At the date of Maldonado's voyage Spain and Portugal were united.

laden with Chinese goods. The crews appeared to be Russian or Hanseatic. Conversation was carried on with them in Latin. They stated that they came from a very large town, situated a little more than a hundred leagues from the sound. In the middle of June Maldonado returned by the way he came to the Atlantic, and on this occasion too the voyage was performed without the least difficulty. The heat at sea during the return journey was as great as when it is greatest in Spain, and meeting with ice is not mentioned. The banks of the river which falls into the haven at Anian Sound (according to Amoretti, identical with Behring's Straits) were overgrown with very large trees, bearing fruit all the year round: among the animals met with in the regions seals are mentioned, but also two kinds of swine, buffaloes, &c. All these absurdities show that the whole narrative of the voyage was fictitious, having been probably written with the view of thereby giving more weight to the proposal to send out a north-west expedition from Portugal, and in the full belief that the supposed sound actually existed, and that the voyage along the north coast of America would be as easy of accomplishment as one across the North Sea.[1] The way in which the icing down of a vessel is described indicates that the narrator himself or his informant had been exposed to a winter storm in some northern sea, probably at Newfoundland, and the spirited sketch of the sound appears to have been borrowed from some East Indian traveller, who had been driven by storm to northern Japan, and who in a channel between the islands in that region believed that he had discovered the fabulous Anian Sound.

Of a third voyage in 1660 a naval officer named DE LA MADELÈNE gave in 1701 the following short account, probably picked up in Holland or Portugal, to Count DE PONTCHARTRIN : "The Portuguese, DAVID MELGUER, started from Japan on the 14th March, 1660 with the vessel le Père éternel, and following the coast of Tartary, i.e. the east coast of Asia, he first sailed north to 84° N.L. Thence he shaped his course between Spitzbergen and Greenland, and passing west of Scotland and Ireland came again to Oporto in Portugal." M. de la Madelène's narrative is to be found reproduced in M. BUACHE'S excellent geographical paper "Sur les différentes idéés qu'on a eu de la

---

[1] The narratives of the Russian voyagers in tho Polar Seas bear a quite different stamp. Details are seldom wanting in these, and they correspond with known facts, and the discoveries made are of reasonably modest dimensions. I therefore consider, as I have said already, that the doubts of the trustworthiness of Deschnev, Chelyuskin, Andrejev, Hedenström, Sannikov, &c., are completely unfounded, and it is highly desirable that all journals of Russian explorers in the Polar Sea yet in existence be published as soon as possible, and not in a mutilated shape, but in a complete and unaltered form.

traversée de la Mère Glaciale arctique et sur les communications ou jonctions qu'on a supposées entre diverses rivières" (*Histoire de l'Académie, Année 1754,* Paris, 1759, *Mémoires,* p. 12). The paper is accompanied by a Polar map constructed by Buache himself, which, though the voyage which led to its construction was clearly fictitious, and though it also contains many other errors—for instance, the statement that the Dutch penetrated in 1670 to the north part of Taimur Land—is yet very valuable and interesting as a specimen of what a learned and critical geographer knew in 1754 about the Polar regions. That Melguer's voyage is fictitious, is shown partly by the ease with which he is said to have gone from the one sea to the other, partly by the fact that *the only detail* which is to be found in his narrative, viz. the statement that the coast of Tartary extends to 84° N.L., is incorrect.

All these and various other similar accounts of north-east, north-west, or Polar passages achieved by vessels in former times have this in common, that navigation from the one ocean to the other across the Polar Sea is said to have gone on as easily as drawing a line on the map, that meeting with ice and northern animals of the chase is never spoken of, and finally that every particular which is noted is in conflict with the known geographical, climatal, and natural conditions of the Arctic seas. All these narratives therefore can be proved to be fictitious, and to have been invented by persons who never made any voyages in the true Polar Seas.

The. *Vega* is thus the first vessel that has penetrated by the north from one of the great world-oceans to the other.

CHAPTER XIV.

Passage through Behring's Straits—Arrival at Nunamo—Scarce species of seal—Rich vegetation—Passage to America—State of the ice—Port Clarence—The Eskimo—Return to Asia—Konyam Bay—Natural conditions there—The ice breaks up in the interior of Konyam Bay—St. Lawrence Island—Preceding visits to the Island—Departure to Behring Island.

AFTER we had passed the easternmost promontory of Asia, the course was shaped first to St. Lawrence Bay, a not inconsiderable fjord, which indents the Chukch peninsula a little south of the smallest part of Behring's Straits. It was my intention to anchor in this fjord as long as possible, in order to give the naturalists of the *Vega* expedition an opportunity of making acquaintance with the natural conditions of a part

' Chukch Land which is more favoured by nature than the
.re stretch of coast completely open to the winds of the Polar
:a, which we hitherto had visited.　I would willingly have
ьyed first for some hours at Diomede Island, the market-place
эned among the Polar tribes, situated in the narrowest part of
ə Straits, nearly half-way between Asia and America, and
эbably before the time of Columbus a station for traffic be-
·een the Old and the New Worlds.　But such a delay would
.ve been attended with too great difficulty and loss of time in
ɒsequence of the dense fog which prevailed here on the
·undary between the warm sea free from drift-ice and the cold
ɿa filled with drift-ice.

SEAL FROM THE BEHRING SEA.
Histriophoca fasciata, Zimm.

Even the high mountains on the Asiatic shore were still
rapped in a thick mist, from which only single mountain
ımmits now and then appeared.　Next the vessel large
ɔlds of drift-ice were visible, on which here and there flocks
' a beautifully marked species of seal (*Histriophoca fasciata*,
imm.) had settled.　Between the pieces of ice sea-birds
ʋarmed, mostly belonging to other species than those which
·e met with in the European Polar seas.　The ice was fortu-
ıtely so broken up that the *Vega* could steam forward at full
)eed to the neighbourhood of St. Lawrence Bay, where the
o o 2

coast was surrounded by some more compact belts of ice, which
however were broken through with ease. First, in the mouth
of the fjord itself impenetrable ice was met with, completely
blocking the splendid haven of St. Lawrence Bay. The *Vega*
was, therefore, compelled to anchor in the open road off the
village Nunamo. But even here extensive ice-fields, though
thin and rotten, drifted about; and long, but narrow, belts of
ice passed the vessel in so large masses that it was not advisable
to remain longer at the place. Our stay there was therefore
confined to a few hours.

During the course of the winter Lieutenant Nordquist endeavoured to collect from the Chukches travelling past as
complete information as possible regarding the Chukch villages
or encampments which are found along the coast between
Chaun Bay and Behring's Straits. His informants always
finished their list with the village Ertryn, situated west of
Cape Deschnev, explaining that farther east and south there
lived another tribe, with whom they indeed did not stand in
open enmity, but who, however, were not to be fully depended
upon, and to whose villages they therefore did not dare to
accompany any of us.[1]   This statement also corresponds, as
perhaps follows from what I have pointed out in the preceding
chapter, with the accounts commonly found in books on the
ethnography of this region.   While we steamed forward
cautiously in a dense fog in the neighbourhood of Cape
Deschnev, twenty to thirty natives came rowing in a large
skin boat to the vessel.   Eager to make acquaintance with
a tribe new to us, we received them with pleasure.   But when
they climbed over the side we found that they were pure
Chukches, some of them old acquaintances, who during winter
had been guests on board the *Vega*.   "Ankali," said they with
evident contempt, are first met with farther beyond St. Lawrence
Bay.   When we anchored next day at the mouth of this bay
we were immediately, as usual, visited by a large number of
natives, and ourselves visited their tents on land.   They still
talked Chukch with a limited mixture of foreign words, lived
in tents of a construction differing somewhat from the Chukches',

---

[1] The enmity appeared, however, to be of a very passive nature and by
no means depending on any tribal dislike, but only arising from the inhabitants of the villages lying farthest eastward being known to be of a
quarrelsome disposition, and having the same reputation for love of fighting as the peasant youths in some villages in Sweden.   For Lieut. Hooper,
who during the winter 1848-9 made a journey in dog-sledges from Chukotskoj-nos along the coast towards Behring's Straits, says that the inhabitants
at Cape Deschnev itself enjoyed the same bad reputation among their
Namollo neighbours to the south as among the Chukches living to the
westward.   "They spoke another language."   Possibly they were pure
Eskimo.

.nd appeared to have a somewhat different cast of countenance.
They themselves would not allow that there was any national
lifference between them and the old warrior and conqueror
ribe on the north coast, but stated that the race about
which we inquired were settled immediately to the south.
Some days we anchored in Konyam Bay (64° 49′ N.L.,
172° 53′ W.L. from Greenwich). We found there only pure
reindeer-owning Chukchees; there was no coast population
living by hunting and fishing. On the other hand the
inhabitants near our anchorage off St. Lawrence Island
consisted of Eskimo and Namollo. It thus appears as if
a great part of the Eskimo who inhabit the Asiatic side
of Behring's Straits, had during recent times lost their own
nationality and become fused with the Chukches. For it is
certain that no violent expulsion has recently taken place
here. It ought besides to be remarked that the name *Onkilon*
which Wrangel heard given to the old coast population driven
out by the Chukches is evidently nearly allied to the word
Ankali, with which the reindeer-Chukch at present distinguishes the coast-Chukch, also that, in the oldest Russian
accounts of Schestakov's and Paulutski's campaigns in these
regions, there never is any mention of two different tribes
living here. It is indeed mentioned in these accounts that
among the slain Chukches there were found some men with
perforated lips, but probably these were Eskimo from the
other side of Behring's Straits previously taken prisoners by
the Chukches, or perhaps merely Eskimo who had been
paying a friendly visit to the Chukches, and who had taken
part as volunteers in their war of freedom. It therefore
appears to me to be on the whole more probable that the
Eskimo have migrated from America to Asia, than that, as
ome authors have supposed, this tribe has entered America
rom the west by Behring's Straits or Wrangel Land.

The tent-village Nunamo, or, as Hooper writes, " Noonah-
none," does not lie low, like the Chukch villages we had
ormerly seen, on the sea-shore, but pretty high up on a
ape between the sea and a river which debouches immediately
o the south-west of the village, and now during the snow-
melting season was much flooded. At a short distance from
he coast the land was occupied by a very high chain of
mountains, which was split up into a number of summits and
whose sides were formed of immense stone mounds distributed
n terraces. Here a large number of marmots and lagomys
had their haunt. The lagomys, a species of rodent that
does not occur in Sweden, of the size of a large rat, is remarkable for the care with which in summer it collects great stores
or the winter. The village consisted of ten tents built without

order on the first high strand bank. The tents differed somewhat in construction from the common Chukch tents, and as
drift-wood appears to be met with on the beach only in limited
quantity, whale-bones had been used on a very large scale in
the frame of the tent. Thus, for instance, the tent-covering
of seal-skin was stretched downwards over the ribs or lower
jawbones of the whale which were fixed in the ground like
poles. These were united above with slips of whale-bones,
from which other slips of the same sort of bones or of whalebone rose to the summit of the tent, and finally, to prevent
the blast from raising the tent-covering from the ground, its
border was loaded with masses of large heavy bones. Eleven
shoulder-blades of the whale were thus used round a single
tent. In the absence of drift-wood, whale and seal bones
drenched in train-oil are also used as fuel in cooking in the
open air during summer; a large curved whale rib was placed
over the fire-place to serve as a pot-holder; the vertebræ of
the whale were used as mortars ; the entrances to the blubber-
cellars were closed with shoulder-blades of the whale; hollowed
whale-bones were used as lamps : slices of whale-bone or pieces
of the under-jaw and the straighter ribs were used for shoeing
the sledges for spades and ice-mattocks, the different parts
of the implement being bound together with whale-bone
fibres, &c.[1]

Masses of black seal-flesh, and long, white, fluttering strings
of inflated intestines, were hung up between the tents, and in
their interior there were everywhere to be seen bloody pieces
of flesh, prepared in a disgusting way or lying scattered about,
whereby both the dwellings and their inhabitants, who were
occupied with hunting, had a more than usually disagreeable
appearance. A pleasant interruption was formed by the heaps
of green willow branches which were placed at the entrance
of nearly every tent, commonly surrounded by women and
children, who ate the leaves with delight. At some places
whole sacks of Rhodiola and various other plants had been
collected for food during winter. As distinctive of the Chukches
here it may be mentioned in the last place that they were
abundantly provided with European household articles, among
them *Remington guns*, and that none of them asked for
spirits.

Most of the seals which were seen in the tents were the common

---

[1] There is still in existence a sketch of a tribe, living far to the south on
the coast of the Indian Sea, who at the time of Alexander the Great used
the bones of the whale in a similar way. "They build their houses so
that the richest among them take bones of the whale, which the sea casts
up, and use them as beams ; of the larger bones they make their doors."
Arrian, *Historia Indica*, XXIX. and XXX.

Phoca hispida, but along with them we found several skins of
Histriophoca fasciata, Zimm., and I even succeeded, though with
great difficulty, in inducing the Chukches to part with the
skin and skull of this uncommon species, distinguished by
its peculiar marking.   The natives appeared to set a special
value on its skin, and parted with it unwillingly.   We had
ourselves, as I have already stated, seen during our passage

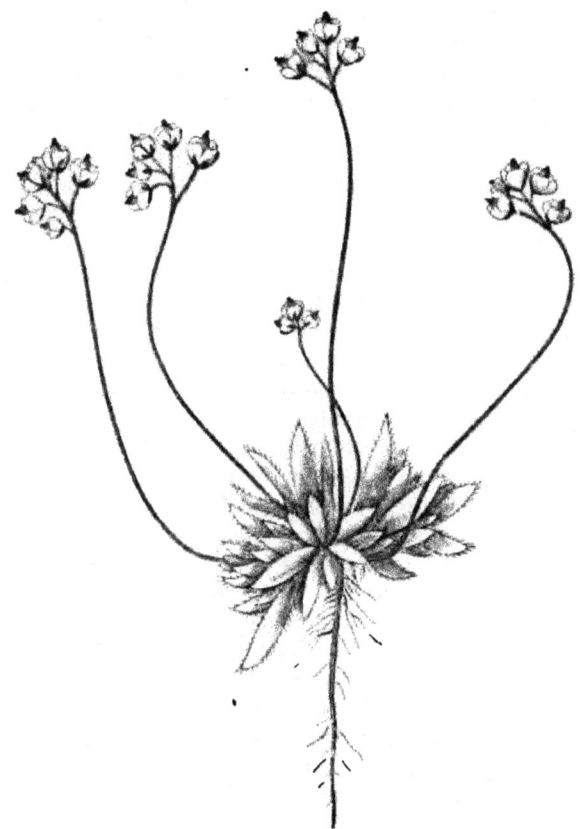

DRABA ALPINA L., FROM ST. LAWRENCE BAY.
Natural size.

from Behring's Straits a number of these seals on the ice-
floes drifting south, but the limited time at our disposal did
not permit us to hunt them.

When we left Pitlekaj, vegetation there was still far from
having reached its full development, but at Nunamo the strand-
bank was gay with an exceedingly rich magnificence of colour.
On an area of a few acres Dr. Kjellman collected here more than

a hundred species of flowering plants, among which were a considerable number that he had not before seen on the Chukch Peninsula. Space does not permit me to give another list of plants, but in order that the reader may have an idea of the great difference in the mode of growth which the same species may exhibit under the influence of different climatal conditions, I give here a drawing of the Alpine whitlow grass (*Draba alpina*, L.) from St. Lawrence Bay. It would not, perhaps, be easy to recognise in this drawing the species delineated on page 260, the globular form, which the plant assumed on the shore of Cape Chelyuskin exposed to the winds of the Polar Sea, has here, in a region protected from them, completely disappeared.

At the rocky headlands there were still, however, considerable snowdrifts, and from the heights we could see that considerable masses of ice were still drifting along the Asiatic side of Behring's Straits. During an excursion to the top of one of the neighbouring mountains, Dr. Stuxberg found the corpse of a native laid out on a stone-setting of the form common among the Chukches. Alongside the dead man lay a broken percussion gun, spear, arrows, tinder-box, pipe, snow-shade, ice-sieve, and various other things which the departed was considered to be in want of in the part of the Elysian fields set apart for Chukches. The corpse had lain on the place at least since the preceding summer, but the pipe was one of the clay pipes that I had caused to be distributed among the natives. It had thus been placed there long after the proper burial.

Anxious as I was to send off soon from a telegraph station some re-assuring lines to the home land, because I feared that a general uneasiness had already begun to be felt for the fate of the *Vega*, I would have willingly remained at this place, so important and interesting in a scientific point of view, at least for some days, had not the ice-belts and ice-fields drifting about in the offing been so considerable that if a wind blowing on land had risen unexpectedly, they might readily have been dangerous to our vessel, which even now was anchored in a completely open road, for the splendid haven situated farther in in St. Lawrence Bay was still covered with ice, and consequently inaccessible. On the afternoon of 21st July, accordingly, when all were assembled on board pleased and delighted with the results of the morning visit to land, I ordered the anchor to be weighed that the *Vega* might steam across to the American side of Behring's Straits. As in all the Polar seas of the northern hemisphere, so also here, the eastern side of the Straits was ice-bestrewn, the western, on the other hand, clear of ice. The passage was at all events a rapid one, so that by the afternoon of the 21st July we were able to anchor in Port Clarence, an excellent haven south of the westernmost promontory of Asia, Cape Prince of Wales. *It was the first time the Vega anchored in a proper haven, since on the 18th August 1878 she left Actinia Haven on Taimur Island.* During the intermediate time she had been constantly anchored or moored in open roads without the least land shelter from sea, wind, and drift-ice. The vessel was, however, thanks to Captain Palander's judgment and thoughtfulness, and the ability of the officers and crew, still not only quite free from damage, but even as seaworthy as when she left the dock at Karlskrona, and we had still on board provisions for nearly a year, and about 4,000 cubic feet of coal.

Towards the sea Port Clarence is protected by a long low sandy reef, between the north end of which and the land there is a convenient and deep entrance. There a considerable river falls into the interior of the harbour, the mouth of which widens to a lake, which is separated from the outer harbour by a sandy neck of land. This lake also forms a good and spacious harbour, but its entrance is too shallow for vessels of any considerable draught. The river itself, on the contrary, is deep, and about eighteen kilometres from its mouth flows through another lake, from the eastern shore of which rugged and shattered mountains rise to a height which I estimate at 800 to 1,000 metres; but it is quite possible that their height is twice as great, for in making such estimates one is liable to fall into error. South of the river and the harbour the land rises abruptly from the river bank, which is from ten to twenty metres high. On the north side, on the other hand, the bank is for the most part low, but farther into the interior the ground rises rapidly to rounded hills from 300 to 400 metres high. Only in the valleys and at other places where very large masses of snow had collected during the winter, were snow-drifts still to be seen. On the other hand, we saw no glaciers, though we might have expected to find them on the sides of the high mountains which bound the inner lake on the east. It was also clear that during the recent ages no widely extended ice-sheet was to be found here, for in the many excursions we made in different directions, among others up the river to the lake just mentioned, we saw nowhere any moraines, erratic blocks, striated rock-surfaces, or other traces of a past ice-age. Many signs, on the other hand, indicate that during a not very remote geological period glaciers covered considerable areas of the opposite Asiatic shore, and contributed to excavate the fjords there—Kolyutschin Bay, St. Lawrence Bay, Metschigme Bay, Konyam Bay, &c.

When we approached the American side we could see that the shore cliffs were formed of stratified rocks. I therefore hoped to be able, at last, to make a rich collection of fossils, something that I had no opportunity of doing during the preceding part of the voyage. But I found, on reaching them, that the stratified rocks only consisted of crystalline schists without any traces of animal or vegetable remains. Nor did we find on the shore any whale-bones or any of the remarkable mammoth-bearing ice-strata which were discovered in the bay situated immediately north of Behring's Straits, which was named after Dr. ESCH-SCHOLZ, medical officer during Kotzebue's famous voyage.[1]

Immediately after the anchor fell we were visited by several very large skin boats and a large number of *kayaks*. The latter were larger than the Greenlander's, being commonly in-tended for two persons, who sat back to back in the middle of the craft. We even saw boats from which, when the two rowers had stepped out, a third person crept who had lain almost hermetically sealed in the interior of the *kayak*, stretched on the bottom without the possibility of moving his limbs, or saving himself if any accident should happen. It appeared to be specially common for children to accompany their elders in *kayak* voyages in this inconvenient way.

After the natives came on board a lively traffic commenced, whereby I acquired some arrow-points and stone fishing-hooks. Anxious to procure as abundant material as possible for instituting a comparison between the household articles of the Eskimo and the Chukches, I examined carefully the skin bags which the natives had with them. In doing so I picked out one thing after the other, while they did not object to me making an inventory. One of them, however, showed great unwillingness to allow me to get to the bottom of the sack, but this just made me curious to ascertain what precious thing was concealed there. I was urgent, and went through the bag half

---

[1] These strata were discovered during Kotzebue's circumnavigation of the globe (*Entdeckungs Reise*, Weimar, 1821, i. p. 146, and ii. p. 170). The strand-bank was covered by an exceedingly luxuriant vegetable carpet, and rose to a height of eighty feet above the sea. Here the "rock," if this word can be used for a stratum of ice, was found to consist of pure ice, covered with a layer, only six inches thick, of blue clay and turf-earth. The ice must have been several hundred thousand years old, for on its being melted a large number of bones and tusks of the mammoth appeared, from which we may draw the conclusion that the ice-stratum was formed during the period in which the mammoth lived in these regions. This remarkable observation has been to a certain extent disputed by later travellers, but its correctness has recently been fully confirmed by Dall. On the other hand, the extent to which the strong odour, which was observed at the place and resembled that of burned horns, arose from the decaying mammoth remains, is perhaps uncertain. Kotzebue fixed the latitude of the place at 66° 15′ 36″. During Beechey's voyage in 1827 the place was thoroughly examined by Mr. Collie, the medical officer of the expedition. He brought home thence a large number of the bones of the mammoth, ox, musk-ox, reindeer, and horse, which were described by the famous geologist Buckland (F. W. Beechey, *Narrative of a Voyage to the Pacific and Behring's Straits, 1825-28.* London, 1831, ii. Appendix).

HUNTING IMPLEMENTS AT PORT CLARENCE.

art with wooden handle for throwing, one-ninth of the natural size. 2. Whale-harpoon with point, one-twelfth. 3. Harpoon-point of bone and nephrite, one-half. 4. Bone leister, one-third. wl, one-half. 6. Harpoon, one-twelfth. 7. Flint dart-point, one-half. 8. Arrows or harpoon-with points of iron, stone or glass, one-eighth. 9. Quiver, one-eighth.

with violence, until at last, in the bottom, I got a solution of
the riddle—a loaded revolver.   Several of the natives had also
breechloaders.   The oldest age with stone implements, and the
most recent period with breechloaders, thus here reach hands
one to the other.

Many natives were evidently migrating to more northerly
hunting-grounds and fishing places, perhaps also to the markets
and play-booths, which Dr. John Simpson describes in his well-
known paper on the West Eskimo.[1]   Others had already pitched
their summer tents on the banks of the inner harbour, or of the
river before mentioned.   On the other hand, there was found in

ESKIMO FAMILY AT PORT CLARENCE.
After a photograph by L. Palander.

the region only a small number of winter dwellings abandoned
during the warm season of the year.   The population consisted,
as has been said, of Eskimo.   They did not understand a word
of Chukch.   Among them, however, we found a Chukch woman,
who stated that true Chukches were found also on the American
side, north of Behring's Straits.   Two of the men spoke a little
English, one had even been at San Francisco, another at
Honolulu.   Many of their household articles reminded us of
contact with American whalers, and justice demands the

[1] *Further Papers relative to the recent Arctic Expedition, etc.*   Presented
to both Houses of Parliament.   London, 1855, p. 917.

tion of the fact that in opposition to what we commonly
ted, contact with men of civilised race appears to have
) the advantage and improvement of the savage in an
ical and moral point of view. Most of them now lived
mer-tents of thin cotton cloth; many wore European
, others were clad in trousers of seal or reindeer-skin and
soft, often beautifully ornamented *pesk* of marmot skin,
hich in rainy weather was worn an overcoat made of
of gut sewn together.   The arrangement of the hair
led that of the Chukches. The women were tattooed with

ESKIMO AT PORT CLARENCE.
After a photograph by L. Palander.

lines on the chin.   Many of the men wore small
ches, some even a scanty beard, while others had
ted the American goatee. Most of them, but not all,
o holes from six to seven millimetres in length, cut in the
ow the corners of the mouth.   In these holes were worn
ieces of bone, glass, or stone (figure 9, page 578). But
rnaments were often removed, and then the edges of the
oles closed so much that the face was not much dis-
, Many had in addition a similar hole forward in the

lip. It struck me, however, that this strange custom was about to disappear completely, or at least to be Europeanised by the exchange of holes in the ears for holes in the mouth. An almost full-grown young woman had a large blue glass bead hanging from the nose, in whose partition a hole had been made for its suspension, but she was very much embarrassed and hid her head in a fold of mamma's *pesk*, when this piece of grandeur attracted general attention. All the women had long strings of beads in the ears. They wore bracelets of iron or copper, resembling those of the Chukches. The colour of the skin was not very dark, with perceptible redness on the cheeks, the hair black and tallow-like, the eyes small, brown, slightly oblique, the face flat, the nose small and depressed at the root. Most of the natives were of average height, appeared to be healthy and

ESKIMO AT PORT CLARENCE.
After photographs by L. Palander.

in good condition, and were marked neither by striking thinness nor corpulence. The feet and the hands were small.

A certain elegance and order prevailed in their small tents, the floor of which was covered with mats of plaited plants. In many places vessels formed of cocoa-nut shells were to be seen, brought thither, like some of the mats, by whalers from the South Sea Islands. For the most part their household and hunting implements, axes, knives, saws, breechloaders, revolvers, &c., were of American origin, but they still used or preserved in the lumber repositories of the tent, bows and arrows, bird-darts, bone boat-hooks, and various stone implements. The fishing implements especially were made with extraordinary skill of coloured sorts of bone or stone, glass beads, red pieces of the feet of certain swimming birds, &c. The different materials

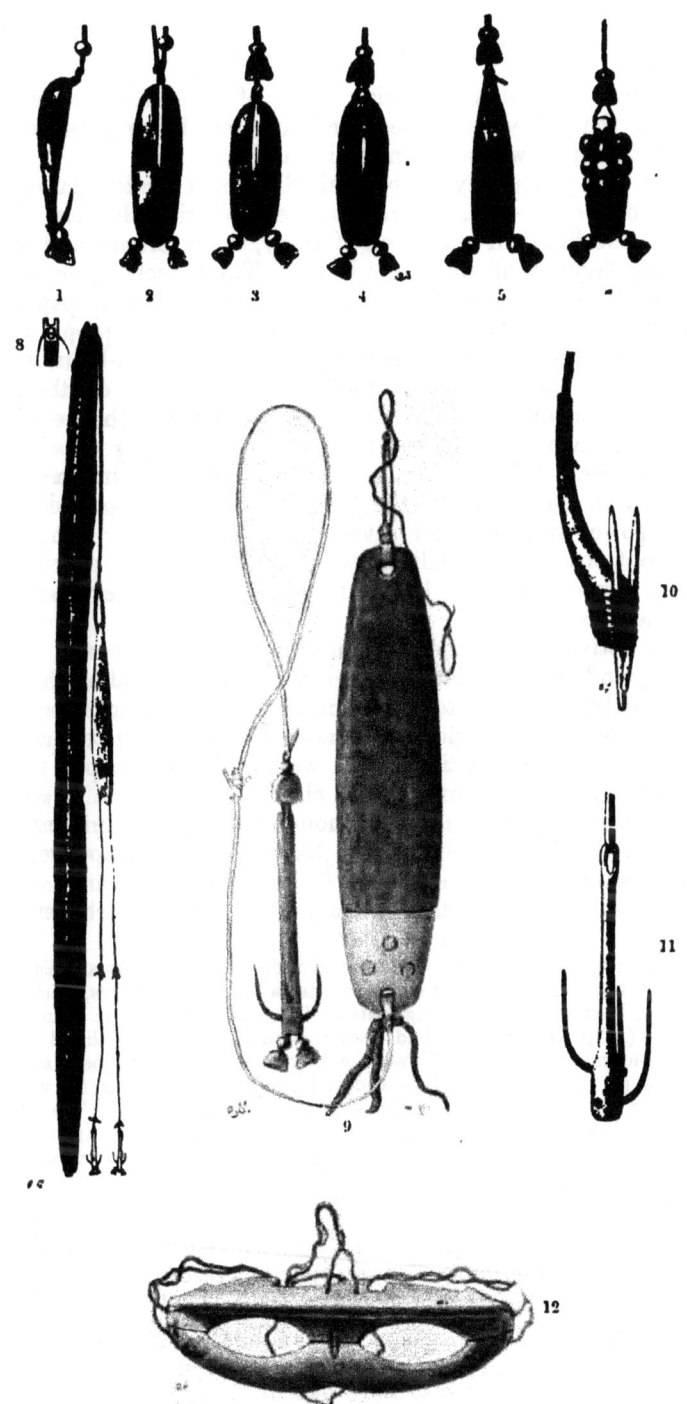

ESKIMO FISHING IMPLEMENTS, ETC.

6. Salmon hooks of stone of different colours, and bone in the form of beetles, one-half of the natural size. 7. Fishing-rod, one-sixth. 8. End of rod. 9. Bone sinker with tufts and fish-hook, one-half. 10. Fish-hook with bone points, one-half. 1. Fish-hook with iron-wire points, one-half. 12. Snow-spectacles, one-third.

were bound together by twine made of whalebone in such a manner that they resembled large beetles, being intended for use in the same way as salmon flies at home.

Fire was got partly with steel, flint, and tinder, partly by means of the fire-drill. Many also used American lucifers. The bow of the fire-drill was often of ivory, richly ornamented with hunting figures of different kinds. Their tools were more elegant, better carved and more richly coloured with graphite [1] and red ochre than those of the Chukches; the people were better off and owned a larger number of skin-boats, both *kayaks* and *umiaks*. This undoubtedly depends on the sea being here covered with ice for a shorter time and the ice being thinner than on the Asiatic side, and the hunting accordingly being better. All the old accounts however agree in representing that in former times the Chukches were recognised as a great power by the other savage tribes in these regions, but all recent observations indicate that that time is now passed. A certain respect for them, however, appears still to prevail among their neighbours.

The natives, after the first mistrust had disappeared, were friendly and accommodating, honourable in their dealings though given to begging and to much haggling in making a bargain. There appeared to be no chief among them ; complete equality prevailed, and the position of the woman did not appear to be inferior to that of the man. The children were what we would call in Europe well brought up, though they got no bringing up at all. All were heathens. The liking for spirits appeared to be less strong than among the Chukches. We learn besides that all selling of spirits to savages is not only forbidden on

[1] Graphite must be found in great abundance on the Asiatic side of Behring's Straits. I procured during winter a number of pieces, which had evidently been rolled in running water. Chamisso mentions in Kotzebue's Voyages (iii. p. 169) that he had seen this mineral along with red ochre among the inhabitants at St. Lawrence Bay ; and Lieut. Hooper states in his work (p. 139), that graphite and red ochre are found at the village Oongwysac between Chukotskoj-nos and Behring's Straits. The latter colour was sold at a high price to the inhabitants of distant encampments. These minerals have undoubtedly been used in the same way from time immemorial, and they are probably, like flint and nephrite, among the few kinds of stone which were used by the men of the Stone Age. So far as is known, graphite came first into use in Europe during the middle ages. A black-lead pencil is mentioned and delineated for the first time by Conrad Gessner in 1565. The rich but now exhausted graphite seam at Borrowdale, in England, is mentioned for the first time by Dr. Merret in 1667, as containing a useful mineral peculiar to England. Very rich graphite seams have been found during recent decades, both at the mouth of the Yenisej (Sidoroff's graphite quarry) and at a spur of the Sayan mountains in the southern part of Siberia (Alibert's graphite quarry), and these discoveries have played a certain *rôle* in the recent history of the exploration of the country.

the American side, but forbidden in such a way that the law is obeyed.

During our stay among the Chukches my supply of articles for barter was very limited; for up to the hour of departure uncertainty prevailed as to the time at which we could get free, and I was therefore compelled to be sparing of the stores. I often found it difficult on that account to induce a Chukch to part with things which I wished to acquire. Here, on the contrary, I was a rich man, thanks to the large surplus that was over from our abundant winter equipment, which of course in warm regions would have been of no use to us. I turned my riches to account by making visits like a pedlar in the tent villages with sacks full of felt hats, thick clothes, stockings, ammunition, &c., for which goods I obtained a beautiful and choice collection of ethnographical articles. Among these may be mentioned beautiful bone etchings and carvings, and several arrow-points and other tools of a species of nephrite,[1] which is so puzzlingly like the well-known nephrite from High Asia, that I am disposed to believe that it actually comes originally from that locality. In such a case the occurrence of nephrite at Behring's Straits is important, because it cannot be explained in any other way than either by supposing that the tribes living here have carried the mineral with them from their original home in High Asia, or that during the Stone Age of High Asia a like extended commercial intercommunication took place between the wild races as now exists, or at least some decades ago existed, along the north parts of Asia and America.

---

[1] Nephrite is a light green, sometimes grass-green, very hard and compact species of amphibolite, which occurs in High Asia, Mexico, and New Zealand. At all these places it has been employed for stone implements, vases, pipes, &c. The Chinese put an immensely high value upon it, and the wish to procure nephrite is said often to have determined their politics, to have caused wars, and impressed its stamp on treaties of peace concluded between millions. I also consider it probable that the precious Vasa Murrhina, which was brought to Rome after the campaign against Mithridates, and has given rise to so much discussion, was nephrite. Nephrite was also perhaps the first of all stones to be used ornamentally. For we find axes and chisels of this material among the people of the Stone Age both in Europe (where no locality is known where unworked nephrite is found) and in Asia, America, and New Zealand. In Asia implements of nephrite are found both on the Chukch Peninsula and in old graves from the Stone Age in the southern part of the country. They have been discovered at Telma, sixty versts from Irkutsk, by Mr. J. N. Wilkoffski, conservator of the East Siberian Geographical Society. In scientific mineralogy nephrite is first mentioned under the name of *Kascholong* (*i.e.* a species of stone from the river Kasch). It has been brought home under this name by Renat, a prisoner-of-war from Charles XII.'s army, from High Asia, and was given by him to Swedish mineralogists, who described it very correctly, though kascholong has since been erroneously considered a species of quartz.

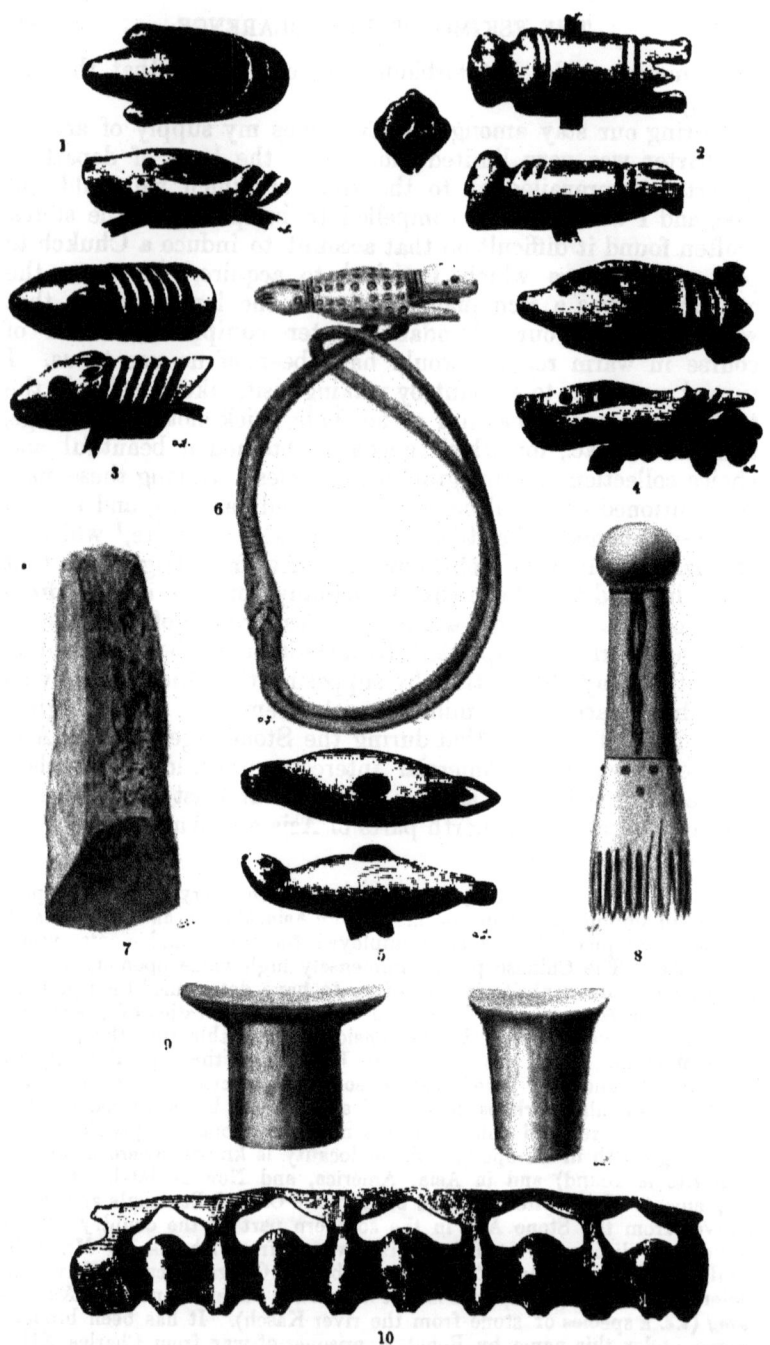

ESKIMO BONE-CARVINGS, ETC.

1.—5. Buttons to carrying-straps, representing heads of the Polar bear, seals, &c., carved in walrus ivory, one-half of the natural size. 6. Carrying-strap with a similar button, carved in the form of a seal, one-third. 7 Stone chisel, one-half. 8. Comb. one-third. 9. Buttons of bone, glass, or stone, to be placed in holes in the lips, natural size. 10. Ivory diadem, two-thirds.

On the north side of the harbour we found an old European or American train-oil boiling establishment. In the neighbourhood of it were two Eskimo graves. The corpses had been laid on the ground fully clothed, without the protection of any coffin, but surrounded by a close fence consisting of a number of tent poles driven crosswise into the ground. Alongside one of the corpses lay a *kayak* with oars, a loaded double-barrelled gun with locks at half-cock and caps on, various other weapons, cloths, tinder-box, snow-shoes, drinking-vessels, two masks carved in wood and smeared with blood (figures 1 and 2, page 581), and strangely-shaped animal figures. Such were seen also in the tents. Bags of sealskin, intended to be inflated and fastened to harpoons as floats, were sometimes ornamented with small faces carved in wood (figure 3, page 581). In one of the two amulets of the same kind, which

ESKIMO GRAVE.
After a drawing by O. Nordquist.

I brought home with me, one eye is represented by a piece of blue enamel stuck in, and the other by a piece of iron pyrites fixed in the same way. Behind two tents were found, erected on posts a metre and a half in height, roughly-formed wooden images of birds with expanded wings painted red. I endeavoured without success to purchase these tent-idols[1] for a large new felt hat—an article of exchange for which in other cases I could obtain almost anything whatever. A dazzlingly white *kayak* of a very elegant shape, on the other hand, I purchased without difficulty for an old felt hat and 500 Remington cartridges.

As a peculiar proof of the ingenuity of the Americans when offering their goods for sale, it may be mentioned in conclusion that an Eskimo, who came to the vessel during our stay in the harbour, showed us a printed paper, by which a commercial house

[1] The Eskimo however, like the Chukches, do not appear to have any proper religion or idea of a life after this.

at San Francisco offered to " sporting gentlemen" at Behring's Straits (Eskimo ?) their stock of excellent hunting shot.

As the west coast of Europe is washed by the Gulf Stream, there also runs along the Pacific coast of America a warm current, which gives the land a much milder climate than that which prevails on the neighbouring Asiatic side, where, as on the east coast of Greenland, there runs a cold northerly current. The limit of trees therefore in north-western America goes a good way *north of* Behring's Straits, while on the Chukch Peninsula wood appears to be wholly wanting. Even at Port Clarence the coast is devoid of trees, but some kilometres into the country alder bushes two feet high are met with, and behind the coast hills actual forests probably occur. Vegetation

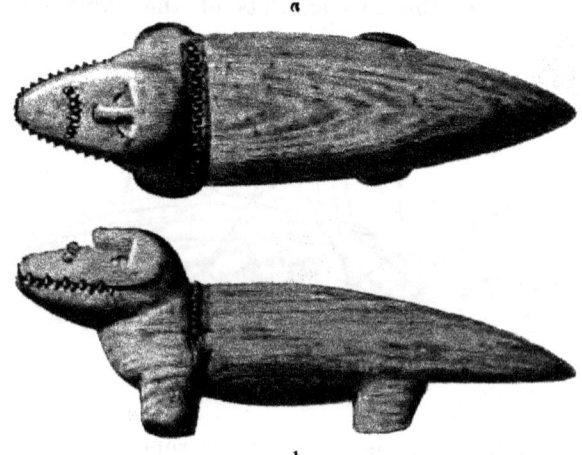

ANIMAL FIGURE FROM AN ESKIMO GRAVE.
a. From above. *b.* From the side.
One-third of the natural size.

is besides already luxuriant at the coast, and far away here, on the coast of the New World, many species are to be found nearly allied to Scandinavian plants, among them the *Linnæa.* Dr. Kjellman therefore reaped here a rich botanical harvest, valuable for the purpose of comparison with the flora of the neighbouring portion of Asia and other High Arctic regions. Dr. Almquist in like manner collected very extensive materials for investigating the lichen-flora of the region, probably before very incompletely known. The harvest of the zoologists, on the other hand, was scanty. Notwithstanding the luxuriant vege-tation land-evertebrates appeared to occur in a much smaller number of species than in northern Norway. Of beetles, for instance, only from ten to twenty species could be found,

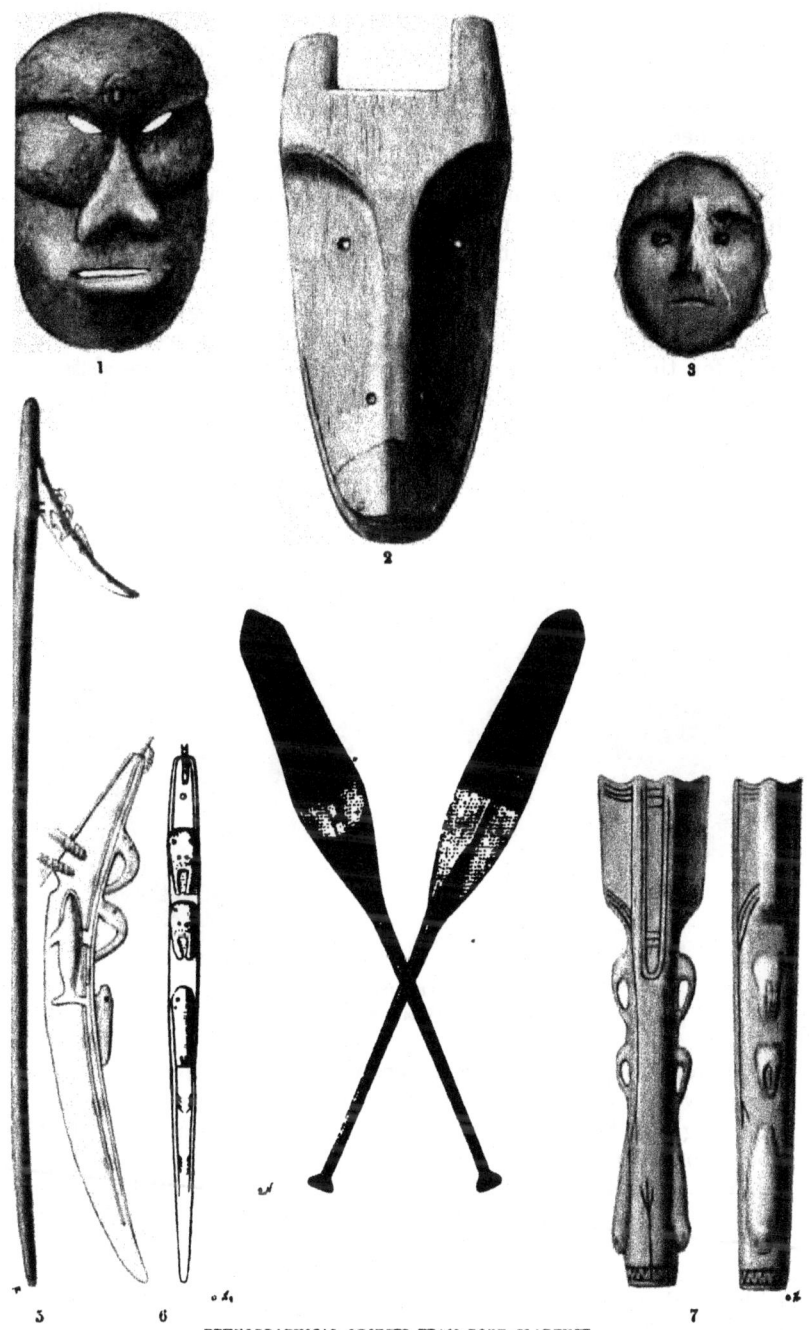

ETHNOGRAPHICAL OBJECTS FROM PORT CLARENCE.

2. Wooden masks, found at a grave, one-sixth of the natural size. 3. Amulet, a face with one eye of enamel, the other of pyrites, from a harpoon-float of sealskin, one-third. 4. Oars, one-nineteenth. 5. Boathook, one-twelfth. 6. The hook of carved ivory. one-fourth. 7. Carved knife handle (?) of ivory, one-half.

mainly Harpalids and Staphylinids, and of land and fresh-water
mollusca only seven or eight species, besides which nearly all
occurred very sparingly. Among remarkable fishes may be
mentioned the same black marsh-fish which we caught at
Yinretlen. The avi-fauna was scanty for a high northern land,
and of wild mammalia we saw only musk-rats. Even the
dredgings in the harbour yielded, on account of the unfavourable
nature of the bottom, only an inconsiderable number of animals
and algæ.

On the 26th July, at three o'clock in the afternoon, we
weighed anchor and steamed back in splendid weather and
with for the most part a favourable wind to the shore of the
Old World. In order to determine the salinity and temperature

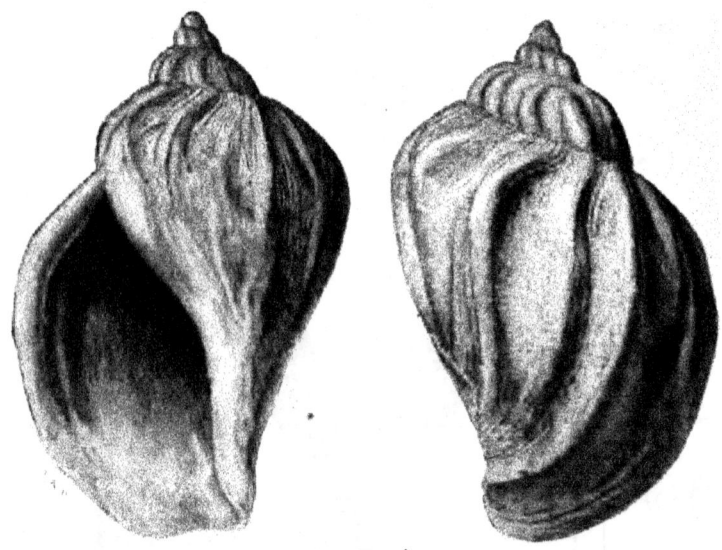

SHELL FROM BEHRING'S STRAITS.
Fusus deformis, Reeve.

at different depths, soundings were made and samples of water
taken every four hours during the passage across the straits.
Trawling was besides carried on three times in the twenty-four
hours, commonly with an extraordinarily abundant yield, among
other things of large shells, as, for instance, the beautiful *Fusus
deformis,* Reeve, with its twist to the left, and some large
species of crabs. One of the latter (*Chionœcetes opilio,* Kröyer)
the dredge sometimes brought up in hundreds. We cooked
and ate them and found them excellent, though not very rich
in flesh. The taste was somewhat sooty.

Lieutenant Bove constructed the diagram reproduced at
page 583, which is based on the soundings and other obser-

vations made during the passage, from which we see how
shallow is the sound which in the northernmost part of the
Pacific separates the Old World from the New. An elevation
of the land less than that which has taken place since the
glacial period at the well-known Chapel Hills at Uddevalla would
evidently be sufficient to unite the two worlds with each other
by a broad bridge, and a corresponding depression would have
been enough to separate them if, as is probable, they were at
one time continuous. The diagram shows besides that the
deepest channel is quite close to the coast of the Chukch
Peninsula, and that that channel contains a mass of cold water,

DIAGRAM,

Showing the Temperature and Depth of the water at Behring's Straits between Port Clarence
and Senjavin Sound.

By G. Bove.

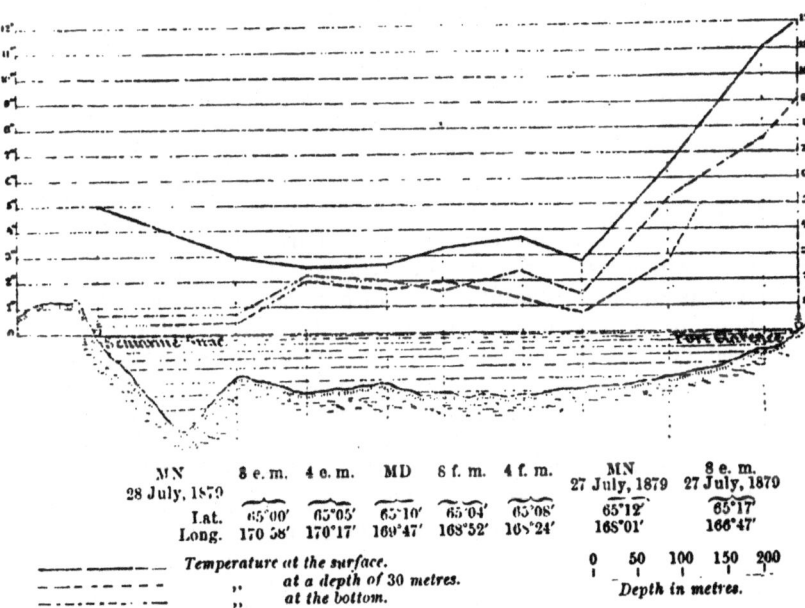

MN 28 July, 1879	8 e. m.	4 e. m.	MD	8 f. m.	4 f. m.	MN 27 July, 1879	8 e. m. 27 July, 1879
Lat.	65°00′	65°05′	65°10′	65°04′	65°08′	65°12′	65°17′
Long.	170 58′	170°17′	169°47′	168°52′	168°24′	168°01′	166°47′

——————   Temperature at the surface.
— — — —   „   at a depth of 30 metres.
—·—·—·—   „   at the bottom.

0   50   100 150 200
Depth in metres.

which is separated by a ridge from the warmer water on the
American side.

If we examine a map of Siberia we shall find, as I have
already pointed out, that its coasts at most places are straight,
and are thus neither indented with deep fjords surrounded with
high mountains like the west coast of Norway, nor protected
by an archipelago of islands like the greater part of the coasts
of Scandinavia and Finland. Certain parts of the Chukch
Peninsula, especially its south-eastern portion, form the only
exception to this rule. Several small fjords here cut into

the coasts, which consist of stratified granitic rocks, and in the
offing two large and several small rocky islands form an archipelago, separated from the mainland by the deep Senjavin
Sound. The wish to give our naturalists an opportunity of
once more prosecuting their examination of the natural history
of the Chukch Peninsula, and the desire to study one of the
few parts of the Siberian coast which in all probability were
formerly covered with inland ice, led me to choose this place
for the second anchorage of the *Vega* on the Asiatic side south
of Behring's Straits. The *Vega* accordingly anchored here on
the forenoon of the 28th July, but not, as was at first intended, in Glasenapp Harbour, because it was still occupied by
unbroken ice, but in the mouth of the most northerly of the
fjords, Konyam Bay.

This portion of the Chukch Peninsula had been visited before
us by the corvette *Senjavin*, commanded by Captain, afterwards
Admiral, Fr. Lütke, and by an English Franklin Expedition on
board the *Plover*, commanded by Captain Moore. Lütke stayed
here with his companions, the naturalists MERTENS, POSTELS, and
KITTLITZ, some days in August 1828, during which the harbour
was surveyed and various observations in ethnography and the
natural sciences made. Moore wintered at this place in 1848-49.
I have already stated that we have his companion, Lieut. W. H.
Hooper, to thank for very valuable information relating to the
tribes which live in the neighbourhood. The region appears to
have been then inhabited by a rather dense population. Now
there lived at the bay where we had anchored only three
reindeer-Chukch families, and the neighbouring islands must
at the time have been uninhabited, or perhaps the arrival of
the *Vega* may not have been observed, for no natives came on
board, which otherwise would probably have been the case.

The shore at the south-east part of Konyam Bay, in which
the *Vega* now lay at anchor for a couple of days, consists of a
rather desolate bog, in which a large number of cranes were
breeding. Farther into the country several mountain summits
rise to a height of nearly 600 metres. The collections of the
zoologists and botanists on this shore were very scanty, but on
the north side of the bay, to which excursions were made with
the steam-launch, grassy slopes were met with, with pretty high
bushy thickets and a great variety of flowers, which enriched
Dr. Kjellman's collection of the higher plants from the north
coast of Asia with about seventy species. Here were found too
the first land mollusca (Succinea, Limax, Helix, Pupa, &c.) on
the Chukch Peninsula.[1]

---

[1] We have already found some land mollusca at Port Clarence, but none
at St. Lawrence Bay. The northernmost *find* of such animals now known

We also visited the dwellings of the reindeer-Chukch families. They resembled the Chukch tents we had seen before, and the mode of life of the inhabitants differed little from that of the coast-Chukches, with whom we passed the winter. They were even clothed in the same way, excepting that the men wore a number of small bells in the belt. The number of the reindeer which the three families owned was, according to an enumeration which I made when the herd had with evident pleasure settled down at noon in warm sunshine on a snow-field in the neighbourhood of the tents, only about 400, thus considerably fewer than is required to feed three Lapp families. The Chukches have instead a better supply of fish, and, above all, better hunting than the Lapps; they also do not drink any coffee, and themselves collect a part of their food from the vegetable kingdom. The natives received us in a very friendly way, and offered to sell or rather barter three reindeer, a transaction which on account of our hasty departure was not carried into effect.

The mountains in the neighbourhood of Konyam Bay were high and split up into pointed summits with deep valleys still partly filled with snow. No glaciers appear to exist there at present. Probably however the fjords here and the sounds, like St. Lawrence Bay, Kolyutschin Bay, and probably all the other deeper bays on the coast of the Chukch Peninsula, have been excavated by former glaciers. It may perhaps be uncertain whether a true inland-ice covered the whole country; it is certain that the ice-cap did not extend over the plains of Siberia, where it can be proved that no Ice Age in a Scandinavian sense ever existed, and where the state of the land from the Jurassic period onwards was indeed subjected to some changes, but to none of the thoroughgoing mundane revolutions which in former times geologists loved to depict in so bright colours. At least the direction of the river appears to have been unchanged since then. Perhaps even the difference between the Siberia where Chikanovski's *Ginko* woods grew and the mammoth roamed about, and that where now at a limited depth under the surface constantly frozen ground is to be met with, depends merely on the isothermal lines having sunk slightly towards the equator.

The neighbourhood of Konyam Bay consists of crystalline rocks, granite poor in mica, and mica-schist lowermost, and then grey non-fossiliferous carbonate of lime, and last of all magnesian schists, porphyry, and quartzites. On the summits of the hills the granite has a rough trachytic appearance, but does not pass into true trachyte. Here however we are already in the

was made by Von Middendorff, who found a species of Physa on the Taimur Peninsula.

After a Photograph by L. Detmider

neighbourhood of the volcanic hearths of Kamchatka, which for
instance is shown by the hot spring, which Hooper discovered
not far from the coast during a sledge journey towards Behring's
Straits. In the middle of the severe cold of February its waters
had a temperature of + 69° C. Hot steam and drifting snow
combined had thrown over the spring a lofty vault of dazzling
whiteness formed of masses of snow converted into ice and
covered with ice-crystals. The Chukches themselves appear
to have found the contrast striking between the hot spring
from the interior of the earth and the cold, snow, and ice on its
surface. They offered blue glass beads to the spring, and
showed Hooper, as something remarkable, that it was possible
to boil fish in it, though the mineral water gave the boiled fish
a bitter unpleasant taste.[1]

The interior of Konyam Bay was during our stay there still
covered by an unbroken sheet of ice. This broke up on the
afternoon of the 30th July, and had almost, rotten as it was,
suddenly brought the voyage of the *Vega* to a termination by
pressing her ashore. Fortunately the danger was observed in
time. Steam was got up, the anchor weighed, and the vessel
removed to the open part of the fjord. As on this account
several cubic feet of coal had to be used for getting up steam, as
our hitherto abundant stock of coal must now be saved, and as
in the last place I was still urged forward by the fear that a
too lengthened delay in sending home despatches might not
only cause much anxiety but also lead to a heavy expenditure
of money, I preferred to sail on immediately rather than to
enter a safer harbour in the neighbourhood from which the
scientific work might continue to be prosecuted.

The course was now shaped for the north-west point of St.
Lawrence Island. A little off Senjavin Sound we saw drift-ice
for the last time. On the whole the quantity of ice which drifts
down through Behring's Straits into the Pacific is not very
great, and most of that which is met with in summer on the
Asiatic side of the Behring Sea, is evidently formed in fjords and
bays along the coast. South of Behring's Straits accordingly I
saw not a single iceberg nor any large block of glacier-ice, but
only even and very rotten fields of bay-ice.

The *Vega* was anchored on the 31st July in an open bay on
the north-western side of St. Lawrence Island. This island,
called by the natives Enguae, is the largest one between the
Aleutian Islands and Behring's Straits. It lies nearer Asia

---

[1] That a fire-emitting mountain was to be found in Siberia east of the
Yenisej is already mentioned in a treatise by Isaak Massa, inserted in
Hessal Gerritz, *Detectio Freti*, Amsterdam, 1612. The rumour about the
volcanoes of Kamchatka thus appears to have reached Europe at that early
date.

than America, but is considered to belong to the latter, for
which reason it was handed over along with the Alaska
Territory by Russia to the United States.   The island is inhabited by a few Eskimo families, who have commercial relations
with their Chukch neighbours on the Russian side, and therefore
have adopted some words from their language.   Their dress also

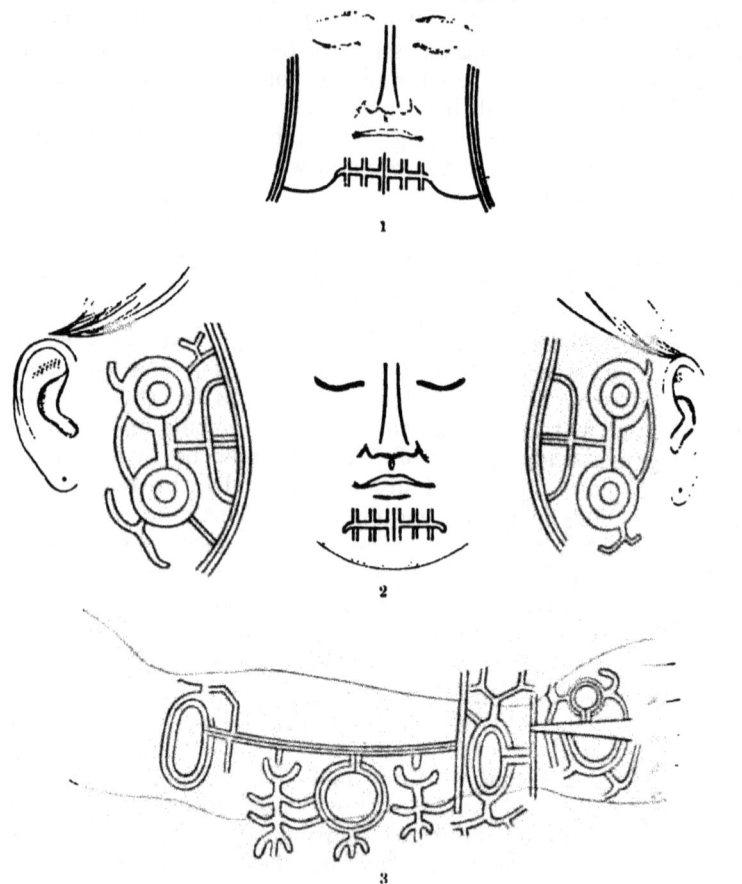

TATTOOING PATTERNS, FROM ST. LAWRENCE ISLAND.
1, 2. Face-tattooing.   3. Arm-tattooing.
After drawings by A. Stuxberg.

resembles that of the Chukches, with the exception that, wanting reindeer-skin, they use *pesks* made of the skins of birds and
marmots.   Like the Chukches and Eskimo they use overcoats
of pieces of seal-gut sewed together.   On St. Lawrence Island
their dress is much ornamented, chiefly with tufts of feathers of
the sea-fowl that breed in innumerable flocks on the island.   It

en appears that gut clothes are made here for sale to other
ibes; otherwise it would be difficult to explain how Kotzebue's
ilors could in half an hour purchase at a single encampment
)0 coats of this kind. At the time of our visit all the natives
ent bareheaded, the men with their black tallow-like hair
ipped to the root, with the exception of the common small
irder above the forehead. The women wore their hair
aited and adorned with beads, and were much tattooed, partly
ter very intricate patterns, as is shown by the accompanying
oodcuts. Like the children they mostly went barefooted and
irelegged. They were well grown, and many did not look ill,
it all were merciless beggars, who actually followed our
aturalists on their excursions on land.

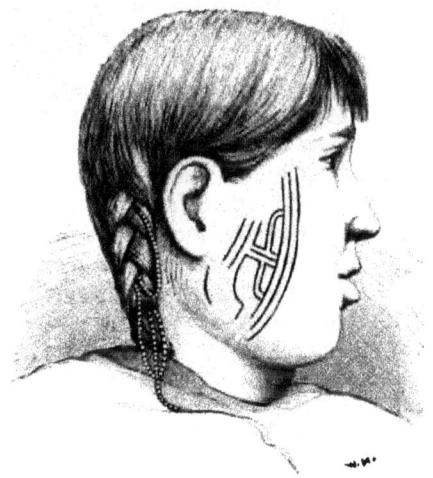

TATTOOED WOMAN, FROM ST. LAWRENCE ISLAND.
After a drawing by A. Stuxberg.

The summer-tents were irregular, but pretty clean and light
its of gut, stretched on a frame of drift-wood and whale-bones.
ie winter dwellings were now abandoned. They appeared
consist of holes in the earth, which were covered above, with
e exception of a square opening, with drift-wood and turf.
uring winter a sealskin tent was probably stretched over
is opening, but it was removed for the time, probably to
rmit the summer heat to penetrate into the hole and melt
e ice, which had collected during winter on its walls. At
veral tents we found large under-jaws of whales, fixed in the
ound. They were perforated above, and I suppose that the
nter-tent, in the absence of other framework, was stretched
er them. Masses of whale-bones lay thrown up along the

shore, evidently belonging to the same species as those we collected at the shore-dunes at Pitlekaj. In the neighbourhood of the tents graves were also found. The corpses had been placed, unburned, in some cleft among the rocks which are split up by the frost, and often converted into immense stone mounds. They had afterwards been covered with stones, and skulls of the bear and the seal and whale-bones had been offered or scattered around the grave.

North-east of the anchorage the shore was formed of low hills rising with a steep slope from the sea. Here and there ruinlike cliffs projected from the hills, resembling those we saw on the coast of Chukch Land. But the rock here consisted of the same sort of granite which formed the lowermost stratum of Konyam Bay. It was principally at the foot of these slopes that the natives erected their dwellings. South-west of the anchorage commenced a very extensive plain, which towards the interior of the island was marshy, but along the coast formed a firm, even, grassy meadow exceedingly rich in flowers. It was gay with the large sunflower-like *Arnica Pseudo-Arnica*, and another species of Senecio (*Senecio frigidus*); the *Oxytropis nigrescens*, close-tufted and rich in flowers, not stunted here as in Chukch Land; several species of Pedicularis in their fullest bloom (*P. sudetica, P. Langsdorfii, P. Oederi* and *P. capitata*); the stately snow auricula (*Primula nivalis*), and the pretty *Primula borealis*. As characteristic of the vegetation at this place may also be mentioned several ranunculi, an anemone (*Anemone narcissi flora*), a species of monkshood with flowers few indeed, but so much the larger on that account, large tufts of *Silene acaulis* and *Alsine macrocarpa*, studded with flowers, several Saxifrages, two Claytoniæ, the *Cl. acutifolia*, important as a food-plant in the housekeeping of the Chukches, and the tender *Cl. sarmentosa* with its delicate, slightly rose-coloured flowers, and, where the ground was stony, long but yet flowerless, slightly green tendrils of the favourite plant of our homeland, the *Linnæa borealis*. Dr. Kjellman thus reaped a rich harvest of higher plants; and a fine collection of land and marine animals, lichens and algæ was also made here. The ground consisted of sand in which lay large granite blocks, which we in Sweden would call erratic. They appeared however not to have been transported hither, but to be lying *in situ*, having along with the sand probably arisen through the disintegration of the rocks.

In the sea we found not a few algæ and a true littoral evertebrate-fauna, poor in species indeed, something which is completely absent in the Polar seas proper. As I walked along the coast I saw five pretty large self-coloured greyish-brown seals, sunning themselves on stones a short distance from land. They belonged to a species which I had never seen in the Polar seas. As there was no boat at hand, I forbade the hunters that accompanied me, though the seals were within range, to test their skill as shots upon them. Perhaps they were females of *Histriophoca fasciata*, whose beautifully marked skin (of the male) I had seen and described at St. Lawrence Bay. The natives had a few dogs but no reindeer, which however might find food on the island in thousands. No *kayaks* were in use, but large *baydars* of the same construction as those of the Chukches.

St. Lawrence Island was discovered during Behring's first voyage, but the first who came into contact with the natives was Otto von Kotzebue [1] (on the 27th June 1816, and the 20th July 1817). The inhabitants had not before seen any Europeans, and they received the foreigners with a friendliness which exposed Kotzebue to severe suffering. Of this he gives the following account :—

"So long as the naturalists wandered about on the hills I stayed with my acquaintances, who when they found that I was the commander, invited me into their tents. Here a dirty skin was spread on the floor, on which I had to sit, and then they came in one after the other, embraced me, rubbed their noses hard against mine, and finished their caresses by spitting in their hands and then stroking me several times over the face. Although these proofs of friendship gave me very little pleasure, I bore all patiently; the only thing I did to lighten their caresses somewhat was to distribute tobacco leaves. These the natives received with great pleasure, but they wished immediately to renew their proofs of friendship. Now I betook myself with speed to knives, scissors, and beads, and by distributing some succeeded in averting a new attack. But a still greater calamity awaited me when in order to refresh me bodily they brought forward a wooden tray with whale blubber. Nauseous as this food is to a European stomach I boldly attacked the dish. This, along with new presents which I distributed, impressed the seal on the friendly relation between us. After the meal our hosts made arrangements for dancing and singing, which was accompanied on a little tambourine." [2]

[1] Kotzebue says that he was the first seafarer who visited the island. This however is incorrect. Billings landed there on the 1st August (21st July), 1791. From the vessel some natives were seen and a *baydar* which was rowed along the coast. The natives however were frightened by some gunshots fired as a signal (Sarytchev's *Reise*, ii. p. 91, Sauer, p. 239). Billings says that the place where he landed (the south-east point of the island) was nearly covered with bones of sea-animals. It would be important to have these thoroughly examined, as it is not impossible that Steller's sea-cow (Rhytina) may in former times have occasionally come to this coast. At all events important contributions to a knowledge of the species of whales in Behring's Straits may be gained here.

[2] Otto von Kotzebue. *Entdeckungs-Reise an die Sud-See und nach der Behring-Strasse, 1815-18.* Weimar, 1821, i. p. 135 ; ii. p. 104 ; iii. pp. 171 and 178.

As von Kotzebue two days after sailed past the north point of the island he met three *baydars*. In one of them a man stood up, held up a little dog and pierced it through with his knife, as Kotzebue believed, as a sacrifice to the foreigners.[1]

Since 1817 several exploring expeditions have landed on St. Lawrence Island, but always only for a few hours. It is very dangerous to stay long here with a vessel. For there is no known haven on the coast of this large island, which is surrounded by an open sea. In consequence of the heavy swell which almost constantly prevails here, when the surrounding sea is clear of ice, it is difficult to land on the island with a boat, and the vessel anchored in the open road is constantly exposed to be thrown by a storm rising unexpectedly upon the shore cliffs. This held good in fullest measure of the *Vega's* anchorage, and Captain Palander was on this account anxious to leave the place as soon as possible. On the 2nd August at three o'clock in the afternoon we accordingly resumed our voyage. The course was shaped at first for Karaginsk Island on the east coast of Kamchatka, where it was my intention to stay some days in order to get an opportunity of making a comparison between the natural conditions of middle Kamchatka and the Chukch Peninsula. But as unfavourable winds delayed our passage longer than I had calculated on, I abandoned, though unwillingly, the plan of landing there. The Commander's Island became instead the nearest goal of the expedition. Here the *Vega* anchored on the 14th August in a very indifferent harbour completely open to the west, north-west, and south, lying on the west side of Behring Island, between the main island and a small island lying off it.

CHAPTER XV.

The position of Behring Island—Its inhabitants—The discovery of the island by Behring—Behring's death—Steller—The former and present Fauna on the island: foxes, sea-otters, sea-cows, sea-lions, and sea-bears—Collection of bones of the Rhytina—Visit to a "rookery"—Toporkoff Island—Alexander Dubovski—Voyage to Yokohama—Lightning-stroke.

BEHRING ISLAND is situated between 54° 40' and 55° 25' N.L. and 165° 40' and 166° 40' E.L. from Greenwich. It is the westernmost and nearest Kamchatka of the islands in the long chain formed

---

[1] On the days after our arrival at Pitlekaj several dogs were killed. I then believed that this was done because the natives were unwilling to feed them during winter, but it is not impossible that they sacrificed them to avert the misfortunes which it was feared the arrival of the foreigners would bring with it.

by volcanic action, which bounds the Behring Sea on the south between 51° and 56° N.L. Together with the neighbouring Copper Island and some small islands and rocks lying round about, it forms a peculiar group of islands separated from the Aleutian Islands proper, named, after the rank of the great sea-arer who perished here, Commander's or Commandirski Islands. They belong not to America but to Asia, and are Russian territory. Notwithstanding this the American Alaska Company has acquired the right of hunting there,[1] and maintains on the main islands two not inconsiderable commercial stations, which supply the inhabitants, several hundreds in number, with provisions and manufactured goods, the company buying from them instead furs, principally the skin of an eared seal (the sea-cat or sea-bear), of which from 20,000 to 50,000[2] are killed yearly in the region. Some Russian authorities are also settled on the island to guard the rights of the Russian state and maintain order. Half a dozen serviceable wooden houses have been built here as dwellings for the officials of the Russian Government and the American Company, for storehouses, shops, &c. The natives live partly in very roomy and in the inside not uncomfortable turf houses, partly in small wooden houses which the company endeavours gradually to substitute for the former, by yearly ordering some wooden buildings and presenting them to the most deserving of the population. Every family has its own house There is also a Greek-Catholic church and a spacious schoolhouse. The latter is intended for Aleutian children. The school was unfortunately closed at the time of our visit, but, to judge by the writing books which lay about in the schoolroom, the education here is not to be despised. The specimens of writing at least were distinguished by their cleanness, and by an even and beautiful style. At "the colony" the houses were collected at one place into a village, situated near the sea-shore at a suitable distance from the fishing ground in a valley overgrown in summer by a rich vegetation, but treeless and surrounded by treeless rounded heights. From the sea this village has the look of a

[1] In February 1871 the right of hunting on these islands was granted by the Russian government to Hutchinson, Kohl, Philippeus & Co., who have made over their rights to the Alaska Commercial Company of San Francisco.
[2] According to a communication made to me by Mr. Henry W. Elliott, who, in order to study the fur-bearing seals in the North Behring Sea, lived a considerable time at the Seal Islands (Pribylov's Islands, &c.) on the American side, and has given an exceedingly interesting account of the animal life there in his work : *A Report upon the Condition of Affairs in the Territory of Alaska*, Washington, 1875: the statement in my report to Dr. Dickson, founded on oral communications of Europeans whom I met with at Behring Island, that from 50,000 to 100,000 animals are killed yearly at Behring and Copper Islands, is thus probably somewhat exaggerated.

northern fishing station. There are besides some scattered houses here and there on other parts of the island, for instance on its north-eastern side, where the potato is said to be cultivated on a small scale, and at the fishing place on the north side where there are two large sheds for skins and a number of very small earth-holes used only during the slaughter season.

Behring Island, with regard both to geography and natural history, is one of the most remarkable islands in the north part of the Pacific. It was here that Behring after his last unfortunate voyage in the sea which now bears his name, finished his long course as an explorer. He was however survived by many of

THE "COLONY" ON COPPER ISLAND.
After a photograph.

his followers, among them by the physician and naturalist Steller, to whom we owe a masterpiece seldom surpassed—a sketch of the natural conditions and animal life on the island, never before visited by man, where he involuntarily passed the time from the middle of November 1741, to the end of August 1742.[1]

[1] Original accounts of the wintering on Behring Island are to be found in Müller's *Sammlung Russischer Geschichte*, St. Petersburg, 1758, iii. pp. 228-238 and 242-268; (Steller's) *Topographische und physikalische Beschreibung der Beringsinsel* (Pallas' *Neue Nordische Beyträge*, St. Petersburg and Leipzig, 1781-83, ii. p. 225); G. W. Steller's *Tagebuch seiner Seereise aus dem Petripaulus Hafen . . . und seiner Begebenheiten auf der Rückreise* (Pallas' *Neueste Nordische Beyträge*, St. Petersburg and Leipzig, 1793-96, i. p. 130; ii. p. 1).

It was the desire to procure for our museums the skins or skeletons of the many remarkable mammalia occurring here, also to compare the present state of the island which for nearly a century and a half has been exposed to the unsparing thirst of man for sport and plunder, with Steller's spirited and picturesque description, which led me to include a visit to the island in the plan of the expedition. The accounts I got at Behring Island from the American newspapers of the anxiety which our wintering had caused in Europe led me indeed to make our stay there shorter than I at first intended. Our harvest of collections and observations was at all events extraordinarily abundant. But before I proceed to give an account of our own stay on the island, I must devote a few words to its discovery and the first wintering there, which has a quite special interest from the island having never before been trodden by the foot of man. The abundant animal life, then found there, gives us therefore one of the exceedingly few representations we possess of the animal world as it was before man, the lord of the creation, appeared.

After Behring's vessel had drifted about a considerable time at random in the Behring Sea, in consequence of the severe scurvy-epidemic, which had spread to nearly all the men on board, without any dead-reckoning being kept, and finally without sail or helmsman, literally at the mercy of wind and waves, those on board on the $\frac{15}{4}$th November, 1741, sighted land, off whose coast the vessel was anchored the following day at 5 o'clock P.M. An hour after the cable gave way, and an enormous sea threw the vessel towards the shore-cliffs. All appeared to be already lost. But the vessel, instead of being driven ashore by new waves, came unexpectedly into a basin $4\frac{1}{2}$ fathoms deep surrounded by rocks and with quite still water, being connected with the sea only by a single narrow opening. If the unmanageable vessel had not drifted just to that place it would certainly have gone to pieces, and all on board would have perished.

It was only with great difficulty that the sick crew could put out a boat in which Lieut. Waxel and Steller landed. They found the land uninhabited, devoid of wood, and uninviting. But a rivulet with fresh clear water purled yet unfrozen down the mountain sides, and in the sand hills along the coast were found some deep pits, which when enlarged and covered with sails could be used as dwellings. The men who could still stand on their legs all joined in this work. On the $\frac{19}{8}$th November the sick could be removed to land, but, as often happens, many died when they were brought out of the cabin into the fresh air, others while they were being carried from the vessel or immediately after they came to land. All in whom the scurvy had taken the upper hand to that extent that they were already lying in bed

NATIVES OF BEHRING ISLAND.

After a photograph.

on board the vessel, died. The survivors had scarcely time or strength to bury the dead, and found it difficult to protect the corpses from the hungry foxes that swarmed on the island and had not yet learned to be afraid of man. On the $\frac{29}{9}$th Behring was carried on land ; he was already much reduced and dejected, and could not be induced to take exercise. He died on the $\frac{19}{8}$th December.

VITUS BEHRING was a Dane by birth, and when a young man had already made voyages to the East and West Indies. In 1707 he was received into the Russian navy as officer, and as such took part in all the warlike enterprises of that fleet against Sweden. He was in a way buried alive on the island that now bears his name, for at last he did not permit his men to remove the sand that rolled down upon him from the walls of the sand pit in which he rested. For he thought that the sand warmed his chilled body. Before the corpse could be properly buried it had therefore to be dug out of its bed, a circumstance which appears to have produced a disagreeable impression on the survivors. The two lieutenants, Waxel and Chitrov, had kept themselves in pretty good health at sea, but now fell seriously ill, though they recovered. Only the physician of the expedition, Georg Wilhelm Steller, was all the time in good health, and that a single man of the whole crew escaped with his life was clearly due to the skill of this gifted man, to his invincible energy and his cheerful and sanguine disposition. These qualities were also abundantly tested during the wintering. On the night before the $\frac{\text{10th December.}}{\text{29th November.}}$ the vessel, on which no watch was kept, because all the men were required on land to care for the sick, was cast ashore by a violent E.S.E. storm. So great a quantity of provisions was thus lost, that the remaining stock was not sufficient by itself to yield enough food for all the men during a whole winter. Men were therefore sent out in all directions to inquire into the state of the land. They returned with the information that the vessel had stranded not, as was hoped at first, on the mainland but on an un-inhabited, woodless island. It was thus clear to the ship-wrecked men that in order to be saved they could rely only on their judgment and strength. At the beginning they found that if any provisions were to be reserved for the voyage home, it was necessary that they should support them-selves during winter to a considerable extent by hunting. They did not like to use the flesh of the fox for food, and at first kept to that of the sea-otter. This animal at present is very scarce on Behring Island, but at that time the shore was covered with whole herds of it. They had no fear of man, came from curiosity straight to the fires, and did not

un away when any one approached.   A dear-bought experience,
however, soon taught them caution; at all events, from 800
to 900 head were taken, a splendid catch when we consider
that the skin of this animal at the Chinese frontier fetched
from 80 to 100 roubles each. Besides, in the beginning of
winter two whales stranded on the island. The shipwrecked
men considered these their provision depôts, and appear to
have preferred whale blubber to the flesh of the sea-otter,
which had an unpleasant taste and was tough as leather.[1]

In spring the sea-otters disappeared, but now there came to
the island in their stead other animals in large herds, viz.
sea-bears, seals, and sea-lions. The flesh of the young sea-
lion was considered a great delicacy.[2] When the sea-otters
became scarcer and more shy and difficult to catch, the shipwrecked men found means also to kill sea-cows, whose flesh
Steller considered equal to beef. Several barrels of their flesh
were even salted to serve as provisions during the return
journey. As the land became clear of snow in the middle of
April, Waxel called together the forty-five men who survived
to a consultation regarding the steps that ought to be taken
in order to reach the mainland. Among many different proposals,
that was adopted of building a new vessel with the materials
supplied by the stranded one. The three ship-carpenters who
had been on board were dead. But fortunately there was
among the survivors a Cossack, SAVA STARODUBZOV, who had
taken part as a workman in shipbuilding at Okotsk, and
now undertook to manage the building of the new vessel.
With necessity for a teacher he also succeeded in executing
his commission, so that a new *St. Peter* was launched on the
$\frac{31\text{st}}{10\text{th}}$ August, 1742. The vessel was forty feet long, thirteen
feet beam, and six and a half feet deep, and sailed as well
as if built by an experienced master of his craft, but on the
other hand leaked seriously in a high sea. The return voyage
at all events passed successfully. On the $\frac{5\text{th September}}{25\text{th August}}$ Kamchatka
was sighted, and two days after the *St. Peter* anchored at
Petropaulovsk, where the shipwrecked men found a storehouse with an *abundant* stock of provisions according to their

[1] According to Müller, whose statements (based on communications by
Waxel ?) often differ from those of Steller. The latter says that the flesh
of the sea-otter is better than that of the seal, and a good antidote to
scurvy. The flesh of the young sea-otter might even compete with lamb
as a delicacy.

[2] To judge by what is stated in Steller's description of Behring Island
(*Neue nord. Beytr.*, ii. p. 290) no one would have dared to attack " diese
grimmigen Thiere," and the only sea-lion eaten during the winter was an
animal wounded at Kamchatka and thrown up dead on the coast of
Behring Island. The fin-like feet were the most delicate part of the sea-
lion.

ideas, which probably were not pitched very high. Next year
they sailed on with their Behring-Island-built vessel to Okotsk.
On their arrival there, of the seventy-six persons who originally
took part in the expedition, thirty-two were dead. At Kamchatka they had all been considered dead, and the effects they
left behind them had been scattered and divided. Steller
voluntarily remained some time longer in Kamchatka in order
to carry on his researches in natural history. Unfortunately
he drew upon himself the ill-will of the authorities, in consequence
of the free way in which he criticised their abuses. This led
to a trial at the court at Irkutsk. He was, indeed, found
innocent, and obtained permission to travel home, but at Zoli-
kamsk he was overtaken by an express with orders to bring
him back to Irkutsk. On the way thither he met another
express with renewed permission to travel to Europe. But the
powers of the strong and formerly healthy man were exhausted
by this hunting backwards and forwards across the immeasur-
able deserts of Siberia. He died soon after, on the $\frac{23rd}{12th}$ November,
1746, at Tjumeu, only thirty-seven years of age, of a fever
by which he was attacked during the journey.[1]

The immense quantity of valuable furs brought home by
the survivors of Behring's so unfortunate third voyage affected
the fur-dealers, Cossacks, and hunters of Siberia much in the
same way as the rumour about Eldorado or about the riches of the
Casic Dobaybe did the Spanish discoverers of middle and southern
America. Numerous expeditions were fitted out to the new
land rich in furs, where extensive territories previously unknown
were made tributary to the Czar of Russia. Most of these
expeditions landed on Behring Island during the voyage out
and home, and in a short time wrought a complete change in the
fauna of the island. Thanks to Steller's spirited sketch of the
animal life he observed there, we have also an opportunity of
forming an idea of the alteration in the fauna which man brings
about in a land in which he settles.

Arctic foxes were found in incredible numbers on the island
during the wintering of the Behring expedition. They not only

[1] According to Müller's official report, probably written for the purpose
of refuting the rumours regarding Steller's fate current in the scientific
circles of Europe. According to the biography prefixed to Georg Wilhelm
Steller's *Beschreibung von dem Lande Kamtschatka, herausgegeben von J.
B. S.* (Scherer), Frankfurt and Leipzig, 1774, Steller had in 1745 begun
his return to St. Petersburg, and was already beyond Novgorod, when he
received orders to appear before the court at Irkutsk. After a year he
obtained permission to travel to St. Petersburg, but when he came to the
neighbourhood of Moscow, he received a new order to return, and for
further security he was placed under a guard. They had travelled a good
way into Siberia, when he froze to death while the guard went into a
public-house to warm themselves and quench their thirst.

ate up everything that was at all eatable that was left in the open air, but forced their way as well by day as by night into the houses and carried off all that they could, even such things as were of no use whatever to them, as knives, sticks, sacks, shoes and stockings. Even if anything had been never so well buried and loaded with stones, they not only found the place but even pushed away the stones with their shoulders like men. Though they could not eat what they found, they carried it off and concealed it under stones. In such a case some foxes stood on guard, and if a man approached all assisted in speedily concealing the stolen article in the sand so that no trace of it was left. When any of the men slept out of doors at night the foxes carried off their caps and gloves, and made their way under the covering. They nosed the noses of the sleepers to find out whether they were dead or living, and attempted to nibble at any who held their breath. As the female sea-lions and sea-bears often suffocate their young during sleep, the foxes every morning made an inspection of the place where these animals lie down in immense herds, and if they found a dead young one they immediately helped each other, like good scavengers, to carry away the carcase. When men were employed out of doors they had to drive the foxes away with sticks, and they became, in consequence of the slyness and cunning with which they knew how to carry out their thefts and the skill which they showed in combining to gain an end which they could not compass as single animals, actually dangerous to the shipwrecked men, by whom they were therefore heartily hated, pursued, tormented, and killed. Since then thousands and thousands of foxes have been killed on Behring Island by the fur-hunters. Now they are so scarce that during our stay there we did not see one. Those that still survive, besides, as the Europeans settled on the island informed me, do not wear the precious dark blue dress formerly common, but the white, which is of little value. On the neighbouring Copper Island, however, there are still dark blue foxes in pretty large numbers.[1]

[1] As early as Schelechov's wintering in 1783-84 the foxes on Behring Island were principally white. During Steller's wintering, over a third of the foxes on the island had a bluish fur (*Neue nord. Beytr.*, ii. p. 277). In the year 1747-48 a fur hunter, Cholodilov, caught on Behring Island 1,481 blue foxes and 350 sea-otters, and the following year another hunter returned with over a thousand sea-otters and two thousand blue foxes, which probably were also caught on Behring and Copper Islands (*Neue Nachrichten von denen neuentdeckten Inseln*, Hamburg u. Leipzig, 1766, p. 20). In the year 1751-53 Jugov caught on the same island 790 sea-otters, 6,844 black and 200 white foxes, and 2,212 sea-bears (*loc. cit.* p. 22). In 1752-53 the crew of a vessel belonging to the Irkutsk merchant, Nikifor Trapeznikoff, caught on Behring Island 5 sea-otters, 1,222 foxes (colour not stated), and 2,500 sea-bears (*loc. cit.* p. 32). It thus appears as if the

Nine hundred sea-otters were killed here by Steller and his companions in 1741-42. The following quotation is taken from Steller's description of this animal which is now so shy at the sight of man :—

"With respect to playfulness it surpasses every other animal that lives either in the sea or on the land. When it comes up out of the sea it shakes the water from its fur, and dresses it as a cat its head with its fore-paws, stretches its body, arranges its hair, throws its head this way and that, contemplating itself and its beautiful fur with evident satisfaction. The animal is so much taken up with this dressing of itself, that while thus employed it may easily be approached and killed. If one strikes a sea-otter twenty times across the back, it bears it patiently, but if its large beautiful tail be struck once it turns its head to its pursuer, as if to offer it as a mark for his club in place of the tail. If it eludes an attack it makes the most laughable gestures to the hunter. It looks at him, placing one foot above the head as if to protect it from the sunlight, throws itself on its back, and turning to its enemy as if in scorn scratches itself on the belly and thighs. The male and female are much attached to each other, embrace and kiss each other like men. The female is also very fond of its young. When attacked she never leaves it in the lurch, and when danger is not near she plays with it in a thousands ways, almost like a child-loving mother with her young ones, throws it sometimes up in the air and catches it with her fore-feet like a ball, swims about with it in her bosom, throws it away now and then to let it exercise itself in the art of swimming, but takes it to herself with kisses and caresses when it is tired."

According to recent researches the *sea-otter*, sea-beaver or Kamchatka-beaver (*Enhydris lutris*, Lin.) is a species neither of the otter nor the beaver, but belongs to a peculiar genus, allied to a certain extent to the walrus. Even this animal, unsurpassed in the beauty of its skin, has been long since driven away not only from Behring Island but also from most of the hunting-grounds where it was commonly killed by thousands, and if an effective law be not soon put in force to keep the hunting in bounds, and check the war of extermination which greed now carries on against it, no longer with clubs and darts but with powder and breechloaders, the sea-otter will meet the same fate which has already befallen Steller's sea-cow. Of the sea-lions (*Eumetopias Stelleri*, Lesson), which in Steller's time were found

eager hunting had an influence not only on the number of the animals but also on their colour, the variety in greatest demand becoming also *relatively* less common than before.

in abundance on the shore cliffs of Behring Island, there are now only single animals there along with the sea-bears (*Otaria ursina*, Lin.); and finally, the most remarkable of all the old mammalia of Behring Island, the great sea-cow, is completely extinct.

Steller's sea-cow (*Rhytina Stelleri*, Cuvier) in a way took the place of the cloven-footed animals among the marine mammalia. The sea-cow was of a dark-brown colour, sometimes varied with white spots or streaks. The thick leathery skin was covered with hair which grew together so as to form an exterior skin, which was full of vermin and resembled the bark of an old oak. The full-grown animal was from twenty-eight to thirty-five English feet in length and weighed about sixty-seven cwt. The head was small in proportion to the large thick body, the neck short, the body diminishing rapidly behind. The short fore-leg terminated abruptly without fingers or nails, but was overgrown with a number of short thickly-placed brush-hairs; the hind-leg was replaced by a tail-fin resembling a whale's. The animal wanted teeth, but was instead provided with two masticating-plates, one in the gum, the other in the under jaw. The udders of the female, which abounded in milk, were placed between the fore-limbs. The flesh and milk resembled those of horned cattle, indeed in Steller's opinion surpassed them. The sea-cows were almost constantly employed in pasturing on the sea-weed which grew luxuriantly on the coast, moving the head and neck while so doing much in the same way as an ox. While they pastured they showed great voracity, and did not allow themselves to be disturbed in the least by the presence of man. One might even touch them without their being frightened or disturbed. They entertained great attachment to each other, and when one was harpooned the others made incredible attempts to rescue it.

When Steller came to Behring Island, the sea-cows pastured along the shore, collected like cattle into herds. The ship-wrecked men, for want of suitable implements, did not hunt them at first. It was only after a thoughtless love of slaughter had driven all other animals suitable for food far from their winter quarters, that they began to devise means to catch the sea-cow also. They endeavoured to harpoon the animal with a strong iron hook made for the purpose, and then drag it to land. The first attempt was made on the 1st June/21st May. 1742, but it was unsuccessful. It was not until after many renewed attempts that they at last succeeded in killing and catching a number of animals, and dragging them at high water so near land that they were dry at ebb. They were so heavy that forty men were required to do this. We may conclude from these particulars that the number of sea-cows killed during the first wintering on Behring Island was not very large. For the first one was killed only six weeks before the shipwrecked men left the island, and the hunting thus fell at a time when they could leave the building of the vessel to occupy themselves in that way only in case of necessity. Besides, only two animals were required to yield flesh-food to all the men for the period in question.

It is remarkable that the sea-cow is so mentioned by later travellers only in passing, that this large animal, still hunted by Europeans in the time of Linnæus, would scarcely have been registered in the system of the naturalist if Steller had not wintered on Behring Island. What Krascheninnikov says of the sea-cow is wholly borrowed from Steller, and in the same way *nearly all* the statements of later naturalists as to its occurrence and mode of life. That this is actually the case is shown by the following abstract, *complete* as far as I know, of what is said of the sea-cow in the only original account of the first hunting voyages of the Russians to the Aleutian Islands, which was published at Hamburg and Leipzig in 1776 with the title, *New Nachrichten von denen neuentdeckten Insuln in der See zwischen Asien und Amerika, aus mitgetheilten Urkunden und Auszügen verfasset von J. L. S * * * (Scherer).*[1] In this book the sea-cow is mentioned at the following places :—

"Ivan Krassilnikoff's vessel started first in 1754 and arrived on the 8th October at Behring Island, where all the vessels fitted out for hunting the sea-otter on the remote islands are wont to pass the winter, in order to provide themselves with a sufficient stock of flesh of the sea-cow " (*loc. cit.* p. 38).

"The autumn storms, or rather the wish to take on board a stock of provisions, compelled them (a number of hunters sent out by the merchant Tolstyk under command of the Cossack Obeuchov) to touch at Commander's Island (Behring Island) where, during the winter up to the $\frac{24}{13}$th June, 1757, they obtained nothing else than sea-cows, sea-lions, and large seals. They found no sea-otters this year" (*ibid.* p. 40).

[1] From this little work, compiled from the original journals (Cf. Coxe, *Russian Discoveries*, 1780, p. vi.) we see that the undaunted courage and the resolution which, matched with other qualities not so praiseworthy, distinguished the *Promyschlenni* during their expeditions of exploration, tribute-collecting, and plunder from the Ob to Kamchatka, did not fail them in the attempt to force their way across the sea to America. It happens yearly that a ship's crew save themselves from destruction in the most extraordinary craft, for necessity has no law. But it is perhaps not so common that an exploring expedition, wrecked on an uninhabited treeless island, builds for itself of fragments from its own vessel, indeed even of driftwood, a new one in order to sail out on the ocean to discover new fishing-grounds or new wild tribes, willing to pay " jassak " to the adventurers. This however happened very frequently during the Russian voyages of discovery and hunting to the Aleutian Islands from 1745 to 1770, and it was remarkable that the craft built in this way were used for years, even after the return from the first voyage.

"They (a Russian hunting vessel under Studenzov in 1758) anded on Behring Island to kill sea-cows, as all vessels are accustomed to do" (*ibid.* p. 45).

"After Korovin in 1762 (on Behring Island) had provided himself with a sufficient stock of the flesh and hides of the sea-cow for his boats .... he sailed on" (*ibid.* p. 82).

In 1772 DMITRI BRAGIN wintered on Behring Island during a hunting voyage. In a journal kept at the request of Pallas, the large marine animals occurring on the island are enumerated, but not a word is said about the sea-cow (PALLAS, *Neue nordische Beyträge*, ii. p. 310).

SCHELECHOV passed the winter 1783-84 on Behring Island, but during the whole time he only succeeded in killing some white foxes, and in the narrative of the voyage there is not a word about the sea-cow (GRIGORI SCHELECHOV *russischen Kaufmanns erste und zweite Reise*, &c., St. Petersburg, 1793).

Some further accounts of the sea-cow have been obtained through the mining engineer PET. JAKOVLEV, who visited Commander's Islands in 1755 in order to investigate the occurrence of copper on Copper Island. In the account of this voyage which he gave to Pallas there is not indeed one word about the sea-cow, but in 1867 PEKARSKI published in the *Memoirs* of the St. Petersburg Academy some extracts from Jakovlev's journal, from which it appears that the sea-cow already in his time was driven away from Copper Island. Jakovlev on this account, on the 27th November, 1755, laid a petition before the authorities on Kamchatka, for having the hunting of the sea-cow placed under restraint of law and the extermination of the animal thus prevented, a thoughtful act honourable to its author, which certainly ought to serve as a pattern in our times (J. FR. BRANDT, *Symbolæ Sirenologicæ, Mém. le l'Acad. de St. Pétersbourg*, t. xii. No. 1, 1861-68, p. 295).

In his account of Behring's voyage (1785-94) published in 1802, Sauer says, p. 181 : "Sea-cows were very common on Kamchatka and the Aleutian Islands,[1] when they were first

[1] The sea-cow does not appear to have ever occurred on the Aleutian Islands; on the other hand, according to Steller, dead sea-cows have sometimes been cast ashore on Kamchatka, where they even obtained from the Russians a peculiar name *kapustnick*, derived from the large quantity of sea-weed found in their stomach. It appears to me that this name, specially distinctive of a graminivorous animal, seems to indicate that on the first arrival of the Russians at Kamchatka the sea-cow actually visited occasionally the coasts of that peninsula. It is probable that in former times the sea-cow was to be met with as far south as the north part of Japan. Some scientific men have even conjectured that the animal may have occurred north of Behring's Straits. This however is improbable. Among the mass of subfossil bones of marine animals which we examined at Pitlekaj the bones of the sea-cow did not appear to be present.

discovered, but the last was killed on Behring Island in 1768, and none has been seen since then."

On the ground of the writings of which I have given an account above, and of various pieces of information collected during this century from the Russian authorities in the region, by the skilful conservator WOSNESSENSKI, the academicians von Baer and Brandt[1] came to the conclusion that the sea-cow had scarcely been seen by Europeans before the $\frac{18}{5}$th November, 1741, when Steller, the day after his landing on Behring Island, for the first time saw some strange animals pasturing with their heads under water on the shores of the island; and that the animal twenty-seven years afterwards, or in 1768, was completely exterminated. The latter statement however is undoubtedly incorrect; for, in the course of the many inquiries I made of the natives, I obtained distinct information that living sea-cows had been seen much later. A *creole* (that is, the offspring of a Russian and an Aleutian), who was sixty-seven years of age, of intelligent appearance and in the full possession of [his mental faculties, stated "that his father died in 1847 at the age of eighty-eight. He had come from Volhynia, his native place, to Behring Island at the age of eighteen, accordingly in 1777. The two or three first years of his stay there, i.e. till 1779 or 1780, sea-cows were still being killed as they pastured on sea-weed. The heart only was eaten, and the hide used for *baydars*.[2] In consequence of its thickness the hide was split in two, and the two pieces thus obtained had gone to make a *baydar* twenty feet long, seven and a half feet broad, and three feet deep. After that time no sea-cows had been killed."

There is evidence, however, that a sea-cow had been seen at the island still later. Two *creoles*, Feodor Mertchenin and Stepnoff, stated, that about twenty-five years ago at Tolstoj-mys, on the east side of the island, they had seen an animal unknown to them which was very thick before, but grew smaller behind, had small fore-feet, and appeared with a length of about fifteen feet above water, now raising itself up, now lowering itself. The animal " blew," not through blowholes, but through the mouth, which was somewhat drawn out. It was brown in colour, with some lighter spots. A black fin was wanting, but when the animal raised itself it was possible, on account of its great leanness, to see its backbone projecting. I instituted a through examination of both my informants. Their accounts

---

[1] Von Baer's and Brandt's numerous writings on the sea-cow are to be found in the publications of the St. Petersburg Academy.

[2] That the hide of the sea-cow was used for *baydars* is evident from the short extract given from Korovin's voyage. On hearing this "creole's" account I inquired whether there were not to be found remaining on the island any very old sea-cow skins that had been used for *baydars*, but the answer unfortunately was in the negative.

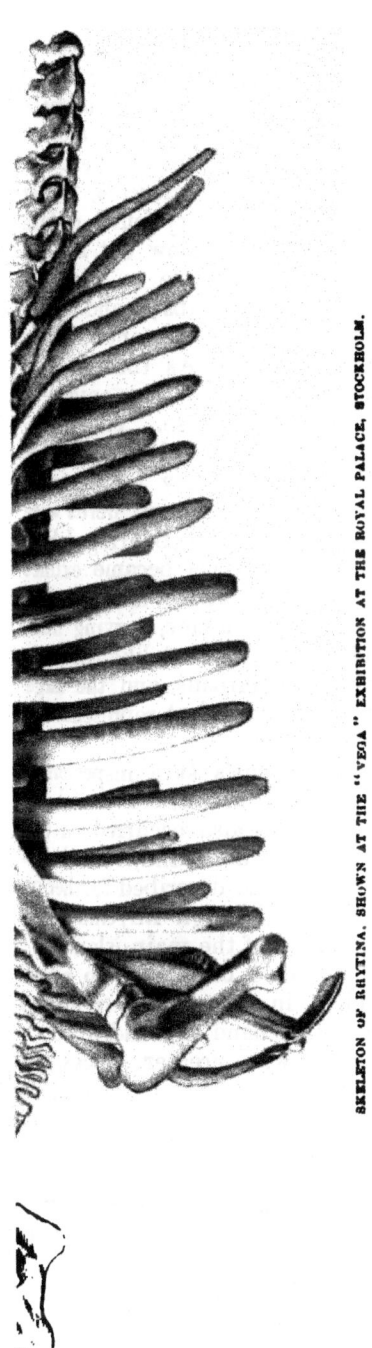

SKELETON OF RHYTINA, SHOWN AT THE "VEGA" EXHIBITION AT THE ROYAL PALACE, STOCKHOLM.

After a photograph.

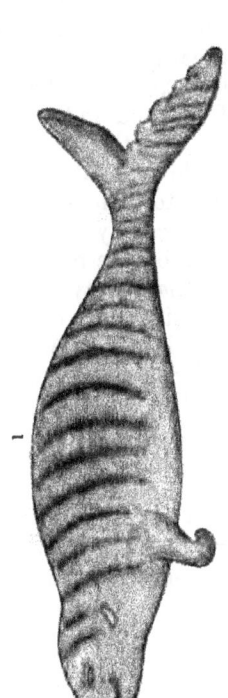

'ORIGINAL DRAWINGS OF THE RHYTINA.

1. Drawing in an old map of the Behring Sea, found by Middendorf (*Sibir. Reise*, iv. 2, p. 889).   2. Sketch by Steller, given to Pallas (PALLAS, *Icones ad zoographiam Rosso-Asiaticam*, Fasc. II.).

agreed completely, and appeared to have claims to be regarded as
trustworthy. That the animal which they saw was actually a
sea-cow, is clearly proved both by the description of the animal's
form and way of pasturing in the water, and by the account
of the way in which it breathed, its colour, and leanness. In
Aüsfurliche Beschreibung von sonderbaren Meerthieren, Steller
says, p. 97, " While they pasture, they raise every fourth or fifth
minute their nose from the water in order to blow out air and
a little water ; " p. 98, " During winter they are so lean that
it is possible to count their vertebræ and ribs ; " and p. 54,
" Some sea-cows have pretty large white spots and streaks,
so that they have a spotted appearance." As these natives
had no knowledge of Steller's description of the animal, it
is impossible that their statement can be false. The death-
year of the Rhytina race must therefore be altered at least
to 1854. With reference to this point it may be remarked
that many circumstances indicate that the Rhytina herds were
rather driven away from the rich pastures on Behring Island
than exterminated there, and that the species became extinct
. because in their new haunt they were unable to maintain the
struggle for existence. The form of the sea-cow, varying from
that of most recent animals, besides indicates that, like the long-
tailed duck on Iceland, the dront of Mauritius, and the large
ostrich-like birds on New Zealand, it was the last representative
of an animal group destined to extinction.

Mr. OSCHE, one of the Alaska Company's skin inspectors, a
native of Liffland and at present settled on Copper Island, informed me that the bones of the sea-cow also occurred on the
western side of that island. On the other hand, such bones
are said not to be found on the small island described further on
lying off the colony on Behring Island, although Rhytina bones
are common on the neighbouring shores of the main island.

This is the scanty information I have been able to collect
from the natives and others resident in the quarter regarding
the animal in question. On the other hand, my endeavours to
procure Rhytina bones were crowned with greater success, and
I succeeded in actually bringing together a very large and fine
collection of skeleton fragments.

When I first made the acquaintance of Europeans on the
island, they told me that there was little probability of finding
anything of value in this respect ; for the company had offered
150 roubles for a skeleton without success. But before I had
been many hours on land, I came to know that large or small
collections of bones were to be found here and there in the huts
of the natives. These I purchased, intentionally paying for them
such a price that the seller was more than satisfied and his neighbours were a little envious. A great part of the male population

now began to search for bones very eagerly, and in this way I collected such a quantity that twenty-one casks, large boxes, or barrels were filled with Rhytina bones; among which were three very fine, complete skulls, and others more or less damaged, several considerable collections of bones from the same skeleton, &c.

The Rhytina bones do not lie at the level of the sea, but upon a strand-bank thickly overgrown with luxuriant grass, at a height of two or three metres above it. They are commonly covered with a layer of earth and gravel from thirty to fifty centimetres in thickness. In order to find them, as it would be too trouble-some to dig the whole of the grassy bank, one must examine the ground with a pointed iron rod, a bayonet, or some such tool. One soon learns to distinguish, by the resistance and nature of the sound, whether the rod stuck into the ground has come into contact with a stone, a piece of wood, or a fragment of bone. The ribs are used by the natives, on account of their hard ivory-like structure, for shoeing the runners of the sledges or for carvings. They have accordingly been

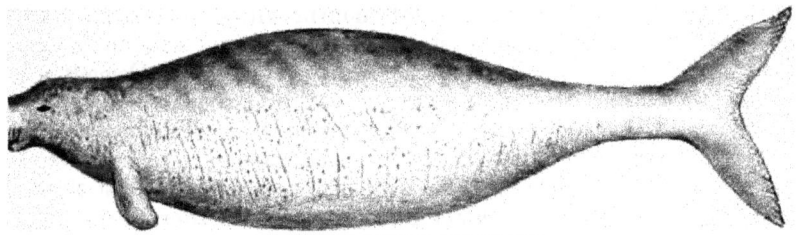

RECONSTRUCTED FORM OF THE SEA-COW.
After J. Fr. Brandt (*Symbolæ Sirenologicæ*, Fasc. iii. p. 282).

already used up on a large scale, and are more uncommon than other bones. The finger-bone, which perhaps originally was cartilaginous, appears in most cases to be quite destroyed, as well as the outermost vertebræ of the tail. I could not obtain any such bones, though I specially urged the natives to get me the smaller bones too and promised to pay a high price for them.

The only large animal which is still found on Behring Island in perhaps as large numbers as in Steller's time is the *sea-bear*.[1]

[1] The number of these animals killed on Behring Island is shown by the following statement given me by Mr. Henry W. Elliott:

In the Year		In the Year		In the Year	
1867	... 27,500	1872	... 29,318	1877	... 21,532
1868	... 12,000	1873	... 30,396	1878	... 31,340
1869	... 24,000	1874	... 31,292	1879	... 42,752
1870	... 24,000	1875	... 36,274	1880	... 48,504
1871	... 3,614	1876	... 26,960		

During the eighteen years from 1862 to 1880 there have thus been shipped from Behring Island 389,462 skins. The catch on the Pribylov Islands

Even it had already diminished so that the year's catch was inconsiderable, when in 1871 a single company obtained for a payment to the Russian crown, if I recollect right, of two roubles for every animal killed, an exclusive right to the hunting, which was accordingly arranged in a more purposelike way. At certain times of the year the killing of the sea-bear is wholly prohibited. The number of the animals to be killed is settled beforehand, quite in the same way as the farmer at the time of killing in autumn is wont to do with his herd of cattle. Females and young are only killed exceptionally. Even the married males, or more correctly the males that can get themselves a harem and can defend it, commonly escape being killed, if not for any other reason, because the skin is too often torn and tattered and the hair pulled out. It is thus the bachelors that have to yield up their skins.

That a wild animal may be slaughtered in so orderly a way, depends on its peculiar mode of life.[1] For the sea-bears are found year after year during summer at certain points projecting into the sea (rookeries), where, collected in hundreds of thousands, they pass several months without the least food. The males (oxen) come first to the place, most of them in the month of May or at the beginning of June. Combats of excessive violence, often with a deadly issue for one of the parties, now arise regarding the space of about a hundred square feet, which each seal-ox considers necessary for its home. The strongest and most successful in fight retain the best places near the shore ; the weaker have to crawl farther up on land, where the expectation of getting a sufficient number of spouses is not particularly great. The fighting goes on with many feigned attacks and parades. At first the contest concerns the proprietorship of the soil. The attacked therefore never follows its opponent beyond the area it has once taken up, but haughtily lays itself down, when the enemy has retired, in order in the arms of sleep to collect forces for a new combat. The animal in such a case grunts with satisfaction, throws itself on its back, scratches itself with its fore-feet, looks after its toilet, or cools itself by slowly fanning with one of its hind-feet, but it is always on the alert and ready for a new fight until it is tired out and meets its match, and is driven by it farther up from the beach.

has been still larger. These islands were discovered in 1786, but the number of animals killed there is not known for the first ten years; it is only known that it was enormously large. In the years 1797-1880—that is in eighty-four years—over three-and-a-half millions of skins have been exported from these islands. In recent years the catch has increased so that in each of the years from 1872 to 1880, 99,000 animals might have been killed without inconvenience.

[1] The traits here given of the sea-bear's mode of life are mainly taken from Henry W. Elliott's work quoted above.   •

One of the most peculiar traits of these animals is that during their stay on land they unceasingly use their hind-paws as fans, and sometimes also as parasols. Such fans may on a

SEA-BEARS.
Male, Female, and Young.
From a water-colour painting by H. W. Elliott.

warm day be in motion at the same time by the hundred thousand at a "rookery."

In the middle of June the females come up from the sea. At the water's edge they are received in a very accommodating way by some strong oxen that have succeeded in securing for themselves places next the shore, and now are bent by fair means or foul on annexing the fair for their harem. But scarcely is the female that has come up out of the water established with seal-ox No. 1, when this ox rushes towards a new beauty on the surface of the water. Seal-ox No. 2 now stretches out his neck and without ceremony lays hold of No. 1's spouse, to be afterwards exposed to a repetition of the trick by No. 3. In such cases the females are quite passive, never fall out with each other, and bear with patience the severe wounds they often get when they are pulled about by the combatants, now in one direction, now in another. All the females are finally distributed in this way after furious combats among the males, those of the latter who are nearest the beach getting from twelve to fifteen consorts to their share. Those that have been compelled to settle farther from the shore must be content with four or five. Soon after the landing of the females they bring forth their young, which are treated with great indifference and are protected by the adopted father only within the boundaries of the harem. Next comes the pairing season, and when it has passed there is an end to the arrangement and distribution into families at first so strictly maintained. The seal-oxen, rendered lean by three months absolute fasting, by degrees leave the "rookery," which is taken possession of by the sea-cows, the young, and a number of young males, that have not ventured to the place before. In the middle of September, when the young have learned to swim, the place is quite abandoned, with the exception of single animals that have remained behind for one reason or other. In long continued heavy rain many of the animals besides seek protection in the sea, but return when the rain ceases. Continuous heat and sunshine besides exert the same influence; cold, moist air, with mist-concealed sun, on the other hand draw them up on land by thousands.

Males under six years of age cannot, like the older males, possess themselves, by fighting, of spouses and a home of their own. They therefore collect, along with young females, in herds of several thousand to several hundred thousand, on the shores between the rookeries proper, some of them close packed next the water's edge, others scattered in small flocks a little farther from the shore on the grass, where they by turns play with each other with a frolicsomeness like that of young dogs, by turns lie down to sleep at a common signal in all conceivable positions.

It is these unfortunate useless bachelors which at the properly managed hunting stations yield the contingent for slaughter. For this purpose they are driven by the natives from the shore

"SEAL-ROOKERY" ON ST. PAUL'S ISLAND, ONE OF THE PRIBYLOV ISLANDS.
After a drawing by H. W. Elliot.

slowly, about a kilometre an hour, and with frequent rests, to the place of slaughter, situated a kilometre or two from the shore. Then the females and the young ones are driven away, as well as the males whose skins are unserviceable. The rest are first stunned with a blow on the head, and afterwards stabbed with a knife.

While the *Vega* steamed down towards Behring Island we met, already far from land, herds of sea-bears, which followed the vessel from curiosity for long stretches. Being unacquainted with the sea-bears' mode of life, I believed from this circumstance that they had already left their summer haunts, but on our arrival at the colony I was informed that this was not the case, but that a very great number of animals still remained at the rookery on the north-eastern point of the island. Naturally one of our first excursions was to this place, situated about twenty kilometres from the village. Such a journey cannot now be undertaken alone and unattended, because even an involuntary want of caution might easily cause much economic loss to the natives, and to the company that owns the right of hunting. During the journey we were accordingly accompanied by the chief of the village, a black-haired stammering Aleutian, and " the Cossack," a young, pleasant, and agreeable fellow, who on solemn occasions wore a sabre nearly as long as himself, but besides did not in the least correspond to the Cossack type of the writers of novels and plays.

The journey was performed in large sledges drawn by ten dogs over snow-free rounded hills and hill-plateaus covered with a rather scanty vegetation, and through valleys treeless as the mountains, but adorned with luxuriant vegetation, rich in splendid lilies, syngenesia umbellifera, &c. The journey was sometimes tedious enough, but we now and then went at a whistling rate, especially when the dog-team descended the steep mountain slopes, or went through the morasses and the clay puddles formed in the constantly used way. The driver was bespattered from top to toe with a thick layer of mud, an inconvenience attending the unusual team, which was foreseen before our departure from the colony, in consequence of which our friends there urged that, notwithstanding the fine weather, we should all take overcoats. The dog-team was kept pretty far from the shore in order not to frighten the seals, and then we went on foot to the place where the sea-bears were, choosing our way so that we had the wind in our faces. We could in this way, without disturbing them, come very near the animals, which, according to the undoubtedly somewhat exaggerated statement made to us on the spot, were collected at the time to the number of 200,000, on the promontory and the neighbouring shores. We obtained permission to creep, accompanied by our guide, close to a herd lying a little apart. The older animals became at first somewhat uneasy when they observed our approach, but they soon settled down completely, and we had now the pleasure of beholding a peculiar spectacle. We were the only spectators. The scene consisted of a beach covered with stones and washed by foaming breakers, the background of the immeasurable ocean, and the actors of thousands of wonderfully formed animals. A number of old males lay still and motionless, heedless of what was going on around them. Others crept clumsily on their small short legs between

SLAUGHTER OF SEA-BEARS.
After a drawing by H. W. Elliott.

the stones of the beach, or swam with incredible agility among the breakers, played, caressed each other, and quarrelled. At one place two old animals fought, uttering a peculiar hissing sound, and in such a way as if the attack and defence had been carried out in studied attitudes. At another place a feigned combat was going on between an old and a young animal. It looked as if the latter was being instructed in the art of fighting. Everywhere the small black young ones crept constantly backwards and forwards among the old sea-bears, now and then bleating like lambs calling on their mothers. The young ones are often smothered by the old, when the latter, frightened in some way, rush out into the sea. After such an alarm hundreds of dead young are found on the shore.

"Only" thirteen thousand animals had been killed that year. Their flayed carcases lay heaped on the grass by the shore, spreading far and wide a disagreeable smell, which, however, had not frightened away their comrades lying on the neighbouring promontory, because, even among them, a similar smell prevailed in consequence of the many animals suffocated or killed in fight with their comrades, and left lying on the shore.[1] Among this great flock of sea-bears sat enthroned on the top of a high stone a single sea-lion, the only one of these animals we saw during our voyage.

SEA-BEARS ON THEIR WAY TO THE "ROOKERIES."
After a drawing by H. W. Elliott.

For a payment of forty roubles I induced the chief of the village to skeletonise four of the half putrefied carcases of the sea-bear left lying on the grass; and I afterwards obtained, by the good-will of the Russian authorities, and without any payment, six animals, among them two living young, for stuffing. Even the latter we were compelled to kill, after

[1] Elliott (*loc. cit.* p. 150) remarks that not a single self-dead seal is to be found in the "rookery," where there are so many animals that they probably die of old age in thousands. This may be explained by the seals, when they become sick, withdrawing to the sea, and forms another contribution to the question of the finding of self-dead animals to which I have already referred (p. 246).

n vain attempting to induce them to take some food. One of them was brought home in spirits for anatomical examination.

The part of Behring Island which we saw forms a high plain resting on volcanic rocks,[1] which, however, is interrupted at many places by deep kettle valleys, the bottoms of which are generally occupied by lakes which communicate with the sea by large or small rivers. The banks of the lakes and the slopes of the hills are covered with a luxuriant vegetation, rich in long grass and beautiful flowers; among them an iris cultivated in our gardens, the useful dark reddish-brown Sarana lily, several orchids, two species of rhododendron with large flowers, umbellifera as high as a man, sunflower-like synanthea, &c. Quite another nature prevailed on the island lying off the haven, regarding which Dr. Kjellman and Dr. Stuxberg make the following statements:—

"Toporkoff Island is formed of an eruptive rock, which everywhere rises along the shore some scores of feet from high-water mark, in the form of steep cracked walls from five to fifteen metres in height, which is different at different places. Above these steep rock-walls the surface of the island forms an even plain; what lies below them forms a gently sloping beach.

"This gently sloping beach consists of two well-marked belts; an outer devoid of all vegetation, an inner overgrown with *Ammadenia peploides*, *Elymus mollis*, and two species of umbellifera, *Heracleum sibiricum*, and *Angelica archangelica*, the two last forming an almost impenetrable thicket fifty metres broad and as high as a man, along the slope. The steep rock-walls are coloured yellow at some places by lichens, mostly *Caloplaca murorum* and *Cal. crenulata*; at other places they are covered pretty closely with *Cochlearia fenestrata*. The uppermost level plain is covered with a close and luxuriant turf, over which single stalks of the two species of umbellifera named above raise themselves here and there. The vegetation on this little island unites a very uncommon poverty in species with a high degree of luxuriance.

"Of the higher animals we saw only four kinds of birds, viz. *Fratercula cirrhata*, a black guillemot (*Uria grylle* var. *columba*), a species of cormorant (Phalocrocorax) and a sort of gull (Larus). *Fratercula cirrhata* lived here by millions. They haunted the upper plain, where they had everywhere excavated short, deep, and uncommonly broad passages to sleep in, provided

---

[1] According to a statement by Mr. Grebnitski, tertiary fossils and coal seams are also to be found on Behring Island, the former north of the colony in the interior, the latter at the beach south of Behring's grave. Also in the neighbourhood of the colony the volcanic rock-masses are under-stratified by thick sandy beds.

with two openings.   From these on our arrival they flew in
large flocks to the neighbouring sea and back.   Their number
was nearly equal to that of looms in the Arctic loomeries.   The
black guillemots and cormorants kept to the cliffs near the
shore.

"The number of the evertebrate land animals amounted to
about thirty species.   The most numerous were Machilis,
Vitrina, Lithobius, Talitrus, some Diptera and beetles.   They
all lived on the inner belt of the shore, where the ground
was uncommonly damp."

Behring Island might without difficulty feed large herds of
cattle, perhaps as numerous as the herds of sea-cows that
formerly pastured on its shores.   The sea-cow besides had chosen
its pasture with discrimination, the sea there being, according to
Dr. Kjellman, one of the richest in algæ in the world.   The
sea-bottom is covered at favourably situated places by forests of
seaweed from twenty to thirty metres high, which are so dense
that the dredge could with difficulty force its way down into
them, a circumstance which was much against the dredging.
Certain of the algæ are used by the natives as food.

In the course of our journey to the hunting place we had an
opportunity, during a rest about halfway between it and the
village, of taking part in a very peculiar sort of fishing.   The
place where we rested was in an even grassy plain, resembling a
natural meadow at home, crossed by a large number of small
rivulets.   They abounded in several different kinds of fish,
among them a Coregonus, a small trout, a middle-sized long
salmon with almost white flesh, though the colour of its skin
was a purplish-red, another salmon of about the same length,
but thick and hump-backed.   These fish were easily caught.
They were taken with the hand, were harpooned with common
unshod sticks, were stabbed with knives, caught with the insect
net, &c.   Other kinds of salmon with deep red flesh are to be
found in the large rivers of the island.   We obtained here for
a trifle a welcome change from the preserved provisions of which
we had long ago become quite tired.   The expedition was also
presented by the Alaska Company with a fine fat ox, milk, and
various other provisions, and I cannot sufficiently value the
goodwill shown to us not only by the Russian official, N. GREB-
NITSKI, a zealous and skilful naturalist, but also by the officials
of the Alaska Company and all others living on the island with
whom we came into contact.

It was my original intention to sail from Behring Island to
Petropaulovsk, in order from thence to put a stop to the under-
takings which were possibly in contemplation for our relief.
This however became unnecessary, because a steamer, which

ras to start for Petropaulovsk as soon as its cargo was on board,
ıad anchored by the side of the *Vega* two days after our arrival.
'he steamer belonged to the Alaska Company, was named
he *Alexander*, was commanded by Captain SANDMAN, and was

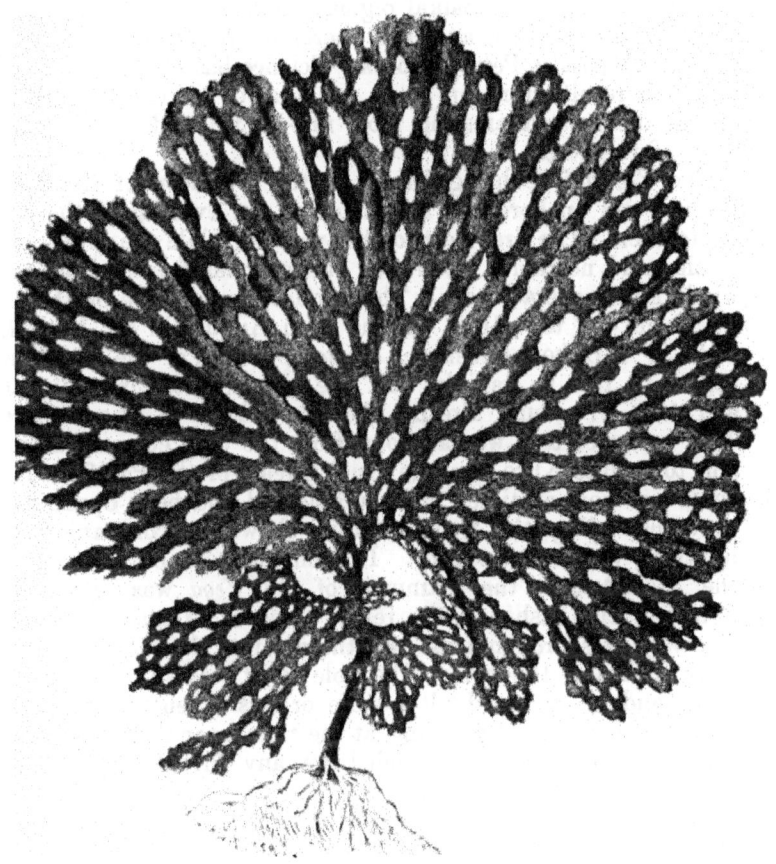

ALGA FROM THE SHORE OF BEHRING ISLAND.
Thalassiophyllum Clathrus, Post. and Rupr.
One-fourth of the natural size.

ıanned almost exclusively by Swedes, Danes, Fins, and
Vorwegians.[1] We found on the *Alexander* two naturalists, Dr.

[1] The first European who welcomed us after the completion of the
forth-east passage was a Fin now settled in California, from Björkboda
rorks in Kimito parish, in which I had lived a great deal when a youth.
Ie was sent by the Alaska Company to do some work on Behring Island.
ıs we steamed towards the colony he rowed to meet us, and saluted us with
ıe cry "är det Nordenskiöld?" ("Is it Nordenskiöld?") His name was
sak Andersson.

BENEDIKT DYBOVSKI and Dr. JULIAN WIEMUT. The former is
a Pole exiled to Siberia but now pardoned, whose masterly
zoological works are among the best contributions which have
been made during recent decades to our knowledge of the
natural conditions of Siberia. His researches have hitherto
mainly concerned the Baikal region. Now he wishes to extend
them to Kamchatka, and has therefore voluntarily taken a
physician's post at Petropaulovsk. Science has reason to expect
very rich results from his work and that of his companions in
one of the most interesting, most mis-known, and least known
lands of the north.

The *Vega* left Behring Island on the afternoon of the 19th
August, and anchored at Yokohama on the evening of the 2nd
September. The first part of the passage, while we were still
in the cold northerly Polar Sea current, was favoured by fair
winds and moderate heat. The surface temperature of the sea
was from $+9°$ to $+10°$. On the 25th August in 45° 15′ N.L.
and 156° E.L. from Greenwich the temperature of the sea-water
began to rise so rapidly that the thermometer in 40° Lat.
and 147° 41′ Long. already showed $+23°·4$ at the surface.
This indicated that we had come from the cold current favourable to us into Kuro-sivo, the Gulf Stream of the Pacific. The
wind was now·at times unfavourable and the heat oppressive,
notwithstanding the frequent rain showers accompanied by
lightning and heavy squalls. In such unfavourable weather on
the 31st August the mainmast of the *Vega* was struck by
lightning, the flash and the report being of excessive violence.
The vane was broken loose and thrown into the sea along with
some inches of the pole. The pole itself was split pretty far
down, and all on board felt a more or less violent shaking, the
man who felt it most standing at the time near the hawse-hole.
The incident was not attended by any further noteworthy
unpleasant consequences.

On our arrival at Yokohama we were all in good health and
the *Vega* in excellent condition, though, after the long voyage,
in want of some minor repairs, of docking, and possibly of
coppering. Naturally among thirty men some mild attacks of
illness could not be avoided in the course of a year, but no
disease had been generally prevalent, and our state of health had
constantly been excellent. Of scurvy we had not seen a trace.

CHAPTER XVI.

Arrival at Yokohama—A Telegram sent to Europe—The stranding of the steamer *A. E. Nordenskiöld*—*Fêtes* in Japan—The Minister of Marine, Kawamura—Prince Kito-Shira-Kava—Audience of the Mikado—Graves of the Shoguns—Imperial Garden at Tokio—The Exhibition there—Visit to Enoshima—Japanese manners and customs—Thunberg and Kämpfer.

YOKOHAMA, the first harbour, telegraph station, and commercial town at which the *Vega* anchored after circumnavigating the north coast of Asia, is one of the Japanese coast cities which were opened to the commerce of the world after the treaty between the United States of America and Japan negotiated by Commodore PERRY.[1] At this place there was formerly only a little fishing village, whose inhabitants had never seen Europeans and were forbidden under severe punishments from entering into communication or trading with the crews of the foreign vessels that might possibly visit the coast. The former village is now, twenty years later, changed into a town of nearly 70,000 inhabitants, and consists not only of Japanese, but also of very fine European houses, shops, hotels, &c. It is also the residence of the Governor of Kanagava *Ken*. It is in communication by rail with the neighbouring capital Tokio, by regular weekly steamship sailings with San Francisco on the one hand, and Hong-Kong, India, &c., on the other, and finally by telegraph not only with the principal cities of Japan but also with all the lands that have got entangled in the threads of the world's telegraph net.

The situation of the town on the western shore of the Yedo or Tokio Bay, which is perhaps rather large for a haven, is not particularly fine. But on sailing in we see in the west, if the weather be fine, Fusiyama's snow-clad, incomparably beautiful volcanic cone raise itself from a cultivated forest-clad region. When one has seen it, he is no longer astonished that the Japanese reproduce with such affection on their varnished wares, porcelain, cloth, paper, sword-ornaments, &c., the form of their highest, stateliest, and also grimmest mountain. For the number of the men who have perished by its eruptions is reckoned by hundreds of thousands, and if tradition speaks truth the whole mountain

---

[1] The Dutch had permission in former times to send some vessels annually to Nagasaki. By Perry's treaty, signed on the 31st March, 1854, Shimoda and Hakodate were opened to the Americans. Finally, by new treaties with the United States and various European powers, the harbours Kanagava (Yokohama), Nagasaki, Hakodate, Niigata, Hiogo, and Osaka, were assigned for commerce with foreigners.

in a far distant antiquity was formed in a single night. Before
we enter Yedo Bay we pass a volcano, active during last year,
situated on the volcanic island Oshima, known in Japanese
history as the place of exile of several of the heroes in the many
internal struggles of the country.

While we sailed, or more correctly, steamed—for we had still
sufficient coal remaining to permit the engine to be used—up
the Bay of Yedo, the coasts were for the most part concealed
with mist, so that the summit of Fusiyama and the contours of
the shore only now and then gleamed forth from the fog and
cloud. The wind besides was against us, on which account it was
9.30 in the evening of the 2nd September before we could
anchor in the haven that had been longed-for for such a length
of time. I immediately hastened on land, along with Captain
Palander, in order to send home a telegram across Siberia
about the fortunate issue of the voyage of the *Vega.* At
the telegraph station I was informed that the Siberian line was
interrupted by inundations for a space of 600 versts, and that
the telegram must therefore be sent by India, whereby the cost
was nearly doubled. The telegraph officials also made difficulties
about taking the foreign gold coin of various kinds which I had
about me. Fortunately the latter difficulty was immediately
removed by the accidental presence of the Russian consul, Mr.
PELIKAN, while I was treating with the telegraph officials. When
he heard that it concerned the sending home of a telegram from
the much-talked-of *Vega* expedition, he immediately offered to
arrange the affair until I had time to operate on the letter
of credit I carried with me from Messrs. James Dickson & Co.
of Gothenburg. Soon after I met with the Swedish consul,
Mr. VAN OORDT, who gave us a large parcel of letters from
home. It was very gladly received by most of us, as, so far
as I know, it did not bring the thirty members of the expedition
a single unexpected sorrowful message. I got, however, soon
after landing, an unpleasant piece of news, viz. that the steamer
A. E. Nordenskiöld, which Mr. Sibiriakoff had sent to Behring's
Straits and the Lena to our relief, had stranded on the east coast
of Yesso. The shipwreck fortunately had not been attended
with any loss of human life, and the vessel lay stranded on
a sandbank in circumstances which made it probable that it
would be got off without too great cost.

As the report of our arrival spread, I was immediately waited
upon by various deputations with addresses of welcome, invitations
to *fêtes,* clubs, &c. A series of entertainments and festivities
now began, which occupied a great part of the time we remained
in this splendid and remarkable country. Perhaps a sketch
of these festivities may yield a picture of Japan during the state
of transition which still prevails there, and which in a decade

FUSIYAMA.

or two will undoubtedly belong to a past and to a great extent
forgotten period, a picture which to future writers may possibly
form a not unwelcome contribution to the knowledge of the
Japan that now (1879) is. Such a sketch would however
carry me too far beyond the subject of this narrative of
travel, and require too much space, on which account I must
confine myself to an enumeration of the festivities, at the head
of which were public authorities, learned societies, or clubs.

On the 10th September a grand dinner was given at the Grand
Hotel, the principal European hotel—and very well kept—of

THE STEAMER "A. E. NORDENSKIÖLD," STRANDED ON THE EAST COAST OF YEZO.
After a Japanese photograph.

Yokohama, by the Dutch minister, Chevalier VAN STOETWEGEN,
who at the same time represents Sweden and Norway in Japan.
The members of the Expedition were here introduced to several
members of the Japanese Government.

We were invited to a *déjeûner à la fourchette*, at one o'clock
P.M. on the 11th September, at the Imperial summer palace
Hamagoten, by Admiral KAWAMURA, minister of marine. At
this entertainment there were present, besides the scientific men
and officers of the *Vega*, and our minister, Herr van Stoetwegen,
several of the ministers and highest officials of Japan. Some

of them spoke one or other of the European languages, others only Japanese, in which case officials of lower rank acted as interpreters, these however taking no part in the entertainment along with the other guests.   It was arranged after the European pattern, with abundance of dishes and wines.   The palace consisted of a one-storied wooden house in the Japanese style of construction.   The rooms, to which we were admitted were provided with European furniture, much the same as we would expect to find in the summer residence of a well-to-do family in Sweden.   It was remarkable that the Japanese did not take

KAWAMURA SUMIYOSHI.
Japanese Minister of Marine.

the trouble to ornament the room or the table to any considerable extent with the beautiful native bronzes or porcelain, of which there is such abundance in the country.   The summer palace was surrounded by a garden which the Japanese consider something very extraordinary, and also on a very large scale. We should call it a small, well and originally kept miniature park, with carefully dressed turf, wonderful dwarf trees, miniature stone bridges, small ponds and waterfalls.   The entertainment was very pleasant, and all, from our intelligent host to the Premier,

Daiyo-daiyin, and the Imperial Prince, SANYO SANITOMI, showed us much friendliness. The latter looked a sickly young man, some years past twenty. He was, however, much older, and had taken a leading part in the most important political transactions since the opening of the ports. Our host, Admiral Kawamura, had more the appearance of a man of science than of a warrior. The modest exterior, however, concealed a great and noble man. For Kawamura, as commander of the Mikado's troops, had with special distinction brought about the suppression of the revolt under the brave Saigo Kichinosuke, who had at the restoration of the power of the Mikado been its heart and sword, but soon after fell before the government he himself contributed to create, and is now, a couple of years after, admired and sung by former friends and by former enemies as a national hero. All the Japanese present at the *déjeûner* were clad in European dress—in black dress coat and white tie. Even the interpreters and attendants wore the European dress. The people, the lower officials, and the servants in private houses are still clothed in the Japanese dress, but do not wear a sword, which is now prohibited. Many of the people have even exchanged the old troublesome Japanese dressing of the hair for the convenient European style.

In the course of conversation after the *déjeûner* the ministers offered to do all they could to make our stay in the country agreeable and instructive. Distinguished foreigners are always well received in Japan, and we are informed that a special committee is appointed to make arrangements for their reception. This has given offence in certain quarters, and shortly before our arrival a proclamation was issued by a secret society, which threatened, if no change were made, to kill one of the ministers and one of the foreigners who were entertained in this, in the opinion of the secret society, extravagant way. One of my Japanese friends promised me a copy of the proclamation, but did not keep his promise, probably because it was impossible for the uninitiated to get hold of the dangerous writing.

On the 13th September a grand dinner was arranged for us by the German Club, the photographer ANDERSEN being chairman. The hall was adorned in a festive manner with flags, and with representations of the *Vega*, in various more or less dangerous positions among the ice, which had been got up for the occasion; the bill of fare had reference to the circumstances of our wintering, &c. A number of speeches were made; the feeling was cheerful and merry.

On the 15th September there was a grand entertainment in Tokio, given by the Tokio Geographical Society, the Asiatic Society of Japan, and the German Asiatic Society. It was

held in the great hall in Koku-Dai-Gaku, a large stone
building surrounded with beautiful trees, which were lighted up
for the occasion by a number of variegated paper lanterns.
Several Japanese ladies dressed in European style took part
in the entertainment. I sat by the side of the chairman,
Prince KITA-SHIRA-KAVA, a young member of the imperial
house, who had served some time in the German army and
speaks German very well. During the disturbances which were
caused by the removal of the residence from Kioto to Yedo
(Tokio), a group of insurgents had seized the prince, then a
minor, who under the name of RINNOJINO-MIYA was chief
priest in a temple, and endeavoured to set him up in opposition
to the Emperor. The plan failed, and in consequence of the
reconciliation at the end of the conflict, which distinguished in
so honourable a way the many involved and bloody political
struggles in Japan during recent years, this adventure was
attended with no other result for him than that the former
chief priest was sent to a German military school. He was
recalled sooner than was intended because he wished to marry
a European, which was considered below the dignity of the
family of the Mikado. After his return he was declared nearest
heir to the throne, in case the Mikado should die without male
heirs, and his name, KITA-SHIRA-KAVA-NO-MIYA, was changed
a second time to YOHI HISHA. The former name was at the
bottom of the speech he made for us at the dinner, and which
he gave me, and the latter, with the addition, "Prince of Japan,"
was on his calling card. The dinner was quite European,
with a large number of speeches, principally in European
languages, but also in Japanese. Before every guest lay a map,
of the form of a fan, with the course of the *Vega* marked upon
it. As a memorial of the feast I received some days after a
large medal in silver inlaid in gold, of which a drawing is given
on pages 628, 629. We were conveyed back to the Tokio
railway station in European equipages, in the same way as we
had been brought to the dinner. During dinner musicians
from the band of the imperial navy played European pieces of
music with great skill, to the evident satisfaction of the
Japanese.

On the forenoon of the 17th September we were presented
at the court of the Mikado in Tokio by the Swedish-Dutch
minister. We were fetched from the railway station by imperial
equipages, consisting of simple but ornamental and convenient *suflett* carriages, each drawn by a pair of beautiful black
horses of no great size. As is common in Japan, a running
groom, clad in black, accompanied each carriage. The reception took place in the imperial palace, a very modest wooden
building. The rooms we saw were furnished, almost poorly, in

European fashion. We first assembled in an antechamber, the only remarkable ornament of which was a large piece of nephrite, which was a little carved and had a Chinese inscription on it. Here we were met by some of the ministers and the interpreter. After a short conversation, in the course of which the interpreter got a sight of the written speech, or more correctly the words of salutation, I was to speak, we were conducted into an inner apartment where the Emperor, clad

THE FIRST MEDAL WHICH WAS STRUCK AS A MEMORIAL OF THE VOYAGE OF THE "VEGA"
Size of the original.

in a uniform of European style and standing in front of a throne, received us. The only thing unusual at our reception was that we were requested at our departure not to turn our backs to the Emperor, and on entering and departing to make three bows, one at the door, another when we had come forward a little on the floor, and one at the place where we were to stand. After we had been presented the Emperor read a speech in Japanese, which was translated

nto French by the interpreter, and of which, before we left
he place, a beautiful copy was given me. I then read my salu-
ation, on which our minister, van Stoetwegen, said a few
vords, and got some words in reply. After leaving the
mperial chamber, we were entertained in the anteroom with
Japanese tea and cigars. The two princes who had taken
art in the entertainment of the 15th came and talked a
ittle with us, as did the minister of foreign affairs. The

THE FIRST MEDAL WHICH WAS STRUCK AS A MEMORIAL OF THE VOYAGE OF THE "VEGA."
Size of the original.

Emperor MUTSUHITO, in whose name reforms have been
carried out in Japan to an extent to which history can
scarcely show anything equal, was born the 3rd November,
1850. He is considered the 121st Mikado of the race of
Jimmu Tenno, the members of which have reigned uninterruptedly in Japan for nearly two thousand years, with varying
ates and with varying power— now as wise lawgivers and mighty
warriors, now for long periods as weak and effeminate rulers,

emperors only in seeming, to whom almost divine homage was
paid, but who were carefully freed from the burden of government and from all actual power. In comparison with this race,
whose first ancestor lived during the first century after the
foundation of Rome, all the royal houses now reigning in
Europe are children of yesterday. Its present representative
does not look to be very strong. During the whole audience
he stood so motionless that he might have been taken for a
wax figure, if he had not himself read his speech. Prince
Kita-Shira-Kava has the appearance of a young lieutenant of
hussars. Most of the ministers have sharply marked features,[1]
which remind one of the many furious storms they have survived, and the many personal dangers to which they have been
exposed, partly in honourable conflict, partly through murderers'
plots. For, unfortunately, a political murder is not yet considered in Japan an infamous crime, but the murderer openly
acknowledges his deed and takes the consequences. Repeated
murderous attempts have been made against the men of the
new time. In order to protect themselves from these, ministers,
when they go out, generally have their carriages surrounded by
an armed guard on horseback.

On the 18th September several of the members of the *Vega*
expedition were invited to a *déjeûner à la fourchette* by Admiral
Kawamura, minister of marine. This entertainment had an interest for us because we were here for the first time received into
a Japanese home. I sat at table by the side of Lady Kawamura.
Even the children were present at the entertainment. Lady
Kawamura was dressed in the Japanese fashion, tastefully but
very plainly, if we except a heavy gold chain encircling the
waist. In other respects the entertainment was arranged according to the European mode, with a succession of dishes and
wines, both in abundance, according to the laws of gastronomy.
When it was over our host offered us an airing in a carriage,
during which I rode with the lady and one of the children, a
little girl about ten years of age, who would have been very
beautiful if she had not been disfigured, in the eyes of Europeans, by the thick white paint that was evenly spread over her
whole face, and gave it a sickly appearance. Lady Kawamura
herself was not painted, nor was she disfigured with blackened
teeth. Most of the married women of Japan are accustomed
after marriage to blacken their formerly dazzlingly white teeth;
but it is to be hoped that this unpleasant custom will soon
disappear, as the women of distinction have begun to abandon

---

[1] At first it strikes a European as if all the Japanese had about the
same appearance, but when one has got accustomed to the colour of the
skin and the traits of the race, the features of the Japanese appear as
various in form and expression as those of Europeans.

it. During this excursion we visited, among other places, the graves of the Tycoons, the imperial garden, and a very remarkable exhibition in the capital.

A number of the Tycoons, or, as they are more correctly called, Shoguns, are buried in Tokio. Their place of sepulture is one of the most remarkable memorials of Old Japan. The graves are in a temple which is divided into several courts, surrounded by walls and connected with each other by beautiful gates. The first of these courts is ornamented with more than two hundred stone lanterns, presented to the temple by the feudal princes of the country, the name of the giver and the date at which it was given being inscribed on each. Some of these peculiar memorials are only half-finished, perhaps an evidence of the sudden close of the power of the Shoguns and the feudal princes in Japan. In another of the temple courts are to be seen lanterns of bronze, partly gilt, presented by other feudal princes. A third court is occupied by a temple, a splendid memorial of the old Japanese architecture, and of the antique method of adorning their sanctuaries with wooden carvings, gilding, and varnishing. The temple abounds in old book-rolls, bells, drums, beautiful old lacquered articles, &c. The graves themselves lie within a separate inclosure.

The common Japanese gardens are not beautiful according to European taste. They are often so small that they might without inconvenience, with trees, grottos, and waterfalls, be accommodated in a small State's department in one of the crystal palaces of the international exhibitions. All, passages, rocks, trees, ponds, yea, even the fishes in the dams, are artificial or artificially changed. The trees are, by a special art which has been very highly developed in Japan, forced to assume the nature of dwarfs, and are besides so pruned that the whole plant has the appearance of a dry stem on which some green clumps have been hung up here and there. The form of the gold fish swimming in the ponds has also been changed, so that they have often two or four tail-fins each, and a number of growths not known in their natural state. On the walks thick layers of pebbles are placed to keep the feet from being dirtied, and at the doors of dwelling-houses there is nearly always a block of granite with a cauldron-like depression excavated in it, which is kept filled with clean water. Upon this stone cauldron is placed a simple but clean wooden scoop, with which one can take water out of the vessel to wash himself with.

The imperial garden in Tokio is distinguished from these miniature gardens by its greater extent, and by the trees, at least at most places, bearing fruit. There is here a veritable park with uncommonly large, splendid, and luxuriantly-growing trees. The public is generally excluded from the garden. At our visit we were entertained in one of the imperial summer-houses with Japanese tea, sweetmeats, and cigars.

Last of all we visited the Exhibition. It had been closed for some time back on account of cholera. We saw here a number of beautiful specimens of Japanese art, from the flint tools and pottery of the Stone Age to the silks, porcelain, and bronzes of the present. In no country is there at this day such a

STONE LANTERN AND STONE MONUMENT.
In a Japanese Temple Court.

love for exhibitions as in Japan. There are small exhibitions in most of the large towns. Many were exceedingly instructive; in all there were to be seen beautiful lacquered wares, porcelain, swords, silk, cloths, &c. In one I saw a collection of the birds and fishes of Japan, in another I discovered some vegetable impressions, by means of which I became acquainted with the

remarkable locality for fossil plants at Mogi, of which I shall
give an account farther on.

On the evening of the 18th September I was invited by the
Danish consul, Herr BAVIER, to a boat excursion up the river
which debouches at Tokio. At its mouth it is very broad and
deep, and it branches somewhat farther up into several streams
which are navigable by the shallow boats of the Japanese with
the present limited development of roads and railways in Japan,
this river and its tributaries form the most important channels
of communication between the capital and the interior of the
country. During our row we constantly met with boats laden

JAPANESE HOUSE IN TOKIO.

with provisions on their way to, or with goods on their way from
the town. The pleasant impression of these and of the remarkable environs of the river is sometimes disturbed by a bad odour
coming from a passing boat, and reminding us of the care with
which the Japanese remove human excreta, the most important
manure of their well-cultivated land. Along the banks of the
river there are numerous restaurants and tea-houses. At long
intervals we see a garden on the banks, which has belonged to
some of the former Daimio palaces. The restaurants and tea-houses
are generally intended only for the Japanese; and Europeans,

although they pay many times more than the natives, are not admitted. The reason of this is to be found in our manners, which are coarse and uncultivated in the eyes of the natives. "The European walks with his dirty boots on the carpets, spits on the floor, is uncivil to the girls, &c." Thanks to the letters of introduction from natives acquainted with the restaurant-keepers, I have been admitted to their exclusive places, and it must be admitted that everything there was so clean, neat, and orderly, that even the best European restaurants cannot compare with them. When a visitor enters a Japanese restaurant which is intended exclusively for the Japanese, he must always take off his boots at the stair else he gets immediately into disfavour. He is received with bended knee by the host and all the attendants, male, but principally female; and then he is almost always surrounded by a number of young girls constantly laughing and chattering. These girls have commonly sold themselves to the restaurant-keeper for a certain time, during which they carry on a life which, according to European standards of morality, is not very commendable. When the time fixed in the agreement has passed, they return to their homes and marry, without having sunk in any way in the estimation of their relatives. But those are unfortunate who, in any of the towns that are not yet opened to foreigners, carry on a love intrigue with a European. They are then openly pointed out, even in the newspapers, as immoral, and their respectability is helplessly gone. Formerly they were even in such cases severely punished.

All women of the lower classes, and even most of the higher, wear the Japanese dress. The more distinguished ladies are often exceedingly beautiful, they have in particular beautiful necks. Unfortunately they are often disfigured by paint, for which the ladies here appear to have a strong liking. The dress of the younger women, even among the poor, is carefully attended to; it is not showy but tasteful, and nearly the same for all classes. Their manners are very attractive and agreeable. The women of the upper classes already begin to take part in the social life of the Europeans, and all European gentlemen and ladies with whom I have conversed on this point agree in stating that there is no difficulty in the way of a Japanese woman leaving the narrow circle to which she was formerly confined, and entering with pleasure and womanly dignity into European society. She appears to be born "a lady."

On the 20th and 21st September the Governor of Yokohama had arranged an excursion for me, Dr. Stuxberg, and Lieut. Nordquist, to the sacred island or peninsula Enoshima, situated at a short distance from the town. We first travelled some English miles along the excellent road Tokaido, one of the few highways in Japan passable in carriages. Then we travelled in *jinrikishas* to the famous image of Buddha (Daibutsu) at Kamakura,[1] and visited the Shinto chief priest living in the neighbourhood and his temple.

The priest was fond of antiquities, and had a collection, not very large indeed, but composed almost entirely of rarities. Among other things he showed us sabres of great value, a head ornament consisting of a single piece of nephrite which he valued at 500 *yen*,[2] a number of old bronzes, mirrors, &c.

JAPANESE LADY AT HER TOILETTE.

We were received as usual with Japanese tea and sweetmeats. The priest himself took us round his temple. No images were to be seen here, but the walls were richly carved and ornamented with a number of drawings and gildings. The innermost wall of the temple was fenced by heavy doors provided with secure locks and bolts, within which "the divine spirit dwelt," or

---

[1] At the close of the twelfth century this now inconsiderable town was the residence of Joritomo, the founder of the Shogun power, and the arranger of the Japanese feudal system.

[2] Five *yen* are about equal to £1 sterling.

A JINRIKISHA.

within which "there was nothing else," as the priest phrased it on another occasion.

Enoshima is a little rocky peninsula, which is connected with the mainland by a low, sandy neck of land. Occasionally this neck of land has been broken through or overflowed, and the peninsula has then been converted into an island. It is considered sacred, and is studded with Shinto temples. On the side of the peninsula next the mainland there is a little village, consisting of inns, tea-houses, and shops for pilgrims' and tourists' articles, among which are beautiful shells, and the fine siliceous skeleton of a sponge, *Hyalonema mirabilis*, Gray. Here I lived for the first time in a Japanese inn of the sort to which Europeans in ordinary circumstances are not admitted. I was accompanied by two officials from the governor's court at Yokohama, and it was on their assurance that I did not belong to the common sort of uncultivated and arrogant foreigners that the host made no difficulty in receiving us.

After we had at our entrance saluted the people of the inn and passed some time in the exchange of civilities, there came a girl, and, in a kneeling posture, offered the foreigners Japanese tea, which is always handed round in very small cups only half full. Then we took off our shoes and went into the guest-chamber. Such chambers in the Japanese inns are commonly large and dazzlingly clean. Furniture is completely wanting, but the floor is covered with mats of plaited straw. The walls are ornamented with songs suitable for the place, or mottoes, and with Japanese paintings. The rooms are separated from each other by thin movable panels, which slide in grooves, which can be removed or replaced at will. One may, therefore, as once happened to me, lay himself down to sleep in a very large room, and, if he sleeps sound, awake in the morning in a very small one. The room generally looks out on a Japanese garden-inclosure, or if it is in the upper story, on a small balcony. Immediately outside there is always a vessel filled with water and a scoop. Generally on one side of the room there is a wall-press, in which the bed-clothes are kept. These, the only household articles in the room, consist of a thick mat, which is spread on the floor, a round cushion for the head, or instead of it a wooden support, stuffed on the upper side, for the neck during sleep, and a thick stuffed night-shirt which serves as covering.

As soon as one comes in the female attendants distribute four-cornered cushions for sitting on, which are placed on the floor round a wooden box, on one corner of which stands a little brazier, on the other a high clay vessel of uniform breadth, with water in the bottom, which serves as a spittoon and tobacco-ash cup. At the same time tea is brought in anew, in the small cups previously described, with saucers, not of porcelain, but of metal.

Pipes are lighted, and a lively conversation commences. Along with the tea sweetmeats are brought in, of which, however, some cannot be relished by Europeans. The brazier forms the most important household article of the Japanese. Braziers are very variable in size and shape, but are often made in an exceedingly beautiful and tasteful way, of cast-iron or bronze, with gilding and raised figures. Often enough, however, they consist only of a clay crock. The Japanese are very skilful in keeping up fire in them without the least trace of fumes being perceptible in the room. The fuel consists of some well-burned pieces of charcoal, which lie imbedded in white straw-ashes, with which the fire-pan is nearly filled to the brim. When some glowing coals are

JAPANESE BEDROOM.

laid in such ashes they retain their heat for hours, until they are completely consumed. In every well-furnished house there are a number of braziers of different sizes, and there are often four-cornered hatches in the floor, which conceal a stone foundation intended as a base for the large brazier, over which the food is cooked.

At meal-times all the dishes are brought in at the same time on small lacquered tables, about half a foot high, and with a surface of four square feet. The dishes are placed in lacquered cups, less frequently in porcelain cups, and carried to the mouth with chop-sticks, without the help of knife, fork, or spoon. For fear of the fish-oils, which are used instead of butter, I never dared to test completely the productions of the Japanese art of cookery; but Dr. Almquist and Lieut. Nordquist, who were more unprejudiced, said they could put up with them very well. The following *menu* gives an idea of what a Japanese inn of the better class has to offer :—

Vegetable soup.
Boiled rice, sometimes with minced fowl.
Boiled fish or raw fish with horse-radish.
Vegetables with fish-sauce.
Tea.

Soy is used to the fish. The rice is brought in hot in a wooden vessel with a lid, and is distributed in abundance, but the other dishes in extremely small portions. After meals, especially in the evening, the Japanese often drink warm *saki*, or rice-brandy, out of peculiar porcelain bottles and small cups set apart for that purpose alone.

During the meal one is commonly surrounded by a numerous *personnel* of female attendants, squatted down on the floor, who keep up with the guest, if he understands their language, a lively conversation, interrupted by salvoes of hearty laughter. The girls remain while the man undresses in the evening, and permit themselves to make remarks on the difference of the *physique* of the Europeans and Japanese, which are not only, in our way of thinking, unsuitable for young girls, but even impertinent towards the guest. The male attendants are seldom seen, at least in the inner apartments. In the morning one washes himself in the yard or on the balcony, and if he wishes to avoid getting into disfavour, the guest will be careful not to spill anything or spit on the mat.

The Japanese tobacco-pipe now in use resembles that of the Chukches, is very small, and is smoked out in a couple of whiffs. A Japanese smokes without stopping a score of pipes in succession. Tobacco-smoking is now very general among high and low of both sexes. It was introduced at the close of the sixteenth century, it is uncertain whether from Corea or from the Portuguese possessions in Asia, and spread with great rapidity. As among us, it here too at first gave occasion to stringent prohibitions, and a lively exchange of writings for and against. In a work by the learned Japanologist, Mr. E. M. SATOW (" The Introduction of Tobacco into Japan," *Transactions of the Asiatic Society of Japan*, vol. vi. part i. p. 68), the following statements among others are made on this subject :—

" In 1609 there were in the capital two clubs whose main delight was to contrive quarrels with peaceful citizens. Upwards of fifty of the members of these clubs were suddenly arrested and thrown into prison ; but justice was satisfied when four or five of the leaders were executed, the rest were pardoned. As these societies were originally smoking clubs, the tobacco-plant came by the bad behaviour of their members into disrepute, and its use was prohibited. At that time tobacco was smoked in long pipes, which were stuck in the belt like a sword, or carried after the smoker by an attendant. In 1612 a proclamation was published in which tobacco-smoking and all trade in tobacco were prohibited, under penalty of forfeiture of estate. The

TOBACCO SMOKERS.
Japanese drawing.

prohibition was repeated several times, with as little success as in Europe."

Mr. Satow further gives the following peculiar extracts from a Japanese work, which enumerates the advantages and disadvantages that are connected with tobacco-smoking:—

"A.—ADVANTAGES.

" 1. It dispels the vapours and increases the energies.
" 2. It is good to produce at the beginning of a feast.

" 3. It is a companion in solitude.

" 4. It affords an excuse for resting now and then from work, as if in order to take breath.

" 5. It is a storehouse of reflection, and gives time for the fumes of wrath to disperse.

" B.—DISADVANTAGES.

" 1. There is a natural tendency to hit people over the head with one's pipe in a fit of anger.[1]

" 2. The pipe comes sometimes to be used for arranging the burning charcoal in the brazier.

" 3. An inveterate smoker has been known to walk about among the dishes with his pipe in his mouth.

" 4. People knock the ashes out of their pipes while still alight and forget to extinguish the fire.

" 5. Hence clothing and mats are frequently scorched by burning tobacco ash.

" 6. Smokers spit indiscriminately in braziers, foot-warmers and kitchen fires.

" 7. Also in the crevices between the floor mats.

" 8. They rap the pipe violently on the edge of the brazier.

" 9. They forget to have the ash-pot emptied till it is full to overflowing.

" 10. They use the ash-pot as nose-paper (*i.e.* they blow their nose into the ash-pot)."

As during our stay at Enoshima as the governor's guests we were constantly attended by two officials from his court, I considered it my duty to show myself worthy of the honour by a liberal distribution of drink-money. This is not given to the attendants, but is handed, wrapped up in paper, and accompanied by some choice courteous expressions, to the host himself. He on his part makes a polite speech with apologies that all had not been so well arranged as his honoured guest had a right to expect. He accompanies the traveller on his departure a shorter or longer distance in proportion to the amount of drink-money and the way in which his guest has behaved.

It is a specially praiseworthy custom among the Japanese to allow the trees in the neighbourhood of the temples to stand untouched. Nearly every temple, even the most inconsiderable, is therefore surrounded by a little grove, formed of the most splendid pines, particularly Cryptomeria and Ginko, which often

---

[1] The Japanese pipes are now so small that no serious results from this disadvantage are to be dreaded. In former times the pipes used were long and probably heavy. The Dyaks of Borneo still use pipes so heavy that they may be used as weapons.

T T

wholly conceal the small, decayed, and ill-kept wooden hut which is dedicated to some of the deities of Buddha or Shinto.

On the 23rd September the Europeans and Japanese of Yokohama gave a dinner and ball for us in the hall of the English club. It was beautifully lighted and decorated. Among other things there were to be seen on a wall portraits of Berzelius and Thunberg, surrounded by garlands of greenery. The latter has a high reputation in Japan. His work on the flora of the

ITO-KESKE.

A Japanese Editor of Thunberg's writings.

country has lately been published in a Japanese edition with a wood-cut portrait, by no means bad, of the famous Swedish naturalist,[1] engraved in Japan; and a monument to his and Kämpfer's memory is to be found at Nagasaki, erected there at the instance of von Siebold.[2] The chairman of the feast was

[1] The work bears the title : *Tai-sei-hon-zo-mei-so* (short list of European plant-names), by Ito-Keske, 1829, 3 vols.

[2] Carl Peter Thunberg, born at Jönköping in 1743, famed for his travels in South Africa, Japan, &c., and for a number of important scientific

Dr. GEERTZ, a Dutchman, who had lived a long time in the country and published several valuable works on its natural productions.

On the 26th September I started for Tokio, in order thence to undertake a journey proposed and arranged by the Danish consul, Herr Bavier, to Asamayama, a yet active volcano in the interior of the country. In consequence of an unexpected death among the European consuls at Yokohama, Herr Bavier, however, could not join us until the day after that which had been fixed for our departure. The 27th accordingly was passed in Tokio among other things, in seeing the beautiful collections

MONUMENT TO THUNBERG AND KAEMPFER AT NAGASAKI.

of antiquities made by the *attaché* of the Austrian legation, Herr H. VON SIEBOLD, son of the famous naturalist of the same name. Japan has also, like most other lands, had its Stone Age, from which remains are found at several places in

works, finally Professor at Upsala, died in 1828. Engelbert Kämpfer, born in Westphalia in 1651, was secretary of the embassy that started from Sweden to Persia in 1683. Kämpfer, however, did not return with the embassy, but continued his travels in the southern and eastern parts of Asia, among them, even to Japan, which he visited in 1690-92; he died in 1716. Kämpfer's and Thunberg's works, together with the great work of von Siebold, who erected the monument to them, form the most important sources of the knowledge of the Japan that once was.

T T 2

the country, both on Yezo and on the more southerly islands. Implements from this period are now collected assiduously both by natives and Europeans, and have been described by H. von Siebold in a work accompanied by photographic illustrations. In general the implements of the Japanese stone folk have a resemblance to the stone tools still in use among the Eskimo, and even in this fruitful land the primitive race, as the bone remains in the kitchen-middens show, lived at first mainly by hunting and fishing.

CHAPTER XVII.

Excursion to Asamayama—The Nakasendo road—Takasaki—Difficulty of obtaining quarters for the night—The Baths at Ikaho—Massage in Japan—Swedish matches—Travelling in *Kago*—Savavatari—Criminals —Kusatsu—The Hot Springs and their healing power—Rest at Roku- riga-hara—The summit of Asamayama—The descent—Journey over Usui-toge—Japanese actors—Pictures of Japanese folk-life—Return to Yokohama.

On the 28th September, early in the morning, accompanied by Lieut. Hovgaard, Herr Bavier, an interpreter, and a Japanese cook skilled in European cookery, I started on a journey to Asamayama. At first we travelled in two very rattling and inconvenient carriages, drawn each by a pair of horses, to the town Takasaki, situated on the great road " Nakasendo," which passes through the interior of the country and connects Tokio and Kioto. This road is considered something grand by the Japanese. In Sweden it would be called an indifferently kept district road. On this road *jinrikishas* are met in thousands, and a great many horses, oxen, and men, *bearing* heavy burdens. but with the exception of the posting carriages, by which, for some years back, a regular communication between Tokio and Takasaki has been kept up, not a single wheeled vehicle drawn by horses or oxen ; and though the road passes through an unbroken series of populous villages, surrounded by well culti- vated rice fields and small gardens, there is not a single work- horse or work-ox to be seen. For all the ground in Japan is cultivated by the hand, and there are few cattle.

Most of the roads in the country consist of foot-paths, so narrow that two laden horses can pass each other only with difficulty. Goods are therefore carried, where there is no canal or river, for the most part by men. The plains are extraordin- arily well cultivated, and we must specially admire the industry with which water-courses have been cut and the uneven slopes changed into level terraces.

The post-horses on Nakasendo were so poor and wretched
лat in Sweden one would have been liable to punishment for
·uelty to animals for using them. They went, however, at a
retty good speed. There were places for changing horses
; regular distances of fifteen to twenty kilometres. The
river besides halted often on the way at some dwelling-house
ι take a couple of scoopfuls of water out of the water-vessel
anding before it and throw them into the horses' mouths and
ɔtween their hind-legs. The opportunity was always taken
lvantage of by the girls of the house to come out and offer
ιe travellers a small cup of Japanese tea, an act of courtesy
лat was repaid with some friendly words and a copper coin.

When we visited any of the peasants' gardens by the way-
de we were always received with extreme friendliness, either on
special dais in the common room looking to the road, or in an
ιner room whose floor was covered with a mat of dazzling white-
ɔss, and on whose walls hung pictures, with songs and mottoes.
he brazier was brought forward, tea and sweetmeats were
лnded round, all with lively conversation and frequent bows.
he difference between the palace of the rich (if we may dis-
ıguish with the name any building in Japan) and the dwelling
˙ the less well-to-do is much smaller here than in Europe.
ᵀe did not see any beggars in our journey into the interior of
ιe country.[1] Nor did the distinction of class appear to be
ι sharp as might be expected in a land where the evils of rank
лd been so great as in Old Japan. We several times saw in
ιe inns by the roadside, people of condition who were travelling
. jinrikishas eat their rice and drink their saki together with
ιe coolies who were drawing their vehicles.

To judge by the crowds of children who swarmed everywhere
ong the roads the people must be very prolific. A girl of
ght or ten years of age was seldom to be seen without
ıother young one bound on her back. This burden did not
ıpear to trouble the sister or attendant very much. Without
ving herself any concern about the child or thinking of its
:istence, she took part actively in games, ran errands, &c.

Even in the interior of the country foreigners are received
ith great friendliness. The lower classes in Japan have also
ason for this, for whatever influence the latest political
ıanges may have had on the old kuge, daimio, and samurai
milies of Japan, the position of the cultivator of the soil is now
uch more secure than before, when he was harried by hundreds
small tyrants. His dress is the same as before, with the ex-
ption, however, that a great proportion of the male population,
en far into the interior, have laid aside the old troublesome way

---

[1] On the contrary, we saw a number of beggars on the country roads in
ɔ neighbourhood of Yokohama.

of collecting the hair in a knot over a close shaven spot on the crown of the head. Instead, they wear their thick raven-black hair cut short in the European style. How distinctive of the new period this change is may be seen from the eagerness with which the Japanese authorities questioned GOLOVIN about the religious and political revolutions which they assumed to have been connected with the change in the European mode of wearing the hair during the commencement of the nineteenth century; for the Russian ambassador LAXMAN, who was highly esteemed by the Japanese, had worn a pig-tail and powdered hair while Golovin and his companions had their hair unpowdered and cut short.[1] When it is warm the workmen wear only a small, generally light-blue, girdle round the waist and between the legs. Otherwise they are naked. They are thus seen to be in many cases strongly tattooed over the greater part of the body. I have not seen the women working naked. They perhaps do so at the warmest season of the year. At least they do not refrain from undressing completely while bathing right in the midst of a crowd of men known and unknown, a state of things which at first, in consequence of the power of prejudice, shocks the European, but to which even the former prude gets accustomed sooner than one would suppose. We even frequently see European ladies drawn in a *jinrikisha* by a youth completely naked with the exception of the blue girdle. Many, especially of the younger men, have besides so well-formed a body, that the sculptor who could accurately reproduce it in marble would at once attain a reputation co-extensive with the globe.

Takasaki is the residence of a governor, with a population of about 20,000 ; but, like most of the towns of Japan, it differs little from many of the villages we passed through. We arrived late in the evening, and there had our first and last experience of an inconvenience of which Europeans often complain in travelling in Japan, and to which they have themselves given occasion by the offensive way in which they not unfrequently behave. We knocked at the door of one inn after another without being received. At one place "the house was full," at another "the rooms were under repair," at a third "the inn people were out," &c. At last we had to apply to the police. When we had shown them our passport, we succeeded with their help in getting a night's lodging with an elderly host, who received us

<hr>

[1] *Voyage de M. Golovin*, Paris, 1818, i. p. 176. Golovin, who was captain in the Russian navy, passed the years 1811-13 in imprisonment in Japan. He and his comrades in misfortune were received with great friendliness by the people, and very well treated by the authorities, if we except the exceedingly tedious examinations to which they were subjected to extract from them the most minute particulars regarding Europe, and particularly Russia.

with a countenance which clearly indicated that he would rather
have hewn us in pieces with one of the two swords he had
formerly as *samurai* been entitled to wear, than received us
under his roof. After our entrance he still turned to the police
official with the cry of lamentation : " Must I then actually
receive these barbarians ? " But we had our revenge in a noble
way. We took off our boots before we entered the room, were so
profuse with talk, civilities, and bows, and on the whole behaved
in such a courteous fashion, that our previously distracted host
not only bade us welcome back, but also gave us a letter of
introduction to the innkeepers at an inn where we were to stay
next, declaring that if we showed this letter we need not fear
any such disagreeable adventure as that just described.

Most of the houses in the Japanese towns are built of pretty
thin, carefully joined timbers. But besides these there are to be
seen here and there small houses with very thick walls, windows
provided with heavy iron gratings, and doors that could be
fastened with large locks and bolts. These houses are fire-
resisting, and are used as storehouses for valuables and household
articles when there is danger of fire. Fires are so common in
Japan that it is supposed that a tenth part of every town is
burned down yearly. The fireman corps is numerous, well
ordered from old times, its members bold and daring. During
our stay overnight at Takasaki we were lodged in such a fire-
proof house, in very large clean apartments with the floor partly
covered with carpets after the European pattern. The walls
were very thick and of brick ; the interior fittings and stairs on
the other hand of wood.

I have just mentioned that we were compelled to resort to the
police in order to obtain quarters for the night. Policemen are
numerous in Japan both in town and country. For the most
part they are taken from the former *samurai* class. They are
clothed in the European style; and walk, with a long stick in a
certain position under the arm, quietly and calmly on the streets
and roads, without, except in cases of necessity, making any
show of their authority. Commonly they are, or appear to be,
young, and all have a gentlemanlike appearance. In a word, they
appear to be equal to the best European police of the present
day, and stand immeasurably above the guardian of the peace, or
rather the raiser of dispeace, as he appeared some decades ago on
the European continent. During the latest revolt the police
were employed by the Government as infantry, and elicited
general admiration by the fire, the gallantry, and the contempt of
death with which they went into action with their old favourite
weapon, the Japanese sword.

A passport is still required for travelling in the interior of the
country, but this is easily obtained at the request of the consul

if health or the wish to prosecute researches be given as the
reason, it being possible perhaps to include common love of
travelling under the latter head. Commercial travelling is not
yet permitted in the interior, nor is the right of settling for the purpose of carrying on business granted to Europeans. The foreign
ambassadors have often entered into negotiations in order to bring
about a change on this point, but hitherto without success, because the Government, as a condition for the complete opening
of the country, require the abrogation of the unreasonable "extra-
territorial" arrangement which is in force, and by which the
foreigner is not subject to the common laws and courts of Japan,
but to the laws of his own country, administered by consular
courts. An alteration in this point may however be brought
about in a short time as Japan will soon be sufficiently powerful
to be able to abrogate all the injurious paragraphs in her treaties
with the civilised countries of Europe. Now, besides, the
ambassadors of the foreign powers, who in former times all acted
together, have divided into two parties, of which one—Russia
and America—wishes, or at least feigns to wish, gradually to free
Japan from all tutelage and to place it on an equality with other
civilised countries; the other again—England, Germany, Holland,
and France—wishes still to retain the guardianship, which
was established by violence, and confirmed by treaty several
years ago.

Shortly before our arrival a quarrel took place between Japan
and the European powers about, as the Japanese themselves said,
a breach of international law, which caused much irritation in
the country. A German vessel coming from Nagasaki, where
the cholera was raging, on the advice of the German minister
broke the quarantine prescribed by the Government, and without
further precautions discharged her cargo in the harbour of
Yokohama. That the cholera in this town was thereby *made worse*
is indeed not only unproved but also undoubtedly incorrect,
though many Japanese in their irritation positively affirmed that
this was the case ; but the words that were uttered by Japan's
fêted guest, ex-President General GRANT,[1] that the Japanese
Government had the right without more ado to sink the vessel,
have left a memory in the minds both of the Government and of
the people, which may in the future lead them to a perhaps
unwise but fully justified exertion of their strength were such
a deed to be repeated.

The first impression of the Japanese, both men and women,
is exceedingly pleasant, but many Europeans who have lived
a considerable time in the country say that this impression is not
maintained, a circumstance which in my belief depends more on

[1] General Grant, as is well known, visited Japan in the autumn of 1879.
He left Yokohama the day after the *Vega* anchored in its harbour.

the Europeans themselves than on the Japanese. For the European merchants are said not to find it so easy to cut gold here with a case-knife as before, and the ambassadors of the Great Powers find it day by day more difficult to maintain their old commanding standpoint towards a government which knows that a great future is before the country, if inconsiderate ambition or unlooked-for misfortune do not unexpectedly hinder its development. Another reproach, that the Japanese can imitate what another has done, but is unable himself to invent anything new, appears on the other hand to be justified in the meantime. But it is unreasonable to demand that a nation should not only in a few decades pass through a development for which centuries have been required in Europe, but also immediately reach the summit of the knowledge of our time so as to be at the same time creative. But it would be wonderful, if the natural science, literature, and art of the nineteenth century, transplanted among a gifted people, with a culture so peculiar and so pervasive, and with an art-sense so developed as those of Japan, did not in time produce new, splendid, and unexpected fruit. The same irresistible necessity which now drives the Japanese to learn all that the European and the American know, will, when he has reached that goal, spur him on to go further up the Nile river of research.

A short distance beyond Takasaki the road to the volcano to which we were on our way, was no longer along Nakasendo, and we could therefore no longer continue our journey in carriages drawn by horses, but were compelled to content ourselves with *jinrikishas*. In these, on the 29th of September, we traversed in five and a half hours the very hilly road to Ikaho, noted for its baths, situated at a height of 700 metres above the sea. The landscape here assumes a quite different stamp. The road which before ran over an unbroken plain, thickly peopled, and cultivated like a garden, now begins to pass between steep uncultivated hills, overgrown with tall, uncut, withered grass, separated by valleys in which run purling rivulets, nearly concealed by exceedingly luxuriant bushy thickets. Ikaho is celebrated for the warm, or more correctly hot, springs which well up from the volcanic hills which surround the little town, which is beautifully situated on a slope. As at the baths of Europe, invalids seek here a remedy for their ailments, and the town therefore consists almost exclusively of hotels, baths, and shops for the visitors. The baths are situated, partly in large open wooden sheds, where men and women bathe together without distinction, partly in private houses. In every bath there is a basin one metre in depth, to which a constant stream of water is conducted from some of the hot springs. The spring water has of course cooled very much before it is used, but is still so hot notwithstanding that I could only with difficulty remain in it a couple of seconds.

In the streets of the town we often met blind persons who walked about very safely without any attendant, only feeling their way with a long bamboo. They blew a short pipe now and then to warn passers-by of their presence. I thought at first that these unfortunates were trying to regain the sight of the eye at the hot springs, but on inquiring whether the water was beneficial in that respect, I was informed that they were not there as seekers after health, but as "massageurs" (shampooers). Massage has been in use in Japan for several centuries back, and therefore persons are often to be met with in the streets offering their services as massageurs, crying in the streets in about the same way as the fruit-sellers in Russia.

The inn where we lodged for the night, consisted as usual of a number of very clean rooms covered with mats, without furniture, but ornamented with songs and mottoes on the walls. One would live here exceedingly well, if like the Japanese he could manage to live wholly on the floor and conform carefully to the indispensable rules, an observance which besides is necessary, because otherwise the inmate is exposed to a very unfriendly reception not only from his host but also from the attendants. An inconvenience in travelling in Japan is the difficulty a European has in accustoming himself to the dietary of the Japanese. Bread they do not use, nor meat, but their food consists mainly of rice and fish, with fowls, fruit, mushrooms, sweetmeats, Japanese tea, &c., in addition. Fish is generally eaten raw, and in that case is said to differ little in taste from our pickled salmon. The food is not unfrequently cooked with fish oils of anything but an agreeable taste. If a traveller wishes to avoid this dietary, he must have his own cook with him on the journey. In this capacity there attended us a Japanese, whose name was Senkiti-San, but who was commonly called by his companions Kok-San (Mr. Cook). He had learned European (French) cooking at Yokohama, and during the journey devoted himself with so great zeal to his calling, that even in the deserts at the foot of Asamayama he gave himself no rest until he could offer us a dinner of five dishes, consisting of chicken soup, fowl omelette, fowl-beefsteak, fowl *fricassé*, and omelette *aux confitures*, all thus consisting only of fowls and hens' eggs, cooked in different ways.

For some years back lucifer matches have been an article of necessity in Japan, and it was pleasing to us Swedes to observe that the Swedish matches have here a distinct preference over those of other countries. In nearly every little shop, even in the interior of the country, are to be seen the well-known boxes with the inscription " Säkerhets tändsticker utan svafvel och fosfor."

But if we examine the boxes more carefully, we find upon many
f them, along with the magic sentence unintelligible to
he Japanese, an inscription indicating that they have been
made by some Japanese manufacturer. On other boxes this is
completely wanting, but the falsification is shown by an unfortunate error in the inscription. It thus appears that the
Swedish matches are not only introduced into Japan on a large
scale, but are also counterfeited, being made with the Swedish
inscription on the box and with a cover resembling that used at
home. The imitation, however, is not nearly so good as the
original, and my Japanese servant bade me therefore, when I
purchased a box of matches, observe carefully that I got one
of the right (Swedish) sort.

Photography also has spread so rapidly in the country that at
many places in small towns and villages in the interior Japanese
photographers are to be met with who put out of their hands by
no means bad work. The Japanese appear to have a great
liking for having their by no means remarkable dwellings photo-
graphed. On several occasions, when we left a place we received
from our host as a parting gift a photograph of his house or inn.
Perhaps this was done with the same view as that which induces
his European brother-in-trade to advertise at great expense.

Between Ikaho and Savavatari, our next resting-place, the
road was so bad that the jinrikisha could no longer be used, we
accordingly had to use the kago, a Japanese sedan-chair made of
bamboo, of the appearance of which the accompanying woodcut gives an idea. It is exceedingly inconvenient for Europeans,
because they cannot like the Japanese sit with their legs crosswise under them, and in course of time it becomes tiresome
to let them dangle without other support by the side of the
kago. Even for the bearers this sedan chair strikes me as being
of inconvenient construction, which is shown among other things
by their halting an instant every two hundred, or in going up a
hill, every hundred paces, in order to shift the shoulder under the
bamboo pole. We went up-hill and down-hill with considerable
speed however, so that we traversed the road between Ikaho
and Savavatari, 6 ri, or 23·6 kilometres in length, in ten hours.
The road, which was exceedingly beautiful, ran along flowery
banks of rivulets, overgrown with luxuriant bamboo thickets,
and many different kinds of broad-leaved trees. Only round
the old temples, mostly small and inconsiderable, were to be
seen ancient tall Cryptomeria and Ginko trees. The burying
places were commonly situated, not as at home, in the neighbourhood of the larger temples, but near the villages. They
were not inclosed, but marked out by stone monuments from a
third of a metre to half a metre in height, on one side of which
an image of Buddha was sometimes sculptured. The recent

graves were often adorned with flowers, and at some of them small foot-high Shinto shrines had been made of wooden pins.

Savavatari, like Ikaho, is built on the slope of a hill. The streets between the houses are almost all stairs or steep ascents. Here too there well up from the volcanic rocks acidulous springs, at which invalids seek to regain health. The watering-place, however, is of less repute than Ikaho or Kusatsu.

While we walked about the village in the evening we saw at one place a crowd of people. This was occasioned by a competition going on there. Two young men, who wore no other clothes than a narrow girdle going round the waist and between the legs, wrestled within a circle two or three metres across drawn on a sandy area. He was considered the victor who threw the other to the ground or forced him beyond the

JAPANESE KAGO.

circle. A special judge decided in doubtful cases. The beginning of the contest was most peculiar, the combatants kneeling in the middle of the circle and sharply eying each other in order to make the attack at a signal given by the judge, when a single push might at once make an end of the contest. In this competition there took part about a dozen young men, all well grown, who in their turn stepped with some encouraging cries or gestures into the circle in order to test their powers. The spectators consisted of old men and women, and boys and girls of all ages. Most of them were clean and well-dressed, and had a very attractive appearance.

Here it was the youth of the village themselves that took part in the contest. But there are also in Japan persons who

carry on these games as their occupation, and exhibit themselves
for money. They are in general very fat, as appears from the
accompanying drawing, which represents the beginning of the
contest, when both the combatants are still watching to get
a good hold.

Next day, the 1st October, we continued our journey to
Kusatsu. The road was uphill for a distance of 550 metres,

JAPANESE WRESTLERS.

downhill for nearly as far, then up again, and ran often without
any protecting fence past deep abysses, or over high bridges of
the most dangerous construction. It was, therefore, impossible
for any wheeled vehicle to traverse it, so that we had to use in
some cases *kagos*, in others riding-horses. Unfortunately the
Japanese high saddle does not suit the European, and if the
traveller prefers a riding-horse to a *kago*, he must, if he does not

carry a saddle with him, determine to ride on an unsaddled
horse, which, with the wretched steeds that are only available
here, soon becomes so unpleasant that he at last prefers to let
his legs hang benumbed from the *kago*. A peculiarity in Japan
is that the rider seldom himself guides his horse. It is commonly led by a halter by a groom running alongside the rider.
These grooms are very light-footed and enduring, so that even at
a rapid pace they are not left behind. Running footmen also
attend the carriages of people of distinction in the towns and the

JAPANESE BRIDGE.
After a Japanese drawing.

mail-coaches on Nakasendo. When there is a crowd before the
carriage they jump down and drive away the people by a
dreadful shouting. From the mail-coach they also blow the
post-horn, not just to the advantage of the ear-drums of the
travellers.

The scenery by the roadside was exceedingly beautiful. Now
it consisted of wild valleys, filled with luxuriant vegetation
which completely concealed the crystal-clear streams purling in
the bottoms; now of level grassy plains or hill-slopes, thickly

JAPANESE MOUNTAIN LANDSCAPE

studded with solitary trees, chiefly chestnuts and oaks. The
inhabitants were fully occupied with the chestnut harvest.
Before every hut mats were spread out, on which chestnuts
lay drying in thick layers. Grain and cotton were being dried
in the same small way as it appeared to us Europeans. On the
plains there stood besides in the neighbourhood of the cabins
large mortars, by which the grain was reduced to groats. On
the hills these tramp-stamps are partly replaced by small mills
of an exceedingly simple construction, introduced by the Dutch.

We passed the 2nd October at Kusatsu, the Aix-la-Chapelle
of Japan, famed like that place for its hot sulphurous springs.
Innumerable invalids here seek an alleviation of their pains.

INN AT KUSATSU

The town lives upon them, and accordingly consists mainly of
baths, inns, and shops for the visitors.

The inns are of the sort common in Japan, spacious, airy,
clean, without furniture, but with good braziers, miniature
tea-services, clean matting, screens ornamented with poetical
mottoes, which even when translated were almost unintelligible to
us, friendly hosts, and numerous female attendants. If the
traveller brings his own cook with him, as we did, he can live
very comfortably, as I have before stated, at such an inn.

The hot springs which have conferred on Kusatsu its importance rise at the foot of a pretty high hill of volcanic origin.
The rocks in the surrounding country consist exclusively of lava

and volcanic tuffs, and a short distance from the town there is an extinct volcano in whose crater there are layers of sulphur.[1] In the immediate neighbourhood of the place where the main spring rises there is a thick solidified lava stream, surrounded by tuffs, which near the surface is cleft into a number of large vesicular blocks. From this point the hot water is conducted in long open wooden channels to the bath-house of the town, and to several evaporating pools, some by the wayside, others in the town, intended for collecting the solid constituents of the water, which are then sold in the country as medicine. The great evaporation from these pools, from the open channels and the hot baths, wraps the town almost constantly in a cloud of watery vapour, while a very strong odour of sulphuretted hydrogen reminds us that this is one of the constituents of the healing waters.

The road between the wells and the town appears to form the principal promenade of the place. Along this are to be seen innumerable small monuments, from a half to a whole metre in height, consisting of pieces of lava heaped upon each other. These miniature memorials form by their littleness a peculiar contrast to the *bauta* stones and *jettekast* of our Swedish forefathers, and are one of the many instances of the people's fondness for the little and the neat, which are often to be met in Japan. They are said to be erected by visitors as thank-offerings to some of the deities of Buddha or Shinto.

I received from a Japanese physician the following information regarding the wells at Kusatsu and their healing power. In and near the town there are twenty-two wells, with water of about the same quality, but of different uses in the healing of various diseases. In the hottest well the water where it rises has a temperature of 162° F. (= 72·2° C.). The largest number of the sick who seek health at the baths, suffer from syphilis. This disease is now cured according to the European method, with mercury, iodide of potassium, and baths. The cure requires a hundred days ; from seventy to eighty per cent. of the patients are cured completely, though purple spots remain on the skin. The disease does not break out anew. A large number of leprous patients also visit the baths. The leprosy is of various kinds ; that with sores is alleviated by the baths, and is cured possibly in two years ; that without sores but with the skin insensible is incurable, but is also checked by frequent bathing. All true lepers come from the coast provinces. A similar disease is produced also among the hills by the eating of tainted fish and fowl. This disease consists in the skin becoming insensible, the nerves inactive, and the patient, who otherwise feels well,

[1] According to the statement of the inhabitants ; I had not time to visit the place.

finding it impossible to walk. It is also cured completely in very severe cases, by baths, ammonia applied inwardly, castor-oil, Peruvian bark, &c. A third type of this ailment is the bone-disease, *kak'ke'*, which is exceedingly common in Japan, and is believed to be caused by unvarying food and want of exercise. It is very obstinate, but is often cured in two or three years with chloride of iron, albumen, change of diet from the common Japanese to the European, with red wine, milk, bread, vegetables, &c. This disease begins with a swelling in the legs, then the skin becomes insensible, first on the legs, next on the stomach, the face, and the wrists. Then the swelling falls, fever comes on, and death takes place. There are besides, certain wells for curing rheumatism, for which from two to three years are required; for eye-diseases and for headache, the latter playing an important part among the illnesses that are cured at Kusatsu. It principally attacks women between twenty and thirty years of age. One of the Kusatsu wells acts very beneficially in this case. Its water is conducted to a special bathing-shed open to the street, intended exclusively for the men and women who suffer from this disease.

Many of the baths at Kusatsu are taken so hot that special precautions must be adopted before one steps down into the water. These consist in winding cotton cloths round those parts of the body which are most sensitive, and in causing the body to perspire strongly before the bath is taken, which is done by the bathers with cries and shouts and with certain movements stirring the water in the basin with large heavy boards. They then all step down into the bath and up again simultaneously at a sign given by the physician sitting at the back of the bathing shed. Without this arrangement it would perhaps be difficult to get the patients to go into the bath, for agreeable it could not be, to judge from the grave faces of the bathers and the fire-red colour of their bodies when they come out.

The baths are under open sheds. Men and women all bathe in common, and in presence of both male and female spectators. They make their remarks without reserve on the diseases of the patients, even if they are of that sort about which one would not speak willingly even to his physician. Often the bath-basin is not fenced off in any way, except that it is protected from rain and sunshine by a roof resting on four posts. In such cases the bathers dress and undress in the street.

In consequence of the situation of Kusatsu at a height of 1050 metres above the sea, the winter there is very cold and windy. The town is then abandoned not only by the visitors to the baths, but also by most of the other inhabitants. Already, at the time of our visit, the number of bathers remaining was only inconsiderable. Even these were preparing to depart.

During the second night that we passed at Kusatsu, our night's rest was disturbed by a loud noise from the next room. It was a visitor who was to leave the place the following morning, and who now celebrated his recovery with *saki* (rice-brandy) and string music.

·The environs of Kusatsu are nearly uncultivated, though the vegetation is exceedingly luxuriant. It consists partly of bamboo thickets, partly of a high rich grass, above which rise solitary pines, mixed with a few oaks or chestnuts.

On the 3rd October we continued our journey to the foot of Asamayama. The road was very bad, so that even the *kago* bearers had difficulty in getting along. It first ran across two

BATH AT KUSATSU.

valleys more than 300 feet deep, occupied with close, luxuriant, bushy thickets. We then came to an elevated plain of great extent covered with unmown grass, studded with beautiful oaks and chestnuts. The plain was not turned to any account, though thousands of the industrious population could find an abundant living there by tending cattle. Farther up the oaks and chestnuts were mixed with a few birches, resembling those at home, and we came next to complete deserts, where the ground consisted of lava blocks and lava gravel, scarcely covered by any grass, and yielding nourishment only to solitary pines. This continued to the place—Rokuriga-hara—where we were to pass the night, and from which the next day we were to ascend the summit of Asamayama.

Rokuriga-hara is situated at a height of 1270 metres above the sea. There was no inn here, nor any place inhabited all the year round, but only a large open shed. This was divided into two by a passage in the middle. We settled on one side of this, making our bed as well as we could on the raised floor, and protecting ourselves from the night air with coverings which our thoughtful host at Kusatsu had lent us. On the other side of the passage our *kago* bearers and guide passed the night crowding round a log fire made on a stone foundation in the middle of the floor. The *kago* bearers were protected from the very perceptible night cold only by thin cotton blouses. In order to warm them I ordered an abundant distribution of *saki*, a piece of generosity that did not cost very much, but which clearly won me the undivided admiration of all the coolies. They passed the greater part of the night without sleep, with song and jest, with their *saki* bottles and tobacco pipes. We slept well and warmly after partaking of an abundant supper of fowl and eggs, cooked in different ways by Kok-San with his usual talent and his usual variety of dishes.

We had been informed that at this place we would hear a constant noise from the neighbouring volcano, and that hurtful gases (probably carbonic acid) sometimes accumulated in such quantities in the neighbouring woods that men and horses would be suffocated if they spent the night there. We listened in vain for the noise, and did not observe any trace of such gases. All was as peaceful as if the glowing hearth in the interior of the earth was hundreds of miles away. But we did not require the evidence of the column of smoke which was seen to rise from the mountain top, which formed the goal of our visit, or of the inhabitants who survived the latest eruption, to come to the conclusion that we were in the neighbourhood of an enormous, still active volcano. Everywhere round our resting-place lay heaps of small pieces of lava which had been thrown out of the volcano (so-called lapilli), and which had not yet had time to weather sufficiently to serve as an under-stratum for any vegetation, and a little from the hut there was a solidified lava stream of great depth.

Next day, the 4th October, we ascended the summit of the mountain. At first we travelled in *kago* over a valley filled with pretty close wood, then the journey was continued on foot up the steep volcanic cone, covered with small lava blocks and lapilli. The way was staked out with small heaps of stones raised at a distance of about 100 metres apart. Near the crater we found at one of these cairns a little Shinto shrine, built of sticks. Its sides were only half a metre in length. Our guide performed his devotions here. One of them had already at a stone cairn situated farther down with great seriousness made some conjurations with reference to my promise to make an extra distribution of red wine, if we got good weather at the top.

As on Vesuvius, we can also on Asamayama distinguish a large exterior crater, originating from some old eruption, but now almost completely filled up by a new volcanic cone, at whose top the present crater opens. This crater has a circumference of about two kilometres; the old crater, or what the old geologists called the elevation-crater, has been much larger. The volcano is still active. For it constantly throws out "smoke," consisting of watery vapour, sulphurous acid, and probably also carbonic acid. Occasionally a perceptible smell of sulphuretted hydrogen is observed. It is possible without difficulty to crawl to the edge of the crater and glance down into its interior. It is very deep. The walls are perpendicular and at the bottom of the abyss there are to be seen several clefts from which vapours arise. In the same way "smoke" forces its way at some places at the edge of the crater through small imperceptible cracks in the mountain. Both on the border of the crater, on its sides and its bottom there is to be seen a yellow efflorescence, which at the places which I got at to examine it consisted of sulphur. The edge of the crater is solid rock, a little-weathered augiteandesite differing very much in its nature at different places. The same or similar rocks also project at several places at the old border of the crater, but the whole surface of the volcanic cone besides consists of small loose pieces of lava, without any trace of vegetation. Only at one place the brim of the old crater is covered with an open pine wood. The volcano has also small side craters, from which gases escape. The same coarse fantasy, which still prevails in the form of the hell-dogma among several of the world's most cultured peoples, has placed the home of those of the followers of Buddha who are doomed to eternal punishment in the glowing hearths in the interior of the mountain, to which these crater-openings lead; and that the heresies of the well-meaning Bishop Lindblom have not become generally prevalent in Japan is shown among other things by this, that many of these openings are said to be entrances to the "children's hell." Neither at the main crater nor at any of the side craters can any true lava streams be seen. Evidently the only things thrown out from them have been gases, volcanic ashes, and lapilli. On the other hand, extensive eruptions of lava have taken place at several points on the side of the mountain, though these places are now covered with volcanic ashes.

After having eaten our breakfast in a cleft so close to the smoking crater that the empty bottles could be thrown directly into the bottomless deeps, we commenced our return journey. At first we took the same way as during the ascent, but afterwards held off to the right, down a much steeper and more difficult path than we had traversed before. The mountain side had here a slope of nearly forty-five degrees, and consisted of a quite loose volcanic sand, not bound together by any vegetable carpet. It would therefore have been scarcely possible to ascend to the summit of the mountain this way, but we went rapidly downwards, often at a dizzy speed, but without other inconvenience than that one now and then fell flat and rolled headforemost down the steep slopes, and that our shoes were completely torn to tatters by the angular lava gravel. Above the mountaintop the sky was clear of clouds, but between it and the surface of the earth there spread out a thick layer of cloud which seen from above resembled a boundless storm-tossed sea, full of foaming breakers. The extensive view we would otherwise have had of the neighbouring mountain ridges from the top of Asamayama was thus concealed. Only here and there an opening was formed in the cloud, resembling a sun-spot, through which we got a glimpse of the underlying landscape. When we came to the foot of the mountain we long followed a ridge, covered with greenery, formed of an immense stream of lava, which had issued from an opening in the mountain side now refilled. This had probably taken place during the tremendous eruption of 1783, when not only enormous lava-streams destroyed forests and villages at the foot of the mountain, but the whole of the neighbouring region between Oiwake and Usui-toge, previously fertile, was changed by an ash-rain into an extensive waste. Across this large plain, infertile and little cultivated, situated at a height of 980 metres above the sea, we went without a guide to the village Oiwake, where we lodged for the night at an inn by the side of the road Nakasendo, one of the cleanest and best kept of the many well-kept inns I saw during our journey in the interior of the country.

Hence I sent a messenger on foot to Takasaki to order a carriage to Tokio. A former *samurai* undertook for a payment of three *yen* (about 12s.) to carry the message. Oiwake is indeed situated on the great road Nakasendo, but it can here only with difficulty be traversed by carriages, because between this village and Takasaki it is necessary to go over the pass Usui-toge, where the road, though lowered considerably of late, rises to a height of 1200 metres. We therefore here used *jinrikishas*, a mode of conveyance very agreeable to tourists, which, though introduced only recently, has already spread to all parts of the country.

Every one with an open eye for the beauties of nature and interest in the life and manners of a foreign people, must find a journey in a *jinrikisha* over Usui-toge pleasant in a high degree.

JAPANESE LANDSCAPE.

The landscape here is extraordinarily beautiful, perhaps unmatched in the whole world. The road has been made here with great difficulty between wild, black, rocky masses, along deep clefts, whose sides are often covered with the most luxuriant vegetation. No fence protects the *jinrikisha* in its rapid progress down the mountains from the bottomless abysses by the wayside. A man must therefore not be weak in the nerves if he is to derive pleasure from the journey. He must rely on the coolie's keen eye and sure foot. On all sides one is surrounded by a confused mass of lofty shattered mountain tops, and deep down in the valleys mountain streams rush along, whose crystal-clear water is collected here and there into small lakes confined between heights covered with greenery. Now the traveller passes a dizzy abyss by a bridge of the most defective construction, now he sees a stream of water rushing down from an enormous height by the wayside. Thousands of foot-passengers, crowds of pilgrims, long rows of coolies, oxen and horses bearing heavy burdens meet the traveller, who during frequent rests at the foot of the steep slopes has an opportunity of studying the variegated life of the people. He is always surrounded by cheerful and friendly faces, and the pleasant impression is never disturbed by the expressions of coarseness in speech and behaviour which so often meet us in Europe.

It is not until the traveller has passed the mountain ridge and descended to a height of only 300 metres above the sea that the road becomes passable for a carriage. While we exchanged, not without regret, our clean, elegant *jinrikishas* for two inferior vehicles drawn by horses, I saw two men wandering from shop to shop, standing some moments at each place, ringing a bell and passing on when they were not attended to. On my inquiry as to what sort of people they were, I was informed that they were wandering players. For me of course they did not ring in vain. For a payment of fifty cents they were ready immediately to show in the street itself a specimen of their art. One of them put on a well-made mask, representing the head of a monster, with a movable jaw and terrible teeth. To the mask was fastened a cloak, in which the player wrapt himself during the representation. He then with great skill and supple tasteful gestures, which would have honoured a European *danseuse*, represented the monster now creeping forward fawningly, now rushing along to devour its prey. A numerous crowd of children collected around us. The small folks followed the representation with great glee, and gave life to the play, or rather formed its proper background, by the feigned terror with which they fled when the monster approached with open mouth and rolling eyes, and the eagerness with which they again followed and mocked it when its back was turned.

. In few countries are dramatic representations of all kinds so much thought of as in Japan. Playhouses are found even in small towns. The play is much frequented, and though the representations last the whole day, they are followed by the spectators with the liveliest interest. There are playbills as at home, and numerous writings on subjects relating to the theatre. Among the Japanese books which I bought, there was for instance a thick one, with innumerable woodcuts, devoted to showing how the first Japanese artists conceived the principal scenes in their *rôles*, two volumes of playbills bound up together, &c.

BURDEN-BEARERS ON A JAPANESE ROAD.
Japanese drawing.

The Japanese pieces indeed strike a European as childish and monstrous, but one must admire many praiseworthy traits in the play itself, for instance the naturalness with which the players often declaim monologues lasting for a quarter or half an hour. The extravagances which here shock us are perhaps on the whole not more absurd than the scenes of the opera of to-day, or the buskins, masks, and peculiar dresses, which the Greeks considered indispensable in the exhibition of their great dramatic masterpieces. When the Japanese have been able to appropriate what is good in European culture, the dramatic art ought to have a grand future before it among them, if the

development now going on is carried out cautiously so that the
peculiarities of the people are not too much effaced. For, in
many departments, and not least in that of art, there is much to
be found here which when properly developed will form a new
and important addition to the culture of the West, of which we
are so proud.

The large Japanese theatres, besides, often resemble the
European ones in their interior arrangement. The partition
between the stage and the space occupied by the spectators is
the same as among us. Between the acts the former is concealed by a curtain. The stage is besides provided with painted
scenes representing houses, woods, hills, &c., supported on
wheels, so that a complete change of scene can be effected in
a few moments. The music has the same place between the
stage and the spectators as at home. The latter, as at home, are
distributed partly in a gently rising amphitheatre, partly in
several tiers of boxes rising one above another, the lowest tier
being considered the principal one. The Japanese do not sit
in the same way as we do. Neither the amphitheatre nor the
boxes accordingly are provided with chairs or benches, but are
divided into square compartments one or two feet deep, each intended for about four persons. They sit on cushions, squatting
cross-legged in the common Japanese fashion. The compartments are divided by broad cross beams, which form the passages
by which the spectators get to their places. During the play
we saw attendants running about with tea, *saki*, tobacco pipes,
and small braziers. For every one smokes during the acts, and
places himself in his crib as comfortably as possible. The piece
is followed with great attention, favourite actors and favourite
passages being saluted with lively applause. Even women and
children visit the theatre, and I have seen the former give their
children suck without the least discomposure among thousands
of spectators. Besides the plays intended for the public, there
are given also a number of other dramatic representations, as
society plays, peculiar family plays intended for the homes of the
old feudal princes, spectacles got up for the Mikado, and some
which have a half religious significance, &c.

On the evening of the 5th October we came to Takasaki,
prepared to start immediately for Tokio. But though the
messenger we sent had duly executed his commission, horses
could not be procured before midnight. We passed the evening
with our former host, who at our first visit received us so unwillingly, but now with great friendliness. We would easily
have reconciled ourselves to the delay, for a Japanese small
town such as Takasaki has much worth seeing to offer a
European, but a great part of the time was wasted in fruitless attempts to get the horse-hirer to let us have the horses

a few hours earlier. In spending time in long conversations mixed with civilities and bows the Japanese are masters. Of this bad habit, which still often makes the European desperate, it will not perhaps be long necessary to complain, for everything indicates that the Japanese too will soon be carried along at the endlessly roaring speed of the Steam Age.

When we had at last got horses we continued our journey, first in a carriage to Tokio, then by rail to Yokohama, arriving there on the afternoon of the 6th October. From this journey I shall only relate an incident which may form a little picture throwing light on life in Japan.

While we halted for a short time in the morning of the 6th October at a large inn by the roadside, we saw half a dozen young girls finishing their toilets in the inn-yard. In passing we may say, that a Japanese peasant girl, like girls in general, may be pretty or the reverse, but that she generally is, what cannot always be said of the peasant girls at home, cleanly and of attractive manners. They washed themselves at the stream of water in the inn-yard, smoothed their artistically dressed hair, which, however, had been but little disturbed by the cushions on which they had slept, and brushed their dazzlingly white teeth. Soap is not used for washing, but a cotton bag filled with bran. The teeth were brushed with a wooden pin, one end of which was changed by beating into a brush-like collection of wooden cords. The tooth-powder consisted of finely powdered shells and corals, and was kept in small, neat wooden boxes, which, along with tooth-brushes and small square bundles of a very strong and cheap paper, all clearly intended for the use of the peasants, were sold for a trifle in most of the innumerable shops along the road. For such stupid regulations as in former times in Europe rendered traffic in the country difficult, and often obliged the countryman to betake himself to the nearest town to buy some horse-shoes or a roll of wire, appear not to be found in Japan, on which account most of the peasants living on a country road seek a subsidiary way of making a living by trafficking in small articles in request among the country people.

Incidents of the sort referred to we had seen so many times before that on this occasion it would not have attracted any further attention on our part, if we had not thereby been reminded that we must look after our own exterior, before we could make our entrance into the capital of Japan. We therefore took from the carriage our basket with linen, shaving implements, and towels, settled down around the stream of water at which the girls stood, and immediately began to wash and shave ourselves. There was now general excitement. The girls ceased to·go on with their own toilet, and crowded round us in a ring in order to see how Europeans behave in such cases, and to give us the assistance that might be required. Some ran laughing and bustling about, one on the top of another, in order immediately to procure us what we wanted, one held the mirror, another the shaving-brush, a third the soap, &c. Round them gathered other elder women, whose blackened teeth indicated that they were married. A little farther off stood men of all ages. Chance had here quite unexpectedly shown us a picture from folk-life of the most agreeable kind. This pleasant temper continued while we immediately after, in the presence of all, ate our breakfast in the porch of the ground-floor, surrounded by our former ministering spirits, now kneeling around us, continually bowing the head to the ground, laughing and chattering. The same fun went on when a little after I bought some living fresh-water fishes and put them in spirit, yet with the difference that the girls now, with some cries, to show their fear of handling the living animals—though fish-cleaning was one of their ordinary occupations—handed over to the men the trouble of taking the fishes and putting them into the spirit-jars. For a worm placed in spirit they feigned the greatest terror, notwithstanding its covering of spirit and glass, and ran shrieking away when any one suddenly brought the jar with the worm near their faces. It ought to be noted to the honour of the Japanese, that although we were by no means surrounded by any select circle, there was not heard during the whole time a single offensive word among the closely-packed spectators, a fact which gives us an idea of the excellent tone of society which prevails here, even among the lowest of the population, and which shows that the Japanese, although they have much to learn from the Europeans, ought not to imitate them in all. In Japan there is much that is good, old, and national to take note of, perhaps more than the Japanese at present have any idea of, and undoubtedly more than many of the European residents will allow.

CHAPTER XVIII.

THE last days at Yokohama were taken up with farewell visits there and at Tokio. An afternoon's leisure during the last day

: spent in the capital of Japan I employed in making an ex-
:ursion in order to dredge from a Japanese boat in the river
lebouching at the town. The Japanese boats differ from the
European in being propelled not by rowing but by sculling.
They have usually a deck above the level of the water, which
s dazzlingly white and laid with matting, like the rooms in a
Japanese house. The dredging yielded a great number of
Anodonta, large Paludina, and some small shells.

During our stay in Japan I requested Lieutenant Nordquist
:o make as complete a collection of the land and fresh-water
:rustacea of the country as the short time permitted. In consequence of the unusual poverty of the country in these animal
orms the result was much smaller than we had hoped. During
: preceding voyage to the Polar Sea I had assisted in making
: collection of land crustacea on Renœ, an island north of the
imit of trees in the outer archipelago of northern Norway. It is
possible to collect there in a few hours as many animals of this
group as in fertile Japan in as many days. There are parts of Japan,
:overed with thick woods and thickets of bushes, where during
: forenoon's excursion one can scarcely find a single crustacean,
although the ground is full of deep, shady clefts in which
masses of dried leaves are collected, and which therefore ought
to be an exceedingly suitable haunt for land mollusca. The
reason of this poverty ought perhaps to be sought in the want
of chalk or basic calcareous rocks, which prevails in the parts of
Japan which we visited.

After the Swedish-Dutch minister had further given us a
splendid farewell dinner at the Grand Hotel, to which, as before,
the Japanese ministers and the representatives of the foreign
powers in Japan were invited, we at last weighed anchor on the
11th October to prosecute our voyage. At this dinner we saw
for the first time the Chinese embassy which at the time visited
Japan with the view of settling the troublesome Loo-Choo affair
which threatened to lead to a war between the two great powers
of Eastern Asia. The Chinese ambassadors were, as usual, two
in number, being commissioned to watch one over the other.
One of them laughed immoderately at all that was said during
dinner, although he did not understand a word. According
to what I was told by one who had much experience in the
customs of the heavenly empire, he did this, not because he
heard or understood anything worth laughing at, but because
he considered it good manners to laugh.

Remarkable was the interest which the Chinese labourers
settled at Yokohama took in our voyage, about which they
appeared to have read something in their own or in the
Japanese newspapers. When I sent one of the sailors ashore
to execute a commission, and asked him how he could do that

without any knowledge of the language, he replied, "There is no fear, I always meet with some Chinaman who speaks English and helps me." The Chinese not only always assisted our sailors as interpreters without remuneration, but accompanied them for hours, gave them good advice in making purchases, and expressed their sympathy with all that they must have suffered during our wintering in the high north. They were always cleanly, tall, and stately in their figures, and corresponded in no particular to the calumnious descriptions we so often read of this people in European and American writings.

From Yokohama the course was shaped for Kobe, one of the more considerable Japanese ports which have been opened to Europeans. Kobe is specially remarkable on account of its having railway communication with Osaka, the most important manufacturing town of Japan, and with Kioto, the ancient capital and seat of the Mikado's court for centuries.

I had already begun at Yokohama to buy Japanese books, particularly such as were printed before the opening of the ports to Europeans. In order to carry on this traffic with greater success, I had procured the assistance of a young Japanese very familiar with French, Mr. OKUSCHI, assistant in Dr. Geertz' chemico-technical laboratory at Yokohama. But because the supply of old books in this town, which a few years ago had been of little importance, was very limited, I had at first, in order to make purchases on a larger scale, repeatedly sent Mr. Okuschi to Tokio, the seat of the former Shogun dynasty, and from that town, before the departure of the *Vega* from Yokohama, to Kioto, the former seat of learning in Japan. The object of the *Vega's* call at the port of Kobe was to fetch the considerable purchases made there by Mr. Okuschi.[1]

Kobe, or Hiogo, as the old Japanese part of the town is called, is a city of about 40,000 inhabitants, beautifully situated at the entrance to the Inland Sea of Japan, *i.e.*, the sound which separates the main island from the south islands, Shikoku · and Kiushiu. Mountain ridges of considerable height here run along the sea-shore. Some of the houses of the European merchants are built on the lower slopes of these hills, with high, beautiful, forest-clad heights as a background, and a splendid view of the harbour in front. The Japanese part of the town consists, as usual, of small houses which, on the side next the street, are occupied mainly with sale or work-shops where the whole family lives all day. The streets have thus a very lively

---

[1] The number of the works which the collection of Japanese books contains is somewhat over a thousand. The number of volumes amounts to five or six thousand; most of the volumes, however, are not larger than one of our books of a hundred pages. So far as can be judged by the Japanese titles, which are often little distinctive, the works may be

pearance, and offer the foreigner an endless variety of remark-
le and instructive pictures from the life of the people. The
iropean part of the town, on the other hand, is built with
itely houses, some of which are situated on the street that runs
ong the shore. Here, among others, are to be found splendid
iropean hotels, European clubs, counting-houses, shops, &c.

Not far from Kobe, and having railway communication with
is Osaka, the largest manufacturing town of Japan, famed for
; theatres and its dancing-girls. Unfortunately I had not time
visit it, for I started for the old capital, Kioto, a few hours
ter the *Vega* anchored, and after I had waited on the governor
order to procure the passport that is still required for travel-
ig in the interior. He received me, thanks to a letter of
troduction I had with me from one of the ministers at Tokio,
an exceedingly agreeable way. His reception-room was part
a large European stone house, the vestibule of which was
stefully fitted up in European style with a Brussels carpet
iy with variegated colours. At our visit we were offered
ipanese tea, as is customary everywhere in Japan, both in the
ilace of the Emperor and the cabin of the poor peasant. The
overnor was, as all the higher officials in Japan now are,
ressed like a European of distinction, but he could not speak

stributed among the various branches of knowledge in the following
ay :

	Number of Works.
History	176
On Buddhism and Education	161
On Shintoism	38
On Christianity (printed in 1715)	1
Manners and Customs	33
The Drama	13
Laws	5
Politics, Political argumentative writings, partly new and privately printed against the recent statutes	24
Poetry and Prose fiction	137
Heraldry, Antiquities, Ceremonies	27
The Art of War and the Use of Weapons	41
Chess	1
Coining	4
Dictionaries, Grammars	18
Geography, Maps	76
Natural History	68
The Science of Medicine	13
Arithmetic, Astronomy, Astrology	39
Handicrafts, Agriculture	43
Notebooks	73
The art of making bouquets (Horticulture ?)	16
Bibliography	9
Various	20
Total	1036

JAPANESE SHOP.

any European language. He showed himself, however, to be much interested in our voyage, and immediately ordered an official in his court, who was well acquainted with English, Mr. YANIMOTO, to accompany me to Kioto.

We travelled thither by a railway constructed wholly in the European style. At Kioto my companion, at my special request, conducted me, not to the European hotel there, but to a Japanese inn, remarkable as usual for cleanliness, for a numerous crowd of talkative female attendants, and for the extreme friendliness of the inn people to their guests as soon as they indicated, by taking off their boots at the door, that it was their intention not to break Japanese customs and usages in any offensive way. A calling card and a letter from Admiral Kawamura, minister of marine, which I sent from the hotel to the Governor of Kioto, procured me an adjutant No. 2, a young, cheerful and talkative official, Mr. KOBA-YASCHI, whose eyes sparkled with intelligence and merry good humour. One would sooner have taken him for a highly-esteemed student president at some northern university, than for a Japanese official. It was already late in the day, so that before nightfall I had time only to take the bath which, at every Japanese inn not of too inferior a kind, is always at the traveller's call, and arrange the dredging excursion which, along with Lieut. Nordquist, I intended to make next day on Lake Biwa.

The road between Kioto and Biwa we travelled the following morning in *jinrikishas*. In a short time there will be communication between these two places by a railway constructed exclusively by native workmen and native engineers. It will be, and is intended to be, an actual Japanese railway. For a considerable distance it passes through a tunnel, which, however, as some of the Europeans at Kobe stated, might easily have been avoided " if the Japanese had not considered it desirable that Japan, too, should have a railway tunnel to show, as such are found both in Europe and America." It is probable, in any case, that the bends which would have been required if the tunnel was to be avoided would have cost more by the additional length than the tunnel, and that therefore the procedure of the Japanese was better considered than their envious European neighbours would allow. There appears to prevail among the European residents in Japan a certain jealousy of the facility with which this country, till recently so far behind in an industrial respect, assimilates the skill in art and industry of the Europeans, and of the rapidity with which the people thereby make themselves independent of the wares of the foreign merchants.

When we reached Lake Biwa we were conducted by Mr. Koba-Yaschi to an inn close by the shore, with a splendid view

x x

of the southern part of the lake. We were shown into beautiful Japanese rooms, which had evidently been arranged for the reception of Europeans, and in which accordingly some tables and chairs had been placed. On the tables we found, on our arrival, bowls with fruit and confections, Japanese tea, and braziers. The walls were formed partly of tastefully gilt paper panels ornamented with mottoes, reminding visitors of the splendid view.

A whole day of the short time which was allowed me to study the remarkable things of Kioto I devoted to Lake Biwa, because lakes are exceedingly uncommon in the south, for they occur only in the countries which have either been covered with glaciers in the most recent geological periods, or, in consequence of the action of volcanic forces, have been the scene of violent disturbances of the surface of the earth. I believed that Lake Biwa would form an exception to this, but I was probably mistaken; for tradition relates that this lake was formed in a single night at the same time that the high volcanic cone of Fusiyama was elevated. This tradition, in its general outline, corresponds so closely with the teaching of geology, that scarcely any geologist will doubt its truth.

After our arrival at the inn we had to wait a very long time for the steamer I had ordered. On this account I thoughtlessly enough broke out in reproaches on my excellent Japanese adjutants, who, however, received my hard words only with friendly smiles, which increased still further my impatience at the loss of time which was thus occasioned. It was not until far on in the day, when I was already out dredging from a small steamer, that I was informed as to the cause of the delay. The Biwa Steamship Company had, at the request of the Governor, intended to place at my disposal a very large boat well provided with coal, but after taking the coal on board it had sunk so deep that it grounded in the mud of the harbour. We had already got far out with the little steamer when the large one at last got off. I was now obliged to exchange vessels in order to be received " in a more honourable way." It was not until this took place that I was informed that I was guest and not master, on which account I was obliged to employ the rest of the afternoon in excusing my former violent behaviour, in which with the help of friendly words, beer, and red wine, I succeeded pretty well, to judge by the mirth which soon began to prevail among my now very numerous Japanese companions.

On the little steamer I had ordered two of my crew whom I had brought with me from the *Vega* to prepare a meal for the Japanese and ourselves. In this way the dinner that had been arranged for us, without my knowledge, became superfluous. I was obliged instead to receive as a gift the provisions and liquors purchased for the dinner, consisting of fowls, eggs, potatoes, red wine and beer, giving at the same time a receipt as a matter of form.

During our excursion on the lake we met with various boats laden with seaweed, which had been taken up from the bottom of the lake to be used as manure for the neighbouring cultivated fields. Partly among these algæ, partly by dredging, Lieut. Nordquist collected various interesting fresh-water crustacea (Paludina, Melania, Unio, Planorbis, &c.,) several sorts of shrimps (a Hippolyte) small fishes, &c. Lake Biwa abounds in fish, and harbours besides a large clumsily-formed species of lizard. In order to make further collections of the animal forms occurring there, Lieut. Nordquist remained at the lake till next day. I, on the other hand, went immediately back to Kioto, arriving there in the evening after nightfall.

After having eaten, along with my two Japanese companions, an unexceptionable European dinner at the inn of the town, kept by Japanese, but arranged in European style, we paid a visit to a company of Japanese dancing-girls.

Kioto competes with Osaka for the honour of having the prettiest dancing-girls. These form a distinct class of young girls, marked by a peculiar variegated dress. They wear besides a peculiar hair-ornament, are much painted, and have their lips coloured black and gold. At the dancing-places of greatest note a European is not received, unless he has with him a known native who answers for his courteous behaviour. After taking off his shoes on entering, the visitor is introduced to a separate room with its floor covered with matting and its walls ornamented with Japanese drawings and mottoes, but without other furniture. A small square cushion is given to each of the guests. After they have settled themselves in Japanese fashion, that is to say, squatting cross-legged, pipes and tea are brought in, on which a whole crowd of young girls come in and, chatting pleasantly, settle themselves around the guests, observing all the while complete decency even according to the most exacting European ideas. There is not to be seen here any trace of the effrontery and coarseness which are generally to be found in similar places in Europe. One would almost believe that he was among a crowd of schoolgirls who had given the sour moral lessons of their governess the slip, and were thinking of nothing else than innocently gossiping away some hours. After a while the dance begins, accompanied by very monotonous music and singing. The slow movements of the legs and arms of the dancers remind us of certain slow and demure scenes from European ballets. There is nothing indecent in this dance, but we learn that there are other dances wilder and less decorous.

x x 2

The dancing-girls are recruited exclusively from the poorer classes ; pretty young girls, to help their parents or to earn some styvers for themselves, selling themselves for a certain time to the owners of the dancing-places, and when the time agreed upon has come to an end returning to their homes, where notwithstanding this they marry without difficulty. All the dancing-girls therefore are young, many of them pretty even according to European ideas, though their appearance is destroyed in our eyes by the tasteless way in which they paint themselves and colour their lips. Unfortunately I had

JAPANESE COURT DRESS.

not time to avail myself of the opportunity which Kioto offers the foreigner of judging with certainty regarding the Japanese taste in female beauty. For here, as at various other Japanese towns, there are a number of girls who have been officially selected as the most beautiful among the youth of the place. The Japanese may visit them for a certain payment, but to Europeans they do not show themselves willingly, and only for a large sum. When this takes place at any time, it is only a dumb show for a few moments, during which no words are exchanged.

The Governor had promised to carry me round next day

see whatever was remarkable in the town. I was not much
lighted at this, because I feared that the whole day would
: taken up with inspecting the whole or half-European
iblic offices and schools, which had not the slightest interest
r me. My fear however was quite unjustified. The Governor
is a man of genius, who, according to the statements of
y companions, was reckoned among the first of the con-
mporary poets of Japan. He immediately declared that he
pposed that the new public offices and schools would in-
rest me much less than the
d palaces, temples, porcelain
id *faïence* manufactories of
.e town, and that he there-
re intended to employ the
ιy I spent under his guidance
showing me the latter.
We made a beginning with the
d imperial palace Gosho, the
ost splendid dwelling of Old
ιpan. It is not however very
·and according to European
eas. A very extensive space
˙ ground is here covered with
number of one-story wooden
ɔuses, intended for the Em-
ɔror, the imperial family, and
ιeir suite. The buildings
·e, like all Japanese houses,
.vided by movable panels into
number of rooms, richly
:ovided with paintings and
.lded ornamentation, but
iherwise without a trace of
ιrniture. For the palace now
ands uninhabited since the
ιkado overthrew the Shogun

NOBLE IN ANTIQUE DRESS.

ɣnasty and removed to Tokio. It already gives a striking
.cture of the change which has taken place in the land. Only the
ιperial family and the great men of the country were formerly
ɔrmitted to enter the sacred precincts of Gosho. Now it
ands open to every curious native or foreigner, and it has
ɣen as an exhibition building been already pressed into the
:rvice of industry. Alongside the large buildings there are
ιveral small ones, of which one was intended to protect
ιe Emperor-deity during earthquakes; the others formed
ay-places for the company of grown children who were then
ɔrmitted to govern the country.

Much more remarkable and instructive than the now deserted imperial palace are the numerous temples at Kioto, of which we visited several. We were generally received by the priests in a large vestibule, whose floor was covered with a fine woollen carpet and was provided with tables and chairs of European patterns. The priests first offered us Japanese tea, cigars, and sweetmeats ; then we examined some valuable articles exhibited in the room, consisting of bronzes, works in the noble metals, splendid old lacquer work, and a number of famous swords dedicated to the temple. These were the only things that our freethinking Governor treated with reverence ; for the rest neither the priests nor their reliques seemed to inspire him with any particular respect.

BUDDHIST PRIEST.

When a valuable Japanese sword is exhibited one touches neither the hilt nor scabbard, and of course still less the blade, with the bare hand, but it is taken hold of either with a gloved hand, or with the hand with a handkerchief or piece of cloth wrapped round it. ' The blade is only half bared, the steel setting is looked at against the light and admired ; on the often exceedingly valuable blades, which are not mounted, but only provided with a wooden case to protect them from rust, the maker's mark is examined, and so on. As among us in former times, the swordsmith's is the only handicraft which in old times was held in high esteem in Japan, and immense sums were often paid for sword-blades forged by famous masters of the art. Among old Japanese writings are to be found many works specially treating of the making of weapons. But since the swordsmen (*samurai*) have now been forbidden to show themselves armed, old Japanese swords are sold in all the towns by hundreds and thousands, often for a trifle. During our stay in the country I purchased for a comparatively limited sum a fine collection of such weapons. Even those who cannot appreciate the artistic forging of the blade, the steel-setting

:mpering, must admire the exceedingly tasteful casting
nbossing of the ornamentation, especially of the guard-
of the sword. They are often veritable works of art,
assed in style and execution.

; not very many years ago since the men who belonged to
:murai class never showed themselves abroad without
armed with two swords. Even schoolboys went armed to
st European schools that were established in the country.
;ave occasion to several acts of violence during the time
succeeded the opening of the ports, for which reason the

:an ambassadors some
after requested that
ig the sword in time
ce should be prohib-
To this the Japanese
iment answered that
ild make short work
the minister who
publish such a pro-
n. Soon after, how-
it gave *permission* to
who desired it to go
it weapons, and the
ig of arms soon be-
so unfashionable that
f the authorities did
t last to issue a distinct
ition of it. During
ay in Japan, accord-
we did not see a
man armed with the
rords formerly in use.
:r we had seen and
:d the treasures in
emple vestibule, we
. the temple itself.
is always of wood,

A SAMURAI.

ornamented with carvings and gilding. If it is dedicated
nto, there are no images in it, and very few ornaments, if
cept a mirror and a large locked press with the doors
ed in, which sometimes occupies the wall opposite the
ce, and in which, as I have already stated, the spirit of the
s said to dwell. The Shinto temples are in general poor.
are so inconsiderable as to look almost like dovecotes.
are often completely deserted, so that it is difficult to
:r them among the magnificent trees by which they were
nded. The entrance to the temple is indicated by a gate

(*torryi*) of wood, stone, or copper, and here and there are ropes, stretched over the way, to which written prayers and vows are affixed.

Even those who have long studied Japan and its literature have very little knowledge of the inner essence of Shintoism. This religion is considered by some a pure deism, by others a belief with political aims, the followers of which worship the departed heroes of the country. Of a developed morality this religion is wholly devoid. In the same way it appears to be uncertain whether Shintoism is a survival of the original religion of the country or whether it has been brought from abroad.

GATE ACROSS THE ROAD TO A SHINTO TEMPLE.

Buddhism was introduced from China by Corea. Its temples are more ornamented than the Shinto temples, and contain images of deities, bells, drums, holy books, and a great quantity of altar ornaments. The transmigration of souls, and rewards and punishments in a life after this, are doctrines of Buddhism. Outside the temples proper there are to be found in many places large or small images in stone or bronze of the deities of Buddha. The largest of these consist of colossal statues in bronze (*Daihutsu*) representing Buddha in a sitting position, and themselves forming the screen to a temple with smaller images.

A similar statue is also to be found at Kamakura, another at
Tokio, a third at Nara near Kioto, and so on. Some have of
late years been sold for the value of the metal; one has in this
way been brought to London, and is now exhibited in the
Kensington Museum. The metal of the statues consists of an
alloy of copper with tin and a little gold, the last named
constituent giving rise to the report that their value is very

BUDDHIST TEMPLE AT KOBE.

considerable. To give an idea of the size of some *Daibutsu*
statues, it may be mentioned that the one at Nara is fifty-three
and a half feet high, and that one can crawl into the head
through the nose orifices.

Nearly all the *Daibutsu* images are made after nearly the
same design, which has been improved from generation to
generation until the countenance of the image has received a

stamp of benevolence, calm, and majesty, which has probably never been surpassed by the productions of Western art. *Daibutsu* images evidently stand in the same relation to the works of private sculptors as folk-poetry to that of individual bards.

As I have before pointed out, the Western taste for the gigantic was not prevalent in Old Japan. It was evidently elegance and neatness, not grandeur, that formed the object towards which the efforts of the artist, the architect, and the gardener were directed. Only the *Daibutsu* images, some bells, and other instruments of worship, form exceptions to this. During our excursion at Kioto we passed an inclosure where the walls were built of blocks of stone so colossal, that it was difficult to comprehend how it had been possible to lift and move them with the means that were at the disposal of the Japanese in former times. In the neighbourhood of that place there was a grave, probably the only one of its kind. · It is described in the following way in an account of the curiosities of Kioto written by a native :—

" Mimisuka, or the grave of the noses and the ears, was erected by Hideyoshi Taiko, who lived about A.D. 1590. When the military chiefs of this famous man attacked Corea with a hundred and fifty thousand soldiers, he gave orders that they should bring home and show him all the ears and noses of the enemies who were killed in the contest, for it was an old practice in Japan to cut off the enemies' heads to show them to the king or the commander of the army. But it was now impossible to bring the heads of the dead Corean warriors to Japan, because the distance was too great. Hideyoshi therefore gave the above order, and the ears and noses, which were brought to Japan, were buried together at that place. The grave is 730 feet in circumference, and is 30 feet high."

Kioto is one of the principal places for the manufacture of *faïence*, porcelain, and *cloisonné*. The productions of the ceramic art are, as is well known, distinguished by their tasteful forms and beautiful colours, and are highly valued by connoisseurs, on which account they are exported on a large scale to Europe and America. The works are numerous and small, and are owned for the most part by families that for a long succession of generations have devoted themselves to the same occupation. The articles are burned in very small furnaces, and are commonly sold in a shop which is close to the place where they are made. The making of porcelain in Japan, therefore, bears the stamp rather of handicraft than of manufacturing industry. The wares gain thereby in respect of art to an almost incredible degree. They have the same relation to the productions of the great

European manufactories that the drawing of an artist has to a showily coloured lithograph. But the price is high in proportion, and the Japanese porcelain is too dear for every-day use even in its own country. Nearly all the large sets of table porcelain that I saw in Japan were, therefore, ordered from abroad. The cups which the natives themselves use for rice, tea, and *saki*, are, however, of native manufacture; but even in a well-provided Japanese household there is seldom so much porcelain as would be required for a proper coffee-party at home.

In the. evening the Governor had invited us to a dinner, which was given in a hall belonging to a literary society in the town. The rooms were partly furnished in European style with tables, chairs, Brussels carpets, &c. The dinner was European in the arrangement of dishes, wines, and speeches. The dishes and wines were abundant and in great variety. The company were very merry, and the host appeared to be greatly pleased when I mentioned that at one of the places which I had seen that day I saw a wall adorned by a motto of his composition. He immediately promised to write a similar one on me with reference to my visit to the town, and when a few moments after he had the first line ready, he invited his Japanese guests to write the second. They tried for a good while with merry jests to hit upon some suitable conclusion, but in vain. Early the following morning Mr. Koba-Yaschi came to me, bringing with him a broad strip of silk on which the following was pencilled in bold, nobly-formed characters:

Umi hara-no-hate-made
Akiva-Sumi-watare,

which when translated runs thus :

" As far as the sea extends
The autumn moon spreads her beneficent light."

According to the explanation which I received the piece points out that the autumn moon spreads her beneficent rays as far as to that place in the high north where we wintered. After the above-quoted verse came the following addition in Japanese: "Written by Machimura Masanavo, Governor of Kioto-Fu, to Professor Nordenskiöld, on the occasion of a dinner given to him during the autumn of 1879." The whole besides was signed with the author's common, as well as his poetical name, and had his seal attached. His poetical name was Rio-San, which may be literally translated "Dragon-Mountain." The poetry of the Japanese is so unlike that of the Western nations that we find it difficult to comprehend the productions

of the Japanese poets. Perhaps they ought more correctly to
be called poetical mottoes. They play a great part in the
intellectual life of the Japanese. Their authors are highly
esteemed, and even in the homes of the poorer classes the walls
are often ornamented with strips of silk or paper on which
poems are written in large, bold, pencil characters. Among the
books I brought home with me are many which contain
collections of the writings of private poets and poetesses, or
selections from the most famous of the productions of Japanese
literature in this department. A roll of drawings which turned
up very often represents the sorrowful fate of a famous poetess.
First of all she is depicted as a representative Japanese beauty,
blooming with youth and grace; then she is represented in
different stages of decay, then as dead, then as a half-decayed

RIO-SAN'S SEAL.

corpse torn asunder by ravens, and finally as a heap of bones.
The series ends with a cherry-tree in splendid bloom, into which
the heroine, after her body had passed through all the stages of
annihilation, has been changed. The cherry-tree in blossom is
considered by the Japanese the ideal of beauty in the vegetable
kingdom, and during the flowering season of this tree excursions
are often undertaken to famous cherry-groves, where hour after
hour is passed in tranquil admiration of the flower-splendour
of the tree. Unfortunately I was so late in getting the
explanation of the beautiful poetical idea that ran through
this series of pictures, some of which were executed with
execrable truth to nature, that I missed the opportunity of
purchasing it.

I was obliged to leave Kioto too early, in order to be present

BURYING PLACE AT KIOTO.

at a *fête*, which was given to us at Kobe by the Japanese, Europeans, and Chinese who were interested in our voyage. The entertainment was held in a Buddhist temple without the town, and was very pleasant and agreeable. The Japanese did not seem at all to consider that their temple was desecrated by such an arrangement. In the course of the afternoon for instance there came several pilgrims to the temple. I observed them carefully, and could not mark in their countenances any trace of displeasure at a number of foreigners feasting in the beautiful temple grove whither they had come on pilgrimage. They appeared rather to consider that they had come to the goal of their wanderings at a fortunate moment, and therefore gladly accepted the refreshments that were offered them.

On the morning of the 18th October the *Vega* again weighed anchor, to proceed on her voyage. The course was shaped through the Inland Sea of Japan for Nagasaki. When I requested of the Governor of Kobe permission to land at two places on the way, he not only immediately granted my request, but also sent on the *Vega* the same English-speaking official from his court who had before attended me to Kioto. The weather was clear and fine, so that we had a good opportunity of admiring the magnificent environs of the Inland Sea. They resemble much the landscape in a northern archipelago. The views here are however more monotonous in consequence of there being less variety in the contours of the mountains. Here as at Kobe the hills consist mainly of a species of granite, which is exposed to weathering on so large a scale that the hard rocks are nearly everywhere decomposed into a yellow sand unfavourable for vegetation. The splendid wild granite cliffs of the north accordingly are absent here. All the hill-tops are evenly rounded, and everywhere, except where there has been a sand-slip, covered with a rich vegetation, which in consequence of the evenness of height of the trees gives little variety to the landscape, which otherwise is among the most beautiful on the globe.

We landed at two places, on the first occasion at Hirosami. Here some fishermen's cabins and some peasants' houses formed a little village at the foot of a high, much-weathered granite ridge. The burying-place was situated near one of the houses, close to the shore. On an area of some hundred square yards there were numerous gravestones, some upright, some fallen. Some were ornamented with fresh flowers, at one was a Shinto shrine of wooden pins, at another stood a bowl with rice and a small *saki* bottle. Our zoologists here made a pretty rich collection of littoral animals, among which may be mentioned a cuttle-fish which had crept down amongst the wet sand, an animal that is industriously searched for and eaten by the natives. Among the cultivated plants we saw here, as many times before in the high-lying parts of the country, an old acquaintance from home, namely buckwheat.

The second time the *Vega* anchored at a peasant village right opposite Shimonoseki. When we landed there came an official on board, courteously declaring that we had no right to land at that place. But he was immediately satisfied and made no more difficulties when he was informed that we had the permission of the Governor, and that instead of the usual passport an official from Kobe accompanied the vessel. Shimonoseki

ENTRANCE TO NAGASAKI.

has a melancholy reputation in European-Japanese history from the deeds of violence done here by a united English, French, Dutch, and American fleet of seventeen vessels on the 4th and 5th September, 1864, in order to compel the Japanese to open the sound to foreigners, and the unreasonably heavy compensation which after the victory was won they demanded from the conquered. Although only fifteen years have passed since this occurred, there appears to be no trace of bitter feeling towards Europeans among the inhabitants of the region. At least we were received at the village in the neighbourhood of which we landed with extraordinary kindness. The village was

situated at the foot of a rocky ridge, and consisted of a number
of houses arranged in a row along a single street, the fronts of
the houses being as usual occupied as shops, places for selling
saki, and workshops for home industry. The only remarkable
things besides that the village had to offer consisted of a Shinto
temple surrounded by beautiful trees and a considerable salt-
work, which consisted of extensive, shallow, well-planned ponds
now nearly dry, into which the sea-water is admitted in order
to evaporate, and from which the condensed salt liquid is
afterwards drawn into salt-pans in order that the evaporation
may be completed. It was remarkable to observe that
several crustacea throve exceedingly well in the very strong
brine.

On the surrounding hills we saw thickets of the Japanese
wax tree, *Rhus succedaneus*. The wax is pressed out of the
berries of this bush with the help of heat. It is used on a
large scale in making the lights which the natives themselves
burn, and is exported bleached and refined to Europe, where it
is sometimes used in the manufacture of lights. Now, however,
these wax lights are increasingly superseded by American kero-
sene oil. The price has fallen so much that the preparation of
vegetable wax is now said scarcely to yield a profit.[1]

We left this place next morning, and on the 21st October
the *Vega* anchored in the harbour of Nagasaki. My principal
intention in visiting this place was to collect fossil plants,
which I supposed would be found at the Takasima coal-
mine, or in the neighbourhood of the coal-field. In order to
find out the locality without delay, I reckoned on the fondness of
the Japanese for collecting remarkable objects of all kinds from
the animal, vegetable, and mineral kingdoms. I therefore hoped
to find in some of the shops where old bronzes, porcelain,
weapons, &c., were offered for sale, fossil plants from the neighbourhood, with the locality given. The first day, therefore, I
ran about to all the dealers in curiosities, but without success.
At last one of the Japanese with whom I conversed told me
that an exhibition of the products of nature and art in the
region was being arranged, and that among the objects exhibited
I might possibly find what I sought for.

Of course I immediately availed myself of the opportunity to
see one of the many Japanese local exhibitions of which I had
heard so much. It was yet in disorder, but I was, at all events,
willingly admitted, and thus had an opportunity of seeing much
that was instructive to me, especially a collection of rocks from
the neighbourhood. Among these I discovered at last, to my

---

[1] Further information on this point is given by Henry Gribble in "The
Preparation of Vegetable Wax" (*Transactions of the Asiatic Society of Japan*,
vol. iii. part i. p. 94. Yokohama, 1875.)

great satisfaction, some beautiful fossil plants from Mogi, a place not far from Nagasaki.

Immediately the following morning I started for Mogi, accompanied by the Japanese attendant I had with me from Kobe, and by another adjutant given me by the very obliging governor of Nagasaki. We were to travel across the hills on horseback. I was accompanied, besides my Japanese assistants and a man from the *Vega*, all on horseback, by a number of coolies carrying provisions and other equipments. The Governor had lent me his own horse, which was considered by the Japanese something quite grand. It was a yellowish-brown stallion, not particularly large, but very fine, resembling a Norwegian horse, very gentle and sure-footed. The latter quality was also quite necessary, for the journey began with a ride up a hundred smooth and not very convenient stone steps. Farther on, too, the road, which was exceedingly narrow and often paved with smooth stones, went repeatedly up and down such stairs, not very suitable for a man on horseback, and close to the edge of precipices several hundred feet deep, where a single false step would have cost both the horse and its rider their lives. But as has been said, our horses were sure-footed and sure-eyed, and the riders took care in passing such places not to pull the reins.

None of the mountain regions I have seen in Japan are so well cultivated as the environs of Nagasaki. Every place that is somewhat level, though only several hundred square yards in extent, is used for growing some of the innumerable cultivated plants of the country, principally rice : but as such easily cultivated places occur in only limited numbers, the inhabitants have by industry and hard labour changed the steep slopes of the mountains into a succession of level terraces rising one above the other, all carefully watered by irrigating conduits.

Mogi is a considerable fishing village lying at the seaside twenty kilometres south of Nagasaki in a right line, on the other side of a peninsula occupied by lava beds and volcanic tuffs, which projects from the island Kiushiu, which at that place is nearly cut asunder by deep fjords. No European lives at the place, and of course there is no European inn there. But we got lodgings in the house of one of the principal or richest men in the village, a maker and seller of *saki*, or as we would call him in Swedish, a brandy distiller and publican. Here we were received in a very friendly manner, in clean and elegant rooms, and were waited on by the young and very pretty daughter of our host at the head of a number of other female attendants. It may be supposed that our place of entertainment had no resemblance to a public-house in Sweden. We did not witness here the tipsy behaviour of some human wrecks, and as little some other incidents which might have reminded us of public-house life in Europe. All went on in the distillery and the public-house as calmly and quietly as the work in the house of a well-to-do country squire in Sweden who does not swear and is not quarrelsome.

Saki is a liquor made by fermenting and distilling rice. It is very variable in taste and strength, sometimes resembling inferior Rhine wine, sometimes more like weak grain brandy. Along with *saki* our host also manufactured vinegar, which was made from rice and *saki* residues, which with the addition of some other vegetable substances were allowed to stand and acidify in large jars ranged in rows in the yard.

When my arrival became known I was visited by the principal men of the village. We were soon good friends by the help *of a friendly reception, cigars and red wine. Among them the physician of the village was especially of great use to me. As soon as he became aware of the occasion of my visit he stated that such fossils as I was in search of did indeed occur in the region, but that they were only accessible at low water. I immediately visited the place with the physician and my companions from Nagasaki, and soon discovered several strata containing the finest fossil plants one could desire. During this and the following day I made a rich collection, partly with the assistance of a numerous crowd of children who zealously helped me in collecting. They were partly boys and partly girls, the latter always having a little one on their backs. These little children were generally quite bare-headed. Notwithstanding this they slept with the crown of the head exposed to the hottest sun-bath on the backs of their bustling sisters, who jumped lightly and securely over stocks and stones, and never appeared to have any idea that the burdens on their backs were at all unpleasant or troublesome.

According to Dr. A. G. NATHORST'S examination, the fossil plants which I brought home from this place belong to the more recent Tertiary formation. Our distinguished and acute vegetable palæontologist fixes attention on the point, that we would have expected to find here a fossil flora allied to the recent South Japanese, which is considered to be derived from a Tertiary flora which closely resembles it. There is, however, no such correspondence, for impressions of ferns are almost completely wanting at Mogi, and even of pines there is only a single leaf-bearing variety which closely resembles the Spitzbergen form of *Sequoia Langsdorfii*, Brag. On the other hand, there are met with, in great abundance, the leaves of a species of beech nearly allied to the red beech of America, *Fagus ferruginea*, Ait., but not resembling the recent Japanese varieties of the same family. There were found, besides, leaves of Quercus, Juglans, Populus, Myrica, Salix, Zelkova, Liquidambar,

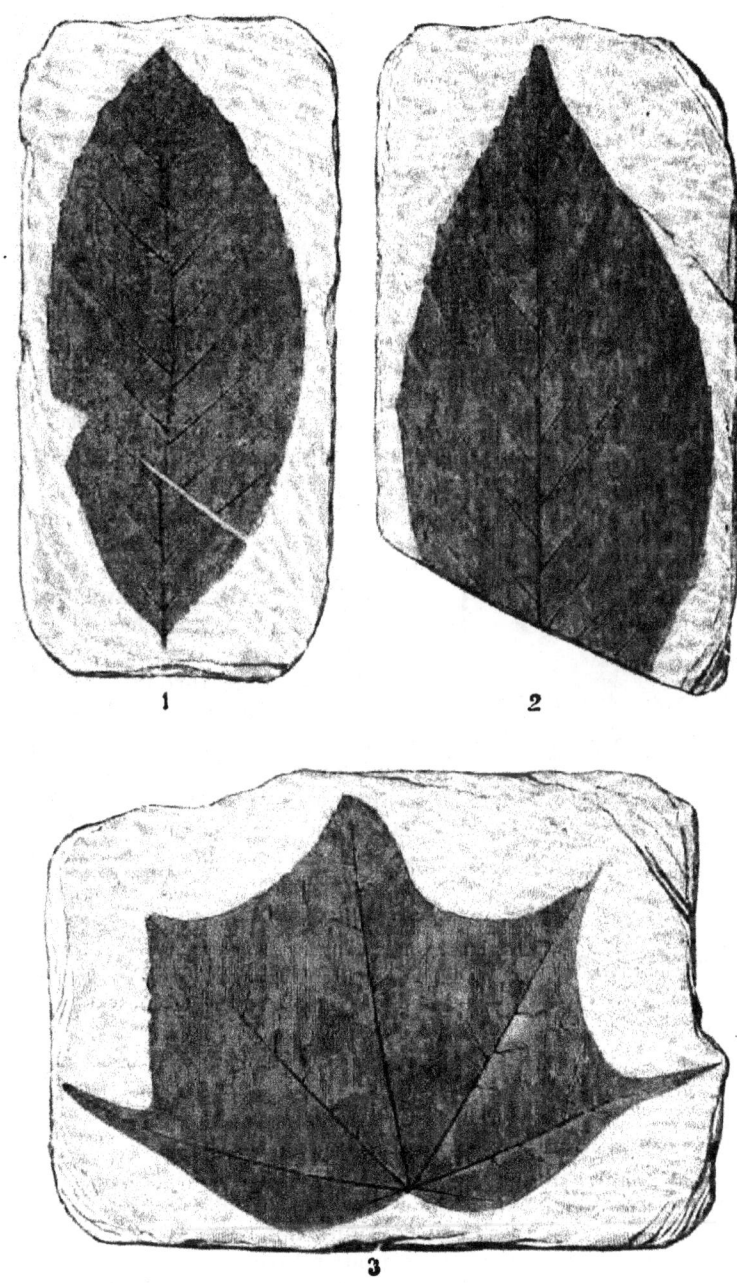

FOSSIL PLANTS FROM MOGI.

1, 2. Beech Leaves (*Fagus ferruginea*, Ait., var. *pliocena* Nath.). 3. Maple Leaf (*Acer Mono*, Max., var. *pliocena*, Nath.).

Acer, Prunus, Tilia, &c., resembling leaves of recent types
from the forests of Japan, from the forest flora of America,
or from the temperate flora of the Himalayas. But as the
place where they were found is situated at the sea-shore,
quite close to the southern extremity of Japan, it is singular
that the tropical or sub-tropical elements of the flora of Japan
are here wanting. From this Dr. Nathorst draws the conclusion that these are not, as has been hitherto supposed, the
remains of a flora originating in Japan, but that they have since
migrated thither from a former continent situated further to the
south, which has since disappeared. Dr. Nathorst's examination
is not yet completed, but even if this were the case, want of
space would not permit me to treat of this point at greater

FOSSIL PLANT FROM MOGI.
Leaf of *Zelkova Keakii.* Sieb., var.
pliocena, Nath.

length. I cannot, however, omit to
mention that it was highly agreeable
to be able to connect with the memory
of the *Vega* expedition at least
a small contribution from more
southerly lands to vegetable palæontology, a branch of knowledge to
which our preceding Arctic expeditions yielded new additions of
such importance through the fossil
herbaria from luxuriant ancient
forests which they brought to light
from the ice-covered cliffs of Spitzbergen and from the basalt-covered
sandstones and schists of the Nour-
soak Peninsula in Greenland, now
so bleak.

After our return from Mogi I
made an excursion to the coal-mine
at Takasami, situated on an island
some kilometres from the town.
Even here I succeeded in bringing together some further
contibutions to the former flora of the region.

After the inhabitants of Nagasaki, too, had given us a grand
parting feast, at which speeches were spoken in Japanese,
Chinese, English, French, German, Italian, Dutch, Russian
Danish, and Swedish, a proof of the mixtures of nationalities
which prevailed there, the *Vega* again weighed anchor on the
27th October, in order to continue her voyage. We now left
Japan to commence in earnest our return, and on our departure
we were saluted by the crews of two English gun-boats anchored
in the harbour, the *Hornet* and the *Sylvia*, manning the yards
and bulwarks. It was natural that the hour of departure, after
fifteen months' absence from home, should be looked forward to

with joy. But our joy was mixed with a regretful feeling that we were so soon compelled to leave—without the hope of ever returning—the magnificent country and noble people among whom a development is now going on which probably will not only give a new awakening to the old cultured races of Eastern Asia, but will also prepare a new soil for European science, industry, and art. It is difficult to foresee what new undreamed-of blossoms and fruit this soil will yield. But the Europeans are perhaps much mistaken who believe that the question here is only that of clothing an Asiatic feudal state in a modern European dress. Rather the day appears to me to dawn of a time in which the countries round the Mediterranean of eastern Asia will come to play a great part in the further development of the human race.

CHAPTER XIX.

Hong Kong and Canton—Stone-polishing Establishments at Canton—Political Relations in an English Colony—Treatment of the Natives—Voyage to Labuan—Coal Mines there—Excursion to the shore of Borneo—Malay Villages—Singapore—Voyage to Ceylon—Point de Galle—The Gem Mines at Ratnapoora—Visit to a Temple—Purchase of Manuscripts—The Population of Ceylon—Dr. Almquist's Excursion to the Interior of the Island.

SOME days after our arrival at Yokohama the *Vega* was removed to the dock at Yokosuka, there to be protected by coppering against the boring mussels of the warm seas, so injurious to the vessel's hull; the opportunity being also taken advantage of by me to subject the vessel to some trifling repairs and alterations in the fitting up, which were desirable because during the remainder of our voyage we were to sail not in a cold but in a tropical climate. The work took somewhat longer time than was reckoned on, so that it was not until the 21st September that the *Vega* could leave the dock and return to Yokohama. It had originally been my intention to remain in Japan only so long as was necessary for the finishing of this work, during which time opportunity could be given to the officers and crew of the *Vega* to rest after the labours and sufferings of the long winter, to receive and answer letters from home, and to gather from the newspapers the most important occurrences that had taken place during our fourteen months' absence from the regions which are affected by what takes place in the world. But as appears from the foregoing narrative, the delay was longer than had been intended. This indeed was

caused in some degree by the difficulty of tearing ourselves
away after only a few days' stay from a people so remarkable, so
lovable, and so hospitable as the Japanese, and from a land so
magnificently endowed by nature. Besides, when the *Vega* was
again ready for sea, it was so near the time for the change of
the monsoon, that it was not advisable, and would not have been
attended with any saving of time, to sail immediately. For at
that season furious storms are wont to rage in these seas, and
the wind then prevailing is so unfavourable for sailing from
Japan to the southward, that a vessel with the weak steam-
power of the *Vega* cruising between Japan and Hong Kong
in a head-wind might readily have lost the days saved by an
earlier departure. On the other hand, in the end of October
and the beginning of November we could, during our passage
to Hong Kong, count on a fresh and always favourable breeze.
This took place too, so that, leaving Nagasaki on the 27th
October, we were able to anchor in the harbour of Hong Kong
as early as the 2nd November.

There was of course no prospect of being able to accomplish
anything for the benefit of science during a few days' stay in
a region which had been examined by naturalists innumerable
times before, but I at all events touched at this harbour that I
might meet the expressed wish of one of the members of the
expedition not to leave eastern Asia without having, during the
voyage of the *Vega*, seen something of the so much talked of
" heavenly kingdom " so different from all other lands.

For this purpose, however, Hong Kong is an unsuitable place.
This rich and flourishing commercial town, which has been
created by England's Chinese politics and opium trade, is a
British colony with a European stamp, which has little to show
of the original Chinese folk-life, although the principal part of
its population consists of Chinese. But at the distance of a
few hours by steamer from Hong Kong lies the large old
commercial city of Canton, which, though it has long been open
to Europeans, is still purely Chinese, with its peatstack-like
architecture, its countless population, its temples, prisons,
flower-junks, mandarins, pig-tailed street-boys, &c. Most of the
members of the expedition made an excursion thither, and were
rewarded with innumerable indescribable impressions from
Chinese city life. We were everywhere received by the
natives in a friendly way,[1] and short as our visit was, it was

---

[1] Yet with one very laughable exception. I wished for zoological purposes to get one of the common Chinese rats, and with this object in view
made inquiries through my interpreter at a shed in the street, where rats
were said to be cooked for Chinese epicures. But scarcely had the question
been put, when the old, grave host broke out in a furious storm of abuse,
especially against the interpreter, who was overwhelmed with bitter

yet sufficient to dissipate the erroneous impressions which a number of European authors have been pleased to give of the most populous nation. One soon saw that he has to do with an earnest and industrious people, who, indeed, apprehend much —virtue and vice, joy and sorrow—in quite a different way from us, but towards whom we, on that account, by no means have the right to assume the position of superiority which the European is so ready to claim towards coloured races.

The greater portion of my short stay in Canton I employed in wandering about, carried in a sedan-chair—horses cannot be used in the city itself—through the streets, which are partly covered and are lined with open shops, forming, undoubtedly, the most remarkable of the many remarkable things that are to be seen here. The recollection I have of these hours forms, as often happens when one sees much that is new at once, a variegated confusion in which I can now only with difficulty distinguish a connected picture or two. But even if the impressions were clearer and sharper it would be out of the question to occupy space with a statement of my own superficial observations. If any one wishes to acquire a knowledge of Chinese manners and customs, he will not want for books on the country, his studies will rather be impeded by their enormous number, and often enough by the inferior nature of their contents. Here I shall only touch upon a single subject, because it especially interested me as a mineralogist, namely, the stone-polishing works of Canton.

It is natural that in a country so populous and rich as China, in which home and home life play so great a rôle, much money should be spent on ornaments. We might therefore have expected that precious stones cut and polished would be used here on a great scale, but from what I saw at Canton, the Chinese appear to set much less value on them than either the Hindoo or the European. It appears besides as if the Chinese still set greater value on stones with old "oriental polishing," i.e. with polished *rounded* surfaces, than on stones formed according to the mode of polishing now common in Europe with plane facets. Instead the Chinese have a great liking for peculiar, often very well executed, carvings in a great number of different kinds of stones, among which they set the greatest value on nephrite, or, as they themselves call it, "Yii." It is made into rings, bracelets, ornaments of all kinds, vases, small vessels for the table, &c. In Canton there are numerous lapidaries and merchants, whose main business is to make and sell ornaments of this species of stone, which is often valued higher

reproaches for helping a "foreign devil" to make a fool of his own countrymen. All my protestations were in vain, and I had to go away with my object unaccomplished.

than true precious stones. It was long so important an article of commerce that the place where it was found formed the goal of special caravan roads which entered China by the Yü gate. Amber also appears to have a high value put upon it, especially pieces which inclose insects. Amber is not found in China, but is brought from Europe, is often fictitious, and contains large Chinese beetles with marks of the needles on which they have been impaled. Other less valuable minerals, native or foreign, are also used, among others, compact varieties of talc or soapstone and of pyrophyllite. But works executed in these minerals do not fetch a price at all comparable to that of nephrite. In the same shop in which I purchased pieces of nephrite carefully placed in separate boxes, I found at the bottom of a dusty chest, along with pieces of quartz and old refuse of various kinds, large crystals, some of which were exceedingly well formed, of translucent topaz. They were sold as quartz for a trifle. I bought besides two pieces of carved topaz, one of which was a large and very fine natural crystal, with a Chinese inscription engraved on its terminal surface, which when translated runs thus : " Literary studies confer honour and distinction and render a man suitable for the court." The other was a somewhat bluish inch-long crystal, at one end of which a human figure, perhaps some Buddhist saint, was sculptured. The polishing of stones is carried on as a home industry, principally in a special part of the town. The workshop is commonly at the side of a small sale counter, in a room on the ground-floor, open to the street. The cutting and polishing of the stones is done, as at home, with metal discs and emery or comminuted corundum, which is said to be found in large quantities in the neighbourhood of Canton.

Large, commodious, well fitted up, but in their exterior very unwieldy river steamers, built after American designs, now run between Hong Kong and Canton. They are commanded by Europeans. The dietary on board is European, and exceedingly good. There are separate saloons for Europeans and Chinese. All over the poop and the after-saloon weapons are hung up so as to be at hand, in case the vessel should be attacked by pirates, or, as happened some years ago, a number of them should mix themselves up with the Chinese passengers with the intention of plundering the vessel.

Hong Kong was ceded to England in consequence of the war of 1842. The then inconsiderable fishing village is now one of the most important commercial cities of the globe. The harbour is spacious, affording good anchorage, and is well protected by a number of large and small granite islands. The city is built on the largest of these on slopes which rise from the shore towards the interior of the island. On the highest points

ie wealthiest foreign residents have built their summer houses
hich are surrounded by beautiful gardens. In winter they live
. the city. We here met with a very gratifying reception both
om the Governor, Mr. POPE HENNESSY, and from the other in-
ibitants of the town. The former invited Captain Palander and
.e to live in the beautiful Governor's residence, gave a dinner,
rranged a stately official reception in our honour, and pre-
nted to the Expedition a fine collection of dried plants from
ie exceedingly well-kept botanical garden of the city, which is
ider the charge of Mr. CHARLES FORD; the latter presented
e with an address of welcome at a festive meeting in the
ity Hall, specially arranged for the purpose and numerously
tended by the principal men of the town. The meeting was
)ened by the Chairman, Mr. KESWICK, with a speech of wel-
ime, after which Mr. J. B. COUGHTRIE read and presented the
ldress, bound in red silk and beautifully illuminated in black,
)ld, and red, with 414 signatures, among which many were by
hinese. The address ended with a hearty congratulation to
; all and a promise of a memorial of our visit to Hong Kong
hich should indicate the way in which the *Vega* expedition
as appreciated there. Some time after our return home
alander and I received from members of the community of
ong Kong a splendid silver vase each.

I here embraced with great interest the opportunity, which
y coming in contact with the principal men of the place
forded, of getting a glance into the political relations which
evailed in this vigorous and promising colony. At first sight
iey appeared to be by no means satisfactory. Peace and
ianimity evidently did not prevail; for dissatisfaction with
e Governor was loudly expressed by many of the Europeans
ttled in Hong Kong. He favoured, they said, the Chinese in
i exceedingly partial way, and mitigated their punishments to
ch a degree that Hong Kong would soon become a place of
fuge for all the robbers and thieves of Canton. At the time
our visit an instructive parliamentary debate on a small
ale was proceeding in the Legislative Council of the city.
ie controversy was carried on with a certain bitterness, but
.th a proper observance of the parliamentary procedure cus-
mary in the mother country. The eloquent leader of the
iposition had evidently, as is usual in such cases, the general
:ling of the Europeans on his side. For they appeared to be
etty well agreed that the only means of protecting themselves
ainst the evil-doers from the great heavenly empire would be
punish them in an inhuman way when they were taken in
e act.

To an outsider it appeared, however, that the Governor not
ly had humanity and justice on his side, but also acted with

a true insight into the future. When he came to the colony
the corporal punishments to which the Chinese were condemned were exceeding barbarous, although mild in comparison
with those common in China—a state of things which the opposition brought forward in defence of the severer punishments.
Prisoners were repeatedly flogged with "the cat," often with the
result that they were attacked by incurable consumption;
they were prepared for the punishment by being subjected for
some time to a starvation-diet of rice and water; they were
branded when they left the prison, &c.   Proceeding on the view
that the greatest security for a colony such as Hong Kong lies
in the affection which is cherished for it by the numerous
native population, the Governor had sought to protect it from
unjust attacks by Europeans.   Considering that too barbarous
punishments are likely rather to promote than to deter from
the commission of crimes, in consequence of the protection the
criminal in such a case may reckon upon from sympathising
fellow-creatures, and that mild punishments are the first condition of a good protective police, the Governor had diminished
the floggings, forbidden the public infliction of the punishment,
given a reprimand in cases where "by mistake" or by an
evasion of the letter of the law extra strokes had been given
to criminals, exchanged "the regulation cat" for the rattan,
abolished the preliminary starvation-diet and the branding,
improved the prisons, &c.   All this was now loudly complained
of by the European merchants, but was approved by the Chinese
subjects in the colony, who were however dissuaded from making
any contrary demonstrations.

When we came afterwards to other English possessions, we
found that the inhabitants were often more or less in conflict
with the authorities, but nowhere was there anything to prevent the opposition from endeavouring to promote their views
by public meetings, by addresses in newspapers and pamphlets.
In this way a pretty active political life arises early, and this
is probably one of the main conditions of the capacity of the
English colonies for self-government, and of their vigour and
influence on the surrounding country.

It will in truth be highly interesting to see what influence
will be exerted on the great neighbouring empire if Mr.
Hennessy's politics with reference to the Chinese settled in
Hong Kong be carried out, and they be converted into fellow-
citizens conscious that they are protected by law in person and
property, that they do not require to crawl in the dust before
any authority, and that so long as they keep within the limits
of the law they are quite safe from the oppressions of all officials,
and in the enjoyment of all the rights and privileges which the
English law confers upon the citizen.

Many of the Europeans settled at Hong Kong were convinced that for another thousand years one would be justified in using the expression regarding China: " Thou art what thou want, and thou wilt be what thou art." Others again stated that contact with Europeans at Shanghai, Hong Kong, and Singapore, and the accounts given by the emigrants returning to China in thousands from California and Australia are by slow degrees changing the aspect of the world in the "heavenly empire," and thereby preparing for a revolution less violent, but as thorough as that which has recently taken place in Japan. If this comes about, China will be a state that must enter into the calculation when the affairs of the world are settled, and whose power will weigh very heavy in the scales, at least when the fate of Asia is concerned. At Hong Kong and Canton the report was current that the far-sighted. Chancellor of the German Empire had taken this factor into calculation in settling his plans for the future.

Already the Chinese took part in the European life. A number of Chinese names, as I have already said, were attached to the address that was presented to me; at the Governor's reception many stout, smiling heads provided with pigtails were seen; and Chinese had taken part in the meetings at which the Governor's scheme of reform was under discussion. There have also existed in the country from time immemorial secret societies, which are said only to wait for a favourable opportunity to endeavour to link their fates to the new paths.[1] The observations that I made at Hong Kong and Canton are, however, too superficial for me to wish to detain my reader with these matters. I accordingly point to the numerous works on these cities published by authors who have lived there as many months or years as I have days, and proceed to sketch the continuation of the voyage of the *Vega*.

Accompanied by the good wishes of many newly acquired friends, we left the harbour of Hong Kong on the morning of the 9th November. It was my original intention to steer our course to Manilla, but the loss of time during our long stay in Japan compelled me to give up that plan. The course was shaped, however, not directly for Singapore, but for Labuan, a small English possession on the north side of Borneo. Its northern extremity (the coal mine) lies in 5° 33′ N. L. and 115° 12′ E. L. England took possession of Labuan on account of the coal-seams which are found there, which are of special importance on account of the situation of the island nearly in the midst of the large, numerous, and fertile islands of south-eastern Asia. It was the coal-seams too that attracted

---

[1] See on this subject W. A. Pickering, "Chinese Secret Societies" (*Journal of the Straits Branch of the R. Asiatic Society*, 1878, No. 1, pp. 63-84).

me to the place. For I wished to see whether I could not, in the neighbourhood of the equator itself, collect valuable contributions towards ascertaining the nature of the former equatorial climate.

We at first made rapid progress, thanks to a fresh and favourable monsoon wind. But when we reached the so-called belt of calms, the wind ceased completely, and we had now to avail ourselves of steam, which, in consequence of the low power of the *Vega's* engine and a strong counter current, carried us forward so slowly that it was not until the 17th November that we could anchor in the harbour of Labuan.

The largest of the islands belonging to the colony has, with a pretty considerable breadth, a length of 10' from N.E. to S.W. It is inhabited by some thousands (3,300 in 1863) of Chinese and Malays, together with a few Englishmen, who are either crown officials or employed at the coal mine. The north part of the island has a height of 140 metres above the sea, but towards the south the land sinks to an extensive sandy plain, closely overgrown with bushy thickets and traversed by low marshes. Most of the inhabitants live along the shore of the harbour which bears the now, or perhaps only for the present, indispensable name for English colonies (which on that account conveys little information) of Victoria. The Governor's fine residence lies at a little distance from the harbour town in the interior of the island, the coal mine on its north side. At the time of our visit the coal company had recently gone into liquidation, and work had therefore been stopped at the mine, but it was hoped that it would soon be resumed. The sandy plain is of little fertility in comparison with the neighbouring tropical lands. It had recently been burned, and was therefore for the most part covered only with bushes, among which stems of high, dried-up, half-burned trees raised themselves, giving to the landscape a resemblance to a northern forest devastated by an accidental fire. In consequence of the fire which had thus passed over the island the plain which, when looked at from a distance appeared to be completely even, was seen everywhere to be studded with crater-formed depressions in the sand, quite similar to the *os*-pits in the *osar* of Scandinavia.[1] On the north side there was sandstone rock rising from the sea with a steep slope six to fifteen metres high. Here tropical nature appeared in all its luxuriance, principally in the valleys which the small streams had excavated in the sandstone strata.

The coal mine is sunk on coal-seams, which come to the surface on the north side of the island. The seams, according to the information I received on the spot, are four in number, with a

[1] Concerning their formation and origin see a paper by K. Nordenskiöld in *Öfversigt af Vet.-akad. Förh.* 1870, p. 29.

thickness of 3·3, 0·9, 0·4 and 1·0 metre. They dip at an angle
of 30° towards the horizon, and are separated from each other by
strata of clay and hard sandstone, which together have a thickness
of about fifty metres. Above the uppermost coal-seam there are
besides very thick strata of black clay-slate, white hard sandstone
with bands of clay, loose sandstone, sandstone mixed with coal,
and finally considerable layers of clay-slate and sandstone, which
contain fossil marine crustacea, resembling those of the present
time. The strata which lie between or in the immediate
neighbourhood of the coal-seams do not contain any other fossils
than those vegetable remains, which are to be described farther
on. Thirty kilometres south of the mine a nearly vertical coal-
seam comes to the surface near the harbour, probably belonging
to a much older period than that referred to above ; and out in
the sea, eighteen kilometres from the shore north of the harbour,
petroleum rises from the sea-bottom. The manager of the mine
supposed from this that the coal-seams came to the surface again
at this place. The coal-seams of Labuan are besides, notwithstanding their position in the middle of an enormous, circular,
volcanic chain, remarkably free from faults, which shows that
the region, during the immense time which has elapsed since
these strata have been deposited, has been protected from
earthquakes. Even now, according to Wallace, earthquakes
are scarcely known in this part of Borneo.

From what has been stated above we may conclude that the
coal, sand, and clay strata were deposited in a valley-depression
occupied by luxuriant marshy grounds, cut off from the sea, in
the extensive land which formerly occupied considerable spaces
of the sea between the Australian Islands and the continent
of Asia. A similar state of things must besides have prevailed
over a considerable portion of Borneo. On that island there are
coal-seams under approximately similar circumstances to those
on Labuan. So far as I know, however, they have not hitherto
been closely examined with respect to vegetable palæontology.

At Labuan fossil plants are found, though very sparingly,
imbedded in balls of clay ironstone from strata above the two
lowermost coal-seams. The upper coal-seams are besides exceedingly rich in resin, which crosses the coal in large veins.
From the thickness and conversion into a hard sandstone of the
layers of sand lying between and above the coal-seams we may
conclude that a very long time, probably hundreds of thousands
or millions of years have passed since these coal-seams were
formed. They also belong to a quite recent period, during which
the vegetation in these regions varied perhaps only to a slight
extent from that of the present time. It is, however, too early
to express one's self on this subject, before the fossils which we
brought home have been examined by Dr. Nathorst.

Coal mining was stopped for the time, but orders were expected by every post to resume work. The road between the mine and the harbour town was at all events pretty well kept, and Mr. COOKE, one of the directors of the company, still lived at the place. He showed me all possible hospitality during the time I remained on the north side of the island for the purpose of collecting fossils. For the rest of the time I was the guest of the acting Governor, Mr. TREACHER, a young and amiable man, who showed me several collections in natural history from Labuan and the neighbouring parts of Borneo, and after our return to Europe sent me a collection of leaves and fruit of the kinds of trees which now grow on the island. I expect that this collection will be very instructive in the study of the fossil plants we brought home with us.

At the steep shore banks on the north coast very fine sections of the sandstone strata, which lie under and above the coal, are visible. While I went along the shore in order to examine these, I visited some Malay huts built on poles. They were surrounded at flood tide by water, at ebb by the dry beach, bare of all vegetation. In order to get inside these huts one must climb a ladder two to two and a half metres high, standing towards the sea. The houses have the same appearance as a warehouse by the seaside at home, and are built very slightly. The floor consisted of a few rattling bamboo splints lying loose, and so thin that I feared they would give way when I stepped upon them. The household articles consisted only of some mats and a pair of cooking vessels. I saw no fireplace ; probably fire was lighted on the beach. I could see no reason why this place should be chosen as a dwelling in preference to the neighbouring shore with its luxuriant vegetation, which at the same time was not at all swampy, unless it was for the coolness which arises from the airy situation on the beach, and the protection which the poles give from the thousands of crawling animals which swarm in the grassy meadows of tropical regions. It is probable also that the mosquitos are less troublesome along the sea-shore than farther into the interior of the country.

Some of my companions saw similar huts during an excursion, which they undertook in the steam launch, to the mouth of a large river debouching on the neighbouring coast of Borneo. Regarding this excursion Dr. Stuxberg gives the following report :

" On the 19th November Palander, Bove, and I, together with two men, undertook an excursion in the steam launch of the *Vega* to the river Kalias debouching right opposite to Labuan. We started at dawn, a little after six o'clock. The course was shaped first north of Pappan Island, then between the many shoals that lie between it and the considerably larger Daat Island, and finally south of the latter island.

" Pappan Island is a small beautiful island, clothed down to high-water mark with a dark green primeval forest. On Daat Island, on the contrary, the primeval forest on the east side has been cut down, and has given place to a new plantation of cocoa-nut trees, the work of a former physician on Labuan, which yields its present owner a considerable revenue.

" We had no little difficulty in finding a way over the sandy bar, which is deposited in front of the river mouth at a distance of a nautical mile and a half to three miles from the coast of Borneo. After several attempts in the course of an hour we at last succeeded in finding the deep channel which leads to the river. It runs close to the mainland on the north side, from Kalias Point to the river mouth proper. At the bar the depth was only a metre, in the deep channel, it varied between 3·5 and 7 metres, in the river mouth it was fourteen to eighteen metres and sometimes more.

" On the south side of the tongue of land, which projects north of the mouth of the Kalias, were found two Malay villages, whose inhabitants appeared to view our passage up the river with curious glances. A crowd of half or wholly naked children began a race along the shore, as soon as they set eyes upon the fast steam launch, probably in order to keep us in sight as long as possible. We now had deep water and steamed up the river without delay. The longed-for visit to some of the Malay villages we thus reserved till our return.

" We steamed about ten or twelve English miles up one of the many winding river arms, when the limited depth compelled us to turn. The vegetation on the mainland, as on the shores of the islands lying near the river-mouth was everywhere so close that it was nearly impossible to find a place where we could land ; everywhere there was the impenetrable primeval forest. Next the mouth of the river this consisted of tall, shady broad-leaved trees, which all had dark green, lustrous, large leaves. Some were in flower, others bore fruit. The greater number consisted of fig-trees, whose numerous air-roots twining close on each other formed an impenetrable fence at the river bank. These air-root-bearing trees play an important *rôle* in increasing the area of the land and diminishing that of the water. They send their strong air-roots from the branches and stem far out into the water, and when the roots have reached the bottom, and pushed their way into the mud, they make, by the close basket-work they form, an excellent binding medium for all the new mud which the river carries with it from the higher ground in the interior. It has struck me that the air-root-bearing trees form one of the most important means for the rapid increase of

the alluvial land on Borneo. Farther up the river there commenced large stretches of a species of palm, which with its
somewhat lighter green and its long sheath-formed leaves was
sharply distinguished from the rest of the forest. Sometimes
the banks on one side were covered with palms only, on the
other with fig-trees only. The palm jungles were not so
impenetrable as the fig-tree thickets; the latter preferred the
more swampy hollows, while the palms on the other hand grew
on the more sandy and less marshy places. Of herbs and
underwood there was nowhere any trace.

"During the river voyage we saw now and then single green-
coloured kingfishers flying about, and a honeysucker or two, but
they were not nearly so numerous as might have been expected
in this purely tropical zone. We saw some apes leaping in pairs
among the trees, and Palander succeeded in shooting a male.
Alligators from one to one and a half metre in length, frightened
by the noise of the propeller, threw themselves suddenly into the
water. Small land lizards with web-feet jumped forward with
surprising rapidity on the water near the banks. This was all
we saw of the higher animals.

"After a run of two hours, during which we examined the
banks carefully in order to find a landing place, we lay to at the
best possible place for seeing what the lower fauna had to offer.
It was no easy matter to get to land. The ground was so muddy
that we sank to the knees, and could make our way through the
wood only by walking on an intermediate layer of palm leaves
and fallen branches. The search for evertebrates did not yield
very much. A half-score mollusca, among them a very remarkable naked leech of quite the same colour-marking and
raggedness as the bark of the tree on which it lived, was all that
we could find here. It struck me as very peculiar not to find
a single insect group represented. The remarkable poverty in
animals must be ascribed, I believe, to the complete absence
of herbs and underwood. Animal life was as poor as vegetation
was luxuriant and various in different places. Over the landscape
a peculiar quietness and stillness rested.

"During our return we visited one of the two Malay villages
mentioned above. It consisted of ten different houses, which
were built on tall and stout poles out in the water at the mouth
of the river, about six to ten metres from the shore. All the
houses were built on a common large platform of thick bamboo,
which was about a man's height above the water. At right
angles to the beach there floated long beams, one end being
connected with the land, while the other was anchored close to
the platform. From this anchored end a plank rose at a steep
angle to the platform. Communication with land was kept up in
this way. The houses were nearly all quadrangular, and contained

a single room, had raised, not flat roofs, and were provided at one of the shorter sides, near one corner, with a high rectangular door opening, which certainly was not intended to be closed, and on one of the long sides with a square window opening. The building material was bamboo, from eight to eleven centimetres in thickness, mostly whole, but sometimes cleft. The roof had a thin layer of palm leaves upon it to keep out the rain. The house in its entirety resembled a cage of spills to which the least puff of wind had always free entrance. The floor bent and yielded much, and at the same time was so weak that one could not walk upon it without being afraid of falling through. One half, right opposite the door opening, was overlaid with a thin mat of some plant; it was evidently the sleeping place of the family. Some pieces of cloth was all the clothing we could discover. Of household articles there was scarcely any trace. Nor were there any weapons, arrows, or bows. The fireplace was in one corner of the room; it consisted of an immense ash-heap on some low stones. Beside it stood a rather dirty iron pot. All refuse from meals, bones and mollusc-shells, had been thrown into the water under the floor; there lay now a regular culture-layer, a couple of feet higher than the surrounding sea-bottom, consisting for the most part of mussel shells. The floor of the room was very dirty and black; it looked as if it had never been in contact with a drop of water. The interior of the whole house struck one as being as poor and wretched as that of a Chukch tent. Its inhabitants appeared scarcely to own more than they stood or walked in, i.e. for every person a large piece of cloth round the waist. Small boats lay moored to the platform. They were nothing else than tree-stems hollowed out, without any separate planks at the sides, at most two to two and a half metres long, and capable of carrying only two men. We had met such a boat a little way up the river, rowed by two youths, and laden with palm-leaves; it was not more than five to eight centimetres above the water, and appeared as if it would capsize with the least indiscreet movement on the part of the boatmen. Some dogs of middle size went about loose on the platform; they were at first shy and suspicious of us, and growled a little, but soon allowed themselves to be caressed.

"Of the natives, the Malays, unfortunately we saw at close quarters only some middle-aged men. When we approached the long floating beams which led to the platform, the women and children fled precipitately out of the nearest houses, and by the time we got to the platform, they had fortified themselves in a distant house, where they sat motionless and cast curious glances at us through a hole. The children showed their fear of us by loud crying, kept up the whole time. When we attempted to approach the fugitives, they hastened farther away. We won their favour with some cigarettes, which Palander distributed among them, and with which they were evidently delighted. They had a serious, reserved, perhaps rather indifferent appearance. A physiognomist would perhaps have had difficulty in saying whether their countenances expressed ferocity, determination, or indifference. It appeared as if it would not be easy to bring forth a look of mirth or gladness on their faces.

"At the Malay villages which we visited, some Chinese had a sago plantation. With some Malays as workmen in their service, they were now employed in loading a vessel of light draught with sago meal, of which they appeared to have a large quantity in store. Another vessel had just taken on board its cargo and was starting. The Chinese here made the same favourable impression on me as their countrymen, whom I had seen before in Japan and Hong Kong, and whom I was afterwards to see at Singapore—the impression of an exceedingly industrious, thriving, contented, and cleanly race."

Labuan strikes me as a very suitable starting-point for a naturalist who may wish to explore Borneo. Surrounded by Europeans, but undisturbed by the distractions of a large city, he would have an opportunity of accustoming himself to the climate, which, though rather warm for a dweller in the North, is by no means unhealthy, to get acquainted with the manners and customs of the natives, to acquire a knowledge of the commonest forms of the luxuriant nature, which would otherwise be apt to overwhelm the northern naturalist; in a word, to make such preparations for the journey as are necessary to secure its success. This region of Borneo appears to be one of the least known parts of the Indian Archipelago, and one need not go far from the coast to come to places which are never visited by Europeans. Labuan itself and its immediate neighbourhood have much that is interesting to offer to the observer, and from thence short excursions may be made with ease and without excessive cost to the territory of the Sultan of Bruni, who is favourable to foreigners, and to the mountain Kini Balu, near the northern extremity of Borneo, which is 4,175 metres high, and visible from Labuan. When, before our arrival at Japan, I arranged the plan of our voyage home, I included in it a visit to this mountain, at whose summit a comparatively severe climate must prevail, and whose flora and fauna, therefore, notwithstanding its equatorial position, must offer many points of comparison with those of the lands of the north. But when I was told that the excursion would require weeks, I had to give it up.

On the 12th November, the *Vega* again weighed anchor to

continue her voyage by Singapore to Point de Galle in Ceylon. Between Labuan and Singapore our progress was but slow, in consequence of the calm which, as might have been foreseen, prevailed in the sea west of Borneo.

Singapore is situated exactly halfway, when a vessel, starting from Sweden, circumnavigates Asia and Europe. We staid here from the 28th November to the 4th December, very hospitably received by the citizens of the town, both European and Asiatic, who seemed to vie with the inhabitants of Hong Kong in enthusiasm for the voyage of the *Vega*. A Babel-like confusion of speech prevails in the town from the men of so many different nationalities who live here : Chinese, Malays, Klings, Bengalees, Parsees, Singhalese, Negroes, Arabs, &c. But our stay was all too short for independent studies of the customs and mode of life of these different races, or of the rich vegetable and animal worlds in the neighbourhood of the town. I must refer those who are interested in these subjects to previous descriptions of that region, and to the abundant contributions to a knowledge of it which have been published by the Straits Branch of the Asiatic Society, which was founded here on the 4th November, 1877.

We arrived at Galle on the 15th December, having during our passage from Singapore had a pretty steady and favourable monsoon. While sailing through the Straits of Malacca strong ball-lightning was often seen a little after sunset. The electrical discharges appeared to go on principally from the mountain heights on both sides of the Straits.

I allowed the *Vega* to remain in the harbour of Point de Galle, partly to wait for the mail, partly to give Dr. Almquist an opportunity of collecting lichens on some of the high mountain summits in the interior of the island, and Dr. Kjellman of examining its algæ, while I myself would have time to visit the famous gem-diggings of Ceylon. The return was as good as could have been expected considering our short stay at the place. Dr. Almquist's collection of lichens from the highest mountain of Ceylon, Pedrotalagalla, 2,500 metres high, was very large ; Kjellman, by the help of a diver, made a not inconsiderable collection of algæ from the neighbourhood of the harbour ; and from an excursion which I undertook in company with Mr. ALEXANDER C. DIXON, of Colombo, to Ratnapoora, the town of gems, where we were received with special kindness by Mr. COLIN MURRAY, assistant government agent, I brought home a fine collection of the minerals of Ceylon.

Precious stones occur in Ceylon mainly in sand beds, especially at places where streams of water have flowed which have rolled, crumbled down, and washed away a large part of the softer constituents of the sand, so that a gravel has been left remaining which contains considerably more of the harder precious stone layer than the original sandy strata, or the rock from which they originated. Where this natural washing ends, the gem collector begins. He searches for a suitable valley, digs down a greater or less depth from the surface to the layer of clay mixed with coarse sand resting on the rock, which experience has taught him to contain gems.[1] At the washings which I saw, the clayey gravel was taken out of this layer and laid by the side of the hole until three or four cubic metres of it were collected. It was then carried, in shallow, bowl-formed baskets from half a metre to a metre in diameter, to a neighbouring river, where it was washed until all the clay was carried away from the sand. The gems were then picked out, a person with a glance of the eye examining the wet surface of the sand and collecting whatever had more or less appearance of a precious stone. He then skimmed away with the palm of the hand the upper stratum of sand, and went on in the same way with that below it until the whole mass was examined. The certainty with which he judged in a moment whether there was anything of value among the many thousand grains of sand was wonderful. I endeavoured in a very considerable heap of the gravel thus hastily examined, to find a single small piece of precious stone which had escaped the glance of the examiner, but without success.

The yield is very variable, sometimes abundant, sometimes very small, and though precious stones found in Ceylon are yearly sold for large sums, the industry on the whole is unprofitable, although now and then a favourite of fortune has been enriched by it. The English authorities, therefore, with full justification, consider it demoralising and unfavourable to the development of the otherwise abundant natural resources of the region. For the numerous loose population devotes itself rather to the easy search for precious stones, which is as exciting

[1] Emerson Tennent says on the subject :—The gem collectors penetrate through the recent strata of gravel to the depth of from ten to twenty feet in order to reach a lower deposit, distinguished by the name of *Nillm*, in which the objects of their search are found. This is of so early a formation that it underlies the present beds of rivers, and is generally separated from them or from the superincumbent gravel by a hard crust (called *Kadua*), a few inches in thickness, and so consolidated as to have somewhat the appearance of laterite or sun-burnt brick. The nellan is for the most part horizontal, but occasionally it is raised into an incline as it approaches the base of the hills. It appears to have been deposited previous to the eruption of the basalt, on which in some places it reclines, and to have undergone some alteration from the contact. It consists of water-worn pebbles firmly embedded in clay, and occasionally there occur large lumps of granite and gneiss, in the hollows under which, as well as in " pockets " in the clay (which from their shape the natives denominate "elephants' footsteps"). gems are frequently found in groups, as if washed in by the current. (E. Tennent, *Ceylon.* London, 1860, i. p. 34.)

GEM DIGGINGS AT RATNAPOORA.

as play, than to the severer but surer labours of agriculture, and
when at any time a rich *find* is made, it is speedily squandered,
without a thought of saving for the times when the yield is
little or nothing. A large number of the precious stones are
polished at special polishing places at Ratnapoora, but the work
is very bad, so that the stones which come into the market are
often irregular, and have uneven, curved, ill-polished surfaces.
Most of them perhaps are sold in the Eastern and Western
Indian peninsulas and other parts of Asia, but many are
also exported to Europe. The precious stones which are
principally found at Ratnapoora, consist of sapphires, commonly blue, but sometimes yellow or violet, sometimes even
completely colourless. In the last case they have a lustre
resembling that of the diamond.[1] Rubies I saw here only in
limited numbers.

The precious stones occur in nearly every river valley which
runs from the mountain heights in the interior of the island
down to the low land. According to a statement by Mr.
Tennent (i. p. 33), the river-sand at many places contains so
much of the harder minerals that it may be used directly
for the polishing of other stones. The same writer, or more
correctly Dr. GYGAX, who appears to have written the rather
scanty mineralogical contributions to Tennent's famous work,
states that a more abundant yield ought to be obtained by
working in the solid rock than by the usual method. This idea
is completely opposed to the experience of mineralogy. The
finest gems, the largest gold nuggets, as is well known, are
never, or almost never, found in solid rock, but in loose earthy
layers. In such layers in Ceylon the abundance of precious
stones, that is to say, of minerals which are *hard, translucent,
and strongly lustrous,* is very great, and enormous sums would
be obtained if we could add up the value of the mass of
precious stones which have been found here for thousands of
years back. Already Marco Polo says of Ceylon : "In ista
insula nascuntur boni et nobiles rubini et non nascuntur in
aliquo loco plus. Et hic nascuntur zafiri et topazii, ametisti,
et aliquæ aliæ petræ pretiosæ et rex istius insulæ habet
pulcriorem rubinum de mundo."

But some one perhaps will ask, where is the mother-rock of
all these treasures in the soil of Ceylon? The question is
easily answered. All these minerals have once been imbedded
in the granitic gneiss, which is the principal rock of the
region.

In speaking of granite or gneiss in southern lands, or at least

---

[1] Diamonds are wanting in Ceylon. And neither gold nor platinum
appears to occur in noteworthy quantity in the gem gravel.

in the southern lands we now visited, I must, in the first place, point out that these rocks next the surface of the earth in the south have a much greater resemblance to strata of sand, gravel, and clay than to our granite or gneiss rocks, the type of what is lasting, hard, and unchangeable. The high coast hills, which surround the Inland Sea of Japan, resemble, when seen from the sea, ridges of sand (*osar*) with sides partly clothed with wood, partly sandy slopes of a light yellow colour, covered by no vegetation. On a closer examination, however, we find that the supposed sandy ridges consist of weathered granitic rocks, in which all possible intermediate stages may be seen between the solid rock and the loose sand. The sand is not stratified, and contains large, loose, rounded blocks *in situ*, completely resembling the erratic blocks in Sweden, although with a more rugged surface. The boundary between the unweathered granite and that which has been converted into sand is often so sharp that a stroke of the hammer separates the crust of granitic sand from the granite blocks. They have an almost fresh surface, and a couple of millimetres within the boundary the rock is quite unaltered. No formation of clay takes place, and the alteration to which the rocks are subjected therefore consists in a crumbling or formation of sand, and not, or at least only to a very small extent, in a chemical change. Even at Hong Kong the principal rock consisted of granite. Here too the surface of the granite rock was quite altered to a very considerable depth, not however to sand, but to a fine, often reddish, clay, thus in quite a different way from that on the coast of the Inland Sea of Japan. Here too one could at many places follow completely the change of the hard granite mass to a clay which still lay *in situ*, but without its being possible to draw so sharp a boundary between the primitive rock and the newly-formed loose earthy layers as at the first-named place. We had opportunities of observing a similar crumbling down of the hard granite at every road-section between Galle, Colombo, and Ratnapoora, with the difference that the granite and gneiss here crumbled down to a coarse sand, which was again bound together by newly-formed hydrated peroxide of iron to a peculiar porous sandstone, called by the natives *cabook*. This sandstone forms the layer lying next the rock in nearly all the hills on that part of the island which we visited. It evidently belongs to an earlier geological period than the Quaternary, for it is older than the recent formation of valleys and rivers. The *cabook* often contains large, rounded, un-weathered granite blocks, quite resembling the rolled-stone blocks in Sweden. In this way there arise at places where the *cabook* stratum has again been broken up and washed away by currents of water, formations which are so bewilderingly like the ridges (*osar*) and hills with erratic blocks in Sweden and Finland that I was astonished when I saw them. I was compelled to resort to the evidence of the palms to convince myself that it was not an illusion which unrolled before me the well-known contours from the downs of my native land. An accurate study of the sandy hills on the Inland Sea of Japan, of the clay cliffs of Hong Kong, and the *cabook* of Ceylon would certainly yield very unexpected contributions to an explanation of the way in which the sand and rolled-stone *osar* of Scandinavia have first arisen. It would show that much which the Swedish geologists still consider to be glacial gravel transported by water and ice, is only the product of a process of weathering or, more correctly, falling asunder, which has gone on in Sweden also on an enormous scale. Even a portion of our Quaternary clays have perhaps had a similar origin, and we find here a simple explanation of the important circumstance, which is not sufficiently attended to by our geologists, that often all the erratic blocks at a place are of the same kind, and resemble in their nature the underlying or neighbouring rocks.

It is this weathering process which has originated the gem sand of Ceylon. Precious stones have been found disseminated in limited numbers in the granite converted into *cabook*. In weathering, the difficultly decomposable precious stones have not been attacked, or attacked only to a limited extent. They have therefore retained their original form and hardness. When in the course of thousands of years streams of water have flowed over the layers of *cabook*, their soft, already half-weathered constituents have been for the most part changed into a fine mud, and as such washed away, while the hard gems have only been inconsiderably rounded and little diminished in size. The current of water therefore has not been able to wash them far away from the place where they were originally imbedded in the rock, and we now find them collected in the gravel-bed, resting for the most part on the fundamental rock which the stream has left behind, and which afterwards, when the water has changed its course, has been again covered by new layers of mud, clay, and sand. It is this gravel-bed which the natives call *nellan*, and from which they chiefly get their treasures of precious stones.

Of all the kinds of stones which are used as ornaments there are both noble and common varieties, without there being any perceptible difference in their chemical composition. The most skilful chemist would thus have difficulty in finding in their chemical composition the least difference between corundum and sapphire or ruby, between common beryl and emerald, between the precious and the common topaz, between the hyacinth and the common zircon, between precious and common spinel; and

every mineralogist knows that there are innumerable intermediate stages between these minerals which are so dissimilar
though absolutely identical in composition. This gave the old
naturalists occasion to speak of ripe and unripe precious stones.
They said that in order to ripen precious stones the heat of the
south was required. This transference of well-known circumstances from the vegetable to the mineral kingdom is certainly
without justification. It points however to a remarkable and
hitherto unexplained circumstance, namely, that the occurrence
of precious stones is, with few exceptions, confined to southern
regions.[1] Diamonds are found in noteworthy number only in
India, Borneo, Brazil, and the Transvaal. Tropical America is
the home-land of the emerald, Brazil of the topaz, Ceylon of
the sapphire and the hyacinth, Pegu of the ruby, and Persia of
the turquoise. With the exception of the diamond the same
stones are found also in the north, but in a common form.
Thus common sapphire (corundum) is found in Gellivare iron
ore so plentifully that the ore from certain openings is difficult
to smelt. Common topaz is found in masses by the hundred-
weight in the neighbourhood of Falun; common emerald is
found in thick crystals several feet in length in felspar quarries,
in Roslagen, and in Tammela and Kisko parishes in Finland;
common spinel occurs abundantly in Åker limestone quarry;
common zircon at Brevig in Norway, and turquoise-like but
badly coloured stones at Vestaná in Skane. True precious
stones, on the other hand, are not found at any of these
places. Another remarkable fact in connection with precious
stones is that most of those that come into the market are not
found in the solid rock, but as loose grains in sand-beds.
True jewel mines are few, unproductive, and easily exhausted.
From this one would be inclined to suppose that precious
stones actually undergo an ennobling process in the warm soil
of the south.

During the excursion I undertook from Galle to Ratnapoora, I
visited a number of temples in order to procure Pali, Singhalese,
and Sanscrit manuscripts; and I put myself in communication
with various natives who were supposed to possess such manuscripts. They are now very difficult to get at, and the collection
I made was not very large. The books which the temples
wished to dispose of have long ago been eagerly bought
up by private collectors or handed over to public museums,
for example, to the Ceylon Government Oriental Library

---

[1] The only considerable exceptions from this are two localities for precious stones in Southern Siberia and the occurrence of precious opal in
Hungary. The latter, however, in consequence of defective hardness
and translucency, can scarcely be reckoned among the true precious
stones

established at Colombo.[1] The collector who remains a considerable time in the region, may however be able to reap a rich after-harvest, less of the classical works preserved in the temples than of the smaller popular writings in the hands of private persons.

We see in Ceylon innumerable descendants of the races who repeatedly subdued larger or smaller portions of the island, or carried on traffic there, as Moormen (Árabs), Hindoos, Jews, Portuguese, Dutchmen, Englishmen, &c., but the main body of the people at all events varies very little, and still consists of the two allied races, Tamils and Singhalese, who for thousands of years back have been settled here. The colour of their skin is very dark, almost black, their hair is not woolly, their features are regular, and their build is exceedingly fine. The children especially, who, while they are small, often go completely naked, with their regular features, their large eyes, and fresh plump bodies, are veritable types of beauty, and the same holds true of most of the youths. Instead of buying in one of the capitals of Europe the right to draw models, often enough with forms which leave much to desire, and which must be used without distinction for Greek or Northern divinities, for heroes or *savants* of the present or former times, an artist ought to make tours of study to the lands of the south, where man does not need to protect himself from the cold with clothes, and where accordingly nakedness is the rule, at least among the poorer classes. The dress which is worn here is commonly convenient and tasteful. Among the Singhalese it consists of a piece of cloth wound round the middle, which hangs down to the knees. The men, who still prefer the convenient national dress to the European, go with the upper part of the body bare. The long hair is held together with a comb which goes right over the head, and among the rich has a large four-cornered projection at the crown. The women protect the upper part of the body with a thin cotton jacket. The priests wear a yellow piece of cloth diagonally over one shoulder. The naked

---

[1] The Catalogue of Pali, Singhalese, and Sanscrit Manuscripts in the Ceylon Government Oriental Library, Colombo, 1876, includes :—

    41 Buddhist canonical books.
    71 Other religious writings.
    25 Historical works, traditions.
    29 Philological works.
    16 Literary works.
     6 Works on Medicine, Astronomy, &c.

According to Emerson Tennent (i. p. 515), the Rev. R. Spence Hardy has in the *Journal of the Ceylon Branch of the Asiatic Society* for 1848 given the titles of 467 works in Pali, Sanskrit, and Elu, collected by himself during his residence in Ceylon. Of these about eighty are in Sanskrit, 150 in Elu or Singhalese, and the remainder in Pali.

children are ornamented with metal bracelets and with a metal chain round the waist, from which a little plate hangs down between the legs. This plate is often of silver or gold, and is looked upon as an amulet.

The huts of the working men are in general very small, built of earth or *cabook*-bricks, and are rather to be considered as sheds for protection from the rain and sunshine than as houses in the European sense. The richer Singhalese live in extensive "verandas" which are almost open, and are divided into rooms by thin panels, resembling in this respect the Japanese houses. The Japanese genius for ornament, their excellent taste and skill in execution, are however wanting here, but it must also be admitted that in these respects the Japanese stand first among all the peoples of the earth.

In the seaport towns the Singhalese are insufferable by their begging, their loquacity, and the unpleasant custom they have of asking up to ten times as much, while making a bargain, as they are pleased to accept in the end. In the interior of the country the state of things in this respect is much better.

Among the temples which I visited in order to procure Pali books was the so-called "devil's" temple at Ratnapoora, the stateliest idol-house I saw in Ceylon. Most of the temples were built of wood; all were exceedingly unpretentious, and without the least trace of style. The numerous priests and temple attendants lived in rather squalid and disorderly dwellings in the neighbourhood of the temple. They received me in a friendly way and showed me their books, of which they occasionally sold some. The negotiation several times ended by the priest presenting me with the book I wished to purchase and positively refusing to receive compensation in any form. On one occasion the priest stated that he himself was prevented by the precepts of his religion from receiving the purchase-money agreed upon, but said that I might hand it over to some of the persons standing round. At two of the priests' houses there was a swarm of school-children, who ran busily about with their palm-leaf writing books and writing implements.

The temples were very different in their arrangements, probably on account of the dissimilar usages of the various Buddhist sects to which they belonged. A temple near Colombo contained a large number of wooden images and paintings of gods, or men of more than human size. Most of them stood upright like a guard round a sitting Buddha. I could not observe any dislike on the part of the priests to take the foreigner round their temples. The key, however, was sometimes wanting to some repository, whose contents they were perhaps unwilling to desecrate by showing them to the unbeliever. This was, for instance, the case with the press which contained the devil's bow and arrows, in the temple at Ratnapoora. The temple vessels besides were exceedingly ugly, tasteless, and ill-kept. I seldom saw anything that showed any sign of taste, art, and orderliness. How different from Japan, where all the swords, lacquer work, braziers, teacups, &c., kept in the better temples would deserve a place in some of the art museums of Europe.

In the sketch of the first voyage from Novaya Zemlya to Ceylon, a countryman of Lidner can scarcely avoid giving a

STATUES IN A TEMPLE IN CEYLON.

picture of "Ceylon's burned up vales." In this respect the following extract from a letter from Dr. Almquist, sketching his journey to the interior of the island may be instructive :—

"Three hours after our arrival at Point de Galle I sat properly stowed away in the mail-coach *en route* for Colombo. As travelling companions I had a European and two Singhalese. As it was already pretty dusk in the evening there was not much of the surrounding landscape visible. We went on the whole night through a forest of tall coco-nut trees whose dark tops were visible far up in the air against the somewhat lighter sky. It was peculiar to see the number of fire-flies flying in every direction, and at every wing-stroke emitting a bright flash. The night air had the warm moistness which is so agreeable in the tropics. Now and then the sound of the sea penetrated to our ears. For we followed the west coast in a northerly direction. More could not be observed in the course of the night, and all the passengers were soon sunk in deep sleep.

" After seven hours' brisk trot we came to a railway station and continued our journey by rail to Colombo, the capital of Ceylon. As there was nothing special to see or do there, I went on without stopping by the railway, which here bends from the coast to Kandy and other places. The landscape now soon became grander and grander. We had indeed before seen tropical vegetation at several places, but of the luxuriance which here struck the eye we had no conception. The pity was that men had come hither, had cleared and planted.

" In the lowlands I saw some cinnamon plantations. Ceylon cinnamon is very dear ; in Europe cheaper and inferior sorts are used almost exclusively, and most of the plantations in Ceylon have been abandoned many years ago. Soon the train leaves the lowland and begins to ascend rapidly. The patch of coast country, where the coco-nut trees prevail, is exchanged for a very mountainous landscape ; first hills with large open valleys between, then higher continuous mountains with narrow, deep, kettle-like valleys, or open hilly plateaus. In the valleys rice is principally cultivated. The hills and mountain sides were probably originally covered with the most luxuriant primitive forest, but now on all the slopes up to the mountain summits it is cut down, and they are covered with coffee plantations. The coffee-plant is indeed very pretty, but grows at such a distance apart that the ground is everywhere visible between, and this is a wretched covering for luxuriant Ceylon.

" At two o'clock in the afternoon we arrived at the station, Perideniya, the nearest one to Kandy. The famous botanical garden lies in its neighbourhood, and there I had to visit the superintendent of the garden, Dr. THWAITES. This elderly, but still active and enthusiastic naturalist is exceedingly interested in botanical research, and very obliging to all who work in that department. He received me in a very friendly manner, and it was due to him that the programme of my visit there was so full.

" A botanic garden in Ceylon must naturally be something extraordinary. Nowhere else can grander or more luxuriant vegetation be seen than here. The garden has been especially famous for the number of different varieties of trees of immense

A COUNTRY PLACE IN CEYLON.

which it can show. Besides, all possible better known plants to be found here, cultivated in the finest specimens. Spices drugs were specially well represented. Here long tendrils of black pepper-plant wound themselves up the thick tree-1s, here the cardamom and the ginger flourished, here the

HIGHLAND VIEW IN THE INTERIOR OF CEYLON.
Coffee Plantations ; Adam's Peak in the back-ground.

tty cinnamon, camphor, cinchona, nutmeg, and cocoa trees 1e a splendid show, here I saw a newly gathered harvest of illa. The abundance of things to be seen, learned, and oyed here was incredible. However, the next day I deter-1ed on the advice of Dr. Thwaites to make a tour up to the

mountain localities proper, in order there to get a better sight of
the lichen flora of Ceylon.

" I now travelled south partly by rail, partly by coach, until in
the evening I found myself lodged at a ' rest-house ' at Ram-
bodde, a thousand metres above the sea, at about the same height
accordingly as that at which trees cease to grow in southern
Norway.   This tropical mountain land reminds one a little, in
respect of the contours of the landscape, of the fells of Norway.
Here too are found league-long deep valleys surrounded by
high mountain summits and ranges with outlines sharply
marked against the horizon.   But here they were everywhere
overgrown with coffee bushes, or possibly with cinchona plants.
The mountain slopes were so laid bare from the bottom all the
way up that scarce a tree was left in sight ; everywhere so far as
the eye could reach only coffee.

" Next day, attended by a Singhalese, I went, or to speak more
correctly, climbed farther up the steep coffee plantations.   At a
height of 1,300 metres above the sea coffee ceases to grow, and
we now found some not very extensive tea plantations, and above
these the primitive forest commences.   At a height of 1,900
metres above the sea there is an extensive open plateau.   Up
here there is a not inconsiderable place, Novara Elliya, where
the governor has a residence, and part of the troops are in
barracks during the summer heat.   One of the mountains
which surround this plateau is Pedrotalegalla, the loftiest
mountain of Ceylon, which reaches a height of 2,500 metres
above the sea.

" I have ascended not so few mountains, but of none has the
ascent been so easy as of this, for a broad footpath ran all the
way to the top.   Without this path the ascent had been impossible, for an hour's time would have been required for every foot
made good through the jungle, so closely is the ground under
the lofty trees covered to the top of the mountain with bushes,
creepers, or the bamboo.   In the evening I returned to my
former night-quarters, where I slept well after a walk of
thirty-six English miles.

" As I felt myself altogether unable the following day to make
any further excursion on foot, I travelled back to Peradeniya by
mail-coach.   During this journey I had as my travelling companion a Singhalese, whom it was a special pleasure to see at
close quarters.   One of his big toes was ornamented with a
broad ring of silver, both his ears were pierced above, and
provided with some pendulous ornament, and one side of the
nose was likewise perforated, in order that at that place too might
he adorn himself with a piece of grandeur.   On his head he had,
like all Singhalese, a comb by which the hair drawn right
upwards is kept in position, as little girls at home are wont to

have their hair arranged. As the man did not appear to know a word of English, it was impossible to enter into any close acquaintance with him.

"At noon on the following day I found myself compelled, by a quite unexpected occurrence, to return precipitately to the coast again. Dr. Thwaites and I had been invited to dinner by his Excellency the Governor. As I was still limping after my long excursion on foot, and besides had not had the forethought to take a dress-suit with me, I considered that, vexatious as it was to decline, I could not accept this gracious invitation, but instead went my way. Thus after six exceedingly pleasant days I came back to Point de Galle and the *Vega.*"

CHAPTER XX.

The Voyage Home—Christmas, 1879—Aden—Suez—Cairo—Excursion to the Pyramids and the Mokattam Mountains—Petrified Tree-stems—The Suez Canal—Landing on Sicily by night—Naples—Rome—The Members of the Expedition separate—Lisbon—England—Paris—Copenhagen—Festive Entry into Stockholm—*Fêtes* there—Conclusion.

DURING our stay in Japan and our voyage thence to Ceylon I had endeavoured at least in some degree to preserve the character of the voyage of the *Vega* as a scientific expedition, an attempt which, considering the short time the *Vega* remained at each place, could not yield any very important results, and which besides was rendered difficult, though in a way that was agreeable and flattering to us, by I may almost say the tempestuous hospitality with which the *Vega* men were everywhere received during their visits to the ports of Japan and East Asia. It was besides difficult to find any new untouched field of research in regions which were the seat of culture and civilisation long before the time when the forest began to be cut down and seed to be sown in the Scandinavian North, and which for centuries have formed the goal of exploratory expeditions from all the countries of Europe. I hope however that the *Vega* will leave lasting memorials even of this part of her voyage through the contributions of Stuxberg, Nordquist, Kjellman, and Almquist to the evertebrate fauna and the sea-weed and lichen flora of East Asia, and by my collections of Japanese books of fossil plants from Mogi and Laquan, &c.

With the new overpowering impression which nature and people exerted on those of us, who now for the first time

3 A

THE SCIENTIFIC MEN OF THE "VEGA."

F. R. Kjellman.   A. Stuxberg.
E. Almquist.   O. Nordquist.

visited Japan, China. India, Borneo, and Ceylon, it was however specially difficult, during a stay of a few days at each place, to preserve this side of the *Vega* expedition. I therefore determined after leaving Ceylon to let it drop completely, that is, from that point merely to *travel home*. Regarding this part of the voyage of the *Vega* I would thus have very little to say, were it not that an obligation of gratitude compels me to express in a few words the thanks of the *Vega* men for all the honours bestowed upon them, and all the goodwill they enjoyed during the last part of the voyage. For many of my readers this sketch may perhaps be of interest as reminding them of some happy days which they themselves have lived through, and it may even happen that it will not be unwelcome to the friends of geography in a future time to read this description of the way in which the first circumnavigators of Asia and Europe were *fêted* in the ports and capitals of the civilised countries. In this sketch however I am compelled to be as brief as possible, and I must therefore sue for pardon if every instance of hospitality shown us cannot be mentioned.

We started from Point de Galle on the 22nd December, and arrived at Aden on the 7th January. The passage was tedious in consequence of light winds or calms. Christmas eve we did not celebrate on this occasion, tired as we were of entertainments, in such a festive way as at Pitlekaj, but only with a few Christmas-boxes and some extra treating. On New Year's Eve, on the other hand, the officers in the gun-room were suprised by a deputation from the forecastle clad in *pesks* as Chukches, who came, in good Swedish, mixed with a few words of the Pitlekaj *lingua franca* not yet forgotten, to bring us a salution from our friends among the ice of the north, thanks for the past and good wishes for the coming year, mixed with Chukch complaints of the great heat hereaway in the neighbourhood of the equator, which for fur-clad men was said to be altogether unendurable.

We remained at Aden only a couple of days, received in a friendly manner by the then acting Swedish-Norwegian consul, who took us round to the most remarkable points of the desolate environs of this important haven, among others to the immense, but then and generally empty water reservoirs which the English have made in the neighbourhood of the town. No place in the high north, not the granite cliffs of the Seven Islands, or the pebble rocks of Low Island on Spitzbergen, not the mountain sides on the east coast of Novaya Zemlya, or the figure-marked ground at Cape Chelyuskin, is so bare of vegetation as the environs of Aden and the parts of the east coast of the Red Sea which we saw. Nor can there be any comparison in respect of the abundance of animal life between the equatorial countries and the Polar regions we have named. On the whole animal life in the coast lands of the highest north, where the mountains are high and surrounded by deep water, appears to be richer in individuals than in the south, and this depends not only on the populousness of the fowl-colonies and the number of large animals of the chase that we find there, but also on the abundance of evertebrates in the sea. At least the dredgings made from the *Vega* during the voyage between Japan and Ceylon gave an exceedingly scanty yield in comparison with our dredgings north of Cape Chelyuskin.

Aden is now an important port of call for the vessels which pass through the Suez Canal from European waters to the Indian Ocean, and also one of the chief places for the export of the productions of Yemen or Arabia Felix. In the latter respect the harbour was of importance as far back as about four hundred years ago, when the Italian, LUDOVICO DE VARTHEMA, was for a considerable time kept a prisoner by the Arab tribes at the place.

In the harbour of Aden the *Vega* was saluted by the firing of twenty-one guns and the hoisting of the Swedish flag at the main-top of an Italian war vessel, the despatch steamer *Esploratore*, under the command of Captain AMEZAGA. The *Esploratore* took part in an expedition, consisting of three war vessels, charged with founding an Italian colony at Assab Bay, which cuts into the east coast of Africa, north of Bab-el-Mandeb, on a track of land purchased for the purpose by Rubbattino, an Italian commercial company. On board was Professor SAPETTO, an elderly man, who had concluded the bargain and had lived at the place for forty years. It was settled that he should be the administrator of the new colony. On board the *Esploratore* were also the *savants* BECCARI and the Marquis DORIA, famous for their extensive travels in the tropics and their valuable scientific labours. The officers of the Italian vessel invited us to a dinner which was one of the pleasantest and gayest of the many entertainments we were present at during our homeward journey. When at the close of it we parted from our hosts they lighted up the way by which we rowed forward, over the tranquil waves of the Bay of Aden with blue lights, and the desert mountain sides of the Arabian coast resounded with the hurrahs which were exchanged in the clear, calm night between the representatives of the south and north of Europe.

The *Vega* left Aden, or more correctly its port-town Steamer Point, on the 9th January, and sailed the following day through Bab-el-Mandeb into the Red Sea. The passage of this sea, which is narrow, but 2,200 kilometres long, was tedious, especially in its northern part, where a strong head wind blew. This caused so great a lowering of the temperature that a film of ice was formed on the fresh-water pools in Cairo, and that we, Polar travellers as we were, had again to put on winter clothes in Egypt itself.

The *Vega* anchored on the 27th January at the now inconsiderable port, Suez, situated at the southern entrance to the Suez Canal. Most of the scientific men and officers of the *Vega* expedition made an excursion thence to Cairo and the Pyramids, and were everywhere received in a very kind way. Among other things the Egyptian Geographical Society sent a deputation to welcome us under the leadership of the President of the Society, the American, STONE PACHA. He had in his youth visited Sweden, and appeared to have a very pleasant recollection of it. The Geographical Society gave a stately banquet in honour of the *Vega* expedition. An excursion was made to the Great Pyramids, and, as far as the short time permitted, to other remarkable places in and around the heap of ruins of all kinds and from all periods, which forms the capital of the Egypt of to-day. During our visit to the Pyramids the Swedish-Norwegian consul-general, BÖDTKER, gave us a dinner in the European hotel there, and the same evening a ball was given us by the Italian consul-general, DE MARTINO. A day was besides devoted by some of us, in company with M. GUISEPPE HAIMANN, to a short excursion to the Mokattam Mountains, famous for the silicified tree-stems found there. I hoped along with the petrified wood to find some strata of clay-slate or schist with leaf-impressions. I was however unsuccessful in this, but I loaded heavily a carriage drawn by a pair of horses with large and small tree-stems converted into hard flint. These lie spread about in the desert in incredible masses, partly broken up into small pieces partly as long fallen stems, without root or branches, but in a wonderfully good state of preservation. Probably they had originally lain imbedded in a layer of sand above the present surface of the desert. This layer has afterwards been carried away by storms, leaving the heavy masses of stone as a peculiar stratum upon the desert sand, which is not covered by any grassy sward. No root-stumps were found, and it thus appeared as if the stems had been carried by currents of water to the place where they were imbedded in the sandy layers and silicified. In their exterior all these petrifactions resemble each other, and by the microscopical examination which has hitherto been made naturalists have only succeeded in distinguishing two species belonging to the family Nicolia, and a palm, a pine, and a leguminous plant, all now extinct. It is possible that among the abundant materials I brought home

. with me some other types may be discovered by polishing
and microscopical examination. Such at least was my
expectation in bringing home this large quantity of stones,
the transport of which to the *Vega* was attended with a
heavy expenditure.

. From Cairo we returned, on the 2nd February, to Suez, and
the following day the *Vega* weighed anchor to steam through the
Suez Canal into the Mediterranean. This gigantic work, created
by the genius and perseverance of LESSEPS, which is unsurpassed by the many marvels of construction in the land of the
Pharaohs, has not a very striking appearance, for the famous
canal runs, like a small river with low banks, through the mono-
tonously yellow plain of the desert. There are no sluices. No
bold rock-blastings stand as monuments of difficulties overcome.
But proud must every child of our century be when he gazes on
this proof that private enterprise can in our day accomplish
what world-empires in former times were unable to carry into
execution. We touched at Port Said for a few hours on the
5th February, after which we continued our voyage to Naples,
the first European port we were to visit.

At Aden and in Egypt I had received several letters and
telegrams informing me that great preparations were being
made at Naples for our reception, and that repeated inquiries
had been addressed to the Swedish consul-general regarding
the day of our arrival, questions which naturally it was not so
easy to answer, as our vessel, with its weak steam-power, was
very dependent on wind and weather. It was hoped that the
Vega might be signalled from the Straits of Messina, but we did
not come to the entrance to the Straits until after sunset. I
therefore ordered the *Vega* to lie to there for some hours, while
Lieut. Bove and I rowed ashore to send off telegrams announ-
ing our arrival in Europe to Sweden, Naples, Rome, and other
places. The shore, however, was farther off than we had calculated, and it was quite dark before it was reached. It was not
without difficulty that in these circumstances we could get to
land through the breakers in the open road quite unknown to
us, and then, in coal-black darkness, find our way through
thickets of prickly bushes to the railway which here runs along
the coast. We had then to go along the railway for a considerable distance before we reached a station from which our
telegrams could be despatched. Scarcely had we entered the
station when we were surrounded by suspicious railway and
coast-guard men, and we considered ourselves fortunate that
they had not observed us on the way thither, for they would
certainly have taken us for smugglers, whom the coast-guard
have the right to salute with sharp shot. Even now we were
overwhelmed with questions in a loud and commanding tone,

but when they saw to what high personages our telegrams were addressed, and were informed by their countryman Bove, who wore his uniform, to what vessel we belonged, they became very obliging. One of them accompanied us back to our boat, after providing us with excellent torches which spread abundant light around our footsteps. They were much needed, for we were now compelled to share the astonishment of our guide that in the darkness we had succeeded in making our way over the rugged hills covered with cactus plants and bushy thickets between the railway and the coast, and along a railway viaduct which we had passed on our way to the station without having any idea of it. It was the last adventure of the voyage of the *Vega*, and my first landing on the glorious soil of Italy.

On the 14th February, at 1 P.M., the *Vega* arrived at Naples. At Capri a flag-ornamented steamer from Sorrento met us; somewhat later, another from Naples, both of which accompanied us to the harbour. Here the Swedish expedition was saluted by an American war-vessel, the *Wyoming*, with twenty-one guns. The harbour swarmed with boats adorned with flags. Scarcely had the *Vega* anchored—or more correctly been moored to a buoy—when the envoy LINDSTRAND, the Swedish-Norwegian consul CLAUSEN, Prince TEANO, president of the Geographical Society, Commander MARTIN FRANKLIN, Commendatore NEGRI, and others came on board. The last-named, who nearly two years before had made a special journey to Sweden to be present at the departure of the *Vega*, now came from Turin commissioned by the Italian government, and deputed by the municipalities of Florence and Venice, the Turin Academy of Sciences, and several Italian and foreign geographical societies, to welcome the Expedition, which had now brought its labours to a happy issue.

After Herr Lindstrand, as King Oscar's representative, had welcomed the Expedition to Europe, and publicly conferred Swedish decorations on Palander and me, and two adjutants of the Italian Ministry of Marine had likewise distributed Italian orders to some of the *Vega* men, some short speeches were exchanged, on which the members of the Expedition, accompanied by the persons enumerated above, landed in the Admiral's steam launch under a salute of twenty-one guns from the Italian guard-ship. On the landing-quay, where a large crowd of the inhabitants of the city was assembled, the Swedish seafarers were received by the Syndic of Naples, Count GIUSSO, accompanied by a deputation from the municipality, &c. Here we were taken, between rows of enthusiastic students, in the gala carriages of the municipality, to the Hotel Royal des Étrangères, where a handsome suite of apartments, along with equipages and numerous attendants, was placed at our disposal. We were there received by the committee in charge of the festivities, Prince BELMONTE and Cavalier RICCIO, who afterwards, during our stay in the city, in the kindest way arranged everything to make our stay there festive and agreeable.

On Sunday the 15th several deputations were received, among them one from the University. A beautifully-bound address was presented by "Ateneo Benjamino Franklin," and a number of official visits were made and received. We dined with the Swedish-Norwegian consul, Clausen. On Monday the 16th an address was presented from "Scuola d'Applicazione per gl'Ingenieri," and from "Neapolitana Archæologiæ, Litterarum et Artium Academia," a song of welcome in Latin, written by Professor ANTONIO MIRABELLI. Then followed a grand dinner given by the municipality of the city in a hall of the hotel, which was now inaugurated and was named the *Vega* Hall, and was on this occasion ornamented with the royal cipher, the Swedish and Italian flags, &c. In the evening there was a gala representation at San Carlo, where the members of the Expedition scattered among the different boxes were saluted with repeated loud cries of "Bravo!"—On Tuesday the 17th the Committee had arranged an excursion to Lake Averno, the Temple of Serapis, and other places famous in a geological and historical respect, situated to the north-west of Naples, Prince URUSOV entertained some of the members of the Expedition to dinner. There was an afternoon musical entertainment at the "Società Filarmonica," where there was a numerous ·attendance of persons moving in the first circles in the city.—Wednesday the 18th, excursion along with the Committee to Pompeii, where the Swedish guests were received by the famous superintendent of the excavations, Director RUGGIERI. Breakfast was eaten with merry jests and gay speeches in a splendid Roman bath, still in good preservation, excavations were undertaken, &c. In the afternoon there was a grand dinner, followed by a reception by the admiral in command, and a festive representation at the Bellini Theatre.—Thursday the 19th, Dr. FRANZ KÜHN, arrived from Vienna, deputed by the Geographical Society there to welcome us. Excursion in company with Professor PALMIERI and the Committee to Vesuvius, which at the time of our visit was emitting thick columns of smoke, was pouring out a stream of lava, and casting out masses of glowing stone. We ascended the border of the crater, not without inconvenience from the heat of the half-solidified lava streams over which we walked, from the gases escaping from the crater, and from the red-hot stones flung out of it. The new railway, not then ready, was inspected, and the observatory visited. We dined with the Committee at the hotel.—Friday the 20th, journey to Rome, where the members of the Expedition arrived at 2 P.M., and were, in the same way as at Naples, received in a festive manner by the Syndic of the city, Prince RUSPOLI, president and director of the Geographical Society, by members of the University, the Scandinavian Union, &c. Carriages met the Swedish guests, in which they were taken past the Swedish-Norwegian minister's hotel, decked with innumerable flags, to Albergo di Roma in the Corso, where a splendid suite of appartments, along with equipages, was placed at the disposal of the Expedition. In the evening we dined with the Swedish minister, and were afterwards received by Prince PALLAVICINI at his magnificent palace.—Saturday the 21st, visit to the Chamber of Deputies, private excursions, dinner given by the Duke NICOLAS of Leuchtenberg, to Nordenskiöld and Nordquist.—Sunday the 22nd, public meeting of the Geographical Society, at which its grand gold medal was presented to Nordenskiöld. In the evening a grand dinner, given by the geographical society, in the Continentel Hotel. Among the toasts which were drunk may be mentioned one to the King of Sweden and Norway, proposed in a very warm and eloquent speech by the Premier, CAIROLI; to Nordenskiöld, by Prince Teano; to Palander, by the Minister of Marine, Admiral ACTON; to the other members of the Expedition, to its munificent patrons, Oscar Dickson and Alexander Sibiriakoff, to Bove, the Italian officer, who took part in it, &c.—Monday the 23rd. Audience of the King. In the evening a grand reception at the Palazzo Teano, where almost all that was distinguished and splendid of Roman society appeared to be assembled.—Tuesday the 24th. Dined at the Quirinal with King Humbert. There were present, besides the King and his suite, the Swedish minister, the members of the *Vega* expedition, Prince Teano, President of the Geographical Society; Commendatore Negri; Cairoli, Premier; Acton, Minister of Marine; MALVANO, Secretary of the Cabinet; Major BARATIERI, and the Italian naval officer, EUGENIO PARENT, a member of the Swedish Polar expedition of 1872-3, and others. In the evening, reception by the English minister, Sir A. B. PAGET, and a beautifully arranged *fête* at the Scandinavian Union, at which a number of enthusiastic speeches were made, and flowers and printed verses were distributed.—Wednesday the 25th. Farewell visits. Some of the members of the Expedition travelled north by rail. Captain Palander made an excursion to Spezzia to take part in a cruise on the large ironclad *Duilio*. The others remained some days longer in Rome in order to see its lions, undisturbed by official *fêtes*.

While the *Vega* lay in the harbour of Naples she was literally exposed to storming by visitors. The crew were on several occasions invited to the theatres there by the managers. Excursions to Pompeii had besides been arranged for them by the consul for the united kingdoms, Clausen, who spared no pains to make the stay of the expedition at Naples honouring to the mother-country and as pleasant as possible to the guests, as well as in arranging the more formal details of the visit. We had besides the joy of meeting in Italy our comrade from the severe wintering of 1872-3, Eugenio Parent, who soon after had the misfortune to be in the tower of the ironclad *Duilio*, when the large Armstrong cannon placed there burst, and the wonderful good fortune to escape with life and without being seriously hurt from this dreadful accident. The only mishap on board the *Vega* during the latter part of her long voyage home occurred besides in the harbour of Naples, one of the sailors who was keeping back an enthusiastic crowd of people who stormed the *Vega*, being thrown down from the bulwarks with the result that he broke an arm.[1]

On the 29th February the *Vega* left the harbour of Naples, but no longer with her staff complete. Doctors Kjellman, Almquist, and Stuxberg, and Lieut. Nordquist had preferred the land route from Italy to Stockholm to the long *détour* by sea, and Lieut. Bove was obliged, by family circumstances, to leave the *Vega* at Naples. We, however, all met again at Stockholm. At our departure from Naples the gunroom *personnel* thus consisted only of me, Captain Palander, and Lieuts. Bruzewitz and Hovgaard.

Through M. A. RABAUT, President of the young, but already so well known Geographical Society of Marseilles, I had received repeated invitations to visit along with my companions the birthplace of Pytheas, the first Polar explorer and the discoverer of the Scandinavian Peninsula. With great reluctance I was compelled to decline this invitation. We had to hasten home, and I wished to save some days for a visit to the fatherland of HENRY the Navigator and VASCO DA GAMA.

We sailed through the Straits of Gibraltar on the 9th March, and anchored in the harbour of Lisbon on the 11th March at 2 P.M. The following day we made an excursion to the beautiful palace of Cintra, situated about five Portuguese miles from the capital. On Saturday we were received in audience by the King, DOM LUIZ, of Portugal, who, a seaman himself, appeared to take a great interest in the voyage of the *Vega*. Later in the day the Swedish minister in Lisbon gave a

---

[1] An accident also happened during the first half of the expedition, the steersman, in backing among drift-ice, having been thrown over the wheel and hurt very seriously.

THE OFFICERS OF THE "VEGA."

E. Bruzewitz.

G Bove.   A. Hovgaard.

dinner, to which were invited the President of the Portugeuse Council, the Minister of Foreign Affairs, the members of the Diplomatic Corps, and others ending in the evening with a grand reception. On Monday the 15th we were present by special invitation at a meeting of the Geographical Society, at which the newly-returned African travellers, BRITO-CAPELLO and IVEN, gave addresses. Here I had besides the great pleasure of meeting the famous African traveller, Major SERPA PINTO. The King at the same time honoured us with decorations, and at its meeting on the 10th March the Portuguese Chamber of Deputies resolved, on the motion of the Deputies ENNES and ALFREDO, to express its welcome and good wishes in a congratulatory address to the *Vega* men.

We weighed anchor again on the 15th March. We were favoured at first with a fresh breeze and made rapid progress, but at the entrance to the Channel we met with a steady head-wind, so that it was not until the evening of the 25th March, considerably later than we had counted on, that we could anchor in the harbour of Falmouth, not, as was first intended, in that of Portsmouth. We thus missed some preparations which had been made at the latter place to welcome us to the land which stands first in the line of those that have sent out explorers to the Polar Seas. We besides missed a banquet which the Royal Geographical Society had arranged in honour of the *Vega* expedition, at which the Prince of Wales was to have presided, and which now, in the midst of the Easter holidays and a keenly-contested parliamentary election, could not be held.[1] Our stay in England, at all events, was exceedingly pleasant. Palander and I travelled on the night before Good Friday to London, where we were received at the railway station by the Swedish minister, Count PIPER, and a large number of our countrymen living in London. Count Piper carried me to my future host, the distinguished Secretary of the Geographical Society and famous Arctician and geographical writer, CLEMENTS R. MARKHAM, who did everything to make my stay in London as pleasant and instructive as possible. Saturday was spent in paying visits. On Easter Sunday Consul-General RICHTER gave a lunch in the Continental Hotel, to which a considerable number of Scandinavians and Englishmen were invited. The same evening we dined with the famous Arctic traveller, Sir ALLEN YOUNG. On Monday we were invited by the Earl of NORTHBROOK, President of the Geographical Society,[2] to his country seat, Stratton, near

[1] Further particulars on this point are given in the Annual Address on the Progress of Geography by the Right Hon. the Earl of Northbrook (*Proceedings of the Royal Geographical Society*, 1880, p. 401).

[2] During our visit to London we had no opportunity of taking part in any of the meetings of the Society, but some time after the Society gave

Winchester.   Here we saw the way—an exceedingly quiet one—
in which an English parliamentary election goes on.   The same
day we paid a visit to Mr. SPOTTISWOODE, the President of the
Royal Society, at his magnificent country seat in the neighbourhood of London.   Here I saw several instructive experiments
with very large machines for the production of light by
electric discharges in highly rarified air.   Wednesday the 31st,
grand dinner at the Swedish minister's, and in the evening of the
same day a Scandinavian *fête* in the Freemasons' Hall, at which
there were great rejoicings according to old northern usages.

We started for Paris on the night before the 1st April.   We
went by Boulogne-sur-Mer, whose Chamber of Commerce had
invited us to a *fête* to celebrate the first landing of the *Vega*
men on the soil of France after the North-East Passage was
achieved.   Several of the authorities of the town and
Dr. HAMY, a delegate from the Geographical Society of Paris
met us in the waiting-room at the station.   Here a breakfast had been arranged, in the course of which we were
presented to a number of eminent persons of the place, with
whom we afterwards passed the greater part of the day in the
most agreeable way.   After making several excursions in the
neighbourhood of the town and paying the necessary official
visits, we partook of a festive dinner arranged by the municipality.   From Boulogne we travelled by night to Paris, arriving
there on the 2nd April at 7 A.M.

Notwithstanding the early morning hour we were received
here at the station in a festive way by the Swedish-Norwegian
Minister and the *personnel* of the Legation, a deputation from
the Geographical Society of Paris, and a considerable number
of the members of the Scandinavian colony in the Capital of
France.   The famous Madagascar traveller, GRANDIDIER,
President of the Geographical Society's Central Committee,
welcomed us, with lively expressions of assent from the surrounding crowd.   We were invited during our stay in the
city to live with our countryman, A. NOBEL, in a very
comfortable villa belonging to him, Rue Malakoff, No. 53, and
I cannot sufficiently commend the liberal way in which he here
discharged the duties of a host and assisted us during our stay
in Paris, which, though very agreeable and honouring to us,
demanded an extraordinary amount of exertion.

Our reception in Paris was magnificent, and it appeared as
if the metropolis of the world wished to show by the way in
which she honoured a feat of navigation that it is not without
reason that she bears on her shield a vessel surrounded by
swelling billows.   It is a pleasant duty for me here to offer

Palander the Founder's Gold Metal (I had in 1869 obtained the same
distinction) and elected me an Honorary Corresponding Member.

my thanks for all the goodwill we, during those memorable days, enjoyed on the part of the President of the Republic, of Admiral LA RONCIÈRE LE NOURY, President of the Geographical Society, his colleague, M. HECHT, M. MAUNOIR, the Secretary of the Society, M. QUATREFAGE, and M. DAUBRÉE, members of the Institute, not to forget many other Frenchmen and Scandinavians. Among the *fêtes* of Paris I must confine myself to an enumeration of the principal ones.

Friday, the 2nd April. Public *séance de réception* by the Geographical Society in the Cirque des Champs Elysée in the presence of a very large and select audience. Admiral La Roncière delivered the speech on this occasion, which I replied to by giving a pretty good account of the Swedish Arctic expeditions, on which the President handed me the large gold medal of the Society "as a proof of the interest which the public and the geographers of France take in the voyage of the *Vega.*" Dined the same day with the Swedish-Norwegian minister, SIBBERN.—Saturday the 3rd. Invitation to a festive meeting of delegates from twenty-eight learned societies in France in the amphitheatre of the Sorbonne.[1] We were greeted by the Minister of Education in a masterly and eloquent speech, after which he conferred upon us, on the part of the Republic, Commander's and Officer's Insignia of the French Legion of Honour. "A reward," as the Minister of the *Republic* expressed himself, "for the blood of the brave and the sleepless nights of the learned." After that an Official dinner and reception by M. Jules Ferry.—On Sunday the 4th an address was presented from the Scandinavian Union, under the presidency of Herr Fortmeijer. In the evening a brilliant entertainment on a large scale given by the Scandinavian Union in the Hotel Continental. Among those present may be mentioned Prince OSCAR of Sweden, the President of the *Fête* Committee, Herr JENSEN, Fru KRISTINA NILSON-ROUZEAUD, the Danish minister, the Swedish embassy, members of the Russian embassy, a large number of Scandinavian artists, many of the principal representatives of the French and foreign press, and lastly, what ought perhaps to have been mentioned first, a flower-garden of ladies, of which every dweller in the north might feel proud.—Monday the 5th. Meeting of the Institute in its well-known hall, with speeches of welcome. Hence we were conducted to a grand festive reception, arranged beforehand to the minutest details by the Municipal Council, in "la Salle des États," situated in that part of the Tuileries where the geographical Congress was held in 1878. The hall

---

[1] These are enumerated in the *Bulletin de la Société de Géographie,* Mai, 1880, p. 463. In the same part (p. 450) there is also a report of the speeches made at the *séance de réception.*

and the ascent to it were richly ornamented with French tri-
colours and Swedish flags, beautiful Gobelins, and living plants.
A number of speeches were made, after which the President of
the Municipal Council, on the part of the City of Paris, presented to me a large artistically executed medal as a memorial
of the voyage of the *Vega*.[1] In the evening a grand dinner
was given by the Société de Géographie, with several eloquent
speeches : for King Oscar (General Pittie), for President Grévy,
for the prosperity of France (Prince Oscar), for the *Vega* expedition (M. Quatrefage), and so on.—Tuesday the 6th. Dinner
given by the President of the Republic, M. Grévy, to Prince
Oscar and the *Vega* men then in Paris.—Wednesday the 7th.
Dinner given to a numerous and select company of French
savants by the then President of the Geographical Society and
of the Institute, M. A. Daubrée.—Thursday the 8th. Dinner
to a small circle at Victor Hugo's house, where the elderly poet
and youthful-minded enthusiast in very warm, and I need not
say eloquent, words congratulated me on the accomplishment of
my task. Reception there the same evening.

Here ended our visit to the capital of France. Thoroughly
exhausted, but bringing with us memories which shall never
pass away, we travelled the following day to Vlissingen, whither
the *Vega* had gone from Falmouth, under the command of
Bruzewitz. We had been compelled to decline warm and
hearty invitations to Holland and Belgium from want of time
and strength to take part in any more festivities. The anchor
was weighed immediately after we came on board, and the
course shaped for Copenhagen. At noon on the 15th we passed
Helsingborg, which was richly ornamented with flags for the
occasion. Already at Kullaberg we had been met by the
steamer *H. P. Prior*, with Lund students on board, and eight
other steamers with deputations of welcome and enthusiasts for
the voyage of the *Vega*, from Copenhagen, Malmö, Helsingborg,
and Elsinore. The number of passengers was stated to be 1,500,
including a number of ladies. Songs were sung, speeches made,
fireworks let off, &c. At night we lay at anchor in the outer
road of Copenhagen, so that it was not until the following forenoon that we steamed into the harbour, saluting the fort with
nine shots of our little cannon, and saluted in turn by as many.
While the *Vega* was sailing into the harbour, and after she had
anchored, there came on board the Swedish Minister, Baron

---

[1] The medal was accompanied by an "extrait du registre de procès-
verbaux du conseil municipal de la ville de Paris," a caligraphic masterpiece illuminated in various colours and gold. The *Conseil municipal* also
ordered a detailed description of the *fête* to be printed, with the title
*Relation officielle de le réception de M. le Professeur Nordenskiöld par le
conseil municipal de Paris le lundi 5 Avril* 1880.

BECK-FRIIS, the Swedish consul-general EVERLÖF, the representatives of the University, of the merchants, and of the Geographical Society under the presidency of the former President of the Council, Count HOLSTEIN-HOLSTEINBORG, to bring us a welcome from the corporations they represented, and accompany us to the Toldbod, where we were received by the President-in-chief, the Presidents of the Communal Authority, and the Bourse, and the Swedish Unions of Copenhagen. We then drove through the festively ornamented city, saluted by resounding hurrahs, from a countless throng of human beings, to the Hôtel d'Angleterre, where apartments had been prepared for us. On the 17th a *fête* was given by the Geographical Society in the Casino Hall, which was attended by the King, the Crown Prince, and Prince John of Glücksborg, and nearly all the distinguished men of Copenhagen in the fields of science, business, and politics. The speech of the *fête* was delivered by Professor ERSLEV. Thereafter a gay and lively banquet was given, at which the Crown Prince of Denmark presided.

The 18th April. Grand entertainment given by the King.—
The 19th April. Magnificent banquet given by the Society of Merchants to the members of the *Vega* expedition at the Bourse, the rooms being richly ornamented with flowers and flags, and with busts and paintings executed for the occasion by eminent artists. Councillor of state MELCHIOR presided, and amongst those present were observed the Crown Prince, the ministers, the speakers and vice-speakers of the *folke-* and *lands-ting*, and a number of the principal scientific and military men and officials. Speeches were delivered by the Crown Prince, state-councillor TEITGEN, Manager of the Great Northern Telegraph Company, Admiral BILLE, Professor, MADVIG, state-councillor Melchior, &c. At another place, an entertainment was given at the same time to the crew. In the evening, *fête* of the students' Union, the Swedish National Union, and the Norwegian Union.

I was obliged to decline an invitation to Lund, because his Majesty, King Oscar, had expressed the wish that we should first set foot on Swedish ground at the Palace of Stockholm.

It was settled that our entry into Stockholm should take place in the evening of the 24th April, but we started from Copenhagen as early as the night before the 20th in order to be sure that we would not, in consequence of head winds or other unforeseen hindrances, arrive too late for the festivities in the capital of Sweden. In consequence of this precaution we arrived at the Archipelago of Stockholm as early as the 23rd, so that we were compelled during the night between the 23rd and 24th to lie still at Dalarö. Here we were met by Commander LAGERCRANTZ who by the King's orders brought our families on the steamer *Sköldmön* to meet us.

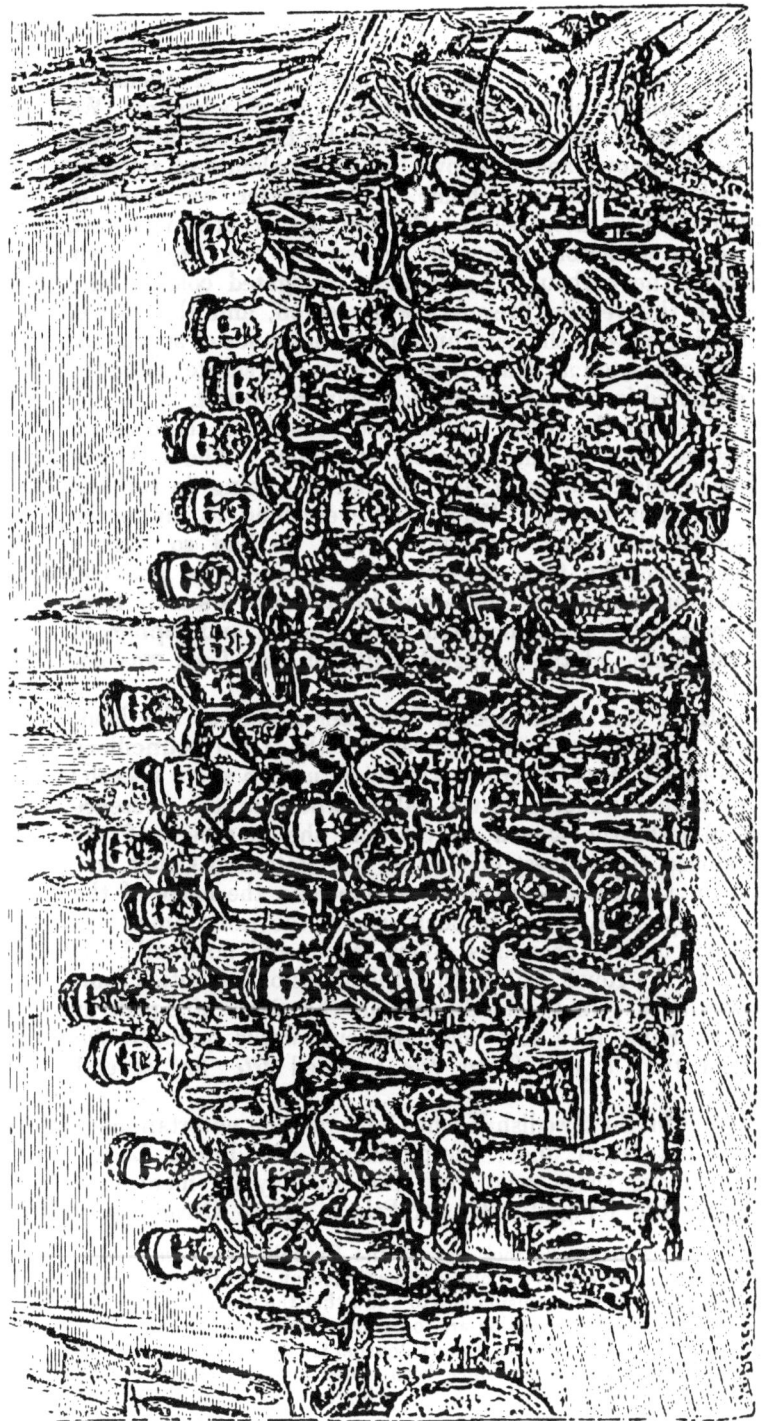

THE CREW OF THE "VEGA."

After a photograph taken at Naples.

On the 24th at 8 A.M. the *Vega* again weighed anchor in order to steam on slowly, past Vaxholm into Stockholm. We met innumerable flag-decked steamers by the way, fully laden with friends, known and unknown, who with shouts of rejoicing welcomed the *Vega* men home. The nearer we came to Stockholm, the greater became the number of steamers, that, arranged in a double line and headed by the *Vega*, slowly approached the harbour. Lanterns in variegated colours were lighted on the vessels, fireworks were let off, and the roar of cannon mingled with the loud hurrahs of thousands of spectators. After being greeted at Kastelholmen with one salute more the *Vega* anchored in the stream in Stockholm at 10 P.M.

The queen of the Mälar had clothed herself for the occasion in a festive dress of incomparable splendour. The city was illuminated, the buildings round the harbour being in the first rank. Specially had the King done everything to make the reception of the *Vega* expedition, which he had so warmly cherished from the first moment, as magnificent as possible. The whole of the Royal Palace was radiant with a sea of light and flames, and was ornamented with symbols and ciphers in which the name of the youngest sailor on the *Vega* was not omitted.

An estrade had been erected from Logaorden to the landing-place. Here we were received by the town councillors, whose president, the Governor, welcomed us in a short speech; we were then conducted to the Palace, where, in the presence of her Majesty the Queen of Sweden, the members of the Royal House, the highest officials of the State and Court, &c, we were in the grandest manner welcomed in the name of the fatherland by the King of Sweden, who at the same time conferred upon us further marks of his favour and goodwill.[1] It was also at the Royal Palace that the series of festivities commenced with a grand gala dinner, on the 25th of April, at which the King in a few magnanimous words praised the exploit of the *Vega*. Then *fête* followed *fête* for several weeks.

On the 26th the Swedish Yacht Club gave an entertainment in the Grand Hotel under the presidency of Admiral Lagercrantz. Among those who were present may be mentioned his Majesty the King, the Crown Prince, Prince Oscar, Oscar

---

[1] Among others to all who took part in the Expedition a *Vega* medal, specially struck, to be worn on a blue-yellow riband on the breast. It may perhaps be of interest for numismatists to know that the medals distributed on account of the *Vega* expedition are to be found delineated in the eighth and ninth parts of the Swedish Family Journal for 1880. To those that are there delineated there have since been added a medal struck by the Finnish Society of Sciences, and the Anthropological-Geographical Society's medal.

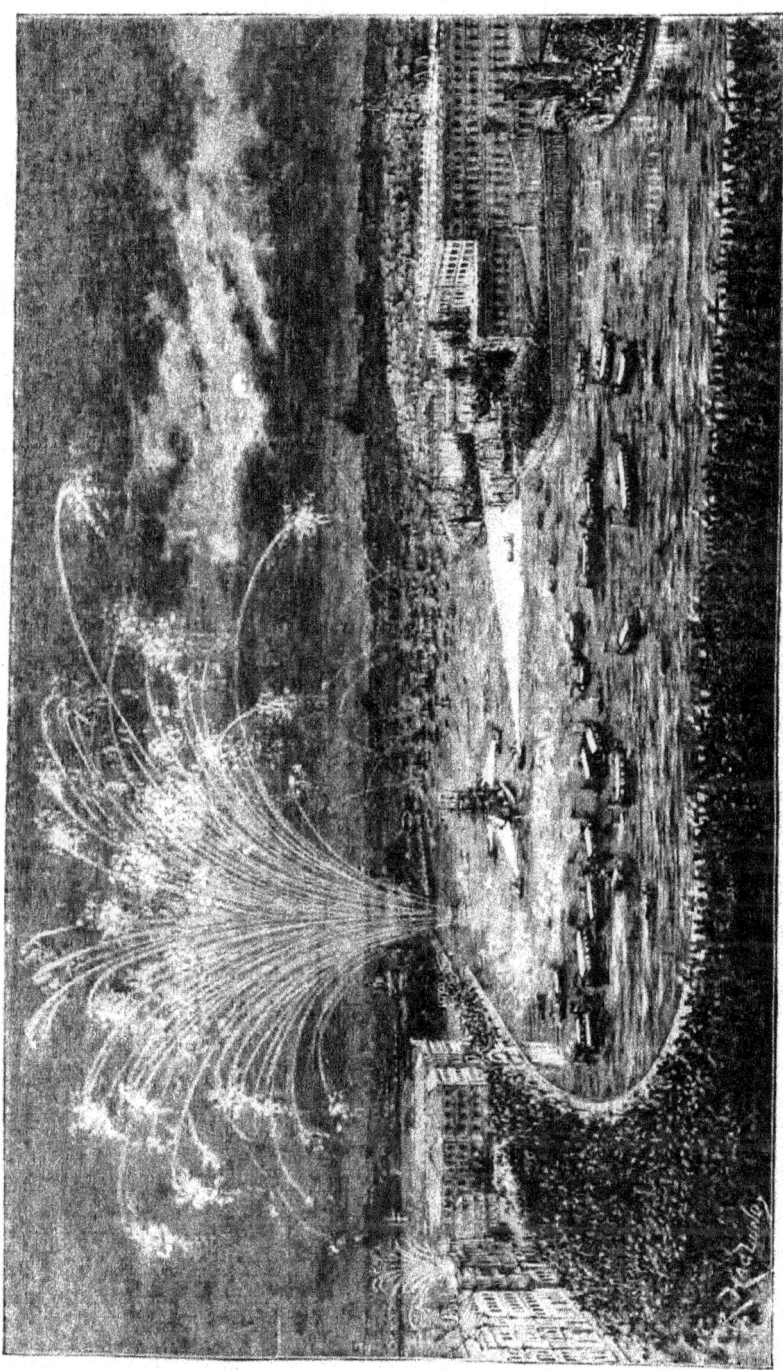

THE ENTRANCE OF THE "VEGA" INTO STOCKHOLM ON THE 24TH APRIL, 1880.

3 B 2

Dickson, and Baron von Otter, Minister of Marine. On the evening of the same day there was a torchlight procession by pupils of the Technical High School. On the 27th there was a gala-play, to which all the *Vega* men were invited. On the 28th at a festive meeting of the Academy of the Sciences, a medal struck on account of the *Vega* expedition was distributed, the meeting being followed by a dinner given at the Hotel Phœnix by the Academy under the presidency of the Crown Prince. On the 30th April and 5th May banquets were given by the Publicist Club, and by the Idun Society, by the Naval Officers' Society to the officers of the *Vega*, and by the Stockholm Workman's Union to the crew. On the 7th and 8th May there were festivities at Upsala, the principal attraction of which consisted of gay, lively, and ingenious carnival representations, in which we received jocular addresses and homage from fantastically dressed representatives of the peoples of different countries and periods.

During this time there were daily received deputations, addresses, and telegrams of welcome, among others from the *riksdag* of Sweden, the *storting* of Norway, and the principal towns of Norway and Finland, from the student corps at Upsala and Helsingborg, from the St. Petersburg Geographical Society, from women in Northern Russia (the address accompanied by a laural wreath in silver), &c. In a word, the Stockholm *fêtes* formed the climax of the remarkable triumphal procession from Japan to Stockholm, which stands unique in the history of festivities. Even after the Expedition was broken up in Stockholm, and the *Vega* had sailed on the 9th May for Karlskrona and Gothenburg, where she was again taken over by the whaling company that previously owned her, the *fêtes* were repeated at these towns. They commenced anew when the *Vega* exhibition was opened with appropriate solemnities by his Majesty the King in one of the wings of the Royal Palace, and when some months after I visited Berlin, St. Petersburg, and my old dear fatherland, Finland.

But I may not weary my reader with more notes of festivities. It is my wish yet once again to offer my comrades' and my own thanks for all the honours conferred upon us both in foreign lands and in the Scandinavian North. And in conclusion I wish to express the hope that the way in which the accounts of the successful voyage of the *Vega* have been received in all countries will give encouragement to new campaigns in the service of research, until the natural history of the Siberian Polar Sea be completely investigated and till the veil that still conceals the enormous areas of land and sea at the north and south poles be completely removed, until man at last knows at least the main features of the whole of the

planet which has been assigned him as a dwelling-place in
the depths of the universe.

Hearty thanks last of all to my companions during the
voyage of the *Vega;* to her distinguished commander Louis
Palander, her scientific men and officers, her petty officers and
crew. Without their courage and the devotion they showed to
the task that lay before us, the problem of the North-East
Passage would perhaps still be waiting for its solution.

ABSTRACT OF THE VOYAGE OF THE VEGA.

	1878.	Distance traversed. English geographical miles
Karlskrona—Copenhagen	June 22—24	144
Copenhagen—Gothenburg	,, 26, 27	134
Gothenburg—Tromsoe	July 4—17	1,040
Tromsoe—Chabarova	,, 21—30	930
Chabarova—Port Dickson	Aug. 1—6	580
Port Dickson—Cape Chelyuskin	,, 10—19	510
Cape Chelyuskin—Preobraschenie Island	,, 20—24	385
Preobraschenie Island—the Mouth of the Lena	,, 24—27	380
The Mouth of the Lena—Irkaipij	Aug. 27—Sept. 12	1,260
Irkaipij—Pitlekaj	Sept. 18—28	235
The Wintering	{ Sept. 28, 1878— July 18, 1879	

	1879.	
Pitlekaj—St. Lawrence Bay	July 18—20	190
St. Lawrence Bay—Port Clarence	,, 21, 22	120
Port Clarence—Konyam Bay	,, 26—28	160
Konyam Bay—St. Lawrence Island	,, 30, 31	90
St. Lawrence Island—Behring Island	Aug. 2—14	900
Behring Island—Yokohama	Aug. 19—Sept. 2	1,715
Yokohama—Kobe	Oct. 11—13	360
Kobe—Nagasaki	,, 18—21	410
Nagasaki—Hong Kong	Oct. 27—Nov. 2	1,080
Hong-Kong—Labuan	Nov. 9—17	1,040
Labuan—Singapore	,, 21—28	750
Singapore—Point de Galle	Dec. 4—15	1,510
Point de Galle—Aden	Dec. 22—Jan. 7, 1880	2,200

	1880.	
Aden—Suez	Jan. 9—27	1,320
Suez—Naples	Feb. 3—14	1,200
Naples—Lisbon	Feb. 29—March 11	1,420
Lisbon—Falmouth	March 16—25	745
Falmouth—Vlissingen	April 5—8	345
Vlissingen—Copenhagen	,, 10—16	632
Copenhagen—Stockholm	,, 20—24	404
Total		22,189

INDEX.

INDEX.

THE END.

Lightning Source UK Ltd.
Milton Keynes UK
UKOW06f0115040717
304607UK00014B/732/P